THE THIRD INTERMEDIATE
IN EGYPT (1100–6

THE THIRD
INTERMEDIATE PERIOD
IN EGYPT

(1100–650 B.C.)

K. A. Kitchen

ARIS & PHILLIPS LTD
Warminster
England

To my Parents
who have so long shared the burden and heat of the day

ISBN 0 85668 298 5

SECOND EDITION WITH SUPPLEMENT

Kitchen, K.A.
  The Third Intermediate Period in Egypt
  (1100-650 B.C.). — 2nd rev. ed.
  1. Egypt — Civilization — To 332 B.C.
  I. Title
  932'.015   DT61

Printed and published in England by ARIS & PHILLIPS Ltd
Teddington House, Warminster, Wiltshire BA12 8PQ.

Contents

NOTE

In this edition an asterisk in the text normally indicates that there is relevant material in the Supplement

PART ONE

Chronology: Twenty-first Dynasty

PART TWO

Chronology: Twenty-second to Twenty-fifth Dynasties

PART THREE

Chronology: Officials of the Realm

PART FOUR

Outline Historical Survey (c. *1100–650 B.C.*)

PROLOGUE

TANITES AND THEBANS

THE LIBYAN DOMINION

THE NUBIAN DOMINION

EPILOGUE

PART FIVE

Excursuses

PART SIX

Tables

I. Dates of Kings

II. Ready-reckoners for Contemporaneous Reigns

III. Royal Genealogies

IV. Chief Dignitaries of the Realm

A. Thebes and South

B. Memphis

List of Maps and Plans

Corrigendum: p.572, line 4 - read standing for kneeling.

Preface

For very many years, no attempt has been made to present a comprehensive, full-scale treatment of the chronology of Late-Period Egypt from the end of the New Kingdom to the resumption of more precise history with the Saite kings from 664 B.C. Despite the growing interest in this formerly much-neglected epoch of Egyptian history, an interest which is marked by an increasing number of monographs and papers on detailed subjects during the last two decades, the chronology has been dealt with in a piecemeal and very summary fashion and with rather unsatisfactory results.

The aims of the present book are simple: to reconstruct the basic chronology of the 21st–25th Dynasties, and therewith to present an historical outline (Part IV) that should incorporate the results gained and serve as a compact, reasonably up-to-date survey of almost five centuries of Egyptian history for a wide scholarly and interested public.

The method of this work is also in principle simple: to classify and survey the main available evidence, and so build up a chronology from mostly first-hand data and on first principles. No useful purpose is served by refuting old works long made obsolete by more recent discoveries, or by merely setting one opinion against another without reference to the underlying facts. However, in matters of controversy, the relevant literature has been weighed, and is adduced as required.

The title 'Third Intermediate Period' – based on the analogy of the well-known First and Second Intermediate Periods – has become quite popular of late as a term for the 21st–24th Dynasties. However, it is my hope that the present work will abolish its own title, so to speak, by demonstrating that the period in question is far from being chaotic (unlike its earlier supposed analogues), and so not merely 'intermediate', but significant in its own right. I would prefer to characterize the overall period as the 'Post-Imperial epoch', subdividing it into the Tanite, Libyan and Nubian periods. For the 25th Dynasty, I have rejected the thoroughly misleading term 'Ethiopian', and instead of (say) 'Kushite' (a more biblical and 'Africanist' term) I have preferred to use 'Nubian', a term that most closely covers the territory involved (unlike 'Sudan', for example, which is rather too wide), and has become well known in recent years, thanks to the intensive archaeological activity in both Egyptian and Sudanese Nubia.

It should be said that this book had its origin almost a decade ago, in two factors. First, the teaching of Egyptian history impelled me to try and produce improved provisional outlines for the 21st and Libyan and Nubian Dynasties, both chronological and historical. Secondly, in 1963, my friend Eric Young (then of the Metropolitan Museum, New York) kindly sent me a copy of the paper he thereafter published in *JARCE* 2 (1963); points of lasting value in his study (recognition of king Osochor; a Year 17 actually 15) compelled me to revise my previous efforts on the 21st Dynasty. Therefrom grew the present entire work, which was already largely complete in 1963/64. Since then, the whole has been revised throughout. In this long interval, on only one point has truly drastic revision so far proved necessary: my German colleagues in particular will doubtless greet with satisfaction my change from a long reign for Amenemope to a long reign for Psusennes I, in the chronology preferred here. But, I may add, the total data pointing to this result are here given full discussion for the first time. It had been intended to have this book (virtually complete in 1964) published in 1966 at the latest (cf. *Orientalia* 35 (1966), 283). For the ensuing 7 years' delay, the author in fairness to himself washes his hands of all responsibility; that, to my regret, must be laid at the door of those responsible for the gross understaffing and excessive work-load of the School of Archaeology and Oriental Studies, especially of the Department of Egyptology, during this period of time.

From those factors which hinder the course of serious scholarship, it is infinitely more pleasant to turn to the congenial activity of thanking those who have given help and encouragement. Among my ever-helpful colleagues in the School of Archaeology and Oriental Studies, my thanks are due to Professor H. W. Fairman for making available copies of important texts, and to Mr. A. R. Millard for reading Part IV and commenting upon cuneiform matters; to Mr. Morris L. Bierbrier, doing further research in this period of Egyptian history, I am indebted for various comments which have been noted wherever appropriate. For communication of various data (and kind permission to quote such, when needed), I am beholden to various colleagues and institutions, in particular to: Bernard

V. Bothmer (Brooklyn Museum); Dr. G. A. Gaballa (Cairo); the Griffith Institute, Oxford, through Miss H. Murray; Mme H. K. Jacquet (Cairo); T. G. H. James (British Museum); Professor J. Leclant (Paris); and Professor H. S. Smith (University College, London). The details are severally acknowledged in the notes to the present work. For kind permission to use the illustration on the cover of this book, I am indebted to Dr. George R. Hughes, lately Director of The Oriental Institute, University of Chicago.

To Messrs Aris & Phillips and their staff, I would express thanks for their willingness to produce this book in their new series on Modern Egyptology, in a form and within a schedule exemplary in these difficult and unstable times. Finally and fundamentally, the dedication of this book only inadequately reflects the lasting debt of gratitude I owe to my parents who, for so many years, have given domestic facility and sacrificial encouragement in my work on this and other projects; to my mother I owe thanks also for statistically checking the whole manuscript prior to press.

Naturally, this work cannot hope to be the final word on so difficult a terrain; but I dare to hope that it may at least provide a basic 'map' of that terrain until future work shall help us to know it better.

K. A. KITCHEN,
Woolton, Liverpool,
June, 1972.

1995 Preface

Introductory.
In the last 23 years since this book first appeared and even in the decade since this Second Edition was first published, interest and work in this complex epoch has in no way diminished. I append some notes on recent issues and discussions.

21st Dynasty.
   §A. For the beginning of our period, K. Jansen-Winkeln has firmly advocated setting Herihor *after* Piankh in Thebes, at the beginning of the 21st Dynasty, and also attributing anonymous regnal dates in Thebes (prior to Amenemope's reign) to the Theban high priests of Amun; see his important paper in *ZÄS* 119(1992), 22-37, especially 22-26, 34-37. However, his reasoning and adduced evidence deserve more rigorous scrutiny than they have been accorded so far.
   His point **1.** (p.23) is that Piankh appears mainly as "general", while Herihor appears mostly as "high priest". This is a mirage that rests on a failure to appreciate the true nature and (limited) extent of the source-material. *Both* men were equally general and high priest alike. In administrative ('secular') contexts, it was their role as military governor ('general') that counted. But in religious and ritual matters, it was their role as high priest that was appropriate. It should be pointed out that almost all of the mentions of Piankh fall into the 'secular' realm; we have no temple relief-scenes of him in ritual roles; in the Nims oracle, he *does* appear in priestly role in the scene, but reverts to 'general' in the affairs in the compressed text below. By contrast, Herihor appears *almost entirely* in the strictly ritual scenes of the Temple of Khons at Karnak, hence the overwhelming number of mentions of him as high priest. In non-temple contexts, he too flaunts his secular titles – vizier, general, in dockets, etc., which (by sheer chance) are currently few in number. In other words, we must consider the nature and quality of data, *not* merely their number. There is no proof here concerning the order of these two men.
   §B. His point **2.** (p.23) is that Piankh's military (etc.) titles link him to the king, while Herihor's do not. This is irrelevant; Piankh's titles could as easily have linked him to the court of Smendes as to that of Ramesses XI. And as Jansen-Winkeln admits, Herihor does bear royally-oriented epithets, and not least the very high-ranking honorific of Fanbearer on the King's Right hand, a clear mark of rank at court. So there is nothing here to decide on the order of Herihor and Piankh.
   §C. His point **3.** (p.23f.) is that Herihor, Pinudjem I and Menkheperre all took royal titles and attributes while Piankh did not – hence he should precede a royally-entitled series, rather than interrupt it. But he makes no attempt to distinguish the *level of usa*ge in each case; – which is both unacceptable and unrealistically schematic. Herihor was 'king' *only in Karnak* and on private funerary effects – *not* in Egypt at large, or even in Theban administration; his "kingship" was a ritual fiction.

The plain facts are documented below, p.251 and cf. 569. In Menkheperre's case, the data are much less: *no* fivefold titulary, only twin cartouches and that almost only on brick-stamps from (again!) Karnak enclosure, plus his fastness at El-Hibeh, and on small votive objects such as the Rio de Janeiro statuette. He was *not* a recognised king throughout Egypt, any more than Herihor. (On year-dates, see below, §Lff.) Only Pinudjem I, of *all* the Theban line of military governors cum high priests, had not only full titles but also public recognition beyond Thebes, as shown by the Koptos stela (A. O. Abdallah, *JEA* 70(1984), 65-72), an Abydos altar and the block reported with those of Psusennes I at Tanis (below, pp.259, 262). But even his pretensions may have been cut back, cf. below pp.570-1, after data noted in the Khons Temple (Weeks, *Temple of Khonsu*, 2, xviii-xix). If Piankh was Herihor's successor in office over the South and distinctly junior to him, there is *no* reason for presuming that he might dare to take royal titles at Herihor's demise (and use of such, almost only in temple-scenes). Furthermore, it was 15 whole years before Pinudjem I felt able (or was allowed?) to assume full royal style! So, the concept of 'royal' continuity adumbrated by Jansen-Winkeln is a non-existent mirage.

§D. His point 4. (p.24) is, again, purely schematic: no bandage-dockets happen to be dated under Piankh, so he has to be set before Herihor merely to provide a continuous series! But, from Year 7 to Year 10 of the *whm-mswt*, 'Renaissance' era, Piankh's span is only 3 years, the shortest incumbency other than the purely ephemeral Smendes II and DjedKhonsefankh (who also had *no* mummy-bandage dockets; only braces on *one* Theban mummy for Smendes II!) So, this point is devoid of value.

§E. His point 5. (p.24) – Herihor and Pinudjem I were builders and restorers in Thebes – founders on the same point (only a 3-year incumbency), and on the fact that Piankh's time seems to have been spent largely in warring against Panehsi in Lower Nubia. There were often time-breaks in work in temples. Thus, Sethos I built and part-decorated the Osireion in Abydos; the 66 years of Ramesses II saw no work there, before Merenptah continued its decoration; and Tuthmosis III's last great obelisk lay unfinished for the whole of Amenophis II's 26-year reign, before Tuthmosis IV completed it. So, a 3-year pause at the Khons-Temple under Piankh engrossed in Nubia is of no significance whatsoever.

§F. His point 6. (p.24) on the non-naming of the Theban high priests in the tomb-robbery papyri is another irrelevance. Those particular juridical enquiries were conducted by high officials from the royal court up north – the vizier and his colleagues – and *not* entrusted to the local power-holder, doubtless to ensure a stricter enquiry, and at the highest legal level. Both Piankh and Herihor were, equally, 'strong man' general and high priest, but this level of enquiry had to be conducted by external assessment.

§G. His point 7. (pp.24-25) is a comparison between the run of titles borne by each of Panehsi, Herihor and Piankh. This is, at best, indecisive and at worst irrelevant. That Herihor as generalissimo (not just general) *had* to be followed by the rest of the Theban high priests also generalissimos is simply being over-schematic; real history is often less tidy. As successor to Herihor, Piankh would have been junior to him, therefore it is little wonder that he is simply 'general', not 'generalissimo', especially if he lasted only 3 years as ruler of the South. Comparisons with Panehsi are irrelevant (a viceroy of Nubia, not high priest and governor of Upper Egypt).

§H. His point **8.** (p.25), that the succession Piankh-Herihor involves us with only one lady called Hrere is the only suggestion of real merit at first sight – that one and the same lady would have been wife of Piankh and mother of Nodjmet, Herihor's wife. This is an economical solution, but falls short of actual proof. The fact remains that we have in the years that followed some 5 or 6 Istemkhebs, probably 4 Henttawys, certainly 2 Maatkares and 2 Nesikhonses, and most likely 2 Tentamuns. So, 2 Hreres would be no problem whatever, if other evidence favours the usual sequence Herihor-Piankh.

§I. In the light of the foregoing observations (and considerations still to follow), our colleague's claim (p.25) that there is "nicht den geringsten Zweifel" ('not the slightest doubt') that Herihor followed Piankh is very optimistic, and is little more than ingenuous fiction. *Against* his proposed reversal of Herihor and Piankh, further points may be noted.

§J. First, the matter of datelines. The Years 5 and 6 in the narrative of Wenamun clearly portray both Herihor and Smendes as contemporary *governors* of South and North respectively – and in no way as kings (no cartouches or titles; no use of 'His Majesty', etc.; and marked failure to link the given regnal years with either person). This stumbling-block cannot be evaded by merely citing Osing's suggestion that the Wenamun narrative is somehow satirical. That judgement is subjective, and not proven. By definition, satire is "the use of ridicule to expose folly or vice", and to satirise is to use this procedure. This does *not* characterise the Wenamun story, and certainly not in relation to either Herihor or Smendes therein. The Years 5 and 6 cannot be those of either Smendes or Herihor except by special pleading, and certainly not of Ramesses XI (far too early). Only as years of *whm-mswt* do they really make any sense. And Piankh then duly follows in Year 7 of that era as the Nims oracle shows. There is no basic problem about Herihor pressing on with the Khons Temple reliefs showing his intended new Barque of Amun, while a Wenamun was out procuring the timber; his death before the barque was completed (if this happened) would be no different from so many other cases in which death prevented a ruler from completing his projects.

§K. Second, to intercalate Herihor as high priest and military governor between Piankh and his son and successor Pinudjem I is bizarre and without any secure parallel, a glaring anomaly. This alone should make one extremely sceptical about the proposed reversal in order of Herihor and Piankh.

And third, there are the anomalies caused by any such reversal. Jansen-Winkeln's view entails assigning at least 10 years rule to Piankh, for whom we have almost *no* monuments, and barely half as much (into 6th year!) for Herihor who left us so much more! This is totally unrealistic, with no datelines whatever for the first 6 years of Piankh's incumbency, – only in the last 3 years.

In short, there is no compelling reason whatsoever to reverse the order of Herihor and Piankh, and very good positive reasons to retain the usual order. Mere novelty does not determine truth.

§L. The other major proposal for our period in Jansen-Winkeln's paper is to attribute anonymous Theban regnal datings to the high priests/military governors in Thebes and Upper Egypt, not to the nationally recognised kings in Tanis. Despite his remarks on p.34, this is not a matter of "dogma", but of patiently observing the overall facts and known Egyptian usages.

The hard fact remains that, for 1000 years before the 21st Dynasty, *nobody* since some Middle-Egyptian nomarchs had ever used personal regnal years unless they were King of Egypt, in reality or by claim (with all the trappings) as in the 2nd Intermediate Period. To claim that the family of military high priests of Amun was Libyan and hence took a quite different view of kingship (Jansen-Winkeln, *ZÄS* 122(1995), 77) is largely wrong on two counts. First of all, that family was *not* purely and exclusively Libyan; that is a gross over-simplification. In fact, by personal names, that family is overwhelmingly Egyptian. Of 10 high priests, only *one* (Masaharta) bore a Libyan name, while only 5 out of Herihor's 19 sons at the Khons Temple bear Libyan-looking names. Of the 7 Tanite kings, only Osochor (Osorkon the Elder) is Libyan by name. In other words, at most, Herihor's family might originally have been of Libyan origin, but had so intermarried with Egyptians that they became predominantly Egyptian in name and outlook, with a Libyan streak in them, so to speak. Or, the family was Egyptian with some Libyan input through intermarriage (perhaps less likely culturally). And secondly, during the *real* Libyan dynasties (22-23), regnal years were used exclusively by. real kings (the two Delta dynasties, and at least one of the two mid-Egypt minor dynastic lines). And *not* by chiefs of the Ma(shwash), high priests, or anybody else in authority. In fact, from the 12th Dynasty to the Ptolemies, *nobody* is known to have used regnal years other than real kings, and certainly no high priests (*e.g.,* not even Harsiese under Osorkon II). It is because of these stark facts that we would need very clear proof indeed that the Theban high priests in the 21st Dynasty used their own independent regnal years in the manner advocated by Jansen-Winkeln.

§M. No such absolutely clear evidence is yet to be found. With only one highly dubious exception, *not a single year-date* is ever expressly attributed to any high priest of Amun at this period. The sole possible apparent exception is the seeming "Year 48 *n* High Priest of Amun, Menkheperre" on a bandage (below, 420, §387:46). Here, Menkheperre is in all likelihood simply following the custom of previous would-be royalties, by using for himself the regnal years of the *real* monarch, the reigning king – so, Hatshepsut using the year-count of Tuthmosis III, and Tewosret annexing the year-count of Siptah, for example. Hence, Menkheperre was in all probability using the year-count of Psusennes I here as his own. This at least has New-Kingdom precedent, which is more than can be said for our colleague's proposal. Previous to this one dubious example, and if the high priests really did use independent regnal years of their own, – why (to avoid ambiguity) did they *never* (in any known case) use the obvious type of formula in their series of dockets and bandages, "Year *x* under (*kher*) or of (*n*) the High priest of Amun, So-&-so"? The schema of the Year 6 mummy-dockets of Herihor is *exactly* like of many ostraca in the 20th Dynasty: Regnal Year *x* <*sc.*, of the King>, – day when such a dignitary came to do this or that. And in those earlier cases, the years are *known* to be those of the reigning king. So, there is *no* factual reason to read these years any differently here, but as those of *whm-mswt*, then of the 21st-Dynasty kings in Tanis. In the evolution of the Theban 21st-Dynasty mummy-bandage texts, the picture is clear. In types A.1 to B.3, the year-date is always at the end; in B.3, the year is explicitly that of the king, and so would likewise have been so in the earlier, less explicit dockets, of the same basic structure. One should note the bandage-docket of linen made by the high priest Masaharta, in a Year 18. Here, Jansen-Winkeln has to admit an exception, that this is *not* a year-date of Masaharta, if he served under his father the shadow-king Pinudjem I. So, why should any of these dates be assigned to the high priests? If, as we would expect, all the year-dates of the Dynasty (Theban and otherwise) belong to the reigns of the Tanite kings, then all difficulties disappear, and in Year 48 of Psusennes I, Menkheperre was at most simply using the old king's year-date as also his own (cf. already, 533-4, §435, below).

§N. Finally, Jansen-Winkeln's denial of any attestations or monuments of 21st-Dynasty Tanite kings in Thebes and Upper Egypt before Amenemope. This is categorically disproved by the former existence of the entirely royal and official stela of King Smendes at Dibabieh in S. Upper Egypt, in which he took the initiative for repair-works in Thebes. The lack of a year-date proves nothing (many Ramesside ceremonial stelae also lack year-dates, as does the official record of the Second Hittite Marriage of Ramesses II, for example, or the Elephantiné stela of Sethos I). Proper attribution of the Theban year-dates to these kings itself witnesses to their acceptance for dating purposes in the South.

In short, there is no scrap of real evidence so far, to assign wholly independent year-dates to the Theban high priests. Near the end of the aged Psusennes I's reign, Menkheperre ventured to use the former's Year 48 as if it were also his. But under Amenemope and onwards, even this tentative move towards further royal pretensions was in due time checked, and the reigning king's name came to be used more explicitly in even the modest bandage-dockets. It is always healthy to have accepted views tested or challenged, and Jansen-Winkeln's paper has certainly served to do this.

His more recent paper on the depletion of the kings' wealth in the Valley of Kings as being due to the Theban authorities drawing upon it rather like a bank-deposit (*ZÄS* 122(1995), 62-78) has much more to commend it, and links in with studies by Reeves and Hornung. Actual explicit proof of robbery of these tombs is very limited; largely to those of Tuthmosis IV (renewed under Haremhab), Tutankhamun (entered not too long after his burial?), and Ramesses VI (within the 20th Dynasty).

The recent paper by A. Niwinski (in I. Gamer-Wallert & W. Helck (eds.), *Gegengabe – Festschrift für Emma Brunner-Traut*, Tübingen, 1992, 235-262) is concerned mainly with the internal affairs of the reign of Ramesses XI and the *whm-mswt*, hence cannot be dealt with in detail here. However, in its later part (258-262) the level of unsupported speculation is too high to be credible. Despite his assertions (260), Ramesses XI continued to be the sole ruler whom people in authority recognised publicly (*e.g.,* Piankh, Nims Oracle; private stela, Year 27, Abydos, *KRI,* VI, 701:15). The *whm-mswt* reflected a redistribution of powers (Smendes in N., Herihor in S.) *under* the king, *not* instead of him. The fantasies about a coup d'état and Tentamun remain such. In civil administration (as noted above), Herihor was *not* king – he also dated by Ramesses XI in his own Khons-Temple oracle-stela! – only generalissimo, vizier and viceroy besides high priest; in no way did he function as 'pharaoh' outside of the walls of the Khons-temple in Karnak.

§O.   From the opening years of the 21st Dynasty, we move to its close. Customarily, the Dynasty is deemed to have ended with a king Psusennes II, successor to Siamun, and himself succeeded by his cousin-in-law, Shoshenq I, founder of a new line of kings (22nd Dynasty). Manetho lists such a king for 14 years (Africanus) or 35 years (Eusebius; Armenian version), better understood as an error for *15 years. In the first-hand sources, there is a king Tyetkheperure (Har)-Psibkhenno (=Psusennes) who fits the bill satisfactorily; see already, pp. 8, 11-13 below. Year-dates for his reign are (so far) few and elusive A Year 12 (below, 432, §390:80) could belong to either Siamun or Psusennes II, while one Year 13 (432, §391:87) could belong to either Siamun, Psusennes II or Shoshenq I. Another Year 13 (423, §391:86) can, however, belong only to Psusennes II or Shoshenq I. And finally, a not-certain Year 5 (or 4) on linen (423, §391:86) made by a Theban high priest Psusennes (after Pinudjem II and before Iuput) would be attributable to the reign of Psusennes II. This docket raises the question as to whether Psusennes the high priest is the same person as Psusennes II the king, or not. See below.

More recently, Dodson sought to resolve the matter by making Psusennes II (both high priest and king) a shadow-contemporary of Shoshenq I (like Pinudjem I with Psusennes I), and so the Year 5(?) would actually be that of Shoshenq I, who would have suceeded Siamun directly, with no reign between Siamun and Shoshenq I. See A. Dodson, *RdE* 38(1987), 49-54. This solution is extremely elegant, and at first sight very alluring. The two Psusennes are one, the date-lines are all accounted-for, and the known relationships of Shoshenq I and Psusennes II Tyetkheperure by marriage of their offspring can all be fitted-in. If there were no other complications one would be inclined to accept it.

§P. But life is not so simple. The first result is to leave a yawning hiatus in Egyptian chronology, of the extent of which Dodson was clearly unaware. If Ramesses II is agreed to have reigned from 1279 to 1213 BC, and as Shoshenq I cannot be placed earlier than 945 BC (on the Assyrian-backed Hebrew synchronism), we have 268 years from the accession of Merenptah to that of Shoshenq I. If we (i) allow (as commonly done, on good first-hand evidence) 10 years Merenptah, 6 years Sethos II, 8 years Siptah+Tewosret, 2 years Setnakht, 31 years Ramesses III, 6 years Ramesses IV, 4 years Ramesses V, 8 (rather than 7) years each for Ramesses VI and VII, 3 years Ramesses VIII (Yr.1 + Book of Sothis), 18 years Ramesses IX, and 28 years Ramesses XI, and follow fashionable prejudice by reckoning Amenmesses at zero (within Sethos II's reign) and Ramesses X at 3 years only, then from Merenptah to Ramesses XI inclusive would total 135 years. Then, for the 21st Dynasty, we have a well-agreed 26 years Smendes, 4 years Amenemnisu, 46 years Psusennes I (yrs.47-48 coregent with Amenemope), 9 years Amenemope, 6 years Osorkon the Elder, and finally 19 years of Siamun, omitting Psusennes II, total only now 110 years. Added to our Ramesside 135 years, this accounts now for only 245 years – leaving a glaring discrepancy of 268-245 = *23 years*. There is no way that this "generation-gap" can be met without an independent reign of Psusennes II. If we allow him 14 years or at most 15 years, then the discrepancy sinks to 8/9 years. This discrepancy can only then be resolved by allowing Amenmesses his sole reign of 3 years and Rameses X a reign of 7 years (Year 8, graffito 1860a), not just 3 years; the remaining year or 2 years could be added to the reign of Ramesses XI/*whm-mswt* (giving 29/30 years and 11/12 years respectively). There is absolutely *no* warrant to lengthen the 21st Dynasty any further, nor any acceptable "dodge" for ruling out a sole reign of Amenmesses and only 3 years for Ramesses X, with 7 to 9 superfluous years that cannot be convincingly attributed elsewhere (excluded for Sethos II, Ramesses III, and IV, for example). To redistribute *23 years* (no independent reign of Psusennes II) would be impossible.

§Q. Also against a shadow-reign for Psusennes II is his inclusion in Manetho's list; the latter simply does not recognise such reigns. Dodson's appeal to the precedent of Queen Hatshepsut (53-54) is invalid. Manetho gives her reign (closely correctly) at 21 years 9 months, but does **not** then give a full 53 years to Tuthmosis III! Instead, we have 30 years 10 months (31 years) wrongly attributed to Amenophis II, to whom belongs the 25 years 10 months (26 years) wrongly given to Tuthmosis III ("Mephramuthosis"), cf. long since, W. Helck, *Manetho,* 1956, p.66 end. In other words, Manetho counted 22 years for Hatshepsut, 31 years for Tuthmosis III alone (totalling 53 years), then Amenophis II 26 years (attributing the coregency to the son, not the father, as is usual in Manetho). Again, Manetho gives an independent reign to Smenkhkare, which is likely (after a brief coregency) and for Amemesses which is possible (despite current fashion). The place of burial of Psusennes II as king is not certainly known; one would expect it to be at Tanis. And Yoyotte (in *Tanis, l'or des pharaons,* Paris, 1987, 136f.) would locate the burial of

Psusennes II in the antechamber of Tanite Tomb III of Psusennes I, identifying shabtis and statuettes found there of a Psusennes beloved of Amun with Psusennes II on typological grounds (like those of Siamun). Dodson's objections to this (*RdE* 38(1987), 54, and in *CdE*63(1988), 232-3) may be ruled out as invalid again – it is commonplace for royalty at least to have more than one type or series of shabti-figures in their burials (one thinks of the faience and wooden series of Sethos I, and (as Dodson himself admits, *CdE*, 233 n.3) the variety used in other cases at Tanis and Deir el-Bahri cache, etc.

§R. What is clear is that Psusennes II (king) could also bear the title of High Priest of Amun, as is indicated by a cane-top of the former Saurma collection (*G3*, 302:IV), in precisely the same way as earlier Tanite kings. At Abydos, we also have an untidy graffito in the name of this king, giving his proper cartouche-titles (but without cartouche-signs), the title of high priest of Amen-Re-Sonter (twice), plus the military title "army-leader" (*hauty*) twice, and the royal epithet, "who makes good laws for [Eg]ypt". A sherd from Umm el-Ga'ab at Abydos also names Tyetkheperure [Psusennes II], *G3*, 302:III. The Abydos graffito may be analysed and set out as follows (utilising improvements from Černý, given by J. von Beckerath, *Handbuch der ägyptischen Königsnamen*, 1984, 99-100, cf. 256):

"King of S & N Egypt, Lord of Both Lands, *Tyetkheperure Setepenre*, <beloved of> Amen-Re-Sonter;

High Priest of Amen-Re-Sonter, Son of Re, Lord of Crowns,

Army-leader, *Psusennes (II) Meriamun*, [LPH?, of] the forces.

High Priest of Amen-Re-Sonter, who makes good laws [for Eg]ypt, the Army-leader,

Pharaoh *Psusennes (II) Meriamun.*"

(The italics used here indicate the uncartouched cartouche-names; this version also corrects implicitly Dodson's transcript, *RdE* 38, 51.)

The occasion for such graffiti and pot(s) at Umm el-Ga'ab is not far to seek: the visit to Abydos by the Great Chief of the Ma, Shoshenq (future Shoshenq I), and his royal master (Psusennes II himself) on the occasion of the inauguration of the Abydene statue-cult of Shoshenq's father Nimlot (text, A.M. Blackman, *JEA* 27(1941), 83-95), following on an oracle of Amun at Thebes.

§S. If Psusennes II Tyetkheperure, the pharaoh, and Psusennes "III", high priest of Theban Amun, were one and the same, then it is easy to concede that Psusennes II as both the reigning Theban pontiff *and* reigning pharaoh would have officiated at Thebes as both high priest and king on behalf of his relative and most powerful man in the kingdom, Shoshenq. While Psusennes II reigned up north and retained his high-priestly title, doubtless the 2nd and 3rd Prophets of Amun would look after strictly Theban affairs. The royal status of Psusennes II/III is no problem – as son of Pinudjem II (grandson of Psusennes I via Menkheperre and Istemkheb C), our man was a great-grandson of Psusennes I in direct line. So, he had a prior claim to the throne over Shoshenq, whose nearest link (to Osorkon the Elder) was that of distant nephew; Osorkon the Elder's links with the line of Amenemope are as yet unknown. Shoshenq thus strengthened his family's position by the marriage-alliance of his son Osorkon with Psusennes II's daughter Maatkare B, a fact long known.   That Psusennes II/III ever made his residence at Abydos (Dodson, *RdE* 38, 52) is a flight of fancy best forgotten.

If we identify Psusennes II/III as one man, what befalls the bandage-epigraph of Year 5? In the light of the formulations of the Abydos graffito, the solution may be simpler than most of us have imagined hitherto.   Namely that the Thebans felt free to cite their man in Tanis by his Theban office as easily as by his assumed Tanite kingship, and so this Year 5(?) is simply of Psusennes II, but content to cite him by his Theban title of High Priest of Amun. This would be the only example (besides the Year 48 *n* Menkheperre, §M above) of a regnal year attributable to a Theban high priest – but *only* because he was already real king as well!

§T.   In one other direction, Dodson has almost certainly solved another longstanding minor riddle of this period. This is the identity of the mysterious Hedjhiq...re, associated with a cartouche of Psusennes II among the copies of Sir J.G. Wilkinson's copies of royal titles. In *GM* 106(1988), 15-19, and *JEA* 79(1993), 267-8, he makes a good case for reading the traces in the questionable cartouche as Hedj-kheper-re [below which one would then restore Setepenre]– *i.e.,* Shoshenq I. We would then have yet another association of Shoshenq I with the outgoing king Psusennes II, in a private graffito.

22nd-23rd Dynasties.

§U. The first major gain since 1986 concerns the formerly elusive Takeloth I. In the tomb of Osorkon II was found the burial of another king, in an outer chamber (2 in Dodson's plan, *CdE* 63(1988), 222, fig.1). The burial in question belonged to a pharaoh entitled Hedjkheperre Setepenre and Takeloth Meriamun. As the only known Takeloth with that prenomen was Takeloth II, this burial was naturally attributed by Montet and everyone since to Takeloth II. However, in 1987, Jansen-Winkeln drew attention (*Varia Aegyptiaca* 3(1987), 253-258, and Abb.1) to a scene in Osorkon II's tomb, in which he is shown adoring Osiris and Udjo (as a uraeus). In substantial agreement with Jansen-Winkeln, the main text may be rendered:

(1) "[Made?] by the King of S & N Egypt, Lord of Both Lands, *Usimare Setepenamun*, Son of Re, Lord of Crowns, *Osorkon II Meriamun*, [to furnish?] the Osiris King (2) *Takeloth Meriamun*, in his Mansion which is [an abo]de of the Sun-disc: "I have caused him to rest in this Mansion, in the vicinity of (3) "Hidden-of-Name" (=Amun), according to the doing by a son of benefactions for his father, [to] furnish the one who made his fortune(?), in conformity with what Horus-Son-of-Isis commanded (4) for his father Wennufer. How pleasant (it is) in my heart, for the Lord of the Gods!"

Above Osorkon II are his cartouches, and: "a son, furnishing the one who created (=begot) him."

§V.   As Jansen-Winkeln pertinently points out, this can only be Osorkon II honouring his father Takeloth I, and burying (reburying?) him in his own tomb ("Mansion"), close to the temple of Amun – which is true of these Tanite royal tombs. Hence, it is but a short step to identify the burial of a Takeloth in Chamber 2 as that of Takeloth I, not II. This attribution gains in likelihood from other data found in this tomb: a shabti of Tashedkhons mother of Takeloth I (Pasenhor stela), and a heart-scarab of 'Takeloth Meriamun' (not Si-Ese); cf. below, 311, nn.381-2. Hence, it was Takeloth I who first used the prenomen Hedjkheperre Setepenre (in imitation of his grandfather Shoshenq I), being followed in this by Takeloth II. The only clear distinction, then, between Takeloth I and II (as both also use the epithet Meriamun) is that Takeloth II uses also the epithet Si-Ese, "Son of Isis", in his second cartouche. A second marker suggested by Jansen-Winkeln (with some reserve) is that Takeloth I has his name spelt with the vertical *t*-sign (Gardiner U 33, *ti* becoming *t*), while Takeloth II and III use the small loaf *t*-sign (X 1), and the rope-tether sign (V 13). This criterion (especially if combined with the use or not of Si-Ese) seems sound. This would suggest attributing to Takeloth I (not II) a donation-stela of Year 9 (from Bubastis), another in Berlin (also from Bubastis) and a fragment in the former Grant collection (references, below, 327, n.263).

This also bears on the high priests of Ptah at Memphis and the Serapeum. There, a block is known bearing the name of a high priest Merenptah and a pair of cartouches hitherto attributed to Takeloth II which, in fact, correspond precisely to those now attributable to Takeloth I (no Si-Ese; tall *t*). Therefore, it seems proper to move this priest back in time to the reign of Takeloth I. If we do so, this removes an anomaly in the sequence of high priests of Ptah. Merenptah can now be set neatly between the end of the line of Shedsunefertem in that office (ending with his grandson Osorkon A), and the installation of his own son Shoshenq D by Osorkon II, (cf. below 192-4). Thus, the line of Shoshenq D each followed-on in office, without Merenptah's intervening. He may have been a brother of Osorkon A, or else totally unrelated to the line of Shedsunefertem.

§W.   Where, then, does this leave Takeloth II? The suggestion has been made that he was really a Theban ruler (D.A. Aston, *JEA* 75(1989), 153), and largely contemporary with Shoshenq III. These are two quite separate issues. The monuments of Takeloth II are, in fact, very sparse at Thebes. Besides the "Chronicle" of his son Prince Osorkon (B), we have little more than his titles in a chapel of the God's Wife, Karomama Merytmut I (below, 323, n.444), two Priestly Annals fragments in the Amun-temple (below, 331 n.486), and the Year 25 stela of his daughter Karoama, one of the college of singers of the Interior of Amun. Bluntly, three fragments and a minor stela do not a Theban king make! Many northern potentates dedicated daughters to the college of Amun's female singers (see Yoyotte, *CRAIBL:1961*, 1962, 43-52), so this item proves nothing. The family links of Takeloth II with Thebes are now considered to be less in number than was once envisaged: perhaps only two daughters married-off to Thebans, not four; cf.

below, 578 §516, correcting 328f., §290. Furthermore, the Theban marriage of a daughter of Takeloth II's son the high priest and governor Nimlot is no more "evidence" that Takeloth II and Nimlot were Theban, than that Shoshenq I was a "Theban" ruler because he appointed his son Iuput as high priest of Amun, and married-off a daughter to one Theban notable, while Iuput did likewise to another (see 288-9, below). Aston's claim that Takeloth II's family relationships with Thebes were somehow different from other Tanite kings (p.140) is spurious. His claim (p.140) that Takeloth II's queen Karomama D lived at Thebes merely because Nimlot C (her son), the military governor of Upper Egypt was high priest there is a clear methodological error. Nor does his list of "Theban" connections (p.141) prove anything more for Takeloth II than identical ones do for any other Tanite king. Thus Iuput son of Shoshenq I might have been buried at Thebes or Abydos – but this would not make of Shoshenq I a Theban king. The poverty of Takeloth II's northern monuments is no more surprising than for (*e.g.*) Osochor and Psusennes II in the 21st Dynasty, or for Osorkon IV in the 22nd (even though Piankhy's stela proves him to be northern). In short, Takeloth II has left *nothing* at Thebes that even remotely proves that he had his seat there. There is not the remotest trace of any burial of his at Thebes – whereas the miscellaneous unidentified bodies in the Tanite royal tombs may include his. In short, whatever he is, Takeloth II is *not* provenly a precursor of the 23rd Dynasty at Thebes (or elsewhere). The title "God, Ruler of Thebes" occasionally used by Takeloth II (Aston, 142) proves absolutely nothing – this precise epithet is used by Shoshenq V *at Tanis* (P. Montet, *Le lac sacré de Tanis,* Paris, 1966, pls.48:40, 52:89, 60:144 & 144*bis*, 64:215, 65:212). Its occurrence in either a prenomen or nomen is immaterial.

There is, in fact, no positive reason whatsoever to remove him from the main line of the 22nd Dynasty in Tanis. Quite the opposite; can one *really* imagine that Takeloth II sat enthroned in Thebes, watching helplessly as the Thebans with impunity repeatedly rejected his son Osorkon B's high-priesthood in favour of their own candidates for years at a time, without even his lifting a royal finger in protest? This does not just strain credulity – it snaps it. The only question is whether Takeloth II's 25 years of reign overlapped with anyone else's. Here, Aston makes much of supposed problems in the spans of genealogies and terms of office. Here, we have no fixed dates either for people's lifespans, or for their terms of office in almost all cases. Hence, his speculations on this point are too subjective to carry much weight; Bierbrier found no basic problem here, in his genealogical work of 1975. Thus, it is misleading to say that three letter-writers of Pharaoh were in office under Osorkon II, and equate this with three *generations* under that king (p.146). One may have served only 6 or 8 years (from a previous reign), his son 15 years, and then his grandson 3 or 4 years (and into a succeeding reign). It is an error to equate generations and terms-of-office. For a sole reign of Takeloth II, the comment "static" (p.143) is a misnomer.

§X.   At times, Aston exaggerates. The 24-year reign of Osorkon II is quite sufficient to cope with the known Theban high priests of Amun for his reign, as pointed out on p. 200 below, and unwisely ignored by Aston (pp.147-8). Smendes III would have died sometime in Osorkon II's reign (by *Year 13?), and have been succeeded by Harsiese A, who quickly claimed royal titles, perhaps in imitation of his possible father Shoshenq II. Harsiese was a truly "Theban" shadow-king: buried in Thebes, with a cult there – unlike Takeloth II! His son was not high priest (K. Jansen-Winkeln, JEA 81 (1995), 137f., fig.4, whose treatment of Dyn. 23 falls with that of the Leahy-Aston chronology, cf. §§AA ff., below). Then comes Nimlot C – again, far better known from posthumous mentions (*e.g.*,by Osorkon B) than from his own term of office. And as foreseen by me (p.200, below, *pace* both Redford and Aston), it is quite possible that Nimlot C soon gave place to his son Takeloth F before the end of Osorkon II's reign, while this Takeloth F then continued into the reign of Takeloth II, until replaced by the notorious Prince Osorkon B (by Year 11). Aston's mention of Harnakht is a mere red herring, as this child "officiated" in Tanis, not Thebes. There is not one scintilla of respectable evidence for arbitrarily extending the reign of Osorkon II by 15/20 years, giving us a really "static" gap – such a total lack of year-dates is no improvement on Aston's grumble about the seeming 22 years "gap" in the narrative of the Chronicle of Prince Osorkon (*JEA 75*, 143). There is a real difference here. For the imaginary extension of the reign of Osorkon II, we have *no* documentation. In Osorkon B's case, the latter passes-over silently the intervening pontificates of his Theban rivals, for whom we *do* have documentation! After all, they *are* his foes and rivals! We have Harsiese B (Years 6 and 12 of Shoshenq III, and Years 8, 18, 19 of Pedubast I), and Takeloth E (Year 23 of Pedubast I and Year 6 of Shoshenq VI [former IV]). For an imaginary static gap of 20 years under Osorkon II, we have nothing. Nor can that gap be assuaged by inserting a Pedubast II before Osorkon IV (p.145), cf. below. In short, a Theban Takeloth II is a mirage, and there is no compelling reason to overlap his reign with that of any other Tanite king – the only result of such a procedure is to create yawning gaps elsewhere.

§Y.   Other rulers require consideration as possible additions to the 22nd Dynasty: (i) was there an unidentified king who reigned between Shoshenq III and Pimay? And (ii) was there a second Hedjkheperre Shoshenq (bearing the additional epithets "God, Ruler of Heliopolis"), distinct from the famous Hedjkheperre Shoshenq I? Various lines of evidence may, it seems, bring these two queries together.

A Great Chief of the Libu, Niumateped (B) is known to have been in office in Year 8 of Shoshenq V, having been preceded by an In-Amun-nef-nebu A in Year 31 of Shoshenq III, and followed by another four such chiefs (cf. below, 490, 599, Table 21). More problematic has been another mention of such a chief Niumatiped (A), author of another donation-stela, dated to Year 10 of Hedjkheperre Shoshenq, "God, Ruler of Heliopolis" (below, 291f., n.278). Yoyotte had wondered if the final epithet might indicate Year 10 of Shoshenq III, not I, as the date of Niumateped A; I had objected that ten years into a new reign was a little late to be confusing the prenomens of Takeloth II and Shoshenq III (below, 291f.n.278). But in various amateur publications, D. Rohl first suggested that Niumateped A and B were perhaps one and the same man, that Hedjkheperre Shoshenq "God, Ruler of Heliopolis" was distinct from Shoshenq I (and much later), and that he was in fact nearer the time of Shoshenq III-V; furthermore, a second burial in the tomb of Shoshenq III at Tanis had canopic jars of this later Shoshenq. That this secondary burial was not Shoshenq I's (as Montet thought) was also mooted by Dodson (*CdE* 63(1988), 229-231). Rohl made the "new" Shoshenq a contemporary of Shoshenq III-V.

But a much neater solution has now been offered by Dodson (*GM* 137(1993), 53-58, esp. 56f., with previous literature). We know from the records of the Apis-burials at Memphis that 52 years elapsed from the accession of Shoshenq III to that of Pimay; and hitherto, most scholars had been content to credit Shoshenq III with that length of reign. Montet had theorised that an "inconnu" might have reigned during the later part of that span (Montet, *Tombeau de Chéchanq III*, Paris, 1960, 8-9, but on mistaken grounds). The highest-attested year-date of Shoshenq III is Year 39 (p. 340, below), so there would be, in fact, room for a 12/13 year reign if Shoshenq III had died in Year 39 or 40. It is the merit of Dodson to have suggested that the "new" Shoshenq (having a date-line with Niumateped of Year 10) would fit in here precisely. This seems to the present writer to be eminently acceptable. Its result for Niumateped (A=B) is to give him a span of 2/3 years under the new king, 6 years under Pimay, and at least 8 years under Shoshenq V, total minimum, 16/17 years in office, probably to be extended slightly back in time in real life. One consequence of the new arrangement (overlooked by both Dodson and Rohl) is that Papyrus Brooklyn 16.205 of a Year 49 followed by a Year 4 must now be attributed to the time of Psusennes I and Amenemope (21st Dynasty), not to Shoshenq III and Pimay (cf. 103, §83 below).

If so, then the 22nd Dynasty had a Shoshenq III (Usimare) followed by a shorter-lived Shoshenq IV (Hedjkheperre, and "God, Ruler of Heliopolis"), then Pimay, then Shoshenq V. The previous Shoshenq IV (on whom, cf. below) is then VI, and the probably fictional (previous) VI becomes VII.

§Z.   So, we gain one king and lose one Chief of the Libu, but without any change in overall chronology. Matters are perhaps different with another suggested addition to the 22nd Dynasty. Pedubast I (Usimare), attested in both north and south, is undoubtedly the Pedubastis, founder of Manetho's 23rd Dynasty (cf. just below); equally, Pedubast III (Seheribre) is outside our period, on criteria offered by Yoyotte. We have still a Pedubast II (Sehetepibenre), attested by monuments found in Tanis and Memphis, and others unprovenanced (pp. 98, 396 below; Habachi, *ZÄS* 93(1966), 69-74, pls.5-6). There is also the Pedubast (*Putubishti*) recorded by the Assyrians as ruler of Tanis in the 7th century BC. The latter may very well be the same as Pedubast II – right place, right name – and in such a guise would also be the

King Pedubast in the Demotic tale about *The Contest for the Breastplate of Inaros* (pp. 455ff., below).

However, in recent studies, A. Leahy would prefer to insert Pedubast II into the main line of the 22nd Dynasty, between Shoshenq V and Osorkon IV. See A. Leahy in Leahy (ed.), *Libya and Egypt, c.1300-750 BC*, London (SOAS/Society for Libyan Studies), 1990, 188f. This is possible in theory, but unlikely in practice. His depreciation of the Pedubast who ruled in Tanis during the Assyrian invasions (188/9) is entirely unjustified, and rests on no positive fact. The prenomen Sehetepibenre is of a type totally foreign to the 22nd Dynasty – *all* of whose kings (from Takeloth I onward) used only the prenomens Usimare, Hedjkheperre or Akheperre with sundry secondary epithets. To insert *this* Pedubast into such a series is wildly improbable. Also, there is very little chronological space to fit in such a ruler for more than perhaps 4 or 5 years at most, given that there is *no* factual basis for removing Takeloth II from the Tanite line, or for overlapping him with anyone else in that line at present (§X above). Furthermore, Leahy ignores the rather special situation at Tanis. We have not only the stonework of this Pedubast, but remains left by other kinglets, of good style: Gemenef-Khons-bak, and the non-Old-Kingdom Neferkare. When Shabako took over Egypt, he is reputed to have slain Bakenranef; and he may possibly have removed any other 'crowned heads' from local rule, leaving in place non-royal chiefs of the Ma, local governors and mayors. At any rate, Osorkon IV and Iuput II are also heard of no more, nor any other local royalties in his time; under Shebitku, we have no data. But by Taharqa's time, there is some reason to posit the reappearance of a local (proto-Saite) dynasty in Sais: Stephinates, Nekauba and Necho I (cf. already below, 145f.), from *c.*685 BC, if not *c.*695 BC. If so, then the local governors of Tanis may have followed suit – *they* had been a seat of kings from long before Sais! The inability of Taharqa to hold back the Assyrian invaders would have weakened his standing among ambitious local princes. The Assyrian occupation gave them scope for local aggrandizement. Hence, a local Tanite dynasty of Gemenef-Khons-bak, Pedubast II and Neferkare (into the earliest years of Psamtek I) makes good sense of the material remains from Tanis. That the Assyrian term *sharru* includes every kind of local mayor, etc. (Leahy, 188/9) is true – but it does *not* exclude local kinglets, where they existed (as in the case of the Saite princes). The style of these Tanite mini-kings is more Saite than Libyan. And finally, the Pedubastis of Tanis in the Demotic tales includes being saved from an Eastern power, involving Assyrians explicitly (in *Egyptians and Amazons,* III::18,27,39) and the ruler *3slstni*, who has (despite Leahy) every likelihood of being Esarhaddon. For Demotic *l* = foreign *r*, cf. also *Combat, Breastplate, Inaros,* XVIII:26, where *3libi* stands for 'Arabian'. The attribution of Pedubast II Sehetepibenre (cf. all the *-ibre* prenomens, from the proto-Saite Dynasty onward!) to the 7th century BC under Assyria's shadow has much more to commend it than an arbitrary insertion into the 22nd Dynasty, as von Beckerath has also noted (*GM* 147(1995), 9,10,13) on similar multiple grounds. The historical geography given on pp. 456-461 below (late Libyan/Nubian to Saite/Persian periods) should be (re)read carefully in this context.

§AA. Now we must turn to the controverted matter of the 23rd Dynasty. The 'Birmingham School' (Leahy, Aston, Taylor) would in effect dismiss the Manethonic data almost completely, and locate some kings actually in Thebes as their base (Pedubast I (Usimare) to Rudamun), along with Takeloth II earlier. The only real reason for this belief is that the majority of these kings' mentions are from (or in) Thebes.   This (despite Leahy's disclaimer, p.185) represents a clear failure to distinguish between a (now lost) distribution of monuments as it was in the 9th-8th centuries BC, and the very different distribution of *surviving and recovered* monuments as it is now.   Especially in the light of the situation for other periods. The data in Manetho have also been badly misunderstood.   Read (again) §102, pp.128-130 below.   First of all, when Manetho's *Epitome* derives a dynasty from a particular place, this is its reputed place of *origin,* not necessarily its capital.   Thus, the 1st and 2nd Dynasties are "from Thi(ni)s", but we know that they created and used Memphis as capital, while still having tombs at Abydos.   The 5th aside, the 3rd to 8th Dynasties are attributed to Memphis, in practice the capital as well as place-of-origin – and certainly capital for the 5th (whether it came from Elephantiné, so Manetho, or Sakhebu, so Papyrus Westcar; perhaps Sakhebu or the like was eventually misunderstood as a *Sekhet (>*Saht)-iebu, 'district of Elephantiné').   In the Middle Kingdom, Thebes was both the home town and capital for the 11th Dynasty; but while Manetho similarly derives the 12th Dynasty from Thebes (cf. Neferrohu's Ameny from the South), its real capital was at Ithet-tawy, its new administrative centre just south from Memphis (the Turin Canon's House of Ithet-tawy).   As with the 12th, so with the 13th Dynasty.   Again, the 18th Dynasty is derived from Thebes, but (from Tuthmosis I onwards) it adopted Memphis as administrative capital, while using Thebes for its necropolis.   The 19th and 20th Dynasties are also described as Theban, whereas the 19th at least we would now regard as from the East Delta.   But its founder Ramesses I had been Theban vizier (for what that is worth).

So, Manetho's *Epitome* derives the 21st Dynasty from Tanis; in the light of Wenamun's narrative, that appears to be true.   And (along with the permanent administrative centre at Memphis) it served as East-Delta capital also, where these kings were buried.   But with the 22nd Dynasty, it is otherwise – point of origin and capitals differ (as with the 1st, 5th, 12th, 13th, 18th, etc. Dynasties).   It is described as Bubastite by origin – while (alongside Memphis) it is clear archaeologically that Tanis was its Delta capital, having also the royal necropolis.

The 23rd Dynasty must be viewed (in Manetho) in this light, and not otherwise. It is derived from Tanis – which for *family* origins is entirely logical, an an offshoot of the 22nd Dynasty – another bunch of kings Shoshenq (VI), Osorkon (III) and Takeloth (III), etc.   But its capital was certainly *not* at Tanis.   Where it was is a matter for investigation. The mere number of references at Thebes in itself proves nothing. As an archaeological site, Thebes still has many surviving buildings, and has produced an unparalleled wealth of other material, from the 11th Dynasty to Roman times. The contrast with the other great centres – Memphis and Heliopolis – could hardly be greater. Heliopolis today is merely a vast dust-pan, marked only by its obelisk, a late Ramesside gateway, and sundry rubble. Yet, almost every king of all Egypt would have been associated with it; Piankhy did not go there for nothing. Memphis, the kingdom's real capital, is now only a colossus, rubble of other statuary, the foundations of the West Hall, and remains of a few minor chapels. Yet we know from inscriptional and classical sources that the temple and town sites of both Memphis and Heliopolis rivalled Thebes. In the Delta, things are largely worse. Tanis is sandy mud-heaps, and a few heaps of granite blocks alone mark the temples within its great precinct. Bubastis is a limited ruin of two New-Kingdom and later temples, an Old-Kingdom structure – and precious little else. And nowhere else in the Delta even reaches this state of preservation or excavation. It is, therefore, in fact unsound to weigh the bulk of Theban remains against those from Memphis and the Delta, when 95% of the latter areas are gone and lost forever, and in part unrecovered. Furthermore, just how much monumental work has the 23rd Dynasty left at Thebes? Merely a minor gate under Pedubast (by a son of Shoshenq III!), one very small temple of Osiris Heqa-Djet, a pair of jambs of Osorkon III, a few blocks and precious little else. Using the Birmingham school's method of argument, one could argue for a sub-dynasty of purely Theban rulers within the 18th Dynasty: Tuthmosis II, Hatshepsut, Smenkhkare, Ay are not famous for their northern monuments. And Shoshenq I left far more at Thebes than anywhere else; his name scarcely occurs at Tanis or Bubastis. Conversely, there is not one scintilla of respectable evidence for any 23rd-Dynasty royal establishment at Thebes, or any royal tomb at Thebes; not one tiny scrap of any funerary equipment of *anyone* from Pedubast I to Rudamun has ever yet come to light. The early Demotic references to a *hwt* of Pharaoh *Wsirtn* under Necho II, Amasis and Darius I in Western Thebes, helpfully given by Leahy in *Egypt and Libya*, 186 (from M. Malinine, *Choix de textes juridiques*, I, Paris, 1953, 88 §6) in themselves prove nothing. In the light of Malinine's translation once (p.87) as "le Sanctuaire" and once (p.88) as "chateau" or a "tombe royale", there is not a scrap of certainty as whether this is the tomb or some other minor chapel (memorial or deity-cult) of a possible Osorkon. The appeal to the occurrence of donation-stelae (Leahy, *Libya & Egypt*, 185) is pointless; the vagaries of discovery-by-chance are no better than those of planned excavation. Chance finds are the very opposite of a systematic sampling of the entire Delta, by their very randomness. All this is clutching at straws.

If not Thebes, where? There is doubtless more than one possibility. Leontopolis still remains a possibility; the burial there of a *Queen* Kama *is* by definition a royal burial, regardless of whether she was linked to Osorkon III or not. Note, again, the details set out, pp. 579f., below. Fudging this point is not helpful. Again, in the

Delta in 728 BC *temp.* Piankhy, his perfectly accurate geo-political map at that point in time gives us two senior pharaohs (note the order on his stela, scene) and two only, in the Delta: Osorkon of Tanis/Bubastis (the basic 22nd-Dyn. fief), and Iuput II, there set in Ta-remu or Leontopolis. The explicit evidence of Piankhy and Queen Kama is qualitatively worth more than many tons of irrelevant temple-masonry at Thebes, only very modestly comparable with what that other Delta-king Shoshenq I erected there. Despite the claims of Spencer and Spencer, Heracleopolis was already the seat of a continuous series of governors (not kings!) from Nimlot C under Osorkon II through to Takeloth, the later Takeloth III, before Rudamun's son-in-law Pef-tjau-awy-Bast finally appeared there as a kinglet. Their statement (*JEA* 72(1986), 200) that no 23rd-Dynasty ruler is acknowledged in the Delta is wrong. We have a donation-stela of Year 23 of Pedubast I (Usimare) from Bubastis, besides a dedication at Memphis in Year 6 (Ewelhon, visiting from Pi-Sekhemkheperre, south of Medum), and another stela (Copenhagen) reported from Memphis, with a land-donation by a chief from Heracleopolis, relating to terrain of a Shoshenq-foundation seemingly in the East Delta (cf. Schulman, *JARCE* 5(1966), 38 & n.17). The suggestion that they were brought to Memphis in antiquity (Leahy, *Libya & Egypt,* 182, following Redford) is simply evading the archaeological evidence. Iuput II (Usimare) was sufficiently important to be dated-by, by a chief of Mendes in Year 21; a bronze hinge, whether from Tell Moqdam or Buto, is also of East-Delta origin. It is significant that Iuput occurs only twice as a royal name, once as the co-regent of Pedubast I (and so, by the explicit double-dateline, contra Leahy, *Libya & Egypt,* 183), and once as this Delta king of Piankhy's time. Despite the sharp remarks by Leahy, *ibid.,* 184, there is *no* guarantee whose Year 11 was used by Harnakht B. If his son Smendes V could date by Iuput II (Year 21), there is no inherent reason why Smendes' father may not already have dated by Year 11 of Osorkon III (except Leahy's hostility to this concept). The alternative, now, would be to identify this Year 11 as pertaining to the "new" Shoshenq IV, direct successor of Shoshenq III, giving a date of *c.* 775 instead of *c.* 776! So, in effect, no difference chronologically.

The accusation that two parallel dynasties in the East Delta, only one being recognised in Memphis, "strains credulity to breaking-point" (Leahy, *Libya & Egypt,* 179) is itself a palpable nonsense in view of the known facts. From the time of Tuthmosis I to that of Takeloth II (some 600 years...), people in Thebes had been dating by kings who lived mainly in Memphis and then Memphis and the East Delta. More specifically, Memphis had had long, intimate links (through the high-priesthood of Ptah) with the family of the 22nd Dynasty ever since the late 21st, and it was the 22nd Dynasty that had originally succeeded to the rule of all Egypt. With the division of the kingship, the Memphite priests merely stayed (in their bull-cult datings, certainly) with dating by the customary dynasty, ignoring the years of the other line. Members of the other line could be dated-by, by whoever recognised them, as in the case of the private texts at Bubastis, Memphis and Mendes. Under Takeloth II and Prince Osorkon B, Theban disenchantment with the ruling Dynasty reached the stage of growing revolt; when the new line declared itself, they (being "agin the Government") eagerly dated by the new and (in their eyes) rival line. Thus, no 22nd-Dynasty datelines ever occurred again after Shoshenq III, and then (after year 6), only with the stubborn Prince Osorkon. So, where is the problem? Significantly, the new line got its sympathisers into power south of Memphis – such as Ewelhon at Pi-Sekhemkheperre under Pedubast I. Then, Osorkon III's own son Takeloth became ruler in Heracleopolis; ever-growing links were forged *with* Thebes, which is *not* the same thing as personally reigning *in* Thebes.

§BB. The old and long discredited idea that Prince Osorkon *must* somehow have been also King Osorkon III (*e.g.,*Leahy, *Libya & Egypt*, 192-3) really does stretch credulity – and well beyond breaking-point. Only by arbitrarily telescoping the reign of Takeloth II into that of Shoshenq III can this be made to work biologically; otherwise his active lifespan becomes incredible. The guesses made by Leahy (pp.192/3) about hiatuses, tentative claims to kingship before becoming king, back-dated years and suchlike desperate expedients condemn themselves. But there is far worse. It is very clear that the Thebans had no qualms whatsoever in accepting either the high-priesthood or the kingship of Osorkon III, wherever he hailed from. That, surely, is agreed. Yet, earlier, they had rebelled against, rejected and refused *Prince* Osorkon at almost every opportunity – typically, on his last known public appearance (Shoshenq III, Year 39), he and a brother descended on Thebes, and "overthrew everyone who fought against them". Yet, on Leahy's hypothesis, we are actually asked to believe that, embarrassingly soon afterwards, the Thebans miraculously forgave the murderous old rogue, and clasped him to their bosoms evermore as High Priest, then as King (as Osorkon III)!! Surely, this is fantasy.

§CC. Two other points about Manetho need to be considered: his treatment of parallel kings and dynasties, and the state of the *Epitome* on the 22nd/23rd Dynasties. First, parallel kings and dynasties. It is very clear that, when the reigns of two rulers overlap, the Manethonic lists attribute the overlapping years (as in coregencies) to only *one* ruler, not both, and often to the new ruler. So, with the reigns of Hatshepsut, Tuthmosis III and Amenophis II in §Q above, for example. With whole dynasties, the matter is quite otherwise. We know today that the Heracleopolitan 9th/10th Dynasties largely overlap the Theban 11th. But that fact does not register in Manetho's king-lists, any more than in their distant precursor, the Turin Canon of Kings. Again, we know that the 13th-17th Dynasties in Thebes paralleled the Hyksos 15th Dynasty, certainly in part, perhaps entirely; but all are listed in Turin, and equally summarised and totalled in Manetho. Then, again, Manetho includes the brief 24th Dynasty (Bakenranef), even though we know that it was entirely contemporary with the 22nd/23rd Dynasties. Hence, the fact that the 23rd and 22nd Dynasties were contemporary in time has no bearing on their listing (originally in full) in Manetho. It is necessary to state this, because of the ill-founded attempt by Leahy (*Libya & Egypt*, 188) to insert the reign of Pedubast II at Tanis as a Tanite 23rd Dynasty in succession to the 22nd Dynasty. We must note (i) the 23rd Dynasty did not need to be later than the 22nd to feature in Manetho; cf. just above. And (ii) as explained at length above, a Tanite origin for the 23rd Dynasty in Manetho does *not* necessarily imply that Tanis was its capital.

§DD.   The other matter in Manetho is the textual state and the nature of his 22nd and 23rd Dynasties.   First their nature.   Neither Leahy and colleagues nor anyone else would deny that his 22nd Dynasty is given as a continuous line of kings, albeit now in summary only.   In Africanus, this is given as 9 rulers, clearly a Shoshenq, an Osorkon, 3 more kings, a Takeloth, and "three other kings".   This compares closely with the Leahy/Aston/Dodson list of 11 kings (cf. Dodson, *GM* 137, 58, retaining Pedubast II & Osorkon IV of L & A's "Dyn. 23 Tanis") as with my list of 10 kings (leaving aside the shadows Shoshenq II and Harsiese).   The first two are clearly Shoshenq I and Osorkon I; the position of the Takelothis does not correspond to either Takeloth I or II, but the year-number is very close to Takeloth I; so, the minor emendation of moving him to third place is just as justified here as are the emendations to the order of Manetho's 18th Dynasty on a far greater scale.   And it is supported by the version in Eusebius.   Then, the other 3+3 kings will correspond to the rest of the 22nd Dynasty with only one omission.   In the 23rd Dynasty, Africanus gives 4 kings, Eusebius but 3 (as in Dyn. 22).   There is not the slightest reason to deny that Petubates (var. Petubastis) at 25 years (Eusebius) is anyone other than our Pedubast I (Usimare) with a known Year 23 (twice); the level of correspondence is exactly like that for Ahmose I in the 18th Dynasty, for example. As Iuput I was entirely co-regent, he does not count.   The Osorthon/Osorcho for 8 years is clearly Osorkon III at <2>8 years.   As long recognised, Psammous and Zet correspond to no attested royal name – but the 10 years for the former is close to what is allowed to Takeloth III, and 31 years for the latter to Iuput II (cf. p. 588 below).   Thus, the only rulers missing would be Shoshenq VI [old IV] and Rudamun. This review of the correspondences gives the lie completely to Leahy's claim that my chronology gives a recension "which is, at almost every point, at variance with Manetho" (*Libya & Egypt*, 178a).   Leahy's attempt to abolish Shoshenq [old] IV, Usimare Meryamun lands him in impossible difficulties, with Year 6 of Shoshenq III, as even his colleague Aston fairly recognises (*JEA* 75(1989), 151-2).   Kings go missing elsewhere in Manetho, so that is no problem on a very small scale here.

§EE.   Leahy objects to the apparent tidiness of the chronology and regimes in Egypt in the 9th-8th centuries BC as presented in this book (*Libya & Egypt*, 178-9,*c*), in "a period which was neither stable nor predictable." The answer is very simple; no-one is predicting anything, and the instability is nothing more than the gradual fragmentation of authority, as it literally fell apart, bit by bit, like a piece of decaying furniture.   There was *no* wholesale chaos.   In *c.* 945-874 BC, we have a unitary monarchy under Shoshenq I to Takeloth I.   The first real crack appears when Harsiese obtains a shadow-kingship at Thebes under Osorkon II.   Theban disenchantment grew apace under the regime of Takeloth II and Prince Osorkon, leading first to the emergence of rival Theban-based high priests.   Shoshenq III proved unable to retain a unified monarchy; a probable sibling Pedubast I split off, founding what Manetho calls the 23rd Dynasty. So, Egypt's citizens could now date by either line. Traditional Memphis stayed with Dyn. 22; anti-Dyn.-22 Thebes and its rebel high priests chose to date by the new line (regardless of where they reigned). During the 8th century BC, coeval with this split, we find the localised chiefdoms of the Ma rapidly emerging into prominence in the Delta: chiefs can be seen in the West (Libu), in Athribis-with-Heliopolis, in Mendes, Pharbaithos and in Busiris from roughly 800 BC onwards; in Sais from *c.* 770 BC onwards, and also in Sebennytos and Pi-Sopd from about 740 BC onwards. In this way, Egypt (in the Delta) was quietly falling to pieces. In Upper Egypt, things moved more slowly at first. Heracleopolis was an apanage of the 22nd Dynasty, seat of its governors of the south. But by the 770s BC onward, it had been taken over by the 23rd Dynasty. Then, in the 750s, the rulers of both Heracleopolis and Hermopolis assumed the rank and style of kings. So, by 730 BC onward, Egypt had two senior lines of kings (22nd/23rd Dynasties), two Upper-Egyptian kings, a permanent princedom in Athribis, a major Chief of the Libu in Sais and the West (later a kingship), and a growing series of locally autonomous chiefs of the Ma over most of the Delta. The political fragmentation was by then complete. This is not artificially "neat", it is strictly historical, based *directly* on our first-hand sources – a hard fact that needs to be recognised.

§FF. Finally the nature of the 23rd Dynasty – a kingly line, or geographically scattered princelings? At one moment Leahy cites (*Libya & Egypt*, 178) the now much-outdated study by Baer (*JNES* 32(1973), 4-25) in favour of much fragmentation of the "23rd" Dynasty; but then, he himself has a unitary line of such rulers in Thebes! (*I.e.,* Pedubast I (+ or – Iuput I), Osorkon III, Takeloth III, Rudamun). What are the facts? First of all, nearly the whole of Manetho's 30 Dynasties are clearly unitary lines of kings, when we can test them by contemporary sources. This is true for the 1st to 13th Dynasaties, the 15th and 17th to 22nd, and 24th to 30th. The 14th and 16th remain enigmatic, because we have no adequate early sources to compare. Hence, with these two unknowns laid aside at present, it has to be admitted that the basic rule for Manetho's dynasties is that they *are* continuous lines when tested by first-hand evidence. So, there is an *a priori* case of considerable weight that the 23rd Dynasty will have been no different. If we consider the first-hand sources for Pedubast I, Shoshenq VI [old IV], Osorkon III, Takeloth III and Rudamun, a remarkable fact emerges. In the genealogies in Thebes, that of the Nebneteru family clearly shows links with Osorkon II (Dyn. 22), then Pedubast (I) and Shoshenq III or VI, then Osorkon III, in three successive generations (below, 211, genealogy). The sequence of Nile-levels and high priests of Amun goes in step with this sequence: a Takeloth serves under Pedubast and Shoshenq VI, while Osorkon III had a Takeloth III as coregent and successor. In the temple of Osiris that they built was found added the names of Rudamun (cf. 123-7 below). So, there can be no serious doubt that Thebes *did* recognise a continuous line of kings, clearly later than Osorkon II. That line of kings began with a Pedubast (up to Year 23) and soon after continued with an Osorkon and two other rulers, while Manetho's 23rd Dynasty likewise began with a Petubastis (25 years), and continued with an Osorkon and two more kings. Leaving aside the ephemeral Shoshenq VI (6 years only), could there be a better fit? Or a clearer straight succession? No scattered fragmentation here. The dating of the Dynasty is also clear; down to the 6th year of Shoshenq III, the 22nd Dynasty has no rivals in Thebes with their own datelines; then comes a double date; then all datelines are of this Manethonically impeccable 23rd Dynasty, which thus ran from early Shoshenq III downwards (but were all gone by Piankhy's time), as perfectly clearly shown below (130-136). The only "scattered" kings are in fact the kinglets of Heracleopolis and Hermopolis – there are none others, bar one. The one, of course, is Iuput II in Leontopolis. If (as I believe) he is indeed the last king of the 23rd dynasty line, then it was indeed a line of Tanite origin (again, in close agreement with Manetho), also based in the Delta. The rest of the matter has already been argued above. Other than the two not unrelated kinglets in Heracleopolis and Hermopolis, there is simply no case for a non-linear 23rd Dynasty, in flagrant contradiction with Manetho.

Thus, none of the points made by either Aston (*JEA* 75(1989)) or by Leahy (*Libya & Egypt*) against the basic presentation made in this volume can in fact be justified under close examination. The claim (Leahy, *Libya and Egypt*, 178, *b*) that the picture presented in this book was "incompatible" with the monumental evidence (as misconstrued by them) is simply not true. A handful of cartouches on some statues and Nile-flood levels, a few blocks and a minor shrine are *not* sound evidence for a "23rd Dynasty" residing in Thebes. There are details on which I gratefully learn from them, and am happy to incorporate – but the facts set out here remain firm, in terms of the 22nd Dynasty (with one new king), and in terms of the linear 23rd Dynasty (wherever it lived, and most unlikely at Thebes).

§GG. Our next concern takes us briefly beyond Egypt's borders, to 'king So' of 2 Kings 17:4 in the Old Testament. Here, two studies have sought to identify the Egyptian ruler involved as Tefnakht of Sais, but not named directly, only through the identification of So as the toponym Sais in one case. The papers are by D.L. Christensen, *VT* 39(1989), 140-153, and by J. Day, *VT* 42(1992), 289-301. While the latter offers a judicious review of the question, courteously expressed, the former combines total lack of understanding of Egyptian matters with unjustified rancour.

We may deal with Christensen's errors first. First, Hosea's appeal to So (king or place) was in 726/725 BC, not 724 (against his p. 141). Second, on his p. 142, the matter of "Nechepso" is irrelevant; and, contrary to Redford and Ray, Nechepso is not merely "Necho" plus epithet (to be confused with Necho I), as he appears as a separate ruler from Necho I in all three recensions of Manetho, and is almost certainly the Nekauba of one fragment (see our p. 146 below). That the Manethonic name could be for *Nekauba (the) Saite is possible – but the epithet would be redundant. Third, there is no likelihood whatsoever of Tefnakht's Horus-name *Sia-ib* being the original of So (Christensen's p. 144), as has been frequently noted. Fourth, his objection that my point that Sais was too distant from Palestine to count is overruled by the meddling of remoter kings of the 25th Dynasty in Palestine (his p. 145) ignores the political situation in 25th-Dynasty Egypt. The whole difference between Pi(ankh)y and his successors Shabako, Shebitku and Taharqa is that they in turn each took up residence *in Egypt*, and governed from Memphis and Tanis, the two traditional capitals of the previous 350 years! Not from distant Napata. In Kawa stala IV, Shebitku reigning in *Memphis* summons prince Taharqa northwards. And members of Taharqa's family were *in Memphis*, when captured by Esarhaddon (cf. p. 392 below). So, Christensen's criticism falls. Fifthly, the longstanding alliance between Egypt and Israel in the 22nd Dynasty *is* relevant – in time of trouble, one would turn to a long-trusted ally (as Mitanni did, under Tushratta, to Akhenaten, and also not realising that circumstances in Egypt had changed). Sixthly, I beg *no* question (C., p. 146) in emphasising the *known* difference between the massive, centuries-old seaport-metropolis of Tanis/Zoan, and the rural backwater of Sais, previously unknown to international politics. For the *known* remains of Tanis, simply see Fig. 3*a*, p. 318 below, once surrounded by a considerable city (huge mounds today). Sais had *nothing* comparable in 725 BC. Sixthly, Christensen has somewhat misunderstood the Old Testament references to Tanis and Memphis in the 8th-7th centuries BC (his p.146). The poetic parallelism of these two cities reflects the political reality of Memphis (administrative centre) plus Tanis (E-Delta residence and port) during the whole period of the 11th to 7th centuries BC, but specifically the 8th-7th centuries BC.

Seventhly, his whole concept of Sais as some kind of powerful capital from 700 BC onwards (p.146ff.) is riddled with error. Sais was merely the seat of a line of Chiefs of Ma, from a Pimay to Tefnakht in our inscriptional sources, who dated themselves by the years of the 22nd Dynasty, until Tefnakht made himself a local king and used his own years. That is *fact*, and not an "assumption" (C, p. 146 end), still less a distortion based on "presuppositions" (p.148 end). Christensen has clearly ignored the textual evidence. Tefnakht originally dated by the years of Shoshenq V of Tanis/Bubastis (22nd Dynasty), as we know from stelae of Years 36 and 38 (p. 355 below). He was still only Prince of the West during Pi(ankh)y's invasion, and the latter gives Tefnakht's *real* titles with great precision as Yoyotte long since proved (cf. 362f., below). Hence, as Tefnakht had publicly recognised the rulers of the 22nd Dynasty down to Year 38 of Shoshenq V, who had been replaced by Osorkon IV shortly before Pi(ankh)y's campaign and was not king then, (i) he only adopted royal titles *after* that campaign, and (ii) having never repudiated Shoshenq V and his line earlier, there is *no* factual reason to imagine him back-dating his years before Pi(ankh)y's invasion. His acknowledgement of Shoshenq V's regnal years proves the opposite (so, refuting Christensen, 151-2). Therefore, Christensen's charge of "distorted... presuppositions" is completely wrong. Furthermore, he appears to be unaware of the other data that belong to the interval between Pi(ankh)y's invasion of Egypt and that by Shabako. We have the dates of Years 21 and 22 (p. 370 below) and 24 (p. 371 below), and most likely of a Year 30 (p.370 & n. 732 below; not superseded by later commentators. From Year 20 to 30 would guarantee a 10-year minimum interval between Pi(ankh)y and Shabako in Egypt (cf. also A. Leahy, *JEA* 78(1992), 235 & n. 79 on this). This compares closely with an 8th year of Tefnakht and 6th year of Bakenranef (7+5 years =12 min.) for this same period.   So, Christensen's attempt to down-date Pi(ankh)y's invasion to about 723 falls before these facts. There is not the slightest possibility of Tefnakht actually *using* royal style *before* Pi(ankh)y's invasion, as the latter's great stela proves conclusively. For the resulting historical sequence (based on direct evidence), see already pp. 142-3 below.

Eighthly, Christensen fails to distinguish between what we know in hindsight now, and what seemed apparent in 725 BC. That Hoshea suddenly realised that "a great new dynasty was emerging in the Delta" (Christensen, 147 end) is romantic fiction. The penetration by a local *West* Delta princeling south to Memphis and further south (and in 728 BC) had nothing whatever to do with events in the Levant (and in 725 BC). The Hebrew king in Samaria would most likely have heard nothing of it. Judah and Israel's links were with the *East* Delta, and more distantly (and only intermittently) with Memphis. An appeal to the 22nd Dynasty in opulent Tanis made more sense then – until it had failed, of course.

Ninthly, talk of Tefnakht's "empire" (Christensen, p. 148) is a semantic nonsense. What aroused Pi(ankh)y was Tefnakht's penetration up the Nile Valley ever closer to Thebes, capital of Amun, Pi(ankh)y's chief god. Christensen's account teems with errors here. There was no operation "by land and sea" (what sea??) And Heracleopolis is in northern Middle Egypt (near the Fayum) – not a city of the Delta! That Tefnakht "was in desperate straits" when he quit Memphis for his fastness in Sais (Christensen, p. 148) is romantic fiction based upon an over-literalistic misunderstanding of Pi(ankh)y's stela, lines 126-144. The fact remains that, alone of all the dynasts, Tefnakht did *not* come and submit to Pi(ankh)y in person – after a suitably flattering message of submission, he suggested that Pi(ankh)y send a messenger to confirm his allegiance. He indeed stood aloof (as pointed out also by Yoyotte *YMM*, 157-8), unlike every other local dynast. At that moment Tefnakht could not know that Pi(ankh)y was shortly thereafter to quit Egypt for distant Nubia, never to return. That would only become apparent several months later, leaving Tefnakht at last free to reaffirm his power southward from Sais towards Memphis, leaving all the East-Delta dynasts still in place. Pi(ankh)y's stay in Egypt was so brief that there is no reason whatever to postulate any involvement on his part with the Levant. The 26th Dynasty had its roots before Necho I (going back to Stephinates, a probable Tefnakht II), and Psammetichus I reigned from 664 BC, not 663 (despite C., p. 151). Tenthly and finally, C. reaches his nadir (152-3) in wrongly confusing the Tefnakht of the 720s BC with Somtutefnakht, Shipmaster of

Heracleopolis in the time of Psammetichus I of the 660s BC, sixty years later. There is not the slightest possibility of identifying these two men as the same – and it is the Shipmaster and general of Heracleopolis (*not* the Prince of the West in Sais) who indubitably appears on the so-called "Piankhy-blocks" from the Temple of Mut in Karnak. This has been common knowledge since F. Ll. Griffiths' time, reaffirmed by Daressy, Kienitz, Stevenson Smith and Yoyotte, not only by the present writer. A ship named after Pi(ankh)y could have been in use long after his death; cf. the long history of the Cunard liner *Queen Mary*, for example.

§HH. Day began with a survey of previous work on So. Thereafter, he argued for the interpretation of So as standing for Sais, and therefore had to dispose of this writer's arguments for So = Osorkon IV. In the sequel, while "Sais" is a theoretical possibility, it is nothing like so probable a solution as Day imagined, nor do his arguments against a personal name of a king (or against Osorkon IV) hold much water.

His first error is his attempt (Day, p.296) to dismiss the Hebrew references to Zoan (Tanis) as irrelevant. Quite the contrary – they are crucially relevant. Tanis and Memphis were Egypt's effective twin capitals from c.1070 BC down to the 26th Dynasty (into 7th century BC) – and that is precisely what is reflected in the parallelism of Isaiah 19:13 (Zoan/Memphis) and other allusions to Zoan (Is. 19:11; 30:4). These contexts presuppose Egyptian leaders functioning in these two cities (19), and envisage Judean envoys going thither (30, cf. 31), regardless of the precise dates of the passages concerned – these will not predate the later 8th century, and shouls not be set after the 7th, given that Tanis lost importance from the 26th Dynasty onwards. What *is* remarkable is that Sais *nowhere* appears in the Hebrew record, never mind as a destination for Hebrew envoys to Egyptian kings! That the Isaiah passages have a Judean origin, not an Israelite one (where Hoshea ruled) is, again, of no importance whatsoever – the geo-political conditions in Egypt remain the same, regardless of which petty kingdom might send there. So, Day's criticisms here are invalid, and merely a red herring.

His second error is to imagine that the greater distance of Sais from Palestine was "more than counterbalanced" by Tefnakht's greater power (p.296f.), and to cite the 26th Dynasty as evidence of "rulers based in Sais" intervening in Palestine (297). The difference in distance from Palestine to Tanis and to Sais, and in the facility of getting there, is considerable. It meant an additional 100 miles sail along the north coast of the Delta, followed by a further 50 miles sail up the unfamiliar west branch of the Nile to penetrate to obscure Sais; any land route was, bluntly, impracticable. Contrast the millennially-familiar route from Palestine across the north coast of the Sinai isthmus, quickly reaching Tanis (or its predecessor Pi-Ramesse, just south), and that by land or boat alike! The 26th Dynasty, moreover, ruled Egypt *from Memphis*, and worked through Tanis, in its Levantine relations. Sais took time to develop, was simply the family seat (its tombs were there), and served for links westward to the Greek world. *No* army ever decamped from Sais, to go to Palestine! All such operations were planned in Memphis, and dispatched from Tanis.

In common with Christensen, Day's third error is to confuse what *we* know in hindsight with appearances as they were in 725 BC. In that year, there was not the slightest evidence that Tefnakht was to become a powerful new ruler.   After Pi(ankh)y's departure, he contented himself with merely extending his realm of the West Delta south towards Memphis; whether he reoccupied it is actually unknown. His successor Bakenranef did so for 5 years, becoming known (later) as the sole king of the 24th Dynasty.   Neither ruler seems to have made *any* attempt to impose his regime on any other local ruler, once Memphis was attained (evidenced for Bakenranef by an Apis-burial). As a local ruler of the large but swampy West Delta, *not* of all Egypt (any more than Osorkon IV), Tefnakht in 725 BC would not have cut any figure of being a "rising star" internationally. While, as noted above, Tanis *was* still an impressive centre and a real capital, ruled by a dynast whose ancestors had been in alliance with Israel before. The real weakness of Osorkon IV would not be apparent until he failed to act. In later days, Tanis again had a series of real local kings: Gemenefhorbak, Pedubast II (celebrated in later tales) and Neferkare; so its political power did not finally end until the early years of the 26th Dynasty. These facts have all been overlooked by Old Testament scholars.

Fourthly, as Day has to admit (297), "the Hebrew text and all the versions are unanimous in treating *So* as as a personal rather than a place name". His escape-route from this obvious fact is still to invent a corruption here, but to push its origin back into the time of the compiler of 2 Kings (297, 300). This is no improvement; the assumption of error where no such assumption is necessary is indeed gratuitous.

Fifthly, Day invents a spurious rule: "The Old Testament elsewhere never abbreviates the names of Egyptian kings". Really? Taharqa is certainly complete (but metathesised as Tirhaqa), as is Neko. But Raamses is abbreviated from Ramesse Me(r)i-Amun (which epithet is *not* omitted in Egyptian), Hophra omits the first part of the name (Wa)hibre, while Shu/ishaq omits the *n* of Shoshenq, a phenomenon known in Egyptian, as is the abbreviation to Shosh. Thus, in principle, Day is wrong; So for Osorkon is simply more of the same – cf. Assyrian Shilkanni, omitting initial *(U), in contrast to Day's wrong presentation on his p.298.   The name of Osorkon IV is so little attested on the monuments that nobody can guarantee that it never was; in fact, final *n* can be found omitted. And not enough Osorkons are known otherwise monumentally to rule out the possibility apodictically, either. The possible *Si* of the time about Osorkon III (p. 342, n. 551 below) may well undermine completely the over-confident claim that the name Osorkon is never abbreviated, although Day is unwilling to accept this possibility.

Sixthly, the emendations needed to force Sais into the Hebrew text of 2 Kings 17:4 are twofold in nature. First of all, there arises the need to emend the text to either <el> *So', el-melek-Misrayim,* or else to *el-So', melek-Misrayim.* Then, there is *no* exact correspondence between Hebrew *So'* and Egyptian Sais (*S3w,* occasionally *S3y*). Only by metathesising the *aleph* and *w/y* can the name made to fit. Possible – but, again, we would be changing the text to fit a preconceived notion.

In the light of the fact (and fact it is!) that historically Sais itself played *no* part in Egyptian-Palestinian relations at any time (Memphis being the real capital, and Tanis the eastern outlet), and that the passages in Isaiah *do* clearly enshrine a concept of Egyptian leaders ensconced in Tanis and Memphis and reachable in Tanis by envoys (regardless of which part of Palestine they came from), there is no warrant whatever to import Sais into 2 Kings 17:4, nor to foist a mantle of imaginary greatness upon the local ruler Tefnakht I; his writ did not run in the E Delta, where Osorkon IV, Iuput II and the chiefs of the Ma all still ruled on regardless until Shabako's triumph at least. All the reasons given below (pp. 372-5, 551) for preferring a personal name So, and for identifying him as Osorkon IV still retain their full validity at the present time.

§II. In the 25th Dynasty, the length of the reign of Shebitku continues to exercise some minds, but not always with much result, especially when there is a failure to take into account all the lines of evidence that we do possess, and also to allow for what we do not possess. The recent paper by L. Depuydt (*JEA* 79(1993), 269-274) is a classic example of this situation. To obtain a "minimal chronology", he merely put together the least coefficient of the attested regnal years of the 25th Dynasty: Taharqa's 26 years (690-664 BC), and Shabako at 14 years are universally admitted to be close to the truth; but for Depuydt, Shebitku's Year 3 is held to give only a 2-year reign, so – hey presto – we have a minimum chronology of Shebitku (*692-690 BC), Shabako (*706-692 BC), and Pi(ankh)y at *728-706 BC (erroneously, as Year 24 is known, and most likely a Year 30 – hence, read *735/729-706 BC, not *728ff. with Depuydt). This petty juggling with a few inadequate figures to produce a "chronology" was all very well 100 years ago, but it will not do today. It ignores too many other facts and factors.

Thus, the 24th Dynasty of Bakenranef at 5 years, preceded by Tefnakht at 7 years (total 12 years) before *705 BC for Shabako's conquest of Egypt would set Tefnakht's assumption of royal style at *717 BC, which implies Pi(ankh)y's raid through Egypt having been not later than *718 or *717 BC, when Tefnakht was exclusively Prince of the West, not king (cf. §GG, 7th point, above). On that basis, 19 years earlier, Pi(ankh)y's own accession would have been in *c.*736 BC, and Depuydt's *728 is, again, totally ruled out. Thus, Pi(ankh)y's reign before Shabako would then indeed have lasted a full 30 years, *736-706 BC, and in fact slightly longer (pp.142-3 below). So, an apparent "minimum chronology" is already a non-starter, even on bare figures.

One factor against having Shabako's conquest of Egypt as late as 705 BC has been the events of 713/712 BC, as seen through the Assyrian records. At that time, Iamani in Ashdod raised revolt against Assyria, digging a moat at his city, and intriguing to gain support from other local rulers, including "Pir'u of Musri" ('Pharaoh of Egypt'), unfortunately not named. Inevitably Sargon II sent forces to crush the revolt, and Iamani "fled to the border of Musri [Egypt] which is at the territory of Meluhha [Nubia], staying there like a thief" – until the king of Meluhha [Nubia] arrested him and handed him over to Assyria. If the 'Pir'u of Musri' was a strictly Egyptian local dynast (such as Osorkon IV), as argued by Spalinger long since (*JARCE* 10(1973), 100) and initially accepted below (p. 583), then it was possible to argue (i) that Iamani had (in 713) intrigued with Osorkon IV, but that within the year that worthy had disappeared, so that Iamani had to flee not merely into an Egypt empty of that ruler but in fact subject to Nubia, whose ruler then turned him in. Hence, Shabako had taken over Egypt in 713/712 BC, at the time the Assyrians were crushing the revolt at Ashdod. Despite Depuydt's attempt to dismiss this scenario and claim that Shabako only took over after 712 ("terminus post quem"), this scenario remains a valid possibility, and cannot be arbitrarily ruled out – if we continue to maintain Spalinger's distinction between the Pir'u and the king of Meluhha. However, this also is open to doubt, see below. Thus, Depuydt's attempt to dismiss 712 BC as bottom date for Shabako's take-over fails to achieve any greater credibility than any other view. And so, a 13-year rule of Shabako over Egypt from 712 BC would last until 699 BC, *and Shebitku would have a 9-year minimum reign.* Any calculation based on a mechanical use of his Year 3 would thus fail, and a so-called "minimal chronology" become merely a false chronology accordingly.

§JJ. However, Depuydt's "minimal" construction fails not only on mere figures; it fails totally to account for other factors, while his five additional points can also be shown to be invalid or indecisive.

(1) Argument about Shabako's dates of contact with Assyria as a distant ruler are pointless; he may already have been in touch with Sennacherib – we have no adequate data, and stock phrases in Assyrian royal records are not a satisfactory basis for argument.

(2) An interval of 10 years or 17 years in transactions in P. Dem. Louvre E. 3228c is of very little consequence, as Egyptian affairs could drag on for years and decades. Cf. the 18-year dispute over a pot of fat at Deir el-Medina, from Year 17 of Ramesses III to Year 4 of Ramesses IV (O. OIC 12073, in Cerny-Gardiner, *Hieratic Ostraca*, I, Oxford, 1957, pls. 77-77A, or *KRI*, VI, 138-9, §A.57). A 'man of the north' is so vague a phrase as to indicate nothing beyond someone from the Delta.

(3) The 50 years for the 25th Dynasty cited from Herodotus is unlikely to have reckoned-in Tantamani; hence, back from 664 BC, it would have begun in 716 BC (as in this book!), not 706. But as Depuydt admits, Herodotus may not be a good chronological source anyway.

(4) The hoary old argument that Shebitku has few monuments, so reigned but briefly will not wash. See already, page 156 below (pyramid comparable with that of Shabako, hence took as many years to build?) And compare the works of Shabako

(380-2 below) and Shebitku (386-7 below), in which both kings worked at both Thebes and Memphis, neither on a large scale.

(5) The supposed "chronological contiguity" from Shabako (over a brief reign of Shebitku) to Taharqa in work at Medinet Habu is another false argument. Considerable time-lapses could and did occur during work on the monuments; cf. already above, §E, refuting the same error by Jansen-Winkeln, with reference to non-work under (*e.g.*) Amenophis II and Ramesses II.

§KK. Then there is a series of important historical factors that Depuydt failed totally to account for, through restricting himself to merely juggling with figures.

(1) Apis-burials. An Apis installed in Year 14 of Shabako died in about Year 4 of Taharqa – after an impeccably normal lifespan of 15/16 years, if Shebitku reigned 12 years. But a totally abnormal and brief 5/6 years, if Depuydt's hyper-minimal dates were to be accepted! Contrast the run of Apis-bulls from Shoshenq III to Psammetichus I averaging 15/16 to 20/24 years, noted p.156 below! A hyper-minimal chronology here produces an unrealistic anomaly, and must therefore be highly suspect.

(2) Before the time of Taharqa's defensive battles against Assyria (677 BC ff.), no 25th-Dynasty ruler got himself into any armed conflict with Assyria except just once, against Sennacherib in support of Hezekiah and his allies in 701 BC (so, both in the Old Testament and Assyrian records, p.385 below). It is remarkable that Shebitku, alone of all the monarchs of Egypt for the first time in 70 years (and never imitated again), took an openly imperialistic titulary, to indicate his intentions. See p.557f. below. And in 701 BC, we find Egypto-Nubian forces flung into the field against Assyria. This only makes sense if it was Shebitku who deliberately did so.

(3) In the same vein, we find prince Taharqa and his brothers summoned by Shebitku at accession to bring an army all the way north from the depths of Nubia (almost 2,000 miles) to the king in Memphis, as Kawa stela IV tells us. For a mere tourist-trip? Hardly! Nobody in antiquity did this kind of thing without serious reasons. And the only major conflict to make such preparation for was that of 701 BC. Hence, all the historical strands come together well, if (i) Shebitku from the start has ambitions in the Levant and showed this in his programmatic titles, (ii) Shebitku intrigued with Hezekiah, Padi and the rest to oppose Assyria (but in his own interest), and (iii) Shebitku promptly raised forces from both Nubia and Egypt (as reflected in Sennacherib's account explicitly). Hence, again, we require a reign of Shebitku for the Manethonic (Eusebian) 12 years, *c.* 702/1-690 BC. There is no place here for artificial "minimal chronologies" based on mere number-juggling, and omitting the data of history.

Finally, one question involving both Shabako and Shebitku. If we admit the historical scenario just sketched, and also Spalinger's view that the Pir'u of Musri has to be a Delta dynast (*e.g.*, Osorkon IV) distinct from the Nubian ruler, then on the interpretation of 713/712 BC noted above, Shabako would have ruled *c.* 714/713 BC to 700 BC, overlapping Shebitku (702-690 BC) by 2 years. This would imply a coregency of the two kings, with Shebitku in effect taking over the reins of power. Such a possibility was foreseen below, pp. 555-557, if but grudgingly, and had the adhesion in some measure of Murnane, Redford and Yurco (there cited). This remains a possible view. There is an alternative. And that is to disallow Spalinger's attempted distinction between Pir'u of Musri and the Nubian ruler. It is, I think, significant that, throughout the 25th Dynasty, its rulers *are* called 'pharaoh' in hieratic and early demotic documents. Thus, in Pi(ankh)y's Years 21 and 22, the datelines of Theban papyri call him already "Pharaoh Piy, Son of Isis, beloved of Amun" (p. 370 below). Then, we find mention of "Year 10, 4th Shomu 30, of Pharaoh Shabako, Son of Isis, beloved of Amun" in P. Louvre E. 3228*e*, line 16, and equally of "Year 3, 1st Peret 10, of Pharaoh Taharqa, Son of Isis, beloved of Amun" in P. Louvre E. 3228*d* (both in M. Malinine, *Choix de textes juridiques en hiératique "anormal" et en démotique*, I, Paris, 1953, pp. 36/37, 44/45). In other words, a Nubian ruler of Egypt was called "pharaoh" right from the beginning – and such a ruler when actually in Egypt (especially at the capital Memphis) would very easily be called "Pharaoh of Egypt", and Pir'u of Musri. Furthermore, the epithet Pir'u was *not* applied to Shilkanni (Osorkon IV) by the Assyrians, even though he was a 'Delta dynast'! So, it is quite possible that Spalinger's distinction in usage is a mirage and should be abandoned. Iamani would have sought to draw in the main ruler of Egypt in 713/712 BC (actually Shabako) – but the Assyrian record does not record that he had any success in trying to "bribe" him, and he may have failed. A Nubian pharaoh in Memphis would have counted as a "pharaoh of Egypt" (cf. our papyrus datelines). But when Iamani fled after defeat, then he had to go far south to the borders of Egypt and Nubia before being able to catch up with the ruler of these lands – and in Lower Nubia, he may then have been arrested and sent on to Assyria by the Nubian ruler (then recognised as such in the Assyrian record). If so, then (as before) 713/712 BC merely becomes the *bottom date* for the Nubian take-over in Egypt, we can at will abandon a theoretical coregency of Shabako and Shebitku, and will have (as before) 715 BC for the date of the renewed Kushite supremacy in Egypt under Shabako (Year 2). This is less constraining.

§LL.   Finally, I have been requested to comment on "trial by television" of Egypt's Third Intermediate Period. Alongside the normal run of investigative scholarship there has run a thin line of would-be problem-solvers who would shift Egyptian (and then also Near-Eastern) history not by decades but by centuries. This began half a century ago with Velikovsky's notorious *Ages in Chaos*. And that is exactly what his results were, based on the wildest guesswork, refusing in principle to acknowledge the simple fact that there *are*, still, large gaps – not in antiquity itself, but in our *knowledge* of it (which is not the same thing). But it is not possible today to drop historical dates by 500 years at a whim. However, in the last two decades, others have wondered if they might down-date Egyptian and Near-Eastern history (for much the same reasons) by a lesser amount, say 250/350 years, having acquired at least a superficial knowledge beyond what Velikovsky had. The first such attempt was launched by P. James and four collaborators, *Centuries of Darkness,* London, 1991. This, in essence, sought to make the 22nd Dynasty overlap about 2/3rds of the 21st Dynasty and most of the 25th Dynasty (see chart, James, p.258), making of Shishak (Rehoboam's opponent) the pharaoh Ramesses III (*ibid.,* p.257). To do this meant "folding up" Mesopotamian chronology, as otherwise the long line of kings of Assyria (having links with New-Kingdom Egypt) presented a fatal obstacle to these chronological gymnastics. The fact is that the James & co. attempt was a brave failure, and broke down badly under the full weight of the total Egyptian and Mesopotamian evidence, and was openly refuted by a body of scholars (especially J.N. Postgate, B.J. Kemp and this writer) in the *Cambridge Archaeological Review* 1/No.2(Oct. 1991), 227-253 *passim.* Their work, therefore, will not be further discussed here.

More recently still, a second attempt has been made (on TV and by book) to sustain such a reduction in dating, by D.M. Rohl, *A Test of Time,* London, 1995, motivated by the same passion for filling "gaps" – this time, by shifting dates downwards and arbitrarily identifying biblical personalities willy-nilly with representations from Egypt and the Levant. The same motive that drove Velikovsky to 'compel' Queen Hatshepsut to become the Queen of Sheba, because he could not otherwise find the latter (it had never dawned on him that no work had ever been done in Yemen to make such an undertaking even possible...). This attempt, too, has no chance of success; we must here summarise why only briefly, but that matters may be clear. Rohl too would drop the 21st Dynasty into being contemporary with the 22nd. Ostensibly because (i) we have no Apis-bull burials between the 20th Dynasty and mid-22nd Dynasty; (ii) because the tomb of Osorkon II (mid 22nd Dynasty) appeared to be overlapped by, and have been built before that of Psusennes I in the 21st Dynasty; and (iii) because the coffin of Sethos I (with a date of Siamun of Dyn. 21) had to have been buried in the Deir el-Bahri cache at Thebes after the last member of the Pinudjem family (bearing bandages dated to Shoshenq I of Dyn. 22).

§MM. But none of these reasons are valid. For, as Rohl knows (his pp. 53ff.), work at the Serapeum was never completed by Mariette and has been recently resumed. Thus, there is no guarantee that the "missing" burials of Dyns. 21-22 will not yet turn up. He also makes no allowance for the possibility that they have been irrevocably destroyed long since. We know of the 'Running of Apis' from the 1st Dynasty – but of *no* burials between this 1st-Dynasty mention and the burials under Amenophis III of the 18th Dynasty 16 centuries later. Do we then collapse 16 centuries of Egyptian history merely to close this gap? Of course not; nor, therefore, for the 21st/early 22nd Dynasties. At Tanis, as has been pointed out long since (*e.g.,* by A. Dodson, *CdE* 63(1988), 221/3), it is most likely that Osorkon II took over an uninscribed royal tomb and had it decorated for himself. If that tomb had originally belonged to either Smendes or Amenemnisu, it would indeed have been built before that of Psusennes I. And at Deir el-Bahri, it is clear that Pinudjem II's last descendant was buried in the cache before the coffin of Sethos I was placed in its entrance – but there is no guarantee that the movement of Sethos I on the same day as the burial of Pinudjem II under Siamun was actually to the cache (cf. already, C.N. Reeves, *Valley of the Kings*, London, 1990, 186-192) – it went there later via the entirely different tomb of Inhapi (where he was temporarily stored on the day of Pinudjem II's burial). In short, none of Rohl's arguments are watertight. And they are clearly contradicted by other, more explicit sources. Thus, we know that Shoshenq I (founder of the 22nd Dynasty) made a marriage-alliance between his son and the daughter of his own contemporary and immediate predecessor Psusennes II at the end of the 21st Dynasty (pp. 60f. below). And that one single line of high priests of Amun held sway in Thebes from the late 20th Dynasty to the late 23rd and into the 25th Dynasty (see lists, Table 13A, pp. 480, 594 below). There is no possibility of overlapping these. The same is true for the continuous line of high priests of Ptah in Memphis, that go through the change from the 21st to 22nd Dynasties (Table 18 below, and §V above). And various genealogies prove that Shoshenq I reigned in the generation following Siamun (Part III below). So, Rohl's overlap is excluded.

There is also no philological alternative to the equation Shoshenq = Shishaq, varying only by an amissible nasal *n*. Rohl's attempted equation with Sessi (short name for Ramesses II and rarely III) is totally false, and ignores what is known of the linguistic facts. These are that as between Egyptian and biblical Hebrew, *s* is always reproduced as *s*, never as *sh* – and *sh* as *sh*, never as *s*. Thus, Hebrew Pi-Beseth is from Egyptian Pi(r)-Baste, Hebrew Phinehas derives from Egyptian Panehesi, and Hebrew Shoshana(t) from Egyptian *sh-sh-n(t)*, and so on. So, Sessi does *not* give Shish(aq), nor can the *q* be arbitrarily added or subtracted at a whim. The omission of Jerusalem from Shoshenq's great list at Karnak means nothing – the city was not stormed or captured; and other Judean-controlled places do appear in it. There is no factual basis for denying that Shoshenq I is the biblical Shishaq. Contrariwise, the apparent Shalim in a Ramesses II name-list at the Ramesseum in his Year 8 may have nothing to do with Jerusalem – its context in the list is too far north.

Of the abuse of genealogies, less said the better. Long genealogies are known to be incomplete at certain points; the Haremsaf in the Hammamat genealogy of Darius I's time was a vizier, not merely a chief of works and is probably *not* the Haremsaf of Shoshenq I (not a vizier). The name Haremsaf is by no means rare, being attested from the Pyramid Age down to Graeco-Roman times (cf., *e.g.*, Ranke *Personennamen*, I, *ad loc.*). And a generation is not 20 years, but 23/25 years – and should **not** be confused with reign-lengths, which are shorter, averaging only 16.6 years (between 13 and 20 years at the outside), cf. my *Documentation for Ancient Arabia*, I, Liverpool, 1994, 57, §56.

§NN. On the Egyptian side, the *coup de grace* is delivered by the evidence linking the forward movement of the Egyptian calendar with the seasonal Nile-flood.

Rohl makes much of a stela of Sobekhotep "VIII" with its account of a late and deep inundation at Thebes, which he would calculate to have happened about 1430 BC, to fit his ultra-low chronology (his pp. 391-3). However, John Baines in *Acta Orientalia* 36(1974), 42, long since indicated that 1650 BC would well fit with a late but high inundation, and in line with normal chronology. So, this monument has nothing to contribute to the matter. In stark contrast, another small text (of the New Kingdom) destroys completely, finally and irrevocably all these ambitious but ill-founded attempts to move Egyptian chronology by centuries. This is the West-Theban graffito No. 862 (W. Spiegelberg, *Ägyptischen und andere Graffiti aus der thebanischen Nekropolis,* Heidelberg, 1921, p.71 & plate), which reads:

"Year 1, 3rd month of Akhet [=Inundation], day 3, (on) this day of the descent made by the water of the great inundation – (under) King of S & N Egypt, *Baienre,* LPH."

Baienre, of course, is Merenptah, son and successor of Ramesses II, and this little text is part of the mass of graffiti left on the West-Theban rocks by the Deir el-Medina work-force and their friends. Here, in the actual season of inundation (on the calendar), they could see the inundation-waters flooding the West-Theban fields – good news for the next farming-year. What matters to us is that this coincidence of the Egyptian calendar only happened at intervals of about 1,460 years, not all the time. It was only 365 days long, so after 4 years it ended a full day early. After about 730 years, the summer months of the calendar had advanced into nature's winter season, and after some 1460 years, the calendar had gone full circle and was temporarily correct again. Within a century, it was visibly slipping away again. Thus, as we know that the calendar was correct in the 2nd century AD, and in the 13th century BC (and before that at about 2700 BC), there can be no doubt that Year 1 of Merenptah in this little text fell in the 13th century BC – and not 250/350 years later, as some would like. All such "revisions" are excluded. The Nile-flood might vary in its timing within July/August/September – but cannot wander all over the rest of the natural year just to please amateur chronologists. The game is up.

§OO. Equally fatal is the Mesopotamian evidence. From Assyria, we have a continuous list of kings from about 1400 BC down to the end in 608 BC. That continuous list can be precisely dated, reign by reign, from 911 BC onwards, as we have the corresponding year-lists of eponym-holders intact from 911 into the 7th century, and dated by a solar eclipse of 763 BC. Furthermore, the eponym-lists are also partly preserved from *before* 911 BC – sufficiently to show that wherever they are preserved, they correspond closely with the King-list, and back it up. Between 1400 and about 1150 BC, the possible margin of error is not more than 10 years *at most.* Furthermore, we have the stratigraphy of the temples and city of Ashur, in which the rebuilding of temples and palaces is certified stratigraphically for the 18th to 7th centuries BC, with royal inscriptions found at various levels and in successive rebuilds – this kind of evidence cannot be changed at will. Cf. in brief, W. Andrae, *Das wiedererstehende Assur,* 2nd ed., Munich, 1977, esp. 141ff. And in parallel with the Assyrian line of kings, we have the successive dynasties of Babylonia, from the Kassites down to Nebuchadrezzar II's line. The Synchronous History and related documents indicate a long series of contacts between contemporary kings of Assyria and Babylon through the centuries – this cannot be telescoped, not even when there are pauses in the relationships. Neither can the like-named kings of Assyria – none of the Adad-niraris, Shalmanesers, etc., are simply repeats of each other, but are separate monarchs. The Assyrian texts of the 13th century BC, for example, are clearly different from those of the 9th or 8th century BC – the earlier are in Middle-Assyrian script and form of language, while the later are in the distinctively different Neo-Assyrian script and language-phase. There is no way of altering this sequence; Tukulti-Ninurta I was *not* identical with Tukulti-Ninurta II, nor Adad-nirari I the same as II! (Rohl, p. 395). This is totally excluded by all the evidence. The attempt to invoke a multiple kingship in Assyria (based on errors by Poebel) has already been tried-on by James & co., and was long since refuted by Postgate (*Camb. Archaeiol., Journal* 1(1991), 244-6). The Assur-uballit of EA letter 16 is explicitly called King of **Assyria** – and is *not* a king of Hanigalbat; Hanigalbat/Mitanni was at that time already ruled by its own series of kings (Sutarna I & II, Artatama I, Tushratta, Kurtiwaza, etc.) Rohl's speculations here are worthless. Likewise, on a supposed anomaly in Babylonian chronology (R., p.395f.), alleging that Shirikti-Shuqamuna had been a brother of Nebuchadrezzar (I), hence Babylonian dating must be altered. However, the original editor of this text (A.R. Millard, *Iraq* 26(1964), 30) pointed out that we certainly have here an easy scribal error of Nabu for Ninurta, and Shiriqti-shuqamuna would have been brother of his immediate predecessor Ninurta-kudurri-usur, not of either Nebuchadrezzar [Nabu-kudurri-usur]. Cf. also A.K. Grayson, *Assyrian and Babylonian Chronicles,* (Texts from Cuneiform Sources, V), New York, 1975, Chronicle 15, pp. 130, 285 on line 21. In such a case, one should always opt for the simpler, more banal explanation; it is almost always the correct one in the end. The **Maat-***kheperu-re* of Cairo CGC 42192 (cf. Jansen-Winkeln, *JEA* 81 (1995), 147, fig.5, pl. 13:2, for the reading) should certainly be for **Heqa-***kheperre* Shoshenq II (with *ibid.*, 148:2), also with J. von Beckerath, *Orientalia* 63 (1994), 84–87, and against N. Dautzenberg, *GM* 144 (1995), 24–29. For Shosenq I in Palestine, cf. also N. Naaman, *Tel Aviv* 19 (1992), 71–93.

Woolton, October, 1995; March, 1996   K. A. Kitchen.

Abbreviations[*]

1. LITERARY

AASOR	*Annual of the American Schools of Oriental Research.*
Aharoni, *LB*	Y. Aharoni, *The Land of the Bible*, 1966.
ANET	J. B. Pritchard (ed.), *Ancient Near Eastern Texts relating to the Old Testament*, 1st ed. 1950, 2nd ed. 1954, 3rd ed. 1969.
ASAE	*Annales du Service des Antiquités de l'Égypte.*
BA	*The Biblical Archaeologist.*
BAR	J. H. Breasted, *Ancient Records of Egypt*, I–V, 1906–7.
BASOR	*Bulletin of the American Schools of Oriental Research.*
BIE	*Bulletin de l'Institut égyptien*, later *Bulletin de l'Institut d'Égypte*
BIFAO	*Bulletin de l'Institut français d'archéologie orientale.*
BiOr	*Bibliotheca Orientalis.*
BMMA	*Bulletin of the Metropolitan Museum of Art, New York.*
BMRAH[3]	*Bulletin des Musées royaux d'art et d'histoire (Bruxelles)*, 3e série.
Brugsch, *Thesaurus*	*Thesaurus Inscriptionum Aegyptiacarum*, 1883–91 (rp. 1968).
BSFE	*Bulletin de la Société française d'Égyptologie.*
CAH[2]	I. E. S. Edwards, C. J. Gadd, N. G. L. Hammond (eds.), *Cambridge Ancient History*, revised (2nd) edition, 1961 ff.
Cairo Cat.	Followed by number, the definitive numbers of objects published in the volumes of the *Catalogue général du Musée du Caire*, 1901 ff.
CdE	*Chronique d'Égypte.*
CPO	R. A. Caminos, *The Chronicle of Prince Osorkon*, 1958.
CRAIBL	*Comptes rendus de l'Académie des Inscriptions et Belles-Lettres.*

G3, G4	H. Gauthier, *Le livre des rois d'Égypte*, III, IV, 1914–15.
HHAHT	Kitchen, *Hittite Hieroglyphs, Aramaeans and Hebrew Traditions*, forthcoming.
IEJ	*Israel Exploration Journal.*
JARCE	*Journal of the American Research Center in Egypt.*
JCS	*Journal of Cuneiform Studies.*
JdE	Journal d'entrée, accession-numbers of objects in Cairo Egyptian Museum.
JEA	*Journal of Egyptian Archaeology.*
JEOL	*Jaarbericht Ex Oriente Lux.*
JNES	*Journal of Near Eastern Studies.*
JPOS	*Journal of the Palestine Oriental Society.*
Kees, *Pr.*	H. Kees, *Das Priestertum im ägyptischen Staat*, 1953, and *Nachträge*, 1958.
Kees, *Hhp.*	H. Kees, *Die Hohenpriester des Amun von Karnak, von Herihor bis zum Ende der Äthiopenzeit*, 1964.
KRI	Kitchen, *Ramesside Inscriptions*, I–VI, 1968 ff.
LAR	D. D. Luckenbill, *Ancient Records of Assyria and Babylonia*, I–II, 1926–7 (rp. 1968).
LB	See Aharoni, *LB.*
LD	C. R. Lepsius, *Denkmäler aus Aegypten und Aethiopen*, Abt. I–VI, 1849–59.
LDT	C. R. Lepsius, *Denkmäler aus Aegypten und Aethiopen, Text*, I–V, ed. by E. Naville, L. Borchardt and K. Sethe.
Leclant, *Recherches*	J. Leclant, *Récherches sur les monuments thébains de la XXVe Dynastie (dite éthiopienne)*, 2 parts, 1965.
Legrain, *Statues*	G. Legrain, *Statues et statuettes de rois et de particuliers.* I–III and Index, 1906–25 (Catalogue général, Musée du Caire).
LES	A. H. Gardiner, *Late-Egyptian Stories*, 1932.
LRL	(1) J. Černý, *Late Ramesside Letters*, 1939, texts; (2) E. F. Wente, *Late Ramesside Letters*, 1967, translations and commentary.
MDIK	*Mitteilungen des Deutschen Archäologischen Instituts, Abteilung Kairo.*
Meyer, *Gottesstaat*	E. Meyer, *Gottesstaat, Militärherrschaft und Ständewesen in Ägypten (Zur Geschichte der 21. und 22. Dynastie)*, in *Sitzungsberichte der Preussischen Akademie der Wissenschaft (Phil.-hist. Klasse)*, 1928.
MIO	*Mitteilungen des Instituts für Orientforschung.*

MMR	G. Maspero, *Les momies royales de Deir el Bahari*, 1889, in *Mémoires . . . de la Mission archéologique française au Caire*, Tome I.
Montet, *Chéchanq III*	P. Montet, *Les constructions et le tombeau de Chéchanq III à Tanis*, 1960 (*La nécropole royale de Tanis*, III).
Montet, *Osorkon II*	P. Montet, *Les constructions et le tombeau d'Osorkon II à Tanis*, 1947 (*La nécropole royale de Tanis*, I).
Montet, *Psus.*	P. Montet, *Les constructions et le tombeau de Psousennès à Tanis*, 1951 (*La nécropole royale de Tanis*, II).
MPON, VI, VIII	*Mitteilungen aus der Papyrussammlung der österreichischen Nationalbibliothek* (*Papyrus Erzherzog Rainer*), *Neue Serie*, VI: A. Volten, *Ägypter und Amazonen*, 1962; VIII: E. Bresciani, *Der Kampf um den Panzer des Inaros* (*Papyrus Krall*), 1964.
NAWG	*Nachrichten von der Gesellschaft* (later, *Akademie*) *der Wissenschaften zu* (later, *in*) *Göttingen, Phil.-hist. Kl.*
OIC	*Oriental Institute Communications.*
OLZ	*Orientalische Literaturzeitung.*
PM	B. Porter and R. L. B. Moss, *Topographical Bibliography of Ancient Egyptian Hieroglyphic Texts, Reliefs and Paintings*, I–VII, 1927–52; 2nd edition, I: 1 ff., since 1960.
PSBA	*Proceedings of the Society of Biblical Archaeology.*
Psus.	See under Montet, *Psus.*
QDAP	*Quarterly of the Department of Antiquities of Palestine.*
RArch³	*Revue Archéologique*, 3ᵉ serie.
RdE	*Revue d'Égyptologie.*
RHJE	*Revue de l'Histoire Juive en Égypte.*
RIK, III	Chicago Epigraphic Survey, *Reliefs and Inscriptions at Karnak*, III, *The Bubastite Portal*, 1954.
RNT	Elisabeth Thomas, *The Royal Necropoleis of Thebes*, 1966.
RT	*Recueil de travaux relatifs à la philologie et à l'archéologie égyptiennes et assyriennes.*
Spiegelberg, *Theb. Graffiti*	W. Spiegelberg, *Ägyptische und andere Graffiti aus der thebanischen Nekropolis*, 1921.
Thiele, *MN*	E. R. Thiele, *Mysterious Numbers of the Hebrew Kings*, 1st ed., 1951; 2nd ed., 1965/66.
TN . . / . . / . . / . .	Temporary numbers (day, month, year; serial) of objects in Cairo Egyptian Museum.
VT	*Vetus Testamentum.*
VTS	*Vetus Testamentum*, Supplement-volumes.
YMM	J. Yoyotte, 'Les principautés du Delta au temps de l'anar-

chie libyenne', in *Mélanges Maspero*, I:4 (1961), 121–
181, 3 pls.

ZÄS	*Zeitschrift fur Ägyptische Sprache.*
ZAW	*Zeitschrift fur alttestamentlichen Wissenschaft.*
ZDMG	*Zeitschrift der Deutschen Morgenländischen Gesellschaft.*
ZDPV	*Zeitschrift des Deutschen Palästina-Vereins.*

2. OTHER CONVENTIONS

DH	Devotee of Hathor (in Part I).
f	denotes names of women.
GW	God's Wife of Amun in Thebes.
HPA	High Priest ('First Prophet') of Amun in Thebes.
HPM	High Priest of Ptah in Memphis.
HPT	High Priest of Amun in Tanis.
LW (S)	Letter-writer of Pharaoh (S. Region).
LXX	Septuagint version of the Old Testament.
MTh	Mayor of Thebes.
2PA, 3PA, 4PA	2nd, 3rd, 4th, Prophet(s) of Amun in Thebes.
V	Vizier.

(...)	Enclose matter not in the original, but inserted in English to give the sense.
[...]	Enclose restorations of matter now lost on the original, or (unrestored) indicate loss, content uncertain.
⟨ ... ⟩	Enclose matter omitted by error anciently from the original.
{ ... }	Enclose matter found in the original which is a dittography or otherwise is superfluous.
⌐ ... ⌐	Enclose matter that is damaged on the original, hence of uncertain reading.

Kings (and some highly-placed homonyms) are numbered with *large Roman numerals* in the customary fashion (I, II, etc.).

Notables (and some of their relatives) are lettered with *capital letters*, to distinguish like-named individuals (A, B, etc.).

Other People are numbered with *small Roman numerals*, again to distinguish like-named individuals from each other (i, ii, etc.).

PART ONE

Chronology
Twenty-first Dynasty[*]

CHAPTER 1

The Basic Sequences of Kings and High Priests of Amun

§1 1. INTRODUCTORY

To the casual eye, the most characteristic feature of the 21st Dynasty is its apparent dyarchy. The line of kings in Tanis in the East Delta is paralleled by the line of army-commanders and high priests of Amun at Thebes as lords of the southland. One might say of these two regions (the north and south halves of the land – delta and valley) that the one half (north) ruled as overlord of the whole only by agreement with the other half (south). Each was confirmed in its fief, under a mutual policy that probably varied from firm alliance to 'live and let live'.

Thus, a reconstruction of the chronological framework and flow of history in this epoch, which is still, hitherto, among the obscurer periods of Egyptian history, must naturally reckon equally with both sets of rulers, and not with the kings alone. This fact has been recognized in Egyptology ever since the 21st Dynasty was first rather dubiously labelled that of the 'priest-kings' long ago.[1] The aim in what follows is to set out the certainties and to outline the limits of the less-certain.

§2 2. HIGH PRIESTS OF AMUN[2]

The fullest single genealogical sequence occurs on the shroud found on the mummy of the high priest commonly termed Pinudjem II: 'The Osiris,

---

1. For early studies of the Twenty-first Dynasty, cf. references given in *MMR*, 640 ff., and *G3*, 230–1. For the term 'priest-kings' among the earlier writers, cf. (e.g.) Miss Amelia B. Edwards, *RT* 4 (1883), 79–87; G. Rawlinson, *Ancient Egypt*, 1893, 297; W. M. F. Petrie, *PSBA* 26 (1904), 39 f.

2. I use indifferently the translation 'First Prophet of Amun' or the description 'High Priest of Amun', for Egyptian *ḥm-ntr tpy n 'Imn*.

3

First Prophet of Amun, Pinudjem (II), justified, son of Menkheperre, the son of King Pinudjem (I) Beloved of Amun.'[3] The rank of Pinudjem II's father Menkheperre as a high priest of Amun occurs on a brace from mummy No. 114 (Pediamun) of the 'second find' at Deir el Bahri.[4] Numerous legends of the high priest Menkheperre name him as 'son of King Pinudjem (I), Beloved of Amun'.[5] Thus far, we have a straight succession of three generations: 'King' Pinudjem I, his son the high priest Menkheperre, and his grandson the high priest Pinudjem II. However, a further high priest Masaharta has also long been known. Like Menkheperre, he is entitled son of 'King' Pinudjem I;[6] but no children (certainly no sons) of his are attested except possibly one daughter who predeceased him.[7] Thus, one may infer that Pinudjem I's first son to serve as high priest was Masaharta who died without heir. This office must then have passed to a second son Menkheperre, and eventually to the latter's son Pinudjem II.

Beyond this point, one finds a high priest 'Pinudjem son of Piankh',[8] and more specifically son of the high priest of Amun, Piankh.[9] Furthermore, this high priest Pinudjem son of Piankh can be identified with the 'King' Pinudjem I in so far as a transitional form of titles is attested at the temple of Khons in Karnak: 'Horus, Strong Bull Beloved of Amun, King of Upper & Lower Egypt (etc., etc.) . . . High Priest of Amun, Pinudjem son of Piankh.'[10] Finally, Piankh was officiating as army-commander or high priest or both in Year 7 of the 'Renaissance Era' under Ramesses XI (the latter's Year 25).[11] In the temple of Khons we also find a high priest Herihor contemporary with Ramesses XI,[12] and known as high priest in Years

---

3. *MMR*, 572; *G3*, 274, 6, I, B. 'Pinudjem Beloved of Amun' is in a cartouche.
4. *G3*, 278, XXIII, E; Daressy, *ASAE* 8 (1907), 31: 114; *RArch³* 28 (1896: I), 75 end: 114.
5. *G3*, 265–6, *passim*.
6. *G3*, 261–2, *passim*.
7. A lady Istemkheb (B), 'daughter of the High Priest of Amun' and entitled 'Chief of the Harim of Min, Horus and Isis in Apu' (Panopolis, Akhmim), *G3*, 263, VIII, on her funerary catafalque published by E. Brugsch, *La tente funéraire de la princesse Isimkheb*, Cairo, 1889. Besides the filiation and titles of Istemkheb already noted, this structure shows friezes of cartouches of 'Pinudjem (I) Beloved of Amun' (Brugsch, pls. IV–VI) and has lines of titles of the high priest of Amun, Masaharta, on its roof-panels (*ibid.*, pl. III). It is, therefore, probable that this item was made for Istemkheb B as daughter of the pontiff Masaharta during the 'kingship' of Pinudjem I. See § 50, below.
8. *G3*, 243–8, *passim*.
9. *G3*, 243, 3, I; 245, V; 246, X, XI, E, H; XIII, B [C].
10. *G3*, 246, D, cf. A (traces of *nsw-bit*).
11. On the 'Renaissance Era' (*wḥm-mswt*) with its Year 1 equal to Year 19 of Ramesses XI, see below, §§ 14 ff.
12. *G3*, 233–5, *passim*.

5 and 6 that can only well be those of the 'Renaissance Era' (*wḥm-mswt*), late in that king's reign, and hardly Years 5–6 of Ramesses XI[13] or Years 5–6 of Smendes I his successor[14] as will be seen below (§ 14). Thus, we have a succession of high priests from Herihor and Piankh in the later years of Ramesses XI down to Pinudjem II, great-grandson of Piankh. To this line may certainly be added a high priest of Amun, Psusennes ('III'), son of Pinudjem, the latter without title.[15] As the sons of Pinudjem I always proudly refer to their father as 'King' Pinudjem (with cartouche), this Psusennes will be a son of Pinudjem II (never more than high priest), not of Pinudjem I – hence he was the successor of Pinudjem II at Thebes. Thus far, a succession of seven high priests seems irrefutable and clear. To these may be added one, possibly two, further names. The first of these is the high priest Nesu-ba-neb-djed or Smendes II.[16] In Thebes itself, Smendes is only entitled high priest in one instance: on the pendants on mummy No. 135 from the 'second find' at Deir el Bahri,[17] in association with the cartouche of Amenemope on its braces. As that cartouche is associated with the name of Pinudjem II on other mummies from this find (e.g. Nos. 38, 81, 113, 124), and Pinudjem II went on into the reign of Siamun, a successor of Amenemope (cf. §§ 3–4, below), Smendes II could be an ephemeral predecessor of Pinudjem II.[18] The second additional name is that of a high priest of Amun, Djed-Khons-ef-ankh, son of 'King' Pinudjem I, known from a single monument now lost. On his filiation and poor attestation, he may – with Masaharta – be a childless predecessor of Menkheperre, but also (like Smendes II) purely ephemeral; see below, § 55 and Excursus C. The resultant succession of Theban high priests of Amun may be listed as follows:

1. Herihor – high priest and 'king', a contemporary of Ramesses XI (Years 5 and 6 of 'Renaissance Era').

13. With Smendes being mentioned in the Wenamun report in this Year 5, it seems hardly likely that he officiated for nearly 25 years under Ramesses XI (if from Year 5 of that king) and then reigned *another* 26 years as himself king, some 50 years all told; as governor in Tanis from whom the high priest's envoy needed authority, he must have been a very high official already of mature years, in his forties or even his fifties (cf. § 64, below) – hence would be over 90 or over 100 at death, if Year 5 of Ramesses XI were intended. Possible, but distinctly unlikely.

14. If Year 5 of Smendes as king were intended in the Wenamun report, one would expect him to be at least called 'Pharaoh Smendes' or king in some form – a mere name with no attribute at all would be unheard-of. Cf. also §§ 14 ff., below.

15. *G3*, 285, I–IV. This Psusennes is here numbered 'III' to distinguish him in discussion as the high priest, from Psusennes I and II as kings, dealt with below.

16. Here numbered II to distinguish him easily from King Smendes (I).

17. *G3*, 271, XXIV, 1, A; Daressy, *ASAE* 8 (1907), 35 f.: 135.

18. For a Theban text concerning an untitled Smendes, probably Smendes II, cf. below §§ 46, 51 (Pylon X); for Tanite data, cf. below, §§ 25, 30.

2. Piankh – high priest, a contemporary of Ramesses XI ('Renaissance Era', Year 7), and was father of:
3. Pinudjem I – high priest, then 'king'; father of three following:
4. Masaharta – high priest.
5. Djed-Khons-ef-ankh – high priest.
6. Menkheperre – high priest, father of at least No. 8 below.
7. Smendes II – high priest, preceding:
8. Pinudjem II – high priest, son of Menkheperre.
9. Psusennes 'III' – high priest, son of Pinudjem II.

Finally, the mummies of the 'second find' at Deir el Bahri also preserve a mention of a high priest Pinudjem 'son of King Psusennes Beloved of Amun'.[19] But this filiation occurs principally alongside similar epigraphs of the high priest Pinudjem II son of Menkheperre,[20] including that on the mummy of Nesikhons A, wife of Pinudjem II.[21] Hence, this filiation is generally accepted today as simply a claim by Pinudjem II to be descended not only from 'King' Pinudjem I but also from the Tanite king Psusennes I.[22]

§3   3. TANITE KINGS

For the pharaohs in Tanis – the 21st Dynasty proper – the picture is initially less clear. All versions of Manetho[23] give seven kings in the following order, whose identifications with kings in the hieroglyphic sources are almost universally agreed, thus:

Manetho	*Monuments*
1. Smendes (I)	1. Hedjkheperre Setepenre, Nesu-ba-neb-djed Beloved of Amun

19. *G3*, 279, XXIV–XXVI.
20. Daressy, *ASAE* 8 (1907), 27 ff.: mummies Nos. 81, 113, 119, 120, 127 (so *G3*; also Černý, *CAH²*, II: 35 (1965), 49, n. 1), and 152 (Daressy, *RArch³* 28 (1896: I), 76). Pinudjem son of Psusennes occurs alone on mummies Nos. 61, 82, 139.
21. Who was buried by Pinudjem II. *MMR*, 579; *G3*, 279, XXV, B, with ref. by error under A.
22. Misled by the double filiation, Naville called Pinudjem son of Psusennes 'Pinudjem II', and numbered the real Pinudjem II as 'III' in his monograph of 1883, *L'inscription historique de Pinodjem III*. Hornung's identification of the high priest Pinudjem son of Psusennes with Pinudjem I as son (-in-law) of Psusennes I in his *Untersuchungen zur Chronologie und Geschichte des Neuen Reiches*, 1964, 102, is surely a slip of the pen.
23. For which cf. conveniently, W. G. Waddell, *Manetho* (bound with F. E. Robbins, *Ptolemy Tetrabiblos*), Loeb Classical Library, 1948, 154–7.

2. Psusennes I   (2?). Akheperre Setepenamun,
                           Psibkhanno I, Beloved of Amun

3. Nepherkheres   (3?). Neferkare Heqa-Waset,
                           Amenemnisu Beloved of Amun

4. Amenophthis   4. Usimare Setepenamun,
                           Amenemope Beloved of Amun

5. Osochor   5. Akheperre Setepenre,
                               [. . .]

6. Psinaches   6. Neterkheperre Setepenamun,
                           Siamun Beloved of Amun

7. Psusennes II   7. Tyetkheperre Setepenre,
                           (Har)-Psibkhenno II, Beloved of Amun.

§ 4   Here, the *identifications* of the Manethonic names and Egyptian nomens of Nos. 1, 2, 4, 7, are transparent. Likewise is the unusual identification of the Manethonic name with the prenomen of No. 3. That Nos. 5 and 6, Osochor and Psinaches, are equivalents in some form of two kings Akheperre . . . and Siamun emerges clearly from data now to be considered. Thus, all seven kings recorded in Manetho are securely attested in first-hand sources.

On fragment No. 3B of the Karnak Priestly Annals, the induction of a priestly scribe Nespaneferhor son of Iufenamun occurred in Year 2 of a king Akheperre Setepenre [name lost]. The next entry records the induction of Nespaneferhor's similarly-entitled son Hori in Year 17 of 'Pharaoh Siamun'.[24] Formerly, the Akheperre Setepenre was taken to be merely a variant of the prenomen of Psusennes I, and the Manethonic name Osochor dismissed as a fiction. However, the results of such a procedure are biologically very improbable. On the Manethonic regnal figures, the span of time from Year 2 of Psusennes I at 46 or 41 years, Nepherkheres at 4 years, Amenemope at 9 years and Siamun at a minimum of 16 years (to his Year 17) would give either 72 or 66 years between the inductions of father and son. On an alternative scheme, of Psusennes I at 26/21 years, Nepherkheres at 4 years, Amenemope at 49 years, and Siamun at 16 years, the period between these inductions becomes a still worse 97/91 years. But when, following Young,[25] the cartouche Akheperre Setepenre in the Annals entry is attributed to Manetho's Osochor, then from Year 2 of Osochor at a Manethonic 6 years of reign (5 years here, from Years 2–6) to Year 17 of Siamun (a further 16 years) gives almost 21 years' interval between the

24. Published by G. Legrain, *RT* 22 (1900), 53–4, cf. 30 (1908), 87–8.
25. E. Young, *JARCE* 2 (1963), 100–1.

inductions. This is a wholly reasonable situation if Nespaneferhor attained to responsible office in his 30s, died before he was 60, and his son Hori was in due time appointed in his 30s also. Hence, the reality of Osochor and the sequence from Osochor to Siamun as set out by Young seems beyond all reasonable doubt. That Osochor and Siamun were close successors of Amenemope follows from the fact that the name of the high priest Pinudjem II is associated at Thebes both with Amenemope[26] and with Siamun, in whose 10th year he was buried.[27]

§ 5   The main *sequence* of kings given by Manetho fits with the first-hand evidence of the monuments with just one possible exception. Thus, Smendes the king is undoubtedly the Smendes who was governor at Tanis under Ramesses XI,[28] and so founder of the 21st Dynasty. As just noted above, Amenemope, (Osochor) and Siamun are contemporaries of the high priest Pinudjem II who sometimes calls himself 'son' (= descendant) of a king Psusennes. Dying in Year 10 of Siamun, Pinudjem II was earlier than Psusennes II, and so his claimed Tanite 'ancestor' was Psusennes I, who was later than Smendes I and earlier than Amenemope. Slight confirmation of this may be seen in the fact that Montet found at Tanis blocks of Psusennes I and Pinudjem I.[29] Also, the burial of Amenemope in the chamber of Queen Mutnodjmet in the tomb of Psusennes I was clearly a secondary burial[30] in the tomb of Psusennes I as an earlier king. In turn, Psusennes II ends the dynasty because his daughter Maatkare B married Osorkon (I), son of Shoshenq I, founder of the next or 22nd Dynasty.[31] This Psusennes would be the Psusennes with prenomen Tyetkheperre whose statue was 'renewed' by Shoshenq I.[32] Finally, the close link between Psusennes I and Nepherkheres (Amenemnisu) is vouched for by their cartouches coupled in pairs on gold bowcaps from the burial of Psusennes I in Tanis.[33]

However, there remains the 'one possible exception'; the doubt and controversy that persist over the order of kings Nos. 2 and 3. Manetho has

26. On mummy No. 124, 'second find', Deir el Bahri (*G3*, 292, II), among others (*G3*, 293, VIII); cf. also below.

27. For Pinudjem II acting in Year 8 of Siamun, cf. *G3*, 294, I–II (the mummies Nos. 133, 124, Deir el Bahri); for Year 10, cf. Černý, *JEA* 32 (1946), 26–30.

28. In the report of Wenamun, cf. (e.g.) *ANET*, 25 ff., Lefebvre, *Romans et contes égyptiens*, 1949, 204 ff.; text, Gardiner, *Late-Egyptian Stories*, 1932, 61 ff.

29. Cf. *BSFE* 6 (1951), 29–30.

30. Cf. Montet, *Psus*, 24–5, 159, 165–6 (replacing the queen), 167–8: 643 (collar of Psusennes I as part of original burial of Amenemope).

31. Nile statue, British Museum No. 8, dedicated by their son the high priest Shoshenq (II), *G3*, 299, 5, II.

32. Cairo Cat. 42192 (Legrain, *Statues*, III, 2 and pl. 1); *G3*, 301, 6, II.

33. Montet, *Psus*, 168, fig. 44 (left), No. 413; pl. 72.

the order Psusennes I – Nepherkheres (Amenemnisu). The genealogy of a Memphite priest published by Borchardt[34] has the order Amenemnisu – Akheperre–Setepena[mun]–Psusennes (twice), which is now generally interpreted as Amenemnisu succeeded by Psusennes I mentioned thrice.[35] As Amenemnisu was in any case ephemeral (only 4 years in Manetho; only one contemporary monument and one later mention), the question of his place before or after Psusennes I does not greatly affect the dynasty as a whole. It interlocks with other considerations, and so is further dealt with below in appropriate places (§ 56; Ch. 12, §§ 151 ff.). Thus, in both lines – Tanite kings and Theban high priests – one can obtain sequences of reigns and pontificates that seem absolutely assured with only one exception (Amenemnisu) and with minor doubts (Smendes II and Djed-Khons-ef-ankh).

34. Borchardt, *Die Mittel zur zeitlichen Festlegung von Punkten der ägyptischen Geschichte und ihre Anwendung*, 1935, 96–112, pl. 2, 2a.

35. e.g. B. Grdseloff, *ASAE* 47 (1947), 207–11.

CHAPTER 2

Correlations and Lengths of Reigns and Pontificates at Both Ends of the Dynasty

§6 1. INTRODUCTORY

The 'monumental' sources of the period do provide a series of links between the kings and high priests, that establish approximately who was the contemporary of whom. However, when one attempts to give precision to these personal synchronisms with lengths of reigns and priesthoods (especially the former), then the picture is less clear. Clashes seem to occur between regnal dates from relics of the dynasty itself and lengths of reigns in the extant versions of Manetho. The family relationships of the two ruling houses likewise offer at first as much trouble as help, but do serve to delimit the possibilities.

§7 2. FROM PINUDJEM II TO THE END OF THE DYNASTY

The key dates are those of Pinudjem II with Siamun which afford a basis for further reconstruction.

The clearest date is given by the text: 'Bandage made by the high priest Pinudjem (II) son of Menkheperre for his lady (*sc.* the goddess) Mut, Year 8 of King Siamun.'[36] Next to this comes the burial of Pinudjem II in 'Year

36. On mummy No. 133 (chantress Har-weben, daughter of Istemkheb), see Daressy, *RArch*³ 28 (1896: I), 77, and *ASAE* 8 (1907), 35; *G3*, 276, XIV. The lady was buried in the time of Psusennes 'III'.

10', which is clearly of Siamun from dockets on the coffins of Ramesses I, Sethos I and Ramesses II which were reburied in the now famous *cache* on the day of Pinudjem II's burial.[37] The establishment of this date means that the 'Year 14', in fragment No. 33 of the Karnak Priestly Annals,[38] which follows the name of Pinudjem II must begin *a new section* and will still refer to the reign of Siamun.[39] The name of Pinudjem II belongs to the entry (date, Year 10–x, now lost) *preceding* that of Year 14, and is probably attributable to an earlier date in the reign of Siamun.

§ 8   At this point a few words need to be written on the identities of Psusennes II and 'III'. Here they are considered to be two separate individuals, principally on one piece of evidence which, it must be emphasized, is itself not flawless. This is the bandage-epigraph read by Daressy as follows: 'Linen made by the high priest Psusennes ("III") son of Pinudjem (II) for his master Amun in Year 5'. In his first publication, Daressy printed the figure without query,[40] but in his second report (in this, followed but not cited by Gauthier) he added '(?)'.[41] Regrettably, so long as these shrouds and bandages from the 'second find' at Deir el Bahri remain lost to science, no verification of the year-figure is possible. If that figure is really 'Year 5' (or any number from 1 to 10), then it is evidence that a separate *high priest* Psusennes ('III') son of Pinudjem II was officiating at Thebes under *king* Psusennes II of Tanis. Given the usage of Pinudjem I as 'king' on earlier dockets, etc.,[42] it is scarcely conceivable that the high priest Psusennes – if he was already the ruling king[43]

37. Černý, *JEA* 32 (1946), 26–30.
38. Legrain, *RT* 22 (1900), 61.
39. In these fragmentary annals (so far as observable), all dates begin a new entry (even in mid-line, e.g. No. 3B, line 3), with only *one* visible exception (No. 38), and this one has the preposition *n* (<*m*), 'in Year *x*'. Young, *JARCE* 2 (1963), 101, had sought to connect the Year 14 of fragment No. 33 with the mention of Pinudjem II; as the latter died in Year 10 of Siamun, the Year 14 would then belong to Osochor, entailing correction of Manetho's figure for his reign from 6 to 16 years. However, as pointed out above, there is *no* connection between Pinudjem II (end of one entry) and the Year 14 (start of another) which thus should be assigned to Siamun. Correction of Manetho here is gratuitous, and had Osochor really reigned 16 years, one might have expected rather more contemporary remains to be known from his reign if it really rivalled in length those of Siamun and Psusennes II and was half as long again as Amenemope.
40. *RArch*³ 28 (1896: I), 77 top, No. 17; in the copy seen by me, the figure quoted as '5' is misprinted with one stroke over three (instead of two over three), which error probably accounts for the figure 'Year 4' published in *BAR*, IV, § 688, before Daressy's second paper in 1907.
41. *ASAE* 8 (1907), 23, No. 17; *G3*, 285, 7, I.
42. *G3*, 248–9, XIX, cf. XX.
43. With real executive supreme power, unlike Pinudjem I, and wholly unlike the entirely 'shadow' kingship of a Herihor.

in his own Year 5 (or, within 1–10) – would (as king) be referred to merely as high priest instead of by his kingly titles. However, if the year-number were in fact to be read as any year from 10 up to 17 or 19, it could be referred to the reign of Siamun. It would then leave open entirely the question as to whether the Psusennes II that followed Siamun on the throne in Tanis was a Tanite or in fact the Theban high priest as 'next-of-kin', making Psusennes II and III just one person as has often been advocated.[44] However, this latter view cannot be assumed as correct[45] until the epigraph just discussed can be validated or disposed of, either by the recovery of the original or by the discovery of fresh data bearing on the point. Until we know any better, the epigraph (and the distinction between Psusennes II and 'III') is provisionally accepted in this work.[46]

§ 9 Returning to chronology in the narrower sense, it is possible to suggest clear limits for the length of time from the death of Pinudjem II under Siamun to the end of the 21st Dynasty. A series of explicit year-dates for Siamun is known after Year 10 when Pinudjem II was buried. Besides the strictly unattributed Year 14 of the Karnak Priestly Annals fragment No. 33 (cf. § 7, above), his Year 16 occurs on a stela published by Munier,[47] and his Year 17 in a graffito at Abydos[48] and, more clearly, in the Karnak Priestly Annals fragment 3B.[49] All extant versions agree in giving but 9 years to the king Psinaches who replaces Siamun in Manetho. As others have done,[50] it is reasonable to suggest that an *iota* has been dropped by copyists, and therefore to emend to ⟨1⟩9 years for Siamun–Psinaches.

44. e.g., by Černý, *CAH*[2], II: 35 (1965), 43; E. F. Wente, *JNES* 26 (1967), 158, 175/6, fig. 1, 2. The two Psusennes are kept separate by (e.g.) Kees, *Hhp.*, 79, by Hornung, *Untersuchungen zur Chronologie und Geschichte des Neuen Reiches*, 1964, 106; cf. Young, *JARCE* 2 (1963), 111.

45. The titles of Tyetkheperre Psusennes II in an Abydos graffito (*G3*, 301, 6, I; Daressy, *RT* 21 (1899), 9–10) prove nothing about his origin, still less that he is identical with the high priest Psusennes 'III'. Other Tanite kings bore the title High Priest of Amun (e.g. Psusennes I, Amenemope, cf. below Part IV, §§ 220, 229, and Part V, Excursus D), and 'army-leader' (*ḥꜣwty*) is a title that he could have borne in Tanis as a prince under Siamun (like the high dignitary Wen-djeba-en-Djed, below, Part IV, § 222).

46. The prenomen Hedj-heqa-. . . .-re given for a Psusennes by Wilkinson, *Materia Hieroglyphica*, V, g, as from a Theban tomb (cf. Petrie, *History of Egypt*, III, 1905, 225; *G3*, 299, I) remains an enigma, if correctly recorded by him. Speculations that it might be a variant prenomen of Psusennes II, or an eventual cartouche of Psusennes 'III' as concurrent with him, are perhaps best left aside at present.

47. In *Recueil Champollion*, 1922, 361–6.

48. *G3*, 295, VII.

49. *G3*, 296, VIII; Legrain, *RT* 22 (1900), 53; 30 (1908), 87.

50. e.g. Young, *JARCE* 2 (1963), 108–9; Hornung, *Untersuchungen zur Chronologie und Geschichte des Neuen Reiches*, 1964, 105; Wente, *JNES* 26 (1967), 176, fig. 2, end. Hornung's further ingenious suggestions (*OLZ* 61 (1966), 441, § 6)

§ 10   The version of Africanus offers 14 years and that of Eusebius 35 years for Psusennes II. The book of Sothis (No. 66) has a misplaced Saites with 15 years, perhaps intended for this king.[51] Contemporary witnesses for Psusennes II are few indeed but perhaps sufficient: besides Daressy's Year 5 already discussed (§ 8 above) and a Year 12 that could equally belong to Siamun,[52] the Karnak Priestly Annals fragment 3B already cited (§ 4 above) has as its third successive entry (after Year 2 of Osochor and Year 17 of Siamun) the Year 13 of a king whose name is entirely lost. Coming after Year 17 of Siamun, this Year 13 can only belong to some subsequent king[53] – either Psusennes II or Shoshenq I[54] – as any following reign would be too late for the series of inductions. Hence, on these limited grounds, one may suggest that the 35 years in Eusebius' version is *15 years plus 20 spurious (cf. 15 years of Sothis: 66), and closely comparable with the 14 years of Africanus which were perhaps rounded up from 14 years and a fraction. The Years 12 and 13 of our Theban sources would agree well with a reign of 14 years plus a fraction. That figure will be adopted here, as there is at present no monumental support for a reign lasting as long as 35 years (or even a midway 25).

§ 11   3. FROM PINUDJEM II BACK TO
          MENKHEPERRE

The pontificate of Pinudjem II stretched back from the initial decade of Siamun's reign to that of Amenemope, thus totally spanning the reign of

that Siamun was a usurper and that 'Psinaches, 9 years' applies to the 'legitimate' Pinudjem II, I find totally unacceptable. Philologically, Psinaches is no more a good equivalent of Pinudjem than of Siamun; and on extant evidence, Pinudjem II *never* claimed any kind of kingship in the first place, nor does any Theban pontificate (even Pinudjem I!) find its way into the list of Manetho. The emendation of 9 to 19 is slight, and only one among many needful emendations to the unevenly corrupted text of our *extant* versions of Manetho; there is no warrant for calling Siamun a usurper, and as Hornung candidly admits, *op. cit.*, 442, Manetho cheerfully accepted the reigns of other 'usurpers' in any case (e.g. Hatshepsut, Amarna kings, Tewosret).

51. As it also misplaces Nepherkheres (Amenemnisu) after Amenophis (Amenemope) as Nos. 65 and 64 respectively.

52. Bandage from mummy No. 65 (P(a)-Amun), Daressy, *ASAE* 8 (1907), 27: 65, *G3*, 285, 7, II. Ambiguity also noted by Young, *JARCE* 2 (1963), 111, and less clearly by Hornung, *Untersuchungen* . . . , 1964, 105, n. 35.

53. As the general rule is for chronological order to be kept in these Annals texts.

54. With the 21 years' interval from Year 2 of Osochor to Year 17 of Siamun (cf. § 4 above), one may compare best an interval of 15 years from Year 17 of Siamun (allowing him 19 years) to Year 13 of Psusennes II, or a little less favourably some 29 years up to Year 13 of Shoshenq I. Reckoning to Year 13 of Osorkon I would give about 50 years, a period between inductions of unlikely length.

Osochor. This fact favours a relatively brief reign for Osochor, and in the absence of any date higher than Year 2 (Annals, 3B), the 6 years given by Manetho may be accepted until we know any differently.[55]

On at least six mummies from the 'second find' at Deir el Bahri,[56] the names of Amenemope and Pinudjem II appear in close conjunction upon braces and bandages. There can be no doubt, therefore, of their contemporaneity for some period at least. One (No. 124) associates Pinudjem II with Year [x]+3 of Amenemope; on No. 38, the date is lost.

Before Pinudjem II must come Smendes II who is also associated with Amenemope, indirectly, on braces and pendants found on mummy No. 135 from Deir el Bahri.[57] As there is no other trace of this high priest (at least, so entitled) at Thebes, and scarcely any evidence on him from elsewhere,[58] a quite short pontificate is probably indicated.

§ 12   Before Smendes II in turn, comes Menkheperre. Here, significantly as we shall see, there is *no* clear, direct correlation between Menkheperre and any named Tanite king in any of the numerous records left by this high priest, although anonymous year-dates are not lacking. These year-dates are easily separated into three groups, each about 20 years apart:

(i)   (a) Year 6, bandage on mummy of Sethos I, naming Menkheperre.[59]
      (b) Year 7, burial-docket on mummy of Sethos I, no agent named.[60]
(ii) (a) Year 25, Maunier Stela, recall of exiles under Menkheperre.[61]
(iii) (a) Year 40, Karnak Priestly Annals, 3A, acts of Menkheperre.[62]
      (b) Year 48, stela of works at Karnak under Menkheperre.[63]
      (c) Year 48 *n* Menkheperre, bandage of Userhatmose.[64]

55. For 6 rather than Young's suggested 16 years, cf. above, n. 50.
56. Nos. 24, 38 (woman Ankhesenmut), 81 (priest Amen-niut-nakht), 82 (scribe of Estate of Amun, Khonsmose), 113 (*imy-st* of ditto, Nesamenope), and 124; cf. Daressy, *ASAE* 8 (1907), 23–33, *passim*.
57. Daressy, *op. cit.*, 35: 135; *G3*, 271, XXIV, 1, A. Amenemope is named on the braces, and Smendes II on the pendants. One might, rather theoretically, argue for different dates of manufacture of braces and pendants and a still later date of burial; but normally, the braces and pendants are the *latest-dated* items on these mummies (unlike some of the bandages), and hence may provisionally be taken as evidence for the general date of burial.
58. For the high priest Smendes son of Menkheperre on bracelets from the burial of Psusennes I at Tanis, see below, §§ 25, 30.
59. *MMR*, 555; *G3*, 263, 3, I.
60. *MMR*, 554–5, fig. 14; *G3*, 264, II.
61. *G3*, 264, III; excellent new edition, von Beckerath, *RdE* 20 (1968), 7–36.
62. *G3*, 265, IV; Legrain, *RT* 22 (1900), 53.
63. *G3*, 265, V; Barguet, *Le temple d'Amon-rê à Karnak*, 1962, 36–8, pl. 32, B.
64. Priest of Mut, scribe of treasury(?); mummy No. 105, Daressy, *ASAE* 8 (1907), 30: 105, and *G3*, 265, VI, where note 2 is mistaken, referring in reality to a different bandage.

These three groups of dates are susceptible of more than one interpretation. The simplest view (I) is just to take the whole series in numerical
order as referring to Years 6–48 of a single reign, which would give Menkheperre a pontificate of at least 42 years. But the fact that, on the Maunier
or 'Banishment' Stela, the events of Year 25 are followed by a Year [lost]
but much less (1–5?) suggests that at least the Year 25 belongs to a reign
different from, and earlier than, a new reign reaching perhaps its Years
1–5. Thus, the Years 6 and 7 of group (i) above would also possibly fall
chronologically after the Year 25 of group (ii). Years 40–48 of group (iii)
would then most likely follow in the same reign as Years 6 and 7, delimiting
the pontificate of Menkheperre as running from the Year 25 of a King
A through the Years 1–7 and perhaps up to 40–48 of a King B, with the
possibility of King A briefly outliving his Year 25, and of some further
ephemeral ruler (King Q) reigning between Kings A and B. This overall
view (II) better accommodates the data of the Maunier Stela than does view
(I). However, it has to be borne in mind that these two options do not
exhaust the theoretical possibilities. For example, one might argue that
Menkheperre served in Years 40–48 of one king, then up to Year 25 of a
second king, and into the first years (up to 7 at most?) of a third king.
Instead of 42 years (view I) or 48+years (view II), his tenure of office on
this view (III) would be 40+ years. But, whatever view be adopted – any
one of these, or any other combination – it is clear that Menkheperre had a
long pontificate of the order of 40–50 years. This is not inconsistent with
his name appearing quite frequently on the mummies of priests buried at
Deir el Bahri, during and soon after his time.[65]

§ **13** But do these theoretical patterns offer any correlations with the
reigns of the kings in Tanis? As Menkheperre's successors-in-office –
Smendes II and Pinudjem II – were both contemporaries of Amenemope,
and Pinudjem II lived on to the 10th year of Siamun, it is evident that

65. Menkheperre's name appears on the braces of mummies Nos. 11 (the priest
Pennesttawy), 13 (braces, pendants of Pairsekheru), 64 (braces of chantress Henttawy), 109 (braces of chantress Djed-< . . . >-es-ankh), and 115 (braces of
priest Aha-nefer-amun), in Daressy, *ASAE* 8 (1907), 22–32, *passim*. These were
probably people who were actually buried during his pontificate. However, three
bodies on which was linen made under Menkheperre were actually buried not earlier
than the pontificate of Pinudjem II whose name appears on their braces: No. 105
(Userhatmose; cf. also, preceding note) with one bandage Year 48 *n* Menkheperre
and another piece – no names – dated to 'Year 1, 4th month of Akhet, Day 1',
presumably of a successor of the king of Year 48; No. 98 (superintendent of recruits
of Estate of Amun, Nespaneferhor), Daressy, *op. cit.*, 30; No. 113 (*imy-st* of Estate
of Amun, Nesamenope), *ibid.*, 31, associated with Menkheperre, Pinudjem II and
King Amenemope. Datable to either Menkheperre or later are Nos. 2 (year-date
lost) and 96, *ibid.* 22, 30.

Menkheperre must in turn be the contemporary *at the latest* of Amenemope and/or his predecessor(s) in Tanis.

It is at this point that conflict arises between two lines of evidence and on how to interpret both of these. On the one hand, a loose piece of mummy-linen from the Deir el Bahri 'second find' bore the legend: 'King of Upper & Lower Egypt, Amenemope; Year 49.'[66] At first sight, this item would appear to be unequivocal evidence for at least a 49-year reign for Amen-emope.[67] On the other hand, all versions of Manetho (even Sothis) are agreed in giving Amenemope only 9 years, and Psusennes I either 46 years (Africanus) or 41 years (Eusebius), favouring attribution of high year-dates such as Years 40, 48, 49, to Psusennes I rather than to Amenemope, despite Daressy's bandage-fragment.[68] Both alternatives must be explored fully if a solution is to be found. Chapter 3 below is entirely given over to precisely this task. But first of all, it is necessary to try to delimit the possible correlations at the beginning of the 21st Dynasty, using the end of the 20th as starting-point. Thereby, the central problem tackled in Chapter 3 can be contained within earlier and later limits.

§ 14   4. THE BEGINNINGS OF THE TANITE AND THEBAN LINES

A. HERIHOR AND SMENDES UNDER RAMESSES XI

That Herihor as high priest of Amun was a contemporary of Ramesses XI is clearly proven by their joint work in the hypostyle hall of the temple of Khons at Karnak, while Herihor appears alone, as 'king', in the peristyle court.[69] That Herihor belongs with the last decade or so of Ramesses XI's reign stems from the fact that among the former's titles at Karnak (the chief ones being those of high priest and generalissimo) there appears that of Viceroy of Nubia. This office and title he could not hold until after Year 17, as one Panehsy is securely attested in that office in Years 12 and 17 of Ramesses XI.[70]

66. *G3*, 293, IV, following on Daressy, *RArch³* 28 (1896: I), 78; *BAR*, IV, § 663, *g*.

67. So understood (e.g.) by Gauthier, *G3*, 292, nn. 3, 5; Young, *JARCE* 2 (1963), 109; Černý, *CAH²*, II: 35 (1965), 43 and n. 5; Kitchen, *CdE* 40/80 (1965), 320–1, *BiOr* 23 (1966), 275–6, and in the first version (1963) of this work.

68. Preferred (e.g.) by Petrie, *History of Egypt*, III, 1905, 223 (implicit); Kees, *Hhp.*, 27–8; Hornung, *Untersuchungen zur Chronologie . . . NR*, 1964, 103–4; Wente, *JNES* 26 (1967), 171–3.

69. See the excellent summary by Černý, *CAH²*, II: 35 (1965), 34–5.

70. Year 12, Papyrus Turin Cat. 1896+2006 (Pleyte-Rossi, *Papyrus de Turin*, pl. 65, etc.), see Gardiner, *Ramesside Administrative Documents*, 1948, 36: 1–5, and

Thus, as he is not in his full range of high offices before Year 17 of Ramesses XI, Herihor's explicitly dated activities can be evaluated with greater certainty. These are few but sufficient. In a Year 5, his underling Wenamun travelled to Phoenicia, first calling in on Smendes at Tanis,[71] while in a Year 6 his dockets of renewal were written on the coffins of Sethos I and Ramesses II.[72] Since, in the Wenamun report, Smendes is *not* a king (having no titles at all) but merely some kind of governor in the north comparable with Herihor in the south, these Years 5 and 6 cannot belong to the reign of Smendes as pharaoh any more than to the Years 5 and 6 of Ramesses XI a generation earlier. As has been evident for some time, the sole acceptable solution for these dates is to attribute them to the 'Renaissance Era' (*wḥm-mswt*). The oracle involving Piankh at Karnak[73] (see just below) is explicitly dated to 'Year 7 of the "Renaissance", 3rd month of Shomu, Day 28, under (titles . . .) Ramesses XI'. Elsewhere, we read of 'Year 1, 2nd month of Akhet, Day 2 (etc.), corresponding to Year 19'.[74] In other words, Year 1 of the 'Renaissance Era' equals Year 19 of Ramesses XI. On this basis, the Year 7 of the Era in the Piankh oracle was in fact also Year 25 of Ramesses XI. Hence, reckoned by this Era, the Years 5 and 6 which attest the activity of Herihor would in turn correspond to Years 23 and 24 of the reign of Ramesses XI. In turn, this also dates Smendes as governor in Tanis to about Year 23 of Ramesses XI (Year 5 of the Era, Wenamun).

§ 15   B. HERIHOR AND PIANKH: LENGTH OF THE ERA
                    AND THEIR PONTIFICATES

Thus, the oracle of Piankh in Year 7 of the Era would follow very closely upon the Years 5 and 6 attesting Herihor. In the scene above the main text, Piankh is called Fanbearer, Viceroy of Nubia, High Priest of Amun,

---

JEA 27 (1941), 23. Year 17, Papyrus Turin Cat. 1896 *rt.* (Pleyte-Rossi, *op. cit.*, pls. 66–7; Möller, *Hieratische Lesestücke*, III, 6–7), see *BAR*, IV, §§ 595–600, and A. M. Bakir, *Egyptian Epistolography from the Eighteenth to the Twenty-first Dynasty*, 1970, pls. 24–5, XXXI.

71. *ANET*, 25–6; Lefebvre, *Romans et contes égyptiens*, 1949, 208, 209, etc.

72. *MMR*, 553, 557, fig. 15; *G3*, 232, 1, I–II.

73. Published by C. F. Nims, *JNES* 7 (1948), 157–62, and pl. 8.

74. Papyrus Abbott, Dockets, 8, A.1, A.19; T. E. Peet, *Great Tomb-Robberies of the Twentieth Egyptian Dynasty*, I, 1930, 128, 131, 132, and II, pl. 23. As is shown by Peet, with this document belong Papyrus BM. 10052 (dated explicitly to Year 1 of the 'Renaissance Era'), Papyrus Mayer A (Years 1 and 2 of the Era), and Papyrus BM. 10403 (Year 2 of the Era), in which *the same groups of people* recur as thieves, etc. Thus, Year 1 of the Abbott Dockets can hardly be divorced from Years 1 and 2 of the Era, and the Year 19 must be that of Ramesses XI. No earlier dating than the second half of his reign is feasible because of Herihor's holding high offices from Year 17 (or after) of Ramesses XI, as noted above.

General and Army-leader (*ḥꜣwty*). In the body of the inscription, he is named once only, as the General Piankh. As a result, opinions have been divided over the true date of the assumption of the high-priesthood by Piankh. The most straightforward reading of this monument is to take it as implying that by Year 7 of the Era, Piankh was in fact High Priest, Viceroy, etc., as well as General, and hence that he had succeeded Herihor in those offices in Year 6 or 7 of the Era. The reference to Piankh simply as General in the inscription below would merely be for brevity's sake, citing him by his real title of power.[75] The opposite view is that this record was actually inscribed at some date *later* than the Year 7 in which the oracle took place, and that Piankh was only really high priest at this (unknown) later date, not at the time of the oracle in Year 7.[76]

The answer to this problem is two-fold: consideration of the monument itself, and examination of external data. On the first count, the whole document is a properly-composed unit, executed at one time. There is no warrant, for example, for believing that the top right-hand corner was especially left blank in Year 7 to be conveniently filled in later. In other words, either the whole record dates to Year 7 in its entirety – the simplest and more natural view – or similarly the whole piece was inscribed on one occasion some time later, but giving the date of the oracle, not that of the inscription.

§ **16**   The sole real objection to treating the whole as having been inscribed in that Year 7 to which it is dated is that, in the inscription below the scene, Piankh is termed General but not High Priest.[77] A secondary objection is that the death of Herihor in Year 6 or 7 of the Era under Ramesses XI would make him as 'king' contemporary with Ramesses XI.[78] But neither objection has any real merit. It is now generally conceded, since the pioneer study by Kees himself,[79] that Herihor's rise to power was very likely as a military man, an army-commander. It is significant and noteworthy that – in sharp contrast to all his New Kingdom predecessors[80]

---

75. The interpretation favoured by (e.g.) Sir A. H. Gardiner, *Egypt of the Pharaohs*, 1961, 305; W. Wolf, *Kulturgeschichte des Alten Ägypten*, 1962, 306–7; Černý, *CAH²*, II: 35 (1965), 36; Kitchen, *BiOr* 23 (1966), 274–5; S. Wenig, *ZÄS* 94 (1967), 134, 138; Wente, *JNES* 26 (1967), 176 and fig. 2, *Late Ramesside Letters*, 1967, 3 f., n. 13; J. von Beckerath, *RdE* 20 (1968), 31 f., n. 8.

76. As favoured (e.g.) by Young, *JARCE* 2 (1963), 112, n. 64 (with reserve); Kees, *Hhp.*, 13–15; Hornung, *Untersuchungen zur Chronologie*, 102, n. 5, and *OLZ* 61 (1966), 439.

77. A point developed by Kees, *Hhp.*, 13–15, esp. 14.

78. A point made by Hornung, *Untersuchungen*, 102, n. 5; *OLZ* 61, 439.

79. Cf. Kees, *Herihor und die Aufrichtung des thebanischen Gottesstaates* (*NAWG*) 1936, e.g. 16, 18 f.; also, Wente, *JNES* 25 (1966), 87 end.

80. During the entire foregoing New Kingdom, not a single High Priest of Amun also holds properly military titles (cf. e.g. in G. Lefebvre, *Histoire des grands*

– Herihor *constantly* couples his military titles ('General(issimo)', 'Army-leader', etc.) with his religious title of High Priest of Amun, as on his Leiden stela and in the temple of Khons in Karnak.[81] This also remained the constant practice of his successors.[82] Furthermore, in the one major group of sources for the high priest Piankh – the Late Ramesside letters edited by Černý and Wente – he appears *par excellence* as 'the general' (of Pharaoh), not only by name[83] but also by customary allusion.[84] It is, there-fore, no surprise to find him mentioned in a compact text by his most characteristic title – and in fact, his title of real, effective power.

Kees made the further point that, if Piankh were indeed high priest in Year 7 on the occasion of the oracle, then he would not have needed the mediation of the oracle by the 2nd Prophet of Amun, Nesamun. However, two points should be noted. First, that the 2nd prophet Nesamun *plays no part at all* in the main text, going entirely unmentioned. Therefore, if (with Kees) his presence in the scene is to be taken seriously, this could be further evidence of the compact nature of the text.[85] If he were acting as intermediary (*ḥm-nṯr wḥm*),[86] it would simply be to transmit Piankh's query to the god, or to confirm the god's own vigorous movement of approval.[87] The second point is that, as *petitioner* in this case, Piankh (even as high priest) would hardly be expected also to be his own inter-

prêtres d'Amon de Karnak, 1929). Only two (Roma-roy and Bakenkhons B, pp. 258, 262) were 'commanders' of forces or recruits of Amun or his estate – purely internal powers over the manpower of the estates of Amun of Thebes, and nothing to do with Egypt's real military forces.

81. *G3*, 233–4; on Year 6 dockets, cf. Wente, *Late Ramesside Letters*, 13 f., n. 13 (vizier, general), also Ostracon Cairo Cat. 25744 in Černý, *Ostraca hiératiques*, 90*.

82. From Piankh to Pinudjem II inclusive (*G3*, *passim*), a point made also by Černý, *CAH²*, II: 35 (1965), 36. For Psusennes 'III', the titles of military stamp are lacking simply because we have no inscriptions indisputably his except for bandage-epigraphs – and these never give military titles, only that of high priest.

83. *LRL*, No. 28 (full titles), No. 40 (general and commander of bowmen), No. 13, *vs.* 10 (no title).

84. *LRL*, No. 28, name and full titles, but in the address-line (*vs.* 16) is simply 'the General of Pharaoh'. Under this latter epithet, Piankh was writer of *LRL*, Nos. 18–22 (all to Tjuroy-Thutmose, Necropolis-scribe), 30 (to Butehamun and others), [32], 34, 35 (this one to Nodjmet). One may also note Ostracon Cairo Cat. 25745 (Černý, *Ostraca hiératiques*, 90*), with most titles, but not high-priesthood, so perhaps showing Piankh serving in 'secular' offices under Herihor, cf. Wente, *LRL*, 3, n. 13.

85. But not needfully, since the *ḥm-nṯr wḥm* is not usually mentioned in the narrative of oracles, at least not in any oracle-text known to me during the 19th to 26th Dynasties.

86. On which function, see Kees, *ZÄS* 85 (1960), 138–43; cf. E. Drioton, *ASAE* 41 (1942), 22–3 on *wḥmw*, and Černý in Parker, *A Saite Oracle Papyrus*, 1962, 32 end.

87. *Hn* translated 'nodded' by Nims, *JNES* 7 (1948), 159; probably 'came for-ward'/'assented', with Černý in Parker, *Saite Oracle Papyrus*, 44–45.

mediary or respondent![88] Finally, if one argues that Herihor only adopted royal titles after Ramesses XI had died, then Piankh could not become high priest until later still, as that title was still retained (in his cartouche) by Herihor as 'king' until he died. As the 'Renaissance Era' lasted to a 10th year,[89] and one would have to allow about a year for all the work in the Khons temple showing Herihor as king, the result would be that the Piankh oracle in favour of the storehouse scribe Nesamun would not have been engraved until at least 4 years after the event. This would surely be an arbitrary and improbable assumption.

§ 17 The secondary reason for assuming an anachronism in the Piankh oracle is no more convincing, i.e. doubt that Herihor would be 'king' under Ramesses XI. This doubt is basically a hangover from late last century, when it was believed that Herihor had actually supplanted Ramesses XI to found a line of 'priest-kings', and it fails to pay due regard to the basically fictional nature of Herihor's kingship. That kingship is entirely restricted to the temple walls within the Karnak precincts[90] and to

88. i.e. as both 'judge and jury', so to speak. In the Papyrus Brooklyn 47.218.3 of Year 14 of Psammetichus I, one may note that Montemhat, 4th Prophet of Amun, still serves as hm-ntr whm (see coloured vignette, Parker, *Saite Oracle Papyrus*, pl. 1) and offers incense before the barque-shrine of Amun, *even though the high priest Harkhebi is also present*. Thus, contrary to Kees, *Hhp.*, 14, the presence of Piankh as high priest would *not* exclude either the presence of (e.g.) the 2nd prophet Nesamun or his possibly functioning as hm-ntr-whm.

89. Černý, *LRL*, 17: 11 (No. 9, Papyrus BM. 10326, *rt.* 6); Wente, *LRL*, 37 (cf. 11–13). This Year 10 cannot be of Ramesses XI himself, because the Necropolis-scribes in that period were Thutmose and Iufnamun (Year 12, cf. Peet, *Great Tomb-Robberies*, I, 97: house-list, Pap. BM. 10068, *vs.*, 7–8), not Thutmose and Butehamun as in *LRL*, No. 9. Nor is it Year 10 of Smendes I, because in that year and Year 11, the scribe Butehamun (along with his son Ankhefenamun) was associated with the high priest Pinudjem I in Spiegelberg, *Thebanische Graffiti*, Nos. 1001 (Year 10), 48, 51, 1021 (on dates as Year 11, not 21, 31, cf. already, Wenig, *ZÄS* 94 (1967), 137–8). And these latter dates do not belong to Psusennes I, or else at 26 years for Smendes, 4 years for Amenemnisu, and 10 years of Psusennes I, Butehamun would be officiating (and climbing around the Theban mountain!) some 40 to 50 years after the *LRL* correspondence in general! Thus, between Year 10 of Ramesses XI and Year 10 of Smendes I, the only realistic date for *LRL* No. 9 is Year 10 of the 'Renaissance Era', equal to Year 28 of Ramesses XI (cf. also Wente, *LRL*, 11–12). This result is clinched by the facts (i) that, in that letter, Thutmose is on campaign in Nubia – a chief activity of Piankh, but not (in our present knowledge) of Pinudjem I; (ii) that other letters correlatable with No. 9 (see Wente, *loc. cit.*) tie in with late Ramesses XI and the Era, not with earlier or later epochs; and (iii) in Theban graffiti Nos. 1285 (esp. *b*) and 1286 of Year 10 (later than the Era), Butehamun 'perpetuates the name' of his father Thutmose, i.e. who is then no longer alive (Černý, *Graffiti hiéroglyphiques et hiératiques de la nécropole thébaine*, 1956, 17–18).

90. The peristyle forecourt of the temple of Khons (*G3*, 234), and a line of text in the great hypostyle hall of the temple of Amun (Barguet, *Le temple d'Amon-rê à*

the funerary equipment of Herihor and his family.[91] That 'kingship' is wholly ignored in *all* everyday and administrative documents of whatever date.[92] There is so far no evidence at all that Herihor's 'kingship' was ever recognized in his lifetime anywhere beyond the cloistered courts of Karnak, nor did any successor ever boast of descent from 'king' Herihor. This is in vivid contrast to the full pharaonic titulary of Pinudjem I (with proper prenomen!) who was recognized not only in Thebes but also in Abydos, Coptos and Tanis itself,[93] and was long commemorated in the titles and genealogies of his descendants, Masaharta, Djed-Khons-ef-ankh and Pinudjem II. The reason for Herihor's adoption of kingly titles is unknown. It was possibly because he was the special representative of the royal power in Nubia and Upper Egypt (a vast realm), or perhaps in order to assure himself of rulership before or with Smendes when Ramesses XI died. This ambition was then thwarted by his own prior decease. There is no valid *a priori* reason against Herihor having been 'king' and dying before Ramesses XI.

§ **18** Finally, two more considerations virtually forbid *any* role of Herihor as either high priest or 'king' after the death of Ramesses XI. With the letter *LRL* No. 9 that is explicitly dated Year 10, 1st Shomu, Day 25 (of the 'Renaissance Era', as indicated above), one should associate several others with the same personnel and their movements, which fall within the same limited span of time (1st month of Shomu). One of these is directed to none other than the General, High Priest of Amun, Viceroy of Nubia, etc., Piankh, with the datelines of 1st month of Shomu, Days 18, 20, 29 (year omitted).[94] On this evidence, not only does Herihor fail to appear as high priest, general, viceroy, etc., under Smendes and after Ramesses XI, but he is also evidently dead and gone by Year 10 of the Era (Year 28 of Ramesses XI) with Piankh occupying all his offices. Second, but less un-ambiguous, is the datum of a bandage inscribed in a Year 1 under the high priest Pinudjem I, found on the mummy of Herihor's wife, 'queen' Nodjmet.[95] This date is of a piece with those of Pinudjem I as high priest

91. As on the second funerary papyrus of his wife Nodjmet, now Pap. BM. 10541, where both have cartouches (*Introductory Guide to the Egyptian Collections, British Museum*, 1930 ed., 81; 1964 ed., 58, Nodjmet only). The provenance of a faience vase (*G3*, 236, XVIII) is uncertain.

92. So, in Year 6 dockets on coffins (*G3*, 232), and in such jottings as Ostracon Cairo Cat. 25744. And when Piankh himself writes to Nodjmet (*LRL*, No. 35), he does so to the Chief of the Harim of Amun, Nodjmet, not to Nodjmet as a 'Queen' or the like.

93. Cf. below, Part IV, §§ 216–19.

94. *LRL*, No. 28; on this point, cf. Wente, *LRL*, 11–12, with details on Nos. 16, 9, 28, etc.

95. See G. Elliott Smith, *Royal Mummies, Cairo Catalogue*, p. 97.

in Years 6, 9, 10, 13, 15, from other bodies, followed by Years 16–19 which record Masaharta as high priest under 'king' Pinudjem I, plus a Year 8 with 'king' Pinudjem I.[96] The solution adopted over the crux of a long reign of 48 or 49 years for either Psusennes I or Amenemope will tend to determine one's interpretation of these two series of dates for Pinudjem I as high priest and as 'king'. Thus, on the hypothesis of a long reign for Amenemope, the Years 1–15 for Pinudjem I as high priest would come under Psusennes I, and his Year 8 as 'king' under Amenemope. On that basis, Piankh could be high priest in the last years of the 'Renaissance Era' and all of the reign of Smendes (up to 26 years in itself). But, on the alternative hypothesis of a long reign for Psusennes I, there is no real escape from dating the second reign (Year 8 with Pinudjem I as 'king') to Psusennes I (or just possibly to Amenemnisu, if he preceded Psusennes), and therefore the first reign involved, with Years 1–15, then 16–19 to Smendes I.[97] Piankh would then *already* have been succeeded by his son Pinudjem I as high priest by Year 1 of the new pharaoh, Smendes, and the whole of *his* pontificate (besides that of Herihor before him) would thus have fallen just within the reign of Ramesses XI, except for a few months at the most.

Hence, the only realistic interpretation of the Piankh oracle is in fact the straightforward one: like any other inscription, it was carved within a reasonably short time of the event commemorated, and in this case actually in Year 7 of the 'Renaissance Era'. By that time, Herihor was dead and all his functions (other than a fictional 'kingship') had passed to Piankh, seen active in Year 10 of the Era, if possibly (on one hypothesis) not for much longer, before his son Pinudjem I succeeded him.

§ **19**   One question that remains to be considered here is whether the 'Renaissance Era' lasted beyond Year 10, and correspondingly the reign of Ramesses XI beyond Years 27 (Abydos stela) and 28 (as equivalent of Year 10 of the Era). As the combined accession date of Ramesses XI and the Era can be calculated to have fallen within the 4th month of Shomu, Days 18–23 inclusive,[98] the dates in Year 10 of the 3rd month of Shomu, Days 18–29 (cf. *LRL*, Nos. 9, 28) would fall barely a month before the change of regnal year from 10/28 to 11/29. Hence, as a *minimum*, it is wisest to allow 28 full years to Ramesses XI (10 full years to the Era), ending at earliest in Year 29/11. But Hornung has noted a Ramesses, son of Uaphres, who is assigned 29 years in the book of Sothis (No. 24), suggesting that this

96. Cf. Chapter 3 below, *passim*, and Excursus B for these datelines.
97. See Chapter 3 just below.
98. See Helck, *Studia Biblica et Orientalia III*, 1959, 128–9, esp. 129. After Day 17 and before Day 24.

could stand for Ramesses XI at 29, or possibly 30 years.[99] One may, therefore, suggest that Ramesses XI and the Era died in his 30th and its 12th
year, after 29 (and 11) full years of reign.

§ 20   If Pinudjem I were already high priest of Amun in Year 1 of
Smendes (on the hypothesis of a long reign for Psusennes I), then Piankh
would have died soon after his last attested activity in Year 10 of the Era
(Year 28 of Ramesses XI). This was perhaps sometime in the Year 11/29,
or about a year before Ramesses XI himself died. Piankh succeeded Heri-
hor in either Year 6 or 7 of the Era. The latest attested date of Herihor is
Year 6, 2nd month of Akhet, Day 7, and probably 3rd month of Peret(?),[100]
Day 15, which would fall in the early and middle parts respectively of
Year 6. In turn, the earliest date for Piankh (the oracle) is Year 7, 3rd
month of Shomu, Day 28, very late in the 7th year and, in fact, barely a
month or so from its end. Hence, one may suggest provisionally that
Herihor may have died early in Year 7, after 6 full years of rule from the
beginning of the 'Renaissance Era' (its Years 1–6 plus a fraction). That 6
years would have been ample for his works in the temple of Khons,
especially those as 'king'. In turn, Piankh would also have had a relatively
brief pontificate of some 4 years, i.e. Years 7–11 of the Era. This would be
quite sufficient to contain his very few monuments.[101] Otherwise, on the
alternative hypothesis (long reign of Amenemope), the Year 1 of Pinudjem
from Nodjmet's mummy would come under Psusennes I (or, Amenemnisu), and then the pontificate of Piankh would cover not only the last 4 or 5
years of Ramesses XI and the Era but also most of the 26 years of the reign
of Smendes I, virtually some 30 years. This is doubtless possible, but
agrees much less well with the extraordinarily few monuments, etc., that
witness to the pontificate and activities of Piankh.

99. Hornung, *Untersuchungen zur Chronologie und Geschichte des Neuen Reiches*,
1964, 100; also Helck, *Untersuchungen zu Manetho und den ägyptischen Königslisten*,
1956, 71. Book of Sothis, Waddell, *Manetho*, 236–7. The identification of No. 24
(R. son of Uaphres) as Ramesses XI at 29 years would be confirmed if No. 23
(Ramesse Iubasse) at 39 years were in fact Ramesses X at 9 years (cf. Parker, *RdE*
11 (1957), 163 f.) pius an otiose 30; cf. also Hornung, *Untersuchungen*, 99, n. 45.
Then, No. 22 (Ramesse-ameno) at 19 years would be Ramesses IX (so also Helck,
Manetho, 71, and Hornung, *op. cit.*, 99, n. 42), and No. 21 (Ramesse-seos) be
Ramesses VIII Sethirkhopshef at 23 years for 3 years (20, otiose), implicit with
Hornung, *op. cit.*, 99. No. 20 (Usimare) at 31 years could be Ramesses III; the
other names may here be left aside at present.
100. Read as Akhet by Daressy, *Cercueils, Cat. Musée du Caire*, 1909, *ad loc.*
101. Abydos stela, Karnak oracle, Ostracon Cairo Cat. 25745, and *LRL*.

CHAPTER 3

The Middle Years of the Dynasty –
Two Hypotheses

§ 21   1. INTRODUCTORY

It is on the middle years of the 21st Dynasty that – apart from family relationships – scholarly controversy has centred in recent years. As mentioned above (§ 13), conflict arises between two lines of evidence and on how to interpret them: an apparent Year 49 of Amenemope on a mummy-bandage, as against Manetho's tradition of 46 or 41 years for Psusennes I and only 9 years for Amenemope. The high priest Menkheperre held office in a reign that reached to years 40, 48, and was the contemporary of Amenemope *at the latest*, and also possibly of one or more of that king's predecessors. The conflict has crystallized into two rival hypotheses: one operating with a long reign of Amenemope (49 years or more) and say 20–26 years for Psusennes I, and the other with a long reign of 46–50 years for Psusennes I and only 9 years for Amenemope.[102] Each in turn must now be explored.

§ 22   2. HYPOTHESIS OF A LONG REIGN FOR AMENEMOPE

A. BASIS

The starting-point is the notorious piece of loose mummy-bandage ('second find' at Deir el Bahri) on which Daressy read: 'King of Upper & Lower Egypt, Amenemope; Regnal Year 49.' No other king of the dynasty is yet attested with a year-date anything like as high attached to his name.

The First Step. This has been to attribute the years 40, 48, 48 with the

102. See references, § 13 above, for adherents of the two views.

24

high priest Menkheperre[103] to the reign of Amenemope. No scholar, so far, is prepared to allow *both* 46/41 years to Psusennes I *and* 49+ years to Amenemope, all told.

The Second Step. This has usually been to attribute Year 25 of the Maunier or 'Banishment' stela (Louvre C. 256) to Amenemope's reign also, but recent work on this stela suggests otherwise.[104]

The Third Step. Menkheperre's successors Smendes II and Pinudjem II were also contemporaries of Amenemope. Thus for this to be possible, Amenemope would clearly have to have outlived Menkheperre and Year 48. If Menkheperre died in Year 48, Smendes II (ephemeral in any case) could have been high priest in Year 49. Associated several times with Amenemope in priestly burials,[105] Pinudjem II would be the contemporary of Amenemope from Year 49 onwards. As one bandage-epigraph[106] associates Pinudjem II with Amenemope in a Year $[x]+3$, one might restore this to read 'Year 53', which would assure an overlap of up to 4 or 5 years between the two potentates.

The Fourth Step. To square this result with Manetho. His 'Amenemope, 9 years' could be emended to 'Amenemope, $\langle 4\rangle 9$ years', and one might infer a co-regency between Amenemope (from Year 50) and Osochor for the first 3 years or so of his 6-year reign. Particularly if he were a son as well as a successor of a long-reigned and aged Amenemope,[107] Osochor himself would have been a man of advancing years when co-regent and thus did not long survive Amenemope as sole ruler.[108]

The Fifth Step. As on this construction Menkheperre did *not* outlive Amenemope (Year 48), the 6th and 7th years with which Menkheperre is associated[109] will be those of Amenemope at the latest, and not of his successor. Hence, the pontificate of Menkheperre lasted at least 42 years during Years 6–48 of Amenemope (but see below).

§ 23   B. CONSEQUENCES FOR THE PREDECESSORS OF
MENKHEPERRE AND AMENEMOPE

The First Step. Pinudjem I was high priest of Amun in Years 1, 6, 9, 10, 13, 15 of one reign; Year 15 appears to be *directly* followed by Year 16 with

103. In the Karnak Priestly Annals, inspection-stela from Karnak, and bandage-epigraph from mummy No. 105 respectively (*G3*, 265, IV–VI).
104. See below, § 23, Second Step.
105. See references, § 11, above.
106. *G3*, 292, 3, II, mummy No. 124 (given as 134); Daressy, *ASAE* 8 (1907), 33: 124, cf. *G3*, 292, n. 5.
107. On the remains of Amenemope as an old man, cf. Derry, *ASAE* 41 (1942), 149.
108. Like Edward VII succeeding the long-reigned Queen Victoria.
109. *G3*, 263–4, 5, I–II.

Masaharta acting as high priest and entitled son of *King* Pinudjem. Masaharta continued in Years 18, 19. Thereafter, in a succeeding reign, King Pinudjem I appears in a Year 8.[110] Once Pinudjem I had become 'king' with *full* titulary (proper prenomen, etc.), he remained king until his death. He is thenceforth proudly mentioned solely as king by his sons and descendants, and was buried with funerary equipment naming him as king. Therefore, his Year 8 date as king is not to be intercalated between his Years 6 and 9 as high priest, but should be attributed to a subsequent reign.[111] Thus, we have one reign of up to 19 years (with Pinudjem I as high priest up to Year 15, and 'king' after it), and a later reign up to whose 8th year Pinudjem I still appeared as a king.[112]

The Second Step. As Menkheperre is already high priest in Year 6 of Amenemope, Masaharta's pontificate cannot be later than Years 16–19 of a previous king – Psusennes I or Smendes I. Likewise the pontificate of Pinudjem I himself cannot be later than the immediately-prior Years 1–15. As Year 25 of the Maunier stela is the date of induction of Menkheperre as high priest (l. 8)[113] and is followed by a section probably dated to an early year of a *later* reign[114] when Menkheperre asked for the recall of exiles, that Year 25 must itself belong to a reign earlier than that of Amenemope. It would be of Psusennes I rather than of Smendes I.

The Third Step. A Dakhla stela of the 22nd Dynasty refers back to Year 19 of a pharaoh Psusennes, who is universally identified with Psusennes I rather than II. Hence, Manetho's figure for Psusennes I might be emended from 46/41 years to 26/21 years (an otiose 20). If one adopts 26 years for Psusennes I, then Menkheperre could have been appointed as successor to Masaharta in Year 25 of Psusennes I (Maunier stela), and his appeal about the exiles would come in an early year of Psusennes I's successor, Amenemnisu or Amenemope. The pontificates of Pinudjem I (Years 1–15) and of Masaharta (Years 16–19 at least) with Pinudjem as 'king' would come in the reign of Psusennes I, while Pinudjem I as 'king' in a Year 8 would be

---

110. *G3*, 248, XIX; cf. Young, *JARCE* 2 (1963), 102, nn. 15, 16, 18.

111. This point has been made by Young, *op. cit.*, 104; Černý, *CAH²*, II: 35 (1965), 44–5; and esp. Wente, *JNES* 26 (1967), 168–70.

112. That, as 'king', Pinudjem I did *not* reckon by his own regnal years is indicated particularly by his change of status being noted in Years 15 and 16 of *one* reign (of an already-reigning king), not by a 'Year 1' of Pinudjem after his high-priesthood in another's Years 1–15. That Pinudjem I as 'king' did not count his own regnal years or have an independent reign is now almost universally admitted.

113. Where the text clearly states 'he (= Amun) established him (= Menkheperre) in the place of his father as high priest of Amun and generalissimo of the south and north', near the end of a paragraph that began with a 'Year 25' date in line 4. This has earlier been seen also by Wente, *JNES* 26 (1967), 168, n. 100, following Kees and with the concurrence of Drs. G. R. Hughes and C. F. Nims.

114. See J. von Beckerath, *RdE* 20 (1968), 17: 8*d*, and 33 and n. 2.

under Amenemnisu or Amenemope (Menkheperre as high priest). Under Smendes I, Piankh would be high priest, following on from the end of the 'Renaissance Era'.

The Fourth Step. The length of pontificate of Piankh under Smendes I would depend on the length of the latter's reign. Manetho gives 26 years, which is possible; emendation to a more modest 16 years has been suggested,[115] which would help with the lack of monumental attestation for both Piankh and Smendes.

§ 24   C. PRELIMINARY TABLE OF RESULTS ON THIS
                             HYPOTHESIS

High Priest	King	Length of Pontificate
Dynasty 20		
Herihor: Years 19–25/ 1–7	Ramesses XI and Era (29/11 years)	Herihor: 6 years
Piankh: Years 25–30/ 7–12		
Dynasty 21		
Piankh: continued Years 1–16/26	Smendes I (16 or 26 years)	
		Piankh: 21/25 or 31/35 years[116]
?	(Amenemnisu, 4 years)?[116]	
Pinudjem I (HP): Years 1–15	Psusennes I (26 years)	
		Pinudjem I (HP): 15/19 years[116]
{ Pinudjem I (King) Masaharta (HP) } : Years 16–19	Psusennes I (26 years)	
Menkheperre: appointed, Year 25	Psusennes I (26 years)	Pinudjem I (King): 18/22 years[116]
	(Amenemnisu, 4 years)?[116]	Masaharta: 8 or 10 years
	Amenemope (52 years)	
(Pinudjem I: king to Year 8)		

115. e.g. by Young, *JARCE* 2 (1963), 108–9.
116. At this juncture in the argument, either position has been allowed for Amenemnisu (i.e. before or after Psusennes I); the placing of his 4-year reign can affect various pontificates in length by that amount, allowed for in this table.

High Priest	King	Length of Pontificate
Menkheperre: Years 6–48	Amenemope (52 years)	Menkheperre: 49 or 53 years[117]
Smendes II: Year 49?	Amenemope (52 years)	Smendes II: 0/1 years
Pinudjem II: (49/50 ff.)	Amenemope (52 years)	
Pinudjem II: continued	Osochor (6 years; 3, co-regent)	
		Pinudjem II: 16 years
Pinudjem II: died, Year 10	Siamun (19 years)	
Psusennes 'III'	Siamun (19 years)	
Psusennes 'III': Year 5(?)	Psusennes II (14 years)	
	Psusennes II (14 years)	Psusennes 'III': up to 24 years

§ 25   3. HYPOTHESIS OF A LONG REIGN FOR PSUSENNES I

A. BASIS

Here, the starting-points are two: the regnal figures for Psusennes I (46/41 years) and Amenemope (9 years) in the extant versions of Manetho, and the identity of the high priest Smendes II at Thebes with the high priest Smendes son of Menkheperre attested on bracelets from the burial of Psusennes I at Tanis.

The First Step. The acceptance of Africanus' figure of 46 years of sole rule by Psusennes I, as a basis upon which to attribute the Years 40, 48, 48 attested with the high priest Menkheperre to the reign of Psusennes I.

The Second Step. To square such high dates as Years 48 and 49 (see next step) for Psusennes I in the first-hand sources with the 46 years of Manetho. This can be done either by emending Manetho's extant entry for '46 years' to (say) '48 years' (if Psusennes I died in Year 49) with von Beckerath,[118] or by assuming that Psusennes I had a co-regent from his Year 47 onwards, with Hornung.[119] Such a co-regency would have lasted

117. Cf. preceding note. On this hypothesis (long reign of Amenemope), one cannot easily attribute the Year 25 of Menkheperre's appointment to Smendes I, because Menkheperre's total pontificate (at 26 years for Psusennes I, 1 year of Smendes preceding, 48 years of Amenemope, and possibly 4 years of Amenemnisu if before Psusennes) would come to 75/79 years! This is hardly likely to commend itself.

118. Tacitly, *OLZ* 62 (1967), 9, where he suggests a 48-year reign for Psusennes I, taking Year 49 as his last year (year of death), followed by Year 1 of Amenemope.

119. Cf. his *Untersuchungen zur Chronologie und Geschichte des Neuen Reiches*, 1964, 103–5.

little more than 2 years (c. Years 47–49), and so the difference between these two views need not amount to more than this 2 years.

The Third Step. To square the Daressy bandage-fragment, 'King Amenemope, Year 49' with a 9-year reign of Amenemope and a 46/48+ years' reign of Psusennes I. To interpret this datum *as it stands* as meaning 'Year 49 (*sc.*, of Psusennes I), Amenemope being co-regent' is, bluntly, unbelievable. It must, rather, be understood as part of a now incomplete legend: [Year *x* of] King Amenemope; Year 49 [of King Psusennes I], or the like.[120] For this reason, Hornung's assumption of a co-regency[121] is probably preferable to von Beckerath's emendation of Manetho from 46 to 48 years.

The Fourth Step. To apply the identification of the high priest Smendes II in Thebes with the high priest Smendes son of Menkheperre known from the burial of Psusennes I in Tanis. The Theban document associates Smendes II with the reign of Amenemope.[122] The Smendes bracelets in Tanis[123] come from the *undisturbed*[124] burial of Psusennes I, so that if the two Smendes are one and the same, the Theban high priest began his pontificate under Psusennes I and continued (if but briefly) into the reign of Amenemope, thus ensuring that the high priest Menkheperre must have died in Year 48 of Psusennes I or very soon after.[125] The brief overlap between Psusennes I and the high priest Smendes (II) might require an extension of the reign of Psusennes I into a 50th (incomplete) year. Smendes II doubtless had a very brief pontificate; his successor Pinudjem II was contemporary with Amenemope, Osochor and Siamun as already seen.[126]

The Fifth Step. To look for the earlier limits of the pontificate of Menkheperre. The Year 25 for the installation of Menkheperre noted on the Maunier stela cannot belong to Psusennes I, but must belong to a pre-

120. See more fully below, Excursus A.

121. *Op. cit.*, but *not* of the 6 years' length erroneously postulated by him, *Untersuchungen*, 104, n. 28 (up to 7 years, in fact, cf. von Beckerath, *RdE* 20 (1968), 30–1), through failure to construe correctly the Year 6 associated with the high priest Menkheperre.

122. Cf. above, §§ 2 and 11.

123. Published by Montet, *Psus*, 149, fig. 54 top right, 154–5, Nos. 598–9 and 600–1; pls. 122, 123–4.

124. This is clear from the descriptions of Montet, e.g. *Psus.*, 21–22, 31, 130 (plaster, largely fallen, that sealed lid and box of outer sarcophagus; rivets that secured lid and body of innermost silver coffin; plaster that sealed roof of W. part of tomb, contrast E. part, p. 32). The bracelets were on Psusennes' body. This disposes of Kees's suggestion (*Hhp.*, 56) that the Smendes bracelets could have got mixed up in Psusennes' burial when Amenemope was reburied in the tomb of Psusennes. In fact, Psusennes' body was left undisturbed, and Amenemope was reburied in an entirely separate chamber adjoining Psusennes (formerly his queen's).

125. Cf. Hornung, *Untersuchungen*, 104–5; Wente, *JNES* 26 (1967), 168.

126. Cf. above, §§ 7, 9, 11.

decessor (see next step), (i) because the Year 25 is followed thereon by an early year of a later king (and Menkheperre did not outlive Psusennes I, cf. above),[127] and (ii) because Year 6 with Menkheperre as high priest[128] *can* be attributed to the reign of Psusennes I (extending his pontificate over years 6–48 of that king), and so also can the early years of the later king of the Maunier stela, which again places its Year 25 in a previous reign.

The Sixth Step. As the Year 25 of the Maunier stela (and Menkheperre's installation)[129] must be of a reign before Psusennes I (see previous step), and Amenemnisu (if rightly placed here) ruled only 4 years, then with von Beckerath[130] one must refer that Year 25 to Year 25 of Smendes I. The early year (1–5?) of a subsequent king can then be referred to either Amenemnisu or Psusennes I, only 2–6 years after the 25th year.[131] Thus, the total pontificate of Menkheperre would have comprised 1 year of Smendes, 48 years of Psusennes I, plus probably 4 years of Amenemnisu between these, a total of either 49 or 53 years.[132]

§ 26   B. CONSEQUENCES FOR THE PREDECESSORS OF
        MENKHEPERRE AND PSUSENNES I

The First Step. Precisely as on the other hypothesis, we have Pinudjem I as high priest in Years 1–15 of one king and then himself 'king' (with Masaharta as high priest) in Years 16–19, and then still boasting the kingly titles in Year 8 of a second king.[133]

The Second Step. As Menkheperre was high priest from Year 25 of Smendes I, continuing on through the reign of Psusennes I (e.g. Years 6–48), then the anterior high-priesthoods of Pinudjem I (Years 1–15) and Masaharta (Years 16–19) can only date to the Years 1–15 and 16–19 ff. of Smendes I, and to no later king.[134] The 'kingship' of Pinudjem I will then also have begun in Year 16 of Smendes I, and have continued to at least Year 8 of either Amenemnisu or (more likely) Psusennes I.[135]

---

127. Unless one assumed a Year 1 to 5 of the later co-regent Amenemope. But the vast interval of a quarter-century from Year 25 of Psusennes I to a date equal to his Years 49–50 or later seems wildly unlikely between the events of Year 25 and those of the subsequent reign all recounted on this one stela.

128. So, in contrast to Hornung, *Untersuchungen*, 104, n. 28, especially as von Beckerath (*RdE* 20 (1968), 30–1) adds a further bandage of a Year 10 with Pinudjem I as only high priest – i.e. from before the pontificates of Masaharta or Menkheperre. Year 6 with the latter is therefore not earlier than Amenemnisu or Psusennes I.

129. Cf. above, § 23, Second Step, and nn. 113, 114.

130. *Op. cit.*, 31; Wente, *op. cit.*, 168.

131. Contrast the alternative rejected in note 127, above.

132. The same as on the alternative hypothesis, cf. § 24 above.

133. See above, § 23, First Step.

134. As already seen by von Beckerath and Wente, *locc. citt.*

135. Psusennes I, Wente, *op. cit.*, 168–70, and von Beckerath, *loc. cit.*

The Third Step. Consequently, Smendes I would indeed have reigned 26 years as recorded in Manetho (guaranteed up to Year 25), which should not be emended to 16 years. With Pinudjem I as high priest in Year 1 of Smendes I, the pontificate of Piankh, which is little-attested in any case, would be over by the death of Ramesses XI, having lasted about 4 years.

§ 27 C. PRELIMINARY TABLE OF RESULTS, SECOND HYPOTHESIS

High Priest	King	Length of Pontificate
Dynasty 20		
Herihor: Years 19–25/ 1–7	Ramesses XI and Era (29/11 years)	Herihor: 6 years
Piankh: Years 25–29/ 7–11		Piankh: 4 years
Pinudjem I: Years 29–30/11–12		
Dynasty 21		
Pinudjem I: continued Years 1–15	Smendes I (26 years)	
		Pinudjem I (HP): 16 years
{ Pinudjem I (King) Masaharta (HP) } : Years 16 ff.	Smendes I (26 years)	
		Masaharta: 10 years
Menkheperre: appointed, Year 25	Smendes I (26 years)	Pinudjem I (King): 18/22 years [136]
	(Amenemnisu, 4 years)?	
Pinudjem I (King): continued, till Year 8 (A or P)	Psusennes I (49 years)	
Menkheperre: continued till Year 48	Psusennes I (49 years)	Menkheperre: 49/53 years [137]
Smendes II: attested	Psusennes I (49 years)	
Smendes II	Amenemope (9 years; 2, co-regent)	Smendes II: 2 years?
Pinudjem II	Amenemope (9 years; 2, co-regent)	
Pinudjem II	Osochor (6 years)	

136. Depending on whether the 4 years of Amenemnisu is reckoned before Psusennes I or later (as well as attributing Year 8 to Psusennes I rather than to an anterior Amenemnisu).

137. See preceding note. The ephemeral pontiff Djed-Khons-ef-ankh (§§ 2, 55, and Excursus C) has been deliberately omitted from these preliminary tables, §§ 24, 27, as he does not affect the chronology.

High Priest	King	Length of Pontificate
Pinudjem II: died, Year 10	Siamun (19 years)	Pinudjem II: *c.* 23 years
Psusennes 'III'	Siamun (19 years)	
Psusennes 'III':	Psusennes II (14 years)	
Year 5(?)	Psusennes II (14 years)	Psusennes 'III': up to 24 years

§ 28   4. THE TWO HYPOTHESES COMPARED: STRENGTHS AND WEAKNESSES

A. INTRODUCTORY

From the outlines given above, §§ 21–27, it should be obvious that it is possible to hold to one or other of two similar but rival hypotheses on the chronology of the first and middle parts of the 21st Dynasty, on the basis of the data utilized above. But is a definite choice between them possible? Any such decision requires a scrutiny of the respective weaknesses, both real *and* imaginary, of the two hypotheses thus far, plus the adduction of additional factors, including such data as can be reliably gleaned on family relationships. With the exception of this last factor (to which Chapter 4 is devoted), that scrutiny must now be applied.

§ 29   B. INDIVIDUAL POINTS

(i) *The Bandage-fragment 'King Amenemope; Year 49'*
This datum has been stigmatized as presenting 'an unusual sequence', because the king's name precedes the date,[138] and has been reinterpreted to mean what in fact it does not say. As it stands, the formula as copied here by Daressy could just possibly be taken as being an abbreviated form of the formula showing the order king + date seen in another bandage-epigraph of this same king:[139] 'King . . . Amenemope Beloved of Amun; linen made by the high priest of Amun, Pinudjem II son of Menkheperre for his lord Amun in Year [x] + 3.' Here, one would have the same basic order – king, the date – as in the criticized docket; the difference could simply be one of drastic abbreviation to king + date, omitting all other details (unless these are lost). On this view, the epigraph as copied could then be cited in favour of the hypothesis of a long reign for Amenemope.

Is there, then, any alternative interpretation that is really viable? First, one may again firmly dismiss the suggestion[140] that 'King Amenemope;

138. e.g. Wente, *JNES* 26 (1967), 173.
139. *G3*, 292, 3, II, etc.
140. Implicitly, Hornung, *Untersuchungen*, 103, and von Beckerath, *OLZ* 62 (1967), 9.

Year 49' is to be taken *on its own* as standing for (accession of) King Amenemope, Year 49 (*sc.* of Psusennes I), etc. Where one has a co-regency of two full and equal kings both having their own regnal years, where in *all* of Egyptian history might one find such an anomaly as the year of *one* king and name of *the other*?[141] Hence, this solution has to be discarded.

However, the highly abbreviated form of just the king's name plus a date (without other details), and the fact that the piece is a mere fragment ('linge tombé') point clearly in another direction for an alternative solution. One may suggest that the full reading was once: '[Year *x* of] King Amenemope; Year 49 [of King Psusennes I]', with the new king's name first. On the standard form of bandage-epigraph as known throughout the 21st Dynasty,[142] one may suggest that the bandage and its text are indeed very incomplete, and once read somewhat as follows: '[Year 3 of][143] King Amenemope, Year 49 [of King Psusennes I; linen made by the high priest of Amun, Smendes II son of Menkheperre[144] for his lord Amun].'[145] This scheme would fit exactly the known structure of bandage-epigraphs. Its sole unusual feature would be the double-dating – a feature which is not unknown in other Late Period texts in the following epoch (Shoshenq III–Pedubast I; Pedubast I–Iuput I; Osorkon III–Takeloth III). No other properly preserved linen epigraph of the 21st Dynasty is abbreviated merely to king + date. Thus, some such restitution as that given above is mandatory; and, a year-date *just on its own* does not follow the king's name.

Thus, if the epigraph in question here is to be taken narrowly as it stands in Daressy's copy, it is just possibly a heavily abbreviated form (otherwise unknown) of a formula otherwise attested with fuller text under Amenemope: King's name – linen made by *x* for *y* – date. One might, therefore, still argue for a long reign of Amenemope from this piece, but not without some difficulty.

It is, however, far preferable to suggest a restoration that is in harmony with nearly all known texts of the species – hence, allowing a long reign for Psusennes I – assuming that a co-regency was once denoted here. This

141. As originally made in *CdE* 40/80 (1965), 321, my point is – within these terms – irrefutable, and has never been answered. Wente's attempt to turn its edge (*op. cit.*, 173) fails, precisely because his comparison of Pinudjem I with regnal years of Psusennes I is *not* a true parallel, seeing that Pinudjem I had no regnal years of his own, whereas both Psusennes I and Amenemope did.

142. See Excursus A, for these formulae in full.

143. If a co-regency be accepted, along with Africanus' figure of 46 full years for Psusennes I, then the latter's Year 47 will be Amenemope's Year 1, and accordingly his Year 49 be Amenemope's Year 3.

144. Or, one might just possibly restore either Menkheperre son of 'King' Pinudjem I, or Pinudjem II son of Menkheperre.

145. Or, for Mut or for Khons, as on some other bandages.

might be unusual, but is by no means impossible. Restoration there must be; Daressy himself termed the piece 'linge tombé'.

One final point: if this datum is to be discarded *entirely* from study of this epoch merely because it does not fit easily into this or that pre-supposition reached on other grounds, then one must *also* be prepared to discard on principle *the whole body* of such epigraphs now uncollated or uncollatable. This, however, is a 'solution' so radical and far-reaching that few are likely to espouse it, given the otherwise extremely limited range of chronological data available for this epoch!

§ **30**   (ii) *The Bandage of King Amenemope, Year* [x]+3
On the hypothesis of a long reign for Amenemope, this document requires a restoration as Year [5]3, which gives this king a reign even longer than the 49 years to be supposed from an emended Manetho; it would desiderate a 3 or 4 years' co-regency with Osochor to allow of the emendation ⟨4⟩9 years in Manetho. This is all possible, but not specially desirable, as Osochor would then have only 2 or 3 years' independent reign out of a total of 6. However, on the hypothesis of a long reign for Psusennes I, the broken numeral might be theoretically restored as any number from [1+]3 to [6+]3, in Years 4 to 9 of Amenemope, depending on what is permitted by the surviving traces[146] in the hieratic original.[147] In this case, the Psusennes I hypothesis is more 'economical' in assumptions than is that for the long reign of Amenemope.

(iii) *The High Priests Smendes*
Here, the hypothesis of a long reign for Amenemope requires the postulate of two separate high priests called Smendes: one in Thebes, between Menkheperre and Pinudjem II (as these were contemporary with Amene-mope and adjacent reigns), and one in Tanis about the time of death of Psusennes I, son of an *unknown* Menkheperre. The latter would have to be a high priest of Amun *in Tanis* (perfectly feasible in principle, cf. Excursus D, below), not Thebes. If the bracelets had been heirlooms (no unknown thing), they might even be construed with Montet as referring back to Smendes I as high priest of Amun in Tanis, son of an unknown Men-kheperre.[148] Against this idea stands the fact that these very bracelets incorporate the monogram and names of Akheperre Psusennes I, and surely, therefore, if made for king Psusennes I should have entitled his

146. If the original could ever be rediscovered!
147. e.g. a Year 7 with four strokes over three as in Möller, *Hieratische Paläo-graphie*, II, No. 620 (upper right), from 'Queen' Nodjmet.
148. Cf. Montet, *Tanis*, 1942, 155, or *Les énigmes de Tanis*, 1952, 153–5.

father as king Smendes, or at least have put his name and title in a cartouche. And Menkheperre is such a rare private personal-name before the Theban high priest of that name, that one hesitates to invoke a new Menkheperre *ex nihilo*.

Thus, with the long-reign-for-Psusennes hypothesis, it makes far better sense to postulate *one* high priest Smendes II son of Menkheperre who briefly succeeded his father in Thebes and saw out the reign of Psusennes I (hence the bracelets). Particularly if (*on either view*) the Theban Smendes II were son of Theban Menkheperre: *two* high priests with identical names, corresponding offices, and separate but identically named fathers (a less usual name at that) – all this seems a very improbable assumption within one limited span of years. Assumption of but one such high priest at the time is a far more 'economical' hypothesis, and favours that of a long reign for Psusennes I.

§ 31   (iv) *Emendations to Manetho*

On the long-reign-for-Amenemope hypothesis, no less than *four* numerical emendations of the extant text of Manetho are required or desirable; in three of these four cases, these emendations run counter to all main versions of Manetho. Compare as follows:

> Smendes I, 26 years: probably 16 years.
> Psusennes I, 46(41) years: to 26 years.
> Amenemope, 9 years: to $\langle 4 \rangle 9$ years.
> Siamun, 9 years: to $\langle 1 \rangle 9$ years.

On the long-reign-for-Psusennes hypothesis, only *one* such emendation is required:

> Siamun, 9 years: to $\langle 1 \rangle 9$ years.

For *both* hypotheses, it is possibly or probably desirable to emend the *order* of kings in Manetho just once, to make Nepherkheres (Amenemnisu) the predecessor of Psusennes I, rather than his successor.[149] This isolated problem, therefore, has no bearing on which hypothesis is to be preferred, whereas the range of numerical emendations (far-reaching with long reign of Amenemope; only one, for Psusennes) clearly favours the thesis of a long reign of Psusennes I as the sounder one.

(v) *Length of Pontificate for Piankh*

On the long-reign-for-Amenemope hypothesis, the tenure of office of Piankh would be 4 or 5 years under Ramesses XI and a further 26 (or 16?)

149. On Amenemnisu, cf. further below, §§ 56, 151–3.

years in the reign of Smendes I – some 20 or 30 years at least, and more
(*c.* 25/35 years) if he also served for 4 years under Amenemnisu to the
accession of Psusennes I. On the alternative view, Piankh's term of office
would have been about 4 years only. The fact that the monuments and
records of Piankh's pontificate are so extraordinarily few[150] for a man shown
as active in the *LRL* would clearly favour a short tenure of office for Piankh
and the long reign hypothesis for Psusennes I. Furthermore, between the
West-Theban activities of Herihor (Year 6 of the 'Renaissance Era') and
those of Pinudjem I (Years 1–15 of Psusennes I) – on the long-reigned-
Amenemope thesis – there would be virtually *a quarter-century gap* in the
records of activities in the Theban necropolis. On either hypothesis, there
is so far little enough from the middle years of the known long reign of 49 years
(regardless of whether it be of Psusennes I or Amenemope), but a further
long gap of about 25 years (and probably more), which the long-reigned-
Amenemope hypothesis would require, seems hardly credible. On this
ground, therefore, the long-reigned-Psusennes hypothesis seems preferable.

§ 32   (vi) *Some Neutral Factors*

(*a*) *Length of Pontificate of Menkheperre.* As already evident,[151] this comes
out at about 49 or 53 years (including the reign of Amenemnisu) on *either*
hypothesis; it therefore neither faults nor favours either.[152]

(*b*) *Ages at Death of Psusennes I and Amenemope.* Hornung appositely
remarked on the advanced age at death of Psusennes I as favouring a long
reign for that king;[153] but the *same* argument can equally be invoked in
favour of a long reign of Amenemope, as his remains were those of an old
man.[154] As correctly pointed out by Wente, however,[155] the undoubted

---

150. As already noted, a stela, an oracle-text, one ostracon, and a bunch of the
'Late Ramesside Letters'.

151. Cf. above, tables in §§ 24, 27.

152. Hornung's former thesis of up to *four* high priests during the long reign of
Psusennes I (cf. *OLZ* 61 (1966), 440 and n. 1) is excluded, because Menkheperre
was appointed *before* the accession of Psusennes I (the antecedent Year 25), and
officiated right up to Year 48. It is worth remembering that Menkheperre was
undoubtedly a *younger* son of Pinudjem I, junior to Masaharta and probably also to
Djed-Khons-ef-ankh (cut off prematurely ?). Likewise, by contrast with Amenemnisu, Psusennes I was very probably a younger son of Smendes I (cf. below, Chapter
5, § 64). Thus, correspondingly, the accessions to office of a younger high priest
and younger king who both lived long resulted in approximately parallel tenures of
some duration. On the other hand, the succession of three high priests of Ptah in
Memphis under Psusennes I probably reflects a normal succession from fathers
to eldest (or, elder) sons, and is not surprising (§§ 151 ff.).

153. *Untersuchungen*, 103.

154. Kitchen, *CdE* 40/80 (1965), 320 and n. 3; Černý, *CAH²*, II: 35 (1965),
43, n. 5.

155. *JNES* 26 (1967), 172–3.

advanced age of *both* monarchs at death[156] has no needful or direct relevance to their respective lengths of reign.

(*c*) *The Place of Amenemnisu.* This is principally an issue between Manetho and the Borchardt genealogy of Memphite priests. *Both* hypotheses will function on the emendation of Manetho's order as desiderated by the Memphite genealogy.[157] Amenemnisu on Manetho's order (after Psusennes I) might be difficult to accommodate with a long reign of Psusennes I ending in a co-regency with Amenemope – unless one reckoned Amenemnisu as the latter's predecessor as co-regent, without a sole reign (unlikely on evidence of Manetho).

None of the three foregoing factors can thus materially settle our problem.

§ 33   5. RESULTS ATTAINABLE

A. ON POINTS CONSIDERED

Ignoring the neutral (and therefore irrelevant) points just noted, it is fair to say that the weight of probability, so far, inclines towards the hypothesis of a long reign for Psusennes I rather than for Amenemope. In its extant transmitted form, point (i), the bandage-fragment 'King Amenemope; Year 49', appears initially to favour a long reign for Amenemope – but, in line with ascertainable typology of such epigraphs, it can be far more reasonably construed as a damaged and incomplete witness for a long reign of Psusennes I; and that without resort to improbable assumptions. Point (ii), another bandage, is modestly in favour of long-reigned-Psusennes hypothesis, while the points (iii) on high priest(s) Smendes, (iv) emendation of Manetho, and (v) pontificate of Piankh, all favour the long-reigned-Psusennes hypothesis very strongly. On five different counts, then, three are strongly and one mildly in favour of that solution, while the first point is probably best so construed (while not free of ambiguity). So far, therefore, the hypothesis of a long reign for Psusennes I undoubtedly seems the better one.

§ 34   B. ADDITIONAL FACTORS

From Western Thebes, one may glean further indications relevant to the present inquest, from data on personnel functioning there.

Thus the Necropolis-scribe Butehamun became partner in that office with his father Thutmose (Tjuroy) within the 'Renaissance Era', and cer-

---

156. Derry, *ASAE* 40 (1940/1), 969, and *ASAE* 41 (1942), 149, respectively.
157. Cf. below, Chapters 4, § 56, and 12, §§ 151–3.

tainly before the death of Herihor (Year 7 of the Era at the latest).[158] However, he is indubitably still active in the attested Years 10, 11, 12, 13 of an unspecified ruler, but in company with Pinudjem I as high priest, in a series of Theban graffiti[159] clearly later than Ramesses XI and the 20th Dynasty. On the long-reigned-Psusennes hypothesis, these graffiti would date to Years 10–13 of Smendes I, so that up to that time, Butehamun would have served for the last 5 years of the 'Era' and some 13 years under Smendes I – 18 years so far. But if, as on the long-reigned-Amenemope hypothesis, these years 10–13 with Pinudjem I as high priest had to be attributed to the reign of Psusennes I, then Butehamun's total service to that point would be 5 years of the 'Era', 26 (or 16?) years under Smendes I, probably 4 years of Amenemnisu, and some 13 years under Psusennes I which would make a grand total of 48 (just possibly, 38) years. This is possible, but long. A further, unpublished, graffito apparently associates a Year 16, the high priest Masaharta, and Butehamun's son Ankhefenamun.[160] On the Psusennes hypothesis, this would be 3 years later, giving 21 years for Butehamun as scribe, when his son was perhaps replacing him; on the Amenemope hypothesis, this would be happening from father to son some 51 (or 41?) years after the former's appearing which would be a rather long span, especially if (for example) one compares the intervals between inductions of priests under Osochor, Siamun and Psusennes II, at intervals of 21 and either 15 or 28 years – but not 40 or 50 years (cf. §§ 4, 10, above). Furthermore, it would be curious to have documentation of Butehamun active in the Era and under Pinudjem I, but a total blank for a quarter-century again under Piankh and Smendes I, as the long-reigned-Amenemope hypothesis would desiderate. This, again, strongly favours the other view.

§ 35 One case (even combined with that of Piankh) might weigh little. But the same phenomenon shows up in other cases. The Superintendent of the Treasury of the Estate of Amenresonter, Panefernefer occurs in *LRL* No. 27 which may be dated roughly to the early years of the 'Era',[161] say up to Years 6 or 7. This same man undoubtedly recurs in two dockets associated with Pinudjem I as high priest in a Year 6, on coffins of Tuthmosis II and Amenophis I.[162] On the long-reigned-Amenemope hypo-

---

158. Cf. Wente, *LRL*, 3.

159. Spiegelberg, *Thebanische Graffiti*, Nos. 1001; 48, 51, 1021 (corrected readings); Černý, *Graffiti hiéroglyphiques et hiératiques de la nécropole thébaine*, 1956, Nos. 1285a-d plus 1286, 1310, 1310a, 1393, etc. Cf. § 16 end, note 89. For Year 13, cf. shroud of Ramesses III, *MMR*, 563-4.

160. *PM²*, I: 2, 594, Nos. 1570-7.

161. Cf. Wente, *LRL*, 9.

thesis, his tenure of headship of Amun's treasury would thus cover *minimally* 5 years (approximately) of the Era, 26 (or 16?) years under Smendes I, 4 years of Amenemnisu, and 6 years of Psusennes I – a period of at least 41 (just possibly, 31) years; again, possible but long – and again with a quarter-century gap in the middle, under Piankh and Smendes I. On the long-reigned-Psusennes hypothesis, the two dates for Panefernefer as active treasurer would cover roughly 5 years of the 'Era' and 6 years under Smendes – barely a dozen years all told, from a career in senior office that could have begun earlier or lasted longer and have spanned (for all we know) up to 20 years or more, without any chronological strain. Again, this is the more natural hypothesis, with no mysterious gaps or further long, silent tenures of office.

Therefore, it seems in order henceforth to give preference to the hypothesis that attributes a long reign to Psusennes I and but 9 years to Amenemope. It remains in the following two chapters to consider the families of the kings and priests of the Dynasty, and to seek to set out possible dates.

162. *MMR*, 545–6, 536–7, respectively.

CHAPTER 4

The Family Relationships

§ 36   1. INTRODUCTORY

This chapter assumes only the two basic sequences of high priests of
Amun and Tanite kings set out above in Chapter 1. Apart from Smendes I
and Psusennes I, we have so far practically no direct evidence on the family
and relationships of the Tanite dynasty; even for these two kings, much
rests on inferences from Theban data. In the family of the Theban high
priests the leading ladies offer the main data and also constitute our greatest
problem, largely through their failure to name those relatives whose ranks
they mention,[163] or to give the rank of those that are named.[164] Given the
desperately confusing nature of the evidence with, for example, at least
three or four Henttawys, four or five Istemkhebs, two Nesikhons, and a
variety of other ladies, I have endeavoured in what follows to group the
material largely under these names, in attempting both to gather together
the relics of particular individuals and to distinguish between homonyms.

§ 37   2. NODJMETS AND HRÈRES

A. NODJMET(S)

One finds this name associated with three high priests of Amun, namely
Herihor, Piankh and Pinudjem I.

163. e.g. the Devotee of Hathor, Henttawy, who claimed to be a King's Daughter,
King's Wife, King's Mother (which kings ?), also mother of a queen and of a God's
Wife of Amun (which ladies ?), besides mother of a Theban high priest and generalis-
simo (which one ?).

164. e.g. in the settlement text of Pylon X, Karnak, wherein a Smendes, Henttawy, and two Istemkhebs occur, all without titles, and likewise the decrees found
with the mummies of Pinudjem II and his wife Nesikhons A. This phenomenon is
seen in most of the amuletic decrees edited by I. E. S. Edwards, *Hieratic Papyri in the
British Museum, 4th Series, Oracular Amuletic Decrees of the Late New Kingdom,*
I, II, 1960.

(i) *With Herihor* (*Alive*)

1. The Leiden stela V 65 shows the Generalissimo and High Priest Herihor with 'the Lady of the House, Chief of the Harim of Amenresonter, Nodjmet'. His figure and the first part of his name have been erased.[165] The simplest assumption is that they were husband and wife, while theoretically they could have been either son and mother or father and daughter.

2. In the forecourt (interior, W. wall, N. end) of the temple of Khons, decorated by Herihor as 'king' (using cartouches), there occurs a scene,[166] in which Nodjmet has queenly epithets,[167] is Chief of the [Har]im of Amenre[. . .], and Chief Queen, beloved.[168] Again, this would suggest that she was wife and 'queen' of Herihor, and that the rows of sons and daughters that follow her are their children.[169]

(ii) *With Piankh* (*Alive*)

3. Among the *LRL* edited by Černý and Wente, No. 35 is directed by 'the General of Pharaoh', i.e. Piankh,[170] to 'the Chief of the Harim of Amenresonter, the noblewoman, Nodjmet', while two others (Nos. 21, 34) from him to other people refer to her without title concerning the same subject-matter. One might expect Piankh to write to his wife or his mother; as a widow of Herihor, Nodjmet would here be Piankh's mother, responsible for certain matters in Thebes while he was away.

(iii) *With Pinudjem I* (*Alive*)

4. In a graffito engraved in the Luxor temple,[171] five men (first one, lost) face to the left, towards Amenre and a woman who correspondingly face right. The first man was the high priest Piankh, already deceased, whose name and titles are preceded by *n kз n*, and followed by *ir.n sз.f sʿnḫ rn.f* 'made by his son who perpetuates his name'. The latter (second man) is given as the vizier, high priest of Amun, generalissimo of the whole

165. Last published in Boeser, *Beschreibung Aeg. Sammlung . . . Leiden*, VI, 1913, 13, pl. 28.

166. *LD*, III, 247a; Champollion, *Notices Descriptives*, II, 228–9; cf. *MMR*, 648–9, and *G3*, 236, XVIII.

167. [*iry-pʿtt*], *wrt-[ḥs]wt, ḥn(w)t tзwy, nbt-⟨bnrt/iзmt⟩, bnrt-mrwt:* '[Hereditary Princess], Rich in Favours, Mistress of South and North, Possessor of ⟨Charm⟩, Sweet of Love'.

168. Latter title, *ḥmt-nsw wrt mr.f*, lit. 'Great King's-Wife whom he loves'.

169. Just as Queen Nefertari with a series of sons and daughters at Luxor (*PM²*, II, 308 (28), III) are known to be the queen and children of Ramesses II.

170. For the explicit identification with Piankh, see No. 28, opening lines, naming Piankh with full titles, and the address-line at end addressed simply to 'the General of Pharaoh' *par excellence*.

171. Published by Daressy, *RT* 14 (1892), 32, cf. *G3*, 245, IX; also, own copy.

land, army-leader (*ḥȝwty*), Pinudjem I. The other three men are sons of Piankh: the 2nd Prophet, Heqa-nefer, the Sem-priest of Medinet Habu(?), Heqa-maat, and the Chief Steward of Amun and prophet of Mut, Ankhef-enmut. Behind Amun, the woman's legend runs: 'May he (i.e. Amun) grant a [long?][172] lifespan within Thebes to the Lady of the House, Chief of the Harim of Amun, Nodjmet.' This graffito implies that Pinudjem I became high priest of Amun while Nodjmet was still alive; he and his three brothers here honour their grandmother (in the company of their dead father), probably soon after Pinudjem's induction as high priest.

§ 38   (iv) *Funerary Effects of Nodjmet(s)*

5. A beautifully-illustrated *Book of the Dead* came into the illicit antiquities' trade in the 1870s. Split into three, one part is Papyrus BM. 10541 (ex Edward VII),[173] one part is in the Louvre,[174] and one in Munich.[175] This document undoubtedly came from the great *cache* near Deir el Bahri; it shows Herihor both as high priest and as 'king' with cartouches,[176] while Nodjmet appears as Osiris, sometimes Lady of the Two Lands,[177] and (in cartouche) as 'King's Mother, Nodjmet'.[178] Once at least, she is curiously entitled what looks like *wbȝ-nsw*, before her cartouche.[179] She is also more fully entitled: 'King's Mother of the Lord of the Two Lands, God's Mother of Khons-the-Child, Chief of the Harim of Amenresonter, chief noblewoman, Lady of the Two Lands, Nodjmet.'[180]

172. Room for a vertical sign, now lost – 'ȝ or kȝ.

173. See A. W. Shorter, *Catalogue of Egyptian Religious Papyri in the British Museum* (*Pr(t)-m-Hrw*), I, 1938, 14–15, No. 10541 and references. The segment in his Pl. V is followed at right by one with Herihor and Nodjmet worshipping, see Budge, *The Book of the Dead, an English Translation* ... , [I], 2nd ed., 1938, pl. X opp. p. 178; two further sections contiguous with each other are shown in the *General Introductory Guide to the Egyptian Collections, British Museum*, 1930 ed., figs. 29 and 206 (the latter only as fig. 21, in 1964 ed.).

174. Cf. Naville, *ZÄS* 16 (1878), 29–30, pl. IV; Pierret, *Recueil des inscriptions inedites du Louvre*, II, 1878, 131 ff.; Naville, *Das Aeg. Todtenbuch, Einleitung*, 108.

175. Shorter, *op. cit.*; *MMR*, 512, n. 1; Wiedemann, *Aegyptische Geschichte*, 1884, 531.

176. See the British Museum portion, sections quoted note 173 above; and the Louvre section as both king and pontiff.

177. Sometimes included, sometimes omitted.

178. Title and name, both within the cartouche.

179. See the cartouche just before Nodjmet's face in solar vignette, *General Introductory Guide, B.M.*, 1964, fig. 21. The title was duly noted by Shorter, *op. cit.*, 14–15, who translated it as 'the Royal Attendant'. But *wbȝ nsw*, 'King's cup-bearer', borne by highly-placed court servants, hardly seems a fitting title for a 'queen', and is not used by women, so far as I know. One may wonder whether the *wbȝ* sign is not here for the similar-looking *ḥmt*, the latter being a sportive ortho-graphy for the more usual *ḥmt* of *ḥmt-nsw*, 'King's Wife'.

180. So, in the Louvre section of the papyrus as quoted by Naville, *ZÄS* 16 (1878), 29.

6. Twin coffins containing her mummy, from the great *cache*.[181] The shroud on her mummy is, again, inscribed for 'the Osiris, Lady of the Two Lands (cartouche:) King's Mother, Nodjmet', like the papyrus, while one bandage bore an epigraph of a Year 1 associated with Pinudjem I (presumably as high priest).[182] The coffins give all the titles attested on her *Book of the Dead* – Chief of the Harim,[183] chief noblewoman, King's Mother (both outside and inside cartouche), and God's Mother (var., King's Mother!) of Khons,[184] plus queenly epithets.[185]

Thus far, practically all the titles of Nodjmet as buried in Western Thebes agree well enough with her having been husband of Herihor and mother of Piankh. All except the additional title of *King's Mother*, which is not properly applicable to her relationship to Piankh, as he never claimed the kingship at all on his known records, or in the filiations of his son Pinudjem I. Because of her iconographic 'context' in the temple of Khons, Nodjmet can hardly be the mother of Herihor as Naville once suggested.[186] Hence, her title can only refer either (i) to her grandson Pinudjem I (in a Year 16 ff.) as a 'King's (Grand)mother', or (ii) to her being actually mother of a Tanite pharaoh, e.g. Smendes I himself (who would thus be Herihor's son),[187] or (iii) to her being in fact a 'King's Mother(-in-law)' if a daughter of hers had married Smendes I or a son of his.[188]

§ 39 (v) *An Additional Papyrus and the Hrēre Problem*

7. Long before it acquired No. 10541 by royal munificence, the British Museum had had a hieratic *Book of the Dead* having but two outline

---

181. Coffins in Daressy, *Cerceuils* (*Cat. Caire*), No. 61024; her mummy, cf. Elliott Smith, *Royal Mummies (Cairo Catalogue)*, No. 61087; initial report, *MMR*, 569 and pl. 19.

182. Shroud, *MMR*, 569. The epigraph is mentioned only by Elliott Smith, *Royal Mummies*, 97, with a regrettable lack of precise detail. The Year 1 would pertain to Smendes I (long reign of Psusennes I), with Nodjmet dying early in her grandson's pontificate thereafter. Alternatively, she would (on long reign for Amenemope) have instead survived 26 years longer (or 30, plus 4 years Amenemnisu) to outlive the first year of Psusennes I with Pinudjem as high priest following on Piankh – possible, but very unlikely, as she would be nearly 100 at death or even more.

183. Often preceded by *ḥr(yt)*, 'Leading Lady'.

184. For once, *G3* (237, C) fails to give all variants, for which Daressy, *Cerceuils*, esp. 41, 49, should be consulted.

185. *iry-pˁtt, wrt ḥst, ḥn(w)t tꜣw ḥr⟨itn⟩*, Daressy, *op. cit.*, 41.

186. *ZÄS* 16 (1878), 30 f.

187. As is suggested by Wente, *JNES* 26 (1967), 174; for omission of Smendes from the line of Herihor's sons in the temple of Khons, he points to the comparable absence of another important and indubitable son, Ankhefenmut A (p. 174 and n. 151) from that same series. This at least allays some of one's doubts about the hypothesis of Smendes I being a son of Herihor.

188. As I had argued in 1962/63, in the first version of this work.

vignettes, No. 10490, belonging to 'the King's Mother (cartouche:) Nodjmet',[189] the daughter of a 'King's Mother, Hrēre' (no cartouche).[190] While the relation of this *Book of the Dead* to the other remains problematic (two copies for one lady?), it seems clear that this 'queen-mother' Nodjmet is identical with the wife of Herihor so far discussed.[191] The title of Hrēre could be for King's Mother(-in-law) in relation to Herihor. Otherwise, with Wente,[192] one must postulate that she mothered both Herihor and Nodjmet who, as full brother and sister, practised consanguineous marriage. Furthermore, Wente draws attention to a further epithet of Nodjmet in this papyrus: *mst kꝫ nḫt*, 'who bore (or, was born of) the Strong Bull'. As Hrēre is described as a 'King's Mother', not as a 'King's Wife' or 'King's Daughter', the passive-mode translation seems excluded, and so this epithet would be a further claim to have mothered a king,[193] as *kꝫ nḫt*, 'Strong Bull', was the standard initial epithet of a pharaoh in the Horus-names of all kings from Tuthmosis I to Osorkon III inclusive. While one might still argue for the relationship being just 'mother-in-law', this phrase would rather favour Wente's view that Herihor and Nodjmet were actually the parents of a Tanite king (Smendes I), rather than merely parents-in-law.

8. As 'Chief of the Harim (of Chantresses) of Amenresonter',[194] a Hrēre sent two letters to Thebes from elsewhere, concerning rations for the necropolis workmen.[195] In other letters, she is mentioned as at Elephantine (No. 2) and also at Thebes (No. 30, written by Piankh), without title, as being someone well-known. Generally, she has been identified with Hrēre, Piankh's grandmother discussed above, albeit with reserves.[196]

189. So, with title usually outside cartouche. Published by Budge, *Facsimiles of the Papyri of Hunefer, Anhai, Kerasher . . . (etc.)*, 1899, pls. 1–10 with transcription and translation; as it was acquired at Thebes in 1894, this papyrus may have come ultimately from the great *cache* a decade or two earlier, before the main body of material was safely recovered and taken to Cairo.

190. Budge, *op. cit.*, pls. 1 and 5.

191. Thus, if one tries to make the queen-mother Nodjmet of Papyrus BM. 10490 into a 'Nodjmet II' as the wife of either Piankh or Pinudjem I, difficulties arise. As wife of Piankh, she would be queen-mother to Pinudjem I – but *her* mother, the 'queen-mother' Hrēre, bears a title that would imply that this Nodjmet had a sister who married a Tanite king (queen-mother-in-law) or else a brother who became Tanite king (Smendes ?). All this is theoretically possible, but lacks corroboration. If 'Nodjmet II' were wife of Pinudjem I, one would be at a loss to explain how she happens to be absent from his monuments – and of whom, then, would she be 'queen-mother'? Especially with Henttawy claiming so many exalted relationships (mothering kings, pontiffs, etc.) at the same general epoch.

192. *JNES* 26 (1967), 173–4.

193. *Ibid.*, 174 and n. 149.

194. *Wrt ḥnrt (šmʿy) n(t) ʾImn-rʿ nsw-nṯrw*.

195. *LRL*, Nos. 38, 39 (latter, restored); var., *šmʿyt* in No. 39.

196. So by me (1962/63 version of this work), by Černý, *CAH²*, II: 35 (1965), 33,

However, as pointed out to me by M. L. Bierbrier, one would expect Piankh to be accompanied to Elephantine and the south by his wife rather than by his aged grandmother; hence, it is probably wiser to postulate the existence of a Hrēre A, mother of Nodjmet (and possibly Herihor), and a Hrēre B, origin unknown, wife of Piankh. The status of Chief of the Harim of Amenresonter would thus apply simply to 'B', and no longer be attested for 'A', Nodjmet's mother whose status in her own right (apart from the epithet 'King's Mother') remains unknown at present.[197]

§ 40   B. NEDJEMMUT AND MUTNODJMET
Despite their outward similarity,[198] these two names, attested for two differently-titled ladies in Thebes and Tanis respectively, should undoubtedly be carefully distinguished from each other.

(i) *'Princess Nedjemmut'*
So far, this lady is attested only in a graffito engraved in the Ramesside forecourt of the Luxor temple,[199] as last adult in a row of four people[200] worshipping four deities.[201] She is entitled 'Bodily King's Daughter whom he loves, [. . .] of Amun,[202] Nedjemmut'. Thus, we know only that she was a daughter of Pinudjem I and attached in some way to the Theban clergy, and should not be confused with her Tanite relative.

(ii) *Queen Mutnodjmet of Tanis*
At Tanis, we find a queen Mutnodjmet closely associated with Psusennes I on objects from his tomb. Montet has repeatedly[203] classed her as the

and by Wente, *LRL*, 14–15, and *JNES* 26 (1967), 173, n. 145. Already, Wente, *op. cit.*, n. 145, had noted the relatively late date of the *LRL* references, remarking that 'there is no positive evidence that the two Hrēres are identical', while I had gone further and envisaged the possibility of the Hrēre of *LRL* having as husband 'either Piankh or a predecessor of Herihor'. See a forthcoming paper by M. L. Bierbrier.

197. Thus, Hrēre A could have been the wife of some high priest before Herihor, but no evidence on the point is available, once Hrēre B is recognized to be separate and later.

198. The former employing an adjective-verb in the *sḏm.f* ('sweet is Mut'), and the latter, an Old Perfective ('Mut is sweet').

199. Published by Daressy, *RT* 14 (1892), 32: LII; cf. *G3*, 245, VIII; own copy.

200. Facing to the right: high priest Pinudjem I, then God's Wife of Amun, Maatkare A (shown small – a girl?), and two other ladies, a Henttawy and Nedjemmut.

201. Facing to the left: two forms of Amun; Mut; Khons.

202. The title is largely broken away, and traces I saw do *not* suit Daressy's printed form; my autopsy and copy agree well with that of Wente, *JNES* 26 (1967), 167–8. I have no suggestion for restoration.

203. e.g. *Psus.*, 102, 178–9; *Les énigmes de Tanis*, 1952, 154; followed by Kees, *Hhp.*, 1964, 22, and Hornung, *Untersuchungen zur Chronologie und Geschichte des Neuen Reiches*, 1964, 103.

mother of Psusennes I, basing himself for evidence exclusively upon the phrase *ir.n*. He cited a gold spouted dish (Inv. 401) which bears in symmetrical facing columns (i) the titles and cartouche of Psusennes, and (ii) *ir.n* the Great Royal Wife, Lady of the Two Lands, Mutnodjmet, interpreting *ir.n* as 'begotten of'.[204] He denied that *ir.n* could be merely a dedication ('made by/for'), and claimed that the spelling *ir.nn* was the rule for that usage at this period.[205] However, this view and its reasons are far from convincing.[206] In other texts of this period, *ir.n* is just as good a spelling as *ir.nn* for the meaning 'made by/for',[207] and thus Montet's interpretation is only one possibility, and does not constitute proof of his view. The remaining evidence points perfectly clearly in another direction. If Mutnodjmet was the mother of Psusennes, why is she NEVER[208] called *mwt-nsw*, 'King's Mother'? Whenever she is associated with Psusennes, it is as *ḥmt-nsw* or *ḥmt-nsw wrt* (+ *tpy n ḥm.f*), or even as *snt-nsw* – as Royal Wife, or (First) Great Royal Wife (of His Majesty) or Royal Sister.[209] The plain and obvious deduction is that Mutnodjmet was in reality the sister-wife of Psusennes I; his queen and not his mother.[210] Mutnodjmet is at once a King's Daughter, Wife and Sister. As wife of Psusennes I

204. *Psus.*, 99, fig. 41, 102. Also bracelets, Nos. 539, 549, *ibid.*, pl. 70; cf. Leclant, *Orientalia* 22 (1953), 411, n. 1.

205. Citing both Herihor, temple of Khons (*LD*, III, 247–8) and objects from Tanis (Inv. 408: *Psus.*, 98, fig. 39).

206. Doubts were already expressed by Leclant, *Orientalia* 22 (1953), 411–12, and on Montet's view of *ir.n* (concerning Smendes II) by Kees, *Hhp.*, 9, n. 2.

207. Notably on the bandages on mummies from the Deir el Bahri *cache*. With *ir.nn* (*G3*, 270: F (= 283: C); 275: V; 277: XVII), compare simple *ir.n* (*G3*, 244: IV; 245: IX (Luxor temple); 263: I; 266: VIII (Luxor); 276: XII–XIV; 277: XV; 285: I–II). '*Ir.n* clearly outnumbers *ir.nn*, even on this summary collection of evidence.

208. Not even in her full titulary, *Psus.*, 164 and fig. 60.

209. The importance of this title *Royal Sister* seems to have been overlooked by Montet and others. If, on his view, Mutnodjmet were mother of Psusennes I and thus wife of Smendes I, then she must also have been *sister* of Smendes. How, in that case, could she truly be *s't-nsw*, 'King's Daughter' – unless *both she and Smendes* were children of Ramesses XI? One could barely escape this (and rescue Montet's view of Smendes I being son of a Menkheperre) by postulating that Smendes and Muntnodjmet were but half-brother/sister – perhaps by the same mother of successive husbands: Smendes by a (first?) non-royal husband and Mutnodjmet by Ramesses XI. But this is almost as large an assumption as that of a royal origin for both Smendes and his supposed wife and both theses may be discarded in the light of the real meaning of Mutnodjmet's titles making her the wife of Psusennes I, not Smendes.

210. So also, Černý, *CAH²*, II: 35 (1965), 51; Kitchen, *BiOr* 23 (1966), 275; Wente, *JNES* 26 (1967), 163–4. A point probably not made hitherto is that a twin tomb like that of Psusennes I and Mutnodjmet at Tanis would be made for a king and queen, *not* a king and his mother (the latter being more properly buried with her husband).

she would thus have been his sister[211] and her royal father would have to be a predecessor of Psusennes who was most likely Smendes, but possibly Amenemnisu or 'King' Pinudjem I.

§ 41 3. THE HENTTAWYS AND TENTAMUNS

The tribe of Henttawys and veritable plague of Istemkhebs are doubtless (at first sight) the greatest bane to the study of this period. However, the margins of doubt regarding their numbers and individuality can be restricted to within quite narrow limits.

A. THE MOTHER OF PSUSENNES I AND DYNASTIC ORIGINS
While queen Mutnodjmet entirely ceases to be a candidate for the role of mother of Psusennes I, her replacement in that distinguished position is not far to seek. On another vessel from the burial of Psusennes I at Tanis,[212] two balancing rows of hieroglyphs have the sign ʿankh as their common *incipit*. On the right run the name and titles of Psusennes I. On the left, we have '(long) live the King's Mother (*mwt-nsw*), Devotee of Hathor Henttawy'.[213] Surely, again, the inference is obvious: Psusennes' mother is this lady Henttawy. It is probably the same woman who occurs with a first cartouche 'Mother of Khons' (*mwt n Ḫnsw*), who is associated with Psusennes I on another vessel.[214] For Montet's suggestion that she was a wife of Psusennes, there is not a scrap of evidence. If this Henttawy was his wife, why is she called *mwt-nsw* ('King's Mother') instead of *ḥmt-nsw* ('King's Wife')?[215] Therefore, it is better to stick to the explicit statement and 'context' which indicate Henttawy as Psusennes' mother.

The further identity of this queen-mother Henttawy is open to two possible interpretations, one to be presented here, and the other below (§ 42).

It has not escaped attention that Psusennes I appears to claim some connection with the preceding, Ramesside, dynasty.[216] Thus, one frag-

---

211. Or just conceivably a half-sister, if sister of another king, e.g. Amenemnisu.

212. Inv. No. 543, Montet, *Psus.*, 152, fig. 56 middle (misinterpreted by Montet as a wife of Psusennes I).

213. Devotee of Hathor, Henttawy, all in cartouche.

214. Inv. No. 399, Montet, *Psus.*, 98, fig. 39.

215. Unless one were driven to the marginal possibility that it was a vessel engraved during, say, a possible co-regency of Psusennes I and Amenemope, and this lady were *mwt-nsw* of the co-regent Amenemope.

216. Montet, *Psus.*, 179–80, and *Énigmes de Tanis*, 1952, 155–6; cf. Leclant, *Orientalia* 22 (1953), 412; Kees, *Hhp.*, 22–3.

mentary block from Tanis bears the cartouche 'Ramesses-Psusennes, Beloved of [Amun]',[217] which recurs on a ring-bezel from the burial of Wen-djeba-en-Djed in the tomb of Psusennes I.[218] Furthermore, in room 3 of his Tanite tomb, Psusennes I made provision for the burial of a prince[219] who was doubtless a son that predeceased him, given the probable long duration of Psusennes' reign. In brief form, this man was called simply 'the King's Son, Ankhefenmut'; but on the end of his sarcophagus were set out his full name and titles, calling him (inter alia): 'Bodily King's Son whom he loves, Ramesses-Ankhefenmut.'[220] These compound names, Ramesses-Psusennes and Ramesses-Ankhefenmut, are wholly in the style of those of the sons and successors of Ramesses III in the 20th Dynasty, and suggest that Psusennes I and his son claimed a link with the Ramessides, a claim which was not taken up by their successors.

Psusennes I could only readily have such a link with the previous dynasty through his mother,[221] the queen-mother Henttawy. One may therefore suggest that, besides his first wife Tentamun, Smendes also[222] married a younger daughter of Ramesses XI, which bond gave him a further, legitimizing claim to the throne as the latter's eventual successor. Psusennes and Mutnodjmet would have been born of this second marriage and so both had Ramesside blood in their veins. So, in time, would the prince Ramesses-Ankhefenmut, if he were their son. The king Amenemnisu who probably reigned but briefly between Smendes I and Psusennes I would then have been an elder half-brother of Psusennes, a son of Smendes by his senior wife, Tentamun, who died childless. To this theory of the origins of the Tanite kings, just one fact may possibly be opposed: the occurrence of the unusual title 'Devotee of Hathor' (Dwȝt-Ḥtḥr) in the cartouche of Psusennes' mother Henttawy is common only to her and to one other Henttawy (associated with Pinudjem I) who was entitled Princess, Queen, King's Mother and to whom we must now turn. If there was but

217. Montet, Psus., 12, fig. 1, top right (cf. p. 11); Énigmes de Tanis, 154, fig. 38.
218. Montet, Psus., 74, fig. 27 (below, left), and 75, No. 714; pl. 53.
219. Tomb-chamber later expropriated, and prince's name erased on walls of room 3 (Psus., 65).
220. Psus., pl. 39, cf. pp. 65/66, 67 (with pl. 38, upper right: Ramesses . . .), 68. It should be particularly noted that, in this case, we here have a compound name 'Ramesses-Ankhefenmut', and not the later title 'King's Son of Ramesses'; the phrases n ḫt.f, mr.f, that intervene between sȝ-nsw and Rʿmss make this absolutely clear, and exclude the latter interpretation, a point not clearly noted by Kees, Hhp., 22–3.
221. A basic point already seen and set forth by Montet, locc. citt., and by Kees, Hhp., 22 f., but erroneously supposing that Mutnodjmet was the link; cf. Kitchen, BiOr 23 (1966), 275.
222. At the inauguration of, or during the course of, the 'Renaissance Era', perhaps.

one Henttawy with the title 'Devotee of Hathor' in her cartouche, then (with Wente) one must make Psusennes I and his wife the son and daughter of Henttawy and a Theban pontiff and grandchildren of Smendes I and Tentamun (see § 42). But in that case, the 'Ramesses' element in the full name-forms of Psusennes I and Ankhefenmut remain an unresolved enigma.[223]

§ 42   B. HENTTAWY, DAUGHTER OF TENTAMUN, APUD
PINUDJEM I

Of Tentamun, we currently have only two records. The first is the report on the misadventures of Wenamun in Syria, where she constantly appears alongside Smendes in Tanis, both of them by name and neither with any titles, in Year 5 of the 'Renaissance Era'.[224] From this, it is fair to deduce that she is Smendes' consort. The second piece of evidence comes from the funerary papyrus[225] of her much betitled daughter Henttawy, who calls herself variously: 'First Chief Queen of His Majesty, etc.' (cartouche:) Devotee of Hathor, Henttawy, born of – *ms.n* – (cartouche:) Tentamun', and 'King's Wife (cartouche:) Devotee of Hathor, Henttawy, born of Queen (cartouche:) Tentamun, *ir.n s3b Nb.sny*', also 'King's Mother, (cartouche:) Devotee of Hathor, Henttawy, born of (cartouche:) Tentamun, *ir.n s3b Nb.sny*'.[226] Most scholars have long since agreed to identify this queen Tentamun as being the consort of Smendes mentioned by Wenamun. Thus, as long ago argued by Lepsius,[227] the final phrase *ir.n s3b Nb.sny*, 'begotten of the Honourable Neb-seny', must name the father of Tentamun, *not* of her daughter the 'King's Daughter' Henttawy. The latter will then have been daughter of Smendes I and Tentamun.

§ 43   Of the Devotee of Hathor[228] Henttawy, we have not only the funerary papyrus, but also her mummy, shroud and coffins, besides sundry men-

223. The occurrence of the element 'Ramesses' in the names of Psusennes I and Ankhefenmut seems not to be discussed at all by Wente in his notable paper, *JNES* 26 (1967), 152–74.

224. Text of Wenamun, Gardiner, *Late-Egyptian Stories*, 1932, 61–76. By Wenamun himself, Smendes and Tentamun are mentioned together no less than 5 times (1 : 4 (p. 61 : 5), 1 : 7 (p. 61 : 9), 1 : 53 (p. 66 : 11), 2 : 35 (p. 70 : 10), and 2 : 39 (p. 71 : 2)), to Smendes alone just once (1 : 15 (p. 62 : 8)); the prince of Byblos twice mentions Smendes alone (1 : 54, 59 (pp. 66 : 13 and 67 : 5)).

225. Stolen from the *cache* at Deir el Bahri and recovered by Mariette; published by him in *Papyrus égyptiens du Musée de Boulaq*, III, pls. 12–21. Commented on by Naville, *ZÄS* 16 (1878), 31–2, and by *MMR*, 688 ff.

226. Cf. conveniently *G3*, 258, Ia, La, b, respectively.

227. Even before the Wenamun papyrus was known (since 1899), in *ZÄS* 20 (1882), 153–4, 158; and by many scholars since its publication.

228. Hereinafter abbreviated to DH.

tions on the monuments from Thebes and elsewhere. On her burial-equipment (as on her papyrus), this lady displays what must surely be the most grandiloquent series of feminine titles for this entire epoch.[229] Leaving aside for the present her priestly and 'economic' benefices, we may note the following:

1. King's Daughter (*s3t-nsw*)
2. Chief-Queen's Daughter (*s3t ḥmt-nsw-wrt*)
3. King's Wife; 1st Chief Queen of H.M. ⎱ royalty
4. King's Mother (var., . . . of Lord of Two Lands)
5. Mother of the Chief Queen

6. Leading Lady, 1st Chief of Harim of Amun
7. Mother of the High Priest of Amun
8. Mother of the Generalissimo of S. and N. ⎱ pontificate
9. Mother of the God's Wife of Amun

Thus, our DH Henttawy claimed to be daughter of a king and his chief queen, in this case Smendes and Tentamun (1, 2). She further claimed to be herself a First Chief Queen, besides being First Chief of the Harim of Amun (3, 6); the latter title suggests that her husband was a high priest of Amun, which would not exclude his also being a king[230] as the first title implies. Her burial at Thebes suggests strongly that her royal husband was a Theban pontiff, not a Tanite king. In that case, Piankh (who never claimed royal status) would be a less likely candidate for being regarded as her husband than Pinudjem I who did become full king.[231]

Much more intricate is the question of her role as mother of King, Queen, High Priest and Generalissimo, and of the God's Wife of Amun. If Piankh (despite his non-kingship)[232] were her husband, she could be mother

229. Conveniently collected in *G3*, 256–7, F–G; 258–9, I–K; Mummy, No. 61090 and coffins, No. 61026, in Elliott Smith, *Royal Mummies*, and Daressy, *Cercueils*, respectively.

230. As is shown, e.g. by the titles of Queen Mutnodjmet in Tanis – an undoubted queen, she is also a First Chief of the Harim of Amun.

231. No later high priest of Amun need be considered; Masaharta was never a 'king', having served as pontiff entirely within the period of the 'kingship' of Pinudjem I, while Henttawy was buried by Menkheperre (cf. mummy-braces, *MMR*, 576–7). Dying as an old woman (Wente, *JNES* 26 (1967), 171, as against Elliott Smith) in Menkheperre's pontificate, she could hardly be his wife. And Menkheperre's claims to 'kingship' were minimal.

232. On his very few known monuments. It is just possible that he might have used the bare title 'King of Upper and Lower Egypt' while high priest (as Pinudjem I did at one stage; cf. *G3*, 246, XI, D). For 'royal' titled relatives of a high priest still without royal titles, cf. the ladies in the graffito including 'princess' Nedjem-mut, § 40 (i) above.

of a 'king', high priest ar d general all in one in Pinudjem I, and of a queen as mother of a wife of his, besides mother of some 'God's Wife', whose identity is unknown.[233]

If Pinudjem I were her husband, then she could be mother of one or more of his sons (e.g. Masaharta, or Menkheperre), which would account for her being termed mother of a high priest and generalissimo. If she were mother of his daughter Maatkare A, she would certainly be mother of the God's Wife of Amun. As mother of a chief queen, she may have had one of her daughters go north to Tanis, to be a wife for either Smendes (in his later years?), Amenemnisu, or Psusennes I. But of which *king* could she be queen-mother? In Thebes itself, only Menkheperre would count. However, his claims to kingship are very limited: the use of ovals, rather than cartouches proper, to enclose his title and name on brick-stamps proves little;[234] but one such stamp from El Hibeh does give him the title 'King of Upper & Lower Egypt'.[235] This *could* account for Hent-tawy's claim, if she were mother of Menkheperre. The only alternatives would be (i) to interpret *mwt-nsw* as King's Mother(-in-law), i.e. doubling with 'Queen's Mother', or (ii) to consider her as actually having been mother of a Tanite *king* as well as queen. The only likely candidates would then be Psusennes I and Mutnodjmet who was probably his sister, as suggested by Wente.[236] This last solution is in some respects highly attractive. The fullest possible value is thereby given to all the titles of Henttawy, and the two DH Henttawys both Tanite and Theban are in fact but one and the same person.[237] Against this solution, one must note that it leaves the usage of the compound names 'Ramesses-Psusennes', 'Ramesses-Ankhefenmut',

233. Lack of data on the God's Wife concerned would be no problem; for the entire 120/140 years of the 21st Dynasty, we know as yet the names of only two such ladies (Maatkare A; a Henttawy). There must have been others.

234. *G3*, 266, XI; 267, XV-269; cf. representations, *LDT*, II, 45, etc.

235. *G3*, 268, XIX, after Prisse d'Avennes, *Monuments égyptiens*, 1847, 5, and pl. 23: 5. The title also occurs, oddly enough, on the coffins of his daughter Istem-kheb, *G3*, 270, Dg.

236. *JNES* 26 (1967), 161–4. Amenemnisu seems excluded, because, if Psusennes I were son of Smendes and Amenemnisu son of Pinudjem and Henttawy, he would hardly have obtained the throne of Smendes while the latter had a son and heir, Psusennes.

237. Not every reason given for the equation by Wente is of equal validity. Thus, the title God's Mother of Khons that pertains to the two possible DH Henttawys of Thebes (*G3*, 257–8) and Tanis (*Psus.*, 98, fig. 39, No. 399; pl. 69) is common not to them only but *also* to other such ladies – so, at Tanis, to Queen Mutnodjmet (*Psus.*, 164, fig. 60) and Princess Istemkheb (*ibid.*, 101, 103, fig. 42), and at Thebes to Nodjmet wife of Herihor (*G3*, 237, E), Istemkheb daughter of Menkheperre (*G3*, 270, D), with usurpation by Nesikhons A (*G3*, 272, XXV). Such a title has no value for Wente's purpose; neither has the supposed Theban reference of the personal name Psusennes (Wente, p. 164).

entirely without rational explanation, and it would be surprising if Smendes and Tentamun (plus lesser wives?) had left no male heir at all.

§ 44   Thus far, the twin questions of the DH Henttawy(s) and the origins of Psusennes I and the 21st Dynasty may be summarized as follows. The DH Henttawy buried at Deir el Bahri was certainly either wife or mother of Pinudjem I, but more likely his wife: (i) if she was wife of Piankh and mother of 'king' Pinudjem I, then the suggested Ramesside affiliations of Psusennes I would not be affected; (ii) if she was wife of Pinudjem I, then her son who was 'king' could perhaps be Menkheperre (who half-heartedly claimed the prefixed kingly title), or it could be for King's Mother(-in-law)[238] (these solutions also would be consistent with the Ramesside affiliation of Psusennes I and his son); (iii) but if she were in fact mother of Psusennes I and his queen, then DH Henttawy's titles of King's Mother (and Queen's Mother) might be more fully accounted for (with Wente). But the Ramesside affiliation would remain entirely unexplained, if not in fact inexplicable[239] and the entitlement of a high priest's daughter as 'princess' (so, Nedjemmut, § 40, (i), above) shows that 'royal' titles were *not* always used with their full literal value. If view (i) be rejected, the present writer would prefer solution (ii), while not being unwilling to accept solution (iii) if the Ramesside question could be compatibly resolved. The status of Henttawy *vis à vis* Pinudjem I must now be more closely examined.

§ 45   C. EVIDENCE ON THE MOTHER AND WIFE OF
PINUDJEM I

This falls under five heads, in descending order of clarity and usefulness.

(i) *Tanis Goblet No. 398*

This golden chalice from the burial of Psusennes[240] is inscribed: 'High

238. As is possible for Hrēre A, in relation to Herihor (if not also Nodjmet in relation to the Tanite line), and certain for Mehtenweskhet A in the 21st–22nd Dynasties (Part II, § 90, below).

239. Smendes I did not specially model his official titles on those of the Ramessides, as apart from the New Kingdom style in general. But if Smendes I claimed no distinctive Ramesside aura himself and Psusennes I (as son of Pinudjem I, grandson of Smendes) was more distant from the Ramessides than was he, then *why* should Psusennes I and his son adopt the additional name 'Ramesses'? On the other side, it may be objected that the Ramesside-affiliation thesis of Smendes and Psusennes means postulating two DH Henttawys. But it is at least possible that (whatever the DH title may mean) the later Henttawy (daughter of Tentamun) followed her stepmother (mother of Ps. I, daughter of R. XI ?) in the particular religious capacity denoted by DH. In any case, DH is not always found in the latter Henttawy's cartouche (Wente, 166 f.).

240. Montet, *Psus.*, 100–1, fig. 41 (p. 99), pl. 70.

Priest of Amenresonter, Pinudjem (I), ⌈justified⌉,[241] son of Piankh, justified; the King's Daughter, Chief of the Harim of Amun, ⌈Lady of the Two Lands⌉,[242] (cartouche:) Henuttawy.' The simplest explanation of this piece is that it names Pinudjem I and Henttawy as husband and wife, before he became 'king' and perhaps before she became Devotee of Hathor,[243] if she is the DH Henttawy buried at Deir el Bahri.

(ii) *Hieratic Graffito, Luxor Temple*[244]

This document would have been invaluable, had it been better preserved. It names 'the High Priest of Amenresonter, Pinudjem I, son of the High Priest of Amenresonter, Piankh, (and) whose mother is the Chief of the Harim of Amun [. . .] Life, Prosperity, Health, [. . .]'. Of the lady's name, Daressy thought to read an initial *ḥ*, with doubt. Subsequently, Černý thought he could see 'fairly certain traces of *ḥnwt* . . .',[245] whereas Wente and Goff considered that (subject to any intervening deterioration) 'it appears . . . that the traces do not support the reading of the name as Henttawy'.[246] Thus, the witness of this document remains indecisive. If it does not read Henttawy, one may wonder whether it once named Hrēre (B), probable wife of Piankh, as mother of Pinudjem I.[247] However, even if it could be read as Henttawy, then – in the light of the Tanis goblet – we might still have to envisage the possibility of Pinudjem I being the son of one Henttawy (a second wife of Piankh; Luxor graffito??), and husband of another (Tanis goblet).

(iii) *Data from Karnak*

First of all, in the temple of Mut, a Sekhmet statue of Amenophis III was given an added dedication by '. . . the Lady of the Two Lands,

241. Written *m tꜣ*. Montet (*Psus.*, 100) took this to imply that Pinudjem I was dead when the goblet was engraved – but Pinudjem I died as *King*, not simply as high priest (his title here), and so Montet's interpretation is excluded. With Leclant (*Orientalia* 22 (1953), 417), it seems better to regard these signs as a simple error (by either the scribe or the engraver) for *mꜣꜥt-ḫrw*. In this type of filiation, the name of Pinudjem I is very often accompanied by this latter epithet while very much alive (e.g. *G3*, 245, VIII, 246–7, *passim*).

242. 'Lady of Justification' (*nbt mꜣꜥt-ḫrw*) is engraved – but a second simple slip, very similar to the first, seems likelier, for *nb(t)-tꜣwy*. So also Kees, *Hhp.*, 36, and esp. Wente, *JNES* 26 (1967), 159 and n. 28, 167.

243. Perhaps in succession to the previous incumbent, her stepmother Henttawy (daughter of Ramesses XI) on the view preferred here. As Wente remarks (*op. cit.*, 166 and n. 87) the DH Henttawy sometimes lacks the title DH in her cartouche, in her funerary papyrus.

244. Published by Daressy, *RT* 32 (1910), 185; cf. *G3*, 246, X.

245. *CAH²*, II: 35 (1965), 47, n. 4.

246. Wente, *JNES* 26 (1967), 160, n. 44.

247. A possibility raised in discussion by M. L. Bierbrier.

(cartouche:) DH Henttawy; she made her monument for her mother Mut, when the King of Upper & Lower Egypt, Khakheperre Setepenamun (i.e. Pinudjem I as king) brought the ram-sphinxes to the Temple of Amun'.[248] As this text dates to the second half of Pinudjem's career (when he had become 'king'), this DH Henttawy is more likely to be his wife than his mother, especially as she shared his Karnak projects.

Secondly, on the façade of the pylon of the temple of Khons, Pinudjem I as high priest is followed by 'the [Hereditary Princess], Great of Favours, Mistress of (all) lands under the sun's disc, [bodily] King's Daughter, [Lady of the Two Lands], (cartouche:) DH Henttawy, may she live!' Again, one may suggest that we here have husband and wife rather than son and mother.[249] Her title of King's Daughter is consistent with that accorded to the presumed wife of Pinudjem I on the Tanis goblet and would reflect her being daughter of Smendes I and queen Tentamun.

(iv) *Medinet Habu Lintel*

Recorded by Daressy, this fragment showed two figures facing each other. At left, looking right, was 'the Hereditary Princess, Great of Favours, Mistress of the Two Lands, Chief of the Harim of Amun, Lady of the Two Lands, (cartouche:) Henttawy', and on the right, facing her, a man over whom was inscribed: 'for the *ka* of the Hereditary Prince and Count, Generalissimo, who pacifies the Two Lands, High Priest of Amenresonter, Pinudjem, justified, son of the High [Priest of Amenresonter, . . .]'.[250] This has been interpreted as Pinudjem honouring a Henttawy as his mother, which is possible if the Luxor hieratic graffito (no. (ii), above) had been readable as Henttawy. But if it is indeed to be read otherwise (as seems likely), then this Medinet Habu Henttawy would have to be the wife of Pinudjem I – if it is Pinudjem I that is intended.[251]

(v) *The Coptos Stela*

On a stela from Coptos,[252] Pinudjem I as King is shown before Osiris;

---

248. *MMR*, 687; other refs., *G3*, 256, E.

249. Insofar as the high priest is, in any case, deputy for the king in the cult, the attribution of queenly titles to the *wife* of this semi-royal pontiff in this scene (cf. Wente, *op. cit.*, 162–3) would be entirely appropriate; depicted, *LD*, III, 250c. A further scene, *LD*, III, 250a (*G3*, 256, C, with erroneous restoration by Maspero; cf. Wente, *op. cit.*, 164–5), adds nothing for our purpose here.

250. Daressy, *RT* 19 (1897), 20; cf. Wente, *op. cit.*, 166.

251. Which is probable, but not certain – the name of Pinudjem's father is lost, so that this piece could belong to either Pinudjem I or II. If the latter, he would presumably be honouring his sister Henttawy, cf. § 46, D (ii), below.

252. Cairo JdE 71902, to be published elsewhere.

behind the king, stands 'the King's Daughter, Leading Lady(??),[253] Chief of the Harim of Amenresonter, chief noblewoman, King's Mother, Lady of the Two Lands, (cartouche:) DH Henttawy, justified'.[254] This document *could* be used to argue that DH Henttawy was the mother of Pinudjem I (one notes the absence of the title 'King's Wife'); or, if she was his wife, that she was mother (or mother-in-law?) of a Tanite king.[255]

In conclusion, it seems most probable that Henttawy daughter of Tentamun was wife of Pinudjem I, rather than his mother. His mother was named in the Luxor graffito, but there her name remains entirely uncertain. If it were Henttawy, then Pinudjem I would be son of one Henttawy and husband of another, but this remains highly speculative.

§ 46 D. OTHER HENTTAWYS IN THE 21ST DYNASTY

Most of the other known Henttawys can, fortunately, be summarized briefly.

(i) *Daughter of Pinudjem I*

A lady who was entitled 'King's Daughter of (cartouche:) Pinudjem I, Beloved of Amun, Chantress of Amun, Flautist of Mut, Henttawy' was buried in a tomb discovered by Winlock.[256] This same personage pretty certainly reappears in one of the hieroglyphic graffiti of Pinudjem I at Luxor, which shows him worshipping two forms of Amun with Mut and Khons, and himself followed by a girl and two women.[257] The first and third of these ladies are each entitled 'Bodily King's Daughter whom he loves', and so originally was the second figure.[258] She was '⌈the bodily King's Daughter whom he loves, Chantress of⌉ Amenresonter, Lord of ⟨the Thrones⟩ of ⟨the Two⟩ Lands, Henttawy, justified'. This lady may readily be identified with Winlock's flautist, and need concern us no further.

253. Poorly shaped sign (probably the sky-sign), possibly for *ḥryt*.
254. The main texts concern only the dedicator of the stela (Wennofer, 2nd prophet of Min), and offer no further information on Pinudjem or Henttawy.
255. Supporting Wente's hypothesis. It could only refer to Menkheperre if his bricks with the title of King were struck early in his pontificate and during the 'kingship' of his father, which seems unlikely. It remains possible that *mwt-nsw* is simply for King's Mother(-in-law), of course. So the evidence of this stela remains indecisive.
256. MMA excavations, 1924–6, *BMMA* 19 (Dec. 1924, II), 22 ff, and *BMMA* 21 (Dec. 1926, II), 19 ff.; Winlock, *Excavations at Deir el Bahri*, 1942, 94 f. On the titles, cf. Kees, *Hhp.*, 53–4, from Hayes.
257. i.e. Maatkare A, and Nedjemmut, cf. above, § 40 (i).
258. So, in Daressy's copy, *RT* 14 (1892), 32; cf. Wente, *JNES* 26 (1967), 162. Most of Henttawy's titles and half of her name were lost when I recopied this text in 1971.

(ii) *The Henttawy of Pylon X*

Under Pinudjem II[259] in Years 6 and 8 of an unnamed king (Amenemope or Siamun), a decree was inscribed on Pylon X (W. wing, N. face)[260] to protect the property-rights of the lady Henttawy daughter of Istemkheb and herself mother of a further Istemkheb (see below). Henttawy had rights to property of a Smendes, who was himself son of an Istemkheb and father of a Nesikhons. Either Henttawy or her mother was a First Chief of the Harim of Amun. Usually, this snatch of genealogy is interpreted so:

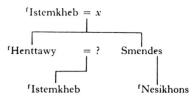

Of these people, it is probable that the Smendes is none other than the previous high priest, Smendes II son of Menkheperre and an Istemkheb. The Henttawy would then be his sister who, as mother of a younger Istemkheb, was married, possibly to Smendes II himself. If so, then the text concerned the property-rights of the widow and her daughter. On this text, see further below, under the Istemkhebs (§ 52, E). This lady Henttawy might well be the same as the lady Henttawy daughter of Istemkheb discovered by Winlock in the same tomb (60) as the like-named flautist-daughter of Pinudjem I. Her titles included that of Chief of the Harim of Amun, and her mother Istemkheb had been First Chief of Amun's Harim.[261]

(iii) *The God's Wife Henttawy*

So far, this lady is explicitly attested only from her ushabti-figurines, and hence cannot be dated precisely.[262] She has sometimes been taken to be

259. Pinudjem (II) son of Menkheperre is named in line 1 of the extracts in Champollion, *Notices Descriptives*, II, 178–9; cf. Gardiner, *JEA* 48, 58 top. Years 6, 8, cf. *ibid.*, 58 (8) and 63 (2).

260. Translated with commentary and references by Gardiner, *JEA* 48 (1962), 57–64; text, *MMR*, 705–6, and Champollion, *loc. cit.*

261. These titles, cf. Wente, *JNES* 26 (1967), 157 and refs.; for Henttawy, these are just visible in photo of coffin, *BMMA*, Dec. 1926, II, 22, fig. 23. However, Wente would identify her as a second daughter of Pinudjem I by an Istemkheb associated with him on bricks from El Hibeh (p. 158) – but it seems highly unlikely that he should have *two* daughters Henttawy. On the seals of Menkheperre in Winlock's tomb 60, see Wente, *op. cit.*, 158, n. 24; they are merely *terminus post quem* for the final closing of this tomb.

262. *G3*, 274, B; see Petrie, *A History of Egypt*, III, 1905, fig. 86, p. 213, and his remarks on style (later than 'queen' Henttawy), p. 215. Cf. also Wente, *op. cit.*, 165, n. 78.

the daughter of an Istemkheb whose title is 'Mother of the God's Wife' on a brick from Higazeh near Qus. When this latter is identified with the wife of the high priest Menkheperre, our Henttawy is then equated with Henttawy daughter of Istemkheb, wife of Smendes II.[263] The correctness of this hazardous assumption turns upon whether or not the God's Wife of Amun in the 21st Dynasty remained celibate (devoted to Amun) as was certainly true later. If so, she is not the wife of Smendes II, and will remain simply an undated God's Wife of Amun of the second half of the 21st Dynasty. If not, the theory would be possible.

(iv) *Others*

No other Henttawys of importance remain to engage our attention here; the girl of this name found by Winlock in another tomb in Western Thebes was seemingly an ordinary citizen of no political consequence.[264]

§ 47   In conclusion, the Henttawys reviewed above may now be listed and lettered for clarity's sake:

Certain:

Henttawy A – (DH) Henttawy, wife of Pinudjem I, as high priest and king; daughter of Smendes I and Tentamun.[265]

Henttawy B – daughter of 'King' Pinudjem I, chantress of Amun, flautist of Mut.[266]

Henttawy C – daughter of Istemkheb (and probably, Menkheperre), sister (and wife?) of Smendes II, alive under Pinudjem II.[267]

Henttawy D – God's Wife, 'Adoratrix', Henttawy, conceivably the daughter of an Istemkheb;[268] remotely possible that she is same as C, but this is highly dubious.

263. For this proceeding, cf. (e.g.) Petrie, *History*, III, 214 (implicit on ushabtis of fig. 86), 210 ('Henttawy II', daughter of Menkheperre); *G3*, 273/4, A/B (implicit); Kees, *Hhp.*, 58. Kees notes that the decree on Pylon X was against 'any scribe of the house of the God's Wife' hiding the decree from Henttawy's descendants, and he inferred that this Henttawy, therefore, was a God's Wife of Amun. This is possible but very uncertain; if the God's Wife were indeed a celibate, it would be ruled out.

264. *BMMA*, Dec. 1926, II, 21–2.

265. Tanis goblet No. 398; pylon, temple of Khons; Sekhmet, temple of Mut; on Coptos stela; burial, Deir el Bahri *cache*.

266. In Luxor graffito with sisters Maatkare A, Nedjemmut, and father; burial, MMA excavations, tomb 60, W. Thebes.

267. Property-decree, Pylon X, under Pinudjem II, Years 6, 8.

268. Ushabtis, published by Petrie and Allen; relation to the mother (Istemkheb) of a God's Wife of Higazeh brick-text is uncertain.

Uncertain:

Henttawy Q – DH Henttawy, mother of Psusennes I, perhaps a daughter of Ramesses XI. She was second wife of Smendes I;[269] otherwise, she would be identical with A, above.

Henttawy Z – mother of Pinudjem I and second wife of Piankh, *if* the Luxor hieratic graffito had read Henttawy.[270] Otherwise, and if Pinudjem's mother's name is different (e.g. Hrēre B), this Henttawy (Z) does not exist.

§ 48 4. THE MAATKARES

Here, at least, only two well-dated personages are of consequence.

A. GOD'S WIFE OF AMUN UNDER PINUDJEM I

For this lady, we have four basic witnesses as follows:

(i) *The Earliest Record*

This probably is the hieroglyphic graffito in the Luxor temple[271] in which (at lesser stature, hence as a girl?) she is shown behind Pinudjem I, being followed by two adults each 'bodily King's Daughter, his beloved', Henttawy B and Nedjemmut. She is entitled there: 'bodily King's Daughter whom he loves, God's Wife of Amun, Lady of the Two Lands, (cartouche:) Maatkare'. In the context of the other two ladies, Henttawy B being known from her burial as explicitly a daughter of Pinudjem, it seems clear that we must understand Maatkare to be also a daughter of Pinudjem I rather than of Smendes I. She was the pontiff's younger daughter on whom he bestowed this ancient office. As the DH Henttawy A, who was most likely the wife of Pinudjem I, claims to be 'Mother of the God's Wife (var., Adoratrix)', it is therefore possible that Pinudjem I appointed his daughter by his Tanite wife (of royal blood) to be God's Wife, rather than either of his daughters by a wife Istemkheb (A, see § 50, below).

(ii) *At Karnak*

Correspondingly, the God's Wife and Adoratrix Maatkare appears on the

---

269. Tanis vessel (399) and bracelets (543/7); possible link between the last Ramesses (XI) and Ramesses-Psusennes, Ramesses-Ankhefenmut.

270. Doubtful trace of Ḥ. . . .; Černý, affirmative, Wente and Goff, sceptical, of this reading.

271. Cited for the other ladies; Daressy, *RT* 14 (1892), 32; *G3*, 252, XXXIVA (where his n. 4 is misleading). On youthfulness of Maatkare, cf. Gardiner, *JEA* 48 (1962), 68–9, and Wente, *JNES* 26 (1967), 167.

pylon of the temple of Khons along with Pinudjem I and Henttawy A, but now at adult height.[272] If the decoration of the pylon and doorway by Pinudjem I came on the eve of his acquisition of full, formal 'kingship' in Year 16 of Smendes I,[273] while the Luxor graffito might be up to a decade earlier, then of course Maatkare would have grown up.

(iii) *Marseilles Statue No. 232*[274]

This gives the titles: 'God's Wife, (cartouche:) Maatkare, Adoratrix (cartouche:) Mutemhat' and less ambiguously as: 'God's Wife, Lady of the Two Lands, (cartouche:) Mutemhat-Maatkare, . . .'. This monument thus indicates that Maatkare as God's Wife actually took an additional cartouche-name, a kind of prenomen, and so was precursor of the ladies of the 23rd–26th Dynasties who regularly took each a prenomen usually compounded with the name of the goddess Mut.

(iv) *Burial*

In the great *cache* were found the coffins, mummy, secondary mummy, papyrus, ushabti-boxes and 150 ushabtis of the God's Wife and Adoratrix, Maatkare also called Mutemhat;[275] the statue just cited shows that just *one* person is intended by these names. Besides her office as God's Wife, these remains attest Maatkare A as a King's Daughter, Daughter of the Chief Queen (*s3t ḥmt-nsw-wrt*), but *not* as herself a Queen or Chief Queen.[276] A source of error has been what I above termed the 'secondary mummy', held to be that of an infant at whose birth Maatkare might have died, and leading to much romantic speculation as to whether the God's Wife had had an indiscreet liaison, or was after all married to the high priest as well as to Amun.[277] However, a recent X-ray has shown that this 'problem-child' was merely a domestic pet,[278] and hence no threat to the assumed celibacy of the God's Wife of Amun at this period.

272. *G3*, 253, D–E–F; *LD*, III, 250b, 248g; Champollion, *Notices Descriptives*, II, 215–16, and in doorway, *LD*, III, 250a. Cf. Wente, *op. cit.*, 162, 164–5; on her titles and epithets, *ibid.*, 162–3.
273. Recalling that Pinudjem I was already using a Horus name and the title 'King of Upper & Lower Egypt' in his dedications on the N. (inner) face of the pylon doorway (*G3*, 246, XI, D; Wente, 163, n. 59).
274. *G3*, 253, H, and references.
275. *G3*, 253, I, to 255, M.
276. The title *s3t ḥmt-nsw-wrt* (or just *s3t wrt*) is clearly written with the *s3*-bird in her funerary papyrus (*G3*, 254, La), whereas elsewhere it is written with egg and *t*, an orthography taken by some scholars as an otiose complement of *ḥmt* in *ḥmt-nsw* (cf. such a spelling in *Psus.*, fig. 60). The correct interpretation (indicated by the papyrus) has been pointed out by Wente, *op. cit.*, 163, n. 58, as against Černý, *CAH²*, II: 35 (1965), 48.
277. Cf. the remarks of Kees, *Hhp.*, 30–1, 34, or Černý, *op. cit.*, 48.
278. Press reports and informal summaries (e.g. *ARCE Newsletter* 77 (April,

As we have so far no evidence for any other God's Wife of Amun in the 21st Dynasty called Maatkare, one may attribute all the foregoing monuments to the one individual without much risk of error.

§ 49   B. DAUGHTER OF PSUSENNES II
Here too, we have some three attestations available.

(i) *Nile Statue*
The key document is a statue of the Nile-god, BM. 8, dedicated to Amun of Karnak by the high priest (cartouche:) Shoshenq, Beloved of Amun, King's Son of Osorkon I, 'whose mother is Maatkare (B), King's Daughter of . . . Har-Psusennes II, Beloved of Amun'.[279] At one stroke, this provides a vital link between the 21st and 22nd Dynasties, long famed: the daughter of Psusennes II was married-off to Osorkon (I), son and heir of Shoshenq I who succeeded Psusennes II.

(ii) *Further Karnak Statue*
A statue from the Karnak *cachette*,[280] dedicated by the same high priest, confirms the link in naming his mother as: 'Prophetess of Hathor, Lady of Dendera, God's Mother of Harsomtus, Maatkare (B), King's Daughter of [Psusennes II].' This document is of particular value in showing that the last Tanite king's daughter had at some stage acquired benefices in the south, at Dendera, bordering on the north of the Thebaid[281]– which bears on the next document.

(iii) *Karnak Inscription*
Finally, there is the property-settlement inscribed on Pylon VII (W. wing, N. face) in favour of a lady called simply 'Maatkare, King's Daughter of Psusennes Beloved of Amun'.[282] Regrettably, she is given no other title,[283]

1971) 7, with misinterpretation of the name Mutemhat) indicate that the secondary mummy is that of a Hamadryas baboon! For animals (pets, etc.) buried with people in the Late Period, cf. the gazelles buried in the Deir el Bahri *cache* (*MMR*, pl. 21B), and with a lady Ankh-Shepenupet (Winlock, *BMMA* 19 (Dec. 1924, II), 30, fig. 35, or his *Excavations at Deir el Bahri*, 1942, 98 and pl. 90).

279. *G3*, 299, II, refs.; text, *MMR*, 735.

280. Cairo Cat. 42194 (Legrain, *Statues*, III, 3–4, pls. 3–4); *G3*, 300, VB, 221.

281. If, as some believe (cf. § 8, above), Psusennes II was in fact the high priest of Amun here termed provisionally Psusennes 'III', and the Year 5 epigraph were read otherwise, then of course Maatkare B would in fact have been daughter not only of the king but of the Theban pontiff, and her tenure of benefices in Dendera would be more expected and less striking. Cf. also note 286 below.

282. Text, *MMR*, 694–5; translation and comments, Gardiner, *JEA* 48(1962), 64–9; other refs., cf. *G3*, 300, V, C, plus 252, XXXIV, B, C (misplaced).

283. An unfortunate practice, shared by the decree on Pylon X, and the 'amuletic decrees' of the period, as already noted.

but this formulation is nearly identical with those that belong indubitably to Maatkare B, daughter of Psusennes II, just considered above. Hence, this document also should most likely be attributed to Maatkare B, daughter of Psusennes II, and not to Maatkare A, daughter of Pinudjem I and contemporary of Psusennes I (as some have thought). Confirmation for this view may be seen in the fact that numerous offspring are foreseen for the Maatkare of this Pylon VII text,[284] whereas in all probability a God's Wife (such as Maatkare A) would remain celibate and have no such expectations. Also, if the Maatkare of Pylon VII were a daughter of Psusennes I, and so probably a later contemporary of Pinudjem I, it might be difficult to explain how she appears with the latter as but high priest on the pylon of Khons at Karnak, much earlier.[285] Finally, this decree concerning Theban property of this Maatkare is of a piece with her holding benefices in nearby Dendera, not least if in fact her father Psusennes II had originally been a Theban pontiff before he was a Tanite pharaoh.[286]

§ 50 5. THE ISTEMKHEBS

The number of Istemkhebs at this epoch is rivalled only by that of the Henttawys already surveyed. Most can be placed, if not always precisely.

A. A WIFE OF PINUDJEM I

At El Hibeh, northern administrative outpost of the Theban pontiffs, brickwork of Menkheperre was noted by Lepsius as overlying, and thus later than, other bricks stamped with the name of Pinudjem.[287] Therefore, the Leading Lady, Chief of the ⌜Harim⌝, Istemkhebit whose name accompanies that of Pinudjem I (as high priest) on the lower El Hibeh bricks[288] is best regarded as a wife of Pinudjem I, perhaps earlier than Henttawy A.[289] However, she cannot possibly be the daughter of Psusennes I (next to be considered).[290] For if, with Wente, Psusennes I were son of Pinudjem I,

284. In lines [2], 4, cf. Gardiner, *op. cit.*, 66, 68.
285. At least on theory (accepted here) of a long reign of Psusennes I, but no problem on the alternative theory (long reign of Amenemope).
286. While Theban interests acquired by a daughter of Psusennes II may be better appreciated if her father had earlier been pontiff, one may also observe that a purely Tanite king could well have installed members of his family as absentee beneficiaries in Upper Egypt as did 22nd Dynasty kings. The Har-element in the nomen of Psusennes II can be omitted (cf. *G3*, 301, 6, I).
287. *LDT*, II, 46.
288. *LDT*, II, 45: 1.
289. With Černý, *CAH²*, II: 35 (1965), 48, n. 8, and Wente, *JNES* 26 (1967), 158.
290. An erroneous identification suggested by Černý, *op. cit.*, 48; nor is Wente's

the latter would have to marry his own granddaughter (!) before Year 16 of Smendes, probably 15 years before the accession of Psusennes I! And even on the view of a Ramesside affiliation of Psusennes I, Pinudjem I as high priest would have to have married the daughter of a much younger cousin. In either case, one may doubt whether the girl would have been more than an infant at the time of Pinudjem's high-priesthood, before his 'kingship'. Hence, while our Istemkheb A was undoubtedly a wife of Pinudjem I as high priest, her own origins remain unknown to us. Wente further suggested that she may have been the mother of Masaharta, who was an elder son of Pinudjem I.[291]

B. A DAUGHTER(?) OF MASAHARTA

From the great Deir el Bahri *cache* a remarkable leather catafalque was recovered bearing the cartouches of 'King' Pinudjem I and the titles of the high priest Masaharta his son – and of 'the daughter of the High Priest of Amun, Chief of the Harim of Min, Horus and Isis in Apu (Panopolis, Akhmim), Istemkheb'.[292] The obvious deduction from this conjunction of data is that *this* Istemkheb was a daughter of Masaharta,[293] who died in the pontificate of her father and the 'reign' of her grandfather, having held a benefice in Panopolis. Nothing else is known of her.

§ 51   C. DAUGHTER OF PSUSENNES I

A flat bowl from the burial of Psusennes I at Tanis names 'the God's Mother of Khons-the-Child, King's Daughter, (cartouche:) Istemkheb, may she live'.[294] She seems self-evidently a daughter of the great Tanite king. However, that was almost certainly not her sole distinction. The later Theban high priest Pinudjem II son of Menkheperre is also termed[295] 'son of Istemkheb, daughter of Wiay' – and claimed further to be 'King's Son of Psusennes (I)'.[296] He could effectively claim descent from Psusennes I only if his own mother (Istemkheb) were a daughter of that king, or if he had a grandmother who was such a daughter. The latter possibility can

identification (*op. cit.*, 158) of this wife of Pinudjem I with the mother of the Henttawy of MMA tomb 60 any better.

291. *Ibid.*, 165, and table, p. 175.

292. Published by E. Brugsch, *La tente funéraire de la princesse Isimkheb*, 1889; *MMR*, 584–9; cf. *G3*, 263, VIII, for further refs.

293. Not of 'King' Pinudjem I, or she would have been called *s3t-nsw*, 'King's Daughter'. Maspero expressed the opinion (*MMR*, 589; cf. Kees, *Hhp.*, 72, n. 7) that this catafalque had been made up from bits of more than one earlier specimen; but this can hardly affect the explicit data of the texts themselves.

294. Inv. No. 403 (Montet, *Psus.*, 101, 103, fig. 42, bottom left; pl. 69).

295. Papyrus from Deir el Bahri, line 33; Daressy, *RT* 32 (1910), 180, 183; *G3*, 278, XXI.

296. *G3*, 279, XXIV–XXVI, and refs.; cf. above, § 2, end.

be excluded, because of the 'generation gap' between Pinudjem I and Psusennes I already observed above on Istemkheb A. Hence, it is in order to identify the mother of Pinudjem II as (i) a wife of Menkheperre (his father), (ii) a daughter of Psusennes I, who was doubtless the lady of Tanis bowl No. 403, and (iii) a daughter of Psusennes I by a lesser wife or concubine, Wiay, and not by his chief queen Mutnodjmet.

To attribute to Menkheperre's wife Istemkheb further relics that are undoubtedly hers is much less easy. The name of an Istemkheb appears linked with that of Menkheperre on bricks from El Hibeh, neither of whom have titles. It seems natural to consider this Istemkheb as his wife.[297] However, little else can yet be safely attributed to her. The great Deir el Bahri *cache* yielded two sets of coffins, *both* sets inscribed for an Istemkheb called daughter of Menkheperre. This ownership is generally admitted for one set, which was later usurped for a Nesikhons.[298] The other set has at times been assigned to Istemkheb *wife* of Menkheperre,[299] – but they too at one point are clearly inscribed for Istemkheb as *daughter* of Menkheperre.[300] It is also significant that this lady's mummy turned up in the *cache*[301] – but *not* that of Menkheperre's wife which (like her husband's body) still remains to be found.[302]

However, in the decree inscribed on Pylon X at Karnak, the Istemkheb named as mother of Smendes (II) and Henttawy (C) was probably our Istemkheb, wife of Menkheperre.[303] Possibly the same lady again may be the First Chief of the Harim of Amun, Istemkheb, who was named as mother of a Chief of the Harim of Amun, Henttawy (C) found by Winlock.[304] Much less certain is the identity of an Istemkheb entitled 'Mother of the God's Wife' on a brick from Higazeh near Qus.[305] She, conceivably, could be the wife of Menkheperre.

297. As in *G3*, 270, C, rather than to the wife of Pinudjem I already named there (so Černý, *CAH²*, II: 35 (1965), 48), as Menkheperre was probably a son of Henttawy A (cf. Wente, *JNES* 26 (1967), 165–6).

298. Set now Cairo Cat. 61030 (Daressy, *Cercueils*, 110–33, pls. 45–9); cf. *MMR*, 577, and *G3*, 272–3.

299. So, *G3*, 270, D (incomplete survey of legends).

300. Cairo Cat. 61031 (Daressy, *Cercueils*, 134 ff., pls. 50–3); 'Istemkheb daughter of Menkheperre', Daressy, *op. cit.*, 147 (troisième tableau) and visible on his pl. 51, middle (top register, 2nd scene from foot). This point is also made by Černý, *CAH²*, II: 35 (1965), 48, n. 9.

301. Cairo Cat. 61093 (Elliott Smith, *Royal Mummies*, 106–7, pl. 80), *MMR*, 577, No. 9; the other coffins, taken over for Nesikhons, contained the latter and a Ramesses (*MMR*, 578–9, Nos. 10–11).

302. And when found, one would expect his wife to be called *s'it-nsw*, 'King's Daughter', in view of her being a daughter of Psusennes I.

303. See above, § 46 (ii).

304. For titles of these ladies, cf. Wente, *JNES* 26 (1967), 157 and n. 16.

305. Known only from *G3*, 269, XXIII.

§ **52**   D. DAUGHTER OF MENKHEPERRE

It is probably entirely by chance that Menkheperre's daughter Istemkheb is at present better attested than his wife of that name, as follows:

(i) An original(?) set of coffins, Cairo Cat. 61030, taken for Nesikhons A (cf. previous paragraph), and replaced by another set.

(ii) A second set of coffins, Cairo Cat. 61031, in which Menkheperre's daughter was actually buried (also cf. above).

(iii) The mummy of this lady (Cairo Cat. 61093) from these coffins.

(iv) Funerary papyrus[306] and other objects from the burial.[307]

(v) As mother of the Chief of the Harim of Amun (4th phyle), 2nd prophetess of Mut, Har-weben, attested by a papyrus[308] and coffins[309] and Cairo Museum, and an epigraph from the shroud of her mummy.[310] Har-weben's bandages included one made in Year 8 of Siamun under Pinudjem II, while the braces on her mummy show that she was buried in the pontificate of Psusennes 'III'.[311] Globally, the *floruit* of these two women, Istemkheb D and her daughter Har-weben, would extend from the middle of the reign of Psusennes I to the time of Psusennes II/III.

The exalted titles of Istemkheb (D) daughter of Menkheperre (as First Chief of the Harim of Amun and holding numerous benefices) and the wealth of her funerary equipment suggest that she was wife of a high priest of Amun. As Smendès II apparently had Henttawy C as wife and was ephemeral, one may rather marry off *this* Istemkheb to Pinudjem II her brother.[312]

Two further references may just possibly apply to this Istemkheb, daughter of Menkheperre and wife of Pinudjem II. One is a bandage-epigraph from the mummy of her niece Nesi-tanebt-ashru: 'linen (for) Min, Horus and Isis, made by the Leading Lady and Chief of the Harim, Istemkheb, in Year 13'. That year could only well pertain to the reigns of either Siamun, Psusennes II or Shoshenq I; possibly to Siamun, if this Istemkheb was wife of Pinudjem II and outlived him.[313] But it remains

---

306. Cf. *MMR*, 576, 577, end.

307. Bronze libation-set, canopic jars, etc. (*MMR*, 589, and pl. 22*b*, *c*).

308. Illustrated (e.g.) by Donadoni, *Egyptian Museum, Cairo*, 1970, 142–3 (but called Tadimut).

309. Cairo Cat. 6273–7, in Chassinat, *La seconde trouvaille de Deir el Bahairi*, 1909.

310. Cf. Daressy, *RArch*[3] 28 (1896, I), 77, No. 133; *ASAE* 8 (1907), 35: 133; *G3*, 273, n. 3.

311. Cf. Daressy, *ASAE* 8 (1907), 35, No. 133.

312. So also Wente, *JNES* 26 (1967), 175, table 1; Kees, *Hhp.*, 68 and *passim*.

313. Epigraph, *G3*, 270, F; 283, C; *MMR*, 579. Otherwise, the Istemkheb concerned would have to be a younger Istemkheb, e.g. the daughter of Smendes II (Pylon X text). But one may note the connection with Min, Horus and Isis in this epigraph, and the fact that, on her discarded coffins (61030, used for Nesikhons), Istemkheb daughter of Menkheperre was Chief of the Harim of these three deities.

possible that the chief lady Istemkheb of this epigraph was a separate person, at present otherwise unknown to us – e.g. the yet-unknown wife of the pontiff Psusennes 'III'?

Another possibility – it is little more – may be that Istemkheb wife of Pinudjem II was also the Istemkheb 'Mother of the God's Wife' named on the Higazeh brick already cited above (§ 51, end). In that case, one might in turn tentatively attribute the God's Wife Henttawy D to the general period of Pinudjem II–Psusennes 'III'.

E. DAUGHTER OF HENTTAWY C (AND SMENDES II?)

This lady is attested solely in the property-decree on Pylon X at Karnak (time of Pinudjem II) already considered.[314] If the usual identifications (also adopted above) be endorsed, then she would be a daughter of Smendes II and granddaughter of Menkheperre and his wife Istemkheb.

In their turn, the Istemkhebs may now be listed and lettered:

Istemkheb A – wife of Pinudjem I as high priest of Amun.
Istemkheb B – daughter(?) of Masaharta as high priest of Amun.
Istemkheb C – daughter of king Psusennes I, wife of Menkheperre, mother of Smendes II and Pinudjem II, grandmother of E.
Istemkheb D – daughter of Menkheperre, wife of Pinudjem II.
Istemkheb E – daughter of Smendes II, granddaughter of C.
Istemkheb F – time of Psusennes 'III' and a 'Year 13' (possibly is same as D or E).

§ 53   6. THE NESIKHONS, NESI-TANEBT-ASHRU, AND RELATIVES

These ladies and their relatives form a clear group, clustering round the person of Pinudjem II.

A. NESIKHONS, WIFE OF PINUDJEM II

This lady is celebrated because of her burial which is securely dated to Year 5 (probably of Siamun) in the great *cache*,[315] her equipment,[316] and the amuletic decree of Amun that she should prosper in the hereafter and do no harm to her husband and relations still on earth.[317] In this decree,

314. Above, § 46 (ii).
315. *G3*, 280–2; Year 5, *ibid.*, 281, C, and Černý, *JEA* 32 (1946), 25–6, 30.
316. *G3*, 281–2; *MMR*, 578–9.
317. Translated by Gunn and Edwards, *JEA* 41 (1955), 83–105, and pl. 20.

her mother is named as Ta-hent-Thuty, while the Pylon X property-settlement names a Nesikhons (usually regarded as the same person) as daughter of (the high priest) Smendes (II). Thus, in marrying her, Pinudjem II married his niece. Her *genuine* titles[318] (i.e. not merely those usurped with her sister-in-law's coffin) include a variety of benefices, besides the rank of First Chief of the Harim of Amun, and the title of Viceroy of Nubia which is its last appearance in Egyptian history.

B. THE CHILDREN OF NESIKHONS A AND PINUDJEM II

These included two daughters, Itawy and Nesi-tanebt-ashru, and two sons, Masaharta B and Tjanefer B.[319] Of these, the only one to leave her mark was Nesi-tanebt-ashru, whose burial was found in the Deir el Bahri *cache*.[320] and who enjoyed various Upper-Egyptian benefices.[321] Her husband is unknown,[322] but her daughter was a further Nesikhons (B) who (unlike her mother?) attained to the rank of Chief of the Harim of Amun (1st phyle), perhaps under Psusennes 'III', or more likely in the earliest years of the 22nd Dynasty.[323]

§ 54 7. OTHER PROMINENT WOMEN IN THEBES

The remaining principal ladies of the age can be dealt with in summary fashion.

A. FAI-A-EN-MUT

This chantress of Amenresonter is recorded as a daughter of the high priest Piankh on a bandage-epigraph from the mummy of Ramesses III,[324] which was cared-for by Pinudjem I as high priest in Years 13 and 15 (i.e. probably of Smendes I).[325] That she was not only a contemporary of Pinudjem I but also married (whether to him or another) may be indicated by her possible identity with the mother of a priest Menkheperre (B) who was buried in tomb 60 excavated by Winlock.[326]

318. Gunn and Edwards, *op. cit.*, 83, n. 4, and corresponding entries, *G3*, 281-2.
319. *G3*, 283, XXX, 2-5; Gunn and Edwards, *op. cit.*, 86, § V.
320. *G3*, 284, B, and n. 1; Gunn, Edwards, 92, n. 19, and refs.
321. Cf. Kees, *Hhp.*, 71-2.
322. For candidates (e.g. 3rd prophet, Djed-Ptah-ef-ankh), cf. Kees, *Hhp.*, 74.
323. Cf. *G3*, 284, XXXI, 2; Nakht-Thuty, grandson of Pinudjem II, *ib.*, 1.
324. *G3*, 243, X; *MMR*, 565.
325. *G3*, 245, V; *MMR*, 563-4 and fig. 19. Bandages made under Pinudjem I in Years 9 and 10 were also used on this mummy; cf. *RNT*, 250: 5-8.
326. Alongside others. For references to Menkheperre's mother, see E. Young, *JARCE* 2 (1963), 107, n. 45; the burial, cf. Winlock, *Excavations at Deir el Bahri*, 1942, 97, 109, pls. 84, 85, and his *BMMA* reports.

B. NAU-NY (OR, 'ENTIU-NY')

This chantress of Amenresonter was also 'bodily daughter of the King, whom he loves',[327] by a lady Tent-nau-bekhenu[328] and buried at Deir el Bahri in the tomb of the 18th-Dynasty queen Merytamun.[329] This filiation suggests that she was a daughter of Pinudjem I by a lesser wife or concubine, as he was the only Theban 'king' of the period.[330] She otherwise does not feature in history.

C. DJED-MUT-ES-ANKH A

This person was entitled Leading Lady, First Chief of the Harim of Amenre, and had a uraeus affixed to the brow of her mummy.[331] The title suggests that she was a wife of a high priest of Amun, who was not earlier than Pinudjem I and probably later.[332] The uraeus could perhaps indicate a claim to 'royal' affiliation – a daughter of Pinudjem I or perhaps of Menkheperre?[333] She is otherwise unknown at present.

D. GAUT-SOSHEN

A daughter of the pontiff Menkheperre, she is known from her funerary papyrus and a coffin.[334] She was entitled Chief of the Harim (3rd phyle) and Chief of the Harim of Montu; her husband was the 3rd prophet of Amun, Tjanefer A.[335]

E. MERYTAMUN

A younger daughter of Menkheperre, to judge from the fact that she was

327. Title on her Osiris-figure (Winlock, *Excavations*, pl. 76, left); on her, cf. also Kees, *Hhp.*, 42–3.

328. Mother named on Nau-ny's *Book of the Dead* (e.g. Winlock, *Excavations*, pls. 78, 79), and also called 'King's Daughter' – but of whom: of Herihor, or a Tanite king? Cf. also Kees, *Hhp.*, 43.

329. Full report, Winlock, *Tomb of Queen Meryetamun*, 1932.

330. Renewal of Merytamun's burial had been conducted under the high priest Masaharta, named with Years 18, 19, on linen used for this purpose (Winlock, *Meryetamun*, 48, 51, 87). Nau-ny's burial was probably some time after these dates, as she died in her seventies.

331. Found in MMA tomb 60; on her, cf. Wente, *JNES* 26 (1967), 157, n. 16 end.

332. The form of title *wrt ḫnrt tpyt n(t) Imn . . .* did not come into use until the time of Pinudjem I onwards; cf. Excursus D, below. This lady could have been a wife of Masaharta, Djed-Khons-ef-ankh, or Menkheperre.

333. The uraeus, of course, might not count for much in this period; cf. the title 'King of Upper & Lower Egypt' on a coffin of Istemkheb (D), daughter of Menkheperre!

334. *G3*, 273, n. 3, end ('Katseshni'); Daressy, *ASAE* 8 (1907), 14, 17, 38, No. 152. Papyrus, Naville, *Papyrus funéraires de la XXIe Dynastie*, II, 1914; cf. Černý, *CAH²*, II: 35 (1965), 45, n. 10; C. de Wit, *BiOr* 10 (1953), 90–4.

335. Kees, *Hhp.*, 68–9, 69, n. 1.

buried in the pontificate of Psusennes 'III';[336] she was another chantress of
Amenresonter, and attached to the cults of Mut and Khons.

F. HAR-WEBEN

This lady was a granddaughter of Menkheperre and Istemkheb, see above,
§ 52, (v).

G. TAYU-HERET

Entitled on her mummy 'Chief of the Harim of Amenre', this lady is sometimes considered to have been the wife of the high priest Masaharta;[337]
on this, we have no evidence either way.

§ 55   8. THE HIGH PRIEST DJED-KHONS-EF-ANKH

This individual is known solely from the reports of Torr[338] concerning a
coffin now lost, which belonged to his son. Torr's account of the filiation
may be modernly transcribed as: '[. . .]re, son of the first prophet of
Amun, Djed-Khons-ef-ankh, son of the Lord of the Two Lands, Pinudjem
(I) Beloved of Amun, first prophet of Amun'.[339] Torr remarks: 'The name
Pa-netchem-Amen-meri was enclosed in a cartouche.' Thus, we would have
a high priest Djed-Khons-ef-ankh, son of 'king' Pinudjem I, and a brother
or half-brother of Masaharta and Menkheperre.

The fact that (as for Smendes II) we have so little record of this high
priest suggests that he too was ephemeral and held that office for only
the briefest interval of time.

But when? As Menkheperre was succeeded in due time (and after a long
pontificate) by his own sons Smendes II and Pinudjem II, Djed-Khons-ef-
ankh would have to precede him. The moment that Pinudjem I moved from
being himself high priest in Year 15 to being 'King' in Year 16, we find his
son Masaharta officiating as high priest. In turn, this suggests that Masaharta was the *first* son to follow his father in office, and so Djed-Khons-ef-
ankh must have come after Masaharta and before Menkheperre – i.e.

---

336. Daressy, *ASAE* 8 (1907), 9, 15, 28: 71; Chassinat, *Seconde trouvaille*, 1909,
Cairo Cat. 6175–6, 6197.

337. So *G3*, 262–3, with query; Kees, *Hhp.*, 47, without doubts, but with no
additional evidence to dispel them.

338. *The Academy* 42/No. 1064 (24 September 1892), 270, middle column, and
given in Excursus C, below; *RArch*³ 28 (1896, I), 297–8. Cf. also *BAR*, IV, § 607,
p. 297, n. *b*, and *G3*, 260, 3.

339. I am not sure that the phrase 'first priest [prophet] of Amen' added after the
cartouche is not Torr's comment rather than his translation of the original; it would
be unique to have this title appended to Pinudjem's kingly titles.

between the other two brothers. One may wonder why Djed-Khons-ef-ankh's son did not succeed his father, rather than Menkheperre doing so. On the one hand it is possible that this son whose coffin Torr saw actually died and was buried in his father's brief pontificate. On the other, it is possible that Djed-Khons-ef-ankh's son was but a child when his father died, and so Pinudjem I chose as successor the dead pontiff's brother Menkheperre as sufficiently an adult and forceful enough to cope with, not only the overall responsibilities of a general and governor of the south-land and as pontiff, but also with the specific troubles that had arisen in Thebes. It is even conceivable that Djed-Khons-ef-ankh met his death and that his pontificate came to a sudden end, as a result of these same troubles in Year 25, although this may be an over-dramatic interpretation of his brief rule. Certainly, in Year 25 and after, Menkheperre had to settle a serious situation in Thebes.[340]

Therefore, in this work, Djed-Khons-ef-ankh is allowed one year as Theban pontiff between Masaharta and Menkheperre.

§ 56 9. KING NEFERKARE AMENEMNISU

In the list for the 21st Dynasty as given in the Epitome of Manetho, a Nepherkheres[341] occurs as third king (reigning 4 years) as successor of Psusennes I, in all versions.[342] At first, no such king was found on the monuments, least of all from this period. Thus, the name was accounted for either by the ingenious suggestion that it stood for a *Kepherkheres (Kheperkhare) representing a personal reign of Pinudjem I[343] or by simply dismissing it as spurious;[344] or the name was simply accepted pending further information.[345]

However, the situation changed dramatically when Montet found two gold bow-caps in the tomb and burial of Psusennes I, with twin cartouches of the latter king and another: King of Upper and Lower Egypt, Neferkare Ruler of Thebes, and Son of Re, Amenemnisu Beloved of Amun.[346] This at once confirmed the existence and provided the identity of 'Nepher-kheres', besides linking him firmly with Psusennes I, in so far as the two

340. The 'Banishment stela', Louvre C. 286; von Beckerath, *RdE* 20 (1968), 1 ff.
341. Inferior variant, Nephelkheres.
342. Waddell, *Manetho*, 154–7; second successor of Psusennes, Book of Sothis, 65 (*ibid.*, 247), with reign of 6 years.
343. e.g. Daressy, *RT* 21 (1899), 12.
344. As put by Montet, *Les énigmes de Tanis*, 1952, 158, or *Psus.*, 185.
345. e.g. *MMR*, 729; Petrie, *History*, III, 223.
346. Montet, *Psus.*, 105, 108, fig. 44, pl. 72; *Les énigmes de Tanis*, 158–9, fig. 39 (p. 156). Cairo, *JdE*. 85886–7.

prenomens and two nomens were grouped together in pairs and not by separate kings. If this were all, then one would simply accept Amenemnisu as (i) the Nepherkheres of Manetho, and (ii) a successor and possible co-regent of Psusennes I.[347]

At this point, a third document was brought into play by Grdseloff.[348] He noted that, in the remarkable priestly genealogy of Berlin published by Borchardt,[349] three generations of Memphite priests contemporary with Akheperre Setepena[mun], Psusennes and Psusennes respectively, were preceded by one contemporary with a king whose name should undoubted-ly[350] also be read as Amenemnisu and not as a variant of Amenemope as Borchardt had thought. Taking the Akheperre and double Psusennes as all referring to Psusennes I, Grdseloff concluded that Amenemnisu was not the successor but the *predecessor* of Psusennes I, that Manetho's order must be corrected on this point, and that Amenemnisu and Psusennes I were perhaps brothers with the latter being briefly co-regent with his elder brother before succeeding him.

As is further indicated below (Pt. III, Ch. 12, §§ 151 ff.), this interpre-tation of the Borchardt genealogy and correction of Manetho is extremely probable, as it is supported by supplementary data on the high priests of Memphis, although an emendation of this document could be used to support the Manethonic order. Therefore, in turn, the order Amenem-nisu – Psusennes I is adopted here. Furthermore, the restoration probably desiderated by the bandage-fragment once thought to be of a Year 49 of Amenemope, and perhaps really from a co-regency of Psusennes I and Amenemope (cf. §§ 25, 29; Excursus A) would hardly allow of a preceding co-regency of Psusennes and Amenemnisu with no independent reign at all of Amenemnisu. This would also favour putting Amenemnisu before Psusennes I.

But the close link between the two kings requires further scrutiny. Had Amenemnisu been the successor of Psusennes, then Amenemnisu would have buried the latter. In that case, the gold-tipped bow with their names so closely linked could have been a funerary gift from Amenemnisu to Psusennes – son to father? – and there would have been no need even to postulate a co-regency.

But with Amenemnisu as predecessor of Psusennes (and the latter having Amenemope as both co-regent and successor), this line of argumentation

347. So Montet, e.g. *Psus.*, 185.

348. *ASAE* 47 (1947), 207–11.

349. Berlin 23673, see Borchardt, *Die Mittel zur zeitlichen Festlegung von Punkten der Ägyptischen Geschichte und ihre Anwendung*, 1935, 96–112, and pls. 2, 2a.

350. Kees had Anthes confirm Grdseloff's reading on the original in Berlin, cf. Kees, *Pr., Nachträge*, 1958, 17.

cannot be neatly transposed and no longer applies. If Psusennes had had the bow made to commemorate his predecessor Amenemnisu, then why was it buried with Psusennes instead of in the tomb of Amenemnisu? If Psusennes I was not king until Amenemnisu's death, then it could not (in its present engraved state) be a gift from Amenemnisu to Psusennes I either. In short, this document makes some sense if the two kings were somehow associated, if even in the briefest of co-regencies, and the bow dated to the time of such a co-regency.[351]

As already seen above,[352] it seems likely that Psusennes I was son of Smendes I and a Ramesside princess or just possibly of Pinudjem I – and so was *not* son of his immediate predecessor. In that case, Amenemnisu died without heir. His association with Psusennes I may reflect that situation: being of mature years,[353] and lacking an heir, he may have associated with himself (before a last illness?) his young brother or cousin Psusennes. Neither relationship is impossible, though I think the former (brother) the more natural. However, if the association of names on the bow-caps merely indicated a wish of Psusennes to link his name with his predecessor's for some reason, then no co-regency need be postulated. One would simply assume that Psusennes I wished merely to emphasize his legitimacy and the continuity of the kingship on this ceremonial object (and perhaps on others?), and that this piece ended up in his tomb as a personal heirloom from his earliest years, and a ceremonial weapon for the hereafter.

351. With Grdseloff, *op. cit.*, 211; Wente, *JNES* 26 (1967), 155–6; Černý, *CAH²*, II: 35 (1965), 42. Wente's reserves (*op. cit.*, n. 4) about a co-regency are understandable – but what alternative is there? Kees's remark (*Hhp.*, 28) that Amenemnisu was buried with Psusennes I is surely a slip of the pen. On the sequence of these kings, it is in order to bear in mind the observations of Young, *JARCE* 2 (1963), 109, n. 50.

352. Above, §§ 41–4.

353. Smendes I was already in the highest position in the north with the 'Renaissance Era' (Year 5, Wenamun); if he were, say, 45 at induction, 56 at his own accession and about 82 at death (§ 64, below), Amenemnisu would be 62–6 during his brief reign. If he were both ill and childless by his 4th year, he may have declared Psusennes his heir and successor, to assure the succession.

CHAPTER 5

Dates, Reigns, and Pontificates

§ 57   1. INTRODUCTORY

Neither the 20th nor the 21st Dynasty can so far offer us any information
from which one may calculate their absolute dates B.C. However, immediately following the 21st Dynasty, the founder of the next line, Shoshenq
I, can be closely dated by a synchronism with the Hebrew monarchy,
whose dates in turn are closely fixed with reference to Assyrian chronology.
Therefore, by defining his date, a terminal date for the 21st Dynasty
becomes possible. Dates can then be offered in turn, for the reigns and
pontificates of the whole Dynasty.

§ 58   2. TOWARDS AN ABSOLUTE DATE FOR THE
END OF THE DYNASTY

A. THE SYNCHRONISM
The essential synchronism is the biblical notice that 'Shishak king of
Egypt' invaded Palestine 'in the 5th year of Rehoboam, king of Judah',
and had to be bought-off from attacking Jerusalem by presentation of its
wealth as tribute.[354] That Shishak was already king of Egypt for some time
prior to Rehoboam's accession is evident from the fact that, during
Solomon's reign, he sheltered the fugitive Jeroboam.[355] Hence, just on the
biblical data, one may see that Shishak's military venture occurred quite
some time after the beginning of his reign.

354. I Kings 14: 25–26; 2 Chronicles 12: 2–12. Synchronisms between the 21st
Dynasty and the Hebrew Monarchy are not sufficiently precise for specific chronological purposes, although of considerable historical interest (cf. below, Part IV,
§§ 231, 235–6).
355. I Kings 11: 40 (cf. 2 Chronicles 10: 2, less explicit).

The selfsame campaign is also attested by the monuments of Shoshenq I, the biblical Shishak.[356] The most imposing of these is his great triumphal relief at Karnak, which adjoins the 'Bubastite gate' and the great forecourt of the temple of Amun, which were all planned and executed as a whole by Shoshenq I. But those great works were never completed: the colonnades were built but never dressed-down and decorated, the gate was built and partly decorated, but never finished (even by Osorkon I thereafter), and even the great triumphal relief may just possibly never have been completely finished.[357] The reason for the sudden cessation of these great works must almost certainly have been the death of the king. It is generally admitted that they were undertaken only from the 21st year of his reign,[358] and there is no reason to believe that he reigned beyond his incomplete 22nd year.[359] Thus, in that year, the Palestinian campaign was commemorated by the great relief, the gateway was built and partly decorated, and the court, colonnades and perhaps a pylon (replaced by that of Nectanebo I, later) were built in rough – then, all work stopped.

In turn, there is no compelling reason to assume that any great interval elapsed between the Palestinian campaign of Shoshenq I and his commemoration of it at Karnak. To assume a delay of even (say) 3 years seems pointless, and hence wholly unnecessary.[360] At the latest, it would have

356. On the campaign of Shoshenq I in Palestine, see below, Part IV, §§ 252 ff., and Part V, Excursus E. A word is in order on the form Shishak compared with Egyptian Shoshenq. Vocalization of the latter is assured by the spelling Shushinqu of the Assyrian records, or Susinqu (Ranke, *Keilschriftliches Material zur altägyptischen Vokalisation*, 1910, 34). With this agrees the original vocalization of the Hebrew as Shushaq (rather than Shishaq), 1 Kings 14: 25 *kethiv*, the *a* being an indefinite vowel; Manetho's *Sesonkhosis* probably shows metathesis. Cf. Meyer, *Gottesstaat*, 513, n. 4; J. Simons, *Handbook for . . . Egyptian Topographical Lists*, 1937, 89, n. 1. The omission of *n* in the Hebrew form faithfully reflects its common omission in Egypt throughout the Libyan period, cf. (e.g.) *G3*, 307, I; 308, IV; 309, XI; 316, XLVIII; 318, C; 321, B; 323, LVIII; 330, A; 364, XVII; 365, XVIII, XIXA; 366, XXII; 367, XXXIII; 369, I; 370, n. 4; 373–4.

357. The figure of the king appears there only in vaguest outline, and is often considered to have been left incomplete. However, through very close study of the king's figure on the original, the Chicago Epigraphic Survey has made out a convincing case to the effect that, in fact, the king's figure was probably modelled in gypsum on the stone, and not intended to be cut in sunk relief like the rest of the scene; see *RIK*, III, 1954, pp. viii–ix. If so, then this relief may indeed have been the sole element of Shoshenq's grand design ever to be completed.

358. Based on Gebel Silsila stela 100, see Caminos, *JEA* 38 (1952), 46–61; it is dated to Year 21, 2nd month of Shomu, ⟨Day 1?⟩, with the king's command to undertake the works at Silsila and Karnak. Cf. *RIK*, III, pp. vii–ix.

359. The versions of Manetho agree in giving 21 years to Shoshenq (except the corrupt Book of Sothis, 34 years). As did Hornung, *Untersuchungen zur Chronologie und Geschichte des Neuen Reiches*, 1964, 24 and n. 4, one may take the 21 years as 21 complete years, plus a few months of an incomplete Year 22.

360. For 3 years' scope (Albright, *BASOR* 130 (1953), 7), and probably much

occurred in the 21st year, before the works at Karnak were inaugurated; but hardly more than a year's delay between the campaign and the commemoration need surely be envisaged, placing it in the 20th year. By roughly the mid-10th century B.C., the 2nd month of Shomu would fall about January; if Shoshenq I invaded Palestine in the spring (a common time for Palestinian wars), then he would have done so – at the latest – in the previous spring, about 9 months earlier than 2nd Shomu of Year 21: probably, therefore, in his Year 20.[361]

§ 59   B. HEBREW DATES

If, then, the Palestinian campaign may be set in about Years 20–21 of Shoshenq I, and it is less likely to have been any earlier (after Years 18/19), and is attributed to the 5th year of Rehoboam, the latter must be defined by the Near Eastern data. This is possible, by establishing a set of interlocking lengths of reigns of Hebrew kings in Judah and Israel, and placing them at definite dates B.C. by an Assyrian synchronism.

Thus, during the first half of the divided monarchy period for Judah and Israel which followed on Solomon's death, one can obtain a closely-integrated series of reigns with regnai years and synchronisms that fit together. For this purpose, it is sufficient to take the period from the death of Solomon – when the reigns of Rehoboam and Jeroboam began (as first kings of Judah and Israel) within but months of each other (1 Kings 12) – to the accession of Jehu of Israel, who slew at one time both his own predecessor, Joram of Israel, and the latter's contemporary Ahaziah of Judah (2 Kings 9). Close attention to the lengths of reigns and to the synchronisms in this period indicates:[362] (i) that Judah initially used the accession-year custom of counting regnal years,[363] (ii) that Israel initially used the non-accession mode of counting regnal years,[364] (iii) that, in synchronisms, each

less, cf. also Hornung, *Untersuchungen*, 24 and n. 3, 29; the nihilism over the 20th year expressed in *RIK*, III, p. viii, n. 9, seems unwarranted, even though Drioton and Vandier had offered no evidence for their adopting Year 20.

361. Unfortunately, we do not know for certain whether Shoshenq used the New Kingdom method of counting the regnal year from his accession-day, or had reverted to the older usage of dating by the civil calendar (1st month of Akhet, Day 1 ff.). Later usage might support the second alternative. In the latter case, one might assume that Shoshenq began his building-programme late in Year 21, and died well on into Year 22 (which became Year 1 of his successor).

362. See E. R. Thiele, *MN*[1], 1951, [2]1965, for full details of the phenomena exhibited by the Old Testament data. Only the barest essentials are presented here.

363. Whereby the interval between a king's accession and next New Year's day was his 'accession-year' (in effect, reckoned to his predecessor), with his Year 1 beginning only at New Year. This was the system usual in Western Asia (e.g. in Mesopotamia). For evidence of its use in Judah, see Thiele, *MN*[1], 20–3, [2]23–6.

364. Whereby the interval between a king's accession and next New Year's day was his 'Year 1' (in effect, annexing the whole year from his predecessor), with his

kingdom reckoned the years of its neighbour in terms of its *own* method, not that of its neighbour,[365] and (iv) that Judah used an autumn New Year (Tishri) and Israel a spring New Year (Nisan).[366] When these conditions are observed for the kings of Judah and Israel from Solomon's death to Jehu's accession, then a closely-woven span of 90 years of interlocking reigns results.[367]

Two links between kings of Israel and kings of Assyria enable us to fix closely the dates of these 90 years. Ahab of Israel was among the opponents of Shalmaneser III at the Battle of Qarqar in 853 B.C.,[368] while his third successor Jehu paid tribute to that king in 841 B.C. As Thiele points out,[369] these dates are, respectively, the *last* year of Ahab and *first* year of Jehu – the 12 years between these two dates are precisely filled by the 12 years of the reigns of Ahaziah and Joram of Israel.[370] On this basis, it is possible in turn to reckon directly back to the accession of Rehoboam in Judah in 931/930 B.C., and to set his 5th year as being in 926/925 B.C.[371]

§ **60** C. DATE OF SHOSHENQ I AND END OF 21ST DYNASTY

On the basis of these figures for Rehoboam, and especially of 926/925 B.C. for his 5th year (running from Tishri to Tishri, autumn 926 to autumn 925), one may suggest[372] that Shoshenq's invasion (and his Year 20–21) occurred in the spring of 925 B.C. during Rehoboam's 5th year.

One may then suggest that a few months later, in January 924 B.C., in the 2nd month of Shomu in Year 21 of Shoshenq I, work was inaugurated at the Silsila quarries (stela 100) and at the Karnak temple for the relief-scene and buildings. One may postulate that Shoshenq died within 12

Year 2 beginning from the New Year. This system obtained principally in Egypt, whence Jeroboam I perhaps took it. On this in Israel, see Thiele, *MN*[1], 20–3, [2]23–6. On this system, a king's true reign is one year less than his highest-attested year; on the other, his highest year gives the true number of years.

365. See Thiele, *MN*[1], 24–8, or [2]25–6. Later, under political pressures, both states switched systems, cf. *ibid.*, 37–41 or 33–8.

366. Thiele, *MN*[1], 29–33, [2]27–32.

367. Thiele, *MN*, for details; cf. Hornung, *Untersuchungen*, 26–8.

368. For the date of Qarqar in 853 B.C., not 854, see Thiele, *MN*[1], 48–53, and [2]46–50.

369. *MN*[1], 53–4, [2]50–1; Hornung, *op. cit.*, 25–6.

370. Ahaziah is attributed 2 years (1 Kings 22: 51), i.e. 1 year real reign on non-accession system; likewise, Joram's 12 years is 11 full years for this reason, and the two kings just fill 12 years.

371. Cf. *MN*[1], Table opposite p. 74; *MN*[2], 56, Table I right half; Hornung, *Untersuchungen*, 28. The oft-quoted alternative chronology of Albright (*BASOR* 100 (1945), 16–22; e.g. Freedman, in Wright (ed.), *Bible & the Ancient Near East*, 1961, 208 ff.) is far inferior to that of Thiele (cf. exposé in *MN*[1], 244–52, 253–4 to 267; omitted in 2nd edition, regrettably). The same is true for the systems of Begrich, Jepsen, and Pavlovsky-Vogt (refs., *CdE* 40/80 (1965), 311, n. 3).

372. With Thiele, *MN*[1], 56, [2]55.

months or so, during his 22nd regnal year, perhaps by the end of 924 B.C. In turn, the 21-and-a-bit years of Shoshenq I would fall during *c.* 945–924 B.C.,[373] and set the end of the 21st Dynasty at *c.* 945 B.C.

§ 61   3. THE REIGNS OF THE TANITE KINGS

Working backwards from *c.* 945 B.C. for the death of Psusennes II, an outline of dates for the whole dynasty can be evolved; on the figures used, see above, Chapter 2.

On the 14 years granted in Africanus' version of Manetho, the reign of Psusennes II would run from 959 to 945 B.C. In turn, Siamun at 19 years (Year 17 attested, and reading Manetho as ⟨1⟩9 years for 'Psinaches') would reign *c.* 978–959 B.C., and before him, Osochor at 6 years during *c.* 984–978 B.C.

With a short reign for Amenemope and a long reign for Psusennes I, Amenemope's 9 years would be *c.* 993–984 B.C. The span allotted to Psusennes I would then depend on the view taken of the Manethonic 46 (var.; 41) years, versus the Years 48, 49, on first-hand documents. If, as seems best, Manetho be held to give the reign of Psusennes I as of 46 sole years prior to a short co-regency with Amenemope,[374] then 'Year 49' would indicate a minimum total reign of 48 years with 2 years of co-regency with Amenemope; Psusennes I would then have reigned altogether *c.* 1039–991 B.C. (993–991 B.C., co-regency with Amenemope).[375]

Prior to Psusennes I, Amenemnisu may be accorded the 4 years of sole rule given him in Manetho, during *c.* 1043–1039 B.C., whether or not he had a few months' co-regency with Psusennes I. The 26 years of Smendes I, founder of the dynasty, would then have covered *c.* 1069–1043 B.C.[376]

373. At the very latest, in *c.* 943–922 B.C., if 2 or 3 years' lapse be assumed between the campaign and the works. The date of 940/939 B.C. suggested by Uphill (*JNES* 26 (1967), 61–2) fails because it is based on a wrong date (961 B.C.) for Solomon, incompatible with clear data from the Divided Monarchy utilized here. For the imaginary eclipse under Takeloth II, see below, Part II, § 148 (also, § 293 (iii), n.).

374. Otherwise, if there were no co-regency with Amenemope, the death and in turn the accession of Psusennes I would fall two years earlier, putting him at *c.* 1041–993 B.C.

375. If one held to my former hypothesis of ⟨4⟩ 9 years for Amenemope in Manetho (emended), invoking a 3-year co-regency with Osochor and 26 years for Psusennes I, then one would date Amenemope *c.* 1033–981 B.C., and Psusennes I at *c.* 1059–1033 B.C.

376. On the alternative hypothesis (cf. previous note), Amenemnisu would reign *c.* 1063–1059 B.C., and Smendes I, *c.* 1089–1063 B.C. (at 26 years). The total difference in dates for beginning of the 21st Dynasty on the two hypotheses is thus 20 years.

Going back to the reign of Ramesses XI and the 'Renaissance Era', his personal reign at 29 years would be *c.* 1098–1069 B.C., and the 'Era' (with Smendes in Tanis) would run during his Years 19–30, at *c.* 1080–1069 B.C.[377]

§ 62 4. THE HIGH PRIESTS IN THEBES

Likewise, corresponding dates may be proposed for the Theban pontiffs. Within the 'Renaissance Era', on the hypothesis of a long reign for Psusennes I, Herihor in Years 1–7 would officiate in *c.* 1080–1074 B.C., and Piankh for 4 years, Years 7–11 (attested in 7 and 10) in *c.* 1074–1070 B.C.[378]

During the 21st Dynasty proper, Pinudjem I would be high priest from the death of Piankh and for the first 15 years of Smendes I, i.e. *c.* 1070–1055 B.C. (15 years), and 'King' from the 16th year of Smendes I to at least the 8th year of possibly Amenemnisu[379] or much more likely of Psusennes I, and perhaps for slightly longer. Year 16 of Smendes I to Year 8 of Psusennes I would be some 22 years, *c.* 1054–1032 B.C., making his total tenure of offices some 37 years at least, all told.[380]

The pontificate of Masaharta began with his father's kingship in Year 16 of Smendes I, *c.* 1054 B.C.; it ended by the 25th year of Smendes I when Menkheperre was installed (*c.* 1045 B.C.) – and if one allows a year between these two for the ephemeral Djed-Khons-ef-ankh (*c.* 1046–1045 B.C.), then Masaharta may be allowed 8 years, *c.* 1054–1046 B.C.[381]

Menkheperre himself then held office throughout the long reign of Psusennes I to Year 48. He may have died in that year, as it is his successor Smendes II who gave burial gifts at the death of Psusennes I. Hence, one may assign the 53 years from the 25th of Smendes I to the 48th of Psusennes I to Menkheperre, *c.* 1045–992 B.C.[382] His elder son Smendes II, though

377. On the alternative hypothesis, Ramesses XI would reign *c.* 1118–1089 B.C., with the 'Renaissance Era' at *c.* 1100–1089 B.C.

378. On the other scheme, Herihor would be *c.* 1100–1094 B.C., and Piankh from 1094 to perhaps 1064 B.C.

379. If (theoretically) Amenemnisu were 4 years sole king and Psusennes his co-regent for another 3 or 4 years.

380. On the other hypothesis, the high-priesthood of Pinudjem I would fall in (at latest) the Years 1–15 of Psusennes I, and his kingship from Year 16 and on into a Year 8 attributable then to Amenemope; if Pinudjem I was also pontiff from the end of Smendes and under Amenemnisu, the net result – 37 years – is identical with that under the preferable hypothesis of the long reign being that of Psusennes I.

381. On the other hypothesis, similarly, Masaharta and his ephemeral brother would still have some 8 years and 1 year, respectively.

382. On the alternative hypothesis, Menkheperre would officiate from a Year 25 (Banishment Stela; here, Psusennes I) and for 47 years of Amenemope, totalling some 49 years.

evidently ephemeral, was contemporary with Amenemope either as co-regent or as sole king. To make Smendes II contemporary with Amenemope as sole king, one may allow Smendes II some 2 years from Year 48 of Psusennes I (Year 2 of Amenemope) to Year 4 of Amenemope at the most,[383] *c.* 992–990 B.C.

Thereafter, we have Pinudjem II, who died and was buried in Year 10 of Siamun, and so would have acted during *c.* 990–969 B.C.[384] – some 21 years. Thereafter, his son Psusennes 'III' would be high priest from *c.* 969 B.C. to perhaps the end of the period, *c.* 945 B.C., some 24 years[385] (especially if he were, in fact, identical with Psusennes II).

The only possibility not envisaged above is that of a personal, sole reign of Pinudjem I as real pharaoh in Tanis; a possibility now increasingly rejected by Egyptologists.[386] Now that we have all the kings in Manetho accounted for, there is no room in that series for Pinudjem I as sole pharaoh in Tanis, unless he be emended into it. Furthermore, the close association between Amenemnisu and Psusennes I would seem to forbid any Theban reigning in between them. The direct sequence from Year 15 with Pinudjem I as high priest to Year 16 with him as a 'king' suggests that he performed under both styles within the one reign of a Tanite king (Smendes I) – and in terms of regnal years of the latter, *without* regnal years of his own. In the light of this situation, then, the Year 8 with which Pinudjem I is associated should indeed be referred to a Tanite king (e.g. Psusennes I) as has been done throughout this work. So, the 'reign' of Pinudjem I remains a purely nominal affair, without a year-count of its own, and overlaps the real reigns of his contemporaries the Tanite kings.

§ 63   5. THE AGE FACTOR

Using the preferred scheme of reigns, pontificates and dates just outlined (on the hypothesis of a long reign for Psusennes I), one may duly sketch an outline of possible relative ages for the principal people concerned.

The high priest Masaharta was heavily-built, and died in middle age or older – aged perhaps 40 or 50 at death.[387] To simplify the presentation of

383. On the other hypothesis, a year or so may be allowed to Smendes II.
384. From *c.* 985 B.C. (other hypothesis) to 969 B.C. (*both* hypotheses), gives 16 years to Pinudjem II, a little less than on the preferred view.
385. Same tenure of office on both hypotheses.
386. Cf. Young, *JARCE* 2 (1963), 101–4; Kees, *Hhp.*, 21; Hornung, *Untersuchungen*, 102, 104; von Beckerath, *Tanis und Theben*, 1951, 98 and n. 530; Gardiner, *Egypt of the Pharaohs*, 1961, 317; Černý, *CAH²*, II: 35 (1965), 44–5; Wente, *JNES* 26 (1967), 155 and n. 2.
387. Description of Masaharta's body, Elliott Smith, *Royal Mummies*, 106, Cairo

ages throughout this section, his age at his death will here be taken as 45 (±5) years old, so that the following calculations may be understood as allowing ±5 years leeway throughout. On the preferred chronology used here,[388] Masaharta would have died at 45 (±5) in *c.* 1046 B.C. If he were born to Pinudjem I when the latter was about 20 (*c.* 1091 B.C.), then Pinudjem I would be about 65 (±5) years old in *c.* 1046 B.C., and would himself (i) have been born *c.* 1111 B.C., (ii) be aged about 41 at induction as high priest in *c.* 1070 B.C., (iii) be aged about 56 at attaining 'kingship' in Year 16 of Smendes I *c.* 1054 B.C., and (iv) be aged about 79 in Year 8 of Psusennes I *c.* 1032 B.C. (earliest date for his decease). From this basis, one may estimate ages for both the predecessors and contemporaries of Pinudjem I, and his descendants and successors.

§ **64**   On the dates just suggested, if Pinudjem I were the eldest (or, second-eldest) son of Piankh and so born to him at 20 or so, then Piankh (i) might be born 20 years earlier still, *c.* 1131 B.C., (ii) have been aged about 57 when he succeeded Herihor in *c.* 1074 B.C., and (iii) have died aged about 61 in *c.* 1070 B.C. Likewise, Herihor if born about 20 years before Piankh (i) could have been born about 1151 B.C., (ii) might be aged about 71 at the beginning of the 'Renaissance Era', *c.* 1080 B.C., and (iii) would have died aged about 77 in 1074 B.C. If, with Wente,[389] one makes Smendes I *also* an elder son of Herihor and Nodjmet, and close in age to Piankh, then Smendes I (i) might be born at or soon after *c.* 1125 B.C., (ii) might be aged about 45 at the beginning of the 'Renaissance Era' *c.* 1080 B.C., (iii) be aged about 56 at his own accession in 1069 B.C., and (iv) would die aged about 82 in *c.* 1043 B.C. In turn, if Neferkare Amenemnisu were the eldest son of Smendes I by his wife Tentamun and born when Smendes was about 20 (*c.* 1105 B.C.), then Amenemnisu would already be aged about 62 at his accession in 1043 B.C., and die aged at least 66 years after a 4-year reign, *c.* 1039 B.C.[390] Then, if the name Ramesses-Psusennes be taken to indicate that Psusennes I was the son of Smendes I by a Ramesside princess (our Henttawy Q)[391] whom Smendes may have married at his election to highest office next to the king at the

Cat. 61092 (no estimate of age); 40 or up to 10/15 years older are (gu)es(s)timates by Young, *JARCE* 2 (1963), 103, and Wente, *op. cit.*, 160, 170.

388. i.e. a long reign of Psusennes I.

389. *Op. cit.*, 174. In any case, with 26 years' reign *after* a decade of rule during the 'Renaissance Era', Smendes I must of necessity belong to the generation of Piankh at earliest, not to that of Herihor.

390. Later and still older, if his 4 years' reign alone were continued by a co-regency with Psusennes I.

391. As a younger daughter of Ramesses XI – of whose family absolutely nothing is otherwise known so far.

inauguration of the 'Renaissance Era', then one may suggest that Psusennes I was born of this marriage soon after 1080 B.C. – say, *c.* 1078 B.C. Then, Psusennes I (i) would be aged about 39 at his accession *c.* 1039 B.C., and (ii) die aged about 87 in 991 B.C.[392] His two eldest sons may have been Ramesses-Ankhefenmut (who predeceased him) and possibly his successor Amenemope. If he were born to Psusennes I when the latter was aged about 20–25, then Amenemope would (i) be aged about 60–65 at his accession as co-regent in 993 B.C., and (ii) be aged about 69–74 at his death in 984 B.C.[393] The remaining Tanite kings can only be reckoned theoretically from this basis.[394]

§ **65** Returning to the Thebans, the length of Menkheperre's pontificate (up to 53 years) suggests that he was a younger son of Pinudjem I, especially if his mother was Henttawy A,[395] who was a younger wife of Pinudjem I than Istemkheb A. Menkheperre (i) could be born *c.* 1080 B.C., (ii) be aged about 35 at his induction in 1045 B.C., and (iii) die aged about 88 in 992 B.C. If Smendes II was born to Menkheperre by Istemkheb C, daughter of Psusennes I,[396] this might have occurred about 1040 B.C., and his brief pontificate have ended with his death at about 50 in *c.* 990 B.C. Pinudjem II (as his younger brother) could thus have been aged about 45 in that year and have died in 969 at about 66 years old. If Psusennes 'III' were his eldest son, he (i) could have been born *c.* 1015 B.C., (ii) may have been aged about 46 when he succeeded Pinudjem II in 969 B.C., and (iii) perhaps died aged about 70 in 945 B.C. If he were also

392. In agreement with the report on his remains as those of an old man at death, Derry, *ASAE* 40 (1940/1), 969.

393. Again, agreeing with his remains being those of an old man at death, Derry, *ASAE* 41 (1942), 149.

394. If one makes Osochor, Siamun, and Psusennes II (if not same as III) each the eldest son of his predecessor – giving maximal likely ages in each case – then one might reckon their theoretical ages as follows: *Osochor* would be (i) about 49/54 at accession in 984 B.C., and (ii) about 55/60 at death in 978. *Siamun* would be perhaps (i) about 35/40 at accession in 978, and (ii) about 54/59 at death in 959 B.C. *Psusennes II* (if not same as III) could be (i) about 34/39 at accession in 959, and (ii) about 48/53 at death in 945 B.C. Then his daughter Maatkare B might have been about 10/20 at her father's accession, and married off to the young Osorkon at almost any time in her father's reign – with her, our estimates become wholly conjectural.

395. If she were about 20 in 1080 B.C., and died and was buried during Menkheperre's pontificate, after 1045 B.C., she would have been over 55 at death, which would agree with more recent findings on her possible age at death, cf. Wente, *JNES* 26 (1967), 171.

396. If Psusennes I were born *c.* 1078 B.C., then his daughter Istemkheb C would not perhaps be born until *c.* 1060 B.C. or later; she might then have been married-off at 15–20 to Menkheperre by *c.* 1040 B.C., for the birth of Smendes II about then.

king as Psusennes II, he would have acceded aged about 56 in 959 B.C.; Maatkare B would then have been a younger daughter of his. Correction or confirmation of these general age-horizons would be welcome; to that end, a modern re-examination of all the royal and priestly mummies is desirable, for which only the scantiest estimates of age-at-death are available.[397]

397. Thus Nodjmet was evidently old at death; cf. indirect remarks on hair and possible marks of changes to senility by Elliott Smith, *Royal Mummies*, 97 top. This would agree with her being probably younger than Herihor, if he died aged about 77 in 1074 B.C., and she died early in Smendes I's reign, say *c.* 1064 – perhaps aged about 82 or so. Smith has nothing definite to say on the age of Maatkare A (pp. 98– 101), but regarded her as relatively young, possibly thinking that she had died in childbirth (a wrong assumption). Her brown hair, with only slight greying, might favour a death-date in middle age. Pinudjem II had traces of 'a short white beard' (Smith, p. 107), probably consistent with the theoretical age-at-death of 66 suggested here. For estimates of age on Wente's scheme, see his paper, *JNES* 26, *passim*; theoretical ages for the alternative scheme of dates (long reign of Amenemope) can also be estimated, but a long pontificate for Piankh would require that he be assigned a younger age at induction; otherwise, Nodjmet's age (for one) would become impossibly high.

PART TWO

Chronology
*Twenty-second to Twenty-fifth Dynasties**

CHAPTER 6

Dynasties 22 and 23: The Kings Involved

§ 66   1. INTRODUCTORY

Over the years, there has often been much confusion as to the identity and number of real kings at this period. Therefore, it is essential first of all to distinguish as clearly as possible between the various kings who have some claim to belong in (or with) these two closely-linked dynasties, and thereby gain a conspectus of the reigns with which the chronology has to be built up.

2. THE SHOSHENQS

 I. Prenomen, Hedj-kheper-re (Setepenre).[1]
 II. Prenomen, Heqa-kheper-re Setepenre.
III*a.* Prenomen, Usimare Setepenamun.
 b. Prenomen, Usimare Setepenre.
 IV. Prenomen, Usimare Meryamun.
 V. Prenomen, A-kheper-re (Setepenre).
 VI. Prenomen, Was-neter-re Setep(en)re.
VII. Prenomen, Sekhem-kheper-re Setepenamun.

Of this series, Nos. I, II, V, are distinct entities, each having a characteristic prenomen and indubitably attested as real kings, not scribal phantoms, by monuments of adequate nature or number. But the individuality or otherwise of Nos. III*a*, III*b*, IV, VI and VII has remained a matter for discussion.

---

1. Bracketed elements are subject to variation; such variables will be noted where appropriate.

Differing solely in the use of either Amun or Re in the complement Setep-en-x, 'Chosen of (the god) x', Nos. IIIa and b have been well discussed long since, and their identity affirmed, by Gauthier,[2] an identity which is now generally accepted. The clearest evidence comes from the Serapeum stelae. One such was made by the chief Pediese son of Takeloth,[3] and is dated to Year 28 of a king Usimare Setepen*amun*, Shoshenq Beloved of Amun, Son of Bast, god, Ruler of Heliopolis. The same man Pediese left two stelae at the burial of the *next* Apis bull, in Year 2 of Pimay, and these both refer back to the birth of that same bull in Year 28 of king Usimare Setepen*re*, Shoshenq Beloved of Amun, god, Ruler of Heliopolis.[4]

This in itself is sufficient to demonstrate the interchangeability of deities, certainly of Amun and Re, in the complement Setepen-x used within the prenomen of one single king.[5] Independent proof of this usage is afforded by the same alternation in the first cartouche of Pimay, wherein Usimare is usually followed by Setepen*amun* as on the Serapeum stelae,[6] but sometimes by Setepen*re* as once on a votive stela in the Louvre.[7] Similarly, the prenomen of the Shoshenq numbered I, Hedj-kheper-re, is usually followed by Setepenre, but can be complemented with Setepen-amun[8] or even Setepenptah[9] (at Memphis). Hence, our IIIa and b may be confidently attributed to one and the same king.

§ 67   This leaves Nos. IV, VI, VII. No. VII is the least satisfactorily attested. If the prenomen has been correctly read upon a Florence stela and the Migliarini scarab,[10] then – as Petrie remarked long since[11] – Sekhemkheperre Setepenamun need be nothing more than a minor variant for Sekhemkheperre Setepenre, the regular prenomen of Osorkon I (§ 69). As for the Tell el Yahudiyeh granite fragment naming the Horus Userpehty,[12]

2. *BIFAO* 11 (1914), 197–216.
3. IM 3749; M. Malinine, G. Posener, J. Vercoutter, *Catalogue des stèles du Sérapéum de Memphis*, I, 1968, No. 21, pp. 19–20, pl. 7.
4. IM, 3697, 3736, to which one may add 4205; *ibid.*, Nos. 22, 23, 24, pp. 21–4, pls. 8–9.
5. Cf. already Gauthier, *BIFAO* 11 (1914), 209–10, adding the variants in cartouches from Karnak.
6. *G3*, 370–2; Malinine, Posener, Vercoutter, *op. cit.*, Nos. 22–5, pp. 21–5, pls. 8–9.
7. *G3*, 372, VI, and n. 4.
8. *G3*, 312, XVII (Theban statue), 316, XLVII.
9. *G3*, 312, XX.
10. See Gauthier, *BIFAO* 11 (1914), 198–205, for full discussion. I find no other trace of his scarab 'BM. 2928' (p. 201).
11. *A History of Egypt*, III, 1905, 253.
12. Birch, *ZÄS* 10 (1872), 122: Petrie, *loc. cit.*

this name has long been known to belong to the Shoshenq here listed as V (Akheperre).[13] Thus, king No. VII had no independent existence, as is now generally admitted.

King No. VI is so far attested solely by a bronze pendant bearing the cartouches: Was-neter-re Setep-⟨en⟩-re, Shosh⟨enq Mery⟩-Amun, god, ⌈Ruler⌉ of Thebes.[14] The *Was* and *neter* signs of the first cartouche are absolutely clear and all the hieroglyphs are well cut; yet, the *spelling* is poor – omission of *n* in the first, and of *nq* and *Mery* in the second, cartouche. Thus we have a choice. Either this is an independent king(let), or else *Was* and *neter* are graphic errors for *Usi(r)* and the *maat*-feather (the *neter* being reversed!), giving in fact Usimare, i.e. simply Shoshenq III of our list.

§ **68**   This leaves us with king No. IV, prenomen Usimare Meryamun. Again, the question arises: was he an independent king, or merely a variant of the known Usimare Setepen-amun/-re, Shoshenq III? Here, one may suggest that we have a separate king. While the Libyan kings can clearly vary the god invoked in the epithet Setepen-*x* (cf. § 66, just above), there is no evidence as yet that they varied the entire epithets Setepen-*x* and Mery-*x*. In the 'imperial' style of titulary, which was retained in the shadow of the Ramessides by the 21st–23rd Dynasties, Meryamun was a sufficiently-distinctive complement for Ramesses III to substitute it for Setepenre in his prenomen (with Usimare) so as both to follow the style of Ramesses II and yet retain his own identity.[15] Therefore, on general principle, one may distinguish here between two kings, i.e. Usimare Setepenamun/re and Usimare Meryamun.

This theoretical distinction gains some support from the few surviving references to Usimare Meryamun Shoshenq (IV). The most important is a Nile level on the Karnak quay: 'Year 6 of Usimare Meryamun, Shoshenq Meryamun, (in) the time of the high priest of Amun, Takeloth.'[16] If this were Year 6 of our Shoshenq 'III' (Usimare Setepenamun/re), this datum on the high priest of Amun would clash with those for *two* other high priests of Amun at this very time! For Nile level text No. 23 is dated to

13. So, on stela published by Daressy, *ASAE* 15 (1915), 144, cf. p. 145.

14. Petrie/UC collection; illustrated in Petrie, *A History of Egypt*, III, 1905, 271, fig. 111, and Petrie, *Scarabs & Cylinders with Names*, 1917, pl. 51, D.

15. Likewise Ruler-of-Heliopolis for Meryamun in his second cartouche; in the less current Horus, Nebty and Golden Horus names, Ramesses III did not imitate his predecessor's usual titles so closely. It is true that Sethos II freely used both Setepenre and Meryamun as complements in his prenomen; but he was the only king ever to use the very distinctive prenomen Usi-kheperu-re, and sometimes used both complements together, and not merely as variants.

16. No. 25, cf. Legrain, *ZÄS* 34 (1896), 114; von Beckerath, *JARCE* 5 (1966), 52.

'Year 6 of Usimare Setepenamun, Shoshenq Meryamun, given life, (in) the time of the high priest of Amenresonter, Harsiese',[17] while Prince Osorkon, son of Takeloth II, also claimed this office during this epoch.[18] That there were two rival pontiffs and factions (Osorkon and adherents versus his opponents, including Harsiese) is clear from Osorkon's own 'Chronicle'; but we have, so far, no evidence for assuming *three* mutually hostile parties. It is, therefore, better to concede the distinction between two different Shoshenqs ('III' and 'IV', Setepenamun/re and Meryamun) each with a separate 'Year 6', as most scholars would accept.[19] Thus, of seven or eight possible Shoshenqs, Nos. III*a* and *b* are one king, VII is non-existent, VI is dubious, and I–V are clear entities (with only minimal doubt on IV).

§ 69   3. THE OSORKONS

   I. Prenomen, Sekhemkheperre (Setepenre);[20] nomen, Osorkon Meryamun.
  II. Prenomen, Usimare Setepenamun; nomen, Osorkon Meryamun, Si-Bast ('Son of Bast').[21]
 III. Prenomen, Usimare Setepenamun; nomen, Osorkon Meryamun, Si-Ese ('Son of Isis').
  IV. Prenomen, Akheperre Setepenamun; nomen, Osorkon Meryamun.

Of this series, Nos. I and IV present no problem, because of their distinctive prenomen in each case. For some reason, Sekhemkheperre was never taken up again by any other pharaoh, while Akheperre was taken over from Psusennes I and Osochor of the 21st Dynasty and more directly from Shoshenq V – but these three kings and this Osorkon are quite distinct from each other.

§ 70   But our Nos. II and III have often proved confusing. The fact that there *are* two separate such kings is made clearly evident by certain genealogies of the Libyan period on statues from Karnak.[22] In particular, that of the Nebneteru-Hor family of royal secretaries shows a Hor (viii) under a king Usimare Setepenamun Osorkon Meryamun and a high priest

---

17. Legrain, *loc. cit.*; von Beckerath, *op. cit.*, 51.
18. Prince Osorkon was active from Year 11 of Takeloth II right through to Year 39 of Shoshenq III; see Part IV of this work, and *CPO*, 172–80.
19. Recently, for example, by von Beckerath, *op. cit.*, 46–47.
20. The Setepenre being occasionally omitted (*G3*, 329, XXIV; 326, XII in retrospect), or perhaps varied with Setepenamun in one case, § 67 above.
21. This epithet being quite often omitted.
22. For which, see below, Part III, Chapter 13, §§ 166 ff.

Harsiese, then Hor viii's nephew Hor (ix) under a king Pedubast (same prenomen), and finally Hor ix's son Nebneteru (iv) under a further king Usimare Setepenamun Osorkon Meryamun.[23] One may tabulate thus:

Hor viii – Usimare Setepenamun Osorkon ('II'): Cairo Cat. 42225.

Hor ix – Usimare Setepenamun Pedubast: Cairo Cat. 42226.

Nebneteru iv – Usimare Setepenamun Osorkon ('III'): Berlin 17272.

This succession is backed up by the genealogy on statues Cairo Cat. 42228, 42229, from which it is evident that a vizier Hor (x), who was a contemporary of a king Usimare Setepenamun, Osorkon Meryamun Si-Ese, god, Ruler of Thebes, was also the great-grandson of the high priest of Amun Nimlot, who was in turn the son of an earlier king Usimare Setepenamun Osorkon Meryamun.[24] Again, one may tabulate the sequence of people and kings:

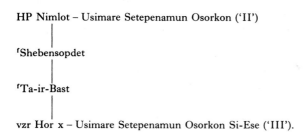

HP Nimlot – Usimare Setepenamun Osorkon ('II')

ʿShebensopdet

ʿTa-ir-Bast

vzr Hor x – Usimare Setepenamun Osorkon Si-Ese ('III').

It will be seen that this second line of evidence adds the distinguishing epithet Si-Ese, 'Son of Isis', to the name of the later of these two kings who were so similarly named, plus the epithets 'god, Ruler of Thebes'. At first sight, this seems a slender basis for establishing a distinction between the two kings, but it is fully confirmed by the other known evidence.

Thus, the statue Cairo Cat. 42211 was dedicated by one Nakhtefmut to his father the 4th prophet Djed-Khons-ef-ankh ii (C) in the time of the kings Osorkon Meryamun Si-Ese and Takeloth Meryamun Si-Ese.[25]

23. See below, Part III, § 177, and references.
24. Below, § 178.
25. Cf. below, § 184.

Through his mother Shepensopdet, this Nakhtefmut was grandson of an earlier king Takeloth, and (on his father's side) great-grandson of a king Harsiese – the latter, as we shall see, was contemporary with the older king Usimare Setepenamun Osorkon. Again, one may tabulate:

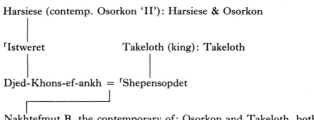

Harsiese (contemp. Osorkon 'II'): Harsiese & Osorkon

ʿIstweret   Takeloth (king): Takeloth

Djed-Khons-ef-ankh = ʿShepensopdet

Nakhtefmut B, the contemporary of: Osorkon and Takeloth, both Si-Ese.

§ 71   In turn, the beginning and end of this sequence tie up with two other lines of evidence. The first is provided by the statue Cairo Cat. 42208 of an earlier Nakhtefmut (A, called also Djed-Thut-ef-ankh, B)[26] who was himself the grandson of the high priest Iuput, son of the king Shoshenq known otherwise as Hedjkheperre[27] (No. I of our list, § 66). On this statue appear the titles of two contemporary kings. It was given by favour of Harsiese Meryamun – but bears also the full titles of:

Horus, Strong Bull appearing in Thebes.
Nebty, Uniting the Two Portions like the Son of Isis – he has joined the
    Double Crown in peace.
Golden Horus, Great of strength, smiting the Mentyu.
King of Upper and Lower Egypt, Usimare Setepenamun.
Son of Re, Osorkon Meryamun.

The same Nebty-name and cartouches[28] occur with this king's commoner Horus-name ('Strong Bull beloved of Truth') on this statue Cairo Cat. 42252 (cache No. 286),[29] and the same basic titulary (with expansions) in a Karnak inscription.[30] Monuments from Bubastis[31] and Tanis[32] offer the same titulary, substituting the vaguer 'enemies' (ḫftyw) for Mentyu in the

26. And paralleled in its genealogical data by statues Cairo Cat. 42206–7.
27. Gebel Silsila, stela 100 (*JEA* 38 (1952), 46 ff.); Karnak (*RIK*, III, pls. 10–11).
28. The Golden Horus name is lost.
29. Cf. Legrain, *ASAE* 5 (1904), 282, and *G3*, 338, XV; on the two Horus-names, cf. Legrain, *ASAE* 6 (1905), 125.
30. Legrain, *ASAE* 5 (1904), 282; *G3*, 337, X.
31. *G3*, 339, XXI.
32. *G3*, 340, XXIII; B. V. Bothmer, H. K. Jacquet-Gordon, *JEA* 46 (1960), 3–11, 12–23, pls. 1–6, 7–8, respectively.

Golden Horus name, and 'Pacifying the Gods with performing truth' as second part of the Nebty-name. On these northern monuments, the king's nomen is commonly Osorkon Meryamun *Si-Bast* ('Son of Bast'),[33] in contradistinction to the epithet *Si-Ese*, 'Son of Isis', used by the later Osorkon. As was noted above (§ 70, beginning), the earlier Usimare Osorkon was contemporary with a high priest Harsiese – just as Osorkon Si-Bast was contemporary with a king Harsiese. Just as the high priest and king Pinudjem (I) are the same person in two successive dignities early in the 21st Dynasty, no one has seen fit to doubt that likewise the high priest and king Harsiese who were contemporary with this Osorkon are but one person. Therefore, of the two Usimare Osorkons, the earlier could be known as Si-Bast and had the full titulary discussed just above.

§ 72   The other line of evidence is in fact the full titulary of the later Usimare Osorkon, the king Si-Ese who was associated with a king Takeloth Si-Ese on the statue Cairo Cat. 42211 (§ 70, end, above). In the temple of Osiris-Ruler-of-Eternity at the East end of Karnak,[34] the *same* association of Osorkon Si-Ese and Takeloth Si-Ese is abundantly attested, and besides the prenomen Usimare (Setepenamun) Osorkon Si-Ese has the following titles:[35]

Horus, Strong Bull appearing in Thebes.
Nebty, Favourite of the Two Lands (*st-ib t3wy*).
Golden Horus, Born of the Gods (*ms-ntrw*).

The Horus-name is shared not only with the earlier Usimare Osorkon, but also with Harsiese and Hedjkheperre Takeloth ('II', § 76 below), not to mention Pinudjem I; it is therefore too banal to be of any use in the present enquiry. But the Nebty and Golden Horus names of Osorkon Si-Ese are *radically* different from those of the earlier Osorkon (Si-Bast) not only in meaning or content but also in structure – they are simpler, reminiscent of the Old and Middle Kingdoms, and thus forerunners of the similarly brief, archaizing style favoured from the 25th and 26th Dynasties onward.

In this temple, this Osorkon is associated with three people: a queen Karoatjet, a daughter Shepenupet, and with Takeloth Si-Ese who had the even more drastically simple titulary of one name repeated, 'Blessing of the Two Lands' (*W3d-t3wy*), as Horus, Nebty and Golden Horus. Here again, the radically simpler style begun by Osorkon Si-Ese is evident.

33. For Osorkon 'II' 's titulary, cf. collected readings by Jacquet-Gordon, *JEA* 46 (1960), 14, n. 1; also below, § 271 and references.
34. Legrain, *RT* 22 (1900), 125–36, 146–9; *PM²*, II, 204–6; publication forthcoming by Canadian expedition under D. B. Redford.
35. *G3*, 384, V.

In terms of the succession of kings, especially Osorkons, one may tabulate the results so far as follows: Usimare Setepenamun, Osorkon Si-Bast, contemporary with Harsiese. Later, a king Takeloth, and also a king Pedubast. Then, a later Usimare Setepenamun, Osorkon Si-Ese with other titles which are clearly distinct from those of Osorkon Si-Bast; Osorkon Si-Ese is closely associated with a king Usimare Takeloth Si-Ese both on a private statue and in a temple, such that they are co-regents.

§ 73   The apparently slender distinction Si-Bast/Si-Ese *does* correspond, therefore, to a *real* distinction between two different kings some generations apart.[36] On this basis, we may now properly attribute a series of monuments to each king.[37]

Chronologically, the most important are the Nile level texts on the Karnak quay. No. 5 is dated to Year 3 of Usimare Setepenamun, Osorkon Meryamun Si-Ese, 'whose mother is the Chief Queen [. . .]', i.e. to the later Osorkon.[38] Equally explicit is No. 13, dated in Year 28 of Osorkon Si-Ese, god, Ruler of Thebes, 'which is Year 5 of his son, [King of Upper & Lower Egypt, . . .], Son of Re, Takeloth Meryamun, Si-Ese, god, Ruler of Thebes'. Here, the epithets Si-Ese and 'god, Ruler of Thebes' are precisely those of the later Osorkon ('III'). This Nile-record, therefore, belongs to Osorkon 'III', not 'II'.

In a recent admirable restudy and republication of all the Nile-level texts, von Beckerath considered that he could see trace of a solar disc, and hence read [Setepen]re, at the end of the destroyed prenomen of the co-regent Takeloth. This may be so. However, he then would restore the entire cartouche as Hedjkheperre Setepenre (as opposed to Usimare Setepenamun), referring the text to Osorkon 'II' and Takeloth 'II', not Osorkon 'III' and Takeloth 'III' as the epithets so clearly require.[39] The clear evidence of the epithets in favour of Osorkon and Takeloth 'III', not 'II', finds support in the following considerations. First, the original reading of the destroyed prenomen could as well have been [Usimare Setepen]re as Hedjkheperre; while not yet otherwise attested, a variation between Setepenre and Setepenamun for Usimare Takeloth would be

36. In all the genealogical monuments so far known to me, I have never yet found an Osorkon Si-Ese to be at an earlier period than any other Usimare Osorkon (whether Si-Bast or unspecified); this situation further suggests that these epithets were not interchangeable between these two kings.

37. Without here attempting, of course, to list *all* their monuments; a working distinction is sufficient for our purpose.

38. With it goes the hieratic graffito at Luxor temple concerning the great inundation that flooded the temple under Usimare Setepenamun, Osorkon Meryamun Si-Ese ('III'); Daressy, *RT* 18 (1896), 181–4 and *ibid.* 20 (1898), 80, cf. *G3*, 382–3, I.

39. J. von Beckerath, *JARCE* 5 (1966), 45.

completely consistent with this same variation in Setepen-*x* exhibited by the prenomens of several other kings in this epoch.[40] Second, the epithet 'god, Ruler of Thebes' is not only proper to Osorkon 'III', but is never found with Osorkon 'II'; while it occurs in the nomen of Takeloth 'III', but only occasionally in the *pre*nomen (*not* the nomen!) of Takeloth 'II'[41] – hence, this Nile-level goes with 'III' not 'II', even on this ground. Third, the epithet Si-Bast is not unknown for Osorkon 'II' in Thebes,[42] and it would not necessarily be replaced by Si-Ese as von Beckerath suggested. Fourth, there is not a scrap of evidence so far for *any* co-regency of Osorkon 'II' and Takeloth 'II', whereas we *do* have two independent witnesses to such an association of Osorkon 'III' and Takeloth 'III'.[43] Therefore, this Nile-level text, again, should be attributed to the known co-regents 'III', not used to 'invent' a co-regency of O. and T. 'II' which is otherwise a pure phantom. Fifth, there is no independent reason to assign a Year 28 to Osorkon 'II', whereas 28 years for Osorkon 'III' is compatible with a possible ⟨2⟩8 years for Manetho's 'Osorcho', in the much-corrupted extant versions of his list for the 23rd Dynasty.[44]

Thus, from virtually every aspect, there is everything to be said for attributing Nile-level text No. 13 to Osorkon and Takeloth 'III', and at present no reason at all to assign it to 'II' – a point that can hardly be over-stressed, in view of the widespread confusion prevailing on this matter.

§ 74 Nile-level texts Nos. 6 and 7 are dated to Years 5 and 6 respectively of an Usimare Osorkon (with no distinguishing epithet) whose mother was the Chief Queen Kamama Meryt-mut.[45] These too can be assigned to Osorkon 'III' rather than 'II', because the mother of Osorkon 'II', Si-Bast, was called Kapes, not Kamama. This is clear from the genealogy

---

40. No less than five kings, so far: Shoshenq I, Shoshenq III, Osorkon I, Iuput (I) and Pimay – the second, third and fourth of these all varying Usimare Setepen-amun with Setepen-re, precisely as here predicated of Takeloth 'III'.

41. Prenomen of Takeloth 'II', *G3*, 354, XIV, and 355, XVI–XVII; on its own, not with cartouche, this epithet is used just once for his father by Prince Osorkon (*RIK*, III, pl. 21, line 7; *CPO*, §§ 129, 261).

42. See *RIK*, III, pl. 16, A, line 17, for Si-Bast in the nomen of Osorkon 'II' as grandfather of Prince Osorkon (*CPO*, §§ 23, 239). This would reduce the validity of von Beckerath's Northern/Theban distinction between use of Si-Bast, Si-Ese (*op. cit.*, 45).

43. Statue Cairo Cat. 42211, and temple of Osiris, §§ 70, 72, above.

44. See below, § 100 and Excursus F; to reduce the reign of Osorkon 'III' to 8 years (von Beckerath, *loc. cit.*) would leave a yawning gap of 20 years in the 23rd Dynasty, and is contradicted by the Year 13 graffito, temple of Khons, of Osorkon Si-Ese, i.e. 'III' (*G3*, 336, IV and n. 1).

45. Spelling of her name is clear in Legrain's and von Beckerath's copies of the texts; it recurs elsewhere.

on the famous Serapeum stela of Pasenhor[46] and the lamentation-text at the Tanite tomb of Osorkon Si-Bast which ends with the cryptic remark, *ir n.f Kȝpws*, 'Kapus did/made (it) for him'.[47]

Also to Osorkon 'III' Si-Ese may be attributed the fine statuette of the kneeling king pushing a barque,[48] the doorjambs from Karnak taken to Berlin,[49] a graffito of Year 13 at the temple of Khons,[50] minor monuments like the Louvre vase D. 34,[51] a bronze plaque from Memphis (Mitrahineh) now in Cairo,[52] and his names on private statuary from Karnak (Cairo Cat. 42211, 42223/4, 42229, etc.).

§ 75   On the other hand, a crowd of monuments equally clearly belong (or refer) to Osorkon 'II' Si-Bast, which it is needless to list in full detail here;[53] suffice it to mention his 'festival hall' (or portal) at Bubastis with text of the Year 22,[54] works at Tanis,[55] etc.

Finally, there are records whose precise attribution remains uncertain. Nile-level records 8 plus 9, 11 and 12 are dated respectively to Years 12 (twice), 21 and 22 of a king Usimare Setepenamun Osorkon Meryamun with no distinguishing epithet, and no name of his mother attached. Thus, theoretically, these four epigraphs could belong to either 'II' or 'III' of our Osorkons. In so far as we have some indubitable Nile-records of Osorkon 'III' and none of 'II', one might be tempted to attribute all to 'III'. But one may on the contrary suggest that the very absence of distinguishing epithets and filiation speaks for attribution to the earlier king ('II'), in whose reign there would be no ambiguity – such only arose with the advent, rather later, of a second king (Osorkon 'III') with closely-similar titles. Certainty is impossible at present.[56]

46. Latest publication, Malinine, Posener, Vercoutter, *Catalogue des stèles du Sérapéum de Memphis*, I, 1968, No. 31, pp. 30–1, pl. 10.

47. Cf. Montet, *Osorkon II*, 71–3, pl. 22.

48. Cairo Cat. 42197; Legrain, *Statues*, III, 1914, 6, pl. 5; Bothmer, *JEA* 46 (1960), 6 n. 2, 10 n. 1, whose reserves on identification of the king can be banished with reference to the epithet Si-Ese.

49. *LDT*, III, 42; *Aeg. Inschriften, Mus. Berlin*, II, 218 (Nos. 2101–2); *G3*, 385, VI.

50. *G3*, 336, IV, with n. 1.

51. Legrain, *RT* 28 (1906), 154; *G3*, 386, XIV.

52. Daressy, *ASAE* 3 (1902), 140; *G3*, 386, XV.

53. Largely in *G3*, 335 ff., and Montet, *Osorkon II*.

54. Naville, *Festival Hall of Osorkon II*, esp. pl. 6: 8.

55. Montet, *op. cit.*, 23–33.

56. The fact that there are two records of Year 12 (Nos. 8 and 9) is of no significance for our chronological purposes, any more than two each for the years 6 (Nos. 34, 35) and 7 (Nos. 36, 37) of Taharqa.

§76   4. THE TAKELOTHS

I. Prenomen, uncertain; nomen, Takeloth.
II. Prenomen, Hedjkheperre Setepenre; nomen, Takeloth Meryamun Si-Ese.
III. Prenomen, Usimare (Setepenamun); nomen, Takeloth (Meryamun Si-Ese).

Of these three, the second stands out most clearly – from the chronicle of his son the high priest Osorkon;[57] from stelae and small objects;[58] and from his burial at Tanis,[59] in the tomb of Osorkon 'II'.[60]

The monuments of No. III link him closely with Usimare Osorkon 'III' (cf. already, §§ 72, 73, above). One document that most probably pertains to 'III' rather than 'II' is Nile-level text No. 4, dated in Year 6 of a king (no prenomen) 'Takeloth Meryamun, Si-Ese, whose mother is Tentsai'.[61] The name of the mother restricts us to either 'II' or 'III' (both kings later than Osorkon 'II'), because the mother of the earlier Takeloth ('I') of the Pasenhor stela is named as Tashedkhons. Unfortunately, the mother of Takeloth 'II' is not known with certainty, so that initially, the Nile-text No. 4 could pertain to either 'II' or 'III'.[62] The same ambiguity of attribution hangs over the wax impression mentioning 'the Crown Prince and Eldest Son (*iry-pꜥt wr, sꜣ smsw*), Takeloth, son of the Lord of the Two Lands, Usimare Setepenamun, Lord of Epiphanies, Osorkon Meryamun, (and) whose mother is [. . .] *n* [. . .]'.[63] If this prince were the future Takeloth 'II' (as son of Osorkon 'II'), he could only be Crown Prince and the eldest son after the death of Osorkon's real first-born son and original crown prince, Shoshenq, who was high priest in Memphis;[64] no such limitation would apply to Takeloth 'III' as crown prince of Osorkon 'III'. A little more helpful is a relief of Amun and Arsaphes which was dedicated to the high priest of Amenresonter and of Arsaphes, etc., the King's Son

57. *RIK*, III; Caminos, *CPO*.
58. e.g. stela of Year 9 (Daressy, *RT* 18 (1896), 52; *G3*, 352, II), and various lesser objects (*G3*, 354–5, XIV–XVII, etc.).
59. Montet, *Osorkon II*, 81–4.
60. A circumstance that indicates that this Takeloth was later than our Osorkon 'II'.
61. Legrain, *ZÄS* 34 (1896), 111; von Beckerath, *JARCE* 5 (1966), 49.
62. Legrain, *ASAE* 7 (1906), 47, n. 5, gives Mut-udj-ankhes as mother of Takeloth II, but for this there is no direct evidence so far. She is named as wife of Osorkon (II) and mother of Nimlot on the Pasenhor stela, but this proves nothing about Takeloth.
63. Restoring either [Te]n[tsai?], or [Ist]en[kheb?]; cf. also, *G3*, 344, XXX, 2; Daressy, *RT* 35 (1913), 133.
64. *G3*, 344, XXX, 1.

Takeloth whose mother was Tentsai.[65] It is very unlikely that the future Takeloth 'II' while a prince ever served as pontiff at either Thebes or Heracleopolis: under his father's reign, we already have at least three pontiffs of Amun – Harsiese, the latter's son (name lost), and Nimlot son of Osorkon 'II' (also ruler in Heracleopolis).[66] But there is ample room for such a prince (Takeloth 'III') as pontiff during some of the 28 years of Osorkon 'III'. Hence, the customary assumption that Takeloth son of Tentsai was actually the last-known king Takeloth ('III'), son of the later Usimare Osorkon ('III') is a realistic view, even if it is not formally proven beyond the last conceivable doubt.

§ **77** However, the real problem of the Takeloths is not to distinguish 'II', Hedjkheperre, from 'III', Usimare (Setepenamun), but rather to find out anything tangible about Takeloth 'I'! Apart from Hedjkheperre (prenomen of 'II'), the only prenomen so far found with a Takeloth is Usimare. As this prenomen is definitely the property of the last known king Takeloth ('III'), two views are possible: either that Takeloth 'I' actually had an individual prenomen differing from those of both 'II' and 'III', which is still unknown to Egyptology, or else 'I' had actually used Usimare as prenomen long before 'III' did. In the former case, practically the *only* cartouche that can *definitely* be attributed to 'I' is the mention of this name in the Pasenhor genealogy. In the latter case, one would need definite criteria to distinguish 'I' from 'III', as has proved possible with Osorkon 'II' and 'III'. Unfortunately, the cartouches which can clearly be attributed to 'III' (Osiris temple, Karnak) already cover most of the permissible variations for one king: he is there as either fully Usimare Setepenamun, Takeloth Meryamun Si-Ese, or else as just Usimare Takeloth![67] The only form not attested there is seemingly just Takeloth Meryamun without Si-Ese – but this form, in turn, is used to some extent by Takeloth II. Thus, even granting the relative dearth of Takelothid monuments, there are simply no criteria to separate between two Usimare Takeloths. Therefore, it is far and away preferable to assume only *one* Usimare Takeloth at present, the known Takeloth 'III', and to attribute all such monuments to him. Monuments and records naming only the name Takeloth, or that name plus Meryamun and/or Si-Ese, could belong to any of 'I', 'II', or 'III', unless there be internal evidence that would combine with external data whereby a definite preference for one or other king could be justified. This could bring a few items into the reign of Takeloth 'I', even in the

65. Gauthier, *ASAE* 37 (1937), 16–24 and pl.
66. For whom, cf. Part III, Chapter 13, §§ 157 ff.
67. Cf. conveniently, *G3*, 390, III.

absence of a prenomen.[68] Recovery of the real, and probably hitherto
entirely unknown, prenomen of Takeloth 'I' is a minor prize that awaits the
spade or epigraphic eye of some future Egyptologist.

§ 78   5. OTHER KINGS

	G3:
I. Prenomen, Hedjkheperre Setepenamun; nomen, Harsiese Meryamun.	348–350
II. Prenomen, Usimare Setepenamun/re; nomen, Pimay Meryamun.	370–373
III. Prenomen, Usimare Setepenamun; nomen, Rudamun Meryamun.	392–393
IV. Prenomen, Usimare Setepenamun; nomen, Pedubast (I) Meryamun Si-Bast/Ese.	378–380
V. Prenomen, Sehetepibenre; nomen, Pedubast (II).	—
VI. Prenomen, Seheribre; nomen, Pedubast (III) Si-Bast	397–398
VII. Prenomen, Usimare Setepenamun/re; nomen, Iuput (I?) Meryamun Si-Bast.	381–382
VIII. Prenomen, unknown; nomen, Iuput (II?).	402:6
IX. Prenomen, Neferkare; nomen, Pef-tjau-awy-Bast.	400–401
X. Prenomen, Neferkheperre Kha-kha(u); nomen, Thutemhat.	401:4
XI. Prenomen, unknown; nomen, Nimlot.	402:5
XII. Prenomen, Menkheperre; nomen, Khmuny(?).	404–405
XIII. Prenomen, Shepseskare Irenre; nomen, Gemenef-Khons-Bak.	—
XIV. Prenomen, Neferkare; nomen, P[. . .].	—
XV. Prenomen, uncertain; nomen, Py Meryamun Si-Ese.	—
XVI. Prenomen, uncertain; nomen, Si/In-beb/redwy?	—
XVII. Prenomen, ?; nomen, . . . Merytawy Penamun.	403:9

§ 79   Of this long list, the first dozen kings are definite and well-established entities, even if their chronology will in due course need discussion.
That there were *two* kings Iuput emerges from the chronology of the
Libyan period, whereby the king Iuput of the time of the Nubian Piankhy
can hardly be the same as the Iuput who was co-regent of Pedubast, the
traditional founder of the 23rd Dynasty! To crush that entire dynasty into
the modest interval between the invasions of Egypt by Piankhy and his
successor Shabako is just not feasible.

68. Cf. below, §§ 95, 96, 270.

Of the three Pedubasts, Usimare belongs squarely within the Libyan period (statue Cairo Cat. 42226, cf. § 70, above) and is attested in both north and south; he would thus be a proper 'national' pharaoh, the Pedubastis, founder of the 23rd Dynasty of Manetho. The monuments of Sehetepibenre are partly of uncertain provenance, but he certainly built at Tanis;[69] it is therefore possible that he is the Pedubast (*Putubišti*) of Tanis who was mentioned by the Assyrians in the 7th century B.C. Finally, Seheribre almost certainly does not belong in the period of the present work at all, but rather to the Persian period, on criteria which have been advanced by Yoyotte.[70]

Most of the other kinglets are either strictly local or almost phantoms. No. IX ruled Heracleopolis in the time of Piankhy. At the same time, No. XI ruled in Hermopolis, where No. X also belongs. One may further attribute to Hermopolis, not with certainty but with probability, No. XII. His sole major monument (stela Louvre C. 100) is from Thebes, but *c.* 730–700 B.C., Thebes and Hermopolis had links, and the traces of his name – circle, sign considered as *mn* by Maspero,[71] and *y* – might be read Khmuny(?), 'the Hermopolitan'. Nos. XIII, XIV, are peculiar to Tanis, and may be local kinglets there, like Pedubast II. The separate existence of Neferkare P . . . is not assured; despite the slight variant Netjerty-khau, he may simply be Pepi II of the Old Kingdom, and hence may not come within the purview of this work. However, a cornice from Athribis with alternating cartouches of Wahibre and Neferkare might well be of Psammetichus I and this kinglet, so he may be a local Tanite of the 7th century B.C. No. XV is a phantom, in so far as he is almost certainly none other than Piankhy, whose name probably ought, in fact, to be read as Py (cf. below, §§ 123, 330). No. XVI is known only from the Khons temple graffiti, and through the courtesy of Mme H. K. Jacquet; the reading of the name is problematical, and it could be an abbreviation or nickname for some better-known king (Iuput I, Osorkon III?); (cf. §§ 302, 303, and references, below). Finally, No. XVII on a piece of stone from Terraneh in the West Delta remains totally obscure; but its orthography would seem to place it well after the period covered by this book.

Thus, in the foregoing list, Nos. I–V, VII–XIV, are clear entities, either

69. Cf. blocks, Montet, *Le lac sacré de Tanis*, 1966, 63–5, Nos. 230–8; see L. Habachi, *ZÄS* 93 (1966), 69–74, for this king.

70. Cf. Yoyotte cited by Habachi, *op. cit.*, 73–4, and references.

71. Cf. Petrie, *A History of Egypt*, III, 1905, 292–3, who originally suggested this reading and interpretation; disapproval voiced in *G3*, 404, n. 2, rests on no new fact, and one may note the statue Cairo Cat. 42212 of Tjanhesret, a priest of Thebes and Hermopolis, who left his statue at Thebes (Karnak), yet dated it by the local king of Hermopolis, Thutemhat. Von Beckerath now reads Pi[ankh]y (*MDIK* 24 (1969), 58–62), with Menkheperre as P's third prenomen.

major (I–IV, VII–VIII) or purely local (V, IX–XIV) kings, belonging in the Libyan and Nubian epochs. No. XV certainly, and XVI possibly, are simply Piankhy and perhaps a known Libyan king. No. VI certainly, and XVII probably, are of Persian period or later, and so will require no further consideration. Further discoveries may well add, of course, to the number of local kinglets of our period.

CHAPTER 7

Dynasty 22: Sequence and Reigns of Kings

§ 80   1. INTRODUCTORY

Manetho retains the tradition that the 22nd Dynasty originated at Bubastis and the 23rd Dynasty originated in Tanis. Correspondingly, the monumental evidence provides two lines of kings dominated by the names Shoshenq, Osorkon and Takeloth, besides a series of lesser princes. Since the individual rulers have been differentiated in the previous chapter, this and the next seek to set these lines of kings in order and to note the lengths of their reigns.

§ 81   2. SERAPEUM DATA

A. MID-DYNASTY

The basis of a succession of kings who were officially recognized at Memphis can be obtained from the Serapeum stelae which commemorated the burials of successive Apis bulls. Louvre stela IM. 3749[72] is dated to Year 28 of Usimare Setepenamun, Shoshenq, No. III of the preceding chapter (cf. § 66, above). On it appear the great chief of the Mā, Pediese and two sons, Pef-tjau-awy-Bast as high priest of Ptah and Takeloth D as a sem-priest.[73] This document links up with both earlier and later personalities.

(i) *Earlier.* Pediese here has the following genealogy.[74]

72. Cf. Yoyotte, *YMM*, 124, § 5, Doc. 3; Malinine, Posener, Vercoutter, *Catalogue des stèles du Sérapéum de Memphis*, I, 1968, No. 21, pp. 19–20, pl. 7.
73. For the high priests of Ptah of Memphis in this period, cf. below, Part III, §§ 155–6.
74. So also, Černý, *JEA* 40 (1954), 23–4, in the context of consanguineous mar-

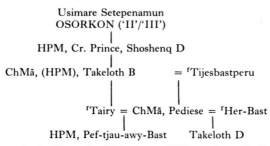

Usimare Setepenamun
OSORKON ('II'/'III')
|
HPM, Cr. Prince, Shoshenq D
|
ChMā, (HPM), Takeloth B   = ʿTijesbastperu

ʿTairy = ChMā, Pediese = ʿHer-Bast
| |
HPM, Pef-tjau-awy-Bast   Takeloth D

In other words, in Year 28 of Shoshenq 'III', we have Pediese as great-grandson of a king Osorkon, who is theoretically either 'II' or 'III' of Chapter 6, above (§§ 69 ff.). The links in this filiation are attested from other sources and enable us to identify the Osorkon as No. 'II'.

Thus, Pediese's grandfather the Crown Prince and high priest Shoshenq D is known from his tomb and burial,[75] a scarab[76] (naming his mother Karama), and reputedly from an Apis-burial at the Serapeum of Year 23 of his father king Osorkon.[77] Also from there, a statue inscribed for Shoshenq calls him explicitly: 'Great Chief Prince of His Majesty, High Priest and Sem of Ptah, Shoshenq justified, great King's Son of the Lord of the Two Lands, Usimare Setepenamun, Son of Re, Lord of Epiphanies, Osorkon Meryamun *Si-Bast*, his mother being Karoma.'[78] The epithet Si-Bast, 'Son of Bast', determines the Osorkon concerned as our Osorkon 'II', not 'III'; the mother, Karama, is well-known as the chief wife and queen from (e.g.) Bubastis[79] of Osorkon 'II' Si-Bast.[80]

Pediese's father, Takeloth B, is also known from his tomb and burial at Memphis,[81] and from other Memphite stone fragments,[82] as contemporary of a king Shoshenq – our 'III', on the basis of the Year 28 stela cited above.

riages. In the genealogy given here, HPM = High Priest (of Ptah) in Memphis; ChMā = Chief of the Mā. Names of kings in capitals.

75. Cf. A. Badawi, *ASAE* 44 (1944), 181 and n. 2; *ASAE* 54 (1957), 154-77, and 16 pls. For this section, cf. also Chapter 12, below.

76. Illustrated, e.g. by Petrie, *History*, III, 253, fig. 103; *Scarabs & Cylinders with Names*, 1917, pl. 50, 22: 5; cf. *G3*, 344, C.

77. Cf. Mariette, ed. Maspero, *Sérapéum*, 1882, 158; *G3*, 336, n. 3 end. To Year 23 of Osorkon II belongs Serapeum stela IM. 3090 (cf. Vercoutter, *MDIK* 16 (1958), 340, n. 16), published by Malinine, Posener, Vercoutter, *Catalogue, stèles, Sérapéum*, I, No. 18; so far as preserved, this stela makes *no* mention of the Crown Prince Shoshenq.

78. Cf. Daressy, *RT* 35 (1913), 142 and n. 3; *G3*, 344, XXX, 1, A.

79. Naville, *Festival Hall of Osorkon II at Bubastis*, 1892, pls. 2–5, 16.

80. By contrast, Osorkon III Si-Ese had a mother Kamama, but not (so far as we know) a wife Karoama or similar; his wife was Karoatjet.

81. Badawi, *ASAE* 44 (1944), 181, n. 2; *ASAE* 54 (1957), 152/8; Pediese's tomb and burial was also found nearby, but regrettably no account *in extenso* of his or Takeloth's burials has yet been published.

82. Daressy, *ASAE* 20 (1920), 169-70.

Pediese's mother, the princess Tjesbastperu, is known from canopic jars in Vienna as a daughter of king Osorkon Si-Bast, i.e. Osorkon 'II', by a lady Istemkheb G.[83] In so far as technically she would be an aunt of her husband, it is generally assumed[84] (probably rightly) that Tjesbastperu was a younger daughter of Osorkon's old age by a lesser wife or concubine, whereas Takeloth B was perhaps eldest son of Shoshenq D, himself eldest son of Osorkon 'II'; there need, therefore, have been no real discrepancy in age between Takeloth and Tjesbastperu, or he could even have been the older. Thus, Pediese was probably grandson and great-grandson of Osorkon 'II' by his mother and father, respectively, and was in high office in the middle of the reign of Shoshenq 'III'.

§ 82 (ii) *Later*. Pediese reappears on stelae of the Year 2 of king Pimay, which commemorate the burial of an Apis that had been inducted 26 years earlier in Year 28 of Shoshenq 'III';[85] relationships, names, titles,[86] etc., all show that the *same* Pediese is involved.

Thus, king Pimay ascended the throne 25 years after Year 28 of Shoshenq 'III'. The Serapeum evidence of itself does not indicate whether any other king came in between these two. The highest year-date unequivocally attested for Shoshenq 'III' is Year 39 from two texts at Karnak.[87] This reduces the maximum interval between his death and Pimay's accession to 14 years, which is still long enough for a brief reign unmarked by an Apis-burial.[88] But two indications, neither of them final, may be urged against assuming the presence of any intervening reign between Shoshenq 'III' and Pimay.

The first and least certain is the dedication on a small statue-group by the 'Chief of the Mā, Pamiu, son of the Lord of the Two Lands, Shoshenq Meryamun'[89] – which could very well be a mention of Pimay as a prince

83. *G3*, 343, 2A, and 347, 4A, with references.
84. e.g. by Daressy, *loc. cit.*, and Kees, *Pr.*, 184, 183 Table, among others.
85. Cf. stelae Nos. 22–5 in Malinine, Posener, Vercoutter, *Catalogue*, I, 21–5, pls. 8–9.
86. e.g. great chief of the Mā; the high-priestly title is given for Pediese in the back-references on Pimay's stelae, but not on that of Year 28 of Shoshenq III.
87. Nile text No. 22, Karnak Priestly Annals No. 7; *G3*, 364, 365, XVII–XVIII.
88. Montet, *Chéchanq III*, 1960, 8–9, would assume precisely such a reign 'd'un inconnu' at this point, but invokes Nile-level text No. 24 following *G3*, 369, II, in reading it as Year 12 (of the 'inconnu') with Year 6 of Pi[may]. However, the latter part is to be read as Year 5 of Pedu[bast] (I), cf. von Beckerath, *JARCE* 5 (1966), 46–7, 51. Montet's suggestion was already rejected by Drioton and Vandier, *L'Égypte*[4], 1962, 672–3; for identification of Year 12 as pertaining to Shoshenq III, cf. below, §§ 106–7. Montet's suggestion of an ephemeral king is possible, but not on the use of this text. But who would this king be?
89. Daressy, *RT* 16 (1894), 48; *Textes et dessins magiques*, 39, pl. XI, No. 9430, Cairo Catalogue.

and son of Shoshenq 'III'.[90] But of course, there is no guarantee that the Shoshenq of this monument is our 'III' rather than any of Nos. 'I', 'II', 'IV' or 'V', and hence no guarantee that his son is the king Pimay.[91]

§ 83 Perhaps more important is Papyrus Brooklyn 16.205,[92] which is dated in Year 4 of one unnamed king and refers back to Year 49 of another. As various factors indicate a date clearly later than Ramesses II and the 19th Dynasty,[93] Parker assumed – probably rightly – that this Year 49 belonged to Shoshenq 'III' (for whom the Serapeum data allow a maximum reign of 52 years), and the Year 4 to Pimay. However, one other possibility might theoretically arise: the long reign of Psusennes I (or, Amenemope) in the 21st Dynasty, up to Year 49, followed by a shorter reign.[94] However, there seems no reason to favour a 21st-Dynasty date for this document. If the 22nd-Dynasty date be retained and preferred, then a Year 49 attributable to Shoshenq 'III' would practically close the gap (now only 4 years at the most) to the accession of Pimay, unless an ephemeral reign be assumed between – an assumption that has, so far, absolutely nothing to commend it. Therefore, it will here be assumed henceforth – pending contrary evidence being found – that Pimay directly succeeded Shoshenq 'III' after the latter had reigned 52 years.

The full length of Pimay's reign is not known for certain. Beyond Year 2 at the Serapeum and the possible Year 4 of Papyrus Brooklyn 16.205, there is only the Year 6 of a votive stela in the Louvre.[95] Pimay's monuments are few, hence he will be allowed just 6 full years here.

§ 84   B. LATER IN THE DYNASTY

One of the Serapeum stelae from Year 11 of Akheperre Shoshenq 'V' gives his names as Akheper{u}⟨re⟩, Son of Re, Shoshe⟨n⟩q, son of Pimay.[96] This in its turn gives the clear succession Pimay – Shoshenq

90. Daressy, *RT* 35 (1913), 137, n. 3. The orthography of the name of this prince (using lion-sign) differs from that of the king Pimay, but this may not signify much.

91. Doubts expressed, cf. *G3*, 370, n. 4. Even if Pimay were a son of Shoshenq III, this would not prevent there having been an elder brother as the *inconnu* of Montet as king before Pimay.

92. Published as Appendix I in Parker, *A Saite Oracle Papyrus from Thebes*, 1962, 49–52, pls. 17–19.

93. Parker, *op. cit.*, 49, on grounds of palaeography and subject-matter; a proper name such as Pasherenese would also favour a later date.

94. Cf. Part I, above, on this matter (Year 49, probably Psusennes I).

95. References, *G3*, 372, VI. Nile-level text No. 24 pertains to Pedubast I, not Pimay; cf. §§ 106–7, below, with von Beckerath.

96. All three names in cartouches. *G3*, 373, X, 11: II; Malinine, Posener, Vercoutter, *Catalogue, Sérapéum*, I, No. 26, pp. 25–6, pl. 9; IM. 3049.

'V'.[97] Dated monuments of Shoshenq 'V' range with certainty up to Year 37, the date of burial of another Apis bull.[98] But beyond this, one may identify a Year 38 as his. A donation-stela at Buto[99] bears a scene of the well-known West-Delta prince Tefnakht, and its unfinished text is dated to 'Regnal Year ⌈reckoned?⌉[100] 38 under the Majesty of the King of Upper & Lower Egypt, Lord of the Two Lands, BLANK, Son of Re, BLANK'.[101]

Tefnakht, of course, was active *after* the reign of Shoshenq 'V'; he was the principal opponent of the Nubian ruler Piankhy whose fleeting conquest of Egypt was perhaps occasioned by fears of Tefnakht penetrating the Thebaid. On his great stela, he names four kings, two in Middle Egypt (Pef-tjau-awy-Bast of Heracleopolis; Nimlot of Hermopolis), and two in the Delta – Osorkon of Bubastis and Re-nefer (i.e. Tanis and region)[102] and Iuput of Tentremu (Leontopolis) and Ta-ayn. There is no sign of Shoshenq 'V' whose reign, therefore, must have ended *before* the invasion of Piankhy and the accession of Osorkon ('IV'). The only other king who reached or surpassed a Year 38 in the Libyan period was the still earlier king Shoshenq 'III' with 52 years (§ 83, above). Therefore, the Buto stela of Tefnakht can definitely be dated to Year 38 of either Shoshenq 'III' or 'V'.[103]

Between these two kings, it is easy to choose. If Year 38 of Shoshenq 'III' were in view, Tefnakht's activities would be rather long-drawn-out: at least the last 15 years of Shoshenq 'III', a minimal 6 years of Pimay, 37 known years of Shoshenq 'V', plus two unknown intervals (i) from the latter's 37th year to Piankhy's invasion, and (ii) between the latter and his own assumption of kingship, plus 7 or 8 years of his own kingship[104] – total, 65 years plus 2 unknown if brief intervals, perhaps up to 70 years. In

97. Assuming no intervening reign; one may note that members of the same family appear on one stela of Year 2 of Pimay (*Catalogue*, No. 25) and on other stelae of Year 37 of Shoshenq 'V' (*ibid.*, Nos. 41, 42). Hence, that interval should not be gratuitously lengthened, and no missing reign need be assumed.

98. *G3*, 373–4; Malinine, Posener, Vercoutter, *Catalogue*, Nos. 31–44, etc.

99. Published by Yoyotte, *YMM*, 152–3, pl. I: 1; cf. Sauneron, *BSFE* 24 (1957), 51, 53–4, figs. 1–2.

100. Either *ḥsb*, 'reckoned', or a mistaken double writing of the 30-sign (hieratic after hieroglyphic); cf. *YMM*, 152, n. 3.

101. Only four out of ten lines of text were ever cut; so, conceivably, the cartouches were to be filled-in afterwards. But as blank cartouches recur on other monuments of the period, they more likely reflect local indifference to which Libyan pharaoh was nominally acknowledged.

102. Cf. *YMM*, 129, n. 2; also § 328, references, below.

103. That the Year 38 pertained to an 'era' (cf. *YMM*, *loc. cit.*) is remotely possible, but rather unlikely – in that case, all reference to a king (other than a deity) could have been dispensed with.

104. As Shepsesre Tefnakht on his Athens stela, *G3*, 409, V. For Tefnakht and Piankhy, cf. below, Chapter 9.

theory this would be possible, but in point of fact, it must be highly unlikely. Hence, it is practically certain that we can, in fact, attribute this
Year 38 to Shoshenq 'V', allowing the latter 37 or 38 years of reign, and a
more natural span to Tefnakht. So far, then, we obtain the following basic
scheme:

22nd Dynasty

OSORKON 'II'
|
SHOSHENQ 'III': 52 yrs.
|
PIMAY: 6 yrs.
|
SHOSHENQ 'V': 37 yrs.   25th Dyn.
|
OSORKON ('IV'): contemporary of Tefnakht and PIANKHY
                          (later, as
                            King)

§ 85   C. THE PASENHOR STELA
To the reign of Shoshenq 'V' belongs a famous chronological key to this
epoch: the Serapeum stela of the Memphite priest Pasenhor B ('Horpasen'
of older works) in the Louvre,[105] from the Apis-burial of Year 37 of this
king. Pasenhor himself was but a God's Father, Prophet of Neit and
Sameref among the Memphite clergy, but his five immediate forebears had
each been Count, Governor of Upper Egypt, Superintendent of Prophets in
Heracleopolis and General.[106] Of this group, the earliest was Nimlot son of
a king Osorkon and the lady Mut-udj-ankhes. The ancestors of this king
Osorkon run back a further nine generations, of whom the last five concern us here and are given just below. Of Shoshenq A's four forebears,
three are simply entitled *mi-nn*, or 'ditto', i.e., they were each a great chief
of the Mā like Nimlot A father of Shoshenq A, while the initial ancestor of
the entire family, Buyuwawa, is entitled merely *Tḥnw*, 'the Libyan'.[107]

This series of names fits very well with the more scattered information
available in first-hand sources from the earlier part of the Dynasty. The
merest essentials of this material may now be put together in order to
bring the main outline of the Dynasty close to completion, and particularly

105. IM. 2846, Malinine, Posener, Vercoutter, *Catalogue, stèles, Sérapéum*, I,
No. 31, pp. 30–1, pl. 10, with earlier bibliography (also, *G3*, 317, n. 1). Main text in
line (after Mariette), Petrie, *History*, III, 230, fig. 94.
106. Pasenhor's father being *ḥЗty-ʿ, imy-r šmʿ, imy-r ḥmw-nṯr n Ḥwt-nni-nsw*,
imy-r mšʿ, his four predecessors being *mi-nn*, 'ditto'.
107. For the full genealogy of Pasenhor and his stela, see Part VI below.

to fit together correctly the kings who were attested on monuments with those given us by Pasenhor and to include others omitted by him.

Shoshenq A = 'Mehtenweskhet A, King's Mother(-in-law?)
|
God's Father, Nimlot A = 'Tentsepeh A, God's Mother
& Ch of Mā |
SHOSHENQ 'I' = 'Karamat A, God's Mother
|
OSORKON 'I' = 'Tashedkhons A, God's Mother
|
TAKELOTH 'I' = 'Kapes, God's Mother
|
OSORKON 'II' = 'Mut-udj-ankhes
┌──┘
Nimlot C = 'Tentsepeh C
|
(Pasenhor B)

§ 86 First, the Count, Governor of Upper Egypt, Superintendent of Prophets in Heracleopolis and General, Nimlot son of king Osorkon, can be readily identified. He duly appears as 'High Priest of Arsaphes, . . . Great Chief of (Pi-)Sekhemkheper(re), General and Army-leader, Nimlot, son of the Lord of the Two Lands, Osorkon Meryamun *Si-Bast*, his mother being Dje(d)-Mut-es-ankh', on a donation-stela dated to Year 16 of king Usimare Setepenamun, Osorkon Meryamun *Si-Bast*[108] – i.e. our Osorkon 'II'. Thus, our Osorkon Si-Bast is the second of the King Osorkons in Pasenhor's royal ancestry, and can henceforth be referred to as Osorkon II, dropping the inverted commas which have hitherto been used to make his numeral provisional. The forms of name Mut-udj-ankhes, Djed-Mut-es-ankh, for Nimlot's mother have virtually the same meaning[109] and may be considered variants of little consequence.

Secondly, this Nimlot is mentioned in inscriptions at Karnak which were left by his descendants: by a son Takeloth,[110] and by Prince Osorkon (B), a maternal grandson.[111] The former names Nimlot C as high priest of Amun, general of Heracleopolis and son of Osorkon II. The latter adds only the title 'Army-leader', but gives the following genealogy (text A, lines 8, 10–12):

108. Cairo JdE. 45327: Daressy, *ASAE* 15 (1915), 141; Iversen, *Two Inscriptions concerning Private Donations to Temples*, 1941, 3–9, pl. 1.
109. i.e. 'Mut ordains that she live' and 'Mut speaks and she lives', respectively. Pasenhor is fond of the *udj*-form of name; among his forebears, Ptah-udj-ankhef is very likely a Djed-Ptah-ef-ankh.
110. Cf. references, Kees, *Hohenpriester*, 113, 138–9.
111. Relationship attested by label-texts to scenes over 'chronicle-texts' of Osorkon, Bubastite portal, *RIK*, III, pls. 16, 17, 20; *CPO*, 14–16.

OSORKON II Si-Bast
|
Nimlot
|
Hedjkheperre Seteperre TAKELOTH 'II' = ⌐Karomama, chief queen
|
Prince Osorkon B, high priest of Amun

This table is the principal evidence that makes Hedjkheperre Takeloth (our 'II') a successor of Osorkon II. The rest of Prince Osorkon's long texts makes it clear that the successor of this Takeloth was the Usimare Shoshenq 'III' who reigned at least 39 years and in fact almost certainly 52 years. Thus, the first text dates to Year 11 of Takeloth (l. 18); the second begins with Year 12 of Takeloth (B, l. 1), turns to Year 15 (B, l. 7 ff.). A list is given of all of Prince Osorkon's benefactions to Amun from Year 11 of his father Takeloth to Year 28 of Usimare Shoshenq 'III'. Then follow the lists which presumably cover the same period. Thus, Year 24 early in the first list will have belonged to Takeloth, while the renewed works that follow in unattributed Years 22–28 would then belong to Shoshenq 'III', with individual mention of Years 23, 24, 25, summation of Years 22–28, and an addendum in Year 29.[112] Prince Osorkon then reappears in Year 39 of this king.[113]

So much for the succession Osorkon II – Takeloth 'II' – Shoshenq 'III'. Year 24 is nearly the highest that has been attested for Takeloth 'II'. An endowment stela for the Chantress of the Abode of Amun, the princess Karama, is dated to 'Year 25 of the King . . . Takeloth, living forever, (and) the High Priest of Amun, Osorkon'.[114] The latter's name is enough to indicate that this is Year 25 of Takeloth 'II' and the pontificate of his son Prince Osorkon, since no other high priest Osorkon is known under any other Takeloth. Hence, Takeloth 'II' may be assigned some 25 years (24 minimum).[115]

§ 87 Now that one may definitely attribute the Nile-level text No. 13 to Osorkon III and Takeloth III,[116] the highest dates left to Osorkon II are

112. For the series of dates, cf. *CPO*, 128, § 199; his consecutive translation, pp. 151–71, gives a convenient conspectus.

113. Nile-level text No. 22 (von Beckerath, *JARCE* 5 (1966), 51) and Karnak Priestly Annals, Legrain, *RT* 22 (1900), 55–6, and *RT* 31 (1909), 6.

114. Legrain and Maspero, *ASAE* 4 (1903), 183, 185–6; *G3*, 353, IX. This recluse was perhaps the second daughter of Osorkon II who appears at Bubastis (Naville, *Festival Hall of Osorkon II*, pl. 4: 1). She was certainly not that king's wife, as Gauthier seemed to think (*G3*, 341, XXIVA).

115. The bandage-fragments Brussels E. 7047*b, c*, of Year 24 with Nespa(u)re and Nesamun and of Year 26 (Nespa(u)re only) probably belong to the reign of Takeloth II, if these names were the Nespare and Nes(er)amun of Cairo Cat. 42221 (so, M. L. Bierbrier; cf. Part III, § 166, below). Capart, *BMRAH³* 13 (1941), 26–9, had referred these epigraphs to the 21st Dynasty, which is unlikely.

116. See above, § 73; this eliminates a spurious Year 28 for Osorkon II.

Year 22 from his festival reliefs at Bubastis[117] and Year 23 reported from the Serapeum.[118] However, certain indications may suggest that Osorkon II probably reigned a little longer beyond Year 23. The Crown Prince Shoshenq D has been linked in early reports with the Apis burial of that year (cf. § 81, above). If this is so, then Shoshenq himself died *after* this burial and *before* his father, dying as high priest of Ptah and buried as such (§ 81, above), the next king being Takeloth 'II'. To allow for this sequence of events, it would seem wise to allot 24 or even 25 full years to Osorkon II, he dying in Year 25 or 26. This would allow for the death and burial of Prince Shoshenq about Year 24, safely after Apis and before his father.

A word is in order at this point on king Harsiese. His contemporaneity with Osorkon II is established by the statue of Nakhtefmut from Karnak (Cairo Cat. 42208) bearing the full titulary of Osorkon II, but given by favour of king Harsiese.[119] This 'king' is generally admitted to be the same man as the high priest of Amun, Harsiese, whose name and titles appear on another Karnak statue (Cairo Cat. 42225) of a Nebneteru, bearing also the cartouches of Osorkon II.[120] Nimlot C, son of Osorkon II who had governed in Heracleopolis up to Year 16, became high priest of Amun after Harsiese, probably also following the latter's son.[121] Hence, the reign of Harsiese – probably as nominal as that of Pinudjem I – was probably contained entirely within that of Osorkon II, shows no regnal years of its own, and is of no direct chronological significance for the main line of 22nd-Dynasty Libyan kings. We now, so far, have the following succession of kings:

—	SHOSHENQ 'I'	⎫
—	OSORKON 'I'	⎬ Pasenhor, prenomens to be
—	TAKELOTH 'I'	⎭ determined
Usimare	OSORKON II Si-Bast: 24 yrs.	HARSIESE, co-ruler
		(10 yrs.??)
Hedjkheperre	TAKELOTH 'II': 25 yrs.	
Usimare	SHOSHENQ 'III': 52 yrs.	
Usimare	PIMAY: 6 yrs.	
Akheperre	SHOSHENQ 'V': 37 yrs.	
	OSORKON ('IV'): contemp. Tefnakht & PIANKHY	

117. *G3*, 336, VII; Naville, *Bubastis*, pl. 42B, or *Festival Hall*, pl. 6: 8.
118. *G3*, 336, n. 3 end, references; Serapeum stela, now Malinine, Posener, Vercoutter, *Catalogue*, I, No. 18, p. 17, pl. 6.
119. *G3*, 348, III, 338, XII; Legrain, *Statues*, III, ad loc.
120. *G3*, 348, II; cf. below, Part III, §§ 177 ff.
121. Whose name is all but totally erased on a monument from Koptos, *G3*, 349, VIII/X; cf. Part III, below, §§ 157 ff.

§ 88   3. EARLIER KINGS OF THE 22nd DYNASTY

A. PASENHOR'S KINGS

As Pasenhor gives no prenomen for any of the kings in his ancestry, these have to be identified with kings who are attested on monuments, on independent grounds. As the parents of his first king, Shoshenq, are non-royal (Chief of Mā and God's Father, Nimlot: God's Mother, Tentsepeh),[122] then that Shoshenq was clearly founder of the Dynasty and the Sesonchis of Manetho who ruled 21 years. Among the Shoshenqs who were attested on monuments and were reviewed in Chapter 6 (§§ 66 ff.), Nos. I, II, IV, VI are all theoretical candidates for identification with the Shoshenq I of Pasenhor and Manetho. That he was, in fact, the No. I, Hedjkheperre, has been accepted since Champollion's day; but it is well to state here the rather limited evidence that actually underpins this axiomatic assumption.

In the first place, Hedjkheperre Shoshenq 'I' had a son, Iuput A, whom he appointed high priest of Amun. This prince accompanies his father in scenes on the Bubastite portal at Karnak,[123] is named in bandage-epigraphs of Year 10,[124] and recurs on Silsila stela 100 of Year 21 of his father,[125] a figure that coincides well with the 21 years for Sesonchis in Manetho.

Secondly, the occurrence of this same Iuput in the genealogies of the Theban family of Djed-Thut-ef-ankh B called Nakhtefmut guarantees the chronological position of Shoshenq and Iuput in relation to later kings.[126]

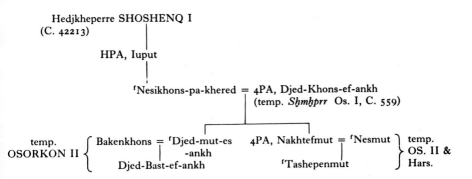

122. The epithet God's Mother for the non-royal mother of a pharaoh corresponds to God's Father for the non-royal father of a king; cf. (e.g.) Gardiner, *MDIK* 14 (1956), 46.
123. *RIK*, III, pls. 10–11; older literature, *G3*, 321, LVI, C.
124. *G3*, 308, VI, VII, and references.
125. Edited by Caminos, *JEA* 38 (1952), 46–61, pls. 10–13.
126. For this family and fuller genealogy, see below, Part III, §§ 183 ff.

Thus, the three Karnak statues of this Nakhtefmut (Cairo Cat. 42206–7–8) offer the genealogy given just above; items derived from the related statues Cairo Cat. 559 and 42213 are so marked. Cairo Cat. 42208 bears the full titles of Osorkon II, and was given by favour of 'king' Harsiese. Cairo Cat. 559 names a king Sekhemkheperre who is otherwise abundantly attested as an Osorkon; as this genealogy clearly puts him earlier than Osorkon II, he will be Pasenhor's Osorkon I.

For Hedjkheperre Shoshenq I, the highest year-date is his 21st, which has already been cited; as has already been set out above (Pt. I, §§ 57–60), he can be allowed 21 full years, dying in the 22nd. For the length of reign of Osorkon I, see next paragraph. To Takeloth 'I' may be attributed 14 years or 15 years (cf. §§ 95–96 below). For him alone can no prenomen be found as yet (cf. § 77 above, §§ 95–96 below). Thus, the predecessors of Osorkon II come out as follows.

Hedjkheperre   SHOSHENQ I: 21 years.
Sekhemkheperre   OSORKON I: (15/35 years?); cf. below.
?   TAKELOTH I: (c. 14/15 years, §§ 95–96).

§ 89   B. THE LENGTH OF REIGN OF OSORKON I

For Sekhemkheperre Osorkon I, Year 36 was for long thought to be the highest-attested,[127] but this is now known to be a misreading for '[Year x, y month of Pere]t, Day 26', leaving at first sight only the Manethonic datum of 15 years.[128] However, certain factors suggest that a 15-year reign is much too short.

In the first place, a Year 33 is reported on linen (along with a Year 3) from the body of a priest buried at the Ramesseum, which had on it braces with a *menat*-tab of Osorkon I.[129] This would clearly date the Year 33 to Osorkon I – Psusennes I is too remote in time, and Shoshenq 'III' much too late; the Year 3 would belong either to Osorkon's co-regent (for whom, see §§ 93–94, below) or be an old scrap from the beginning of his own reign. This Year 33 suggests a minimum reign of 32 years and that Manetho's figure should indeed be taken as a corruption of 15 from 35 years.

Secondly, in favour of a long reign, one may note the sequence of high priests of Amun. Osorkon's heir, the high priest Shoshenq 'II', served under his father, and (as the latter was succeeded by Takeloth) predeceased his father. As high priest, he was succeeded by Iuwelot, his brother, by a

127. Following the reading of Petrie, *History of Egypt*, III, 1905, 241, of a stela then in his collection and now in University College, London.
128. See H. K. Jacquet-Gordon, *JEA* 53 (1967), 63 ff.
129. Cf. Quibell, *The Ramesseum*, 1898, 10–11. The present whereabouts of the inscribed linen is unknown.

Year 5 that can only belong to the following king (Takeloth 'I'). Iuwelot was only a youth in Year 10 of Osorkon I, and in the responsible positions of high priest, army-commander and effective governor of southern Upper Egypt, he is more likely to have been so appointed 25 years later, aged about 40, than 5 years later at hardly 20, when he was still a callow youth.[130]

Thirdly, as co-regent of Osorkon I (§§ 93–94 below), Shoshenq 'II' died aged 'about fifty'.[131] If so, and if he were eldest son of Osorkon I (born when latter was about 20), then Osorkon I died aged about 70 or more. If he were married, therefore, to Shoshenq's mother Maatkare B while he was about 18 or 19, and under Psusennes I not later than c. 945 B.C., there would be about 50 years' interval from his marriage to his death – 21 years of Shoshenq I, 30+x years of his own reign, and perhaps a year or so of Psusennes II. If Maatkare B had been a second wife of Osorkon, not his first, he may have been a little older. At any rate, a long reign of 32–35 years fits well, while a 15-year reign seems too short.[132] If by any chance the marriage of Osorkon and Maatkare had been arranged by Shoshenq I in his *own* reign, after the death of Psusennes II, then a long reign of Osorkon I is virtually inevitable; but so late a marriage-date may be too late.

Fourthly, the series of 3rd Prophets of Amun, and even more of 4th Prophets, is only easily accommodated within a long reign of Osorkon I, and would border on the unrealistic if crammed into a 15-year reign for that king.[133]

No longer on the basis of the Petrie stela, but on the four-fold basis given above, therefore – Year 33 bandage in a burial under Osorkon I, sequence of high priests of Amun, age-relationships of the early 22nd Dynasty, and sequences of 3rd and 4th prophets of Amun – a reign of 35 years for Osorkon I is herewith adopted unless and until we can know any better.

§ **90** C. LINKS BETWEEN SHOSHENQ I AND THE 21ST DYNASTY
A further area which is in need of clarification is the ancestry of Shoshenq I, and more especially his possible relationships with the 21st Dynasty and

---

130. Cf. § 96 below, also Part III, §§ 157 ff.

131. So, Derry, *ASAE* 39 (1939), 549–51; for 'Shoshenq II', see §§ 93–4 below.

132. So short a reign would make Osorkon I about 55 at accession, about 34 at Shoshenq I's accession, and so possibly have married Maatkare B, daughter of Psusennes II (reigning 14 years) right at Psusennes' accession or even before it – perhaps hardly likely.

133. Cf. general account, Part IV, § 266, and lists of these prophets, Part VI below.

other notables of the time. The immediate ancestry of Shoshenq I given on the Pasenhor stela is confirmed by three sources: a family monument from Abydos,[134] a stela seen in trade,[135] and data concerning the contemporary high priests of Ptah in Memphis. The first item records a foundation at Abydos in favour of the deceased Chief of the Mā, Nimlot, son of a Chief of the Mā, Shoshenq (A), and his wife Mehtenweskhet (l. 24); Nimlot is often called simply 'son of Mehtenweskhet' (ll. 3, 10, 18, 20, 22, 24, 25). Acting for his father Nimlot, 'his son' Shoshenq (B) appears in line 1, being addressed by the unnamed king (ll. 5–6). It is precisely Nimlot A son of Shoshenq A and Mehtenweskhet who is given as father of Shoshenq I by the Pasenhor stela; thus our Shoshenq B is none other than the future king Shoshenq I, gaining favours from the reigning king for his own father's cult; that pharaoh would be Psusennes II. This picture is supplemented by the second item. The stela seen by Daressy names 'the Great Chief of Foreigners, Chief of Chiefs, Shoshenq justified, son of the Great Chief of Foreigners, Nimlot justified, his mother being the daughter of a Great Chief of Foreigners, Tentsepeh, justified for eternity'. Adding the name of Tentsepeh, wife of Nimlot and mother of the future Shoshenq I precisely as on Pasenhor's stela, this document agrees with the Abydos monument.[136]

On Pasenhor's stela, Mehtenweskhet is, curiously, called *mwt-nsw*, 'King's Mother'. This cannot refer to Shoshenq I, unless it be understood as 'King's (grand)mother'. For this, there seems little warrant, and a different solution seems more attractive. It is possible that in the previous, 21st, Dynasty, this title may stand for 'King's Mother(-in-law)'.[137] If that applied here, then one may suggest that a daughter of Shoshenq A and Mehtenweskhet (sister of Nimlot, aunt of Shoshenq I) was actually married-off to a pharaoh of the 21st Dynasty. The following picture would then emerge.

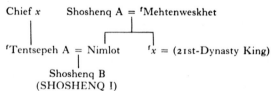

Chief *x*   Shoshenq A = ⸢Mehtenweskhet

⸢Tentsepeh A = Nimlot   ⸢*x* = (21st-Dynasty King)

Shoshenq B
(SHOSHENQ I)

134. Published by Blackman, *JEA* 27 (1941), 83–95 and pls. 10–12.

135. Daressy, *ASAE* 16 (1917), 177.

136. We do not know the name of Tentsepeh's father; if he were actually the chief Shoshenq A, then she and Nimlot A would have been at any rate half-brother/sister, but could even have been full brother and sister. However, she is perhaps the daughter of some other Libyan chief.

137. Cf. for example, Part I, above, §§ 43–4; besides Henttawy A, this may apply to Nodjmet (§ 38 end) and very likely to Hrēre A (§ 39).

The names Tentsepeh and Mehtenweskhet recur on a monument of Shedsunefertem A, high priest in Memphis about this time,[138] namely the statue Cairo Cat. 741, and previously they have been considered identical with the ladies bearing these names who have been discussed just above. As will be seen below, these identifications are highly unlikely.

Cairo Cat. 741 is a statue-group of a man and woman; the text on the back indicates that they are Shedsunefertem A with his *mother* (not wife) Tapeshenese.[139] In this text, after the name and titles of Shedsunefertem and introductory 'he says', one may read:

(5) *nfr.wy mwt ḥpt.s sꜣ.s, t⟨w⟩t.s wbn im.st,*
    nb-im(ꜣ), bnr{t}-mrwt,
bs ḫꜣ[t](6) wrt-ḥ⟨nr⟩t tpyt n(t) Ptḥ, ḥm-nṯr n Mwt, Tꜣ-pš-n-ꜣst:
    – sꜣt.s[140] wn ḥr st.s –
sꜣt.s (for sꜣt nꜣ?)[141] wr ꜥꜣ [n Mꜥ](7)w,
    wrt-ḥ⟨nr⟩t tpyt n(t) Ptḥ, ḥm-ntr n Mwt, Mḫt-n-wsḫt,
sn(t) n[142] sꜣt[143]-nsw n nb-tꜣwy, [wrt-](8) ḥn⟨r⟩t tpyt n(t) Ptḥ,
    ḥm-nṯr – Tnt-spḥ – n Pr-Mwt [. . .].

(5) 'How beautiful is a mother who embraces her son,
       her image who shone forth from
             her,
  (he, a) possessor of charm, sweet of love,
who conducted the burial of (6) the First Chief of the Harim of Ptah,
       Prophetess of Mut, *Tapeshenese*:
    – her daughter remaining on her seat –
{her daughter}, ⟨the daughter of⟩ the Great Chief [of the Mā] (7),
First Chief of the Harim of Ptah, Prophetess of Mut,
            Mehtenweskhet,

138. As shown by his occurrence with the cartouches of Shoshenq I on an embalming-table for the Apis bulls, Brugsch, *Thesaurus*, 817, 948 f. Shedsunefertem is there named as son of Ankhefensekhmet.

139. Daressy, *RT* 18 (1896), 46: 1; Borchardt, *Statuen und Statuetten*, III, 67–9 (esp. 68); cf. Kees, *ZÄS* 87 (1962), 140–2. The real relationship between Shedsunefertem and Tapeshenese was pointed out by Kees, *Pr.*, 176, and *ZÄS* 87 (1962), 141, n. f; he (n. i) would prefer to take her name as Tashepenese.

140. Kees, *op. cit.*, 140, 141, note k, regarded *sꜣt.s* as an error either for 'she is a daughter (who is in her place)' or for 'her mother', *mwt.s*.

141. So by implication Kees, *op. cit.*, 140, in his translation; the poorly shaped horizontal stroke would probably allow of either reading – a cursive *s* or equally slipshod *n*.

142. Read *sn(t) n*, not *sn(t).s*, on collation by Kees (p. 141, n. 1).

143. So clearly the text; but Kees silently emends to *sꜣ-nsw*, referring it to Nimlot.

sister of the King's Daughter of the Lord of the Two Lands,
First Chief (8) of the Harim of Ptah, Prophetess of Mut's
Temple,
Tentsepeh, [. . .].'

Daressy and Kees[144] saw here evidence of a marriage-alliance between the powerful Great Chiefs of the Mā and the high priests of Ptah in Memphis – which seems assured – but proceeded to identify the Mehtenweskhet of this statue with the like-named wife of the great chief Shoshenq A, father of Nimlot and grandfather of Shoshenq I. This equation seems to be ruled out on two grounds. First, the title First Chief of the Harim of a deity properly belongs to the wife or officiating daughter of a high priest of that deity – and the wife of the Libyan chief Shoshenq A never had these relationships.[145] Secondly, the only way of easily placing the Mehtenweskhet of Cairo Cat. 741 a generation before Tapeshenese (latter, in Nimlot's generation) is to make her the *mother* of Tapeshenese – which is only possible if one emends *śśt.s* 'her daughter' to *mwt.s* 'her mother' in line 6 after the name Tapeshenese. This is possible,[146] but so drastic an emendation is neither desirable nor perhaps even necessary.

Instead, one may more simply place the Mehtenweskhet of Cairo Cat. 741 in the generation *after* Tapeshenese, and therefore in the same generation as Shedsunefertem and Shoshenq I. She was daughter of a Libyan great chief, became a First Chief of the Harim of Ptah – surely, by marrying the high priest, Shedsunefertem – and thus was in fact not daughter but daughter-in-law of his mother Tapeshenese, characteristically expressed as 'daughter' in the imprecise Egyptian terminology for family relationships. Thus, Cairo 741 would indeed reflect a marriage-alliance between the Libyan great chiefs and the high priests of Memphite Ptah, but Shedsunefertem probably married a daughter of Nimlot and sister of the future Shoshenq I.[147]

However, this leaves us with the Tentsepeh of Cairo 741. She is described (i) as a princess (King's Daughter of the Lord of the Two Lands), (ii) as also First Chief of the Harim of Ptah, and (iii) as having Mehtenweskhet as her sister. One may infer from (i) and (ii) that a Tanite

144. Daressy, *RT* 18 (1896), 46; Kees, *op cit.*, 142.
145. Unless, *in extremis*, one assumes that Mehtenweskhet had been the daughter of a Memphite high priest married-off to Shoshenq A; she could then have been First Chief of Ptah's harim before her marriage – rather far-fetched.
146. On the original, this would imply an error of one bird (duck) for another (vulture) – not impossible, but not a particularly likely error.
147. One could postulate that Shedsunefertem married Mehtenweskhet as having been a daughter of Shoshenq B (Shoshenq I), but this might be less easy in terms of relative ages.

king married-off his daughter Tentsepeh to a high priest of Ptah, whereby she became a Chief of the Harim of Ptah – and if, in fact, she had thus also married Shedsunefertem, then she would in Egyptian terms rank as 'sister' to Mehtenweskhet.[148] The Tanite king concerned may well have been Psusennes II, one of whose daughters (Maatkare B) was married-off to the young Libyan prince Osorkon, son of Shoshenq I.

§ 91   These results for Cairo 741, set against the background of the other documents discussed, present a striking picture of the interrelationships linking the Tanite royal house, the high priests of Ptah in Memphis, and the Libyan great chiefs of the Mā during the closing decades of the 21st Dynasty.

Thus, under Siamun, the high priest Pipi B had expressed his loyalty to the Tanite throne by adopting a 'loyalist' surname,[149] and his son and grandson (Asha-khet B, Ankhefensekhmet A) were allowed in turn to succeed him in office under Siamun and Psusennes II. Such was the favour enjoyed by this family that Shedsunefertem was able to marry Tentsepeh, who was probably a daughter of Psusennes II. On the other side, good relations had also developed between the Memphite pontiffs and the Libyan great chiefs in Bubastis, the great city that lay *en route* between Memphis and Tanis, twin capitals of the 21st Dynasty, and whose cults had many links with those of Memphis.[150] So, at some point in time, Shedsunefertem married also Mehtenweskhet, daughter of one of these chiefs – perhaps Nimlot – making him the brother-in-law of Shoshenq B, who eventually became king Shoshenq I. As with the multiple wives of the

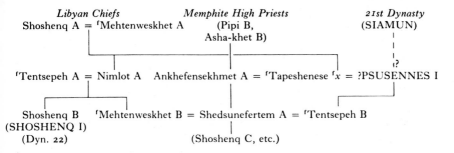

148. This solution disposes of the difficulties felt by Kees, *ZÄS* 87 (1962), 141, over *sʾt-nsw* (or *sʾ-nsw* to which he would emend it). In the New Kingdom it had become customary for Egyptians to call a wife a 'sister'; two wives, therefore, might easily be termed 'sisters'.

149. A practice common in the Ramesside epoch, but almost unknown in the 21st Dynasty.

150. Bast of Bubastis with Sekhmet of Memphis; Nefertum in both cities.

Theban pontiffs (cf. Pinudjem II), so here each wife was diplomatically allowed to be First Chief of the harim of her husband's patron deity. Thus, through the Memphite high priests, the Libyan chiefs and Tanite kings were already 'in-laws' before the 21st Dynasty had ended.

One other well-known link between the 21st and 22nd Dynasties has been noted already (§§ 5, 49, above): that Maatkare B, daughter of Psusennes II, last king of the 21st Dynasty, married the eventual Osorkon I, son of Shoshenq I (founder of the 22nd Dynasty), and mothered a prince Shoshenq, who became high priest of Amun. This personal link confirms the last and first rulers of the two dynasties.

§ 92   4. LESSER KINGS

To complete the 22nd Dynasty, only three matters remain to be considered: the identities and reigns in each case of 'Shoshenq II', Takeloth 'I' and Osorkon 'IV'.

A. OSORKON IV

The simplest case is that of Osorkon IV. As noted in § 84 above (cf. §§ 149, 316 (iii), 333–336, below), Shoshenq V had been followed in the rule of Tanis and Bubastis by a king Osorkon by the time of Piankhy's invasion of Egypt. As this Osorkon succeeds Shoshenq V in the rule of those districts (Tanis, Bubastis) most closely associated with the *22nd Dynasty*,[151] it should be absolutely crystal clear that Osorkon IV belongs to the *22nd* Dynasty (NOT the 23rd which was reigning elsewhere) and was the last king of the 22nd Dynasty.

Sekhemkheperre was Osorkon I, and Usimare surnamed Si-Bast was Osorkon II, and both reigned generations before the general date of Piankhy's Osorkon IV; so he is neither of these. Likewise, Usimare Osorkon III Si-Ese can be ruled out – he *never* reigned at Tanis or Bubastis (entirely absent from these sites), and he was *not* the last king of either Libyan line: he was succeeded by a co-regent Takeloth 'III' and he by a Rudamun (cf. §§ 100, 101 below). There is no room for 28 years of Osorkon III Si-Ese plus the reigns of his two sons between the conquests of Piankhy and Shabako; these three kings belong to the 23rd Dynasty (cf. Ch. 8), and so Osorkon IV is separate from these.

---

151. As is clear from the Piankhy stela; in the Libyan epoch, it is the 22nd Dynasty that almost exclusively left its mark in Tanis and Bubastis. Of the 23rd Dynasty, we have only one private donation-stela of Pedubast I (Year 23, formerly misattributed to Takeloth I) from Bubastis and nothing certain from Tanis.

Monumentally, this leaves just one Osorkon unaccounted for, in § 69, above: Akheperre Setepenamun, Osorkon Meryamun. These cartouches occur on a glazed ring at Leiden of unknown provenance,[152] and can reasonably be attributed – without final proof – to our Osorkon IV. He would, then, at his accession, merely have adopted the prenomen of his immediate predecessor (and father?), Shoshenq V. No other monuments can yet be attributed to his reign with any confidence, except perhaps a silver-gilt aegis in the Louvre,[153] which names a king Osorkon and the 'God's Mother (cartouche:) King's Wife, Tadibast'. As the mothers of Osorkon I, II, III are all known and are different (Karamat, Kapes, Kamama), it is probable that this lady was wife of Shoshenq V and mother of Osorkon IV Akheperre[154] – or less probably, that she was wife of Osorkon IV simply bearing the cult-title 'God's Mother' (of Khons).[155]

§ 93   B. 'SHOSHENQ II'

For the title 'Shoshenq II', there are in theory two or three possible contenders. Usimare Meryamun (Shoshenq No. IV, §§ 66, 68, above) can be eliminated because he belongs to the 23rd Dynasty and to the time of Shoshenq III (cf. § 99, below). The existence and placement of No. VI, Was-neter-re, remains dubious and obscure (§§ 66, 67, above), so he may be left aside for the moment. Sekhemkheperre has already been eliminated as spurious (above, § 67). This leaves technically two other Shoshenq 'kings'. One is the high priest of Amun, Shoshenq C, son of Osorkon I by the 21st-Dynasty heiress Maatkare B (§§ 5, 49, 91 end, above). Both on the British Museum 'Nile' statue and in the texts of the former Alnwick Besfigure,[156] this pontiff has his name in a cartouche, as Shoshenq Meryamun. The other person is the king Heqa-kheper-re Shoshenq whose burial Montet discovered at Tanis in the vestibule of the tomb of Psusennes. I.[157]

Various minor pieces of evidence might suggest a date for Heqakheperre Shoshenq quite early in the 22nd Dynasty.[158] His burial-goods included a pectoral which had originally been inscribed for 'the Great Chief of the Mā, Chief of Chiefs, Shoshenq, son of the Great Chief of the Mā, Nimlot, justified',[159] and a pair of bracelets of Shoshenq I as king,[160] but no later

152. G3, 399, 2, I, with references; conveniently reproduced in Petrie, History, III, 264, fig. 107.
153. G3, 399, 2, II, 400, IV, and references.
154. Cf. use of mwt-nṯr throughout for royal mothers on the stela of Pasenhor.
155. Like, for example, Queen Mutnodjmet of the 21st Dynasty.
156. Legrain, RT 30 (1908), 89; G3, 331, E.
157. Montet, Psus., 36–63 with illustrations.
158. Cf. already on this point, Montet, Psus., 61–3.
159. Ibid., 43–4, fig. 13 centre, colour-pl., and pl. 28.
160. Ibid., 45, fig. 13, colour-pl., and pl. 29.

objects. As the Great Chief Shoshenq is none other than Shoshenq I before his accession,[161] these objects would – even as heirlooms – seem to link the 'new' Shoshenq with the beginning of the 22nd Dynasty. The absence of objects from later in the Dynasty, while not decisive, would point in the same direction. However, it must be admitted that these considerations are very fragile.[162] Thus, the burial of Osorkon II's son Harnakht contained objects naming the 21st-Dynasty king Amenemope[163] and a King's Son of Ramesses Pashedbast (linked with Osorkon I?).[164] The burial of Takeloth II contained a jar, etc., of Osorkon I,[165] and an ushabti of Tashedkhons, mother of Takeloth I;[166] that of Shoshenq III contained a scarab and a canopic jar (mere reuse?)[167] of Shoshenq I.[168] Thus, a relatively 'late' burial could be marked by heirlooms of relatively much earlier dates. Therefore, the absence of any objects later in date than Shoshenq I from the burial of Heqakheperre Shoshenq does *not* necessarily prove that he was a direct successor (real or intended) of Shoshenq I or Osorkon I. From his prenomen, one cannot draw any firm conclusion except this: from Osorkon II onwards, the 22nd and 23rd Dynasties showed practically *no* originality in their choice of prenomens – a confusing series of Usimares and a couple each of Hedjkheperres and Akheperres (neither original), almost nothing more. Only at the *beginning* of the 22nd Dynasty do we find any originality. Shoshenq I boldly took the prenomen of Smendes I, thereby proclaiming himself a new Smendes, at one stroke marking continuity with the past and a new beginning. Osorkon I took an entirely original prenomen (Sekhemkheperre) on the same basic model as his father's. The prenomen Heqakheperre is equally original and, again, on the same model. Hence, for this reason as much as for the early heirlooms, it seems best to connect this Shoshenq with the epoch of Shoshenq I and Osorkon I. If Osorkon I was married to Maatkare B in the reign of

161. So by comparison with the Pasenhor genealogy and related documents (§§ 90–1, above). Montet's doubts (*ibid.*, 44, n. 1) are groundless, particularly as he overlooked these data.

162. The re-use of building-materials, sarcophagi, etc., of the 12th–13th, 18th–20th Dynasties does not enter into this discussion, as these were mere 'scrap' for re-use, not dynastic heirlooms.

163. Montet, *Osorkon II*, 66, fig. 21: 88, and pl. 60.

164. *Ibid.*, 66, fig. 21: 87, and pl. 58. Gauthier, *ASAE* 18 (1918), 245, would make such a person son of Osorkon I, but this is not certain.

165. *Ibid.*, 82, 84, and pl. 46.

166. *Ibid.*, 84, fig. 25 centre-left (p. 80), pl. 56 upper right. Tashedkhons as mother of Takeloth I, cf. Pasenhor stela.

167. Montet, *Chéchanq III*, 76, suggested that perhaps Shoshenq I himself had been reburied in this tomb. This seems doubtful; if true, then of course these remains would be directly of his burial and not mere heirlooms with Shoshenq III.

168. *Osorkon II*, 59; *Chéchanq III*, 76, pl. 49.

Psusennes II her father, and himself (21 years of Shoshenq I intervening) had a long reign of *c.* 35 years, then late in his reign he may well have felt aged enough to need a co-regent to assume the more onerous burdens of kingship. That co-regent, a man of mature years,[169] predeceased him, so that the throne went to Takeloth I.

§ 94   This brings us back to that other Shoshenq, who was high priest of Amun and Army-Chief under his father Osorkon I, and whose mother was Maatkare B. He called himself Shoshenq Meryamun, using a cartouche. While it is theoretically possible that Osorkon I had two sons Shoshenq, one a high priest with royal pretensions (born of an heiress) and one who became his intended successor, though he outlived them both, yet it would seem altogether much more realistic to assume just *one* such son: Shoshenq his principal and eldest son, borne by the heiress Maatkare, pontiff in Thebes, with expectations on the throne (hence, cartouche while yet pontiff), and finally full co-regent and intended successor of his father though he died before him in the prime of life.[170]

There is perhaps additional reason to believe that this co-regent never outlived his father, if indeed he were the former Theban pontiff. This is provided by the former Alnwick Bes-figure. This was dedicated by the high priest of Amenresonter Harsiese (and his lesser brother, an ordinary priest Osorkon),[171] given as son of the pontiff and army-chief (cartouche:) Shoshenq Meryamun. Had Shoshenq ever become sole king, one might have expected Harsiese to have called himself King's Son of the Lord of the Two Lands Shoshenq, in the style of the age, like his father. But if Shoshenq had been high priest for many years and only briefly co-regent, never knowing sole rule as pharaoh, then Harsiese's filiation as from a 'semi-royal' pontiff is natural and would emphasize his own high-priest-hood following from father to son, which was an important concept in Thebes at that time. Furthermore, had Shoshenq 'II' ever ruled as sole king, then one might expect that he would be succeeded not by his shadowy brother Takeloth (I) but by Harsiese – and the latter's purely nominal 'kingship' would not have needed to await the reign of Osorkon II; in fact, there would have been no Osorkon II.

169. Cf. remarks on the mummy of Shoshenq Heqakheperre: Montet, *Psus.*, 40, following Derry, *ASAE* 39 (1939), 549–51, 'about fifty'. I see no reason whatever to suppose that Heqakheperre should be a mere variant of Hedjkheperre, i.e. Shoshenq I (a speculation briefly mooted by Gardiner, *Egypt of the Pharaohs*, 1961, 448).

170. A view already taken by several scholars previously, e.g. Montet, *Psus.*, 63, or Drioton & Vandier, *L'Égypte*⁴, 1964, 530, 536, etc.

171. See *G3*, 331, n. 2, and now B. J. Peterson, *Orientalia Suecana* 19/20 (1970/71 [1972]), 17–18, § XXVII.

Hence, the title of Shoshenq II can with considerable plausibility be accorded to the son of Osorkon I who first served as pontiff in Thebes, probably for most of his father's reign, and then as full co-regent for a brief span at the end of his father's reign, though he died before Osorkon I. His chronological significance is *nil*; his being 'II' removes doubt on numbering III–V.

§ 95   C. TAKELOTH I

So far, only *one* clear, unequivocal mention of Takeloth I (as distinct from II, Hedjkheperre, and III, Usimare) has been isolated: that in the famed genealogy on the Pasenhor stela.[172] No other unambiguous evidence of his existence has so far been found. There seems no warrant to attribute to him as prenomen the Usimare that belongs to Takeloth III.[173] Hence, one must rather expect that, some day, a 'new' prenomen of a Takeloth may be found, and that this will be the real Takeloth I.

In the meantime, some possible or alleged monuments of this reign may here be reviewed. From the burial of Osorkon II at Tanis was recovered a heart-scarab[174] inscribed for a Takeloth Meryamun (no Si-Ese), a limited combination not commonly found with Takeloth II or III.[175] Unless one attributes this scarab to Takeloth II as a burial gift in his own name for his father, one may suggest that it is a 'left-over' from Takeloth I; there can be no certainty on the point.

A monument commonly attributed to Takeloth I and alleged to attest his 23rd regnal year can be totally rejected on two grounds. This is a donation-stela in Florence, read originally as belonging to the 23rd year of an Usimare Setepenamun Takeloth Meryamun.[176] If this were so, it would in any case belong to Takeloth III, not I. However, a second and final point rules out even this attribution. Scrutiny of this stela simply on a good photograph[177] shows clearly beyond all possible cavil that it belongs, in fact, to the 23rd year of Usimare Setepenamun, *Pedubast* Meryamun Si-Bast – i.e. to Pedubast I of the 23rd Dynasty, and has no bearing whatsoever on any Takeloth of either 22nd or 23rd Dynasty.[178] The nomen, in

172. Cf. already §§ 76–7, above.

173. Cf. § 77, above; thus Year 7 of Usimare Takeloth should be assigned to Takeloth III; *G3*, 333, 3, I, and n. 3.

174. Montet, *Osorkon II*, 59, fig. 20: 88 (p. 65), and pl. 58.

175. Cf. *G3*, 352, 2; Montet, *Osorkon II*, 82–3, figs. 26–7, pl. 56 centre-rt.

176. Florence No. 7207 (Schiaparelli 1806); cf. *G3*, 333, n. 3 and 390, II, with references.

177. Such as that kindly supplied to me by the authorities of the Florence Museum, whose help it is a pleasure to acknowledge here.

178. This result has now been fully corroborated by the admirable publication of this stela by Caminos, *Centaurus* 14 (1969), 42–6, pls. 1–2, which appeared after my own (unpublished) investigation.

fact, corresponds to that attested for Pedubast I on a damaged stela in Copenhagen.[179]

§ **96** The only remaining records that can be referred to the reign of Takeloth I are Nile-level texts at Karnak whose authors do not even deign to name the pharaoh.

No. 16 dates to a Year 5, naming the high priest of Amun Iuwelot, son of a king Osorkon. The extensive genealogy of Djed-Thut-ef-ankh called Nakhtefmut shows clearly that the high priest Iuwelot was in the same generation as a daughter of the 4th prophet of Amun, Djed-Khons-ef-ankh A, who served under Osorkon I (Sekhemkheperre). Iuwelot, therefore, was a son of Osorkon I, not of II, III, or IV.[180] According to the so-called *stèle de l'apanage*, Iuwelot was but a youth in Year 10 of his father Osorkon I. Hence, the Year 5 in which he was high priest cannot well be that of Osorkon I, but must belong to a successor: Takeloth I, as Shoshenq II probably never reigned either alone or that long.[181] Three more such texts (Nos. 17, 18, 19) are dated to Years [*lost*], 8, and 13 or 14 under a high priest Smendes, son of king Osorkon, just like Iuwelot. That the dates belong to the same reign and that Smendes was a brother and direct successor-in-office of Iuwelot, is not yet susceptible of outright proof.[182] Along with the damaged Nos. 20, 21, these texts of Iuwelot and Smendes agree in not naming the king whose years are given, in complete contrast to *all* the other Nile-level texts which give either the date with the king's name (and perhaps epithets), or else add the high priest's name after that of the king, but never omit the king. Therefore, Years 8 and 13/14 with Smendes (III) should be regarded as following Year 5 with Iuwelot, and the whole most probably should be referred to the reign of Takeloth I. It is regrettable that No. 19 of Smendes has lost its date, and that Nos. 20, 21 preserve neither year nor pontiff; knowledge whether they were dated outside or within the series covering Years 5–14 would have been valuable. However, on this basis, one may assign Takeloth I a reign of not less than 14 or

179. See photo in O. Koefoed-Petersen, *Recueil des Inscriptions Hiéroglyphiques, Ny Carlsberg (Bibliotheca Aegyptiaca, VI)*, 1936, pl. V, No. 917, line 1. Likewise stela published by A. R. Schulman, *JARCE* 5 (1966), 33 ff., and pl. 13: 2.

180. More detail, cf. Part III, below, on high priests of Amun (§§ 157 ff.) and the Djed-Thut-ef-ankh family (§§ 183 ff.).

181. One may also, I think, exclude the reign of Osorkon II – we already have at least *three* high priests of Amun within his reign: Harsiese who became 'king', Harsiese's son (name lost), and Nimlot C, son of Osorkon II. And there is just a possibility of Nimlot's son Takeloth for a fourth. It hardly seems realistic to squeeze in two more.

182. e.g., no text as yet names Smendes III explicitly son of king Osorkon I in the way that we can discover for Iuwelot, rather than son of Osorkon II, III or IV.

(for safety) 15 years. Finally, Papyrus Berlin 3048, dated to Year 14 of a Takeloth, might also belong to the reign of Takeloth I; Takeloth II would also be possible.[183]

183. Published by G. Möller, *Zwei ägyptische Eheverträge aus vorsaïtischer Zeit*, 1918, 3 ff. Cf. comment on this document (on vizier Hory), below, references to § 298 end.

CHAPTER 8

Dynasty 23: Sequence and Reigns of Kings

§ 97 1. INTRODUCTORY

The foregoing chapter exhausts the known kings that can be definitely attached to the main line of the 22nd Dynasty. But a *second* series of Libyan pharaohs, constituting a 23rd Dynasty (whose memory survives imperfectly in Manetho), can still be constructed from the remaining kings set out in Chapter 6 above: a IVth Shoshenq, a IIIrd Osorkon, a IIIrd Takeloth, and some kings in § 78. Beyond these in a main succession, further 'local' extensions of the 22nd/23rd Dynasties can be placed, leaving only one or two minor kinglets floating still in time and space.

§ 98 2. PEDUBAST I, IUPUT I, SHOSHENQ IV

The starting-point of the Dynasty[184] must be king Usimare Setepenamun, Pedubast Meryamun. In the Nebneteru genealogy,[185] Hor viii is a contemporary of Usimare Osorkon II and the pontiff Harsiese; his nephew in the next generation, Hor ix, is contemporary with king Usimare Pedubast; and in the next generation, Nebneteru iv son of Hor ix is in turn a contemporary of Usimare Osorkon III – (see § 70, above). This series indubitably makes Pedubast an eventual successor of Osorkon II and a predecessor of Osorkon III. However, even if one allows that the father of Hor ix was a younger brother of Hor viii, and that Nebneteru iv might in turn have been a younger son of Hor ix, it would be biologically unrealistic,

---

184. Begun by Manetho with a 'Petubates' or 'Petubastis'.
185. See below, Part III, §§ 177 ff., with reference to Cairo Cat. 42226 and related material.

hence very unwise, to put Pedubast's reign much more than a generation or so after Osorkon II's time, say 20–60 years at the outside. However, the date of Pedubast in relation to the 22nd Dynasty must be considered after the reconstruction of his dynasty as an entity (cf. § 103, below).

Certain dated records of Pedubast are of special value at this point. In his 8th year, alongside the obscure vizier Paentyefankh, fragment No. 2 of the Karnak Priestly Annals mentions a high priest of Amun called Harsiese.[186] Then, Nile-level text No. 26 equates the 16th year of Pedubast with 'Year 2 of King of Upper & Lower Egypt, Iuput Meryamun'.[187] Nile-level texts Nos. 27 and 28 are dated to the 18th and 19th years of Pedubast in the time of the pontiff [Harsi]ese, while No. 29 is dated to his 23rd year but in the time of the high priest Takeloth.[188] Taken with other data, this material makes the reconstruction of nearly the whole dynasty readily possible.

First, Pedubast had a minimum reign of 22 or 23 years.[189]

Secondly, he had as co-regent a king Iuput Meryamun from his own 15th year (Year 16 = Year 2). Now, a donation-stela at Mendes is dated to 'Year 21 of Pharaoh Iuput' by Smendes son of Harnakht, the ruler of that city. The list of rulers of Mendes makes it impossible to identify the Iuput (I) of this stela[190] with the king Iuput (II) mentioned by Piankhy; therefore, we have here Year 21 of the earlier Iuput (I), i.e. of Pedubast's co-regent. This would make Iuput I Pedubast's successor with a minimum total reign of 20/21 years, and a sole reign of 10–12 years.[191] Manetho gives 40 or 25 years to Pedubast; the former figure seems grossly exaggerated, but the latter is close to Year 23 which is attested at first hand. On this basis, a 25-year reign may here fitly be assigned to Pedubast I, as being very close to reality. If Iuput I in turn be allowed 21 full years (dying in a 22nd year), then his sole reign after Pedubast's death would be some 10 years. Two or three monuments may perhaps be attributed to his reign: a statue-base of Usimare Setepenamun, Iuput Meryamun Si-Bast from Tell el Yahudieh,[192] a glazed plaque now in Brooklyn Museum,[193] and a bronze

186. Legrain, *RT* 22 (1900), 52, plus *RT* 26 (1904), 88, n. 1 on line 3 end.

187. Legrain, *ZÄS* 34 (1896), 114; von Beckerath, *JARCE* 5 (1966), 52. On Iuput, cf. *G3*, 381, nn. 1, 3, references, esp. Daressy, *RT* 30 (1908), 203.

188. Legrain, *ZÄS* 34 (1896), 114, and von Beckerath, *op. cit.*, 52.

189. Besides the Nile text No. 29, there is the Florence stela 7207.

190. For this stela, see Yoyotte, *BSFE* 25 (1958), 21 and fig. 3, and *YMM*, 125, Document 10, 132. For the rulers of Mendes, cf. *YMM*, 132, Kitchen, *JARCE* 8 (1970/71), 61–3, and below, Part VI.

191. A figure reducible by any years of Pedubast I beyond Years 22, 23, but which could be lengthened by any years of Iuput beyond his 21st.

192. Naville, *City of Onias & Mound of the Jew: Tell el Yahudiyeh*, 10–11 and pl. 1; *G3*, 382, II.

193. No. 59. 17; cf. Sotheby's sale of Hood Collection, *Catalogue*, 1924, with plate.

door-hinge apparently from Tell Moqdam (Leontopolis) bearing identical titles of the king along with mention of the Chief Queen, Tent-kat [. . .], and some obscure epithets.[194] While this series of works could belong in theory to the Iuput II mentioned by Piankhy, the latter was but a minor kinglet compared to the kings of the early 23rd and early-to-middle 22nd Dynasties, and so – having already the Karnak datum and Mendes stela – it is better to attribute them at present to Iuput I. If this is so, then one may say that in his cartouche-titles, Iuput I servilely followed those of his senior colleague Pedubast I exactly and completely.

§ 99   Thirdly, the high priests of Amun who were associated with Pedubast take us a step further. (For the bearing of the high priest Harsiese, cf. below §§ 103 ff., and Pt. III, §§ 157 ff.) By Year 23 of Pedubast, a Takeloth had succeeded Harsiese as high priest (Nile level No. 29). Just such a Theban pontiff, Takeloth, appears in Nile-level text No. 25, which is dated to Year 6 of Usimare Meryamun, Shoshenq (IV) Meryamun. As this king is with virtual certainty *not* to be identified with any other Shoshenq (cf. above, § 68), one may infer that this particular Shoshenq was a successor of Pedubast I and Iuput I, and that the high priest Takeloth officiated from at least the 23rd year of Pedubast I through to the 6th year of Shoshenq IV, i.e. at least 18 years on the reckoning adopted above for Pedubast and Iuput, plus 5 years of Shoshenq IV. It is very possible (in this writer's mind, highly probable) that this Takeloth was identical with the pontiff Takeloth son of the former high priest Nimlot son of Osorkon II, attested by a small chapel found at Karnak.[195] Takeloth would then have been a grandson of Osorkon II, a point which may be of possible chronological value. On the other hand, it is also possible that the pontiff Takeloth son of Nimlot had directly succeeded his father, being in turn replaced by Prince Osorkon (B) under Takeloth II; in that case, Nimlot's son would have nothing to do with our later pontiff Takeloth, but the latter would still be the link between the reigns of Pedubast I and Iuput I on the one hand and that of Shoshenq IV on the other.[196]

Otherwise, Shoshenq IV is barely attested monumentally. A Cairo scarab and the cone of an official Hor could pertain to either Shoshenq III or IV;[197] a lintel and fragment 18 of the Karnak Priestly Annals may really

---

194. Daressy, *RT* 30 (1908), 202–3; *BIFAO* 30 (1930), 626 f.; cf. Yoyotte, *BIFAO* 52 (1953), 190, n. 1.

195. Cf. Leclant, *Orientalia* 20 (1951), 462–3 (where read Usimare Setepenamun, not Meryamun, as prenomen of Osorkon); Kees, *MIO* 2 (1954), 361; differently, Kees, *Hhp.*, 113, 139–40.

196. See further Part III, §§ 157 ff.

197. Newberry, *Scarabs*, 185, pl. 37: 16; *G3*, 370, VI. Cones, Davies & Macadam,

commemorate Ramesses III.[198] As no other monuments of Shoshenq IV
are yet known, it is proposed here to allow him simply 6 full years as being
sufficient.[199]

§ 100 3. OSORKON III TO IUPUT II

At this point, the Nebneteru genealogy indicates how the Dynasty continued. Hor ix, contemporary of Pedubast, had a son, Nebneteru iv, who in
turn was contemporary with the king Usimare Setepenamun, Osorkon III,
who elsewhere has the surname Si-Ese. To this king belong the Nile-level
texts Nos. 5, 6, 7, of the 3rd, 5th and 6th years, while Nos. 8–12 of Years 12
(twice), 21, 22, could belong to Osorkon II or III (cf. §§ 73–75, above). As
also set out above (§ 73), No. 13 should be attributed to Osorkon III (not
II), Year 28, this being Year 5 of his co-regent Takeloth (III); No. 14 of a
Year 29 of 'Usimare Setepenamun' may also belong to him. These two
documents would imply 28 full years' reign plus a fraction for Osorkon III,
comparable with Manetho's 'Osorcho' for whom one can suggest ⟨2⟩8
years. Prior to the co-regency, Osorkon III would have had 23 years of sole
reign.

The co-regency of Osorkon III and Takeloth III is in any case established clearly by their joint work in the temple of Osiris-Ruler-of-Eternity
at Karnak (§ 72, above), and reason has already been given to indicate that,
before becoming co-regent, Takeloth had been Theban pontiff as Takeloth
son of the lady Tentsai (§ 77, above), and as king, in the year of his father's
death, a supplementary Nile text was inscribed for 'Year 6 of King . . .
Takeloth (III) Meryamun, Si-Ese, whose mother is Tentsai' (No. 4). As
high priest, he must have been a successor (ultimate, rather than direct?) of
that Takeloth who is attested under Pedubast I and Shoshenq IV.

Unfortunately, direct evidence on the length of reign of this Takeloth
after his father's death is sparse.[200] The Florence stela is of Year 23 of

A Corpus of Inscribed Egyptian Funerary Cones, 1957, Nos. 25, 26; G3, 370, V,
wrongly refers the title ḥm-nṯr to the cult of Shoshenq.
198. Legrain, RT 22 (1900), 58, 148; G3, 369, III, 370, IV.
199. The fact that Manetho has no Shoshenq here appears to give Kees pause
(Hhp., 139) – but needlessly, I think, because the names for the 23rd Dynasty in
our extant versions of Manetho (other than the obvious Pedubast and Osorko(n
III)) are practically worthless and also omit Iuput I (who indubitably belongs here),
Takeloth III and Rudamun, unless any of these are the enigmatic Zet. The '40
years' for Pedubast in Africanus might conceivably represent 25 years of Pedubast I
himself, plus 10 years for Iuput I, plus 5 years for Shoshenq IV. At least his total of
89 years for the whole Dynasty does agree well with the approximately 90 years
suggested in § 101 below.
200. I see no warrant at all for Kees's assumption (Hhp., 147) that Takeloth III
reigned only in Thebes, not in Lower Egypt – his monuments go as far north as

Usimare Pedubast, not Takeloth (cf. § 95, above), and so does not help here. However, we shall see later (Chapter 11, §§ 143–145) that a very probable 'Year 19' can be attributed to this king; hence, he may be given some 20 years total, and about 15 years of sole reign following his 5-year co-regency.

§ 101 At least two further rulers can be attributed to the 23rd Dynasty: Rudamun and Iuput II. On a large reused block found at Medinet Habu, the 'Lord of the Two Lands Rudamun' is called 'King's Son of the Lord of the Two Lands, Osorkon, justified, possessing reverence'.[201] The Osorkon concerned must be Osorkon III, for the cartouches of Usimare Rudamun Meryamun occur in the temple of Osiris which had been built and largely decorated by Osorkon III and Takeloth III.[202] The latter king would thus have been succeeded by his brother. In its full form, Ruda-mun's prenomen was the dismally inevitable Usimare Setepenamun.[203] It is highly probable that the Horus-name Neb-maat and Nebty-name Heken-em-maat belonging to a king Usimare in the Osiris-temple already men-tioned should be attributed to Rudamun,[204] as they differ from the known Horus and Nebty names of both Osorkon III and Takeloth III. But the Memphite statuette of this epoch which belonged to a king Usimare could belong to any one of eight or nine kings of the Libyan period.[205] Again, Rudamun is often thought of as a Theban kinglet, but there is no proof and no warrant for this assumption – his three or four mentions in Thebes is but the same accident of survival of Theban data rather than of Delta data, much as for his predecessors who undoubtedly lived in the Delta. The length of Rudamun's reign is still unknown, as no year-dates of his have so far been found. The relative paucity of monuments and the fact that he was a brother, not a son, of his predecessor both probably suggest a quite short reign. From a coffin-fragment belonging to a great-grandson [Pedi]amen-neb-nesttawy, we learn that a daughter of Rudamun called Ir-Bast-udja-nefu was the wife of Pef-tjau-awy-Bast, local king in Hera-cleopolis;[206] this worthy, therefore, was in all probability a contemporary (a slightly younger contemporary?) of Rudamun. As this same king Pef-tjau-awy-Bast was also a contemporary of Piankhy, this gives us a further

Abydos, the whole of the Dynasty is northern, and this position cannot rest on the wreckage of Manetho.

201. Daressy, *RT* 19 (1897), 20–1; *G3*, 392, 5, I.
202. *G3*, 392, 5, II.
203. Vase in the Louvre, *G3*, 392, 5, III, references.
204. Cf. long since *G3*, 394, 6, and esp. n. 4.
205. *G3*, 393, V, and n. 2.
206. Berlin 2100 (*LD*, III, 284*a*; *Aegyptische Inschr.*, *Berlin*, II, 540; *G3*, 392–3, IV, 393, n. 1, 401). Cf. §§ 108, 319, for this local king.

chronological indication – namely, that the reign of Rudamun probably did not long precede the invasion of Piankhy.

However, besides the petty kings of Hermopolis and Heracleopolis, Piankhy mentions as contemporary of Osorkon IV of Bubastis/Tanis, not Rudamun but a king Iuput (II).[207] As the only Delta pharaoh to be named alongside Osorkon IV of the 22nd Dynasty, this Iuput II must in turn be regarded as (so far) the latest-known representative of the 23rd Dynasty, and thus a successor – probably a direct successor – of Rudamun. The main line of the 23rd Dynasty may therefore now be set out as follows:

1. Usimare Setepenamun, Pedubast I: 25 years.
2. Usimare Setepenamun, Iuput I: 21 years. (Co-regent, 11 years.)
3. Usimare Meryamun, Shoshenq IV: 6 years.
4. Usimare Setepenamun, Osorkon III: 28 years.
5. Usimare Setepenamun, Takeloth III: (? years; 5, minimum; 19/20 years?)
6. Usimare Setepenamun, Rudamun: (? years, no dates – brief?)
7. ?, Iuput II:[208] (? years, no dates).

For the whole dynasty, remembering that all but 10 years of the reign of Iuput I were spent as co-regent, this gives us a total of 69 years from the accession of Pedubast I to the death of Osorkon III. To these 69 years must be added the three unknown figures for the sole reigns of Takeloth III, Rudamun and Iuput II. If the first reigned *c.* 20 years, 15 alone (§§ 143–145, below), and the second only a few years, plus an unknown amount for Iuput II, an additional 20 years would be an absolute minimum to add to our basic 69 years – in other words, the 23rd Dynasty lasted *at least 90 years* all told, and any chronology that fails to allow for this fact must be discarded.

At this point, three aspects of the 23rd Dynasty remain to be considered: its location in Egypt, its chronological relationship to the 22nd Dynasty (and the 25th),[209] and the local sub-kings at its end.

§ **102** 4. GEOGRAPHICAL LOCATION OF THE 23rd DYNASTY

Manetho derives the 22nd Dynasty from Bubastis and the 23rd from Tanis. It should be emphasized that these are *not* necessarily the capitals used by

207. Piankhy stela (*Urk III*, 1 ff.), lunette and lines 18, 99, 114; *G3*, 402, 6.
208. So far, no other references to Iuput II are known, hence his prenomen is unknown – unless the three monuments of an Usimare Iuput be attributed to him rather than to Iuput I.
209. In relative terms; absolute dates B.C. are dealt with in Chapter 11.

these dynasties, but merely their *towns of origin*. Manetho, for example, calls the 12th Dynasty Diospolite or Theban, which correctly defines its place of origin; but that dynasty in fact reigned from Ithet-tawy in the north as its capital. His statements here should be regarded in exactly the same way. Thus the 22nd Dynasty will have come from Bubastis,[210] but it took over (with the accession of Shoshenq I) the old 21st-Dynasty capitals of Tanis and Memphis, especially Tanis, and retained these till almost the very end.[211] Thus, in turn, the 23rd Dynasty will have originated in Tanis – i.e. as an offshoot of the 22nd Dynasty which was already there – but the new dynasty did not itself necessarily *reign* also from there. In fact, in strong contrast with the attestation of most 22nd-Dynasty monarchs in Tanis, practically *nothing* has been found there of the 23rd Dynasty – which would be passing strange if it were their real capital. The Tanite origin of Pedubast I might conceivably be illustrated by one monument: a bronze torso (Stroganoff collection)[212] is attributed to Tanis by Petrie.[213] But the supposed Tanite provenance of this piece is mentioned neither by Wiedemann who first published it,[214] nor by Gauthier or others.[215] The blocks attributable to a king Pedubast at Tanis belong, in fact, not to Usimare Pedubast I but to Sehetepibenre Pedubast II, local king there in the 7th century B.C. under the Nubians and Assyrians.[216] No other 23rd-Dynasty king appears at Tanis at all.

Rather, it is Piankhy's stela which gives us a clue to the real location of the residence of the 23rd Dynasty, by locating its last-known king, Iuput II, at Taremu (Leontopolis) which is now Tell Moqdam.[217] As noted above (§ 98), a bronze door-hinge of Iuput (I) and his queen was found there. One may suggest that, for reasons not wholly clear,[218] a 22nd-Dynasty pharaoh in Tanis had to take as co-regent and in effect as co-ruler,

210. Contrary to popular belief, the Serapeum stela of Pasenhor ('Horpasen') does *not* imply that the 22nd Dynasty came from Heracleopolis to assume the throne of Egypt. That link in the stela does not antedate Nimlot C, son of Osorkon II. The other Nimlot (A, father of Shoshenq I) is entitled simply God's Father and Great Chief, without any location. Nor does any other monument link either Nimlot A or his forebears with Heracleopolis. During the 22nd Dynasty, interest in that town was strategic and religious – nothing more.

211. Well illustrated by the frequent 22nd-Dynasty royal burials in Tanis – Shoshenq II, Osorkon II, Takeloth II, Shoshenq III – and their major works there, e.g. by Osorkon II, Shoshenq III and V.

212. Wiedemann, *RT* 8 (1886), 63–4; *G3*, 380, VIII.

213. *History*, III, 262, with erroneous historical conclusions.

214. *Op. cit.* (last note but one).

215. e.g. it does not come under Tanis in *PM*, IV.

216. Montet, *Le lac sacré de Tanis*, 1966; and esp. L. Habachi, *ZÄS* 93 (1966), 69–74.

217. On these identifications, see esp. Yoyotte, *BIFAO* 52 (1953), 179–90.

218. Cf. § 297 below.

Pedubast I. When in due time Pedubast I took a co-regent of his own (Iuput I), the result was in fact two parallel lines of kings. The senior line, 22nd Dynasty, continued to hold Tanis, which had long been the Delta capital, and Bubastis the old family seat – and did so, right down to and including Osorkon IV. The other branch, 23rd Dynasty, may therefore have adopted nearby Leontopolis for its own residence. Leontopolis had connections with Bubastis from the 22nd Dynasty onwards.[219] Harmose, royal secretary of Osorkon II,[220] had his name on a statue usurped there by his master, and probably on a block found in debris (reused?) in a tomb at Tell Moqdam. One chamber of that tomb had contained the burial of a queen, Kama(ma).[221] The spelling of her name which admittedly is defective does not agree very well with the name of Karomama, queen of Osorkon II, and the like-named queen of Takeloth II, but it would be an easy abbreviation for Kamama, queen-mother of Osorkon III of the 23rd Dynasty, who was presumably the wife of one of his predecessors. This would be further good evidence for Leontopolis as residence of the Dynasty, with its royal family being buried there just as the 22nd Dynasty was buried at Tanis. On the religious plane, Bast and Mihos of Bubastis were honoured at Leontopolis from at least the 26th Dynasty onwards.[222]

In Lower and Middle Egypt, inscriptions were commonly dated by the senior line of kings (22nd Dynasty), but sometimes by those of the 23rd Dynasty.[223] Both Dynasties were thus recognized throughout Egypt, and the 23rd Dynasty should *not* be regarded as a merely Theban line. Once the practical independence of the 23rd Dynasty was clearly established, the Thebans dated by its kings precisely because they could then ignore the senior line of kings, with whom they were in disagreement from the time of Takeloth II and Prince Osorkon. Both Libyan dynasties reigned in the Delta and enjoyed a comparable status throughout Egypt. By contrast, the petty 'kings' in Hermopolis and Heracleopolis at the end of the Libyan epoch were purely local rulers.

§ 103   5. DATE OF THE 23rd DYNASTY IN TERMS OF THE 22nd DYNASTY

Various lines of evidence bear on this question. In Upper Egypt, at Thebes, the official monuments – temples – owe their decoration to kings of the

219. Cf. Yoyotte, *BIFAO* 52 (1953), 191 and references.
220. For whose monuments, cf. Barguet, *Mélanges Maspero*, I: 4, 1961, 1–10, and Yoyotte, *BIFAO* 52 (1953), 191, n. 6.
221. Gauthier, *ASAE* 21 (1921), 25, 26; Yoyotte, *loc. cit.*
222. Yoyotte, *op. cit.*, 191 and n. 2.
223. Cf. various monuments cited in Part IV, Chapters 20–1, below.

22nd Dynasty from Shoshenq I down to Takeloth II (via Prince Osorkon) inclusively. Private monuments (for example, statues at Karnak, epigraphs in burials) extend from Shoshenq I down to Osorkon II and Harsiese, and possibly to Takeloth II.[224] The Nile-level texts, which hold an intermediate place, extend from Shoshenq I (No. 1, Year 6) on through the reigns of Osorkon I (No. 2, Year 12) and implicitly Takeloth I (Nos. 16–19, Years 5–14; cf. §§ 95–96, above), possibly under Osorkon II (Nos. 8–12, Years 12–13, 21–22; unless of Osorkon III) to the 5th year of Takeloth II (No. 3) and the 6th year of Shoshenq III (No. 23, high priest Harsiese). Thereafter, only one isolated Nile-text is dated by the 22nd Dynasty, No. 22 of Year 39 of Shoshenq III by the high priest Prince Osorkon. Similarly, the Karnak Priestly Annals[225] run from the 2nd and 13th years of Shoshenq I (fragment 4) via Years 1 and x of Osorkon I (fragments 17–34–37, 35), Osorkon II(?) (fragment 5, l. 1; Fitzwilliam No. 391) and Harsiese (No. 23) to the reign of Shoshenq III (fragment 5, first vertical line). Then, again, there is one isolated entry for his Year 39 made by Prince Osorkon (No. 7). The other clear mentions of this king have no dates preserved (Nos. 11, 19(?), 32, 44; Fitzwilliam No. 391). Fragments offering only a prenomen Usimare Setepenamun (e.g. Nos. 5, horizontal lines 2, 3; Nos. 6, 28; Fitzwilliam No. 392) could, of course, belong at first blush to any one of eight kings of this general period!

But once the reign of Shoshenq III is reached, *almost no further mention occurs of 22nd-Dynasty kings in Thebes.* So far, we have *no* definite Theban monuments of Pimay, Shoshenq V, or Osorkon IV.

Instead, the 23rd Dynasty obtains recognition at all levels. A text on the gateway of Pylon X at Karnak is dated under Pedubast I; so are the Nile-level texts Nos. 26, 27–28, 29, to his Years 16, 18–19, 23. Private statues can bear his name (e.g. Cairo Cat. 42226). The Karnak Priestly Annals, fragments 1 and 2, record his Years 7 and 8. Nile text No. 26 equates his Year 16 with Year 2 of Iuput I, a king who is known also by Theban graffiti. No. 25 dates to Shoshenq IV. At Karnak, the little temple was built and decorated in the names of Osorkon III and Takeloth III. Their names occur on private statuary of Theban dignitaries, and Nile-level texts are duly dated by their reigns (Nos. 5–7, 13, 4). In turn, Rudamun's name recurs in the Osiris temple of his precursors, and on other Theban fragments; only Iuput II is so far missing – as yet, securely attested solely on Piankhy's stela in any case.

The basic picture presented by all these sources together is consistent

---

224. See next note but one.
225. Legrain, *RT* 22 (1900), 51–63 *passim*, and for Fitzwilliam Museum fragments, Daressy, *RT* 35 (1913), 131–2.

and clear. In the Delta, both lines of kings were recognized as legitimate rulers, even if it was with varying emphasis. In Thebes, the 22nd Dynasty is recognized down to, and including, Shoshenq III – but thereafter, the Thebans ignored the senior line, and dated solely by the 23rd Dynasty, from Pedubast I to at least Rudamun. On this overall evidence, therefore, the 23rd Dynasty would have begun and have been accepted in Thebes by the reign of Pimay, or in the course of the reign of Shoshenq III. However, the facts permit one to go one step further.

The first factor is that, *after* *Year 6* of Shoshenq III with mention of the high priest Harsiese, the only other surviving dates of that reign are *those given by Prince Osorkon*. These are Years 22–28, 29, in his 'Chronicle' texts, and 39 in the Nile-texts and Priestly Annals. In other words, whereas Prince Osorkon seemingly never dated by, or accorded any open recognition to, the 23rd Dynasty, only by and to the years of the 22nd Dynasty (Shoshenq III), the Thebans generally accepted the 23rd Dynasty (spiting the 22nd) and could have dated by that Dynasty at any time after the 6th Year of Shoshenq III. The facts (i) that the Thebans dated down to Year 6 of Shoshenq III even when Osorkon's opponent Harsiese held power there, and (ii) that a few monuments and traces at Thebes other than those of Prince Osorkon are inscribed in the name of Takeloth II,[226] suggest clearly that the 23rd Dynasty did not exist until the end of Takeloth's reign or, better, until after Year 6 of Shoshenq III, prior to which date there was no alternative dynasty by which to date. Thus, with this date, we have a practical upper limit for the date of the 23rd Dynasty.

§ 104   The second factor is the control imposed by the Theban dated genealogies (utilized in §§ 70, 98, above). Three successive generations (a man Hor viii, his nephew, the latter's son) correlate with Osorkon II, Pedubast I, and Osorkon III. This sequence would allow the 23rd Dynasty to begin soon after Osorkon II (e.g. under Takeloth II), or if Hor viii's nephew was the younger son of Hor's brother (or his brother were a younger brother, anyway), rather later, e.g. with Shoshenq III. Adoption of the latter alternative is supported not only by the data adduced in § 103 above, but also by further genealogical data (cf. in part, § 70, above).

226. His Year 11 occurs in a text of a priest Harsiese (*G3*, 352, IV, and *BAR*, IV, §§ 752–4, with references; in Louvre), and probably Karnak Priestly Annals, fragments 26–7 (*G3*, 352, V; conjectural). His Year 25 dates a stela of princess Karoama (*ASAE* 4 (1903), 183). Other traces include a line of text at the Temple of Ptah (*G3*, 354, X), a reused block in the later temple of Osiris-Ruler-of-Eternity (*G3*, 354, XI) – both distinguished by the Horus-name from Takeloth III – and a leather band from a mummy, Berlin 6964 (*Aeg. Inschr.*, II, 539). This series of documents virtually rules out the recognition and (in Theban terms) even the existence of the 23rd Dynasty under Takeloth II.

From the statues Cairo Cat. 42228–9, we have a vizier Hor x, contemporary of Osorkon III, grandson-in-law of Takeloth II and directly great-great-grandson of Osorkon II through two female links and the pontiff Nimlot C. As Takeloth II was himself both son and successor of Osorkon II, there can be no real interval between these two kings, but there would have to be a full generation between Takeloth II and Osorkon III; there, as contemporary of the earlier years of Shoshenq III, one may locate Pedubast I. Thus, consideration of *both* genealogies – of Hor viii and Hor x – sets definite limits of credibility within which the beginning-date of the 23rd Dynasty must be set. That of Hor x indicates up to two generations at least between Osorkon II and Osorkon III: enough for Takeloth II followed by (Shoshenq III and) Pedubast I. But that of Hor viii warns us that the interval between Osorkon II and III *will not be more* than the time spanned by a man, his nephew, and that nephew's son, i.e. three generations (one, younger) or about 70 years or so. Thus, if Osorkon II were reigning about 870/850 B.C., Osorkon III should begin within a few years of *c.* 780 B.C.– and Pedubast I in between would be *c.* 820/800 B.C. approximately. The question of absolute dates B.C. is dealt with in the proper place below (Chapter 11), but these rough figures will serve to point out the implications of the data here discussed. And one thing here should be absolutely crystal clear. Because of these genealogies and the data in § 103, a date for the *beginning* of Pedubast I and the 23rd Dynasty as late as the time of Shoshenq V[227] (*c.* 760 B.C.) is firmly excluded. Such a date would set Osorkon III at *c.* 730 B.C., and certainly *some 120 years*[228] after Osorkon II. This is virtually a biological impossibility for the genealogy of Hor x and certainly so for that of Hor viii. In modern terms, few who witnessed the coronation of Elizabeth II in 1953 are likely to have had a grandfather or a great-uncle who could have witnessed that of Queen Victoria some 115 years before. Hence, the two Hor genealogies go with the other data in beginning the 23rd Dynasty with Shoshenq III.

§ **105**   A third factor is the length of time occupied by the 23rd Dynasty prior to the invasion of Piankhy. He knew nothing of Rudamun, Takeloth III, Osorkon III, Shoshenq IV, Iuput I, or Pedubast I – all were dead and

227. Such as supposed by Albright, *BASOR* 130 (1953), 10, and repeated most recently by Parker in the table (p. 25) of his otherwise excellent contribution to J. R. Harris (ed.), *The Legacy of Egypt*, 1972. Canonization of this ultra-late (and erroneous) date in such a standard reference-work will doubtless perpetuate its use by non-Egyptologists for a further generation.

228. Osorkon II being separated from Osorkon III by: 25 years of Takeloth II, 52 years of Shoshenq III, 6 years of Pimay, initial years of Shoshenq V (to accession of Pedubast I), 25 years of Pedubast I, and 16 years of Iuput I (sole) and Shoshenq IV combined – a grand total of over 122 years altogether.

gone by his time; their successor was Iuput II. Thus, all these reigns prior to Iuput II are prior to Piankhy. As shown above (§ 101), the 23rd Dynasty from just Pedubast I to Osorkon III lasted at least 69 years, to which the reigns of Takeloth III and Rudamun must be added (probably making the total c. 90 years). Even if one misattributed the Nile-level text No. 13 to Osorkon II and Takeloth II instead of to Osorkon III and Takeloth III, so as to take 20 years off Osorkon III, the $49 + x$ years still left simply will *not* fit inside the 37-year reign of Shoshenq V. And as the 23rd Dynasty cannot be reduced in this way, in any case, its real 70–90 years can still less be crushed into the reigns of Shoshenq V and early Osorkon IV, prior to Piankhy. Some 90 years before the *last* possible year of Osorkon IV (c. 715 B.C.) would set the accession of the 23rd Dynasty at c. 805 B.C., and as Piankhy's invasion was several years before, about 810/820 B.C. becomes more likely. We are thus, again, brought back to early in the reign of Shoshenq III, about 30 years or so after the death of Osorkon II, c. 850 B.C. in a round figure. These rough dates B.C. are here used simply because they may be easier to visualize. The same result obtains by reckoning reigns *without* dates. Thus, before Piankhy, x years for Takeloth III and Rudamun, 28 for Osorkon III, 16 for Iuput 1 (*after* co-regency) and Shoshenq IV combined, and 25 years for Pedubast I given a total of $69 + x$ years. The parallel 22nd Dynasty before Piankhy has Shoshenq V at 37 years, Pimay at 6 years, and Shoshenq III at 52 years – totalling 95 years. By this, Pedubast I would begin to reign in the year $26 - x$ of Shoshenq III, assuming that Osorkon IV and Iuput II had ascended their thrones together on the eve of Piankhy's invasion. (This is an unsupported and minimal assumption.) The amount x could be up to 20 years, *not* going back beyond Year 6 of Shoshenq III. Thus, the overall length of the 23rd Dynasty before Piankhy leads back, again, to the same starting-point: the first part of Shoshenq III's reign.

§ **106** While the total convergence of all lines of data, so far, to give the early part of Shoshenq III's reign for the start of the 23rd Dynasty is in itself a valuable fact, it is still not an *exact* synchronism. Can we do better? Most probably we can, on the basis of one piece of evidence hitherto rigorously excluded from consideration because of its possible ambiguity unless other evidence has been properly correlated first. This is the well-known Nile-level text No. 24 which can be read:[229] 'The Inundation: Year 12 which is Year 5[230] (of) the King of Upper & Lower Egypt, Usimare [Setepen]amun, Son of Re, Pedu[bast] (I), [Si]-Ese, Meryamun, given life

229. See von Beckerath, *JARCE* 5 (1966), 46–7, 48, 51.
230. See von Beckerath, *loc. cit.*

forever; High Priest of Amenresonter, Harsi[ese].' The reading of the king's nomen as Pedubast, not Pimay, was first pointed out by Daressy,[231] and is fully borne out by von Beckerath, who considered that the second regnal year was (though damaged) '5' rather than '6' with Legrain.[232] Thus, we have a double date of Year 5 of Pedubast I with a senior pharaoh in his Year 12; self-evidently, this co-ruler cannot be Pedubast's own later associate Iuput I (beginning only from Year 15 of Pedubast) – he can only be a king of the 22nd Dynasty. And, by simple arithmetic, if Year 5 of Pedubast is Year 12 of another ruler, the accession (Year 1) of Pedubast I will have fallen in Year 8 of the unnamed ruler. Who, then, is the unnamed ruler whose 8th year saw the accession of Pedubast I, and so the beginning of the 23rd Dynasty?

§ **107**   As seen above, genealogical reasons exclude a date as late as the 8th year of Shoshenq V. Attestation of Takeloth II in Thebes and the genealogical data would also tend to exclude a date as early as the 8th year of Takeloth II – Thebes accepted him without demur until the 11th–15th years (chronicle of Prince Osorkon). Pimay did not, so far as we know, ever reach an 8th or 12th year. Hence, the one solution left is the 8th year of Shoshenq III.

This date suits the combined total evidence perfectly. First, it comes just 2 years after the last *general* Theban date for this king (i.e. not merely by Prince Osorkon), his Year 6 with the pontiff Harsiese; it is the last non-Prince-Osorkon dateline of the senior line of kings yet known to us from Thebes. Second, giving the date ('Year 12') and no name, this dateline is transitional – preceded in time by full datelines of the 22nd Dynasty (before the 23rd existed), and followed by datelines of the 23rd Dynasty that omitted not merely the *name* of their 22nd-Dynasty contemporaries but all reference to them *at all*. Third, the pontificate of Harsiese, high priest under Pedubast in this double-dated text is identically that of the Harsiese who was in office in Year 6 of Shoshenq III, now just 2 years before; furthermore, the later activity of Prince Osorkon dovetails well with that of Harsiese.[233] Fourth, the requirements of the rest of Theban dating practice are now met; after this datum, all other records are in the names of the 23rd-Dynasty kings (apart from Prince Osorkon's). Fifth, the genealogical data are amply satisfied, as Pedubast comes to his throne very soon after Takeloth II's death, and is a generation ahead of the accession of Osorkon

231. *ASAE* 15 (1915), 147.
232. Von Beckerath, *loc. cit.*
233. See 'ready-reckoner' for this period, Part IV below, Table 6. The two pontiffs only once occur in the same year (25 of Shoshenq III, 18 of Pedubast I), perhaps in close succession.

III and behind the death of Osorkon II. Sixth, the roughly 90 years of the 23rd Dynasty run very satisfactorily from the 8th year of Shoshenq III down to about the 3rd year of Osorkon IV, i.e. to just after the death of Shoshenq V. The invasion of Piankhy could then come at any time after that point, assuming only the accession of Iuput II.

Therefore, in calculating the dates for the Libyan dynasties in years B.C. (cf. Ch. 11, below), the 23rd Dynasty may be deemed to have commenced in the 8th year of Shoshenq III, and be dated accordingly.

§ 108 6. LESSER KINGLETS OF THE PERIOD

On his famous stela, Piankhy records not two, but four, pharaohs in Egypt in his time. Two were the representatives of the main lines already dealt with (Osorkon IV, Iuput II), in the Delta. The other two are both Upper-Egyptian. At Heracleopolis, the long series of governors was succeeded by a kinglet Pef-tjau-awy-Bast. As son-in-law of Rudamun (§ 101, above), he would well fit in as contemporary of Iuput II and Piankhy. His own monuments attest his 10th regnal year, his prenomen Neferkare, and more of his family (cf. § 319 end, below). Prior to his reign, a long series of governors of Heracleopolis is known, down to Hem-Ptah B, father of the priest Pasenhor whose famous stela accompanied the burial of an Apis bull in Year 37 of Shoshenq V. One may best date Pef-tjau-awy-Bast after that date. After this local pharaoh, a gap occurs in our knowledge of rulers at Heracleopolis until the advent of Pediese and a new family, later in the 25th Dynasty (cf. further, Pt. III, Ch. 14, below).

§ 109 Further south, at Hermopolis, Piankhy's fourth king was a Nimlot. His Libyan name suggests a connection of some kind with the 22nd or 23rd Dynasty, and perhaps that he had been installed in Hermopolis by one of these lines. Two other kings can be attributed to the local kingdom of Hermopolis. The first is Thutemhat, who may have been either a predecessor or a successor of Nimlot, by whose favour the priest Tjaen-hesret ('man of Hermopolis') received a statue, set up in Karnak (Cairo Cat. 42212). Tjaenhesret was the son of a 4th prophet of Amun, Nakhtef-mut, and grandson of another, Djed-Khons-e[f-ankh]. This filiation occurs twice in the well-known Djed-Thut-ef-ankh/Nakhtefmut family (Pt. III, §§ 183 ff., below): once in the period Osorkon I–II, and once in the time of Osorkon III and Takeloth III. While Theban pontiffs with royal blood in their veins might have pretensions (Harsiese), a genuinely independent king of Hermopolis as early as Osorkon II is otherwise anomalous and unheard-of. This was not so by the time of Takeloth III or later, when the Libyan kingship had long been split between Tanis and Leontopolis, and Piankhy records a four-fold kingship. Hence, this Thutemhat may be considered as the immediate predecessor or successor of Nimlot; if Nimlot were directly linked with the main house, perhaps Thutemhat was a successor. A third kinglet who might be attributable to Hermopolis, with its Theban links, is Menkheperre ⌈Khmuny⌉ (cf. § 79 above). The name of his daughter Mutirdis and the style of his stela would not be inconsistent with making him a successor of Nimlot and Thutemhat, early in the 25th Dynasty.

§ 110 Finally, there remain a handful of lesser or doubtful names. For Pedubast II, Gemenef-Khons-Bak, and Neferkare at Tanis, and the much later Pedubast III, see already §§ 78-79 above.

The one doubtful name of any moment is the possible Was-neter-re Shoshenq VI. His very existence remains open to question; he might just possibly be an ephemeral successor of Iuput II, and is therefore conjecturally placed in that position until we know any better.

CHAPTER 9

Dynasties 24 and Early 26

§ 111   1. INTRODUCTORY

Manetho attributes only one king to the 24th Dynasty: Bocchoris with
6 years, the Bakenranef of the monuments. But the monumental evidence
indicates that he had predecessors in the rule of Sais, culminating in
Tefnakht who took full royal titles. Less clearly recognized are Bocchoris'
successors at Sais, ending with Necho I (father of Psammetichus I) whom
Manetho counts as the early part of his 26th Dynasty.

§ 112   2. TEFNAKHT, BAKENRANEF AND NUBIA

These two rulers form the essential link between the 22nd/23rd Libyan
Dynasties and the 25th Nubian Dynasty, helped out by Western Asiatic
evidence.

The earliest dated records of Tefnakht at present are two donation
stelae communicated by Yoyotte in his epoch-making study of the Delta
princedoms. The first (from Buto, by its content) is dated to a Year 36 of a
ruler left unmentioned, and commemorates a donation of land by 'the
Great Chief of the Mā, the Army-leader, Tefnakht', who is in addition
entitled 'Great Chief of the Libu' in the scene on the stela.[234] The second
stela, still at Buto, dates to Year 38 of a king, whose cartouches are left
blank, for a donation by 'the Great Chief, Army-leader, Great Chief
of the Libu, Prophet of Neith (i.e. of Sais), of Edjo (i.e. of Buto) and
of the Lady of Imau (Hathor of Kom el Hisn), . . . *Mek*-prince of Pehut
and of Kahtan, Ruler of the Provinces of the West, Te⟨fnakht⟩.[235] As we

234. *YMM*, 153–4, § 48.
235. *YMM*, 152–3, § 47, pl. I: 1.

have seen above (Ch. 7, § 84), these high year-dates can belong only to Shoshenq III or V. For practical purposes only Shoshenq V fits the case.

This powerful prince Tefnakht is visibly the same individual as that Tefnakht who secured the support of most of the Delta and Middle Egyptian chiefs and clashed with Piankhy, as reported on the latter's great stela of his Year 21. As ably demonstrated by Yoyotte,[236] this stela presents a picture which is closely accurate, of the hierarchy of chiefs and rulers – four 'pharaohs', the 'hereditary prince' of Athribis, the four principal chiefs of the Mā, and lesser chiefs and mayors. Outside of all these was Tefnakht, who is accorded a series of territorially-significant titles that indicate his rule of the West Delta all the way from Memphis to the Mediterranean.[237] Throughout, there is a striking correspondence between the powers and dignities of Tefnakht as transmitted to us by Piankhy's stela and by his own stelae.[238]

From this fact, it follows that Tefnakht's assumption of *royal* titles – Horus, Nebty, etc., cartouches – took place *after* Piankhy's invasion of Egypt and withdrawal to Nubia.[239] A stela of Year 8 of Tefnakht as king[240] indicates an official reign of 7 years at the least. The normal inference would be that Tefnakht adopted royal style soon after Piankhy's return south, erecting this stela in his 8th regnal year thereafter. It is theoretically possible to argue that Tefnakht adopted royal style after Piankhy's retreat, but reckoned his regnal years from some point *before* Piankhy's invasion; by this means, a later date for Piankhy's invasion is obtained, relative to the reigns of Tefnakht and Bakenranef. At the lowest extreme, one might argue that Piankhy's invasion came 7 years after a significant point for

236. *YMM*, 128–9, § 7.
237. For details, cf. below, Part IV, § 324.
238. *YMM*, 154–7, §§ 49–55, on these titles. The demonstrable accuracy of Piankhy's stela on this topic thus rules out absolutely the wild speculations by Goedicke (*BASOR* 171 (1963), 65) that Tefnakht's non-royal titles on the Piankhy stela were 'either indignities inflicted by' Piankhy 'or the result of misinformation' from Tefnakht's rivals. Alas, nothing could be less true. Also, Goedicke's ascription of further titles to this Tefnakht such as General of Heracleopolis from 'another inscription of Piankhy' (*ibid.*, 65, n. 11 end) is equally mistaken: the 'Piankhy blocks' from the temple of Mut at Karnak are pretty certainly contemporary with Psammetichus I almost a century later, and mention Somtutefnakht, an entirely distinct personage, cf. below, Part III, Chapter 14.
239. Otherwise, given the meticulous accuracy of Piankhy's account in all other prosopographical matters, his stela would have accorded royal style and titles to Tefnakht just as to the other 'pharaohs' (e.g. Nimlot who stoutly opposed Piankhy). This fact alone suffices to rule out Albright's suggestion (*BASOR* 141 (1956), 25) that Piankhy's invasion ended Tefnakht's rule and heralded Bakenranef's reign. A minimal chronology gained by these means is worthless.
240. The Athens stela; *G3*, 409, V.

Tefnakht, so we have a stela of 'Year 8' which was when Tefnakht adopted royal style. Thus, between the ordinary view and an ultra-late-date view, there would be up to 7 years of possible divergence. Is it possible to choose between these views?

The basic facts to start from are that Tefnakht as contemporary of Shoshenq V was still Prince of the West, not a king, as is shown by his donation-stelae of Years 36, 38 of that pharaoh; and that he continued as a non-royal Prince of the West contemporary with Osorkon IV and Iuput II down to and during the time of Piankhy's invasion. No circumstance had induced him to become a 'pharaoh' so far. But after that invasion, he *did* make himself a pharaoh – why? Two interrelated reasons suggest themselves. First, the representatives of the old Libyan dynasties, in particular Osorkon IV of the senior line, had not only submitted themselves to Piankhy but were at will dismissed by him as ritually unclean[241]– a humiliation that no real pharaoh of former times would have readily incurred. These 'kings' were now seen for what they really were – not real kings to whom all Egypt might owe allegiance, but just local chiefs like the rest, distinguished only in having inherited the trappings of royalty from more glorious predecessors. By contrast, Tefnakht alone had never kissed the foot of the conqueror, but as ruler of a realm that was as solidly united as it was extensive, he had remained proudly aloof and independent in Sais.[242] He deigned to go on oath to the Nubian's envoys, but not to bow to Piankhy in person, unlike those discredited shadows, Osorkon IV and Iuput II. Secondly, Piankhy made no attempt to settle in Memphis and take up effective rule of all Egypt, but simply sailed back to Nubia, content to have the submission of the local dynasts, and to retain the rule of Thebes – leaving a power-vacuum behind him in the north. As soon as this was clear to Tefnakht, he declared himself the new pharaoh in the north and reckoned his regnal years from that point, i.e. either from Piankhy's departure or from his own formal 'accession', two events which were probably close in time in any case. The Athens stela was then erected in the 8th year after his own accession.

If one adopts the alternative view, that Tefnakht reckoned his years from some point in time up to 7 years *before* Piankhy's invasion, what could the chosen starting-point possibly have been? It cannot have been the death of a previous Libyan pharaoh, such as Rudamun or Shoshenq V, precisely because Tefnakht remained Prince of the West, not king, under their successors Iuput II and Osorkon IV until the coming of Piankhy. There simply is no discernible event from which we may consider him to

241. Piankhy's stela, lines 148 ff., e.g. *BAR*, IV, § 882.
242. Note Yoyotte's observations, *YMM*, 158 top.

have appropriately dated in this way.[243] Therefore, we may proceed on the much more natural assumption that Tefnakht became king in Memphis after Piankhy's departure and dated from then.

§ 113 Tefnakht's predecessors need not detain us long. Most significant has been Yoyotte's publication[244] of the 'talisman of Osorkon', a faience amulet inscribed in favour of 'the Great Chief of the Mā, Army-leader, Prophet of Neith, Prophet of Edjo (and of) the Lady of Imau, Osorko(n)', connecting therewith the ushabtis of 'the Great Chief of the Mā, Osorkon'.[245] These titles are so close to those borne by Tefnakht that, as Yoyotte has inferred, we must see in this Osorkon a precursor of Tefnakht. Leaving Memphis aside, this prince already ruled the main core of Tefnakht's princedom of the West, and it is very possible that this Osorkon was Tefnakht's immediate predecessor, and thus probably a contemporary of Shoshenq V's middle years.

A still earlier prince of Sais(?) may be the Chief of the Mā, Pamiu or Pimay, son of the Lord of the Two Lands Shoshenq⟨Mery⟩amun, who dedicated a statue-group found at Sais. It is possible that this was the future king Pimay as a son of Shoshenq III, although there is no certainty on the point (cf. above, § 82 end). If this were the future king as governor of Sais, then one may posit one or two unknown rulers of Sais between him and Osorkon, the precursor of Tefnakht.

§ 114 In the version of Africanus, Manetho gives Bocchoris 6 years, a figure that agrees well with the date of 'Year 6' of Bakenranef attested for the burial of an Apis bull that probably died late in Year 5.[246] The burial (allowing for 70–75 days of embalming) would have been undertaken early in Year 6. There is every probability that this was the same Apis-burial that was dated also to Year 2 of Shabako.[247] This would mean that

243. Goedicke's claim (*BASOR* 171 (1963), 65, n. 14) that ante-dating of regnal years 'was by no means rare' cannot be taken seriously. During the first 25 dynasties (two-and-a-half millennia) of Egyptian history, the sole *certain* case is the attribution of the years of the Amarna pharaohs to Haremhab – and that by the Ramessides, not by Haremhab himself ('Mes-inscription'). There is *no* reason to assume this practice for Psammetichus I who would date in Sais from his father's death and as Assyrian vassal was effective ruler there from c. 663 B.C., his own 2nd year; thereafter, his 3rd and 4th years are reported (*G4*, 66,i, 67, II). There is no warrant here for assuming ante-dating – or for the rest of Egyptian history, either.

244. *BSFE* 31 (1960), 13–22, esp. 15–18 and figs. 1–2.

245. University College collection, London; Petrie, *Shabtis*, pls. 11, 18, 45, Nos. 475–6, and Yoyotte, *op. cit.*, 16, 18, fig. 3.

246. Stelae, Malinine, Posener, Vercoutter, *Catalogue des stèles du Sérapéum de Memphis*, I, 1968, Nos. 91–107, and cf. Vercoutter, *MDIK* 16 (1958), 341, E.

247. See paper by Vercoutter, *Kush* 8 (1960), 62–76, esp. 65–9. The wall-inscription of Shabako's Year 2 was in the same chamber as the Apis burial of Year 6

early in Bakenranef's Year 6, and before the vault of Apis had been finally closed, Shabako had gained control of Memphis. The final elimination of Bakenranef by Shabako must swiftly have followed. Thus, Bakenranef ruled in fact for 5 years and a fraction; Manetho's 6 years is a rounded-up figure. One may therefore reckon at least 12 years (7 of Tefnakht as king; 5 of Bakenranef) between Piankhy's invasion of Egypt and the reconquest by Shabako. It is noteworthy that the Serapeum epigraph of Shabako dates to his Year 2, not Year 1. He therefore spent his first year confirming his rule in Nubia, and only marched into Egypt in his 2nd year. No record of Year 1 of Shabako has yet been found in Egypt, but several of Years 2 and 3: Year 2, Nile-level text No. 30 at Thebes,[248] the Serapeum epigraph, and a donation-stela from Horbeit (Pharbaithos);[249] Year 3, another donation-stela, from Bubastis,[250] etc. Shabako's control of Egypt was thus complete in Years 2 and 3. If his reconquest of Egypt came in Year 2, which would have been 12 or more years after the invasion by Piankhy, then his accession in Nubia would have occurred 11 or more years after that event. Piankhy's stela is dated to New Year's Day (1st month of Akhet; day omitted, probably 1) of his Year 21, so the campaign to Egypt was probably in Year 20; hence, his death a minimum of 11 years later guarantees Piankhy a total reign of 31 years, perhaps slightly more. One may tabulate as follows:

Nubia	*Egypt*
Piankhy, Year 19–*x*	Death of Shoshenq V; accession of Osorkon IV
	Unknown interval
Piankhy, Year 19	Tefnakht expands southward, opposed by Nubian garrisons
Piankhy, Year 20: invasion of Egypt	Defeat of Tefnakht and chiefs.
Piankhy, Year 21, stela	Tefnakht becomes king; Year 1.
	Reigns at least 7 years (Year 8, stela)
Piankhy dies after Year 31 (32 or slightly later); accession of Shabako, Year 1	Bakenranef then reigns 5 years; death of Apis, Year 5.

of Bakenranef, cf. *ibid.*, 65 and n. 25. As Vercoutter observes, (i) there is no other monument from a separate burial of Year 2 of Shabako, (ii) one would have to suppose a burial of two bulls in one vault (as Mariette did), and (iii) the extreme closeness of dates, not more than a year apart (if Shabako *had* taken Egypt in Year 1 rather than 2) is too coincidental to favour the assumption of a further ephemeral Apis bull who lived less than a year.

248. Legrain, *ZÄS* 34 (1896), 114–15; von Beckerath, *JARCE* 5 (1966), 52.
249. Louvre E. 10571, *G4*, 13, II; on its provenance, cf. Leclant and Yoyotte, *BIFAO* 51 (1952), 27.
250. *YMM*, 134, n. 2; Shehata Adam, *ASAE* 55 (1958), 307 (without date).

Shabako, Year 2: goes North to re-
conquer Egypt: completes Apis-
burial, vanquishes Bakenranef
    Henceforth, Shabako king of Egypt and Nubia.

The only unknown quantities here are (i) the interval between the accession of Osorkon IV and the invasion of Piankhy which was perhaps quite
short (cf. Ch. 11, below), and (ii) any further years of Tefnakht beyond
his Year 8 (which would lengthen Piankhy beyond Year 32) – this, too,
was probably very short, and possibly nil. We therefore begin to obtain a
clear interrelationship of the Libyan, Nubian and Saite dynasties.

§ 115   3. ASSYRIAN DATA

Valuable hints towards establishing the absolute chronology of the transitional period from the 22nd to 25th Dynasties – from Osorkon IV to
Shabako – are furnished by Assyrian records under Sargon II. In the year
716 B.C., Sargon II's forces reached the 'River of Egypt' (Wadi el Arish),
and he received a present of twelve large horses from 'Shilkanni king of
Musri'.[251] As Musri is Egypt and not Winckler's imaginary North-Ara-
bian toponym,[252] Shilkanni is an Egyptian king and must be an (O)sorkon[253]
– in fact, Osorkon IV (Akheperre) of Tanis and Bubastis, the ruler closest
to Egypt's Palestinian border.[254] This datum immediately puts the death of
Shoshenq V in, or preferably *before*, 716 B.C. We thus have a basis for
minimal dates for the 22nd Dynasty (cf. Ch. 11).

    Thereafter, in 712 B.C., Sargon's generals invaded Philistia to suppress
the revolt of Iamani at Ashdod.[255] Iamani fled to Egypt, 'which now belongs to Nubia' (*Meluḫḫa*), but the Nubian king (according to the Display
Inscription) sent back Iamani in chains to the Assyrians. Other texts refer
more briefly to 'Pir'u king of Musri' ('Pharaoh king of Egypt') from whom
Ashdod and its allies had sought help in vain.[256] This ruler of Egypt *and
Nubia* cannot possibly have been either Osorkon IV of the 22nd Dynasty

251. For the date 716 B.C., and the texts, see H. Tadmor, *JCS* 12 (1958), 77 f.
    252. For ample refutations of the supposed North-Arabian Musri, see von Bissing
RT 34 (1912), 125 ff.; Olmstead, *Western Asia in the Days of Sargon*, 56–70 and
nn. 34 ff.
    253. On the phonetics of this identification, see Albright, *BASOR* 141 (1956),
24.
    254. And definitely *not* Osorkon III (Usimare, Si-Ese) at Leontopolis, much too
early in time, and further away from the Sinai border.
    255. On this date, see Tadmor, *JCS* 12 (1958), 79–84, 92–3.
    256. Texts, cf. (e.g.) *LAR*, II, §§ 62–3, 193–5; *ANET*, 286–7.

(or Iuput II) or Tefnakht and Bakenranef of the 24th Dynasty, none of whom ruled any further south than Memphis. None of these could *ever* be termed a king of Nubia. Only the 25th Dynasty will fit this definition – in the event it must have been either Piankhy or Shabako. Between these two kings, it is easy to choose. Piankhy reigned in Napata, and in Egypt was content to rule only as far north as the Thebaid, with Middle-Egyptian princelings as nominal vassals – until Tefnakht began to take over Upper Egypt and threatened to advance south towards Abydos and Thebes. Piankhy briefly ruled all Egypt *only* in his 20th year, when this expedition reached Memphis and Athribis, and Tefnakht who was ensconced in Sais made nominal submission. This was the *only* moment in time when an Assyrian envoy could have met Piankhy – and there is no particle of evidence for supposing *any* Egypto-Assyrian contact during Piankhy's brief sojourn in Lower Egypt. After his triumph, Piankhy swiftly returned south to Thebes and to Nubia, never, so far as we know, to be seen in Egypt proper again. Thus it could hardly be he who returned fugitives to Assyria. Therefore, the inevitable choice for Sargon's Pharaoh of Egypt and Nubia in 712 B.C. is Shabako, in the latter's Year 2 at earliest, but possibly in some later regnal year. That Shabako actually did have relations of some kind with Assyria is indicated by a sealing of his from some long-perished document found by Layard at Nineveh.[257]

Therefore, we can say that Shabako must have gained control of Egypt (in his Year 2) *by 712 B.C.* *at the very latest.* This in turn implies that Bakenranef was displaced by 712 B.C., that he began to reign 5 years earlier in 717 B.C. or earlier, and that at least 7 years earlier Tefnakht had adopted kingship in 724 B.C. or earlier, putting Piankhy's invasion of Egypt in 724 B.C. *at the latest.* In turn, the accession of Osorkon IV (and death of Shoshenq V) would probably be 725 at latest.

Furthermore, as it was Shilkanni, Osorkon IV, and not Shabako who dealt with the Assyrians in 716 B.C., one may suggest that in 716 Shabako had not yet taken over all Egypt. Hence, one may narrow down the date of Shabako's conquest of Egypt in his 2nd year to within the 4 years 716–712 B.C., and the death of Bakenranef likewise. This in turn sets narrow limits within 4 years' range for the accession of Bakenranef (721–717 B.C.), the minimal 7 years of Tefnakht as king (from 728/724), the invasion of Piankhy (728/724 at latest), and the death of Shoshenq V (probably 729/725 at latest). A closer definition (Ch. 11, below) must await the consideration of data on the Saite successors of Bakenranef and especially for the 25th Dynasty.

257. References, Tadmor, *JCS* 12 (1958), 84, n. 252; H. von Zeissl. *Äthiopen und Assyrer in Ägypten*, 1944, 22, n. 84.

§ 116   4. LOCAL SAITE RULERS

At Sais, between Bakenranef and Psammetichus I, Manetho begins his 26th Dynasty with the following four 'kings':

Ammeris (Ameres) the Nubian, 12 (var., 18) years.[258]
Stephinates, 7 years.
Nechepsos, 6 years.
Necho (I), 8 years.

When Shabako vanquished Bakenranef and took over Sais, it is reasonable to assume that he appointed there a governor of his own choosing – and for such a key post, perhaps a Nubian commander. Some such person may well be reflected by the mysterious 'Ammeris the Nubian' with 12 or 18 years found in two of Manetho's versions.[259] Then, probably after Shabako, under Shebitku or Taharqa, when a new local ruler had to be appointed in Sais, a member of Bakenranef's family perhaps obtained the post – the Stephinates of Manetho, perhaps a 'Tefnakht II'. He and his successors re-established a Saite dynasty (like Osorkon, Tefnakht and Bakenranef earlier), until Necho I under Assyrian patronage ruled Sais, Memphis and a large West-Delta kingdom.

§ 117   These kings are perhaps best considered in reverse order. The last and best-attested is Necho I, who was probably slain by Tantamani and who died in 664 B.C.[260] Prior to this, when reconquering Egypt in 667/666 B.C., Assurbanipal had reinstalled the various local princes who had been confirmed or established by his father Esarhaddon, including specifically Necho of Sais and Memphis;[261] he also appointed Necho's son in Athribis. According to the Babylonian chronicle,[262] Esarhaddon invaded Egypt in his 7th and 10th years, 674 and 671 B.C. He was repulsed at first and then met with success. Thus, Necho's appointment to Sais and Memphis as Assyrian vassal would fall in 671 B.C. If Manetho's 8 years be correct,

258. In Eusebius and Armenian version, omitted by Africanus. I render the Greek 'Ethiops' as Nubian, as geographically more accurate.
259. I see no merit whatever in Rowton's speculation that Ammeris is Tantamani and scepticism over Psammetichus I's predecessors, in *JEA* 34 (1948), 60. His identification is wrong date and dynasty.
260. Cf. also § 138 below. The accession of Psammetichus I and the 26th Dynasty of modern histories occurred in 664 B.C. (Parker, *MDIK* 15 (1957), 208–12), hence Necho I died in that year or earlier.
261. *LAR*, II, §§ 771–4, 902–5; *ANET*, 294, 295. Esarhaddon died in his 12th year (669 B.C.) on his way to Egypt.
262. e.g. *ANET*, 302b, 303b.

then one may suggest that Necho I began to reign as local king in Sais in 672 B.C., and had his rule confirmed and extended by Esarhaddon in 671 B.C. So short a reign for Necho I, followed (in Sais) by the very long reign of his son Psammetichus I (54 years) would suggest that his death had been premature – which would fit his being killed by Tantamani. Hence, we may retain Manetho's figure of 8 years for Necho I as probably correct. Original monuments of Necho I are but few;[263] a glazed statuette of Horus gives his full cartouches with prenomen Menkheperre.[264]

Necho's predecessor Nechepsos has often been identified[265] with the King of Upper and Lower Egypt, Nekau-ba, who was named on a broken *menat* amulet;[266] his prenomen (if any) remains unknown.[267] Manetho gives him 6 years – 678–672 B.C., if correct – but this is probably too short and may be for 16 years (i.e. 688–672 B.C., cf. just below).

Then there is 'Stephinates', to whom Manetho assigned 7 years. Unlike Necho I and Nekau-ba, we have no monument that can yet be assigned to him with certainty. Helck[268] considered Stephinates to be a possible equivalent of the name Tefnakht, and identified him with the famous Tefnakht who preceded Bakenranef. But it is simpler to retain this Stephinates as a local ruler at this point, whose Egyptian name is unknown or preferably as a 'Tefnakht II', as Petrie long ago suggested.[269] A 7-year 'reign' in Sais would run during either 685–678 (6 years for Nekau-ba) or better at 695–688 (16 years for Nekau-ba).

Finally, Ammeris could then precede all these kinglets as Nubian ruler of Sais under the conqueror Shabako, from his conquest of Egypt within 716–712 B.C. down to either 685 or 695 B.C. This would give Ammeris either 31/27 or 21/17 years respectively. The shorter span is more realistic and closer to the Manethonic figure of 12 or 18 years, uncertain as the latter may be. Hence, 16 rather than 6 years for Nekau-ba seems preferable and is adopted here.

§ 118   For the principality of Sais, we may give a first tabulation:[270]

263. On Necho I, see Yoyotte, 'Néchao', in *Supplément au Dictionnaire de la Bible*, VI, 365.
264. Petrie, *Scarabs & Cylinders with Names*, 1917, pl. 54: 25, 5. 1.
265. e.g. by Petrie, *History of Egypt*, III, 1905, 318–19; *G3*, 414, 4; von Zeissl, *op. cit.*, 56, etc.
266. *G3*, 414; *RT* 8 (1886), 64.
267. Conceivably the Iribre or Menibre of various scarabs, beads, etc., *G3*, 414–16.
268. *Untersuchungen zu Manetho*, 1956, 48, with other Greek forms.
269. Petrie, *History*, III, 317–18. However, the supposed prenomen Wahibre is unlikely and very problematical; one may prefer the Menibre or Iribre already cited.
270. For more precise dates, see below, Chapter 11, and Part VI, Table 4.

(Early 8th century): Pimiu/Pimay, under Shoshenq III?

(Early 8th century): One or two further governors, unknown.

Mid-8th century: Osorkon, Chief of Mā.

Later 8th century: Tefnakht, as Chief of Mā.

c. 728/4–721/717: Tefnakht as king, after Piankhy's invasion of c. 728/724.

c. 721/717–716/12: Bakenranef, king (Dynasty 24).

c. 716/712: Shabako, Year 2, reconquers Egypt.

c. 716/712–695: Ammeris, Nubian governor.

695–688: Stephinates ('Tefnakht II'?), 7 years.

688–672: Nekau-ba (Nechepsos), ⟨1⟩6 years.

672–664: Necho I, 8 years.

CHAPTER 10

Dynasty 25: Nubian Rulers

§ 119   1. INTRODUCTORY

Accurate dates that are generally accepted do not begin in Egypt until the 26th Dynasty, 664–525 B.C., formerly 663–525 B.C.[271] For this reason, and because the problems attending on late Dynasties 22/23 plus 24 are inseparable from issues affecting the 25th or Nubian Dynasty, the latter has been included in this book as part of the 'Third Intermediate Period' *chronologically*, even though in other respects (e.g. art) it would be better considered as an age of transition between the Libyan and Saite epochs.

§ 120   2. SUCCESSION OF NUBIAN KINGS

The succession of Nubian rulers connected with Egypt is clear and virtually beyond dispute, down to and including Tantamani. For the 25th Dynasty proper, Manetho's Sabacon, Sebichos and Tar(a)cos have long been recognized as the Shabako, Shebitku and Taharqa (or, Taharqo) of the monuments. Manetho's sequence of kings is easily confirmed from the monuments. That Shebitku was Taharqa's immediate predecessor is clear from Kawa stela IV (esp. l. 8) of Year 6 of Taharqa.[272] For the closeness in time of Taharqa and Tantamani ('Tanutamun'), one notes that these two kings are closely associated in the decoration of the little temple of Osiris-Ptah at Karnak,[273] and that the God's Wife of Amun Shepenupet

---

271. For 664 (*not* 663), see Parker, *MDIK* 15 (1957), 208–12, and Hornung, *ZÄS* 92 (1965), 38–9.
272. Macadam, *Temples of Kawa*, I, 1949, pls. 7/8.
273. *PM*, II, 95; *PM²*, II, 278; Mariette, *Monuments Divers*, pls. 79–86.

II (daughter of Piankhy) was a contemporary of Taharqa,[274] while a Cairo statue of her high steward Akhamenerou bears the cartouche of Tantamani.[275] The succession Taharqa–Tantamani is clearly indicated by the annals of Assurbanipal of Assyria who in Egypt first fought *Tarqu* (Taharqa) and then 'his sister's son' UR-*damani*, perhaps to be read Tanatamani.[276] Shepenupet II, contemporary of Taharqa, was also sister of Shabako[277] and daughter of Piankhy.[278] These relationships put Piankhy and Shabako by age in that order, and these two will in turn precede the series Shebitku–Taharqa–Tantamani.

Piankhy's predecessor was Kashta. Their sequence by generation (and so, also, by succession) is indicated by some doorjambs which were found at Abydos from a tomb or chapel of the princess Peksater;[279] she is named as daughter of Kashta and Pebatma,[280] and royal wife of Piankhy. On Kawa stelae IV (l. 17) and VI (l. 22), Taharqa refers back to a king Alara as having committed the concerns of his grandmother to Amun. Taharqa was a brother of Shepenupet II (to whom he gave his daughter Amenirdis II as heiress).[281] As Shepenupet II was daughter of Piankhy, so Taharqa was a son of Piankhy. A grandmother of Taharqa would thus be of the same generation as Kashta, while her contemporary Alara would then possibly be the brother and predecessor of Kashta.[282] We thus gain a full series of named Nubian kings: Alara, Kashta, Piankhy, Shabako, Shebitku,

274. Temple of Osiris Neb-ankh in precinct of Amun, Karnak; see Jéquier, *Les temples ramessides et saites*, pl. 79: 3.

275. Cairo *JdE* 37346, cf. Leclant, *JNES* 13 (1954), 155–6, pl. III, Vc.

276. The sign UR may be read Tan/Tana, if one notes the analogy of KAL being read as Kala (K.-H. Deller, *Orientalia* 31 (1962), 17: 173); cf. von Soden and Röllig, *Das akkadische Syllabar*, under 310, Tàn. For earlier suggestions on the reading, cf. von Zeissl, *Äthiopen und Assyrer in Ägypten*, 1944, 47, following Struve, *ZÄS* 62 (1927), 65, who took UR-*damani* as Tašdamani for *Taltamani*; cf. Vycichl, *Kush* 6 (1958), 177, d. The text, cf. *LAR*, II, §§ 775–8; *ANET*, 295.

277. Shepenupet II as adoptive 'daughter' of Amenirdis I, cf. *G4*, 25–7. As sister of Shabako, Mariette, *Karnak*, pl. 45d, cf. *G4*, 20.

278. Statue, Roeder, *Mélanges Maspero*, I, 433 ff.; another, Leclant, *ibid.*, I: 4 (1961), 85, fig. 6; cf. Greene, *Fouilles à Thèbes*, 1855, pl. 8: 1, *G4*, 26–7, and Yoyotte, *RdE* 8 (1951), 219, n. 1.

279. *G4*, 10; Amélineau, *Les nouvelles fouilles d'Abydos* (1895/96), 52–3; Legrain, *RT* 22 (1900), 142.

280. Pebatma was sister as well as wife of Kashta, cf. statue of the other daughter Amenirdis I (Cairo Cat. 42198). For the variants of the name Pebatma/'Pe-ab-ta-mery', cf. Leclant and Yoyotte, *BIFAO* 51 (1952), 36.

281. From the Adoption Stela of Nitocris, lines 3–4 (Caminos, *JEA* 50 (1964) 74 and pl. 8); Amenirdis II in line 16 (p. 75, pl. 9).

282. Alara is also named on Kawa stela IX, 54, of Aman-nete-yerike (the Tabiry stela), and probably as Piankh-Alara by Nastaseñ; cf. Macadam, *Temples of Kawa*, I, 1949, 121–3, and Dunham and Macadam, *JEA* 35 (1949), 141, No. 5. Alara's daughter Tabiry (by Kasaqa) married Piankhy.

Taharqa, and Tantamani. Their nameless predecessors and purely Nubian successors fall beyond the purview of this work.[283]

§ 121   3. ROYAL FAMILY OF NAPATA

The most essential family relationships are briefly documented just above; a few more may be added here.[284] The parentage of Tantamani is not absolutely certain; the 'Rassam Cylinder' of Assurbanipal calls him 'son of Shabaku', while Cylinder B makes him 'the son of his (Taharqa's) sister', cited above. It would be possible for Tantamani to have been a son of Shabako by an elder sister of Taharqa.[285] This solution, however, would make Tantamani the son of an uncle/niece marriage; and most scholars prefer – perhaps correctly – to take the Assyrian 'Shabaku' as intended (or an error) for Shebitku. As the latter was a brother of Taharqa, Tantamani would then have been the offspring of a brother/sister match precisely like the marriages of Alara and Kasaqa, Kashta and Pebatma, Piankhy and three of his five wives, and Taharqa and two wives.[286] So,

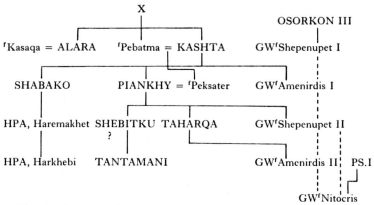

GW = God's Wife of Amun
HPA = High Priest of Amun
Kings in capitals; adoptive relationships, shown by broken lines.

283. Early burials, Dunham, *El Kurru*, 1950; later Napatan kings, cf. lists in Shinnie, *Meroe*, 1967.

284. For the further ramifications of the Nubian royal family, see particularly Dunham and Macadam, *JEA* 35 (1949), 139–49; also, Table 11 in Part VI below.

285. If no eligible brother of Taharqa outlived the latter, then his throne might presumably still pass to Tantamani if the latter were a cousin of Taharqa. But a son of the elder brother (i.e. Shebitku) would be the more eligible (cf. Macadam, *Temples of Kawa*, I, 125).

286. For all these marriages, cf. Dunham and Macadam, *JEA* 35 (1949), 149 Table, with its preceding list, and Macadam, *Kawa*, I, 120 ff.

provisionally, I adopt this latter solution here.[287] Shabako's son Hare-makhet and grandson Harkhebi each in turn became high priest of Amun (§ 157 ff.). The most essential relationships can be set out as above; for a fuller table, see Part VI.

§ 122   4. LENGTHS OF REIGNS OF NUBIAN KINGS

A. ALARA TO PIANKHY INCLUSIVE

The reign of Alara (like those of his nameless predecessors) is of unknown length, likewise that of Kashta, as no year-dates are so far known for any of these kings. As Piankhy son of Kashta reigned for at least 31 years (see § 114, above), one may suggest that he began to reign as a relatively young man, succeeding a father (Kashta) who had died possibly in middle age after a fairly short reign, perhaps following Alara who might have had an 'average' reign. Any figure for Kashta or Alara is bound to be guesswork; 20 years for Alara and about a dozen for Kashta may well meet the case, and is adopted here.

We have no evidence that Kashta ruled any part of Egypt north of Aswan, where a broken stela of his was found.[288] His reign perhaps marked the first phase of Nubian expansion northwards to reach Upper Egypt; thereafter, Piankhy obtained ascendancy as far as the Thebaid and in his 20th year sought to ward off the threat of Tefnakht. It is noteworthy that, the Aswan stela apart, Kashta's name occurs in Egypt almost solely in filiations in the inscriptions of his offspring which were engraved under his successors. Just as the throne and kingship passed from brother to brother initially, so it was doubtless Piankhy who installed his *sister*, Amenirdis I, as God's Wife (heiress-apparent) with Shepenupet I – not Kashta, his daughter.[289]

§ 123   The one generally-accepted year-date of Piankhy is Year 21 on his great stela. However, a minimum of 31 years is assignable to him on the

287. Refusal of this solution by von Zeissl, *Äthiopen und Assyrer in Ägypten*, 47, is based partly on assertions that are erroneous (e.g. that Taharqa was not son of Piankhy), and hence require no further refutation here.
288. On which see Leclant, *ZÄS* 90 (1963), 74 ff., with earlier literature.
289. So, despite von Zeissl, *op. cit.*, 68, whose contrary reasons are wholly inadequate. Thus, that Amenirdis I names her father Kashta in her inscriptions does *not* prove that Kashta installed her in Thebes. Shepenupet II, daughter of Piankhy, was still alive as late as Year 9 of Psammetichus I, 656 B.C., some 60 years after her father's death; she is most unlikely to have been installed by Piankhy, more likely by Shabako or Shebitku. That Amenirdis I was at Thebes before Piankhy's great Egyptian campaign is most likely – but that gives us 20 years of Piankhy's reign in which he could instal her in Thebes.

external evidence which is outlined above (§ 114). To these factors, a little more can be added. First, there are three documents dated by the reign of 'Pharaoh Py, Si-Ese Meryamun'– two papyri of his Years 21 and 22, most probably Theban, and the lesser Dakhla stela of Year 24. There is good reason to view Py as the real reading of Piankhy[290] and to attribute all three documents to Piankhy's reign.[291] Second, a fragmentary bandage from Western Thebes bears an obscure date of Sneferre Piankhy. The visible traces indicate 'Regnal Year 20', a patch and trace (the latter compatible with a '10'), and a shallow sign perhaps an otiose *t*.[292] In other words, we here have a date higher than Year 20 of Piankhy, and very possibly Year 30 – which would fit very well with the 31 years' minimum reign which has been already inferred on independent grounds.

The mention of Sneferre raises the question of the prenomens of Piankhy. He preferred simply his nomen 'Piankhy', sometimes with complements such as Si-Bast, Si-Ese, Meryamun, to the use of a prenomen; he is thus, Piankhy, on his great stela. He used the common prenomen Usimare (as at Gebel Barkal) and subsequently Sneferre.[293] There is certainly no room for a second king Piankhy, and so both prenomens must belong to the one ruler.

§ **124** This raises the question of whether Shabako and Shebitku also used more than one prenomen. The alternate prenomens Neferkare and Wahibre have been cited for Shabako[294] from a cornice-fragment from Athribis and a sistrum-handle from Bubastis.[295] But if this were so, it is surprising that the supposed second prenomen Wahibre occurs so rarely. The location of these two occurrences, in or bordering the former domains of the 22nd Dynasty, suggests another explanation: namely, that these pieces indicate an association between two local kings – Psammetichus I in his earliest years, and a kinglet of Tanis/Bubastis, who was very possibly

290. Cf. Leclant, *OLZ* 61 (1966), 552, arguing that the sign 'ankh' was simply an ideogram or complement.
291. On the identification of Py as Piankhy, and publication of datelines of the documents, esp. Dakhla stela, see Parker, *ZÄS* 93 (1966), 111–14, and J. J. Janssen, *JEA* 54 (1968), 165–72.
292. British Museum No. 6640; Greene, *Fouilles à Thèbes*, 1855, pl. 8: 3, 3a; I owe details of the traces to the kindness of Mr. T. G. H. James, although the interpretation offered is mine. Certainly, the traces with a clear blank next to the bottom 10-sign excludes the Year 40 suggested by Petrie, *History of Egypt*, III, 1905, 290.
293. Cf. Reisner, *ZÄS* 66 (1931), 94–7, on Piankhy's titles; sequence of monuments, cf. also § 329 below.
294. Cf. von Zeissl, *Äthiopen und Assyrer in Ägypten*, 14, after Reisner, *JEA* 6 (1920), 64.
295. Cf. Yoyotte, *RdE* 8 (1951), 221: 37 and n. 3; Berlin 8182, in *ZÄS* 21 (1883), 23.

the Neferkare of Tanis whom Montet isolated for this general period. Erasure of the Neferkare subsequently might indicate the suppression of such a possible rival by Psammetichus I.[296] Alternate prenomens of Shabako remain a possibility, but this other explanation is perhaps preferable.

The evidence for twin prenomens of Shebitku is hardly much more extensive. From the row of horse-graves associated with his burial at El Kurru, came a faience cartouche Menkheperre and a faience necklace of identically-styled, alternating cartouches Djedka(u)re and Menkheperre.[297] Here, at least, Djedka(u)re can only be Shebitku, which leaves Menkheperre to be accounted for. One might possibly assume amuletic use of the old prenomen of Tuthmosis III, but this lacks substantiation. One might assume that it was truly an alternative prenomen of Shebitku, but – even allowing for the limited number of his monuments – it is curious that (as with Shabako) this alternative cartouche is so very little used otherwise. There remains the possibility that Menkheperre is the cartouche of some vassal-prince. Two local princes bearing this prenomen are known: Necho I of Sais, and ⌈Khmun⌉y probably of Hermopolis. Necho I can be excluded on date – he is (at 672 B.C.) 20 years too late, if Taharqa began to reign 26 years before Tantamani and Psammetichus I at c. 690 B.C. (cf. below, and Ch. 11). ⌈Khmun⌉y is at least a possibility, as his date is not fixed beyond the Nubian period in general.

In short, Piankhy definitely had two prenomens, but preferred his nomen to either. There is no compelling evidence for crediting his successors with two prenomens each, but no decisive evidence against this, either. In this work, twin prenomens will not be assumed except for Piankhy for whom it is certain; three are possible (above, §79, n. 71).

§ 125   B. SHABAKO

For the reign of Shabako, the extant versions of Manetho give either 8 years (Africanus) or 12 years (Eusebius and Armenian) – both palpably wrong, as are the figures for Taharqa (18, var. 20 years, instead of 26).[298] For, the British Museum statue (24429) of a man Ity is clearly dated to Year 15, 11th day of the month Pauni, of Shabako.[299] In older terms, this would be Year 15, 2nd month of Shomu, Day 11, or in the 10th month of

296. Cf. below, § 357 and n. 904, also YMM, 179, n. 1.
297. See Dunham, El Kurru, 1950, 113 (Ku. 209: 19-4-71) and pl. 68: A2.
298. I see no point in juggling endlessly with all Manethonic figures as at present transmitted, as done by Rowton, JEA 34 (1948), 60–1. With him, I would agree that Manetho's figures in their original form were no doubt of the greatest value; but all too often, the extant text is all too obviously much corrupted. Cf. Helck, Untersuchungen zu Manetho, 1956, for many details, and Excursus F below.
299. Published by Leclant, Enquêtes sur les sacerdoces ... XXVe Dynastie, 1954, 15, 16, 18, and pl. V.

the civil calendar, which would have been late in the 15th year if the 25th Dynasty were dating its regnal years thereby. Thus, Shabako had a minimum reign of 14 years and a good fraction, and could have reached his 16th year, giving him 15 years. As Shabako conquered Egypt only in his 2nd year (§ 114 above), this means an absolute minimum of 13 years of rule in Egypt, and possibly 14 years.

As has already been set out above (§ 115), Shabako's conquest of Egypt (and his Year 2) must fall within the years 716–712 B.C. Hence, his absolute minimum reign of 13 years in Egypt would come within the limits 716/712–703/699 B.C., or at 14 years, down to 702/698 B.C. One may further suggest that it would be more prudent to assume that Shabako did not take over Egypt in 716 B.C. right on top of Osorkon IV's submission to Sargon II, or in 712 B.C. immediately before he had to extradite Iamani to that same ruler. Hence, one may suggest the closer limits of 715–713 B.C. as more realistic for the Year 2 of Shabako in Egypt (716–714, accession in Nubia), and hence place his death either within 702–700 B.C. after 13 years, or in 701–699 B.C. after 14 years. A closer date can only be suggested after consideration of the reigns of his successors.

§ 126   C. SHEBITKU

(i) *Lack of Official Dates*
For the reign of Shebitku, explicitly dated Egyptian inscriptions are still inadequate. The highest known date for his reign is Year 3 in Nile-level text No. 33 at Karnak. As Taharqa ascended the throne in 690 B.C.[300] and Shabako died within the extreme limits of 703/698 B.C. (cf. just above), it is unimpeachably clear that Shebitku must have reigned for not more than 13 years[301] and *not less than 8 years*. Therefore, this low date of Year 3 is of not the slightest value in estimating the length of his reign.

(ii) *Assyrian Evidence*
Further data suggest still closer limits for defining the date of Shebitku's accession. One is from Assyria. In the narrations of his third campaign, which was waged in Phoenicia and Palestine in 701 B.C., Sennacherib tells[302] how, when he had cowed Phoenicia and captured the rebel king

300. Cf. §§ 130-1, and Chapter 11, below.
301. Unless one combines with this datum Macadam's hypothesis of a 6-year co-regency of Shebitku with Taharqa in the latter's first 5 or 6 years, which would lengthen Shebitku's reign to 18 or 19 years – a highly unrealistic result; cf. §§ 132-7 below.
302. Texts, cf. Luckenbill, *Annals of Sennacherib*, 1924, 29-34 (esp. 31-2), *LAR*, II, §§ 240, 309-12; *ANET*, 287-8.

of Ascalon, he was confronted by the allied forces of Ekron and of Egypt and Nubia (*Meluḫḫa*), Hezekiah of Judah being a party to the league. This Egyptian intervention in Palestine against Assyria represents a radical new departure in 25th-Dynasty foreign policy. The last occasion on which Egypt had actively interfered here had been back in 720 B.C., when Osorkon IV or some other Delta ruler had sent out his commander Re'e to help Hanno of Gaza against Sargon II;[303] in 716 B.C., Osorkon IV did not dare oppose Sargon on the borders of Egypt itself. Then, in 712 B.C., when Sargon's forces were subduing Ashdod, Shabako (§ 115, above) remained a friendly neutral towards Assyria – unlike his Libyan predecessor in 720 B.C.– in so far as he complied with the Assyrian demand for extradition of the fugitive Iamani of Ashdod. Egypto-Assyrian diplomatic contacts under Shabako may perhaps be further illustrated by the seal-impression of that pharaoh from Nineveh.

Now, in 701 B.C., all is suddenly changed. From being a neutral (and possibly a friendly neutral), Egypt has moved over to the offensive, supporting with troops the kings of Ekron and Judah against Assyria. New policies, in a basic situation virtually unchanged, are commonly the mark of new men. Therefore, the drastic change of policy in Egypt at this time may well imply the death of Shabako (who had been neutral) and the accession of a new king, Shebitku, who favoured direct intervention in Palestine. On *this* basis, Shebitku's accession would fall not later than early in 701 B.C., possibly in the latter part of 702 B.C., if one allows for prior parleys between the new king and the emissaries of the anti-Assyrian Palestinians who were seeking his help. If this happened in 701, then (on minimum 14 years total reign, 13 in Egypt) Shabako would have acceded in Nubia in 715 B.C. and taken Egypt in 714 B.C.; on a 15-year total reign, and 14-year Egyptian reign, Shabako would have acceded to the Nubian throne in 716 B.C., and taken over Egypt in 715 B.C. If, on the other hand, Shebitku had come to power in 702, then on the minimum figures (14 years, 13 in Egypt) Shabako would rule Nubia from 716 and Egypt from 715; on the maximum figure (15 years, 14 in Egypt), he would have ruled in Nubia from 717 and taken over Egypt in 716 B.C.

There is little to choose between all these alternatives, none more than a year or two apart. Here, to allow for political intrigue between the new king and his would-be allies (plus readying his forces), it will be assumed that Shabako reigned for 14 years all told (13 in Egypt) and died well on in his 15th year; by this means, his conquest of Egypt will have occurred in *c.* 715 B.C., safely after the Shilkanni-incident, and his original accession in

303. *LAR*, II, § 55; *ANET*, 284/5; cf. Tadmor, *JCS* 12 (1958), 35, 37/8. On Re'e, cf. Borger, *JNES* 19 (1960), 49–53.

Nubia in 716 B.C. Consequently the reign of Shebitku was not less than 11 years (if it began in 701 B.C.), and was quite probably 12 years if it began – as suggested here – in 702 B.C. While there is nothing in favour of Africanus's figure of 14 years for Shebitku, devotees of Manetho will perhaps welcome the agreement between the 12-year reign proposed here for Shebitku and the figure of 12 years accorded him in the other manuscripts of Manetho (Eusebius, Armenian).

(iii) *Indirect Egyptian Data*

The fact that at present the known monuments of Shebitku are fewer than those of Shabako means little, is very easily exaggerated (contrast outline, below, §§ 347 alongside 342–343), and proves nothing as to length of reign. Shebitku's pyramid at El Kurru is comparable with that of his predecessor, for example.

The sketchy history of the Apis bulls at Memphis during the 25th Dynasty would also imply that Shebitku was not an ephemeral ruler. An Apis bull installed in the 14th year of Shabako and dying in about the 4th year of Taharqa would, on the dates suggested above, have lived for 16 years (last year of Shabako, 12 of Shebitku, 3 of Taharqa). This corresponds strikingly well with the average life-span of 16/17 years for pre-Ptolemaic Apis bulls (19 years for Ptolemaic ones) which was worked out by Vercoutter.[304] In more detail, one may compare this figure with those for the lives of other individual bulls of the Libyan and Nubian periods.[305] One born in Year 28 of Shoshenq III was buried in Year 2 of Pimay, aged 26 years; the next died in Year 11 of Shoshenq V, aged about 15 years; the next died in Year 37 of Shoshenq V, aged 16 years; its successor died in Year 5 of Bakenranef, aged not less than 13/14 years (on data set out so far) and probably a year or two older; the next died in Year 14 of Shabako, aged (from his Year 2) some 12 years; one installed about Year 4 of Taharqa died in Year 24, aged about 20 years; its successor, of Year 26, died in Year 20/21 of Psammetichus I, aged 21 years. Of these, three died notably older than 16 years, two or three at 15/16 years or approaching this, only one at but 12 years. Hence, again, 12 years for Shebitku and 16 years for the bull that completely spanned his reign fits perfectly – any reduction would tend

---

304. Vercoutter, *MDIK* 16 (1958), 340–1.

305. For these Apis bulls, see (i) Vercoutter, *loc. cit.*; (ii) Vercoutter, *Kush* 8 (1960), 68–9 (25th Dynasty bulls); (iii) Table of Apis Bulls, Part VI below. The interval from Year 37 of Shoshenq V to Year 5 of Bakenranef includes: last year (37/38) of Shoshenq V, plus a year or so for accession of Osorkon IV followed by Piankhy's invasion, plus 7 years of Tefnakht as king, plus 4 or 5 years of Bakenranef – a minimum, as Piankhy's invasion need not have followed directly upon the accession of Osorkon IV.

to be a deviation from norm, perfectly possible, but not to be looked for.

§ 127 (iv) *Kawa Stelae*

From the Kawa stelae IV and V,[306] we learn that Taharqa was a youth in Nubia when, aged 20, he was summoned north to Thebes with other royal brothers by the king, Shebitku – and they came north *with an army*, thereafter accompanying the king to Lower Egypt. Shabako, brother of Piankhy, had been the uncle of Shebitku, Taharqa and their brothers, having no known closer connection with them. It seems that, as soon as he was settled on the throne, Shebitku swiftly surrounded himself with his own brothers (who were the same generation as himself)[307] and for some reason began to collect together military forces. Is it too much to postulate the following sequence of events?:

1. Ekron and other petty states reject Assyrian rule and prepare against attack.
2. Death of Shabako (neutral) and accession of Shebitku.
3. Ekron and allies appeal for help to the new young pharaoh.
4. Shebitku decides in favour of an active role in Palestine and gathers his forces.
5. He at the same time summons his brethren (including Taharqa) from Nubia, together with an army; they meet in Thebes and proceed to Lower Egypt.
6. Egyptian and Nubian forces join up with those of Ekron, etc., in Palestine against Assyria; in 701 B.C., Sennacherib claims to defeat them at Altaku (Eltekeh).

This would abundantly explain why an army-force was moved from Nubia down into Egypt; Sennacherib expressly states that both Egyptian and Nubian forces were at Eltekeh. And it was commonplace for royal princes to accompany Egyptian armies when they campaigned in Syria–Palestine.[308] The sons of the Egyptian Delta rulers (*mare-šarrani*) are also explicitly mentioned by Sennacherib. Therefore, it is on these general grounds very probable that Taharqa and his princely brothers accompanied

306. Published by Macadam, *Temples of Kawa*, I, 1949; on his interpretation, cf. §§ 132 ff., below.

307. Cf. in some measure, the interaction of different generations with Rehoboam, his elders and his 'buddies' in 1 Kings 12: 6–14. That Taharqa came with an army and *slew* Shebitku, as late classical sources suggest, is manifestly false; on this point and the lateness of such sources, cf. J. M. A. Janssen, *Biblica* 34 (1953), 25 and n. 2.

308. e.g. sons of Ramesses II; *KRI*, II/3, 1970, 141, 144–5, 171, 174, 180, 183, 188, 191, and elsewhere.

their forces to Eltekeh in 701 B.C.[309] and quite possible that he himself was his brother the pharaoh's representative, nominally in command but supplied with generals to do the real tactical planning.

If Shabako had died in his 16th year, early in 701 B.C., it is possible that events 3–6 listed above could fit into 701 B.C., assuming that the clash with Assyria took place in the latter part of 701 B.C. But if (as suggested earlier) Shabako's death occurred well on in his 15th year, in 702 B.C., then the Assyrian clash could have come in the spring to summer of 701, and the sequence of events be a little less congested. Again, this may favour the 702 date for the accession of Shebitku which is adopted provisionally here.

§ **128** (v) *Old Testament Data*

Finally, the Old Testament reports a campaign of Sennacherib in Palestine.[310] As it stands, the main Hebrew account in 2 Kings and Isaiah is reasonably plain and straightforward, and is closely comparable with Sennacherib's accounts of his campaigns of 701 B.C.[311] One point apart, the Assyrian records for 701 B.C. and the Hebrew accounts agree sufficiently closely that they may well be regarded as all referring to one and the same war in 701 B.C.

(vi) *Taharqa and Shebitku*

The one point apart is the presence of Taharqa, called 'king of Kush' or Nubia, 2 Kings 19:9, Isaiah 37:9. From considerations in § 127 above and § 132 below, it should be obvious that *there is no reason whatever* to doubt that Taharqa could have been present at Eltekeh in 701 B.C., and a slight presumption in favour of him and possibly some of his brothers actually being with their armies there, then. Aged 20 or 21, Taharqa could well have been titular head of the expedition, with generals to advise him. One may note that the Assyrian accounts never state that the pharaoh came in

---

309. H. von Zeissl, *Äthiopen und Assyrer in Ägypten*, 23, 25, 26, would very plausibly suggest that the Egyptian army came in two forces or divisions – one defeated at Eltekeh, and a reserve-force that came up with Taharqa in person. This would correspond very well with the long-known custom of the pharaohs of deploying their forces in Palestinian campaigns in several distinct divisions – cf. Sethos I, Year 1 (Beth-Shan stela, *KRI*, I/1, 1969, 12); Ramesses II at the Battle of Qadesh (*KRI*, II/1–3, 1969–70, 2–147; Gardiner, *Kadesh Inscriptions of Ramesses II*, 1960, *passim*); Shoshenq I or 'Shishak', cf. §§ 252–8 and Excursus E, below.

310. 2 Kings 18–19; Isaiah 36–7; 2 Chronicles 32.

311. Despite much contrary fumbling by Old Testament scholars (of which a particularly jejune example is afforded by B. S. Childs, *Isaiah and the Assyrian Crisis*, 1967); for a reasonable outline, cf. below, § 346. It is not certain that Sennacherib's account is strictly chronological; he first deals with Ekron and the Egypto-Nubian forces, and then devotes a whole section of his narrative to Hezekiah in particular. Cf. W. J. Martin, *VTS* 17 (1969), 179–86, esp. 183–4.

person – this would agree with him having delegated the expedition to a brother such as Taharqa. The *sole* difficulty resides in just two Hebrew words: *melek Kuš*, 'king of Kush'. Taharqa's reign of 26 years ended in 664 B.C., and therefore did not begin until 690 B.C. (§§ 130–131, below), and certainly not as early as 701 B.C. Faced by this awkward fact, confused by the real problems of Late-Egyptian chronology, and (since 1949) mesmerized by Macadam's ingenious but erroneous views of 25th-Dynasty chronology (making Taharqa 9 years old in 701 B.C.), Old Testament scholars have produced all manner of theories to explain this little Hebrew phrase.[312] The two favourite explanations have been either to dismiss the phrase as an 'obvious' anachronism if only 701 B.C. is in view,[313] or else to invent a second, much later campaign by Sennacherib in Palestine after 690 B.C. (after Taharqa's undoubted accession), with the assumption that the Old Testament writers have telescoped the accounts of two campaigns into one.[314] But, in point of fact, neither hypothesis is necessary.

In the first place, no respectable evidence whatever has yet been produced from either Assyria or Egypt in favour of a second Palestinian campaign by Sennacherib or of a later clash between Egyptian and Assyrian forces; nor do the Hebrew texts really agree with a 'telescoping' theory. The sole 'evidence' is those two words, *melek Kuš*. In the past, Old Testament scholars have often shown little scruple in excising odd words and phrases that got in their way – they could as easily remove this one as a 'gloss' and be troubled by it no more. However, emendation should be the last, not the first, resort, and other avenues must yet be explored.

§ **129**   In the second place, it is totally needless to talk of 'anachronism' here. Taharqa was not king in 701 B.C., but he certainly was during 690–664 B.C., for a quarter of a century. In considering the Hebrew text, it should be carefully noted that the phrase 'Tirhakah king of Kush' is *not* reported speech of 701 B.C., but belongs to the words of the later narrators, either the writer of Kings or the prophet Isaiah. There is no difficulty whatever in assuming that the existing narrations were drawn up at a date

312. L. L. Honor, *Sennacherib's Invasion of Palestine*, 1926, reviews some 6 theories of the course of Hezekiah's rebellion against Assyria. For recent surveys of the problem, cf. (e.g.) H. H. Rowley, 'Hezekiah's Reform and Rebellion' in his *Men of God*, 1963, 98–132 (earlier, *Bull., John Rylands Library* 44 (1962), 395–431); S. H. Horn, *Andrews University Seminary Studies* 4 (1966), 1–28; J. Bright, *History of Israel*[2], 1972, 296–308.

313. e.g. Rowley, *Men of God*, 109–26 (*Bull. JRL*, 407–25), cf. 108, n. 2 (406, n. 1).

314. For adherents of this view, cf. references in Rowley, *Men of God*, 108, n. 1 (*Bull. JRL*, 405, n. 4), to which add Horn and Bright, *op. cit.*

after 690 B.C., when it was one of the current facts of life that Taharqa was king of Egypt and Nubia. Therefore, he was called by the kingly title for immediate identification, even in referring back to his activities of earlier days. The terminology one may choose for this mode of reference – e.g. prolepsis or the like – matters little. What does matter is that two points should be clearly understood: (i) such a mode of reference is NOT an anachronism in any ordinary sense, i.e. a 'mistake' by the ancient writer; (ii) precisely this mode of reference is well-nigh universal in the linguistic usage of mankind, from Taharqa's day to ours. If in current speech one says that Queen Elizabeth was born in 1926, this is precisely like saying that king Taharqa was in Palestine in 701 B.C.; only a fool and a pedant would seek to 'correct' the first statement, and therefore there is no reason to 'correct' the second where equally the identification of the individual mentioned is the reason for the use of the subsequently-acquired title. What is more, Taharqa and his scribes used *precisely* this mode of reference in his own inscriptions. In Kawa stela IV itself, we read:[315] 'Now *His Majesty* was in Nubia, being a goodly youth and a king's brother pleasant of love, and he came north to Thebes among the goodly youths whom His Majesty King Shebitku had sent to fetch from Nubia.' Taharqa was *not* a king when he was thus summoned as a youth from Nubia; but in Egyptian, the phrase *ḥm.f* 'His Majesty' is applicable *solely* to kings and gods. But, of course, when the Kawa text was drawn up, more than a decade after the event (*exactly* like 2 Kings and Isaiah), Taharqa as reigning king was – even as a prince – referred to by the later title, being now known as king.[316] No one has ever alleged an 'anachronism' here.

Furthermore, the view that the offending phrase 'Tirhakah king of Kush' is a phrase from the pen of the narrators from after 690 B.C. has direct support from the Hebrew text itself. For as a sequel to the Assyrian withdrawal from Palestine, both Kings and Isaiah include a final note on Sennacherib's violent end, when he was murdered by his sons (2 Kings 19:37; Isaiah 37:38). This event did not occur until 681 B.C. – virtually a decade after Taharqa's accession as king. This final notation on Sennacherib, therefore, gives us the earliest date – 681/680 B.C. – for the present Hebrew narratives, at which time one would *expect* Taharqa to be called king of Egypt or Nubia or both, and all reason for talking of 'anachronism' simply vanishes. Old Testament scholars must now go elsewhere, if

315. Macadam, *Kawa*, I, 15; pls. 7/8, lines 7 ff.; cf. Leclant and Yoyotte, *BIFAO* 51 (1952), 19–20.
316. Nor is this example unique; thus, on the Late-Middle-Kingdom stela Cairo JdE 52453 (Lacau, *Une stèle juridique de Karnak*, 1949), one Sobeknakht is referred to proleptically as Count of El-Kab at a point *before* he actually had acquired that office.

they are still in search of the 'errors' and 'anachronisms' so dear to the hearts of some.

§ 130 D. TAHARQA

(i) *Length of Reign*

As noted above, the 26th Dynasty began in 664 B.C. (§ 119). In official reckoning, its immediate predecessor was Taharqa, as is shown by the Serapeum stela Cat. 192 (IM. 3733)[317] which records that an Apis bull who was born and installed (4th month of Peret, Day 9) in Year 26 of Taharqa died in Year 20 of Psammetichus I (4th month of Shomu, Day 20), having lived 21 years.[318] This document would give Taharqa a reign of 26 years and a fraction, in 690–664 B.C.

However, the data furnished by this stela are not so straightforward as they seem.[319] The dates of the death and burial of this Apis are precise to the day, likewise that of its installation: 4th month of Peret, Day 9, to be understood[320] as Year 26, the year given for its birth without mention of month and day. The scribe who drew up this official epitaph evidently knew that the bull had been installed on 4th Peret 9, but was unable to find out its date of birth.[321] He assumed Year 26, and left its age at the round number of 21 years. As an afterthought, following the text proper, someone has hastily scratched the almost illegible entry, '20 year(s), 1(??) month, 4(??) days'.[322] Dying on 4th Shomu 20, this bull outlived the 20th anniversary of its installation (4th Peret, 9) by 4 months and 11 days.[323]

317. Latest editions of this stela (old no. 190), Parker, *Kush* 8 (1960), pl. 38 to p. 268, and especially Malinine, Posener, Vercoutter, *Catalogue des stèles du Sérapéum de Memphis*, I, 1968, No. 192, p. 146, pl. 52.

318. Strictly, 19 years, 11 months and 19/20 days from start of (incomplete) Year 27 of Taharqa to death in Year 20 of Psammetichus I; only 15 days short of the 21st year, if the 20th year is made up by the 26th full year of Taharqa. The 21 years exactly is evidently a round number, but close to the truth.

319. See Parker, *Kush* 8 (1960), 267–9 (apud Schmidt, *Kush* 6 (1958), 121–30), and Vercoutter, *Kush* 8 (1960), 72–6.

320. When two dates in the same regnal year are given, the year-number can be omitted as superfluous in the second reference (Vercoutter, *op. cit.*, 73, n. 65; Parker, *op. cit.*, 268–9), a usage known both in these Serapeum texts and in earlier times.

321. I see no merit in Vercoutter's suggestion (*op. cit.*, 75–6) that the date given as that of installation is an error for the birth-date; we know nothing of the scribe's sources, and a graphic error in terminology is in the highest degree unlikely (*ms.tw.f; šn.tw.f*).

322. One notes in the new *Catalogue, Sérapéum*, p. 146, the remark that 'this graffito did not exist when the photograph reproduced by Mariette was taken' – which would appear to cast doubt on the authenticity of this 'graffito'.

323. Perhaps the almost illegible summation was to record the lifetime of the bull since induction; but if modern, its testimony is worthless.

The actual date of birth of this bull remains uncertain. If it had been born very early in Year 26 of Taharqa, it would *at the most* have been 7 months, 8 days old at its installation on 4th Peret 9.[324] But, as Vercoutter points out,[325] Apis bulls were not normally installed below the age of about 9 months – this one would be 2 months too young. However, as the scribe acting in Year 21 of Psammetichus I did not know the birth-date of this bull, his 'Year 26' for this event may be an inference from the known installation-date of Year 26, 4th Peret 9, and nothing more. Therefore, we are at liberty to postulate that this Apis was in all probability born in Year 25 and that the precise record of this fact was not available to the scribe.

§ **131**   Nor does this end the matter. For the previous Apis bull died in Year 24 of Taharqa, and was buried in 4th Peret 23 of that year.[326] This leaves an interval of about 2 years until the installation of the next bull in Year 26 of Taharqa, the one whose birth-date could not be fully ascertained in Year 21 of Psammetichus I. However, this apparent anomaly is by no means unparalleled, is susceptible of at least two constructions and of a possible explanation.[327] Thus, long ago, Posener noticed an apparent gap of 4 years between the death of one Apis in Year 23, 3rd Peret 6, of Amasis and the birth of the next known bull in Year 27 of Amasis, well within the 26th Dynasty.[328] And according to an unpublished manuscript of Mariette which was rediscovered by Vercoutter, the seven intervals between 8 Ptolemaic Apis-bulls, from their death to their successor's birth, varied in length from 1 year or less to over 3 years (under Soter II). As Vercoutter noted,[329] this may be due either to errors of interpretation by Mariette or to different customs under the Ptolemies. But seven such errors in a row seem rather too many, while the variations in length of interval hardly seem consistent with a deliberate new practice.[330] Thus, the apparent interval of 2 years between the burial of one Apis and the installation of another in Years 24–26 of Taharqa is not unique in the light of later usage, however it

324. Parker, *op. cit.*, 268–9 and n. 7.
325. *Op. cit.*, 74; this is in relation to the new bull's procreative potency, *ibid.*, nn. 68, 69.
326. Stela in Louvre, IM. 2640, cf. Vercoutter, *op. cit.*, 71 and n. 52; now in Malinine, Posener, Vercoutter, *Catalogue, Sérapéum*, I, No. 125.
327. It would, therefore, be rash indeed to emend the 'Year 26' of the Serapeum Stela *Cat.* 192 to 'Year 24' to reduce Taharqa's reign by 2 years, particularly as the installation-date of the bull concerned was available in proper, detailed form.
328. Posener, *La première domination perse en Égypte*, 1936, 34–5.
329. See Vercoutter, *MDIK* 16 (1958), 341–2.
330. It is possible that there was no Apis bull at all for most of the reigns of Xerxes I and Artaxerxes I (cf. Vercoutter, *op. cit.*, 343–4), and of course Egypt was then under foreign rule and in intermittent conflict with those rulers.

might be explained. Furthermore, the 2 years' interval is from the death of one bull to the installation of the next – not to its birth, which would shorten the true interval to less than a year and a half.

Two constructions are possible to explain this interval. One may assume that the new bull was about 9 months old at its installation in Year 26, and was thus born late in Year 25, barely 1 year and 2 or 3 months after its predecessor's burial – a gap comparable with the shorter gaps between Ptolemaic bulls. On a reign of 26 years that ended in 664 B.C., Taharqa's 24th year would begin about February 667 B.C., and the Apis that then died would be embalmed and buried in about July–September, 667 B.C. The next bull would be born about December 666 B.C. in Year 25, if it were installed some 9 months later than this, in September 665 B.C., Year 26. The delays in finding a new Apis bull could reflect political events[331]– it was in 667 B.C. that Assurbanipal's forces first invaded Egypt,[332] and unrest continued after their conquest.[333]

Following Vercoutter's observation that a future Apis was frequently born very soon after its predecessor's death, the other construction is to assume that a new Apis calf actually *was* found in 667 B.C. (Year 24) before the Assyrian invasion, but that it was not ceremonially installed until nearly 2 years later – again, because of the political situation in 667–666 B.C. Either construction is possible and both assume that the scribe who drew up the epitaph 20 years later had no record of the precise birth-date of this Apis.[334] He only had the date of its installation in Year 26 (4th Peret 9), and so guessed at Year 26 for its birth (possibly only a couple of months out). The delay between the burial of one Apis and either the finding or installation of the next has a sufficient explanation in the troubled times of the Assyrian attacks.[335] The net result of this long but necessary inquest on one epitaph is that we have indeed, for the present, no reason to doubt that Taharqa reigned in fact for 26 years and a fraction, no more and no less, during 690–664 B.C.

331. Or merely the difficulty met by the priests in finding a calf that had the right markings to qualify it as the new Apis – perhaps they became increasingly strict on markings in the Late Period (with its great emphasis on the animal-cults) and hence had more trouble in finding an appropriately-marked animal.

332. In the official first year of Shamash-shum-ukin of Babylon (*ANET*, 303*b*), which is 667 B.C.; cf. Ebeling & Weidner, *Reallexikon der Assyriologie*, II, 414–15. One might hazard the suggestion that the Assyrian invasion perhaps occurred soon after the burial of Apis that year (Oct/Nov.?).

333. Note the passage, *ANET*, 294/5.

334. Record lost in disturbances of the Assyrian invasions?

335. Vercoutter's query (*Kush* 8 (1960), 73) whether the priests would have installed the new Apis in Taharqa's name if he were absent seems unnecessary; no one else was the acknowledged pharaoh of *all* Egypt as Taharqa had then been for a quarter-century – certainly not the Assyrians.

§ 132 (ii) *A Co-regency with Shebitku?*

While it is clear that Taharqa ascended the throne in 690 B.C., not all are agreed that he found it vacant in that year. In his splendid volumes on the Kawa inscriptions,[336] rich in their content and scholarly treatment alike, Macadam presented a new low chronology of the 25th Dynasty based largely on the hypothesis of a 5 or 6 years' co-regency of Taharqa with his predecessor Shebitku. From the Kawa stelae IV and V (cf. § 129 above), it is clear that Taharqa left Nubia as a youth of 20 with his brothers and an army, having been ordered by Shebitku to join him at Thebes, whence they went to Lower Egypt. Setting this late in Shebitku's reign (rather than at its beginning), Macadam suggested that Shebitku immediately associated Tarharqa with him in the kingship, but that Taharqa was not crowned until after Shebitku's death,[337] to allow for Kawa V, 15. Therefore, if Taharqa at 20 years old became co-regent in 690 B.C., he would be born in 710 B.C.[338] and be only 9 years old in 701 B.C. and thus almost certainly *not* be present at the battle of Eltekeh in that year. In his Year 6 (685 B.C.), Taharqa became sole king, and commemorated four 'wonders' in that same year on his stelae: taken by Macadam to be the high inundation of the Nile, a rainstorm in Nubia, Taharqa's coronation, and the visit to Egypt by the queen-mother whom he had long since left in Nubia.

This ingenious scheme has found a large and highly uncritical following among Old Testament scholars,[339] but has found very little acceptance among Egyptologists.[340] In point of fact, the objections to Macadam's

336. *The Temples of Kawa*, I, Oxford, 1949, plates and text.
337. *Ibid.*, 17, n. 17; 19.
338. The dates given by Macadam are 689, 709, but it must be remembered that these are based on the erroneous date 663 B.C. for start of the 26th Dynasty, and hence have to be corrected upward by one year as is done here.
339. e.g. Albright, *BASOR* 130 (1953), 9, 11 (table); Rowley, *Men of God*, 1963, 121; Horn, *Andrews University Seminary Studies* 4 (1966), 1–28; J. Gray, *I & II Kings*, 1964, 37, 602–6, 616, 623–4, etc., and ²1970, 660–1 (expressing scepticism); Bright, *A History of Israel*, 1960, 270, 282–7, and ²1972, 284–6, 291, 296–308. Horn's paper is little more than a re-work of Macadam's views applied to Hebrew history; neither he nor Bright faces up to the facts and arguments set out by Leclant and Yoyotte, *BIFAO* 51 (1952), 15–27, the documented warnings given by me (e.g. *Ancient Orient & OT*, 1966, 82–4) on the general rejection of Macadam's views by Egyptology as a whole. From this general stricture about Old Testament scholars ignoring Egyptian evidence, I would except J. Gray, *I & II Kings²*, 1970, 660–1, who has understood and applied some of the data offered by Leclant, Yoyotte and others.
340. e.g. Leclant and Yoyotte, *BIFAO* 51 (1952), 15–27; J. M. A. Janssen, *Biblica* 34 (1953), 26; Schmidt, *Kush* 6 (1958), 121–30, a study carefully avoided by OT scholars; Drioton & Vandier, *L'Égypte⁴*, 1962, 564, 572 table, 677; Sir A. H. Gardiner, *Egypt of the Pharaohs*, 1961, 344, 450; E. Hornung, *Grundzuge der ägyptischen Geschichte*, 1965, 128–9; Kitchen, *Ancient Orient and Old Testament*, 1966, 82–4; H. De Meulenaere in *Fischer Weltgeschichte 4, Die Altorientalischen*

hypothesis, for all its initial attractions, seem absolutely fatal for the varied reasons which are now to be considered.

1. Taharqa *cannot* have been as young as 20 years of age in 690 B.C., because he could not have been born so very late as 701 B.C. This is because his father Piankhy (§§ 120–121) had died (succeeded in Nubia by Shabako) *not later than 713 B.C.* and possibly as early as 717 B.C.– i.e. from 3 to 7 years *before* 710 B.C. and the supposed birth-date of Taharqa.[341] Reason has been given above for more precisely attributing Shabako's accession to the year 716 B.C. (§ 126, ii, end), thus leaving an interval of 6 years between the death of Piankhy and the birth of Taharqa. The only conceivable means of saving Macadam's scheme in the teeth of this evidence would be to invent ad hoc a 6 or 7 years' co-regency of Piankhy and Shabako for which no particle of evidence is yet forthcoming;[342] it is far easier simply to give up an obviously erroneous thesis. And in fact, there is no warrant either for assuming that Taharqa came north only towards the latter end of Shebitku's reign. The very opposite view makes far better sense. Thus, if Piankhy died 14 or 15 years (Shabako's reign) before the accession of Shebitku, Taharqa could hardly be any less than 15 or 16 years old at the latter event and would certainly be 20 by Shebitku's 4th or 5th regnal year, and nearer 30 than 20 by the end of Shebitku's reign, 8 years later. Furthermore, we have no *a priori* reason to assume that Taharqa was born so late as Piankhy's last months of reign and of life, or that he was necessarily the youngest of the royal brood of brothers.[343] In other words, if one admits that Taharqa was 20 years old *at Shebitku's accession*, he was probably the eldest of a small group of brothers, and even so born only 5 or 6 years before his father's death – quite late enough in these circumstances. He and they were thus summoned north, with an army, by the new king who wanted to have his brothers with him and doubtless to share in his administration.[344] It is therefore virtually impossible and certainly in the highest degree unrealistic to assume that Taharqa was

Reiche III, 1967, 244; W. Helck, *Geschichte des alten Ägypten*, 1968, 238–40. None of these scholars accept the imaginary co-regency.

341. Macadam had erroneously allowed only 12 years to Shabako, whereas BM 24429 *proves* that he reigned 14, possibly 15 years, as pointed out by Leclant and Yoyotte, *op. cit.*, 25.

342. It should be noted that the occurrence of *ankh-djet*, 'living forever', after Piankhy's cartouche on the BM statue 24429 of Year 15 of Shabako proves nothing; cf. Leclant, *Enquêtes sur les sacerdoces . . .* , 1954, 23 and references. Furthermore, this reference is to the cult of a *ḳny(t)* of Piankhy, such as is customary for the cult of *dead* kings. On this, cf. Helck, *Materialen zur Wirtschaftgeschichte des Neuen Reiches*, I, 1961, 119 ff.

343. His prominence in the group might suggest the opposite.

344. But not as an electoral college as much later under Aspelta; cf. Leclant and Yoyotte, *BIFAO* 51 (1952), 18 and n. 2.

only 20 years old in 690 B.C. and was born in 710 B.C. It would be entirely realistic to have him aged 20 in 702 or 701 B.C.

§ **133** 2. The fact that Taharqa was distinctly older than 20 in his first
regnal year in 690 B.C. (in fact 31 or 32) means in turn that Macadam's
interpretation of a key phrase in the stela Kawa IV, 11–13, is now excluded,
and that the interpretation of Leclant and Yoyotte must be accepted.[345]
Speaking of a Kawa temple, Taharqa says that he 'recalled this temple
(l. 13) which he saw as a youth in the first year of his reign' (*lit.*, appearing).
This sentence is ambiguous, as Macadam himself first noted, and as the
following punctuations indicate:

A: 'he recalled this temple, which he saw as a youth in the first year of his
reign'.
B: 'he recalled this temple, which he saw[346] as a youth, in the first year of
his reign'.

Macadam adopted rendering *A*, which implies that Taharqa saw the
temple as a youth in what became his first regnal year;[347] this was when he
came from Nubia aged 20 (Kawa V). As in cold fact he was *not* a mere
youth or aged but 20 in 690 B.C., this interpretation cannot be retained.
Instead, we must adopt rendering *B*, which indicates (i) as a youth,
Taharqa (aged 20, on his way to Egypt, *c.* 702 B.C.) had seen the temple,
and now in his first regnal year rather later in life (690 B.C.) he (ii) recalled having seen it and planned to work on it.

In this case, interpretation *B* is a good example of a noteworthy difference between English and Middle-Egyptian syntax. We would have
said today, 'he recalled this temple in the first year of his reign, which he
saw (had seen) as a youth'. But Middle Egyptian often prefers to leave an
adverb or adverb-phrase or equivalent to the end of a sentence in a manner
quite foreign to English.[348] And it is known that the 25th Dynasty liked to

345. See Leclant and Yoyotte, *op. cit.*, 20 f.
346. i.e. 'had seen'.
347. Macadam, *Kawa*, I, 18, n. 30.
348. Random Middle-Egyptian examples of the Middle and New Kingdoms
include: (i) Sinuhe B, 1–2 (R, 24–5), 'I heard his voice as he was speaking, I being
near (*sc.* him), at a distance (*sc.* from main body of camp)'; cf. A. De Buck, *Studies
in Honour of F. Ll. Griffith*, 1932, 58–60. (ii) Tuthmosis III, Gebel Barkal stela,
17 (*Urkunden IV*, 1233: 17), 'never was the like done by (any) king, since the (time
of the) god, of those who had previously assumed the White Crown'. (iii) *Ditto*,
29 end (*Urk. IV*, 1237: 7), 'There hewed them (*sc.* timbers) my army, in Kush,
who were there in millions'. (iv) Armant stela (*Urk. IV*, 1246 end), 'His Majesty
entered, on this path which becomes very narrow, at the head of his army'. And so
on.

follow ancient models in its inscriptions[349] and other works. Hence, both on the real *curriculum vitae* of Taharqa himself and on the Nubian use of older modes of expression, interpretation *B* is both correct and preferable, and the support of this passage for a co-regency vanishes.

§ 134   3. On Macadam's hypothesis, acute difficulties arise over the status of Taharqa during the supposed co-regency. In Kawa stela V, 15, Taharqa states with crystal clarity: 'I received the crown in Memphis *after the Falcon flew to heaven*', i.e. after Shebitku's death, expressed in the traditional manner. As has already clearly been seen by Leclant and Yoyotte,[350] that event coincides with the asseverations of Kawa stela IV, 11–13: 'His Majesty's heart was sad about it,[351] until His Majesty appeared as King, crowned (or: appearing) as King of Upper & Lower Egypt. (When) the Double Crown was established upon him and his name became the Horus Qa-khau, (then) he recalled this temple, which he had seen as a youth, in the first year of his reign.' Here, Taharqa appeared as king *when he was crowned and took a Horus name*. This corresponds to Kawa V, 15, already cited, and is clearly a crowning of the king, with giving of proper full titulary, *after* Shebitku's death – which event Macadam placed in Taharqa's 6th year, but which these texts (especially Kawa IV) and contemporary monuments would place in Taharqa's 1st year, thereby almost completely eliminating a co-regency. There can be no question whatever of Taharqa being crowned and enjoying the Horus name and other kingly attributes only as late as his 6th years onward. For we have a whole series of monuments, dated works, for his 2nd to 5th years that show he was full king, Horus-name Qa-khau and all, from his 2nd year onwards at least. Thus, Kawa stela III records a whole series of donations by Taharqa as king to the Kawa temple in Years 2–5 (not 6–8).[352] Taharqa appears as full king on two stelae of Year 3 from Medinet Habu, which record restorations there.[353] A series of papyri, private records, bear dates in Years 3, perhaps 4, and certainly 5;[354] two Nile-level texts at Karnak then follow in Year 6.[355] As Schmidt had correctly concluded, any co-regency (certainly, with an uncrowned

349. e.g. Macadam, p. xiii; Gardiner, *Egypt of the Pharaohs*, 340; Schott, in *Beitrage zur ägyptischen Bauforschung und Altertumskunde (Festschrift fur H. Ricke)*, Heft 12, 1971, 65, 66, 72.

350. *BIFAO* 51 (1952), 24; cf. also Schmidt, *Kush* 6 (1958), 123–7.

351. The ruinous state of the Kawa temple.

352. Published by Macadam, *Kawa*, I, 4–14, pls. 5/6.

353. Carter and Maspero, *ASAE* 4 (1903), 178–80; Gauthier, *ASAE* 18 (1918), 190; cf. Schmidt, *op. cit.*, 127, and n. 31.

354. References, Leclant and Yoyotte, *op. cit.*, 24, n. 3; Schmidt, *op. cit.*, 127, nn. 34, 35.

355. For which see von Beckerath, *JARCE* 5 (1966), 47–8, 53, Nos. 34–5 – not Years 5 and 6 (as read by Legrain, *ZÄS* 34 (1896), 115, and others).

Taharqa) could only have been for a brief period in his Year 1; and in fact, Kawa IV, 11–13, as dealt with above, would ultimately exclude even Year 1.

§ **135**   4. Macadam estimated that his supposed co-regency lasted to the 6th year, because it was only in Year 6 that Taharqa first recorded that he built a new temple at Kawa,[356] and because he considered Taharqa's four 'wonders' to include his coronation and the queen-mother's visit – events dated to Year 6 at the latest by Kawa V and parallels – besides the great inundation of Year 6, and the Nubian rainstorm.[357] This raises the question of the validity of Macadam's interpretation of the four wonders. Here, again, serious objections beset his thesis, alternatives can be offered that cope better with the total facts, and this without any need to invent a co-regency.

First, Leclant and Yoyotte have pointed out that in Kawa V – a copy of the Great Text of Year 6 – one should translate merely 'four wonders', not 'these four wonders', on both orthographic and syntactical grounds.[358]

Secondly, they point out that the 'four wonders' in the third main section of the text (*c*) cannot convincingly refer back to items in the section of text (*b*) *preceding* this phrase. This fact would automatically exclude two of Macadam's wonders, namely the great inundation of Year 6 and the rainstorm in Nubia. For, in two copies of the Great Text of Year 6 (the Coptos and Mataanah stelae), that second section (*b*) is *not* followed by the one (*c*) on the 'four wonders'.[359] Therefore, these 'four wonders' must be sought *within their own section*. As Taharqa's coronation and assumption of royal style occurred long before Year 6 (in Year 1, in fact, cf. § 134 above), the third of Macadam's list of wonders is excluded. Furthermore, the account of the queen-mother's visit is placed, not in close association with references to the 'four wonders', but after the intervening section on Taharqa's summons from Nubia as a youth, acceptance at the court of Shebitku,[360] and eventual accession. These are a fitting prologue to the account of Taharqa seeing his mother after many years away in the north – but they also separate her visit effectually from the account of the 'four wonders'. Therefore, her visit to the north, though noteworthy, was not one of the 'four wonders' either.

§ **136**   Thirdly, a re-examination by Leclant and Yoyotte of the section on the four wonders (Kawa V, 10–13) and its predecessor (Kawa V, 5–9) suggests a different identification for these.[361]

In themselves, the great inundation of Year 6 and the rainstorm in

356. Macadam, *Kawa*, I, 19, n. 30.   357. *Ibid.*, 19–20.
358. *BIFAO* 51 (1952), 16.   359. *Ibid.*, 16, 22.
360. For improved renderings of the passages Kawa IV, 7–9, and V, 13–15, see *ibid.*, 17–20, with detailed discussion.
361. See *ibid.*, 22–4.

Nubia were considered 'wonders' and are so termed in *all* four texts (long and short versions) of the Year 6. But just as a deficient inundation can mean famine, so an unusually-high inundation can have (or be linked with) ill-effects.[362] With Leclant and Yoyotte, Taharqa's words in Kawa V, 10–13, may best be taken as follows: 'And His Majesty said, "My father Amen-re, Lord of the Thrones of the Two Lands, has wrought for me four goodly wonders within a single year, in the 6th year of my reign ('appearing') as king. The like [has not been seen] since the (time of the) ancestors. The inundation came as a cattle-thief and it flooded this entire land; the like was not found in writing from the time of the ancients, and none said, 'I have heard (of such) from my father'. (But) he (= Amen-re) has given me good cultivation throughout, he has destroyed the vermin and snakes within it, he has kept away the locusts, and he has not allowed the South winds to reap it. (Thus) I have reaped for the Double Granary an incalculable harvest of Upper-Egyptian and Lower-Egyptian barley and (of) every seed that grows upon the earth." ' Again with Leclant and Yoyotte,[363] the four matching clauses . . . given, . . . destroyed, . . . kept away, . . . not allowed, must have Amen-re as their subject (not the inundation), as he might be credited with keeping off locusts and the South wind – but the inundation certainly could not.[364]

Therefore, the four wonders may be taken as these fourfold benefits of Amun whom the king considered had graciously eliminated the possible evils that could accompany an extra-high inundation of the Nile, allowing of good cultivation. The result was good harvests and prosperity, while the years before Year 6 may well have been marked by low Niles.[365] Difficulties in these early years followed by the blessings of Year 6 may help to explain both why Taharqa did not build at Kawa until Year 6 (nor his mother visit him till then), and why the grateful king in Year 6 then launched his building-programme at Kawa (and his mother felt able to visit him). In any case, Kawa stela III shows clearly that Taharqa gave constant attention to the furnishing of the existing Kawa temple right through Years 2–6. And Kawa V, 17–18, states explicitly that Taharqa's mother came to visit him, now king, only 'after a period of years', without specifying reasons for that interval.[366] Such a phrase would be much more

362. Note particularly *ibid.*, 23, n. 3, with references; and, in another context, G. Hort, *ZAW* 69 (1957), 91 ff.; *ZAW* 70 (1958), 50.

363. *Ibid.*, 22; so rendered also by Janssen, *Biblica* 34 (1953), 28, and by De Meulenaere, in *Fischer Weltgeschichte*, 4, 1967, 243.

364. For Amun as master of the waters and giver of the inundation at this period, cf. Leclant, *Recherches*, 1965, 240–6.

365. Cf. Leclant and Yoyotte, *BIFAO* 51 (1952), 23 and nn. 2, 3.

366. One may note here that Bright's assertion that Taharqa had hitherto 'never

appropriate for a real span of years up to 16 or 17 years (11 or 12 of Shebitku, 5 of Taharqa) than merely the first 5 years of Taharqa during the imaginary co-regency.

§137 5. Finally, one may note that Macadam posited an 'association' or possibly a co-regency between Shabako and Shebitku during the latter's first 2 years, basing himself on Nile-level text No. 33 at Karnak,[367] which has been understood to mean that Shebitku was crowned as late as his 3rd year and at Karnak. However, while one *may* read this into the text if one desires it earnestly enough, there is no reason whatever to do so. The text may be rendered:[368] 'Year 3, x[369] month of Shomu, Day 5, under the Majesty of . . . (titles) . . . Shebitku, beloved of Amen-re, Lord of the Throne(s) of the Two Lands, [. . .]. Now, His Majesty appeared in the Temple of Amun,[370] (when) he (= Amun) granted to him that he should appear with the two serpent-goddesses/to the Two Lands,[371] like Horus on the throne of Re. His father Amun the great has accorded him an exceedingly great inundation. Great is the inundation in his time. 20 (cubits), 2 palms.' 'To appear', with or without complement 'as king' can, of course, mean the accession and initial crowning of a pharaoh; so, in Kawa IV, 11–12, to go no further. But this verb *ḫꜥi* applies to *any* official 'epiphany' or official manifestation of the king, to his 'public appearances' to use a modern approximate equivalent.[372] Also, the first month of Shomu, days 1–5, are the date of a festival of Amen-re of Karnak which has been well-attested from the 18th Dynasty (Tuthmosis III, Amenophis II), through the 20th (Ramesses III) and 22nd (Osorkon II, Takeloth II) to the Ptolemaic period (Bentresh stela).[373] In the 3rd year of Shebitku, this

been separated from his mother in Nubia' when aged 20 and that Taharqa was only 'an untried youth' at 20 (*History of Israel*[2], 1972, 298, and n. 9) goes beyond what the Kawa stelae actually say. As regards the youthfulness of Taharqa, he and his friends were trusted by Shebitku to bring an army well over 1,000 miles down the Nile valley (including some very difficult stretches) to Thebes and Memphis. As I have stated elsewhere, there is no reason to doubt that Taharqa at Eltekeh had generals and advisors with him (a point evaded by Bright). Youthfulness is no bar to military activity in the ancient Near East; cf. K. C. Seele, *The Coregency of Ramses II with Seti I.*., 1940, 27, 36–7, who saw no difficulty in young pharaonic princes going to war.   367. Macadam, *Kawa*, I, 19, 20.

368. Following new copy of von Beckerath, *JARCE* 5 (1966), 53 (cf. also Leclant, *Recherches*, 1965, 243).

369. Number omitted, but probably (with Leclant) to be taken as '1st'.

370. Legrain had here *m nsw*, 'as king'– this phrase is not present in von Beckerath's new copy.

371. Just possibly: 'He gave him his crown with two uraei'. For this spelling of *tꜣwy*, cf. Erman & Grapow, *Wörterbuch der Aegyptischen Sprache*, V, 217.

372. Cf. D. B. Redford, *History and Chronology of the Eighteenth Dynasty of Egypt*, 1967, 19–22, 25, 27.

373. See references in Schott, *Altägyptische Festdaten*, 1950, 104–5, Nos. 139–46.

feast evidently coincided with the inundation – and with a visit to Amun of Karnak (on his feast-days) by the king in person (perhaps even on his accession anniversary?), but we have no warrant whatever for assuming that Shebitku had remained uncrowned for 2 whole years after his accession.[374] As is clear from assured co-regencies in the 12th,[375] 18th,[376] and 22nd/23rd Dynasties,[377] a co-regent in Egyptian usage was given *all* the attributes of kingship – crowns, titulary, regnal years, etc. – at his initial accession *as co-regent*, and was crowned then; he needed *no* further induction or coronation at the senior co-regent's death. Hence, there is neither clear evidence nor any necessity to assume a co-regency between Shabako and Shebitku, or between any of the Nubian rulers from Alara down to Taharqa; and there is no warrant whatsoever for assuming *any* recrowning of a real king at the end of a normal co-regency. What is more Taharqa's own words in Kawa V, 15, go with this situation perfectly: he was crowned and given his pharaonic titles at the death of Shebitku, because it was after the death of Shebitku that he first became king. Let this point be understood clearly, once and for all: there is *no* co-regency of Shebitku and Taharqa mentioned anywhere in the Kawa inscriptions. A co-regency was one possibility based on Macadam's *interpretation* of those texts, and a co-regency features nowhere in the texts themselves. Furthermore, reconsideration of those very texts plus setting Nubian dates in their wider context of Late Libyan and early Saite chronology, combined with precise Assyrian evidence, virtually rules out such an assumed co-regency completely.

Let it be recalled in closing, that the accession of Shabako is *independently fixed* to 717–712 B.C. at the extremes, and is most likely to be in 716 B.C.; that his death and the accession of Shebitku is correspondingly fixed within 703/702 B.C. to 699/698 B.C. at the extremes, and is most likely 702 B.C., perhaps 701 B.C. Taharqa's accession *as a full king* came in 690 B.C. Therefore, *if* Shebitku had ever had a co-regency with Taharqa of 5 or 6 years, it would have to be added to a minimum reign of 11 or 12 years – making his total reign up to 18 years. And 20 years, if the Shabako–Shebitku co-regency were added. This range of figures goes quite beyond all reality on our current knowledge of the monuments and activities of the 25th Dynasty and stands self-condemned. So, once again, ludicrous results

374. Any more than one should assume Taharqa was co-regent uncrowned for six years; and once crowned, an Egyptian king needed no second enthronement.

375. e.g. Amenemhat I and Sesostris I (W. K. Simpson, *JNES* 15 (1956), 214 ff.).

376. e.g. Tuthmosis III and Amenophis II (R. A. Parker in *Studies in Honor of John A. Wilson*, 1969, 75–82).

377. Pedubast I and Iuput I; Osorkon III and Takeloth III, Chapter 8 above.

are to be avoided only if the imaginary co-regency of Macadam be definitively abandoned.[378]

Thus, Macadam's scheme was ingenious but fails to fit the total facts. The foregoing close criticism of that scheme, of course, does not touch at all the vast and solid gains represented by Macadam's epoch-making publication of the Kawa texts; his treatment of the relationships of the Nubian royal family[379] has brilliantly stood the test of time for the most part, and we all remain forever in his debt.

E. TANTAMANI

§ 138 Finally the reign of Tantamani may briefly be reviewed. As we have already seen (§§ 130–131, above), however its exact details be interpreted, the Serapeum stela Cat. 192 (old 190, IM. 3733) indicates that Psammetichus I reckoned his years in direct succession to Taharqa, and so did not recognize any intervening reign of Tantamani. In other words, the reigns of Tantamani and Psammetichus I ran concurrently, in Upper and Lower Egypt respectively, from the death of Taharqa. But more locally, in the West Delta, Psammetichus I was also successor to his own father Necho I. It seems that Necho I perished in 664 B.C., when Tantamani briefly reconquered Egypt from the Assyrians and their *protégés* of whom Necho I was the chief.[380] Thus, coincidentally, the reigns of Taharqa in Nubia and of Necho I in Sais ended within months of each other, so that the reigns of Tantamani in the south and of Psammetichus I (in Sais or as a fugitive) likewise began in the same year.[381]

§ 139 It has long been recognized as significant that the latest year-date of Tantamani in Upper Egypt is a Theban stela of his 8th year,[382] while the earliest recognition of Psammetichus I in Thebes is in his 9th year, when his daughter Nitocris arrived at Thebes to be adopted as God's Wife of Amun, elect.[383] The interval between the 3rd month of Peret in Year 8 of

378. Thus, the rejection of the hypothetical co-regency by the majority of Egyptologists stands upheld and fully justified. It is to be hoped that their Old Testament colleagues (following Gray's lead, *I & II Kings*[2], 1970, 660–1) will review their position in the light of the full facts, cease to shout 'anachronism' where none exists, and will no longer be bound by a co-regency hypothesis that flies in the face of so much contrary evidence; they have everything to gain thereby.

379. *Kawa*, I, 119–30; with Dunham, *JEA* 35 (1949), 139–49.

380. As noted (e.g.) by Yoyotte, 'Néchao', in *Supplément au Dictionnaire de la Bible*, VI, col. 365; on Necho I, cf. also § 117 above.

381. There is no warrant for assuming (cf. Goedicke, *MDIK* 18 (1962), 48) that Psammetichus I either dated from his installation in Athribis (666/5) or practised any form of later 'ante-dating'.

382. Legrain, *ASAE* 7 (1906), 190, 226–7; *G4*, 43, III.

383. Nitocris adoption stela (Caminos, *JEA* 50 (1964), 74, pls. 8–9).

Tantamani (also, of Psammetichus in the north) and the 2nd month of the next Akhet, in Year 9 of the Saite king (also, of Tantamani in Nubia) is but 6 months and a few days; within that time were doubtless concluded the negotiations that finally attached Thebes to the northern king's *régime*. Thereafter, Tantamani was doubtless recognized only in Nubia.

Some have considered that, at the start of his reign, Tantamani was co-regent with Taharqa, at least briefly. This is perhaps just possible; in the little temple of Osiris-Ptah at Karnak, one wall has two identical sub-scenes, one of Taharqa and one of Tantamani.[384] A lintel has decoration symmetrically attributed to the two kings.[385] Further evidence for a brief co-regency has been alleged in the text of Tantamani's 'dream stela'.[386] Here, it is clear that the phrase 'Year 1 of his being caused to appear as king' implies Tantamani's accession. But its expression which is impersonal and passive does not tell us who caused him so to appear – this may as easily be a god (Amun?) as Taharqa. The new king then had a dream of which he relates the features and interpretation. Then the text continues: 'When His Majesty appeared on the Horus-throne in this year, he proceeded from where he was, like Horus from Chemmis. . . .' This, surely, is merely a reference back to his accession, and does not of itself imply a co-regency. In any case, if Schäfer's co-regency view were retained, the difference would not be more than a few months, leaving the basic chronology of this reign virtually untouched. One might then attribute the decoration of the two kings in the Osiris-Ptah chapel to that brief period. Otherwise, without a co-regency, one may simply suggest that Tantamani continued his predecessor's work in building and decorating the chapel, and associated the newly-deceased Taharqa with himself in two scenes (wall and lintel), as though to claim the dead king's sanction for his own kingship in Thebes. Tantamani's first concern was to assure himself of the kingship by going from wherever he was (Thebes?) to Napata, the Nubian capital, to obtain recognition there.[387] Thence he returned to Elephantine and Thebes before going north to seize Memphis and the Delta. Thus, we may put Tantamani's known reign in Nubia and Upper Egypt into the 8 years from 664 to 656 B.C., at which latter date Psammetichus I gained recognition by the Thebans, an act which was sealed by the acceptance of his daughter as chief lady elect in the cult of their god Amun.

384. Mariette, *Monuments Divers*, pl. 87.
385. *Ibid.*, pl. 83.
386. Schäfer, *ZÄS* 35 (1897), 67–9; von Zeissl, *Äthiopen und Assyrer*, 48; *BAR*, IV, p. 469a.
387. A move surely needless if he were already co-regent, unless he had not been to Napata in the interim.

CHAPTER 11

Dates for the Twenty-second to Twenty-fifth Dynasties

§ 140   1. INTRODUCTORY

Now that the basic data for these dynasties has been surveyed, we may now endeavour to translate the results into dates B.C. In Part I of this work, it was possible to set a close date for the end of the 21st Dynasty and accession of Shoshenq I of the 22nd Dynasty: 945 B.C.[388] Similarly, the official end of the 25th Dynasty in Egypt is set at 664 B.C., and the reign of Taharqa at 690–664 B.C. Thanks to Assyrian synchronisms, Osorkon IV is attested in 716 B.C., and the reconquest of Egypt by the 25th Dynasty to 716–712 B.C. (probably 715 B.C.). A change of Egyptian policy towards Assyria which was visible in 701 B.C. suggests a change of kings (i.e. Shabako to Shebitku) in 702/701 B.C. The rest of the interrelated sets of kings may now be fitted into the framework defined by 945 B.C., 716–712 B.C., 702/701 B.C., and 690–664 B.C.

§ 141   2. THE 25th DYNASTY AND LINKS WITH ITS PREDECESSORS

A. THE 25TH DYNASTY PROPER
After Taharqa in 690–664 B.C., Tantamani was recognized in Upper Egypt to his 8th year and a few months longer, i.e. to 656 B.C. From that year, as noted, the 9th of Psammetichus I (as of Tantamani), the Thebans switched allegiance to the 26th Dynasty in Sais. As seen in the previous chapter, Shebitku most probably became king in 702 or 701 B.C., reasons

388. Or possibly 944; details, see above, Part I, §§ 58–60.

being given for 702 (§§ 126–127, above). Before him, Shabako reigned not less than the 14 years, adopted here, and perhaps for 15; he would then reign *c.* 716–702 B.C., or within a year or so of those dates. In his 2nd year he became master of Egypt, supplanting Bakenranef; this would fall in 715 on the dates here adopted.

§ **142** B. LINKS WITH THE 24TH DYNASTY

Shabako's conquest of Egypt in 715 B.C. terminated Bakenranef's reign in its incomplete 6th year. Hence Bakenranef would have reigned 5 years and a fraction during 720–715 B.C., constituting Manetho's official 24th Dynasty. Before him, Tefnakht reached an 8th year as king, guaranteeing him a 7-year reign (perhaps more), at 727–720 B.C. As has been seen above (§§ 112–114), Tefnakht assumed formal kingship *after* Piankhy's invasion of Egypt, and probably very soon after it. Therefore, one may place Piankhy's invasion – and his 20th year – not later than about 728 B.C. Ending in 716, his total reign would then cover 31 years, *c.* 747–716 B.C. As noted above (§ 122), no figures exist for Alara or Kashta, but one may suggest an average reign for the former and (in view of Piankhy's longer reign) a shorter reign for the latter. Thus, some 12 or 13 years for Kashta would set him at *c.* 760–747 B.C., and about 20 years for Alara at roughly 780–760 B.C. For the precursors of Tefnakht and the successors of Bakenranef at Sais, see above, Chapter 9; with Shabako in Egypt from 715, Ammeris in Sais would not begin before that date.

§ **143** C. LINKS BETWEEN THE 22ND/23RD AND 24TH/25TH
DYNASTIES

Here, a piece of evidence which has been hitherto left on one side may now be more profitably evaluated.

In the Wadi Gasus, above and to the right of a well-known scene depicting Psammetichus I and the God's Wives of Amun, Nitocris and Shepenupet II, before Amenre, there is preserved a curious graffito. It has 'Year 12' above the name and title of 'Adoratrix of the God, Amenirdis, may she live', and similarly beside and behind it, 'Year 19' above 'the God's Wife, Shepenupet, may she live'.[389] At first sight, this document is highly ambiguous. *If* the year-dates pertain to the Adoratrix and God's

---

389. Originally published by Schweinfurth and Erman, *Alte Baureste und hieroglyphische Inscriften im Uadi Gasus mit Bemerkungen . . .*, 1885. Closely studied by Leclant, and given preliminary re-edition by Christophe, *BIE* 35 (Session 1952/ 53: 1954), 141–52; they were able to verify that the dates are definitely Year 12 (not 13 or 20) and Year 19; to Professor Leclant, I owe thanks for a print of the inscription, and for confirming that '13' is a misprint for '12' in his invaluable *Recherches*, 1965, 383.

Wife – as Egyptologists have tended to assume – then an Amenirdis became associated with a Shepenupet in the latter's 8th Year of office. *A
priori*, this could refer to either of two pairs: Amenirdis I adopted by
Shepenupet I, or Amenirdis II adopted by Shepenupet II. As the dates of
the 'reigns' of the God's Wives of Amun are uncertain even to a decade in
the 25th Dynasty, such year-dates would not be very useful. For example,
if Taharqa appointed his daughter Amenirdis II to be heir of Shepenupet
II in his own first year, this graffito would date to her (and his) 12th year,
and to a later year of his if her appointment were later. Correspondingly,
Shepenupet II would have been God's Wife of Amun for 7 years before
Taharqa's accession (at the earliest). This would fall in the middle of
Shebitku's reign and in turn would imply that she was *at that time* made
heiress to Amenirdis I. This is probably ruled out by the fact that Shepenupet II refers back to having received *her* inaugural testament from 'her
father and her mother',[390] i.e. Piankhy her real father, and probably
Amenirdis I, her adoptive mother and predecessor-in-office. If so, our
graffito cannot be referred to 'reigns' of Shepenupet II and Amenirdis II.

One may then turn to the option Shepenupet I and Amenirdis I. This
would mean that Piankhy had installed Amenirdis I 7 years after Shepenupet I had been installed by her father Osorkon III, not later than the
latter's 24th year, when Takeloth III became his co-regent and under
which triple *régime* (Osorkon III, Takeloth III, Shepenupet I) the little
Osiris-temple was built at Karnak. Therefore, *at the latest*, Piankhy would
have had Amenirdis I adopted by Shepenupet I in her own and Takeloth
III's 8th year. This is theoretically possible; the prominence of Amenirdis
I over against Shepenupet I would not be unparalleled, as von Zeissl also
remarked in another connection.[391]

§ **144** However, the general assumption that these two year-dates actually
belong to these ladies at all has been challenged by Christophe. As he says,
in no other case do we ever find regnal years attributed to the God's Wife of
Amun at this period[392] – or, one may add, at any other. And indeed, the
only women throughout Egyptian history who ever had regnal years were
those who in fact became female pharaohs: Nitokert, Sobeknofru, Hatshepsut and Tewosret. Even here, the latter two did not have sole reigns
with regnal years of their own, but used or took over those of the kings
with whom they reigned. For all their outward trappings of royalty (car-

390. Adoption stela of Nitocris, lines 15–16 (Caminos, *JEA* 50 (1964), 75); cf.
Yoyotte, *RdE* 8 (1951), 229, n. 4.
391. *Äthiopen und Assyrer in Ägypten*, 67.
392. *BIE* 35 (1954), 143.

touches, 'female Horus', perhaps jubilee-rites), the God's Wife of Amun never aspired to real pharaonic powers in the 23rd–26th Dynasties.[393] Therefore, it seems wise – with Christophe – to conclude that in fact we have here the regnal years 12 and 19 *of two unnamed kings*, each perhaps associated with one of the God's Wives named. In favour of this interpretation, I would cite a striking parallel from the records of a God's Wife of a far earlier day. At Serabit el Khadim in Sinai was found a stela headed: 'Year 11 under the majesty of' above the main scene in which appears 'the God's Wife, Neferure, may she live', and her steward Senmut.[394] Of young Neferure, *one* thing is certain – she never reigned, apparently never even became a queen, but perhaps died while still a child.[395] In fact, all agree that this 'Year 11' is simply the Year 11 of Tuthmosis III and Hatshepsut. Hence, one may well expect the dates of the Wadi Gasus graffito to be those of kings in a like manner.

However, even if this point be granted, one other possibility has to be noted. Namely, that we have here not one graffito with double dating, but two single, separate graffiti in close mutual proximity. Were this the case, these two lines of text would lose virtually all special historical value. The 'Year 12 – Amenirdis' could then be referred to Year 12 of Shabako with Amenirdis I, like text No. 187 in Wadi Hammamat naming these two,[396] while 'Year 19 – Shepenupet' might well refer to Year 19 of Taharqa and to Shepenupet II, merely confirming their known contemporaneity. But is such a division into two graffiti correct? Probably not. For the 'Year 19' was put on exactly the same level as the 'Year 12' as if to be closely symmetrical, while the *same* blank space (equivalent to about one group) was left between the date and name and title in each case. In other words, it *does* seem that both columns of dates and names were written at the same time as part of one and the same graffito.

If so, then we have here *two contemporary kings*, one of whom began his reign in the other's 8th year. Who can these be? Some solutions can be quickly eliminated. If the ladies concerned were Shepenupet II and Amenirdis II (daughter of Taharqa), either Taharqa or Psammetichus I would be involved. But in Years 12 or 19, Taharqa shared neither a co-regency nor the rule of Upper Egypt with anyone. Nor was Psammetichus I in his Year 12 contemporary with Year 19 of any other monarch in Upper

393. Cf. outline of role of God's Wife of Amun at this period by Leclant, *Recherches*, 1965, 374–86.

394. Gardiner, Peet, Černý, *Inscriptions of Sinai*, I², pl. 58, and II, 151–2, No. 179. The numeral is oddly written with eleven strokes instead of 10 plus 1.

395. On Neferure, cf. Kitchen, *JEA* 49 (1963), 38–40.

396. Couyat and Montet, *Inscriptions hiéroglyphiques et hiératiques du Ouadi Hammamat*, 96 and pl. 35.

Egypt; Tantamani was by then ruler only in Nubia, and his years in any case were in step with those of Psammetichus I, not 8 years ahead. So, this graffito does not belong to Shepenupet II and Amenirdis II.

A solution Amenirdis I/Shepenupet II is no better. We have no evidence that Amenirdis I survived the reign of Shebitku, still less that he ever attained a 19th year. Nor in his 12th year could he possibly be co-regent with Shabako in an imaginary 19th year of the latter. Nor under these monarchs would the years of some Delta princeling be counted with a Nubian God's Wife of Amun under a Nubian pharaoh. Nor in turn can a 12th year of Shabako be equivalent to anyone else's 19th year – least of all Piankhy whose 20th year fell at least a dozen years (reigns of Tefnakht and Bakenranef) before the 2nd year of Shabako, let alone his 12th!

§ 145   Thus, as before, we come back to one possible solution: that this graffito commemorates Shepenupet I and Amenirdis I, as Christophe also concluded.[397] For, 'Year 12' associated with Amenirdis I could be that of a Nubian king – in fact, of Piankhy who installed her – and 'Year 19' with Shepenupet I would belong to a king of her family (23rd Dynasty), which had long been recognized in Thebes. In his 20th year, 728 B.C., Piankhy found Iuput II reigning, but there is no warrant for extending that ruler's reign back in time to a point 7 years before Piankhy's accession in 747 B.C., i.e. to 754 B.C. (a span of 26 years). Such a date for the accession of Iuput II is ultimately excluded by the high date it would require for founding of the 23rd Dynasty (c. 840 B.C.), and through its link with Shoshenq III for the founding of the 22nd Dynasty (then c. 968 B.C., a wholly impossible date). Nor is there any reason to assign 19 years to Rudamun, predecessor of Iuput II. Going earlier, we cannot refer the Year 19 to Osorkon III, father of Shepenupet I, as equivalent to Year 12 of Piankhy, because then the latter's Year 20 and his famous Egyptian campaign would fall into the 27th year of Osorkon III! Piankhy's Delta pharaohs would then have been Shoshenq V and Osorkon III, not the quite different Osorkon IV (Dynasty 22) and Iuput II actually mentioned by him. So, there is one solution left: Year 19 of Takeloth III, co-regent and eventual successor of Osorkon III, some 13 years after the latter's death. The 8 years' interval between the 12th year of Piankhy and his 20th would be quite sufficient time to accommodate the last year or so of Takeloth III, the ephemeral reign of Rudamun and the accession of Iuput II before Piankhy's invasion of Egypt.

This now gives us the scheme below (with Piankhy's Year 12, 736 B.C., dating Year 19 of Takeloth III to that year).

397. *BIE* 35 (1954), 149 ff.; he also excludes the other 'solutions' (146–9), if on less cogent grounds.

	777 B.C.: accession of Osorkon III
	754 B.C.: Takeloth III, co-regent, O. III
	750 B.C.: Year 5 T. III = Year 28 O. III
Accession of Piankhy	747 B.C.: Year 8 of Takeloth III
Piankhy extends his rule to Thebes, instals Amenirdis I, date unknown.	
Year 12 of Piankhy	736 B.C.: Year 19 of T. III (W. Gasus)
	Brief reign, Rudamun
	Accession of Iuput II
Year 20, Piankhy invades Egypt	728 B.C.: Iuput II of 23rd Dynasty
Year 21, Great Stela	727 B.C.: Tefnakht king in West Delta
	720 B.C.: Bakenranef succeeds
Year 32, Piankhy dies; Year 1 of Shabako	716 B.C.: Bakenranef, Year 5
Year 2, Shabako invades Egypt	715 B.C.: End of Bakenranef
	25th Dynasty rules all Egypt

§ 146   3. DATES FOR THE 22nd AND 23rd DYNASTIES

The results attained in § 145 enable us now to set up a series of ultimately interlocking data:

(i) Accession of Shoshenq I in 945 B.C., on Near-Eastern evidence.

(ii) The series of reigns of kings of the 22nd and 23rd Dynasties, the lengths of most of which have been fairly closely determined.

(iii) The link between the 22nd and 23rd Dynasties whereby the latter is begun by Pedubast I in Year 8 of Shoshenq III.

(iv) Links between the Libyan, Nubian, and Saite lines: Piankhy, Takeloth III, Iuput II, Osorkon IV; Shabako and Bakenranef.

(v) An Apis living from Year 37 of Shoshenq V to Year 5 of Bakenranef.

(vi) Near-Eastern correlations of Osorkon IV.

First of all, the upper limits of the 22nd Dynasty must be fixed. Shoshenq I reigned 21 years,[398] acceded in 945 B.C. (not earlier), and so can be set at 945–924 B.C. At 35 years, Osorkon I would reign 924–889 B.C. Shoshenq II was almost certainly only a co-regent, and so does not affect the dates of the Dynasty. Takeloth I can be given a minimum of 13 years,

---

398. This figure and all other regnal figures used here are those already set forth in Chapters 6 to 10 above, unless otherwise commented upon.

and more probably 14 or even 15; this would permit a reign from *c.* 889 to within 876–874 B.C. In turn, Osorkon II has at least 22 years, perhaps up to 24 years. The consequent limits for his reign might then be *c.* 876/874 to *c.* 854/850 B.C.[399] To Takeloth II can be attributed 25 years, which would be about 854/850 B.C. to *c.* 829/825 B.C. This latter date would also be that for the accession of Shoshenq III.

One may then turn to the lower limits, which are provided by Piankhy and the 23rd Dynasty. As seen just above (§ 145), the 12th year of Piankhy in 736 B.C. is the 19th year of Takeloth III. If the latter be allowed a round 20 years, he will have reigned 754–734 B.C. One may allow, say, 3 years for the ephemeral Rudamun (*c.* 734–731 B.C.), so as to have Iuput II reigning shortly before Piankhy's raid through Egypt in 728 B.C. Iuput may have lasted until Shabako in 715, or have been by then succeeded by some further ephemeral kinglet (Shoshenq VI? – If the latter existed). Takeloth III was co-regent with Osorkon III from the latter's Year 24, his father having reigned 28 years; Osorkon III may thus be set at 777–749 B.C. Before him, Shoshenq IV at 6 years would be 783–777 B.C. Before him, Iuput I at 21 years would be 804–783 B.C. The latter was co-regent with Pedubast I from the latter's 15th year, and Pedubast I reigned about 25 years; these would be *c.* 818–793 B.C., completing the 23rd Dynasty.

§ **147**   However, the accession of Pedubast I can be fixed precisely to the 8th year of Shoshenq III of the 22nd Dynasty (Nile-level text No. 24) – and that year is 818 B.C. or very close thereto. This is important in two directions: upward, to link up with the dates for the earlier 22nd Dynasty from Shoshenq I (945 ff.) downward, and in turn downward for Shoshenq III and his successors to the time of Piankhy again, as a check on the chronology adopted for the 23rd Dynasty.

To tackle the upward link first, a Year 8 of Shoshenq III in 818 B.C. would put his accession in 825 B.C. The 25-year reign of Takeloth II would then fall in 850–825 B.C., and the 22–24 years of Osorkon II from 874/872 B.C. This would leave the 15–17 years in 889 B.C. (death of Osorkon I) to 874/872 B.C. for Takeloth I, which is ample. One may there-fore provisionally assign some 15 years to Takeloth I and 24 years to Osorkon II; thus, the dates for the Dynasty correspond well, whether one reckons downward from Shoshenq I (§ 146) or upward from Shoshenq III, linked to the 23rd and 25th Dynasties.

Turning to the second half of the 22nd Dynasty, Year 8 of Shoshenq III in 818 B.C. would put his entire 52-year reign in 825–773 B.C. Then

---

399. Harsiese as king had no sole reign, and so does not affect the chronological sequence of kings.

Pimay at 6 years would reign 773–767 B.C., and Shoshenq V at 37 years in 767–730 B.C. – ending his reign and allowing the accession of Osorkon IV just nicely about 2 years before the invasion of Piankhy in 728 B.C. Osorkon IV then reigned on until 716 B.C. (Shilkanni of Sargon II), and may have died soon after – say, *c.* 715 B.C.

This series of dates also fits perfectly the resulting lifespan of the Apis bull inducted in Year 37 of Shoshenq V and dead in Year 5 of Bakenranef, buried in his Year 6, Year 2 of Shabako (715 B.C.). This would give the bull a span of 16 years – precisely the average for Apis bulls at the time (cf. above, § 126, (iii) and references). Thus, we now obtain a complete series of dates for all the principal kings of the 22nd–25th Dynasties. For the petty kings of Middle Egypt, only estimates can be made; no regnal years are known, except Year 10 for Pef-tjau-awy-Bast. (See Table 16 in Part VI.)

§ 148 4. SUPPLEMENTARY POINTS

A. A SUPPOSED ECLIPSE UNDER TAKELOTH II

In 1953, Albright revived the theory that the 'chronicle' of Prince Osorkon contains mention of an eclipse in Year 15 of Takeloth II, an eclipse of the moon. He suggested the eclipse of 822 B.C., which would place the accession of Takeloth II in 836 B.C., some 14 years later than the dates set out above. So low a date is impossible on strictly chronological grounds. Upward, it would bring the accession of Shoshenq I down to 931 B.C., which cannot be squared with the Near Eastern data properly treated.[400] Downward, the irreducible total of 106 years from the 15th year of Takeloth II to the 38th and death of Shoshenq V (11, 52, 6, 37, years) reckoned from 822 B.C. runs down to 716 B.C. – far too late, by over a decade! By 712 *at the very latest*, Shabako was ruler of all Egypt and Nubia (cf. Sargon II), which event (his conquest) was preceded by 5 years of Bakenranef and 7 years of Tefnakht to set the conquest of Piankhy minimally in 724 B.C. – when Shoshenq V was already dead and gone, whereas on Albright's erroneous chronology, he would have 8 more years to live! In short, Albright's entire Late Period Egyptian chronology must now be discarded; it rested on too-low dates partly inspired by Macadam's erroneous co-regency of Taharqa, and on inaccurate regnal years – and made *no use whatever* of the genealogical data that are vital to a right relative chronology of the 22nd with 23rd Dynasties.

400. Albright, *BASOR* 130 (1953), 4–11, cf. *BASOR* 141 (1956), 26–7. His figures for reigns include several errors (Takeloth I's 23rd year is actually Pedubast I; co-regency of T.II with O.II is T.III/O.III).

However, it must further be objected that in fact the 'chronicle' *does not mention an eclipse at all.* It says literally: 'In Year 15, . . . not did the sky swallow the moon (*n sdm.f*) . . . a great convulsion broke out in this land' – i.e. although there was *no* premonitory eclipse, yet disaster came. But Albright reversed the plain meaning of the text completely, by inserting gratuitously a word that is not in the original at all, translating 'the sky not having swallowed the moon (completely)'. Breasted and Borchardt had translated 'before the sky / the sky had not yet . . . swallowed the moon' – but as Parker pointed out to Albright, and likewise Caminos subsequently,[401] one should in that case expect the *n sdmt.f* construction, not the narrative-past *n sdm.f* form. In other words, the eclipse is simply not in the text, and not relevant therefore to the chronology of the 22nd Dynasty, and dates based upon it must be discarded.

§ **149**   B. KING SO

In 725 B.C., Hoshea of Israel sought help from 'So, king of Egypt' (2 Kings 17: 4). Chronologically, this date falls into the reigns of Osorkon IV of Tanis/Bubastis, Iuput II of Leontopolis, and Tefnakht of Sais. Of the three, Osorkon IV is by far the best candidate for 'So' on all grounds: historical, geographical, textual, political, etc. (For full discussion, see Part IV below, § 333.)

§ **150**   C. CONCLUSION: POSSIBLE ADJUSTMENTS

While I believe the scheme offered in this book to be very close to the truth, it is perfectly possible that future discoveries may require modifications. Despite the close dating achieved, the present scheme is flexible enough to adjust. If slightly higher year-dates are found for one or two kings, there is room to shorten reigns such as Takeloth I or Osorkon II nearer to their minimal lengths, to compensate. If Tefnakht reigned a little more than 7 years, prior dates could thus be raised correspondingly for the 23rd and second half of the 22nd Dynasties; a great lengthening of his reign is unlikely because of the Apis that spanned from Shoshenq V to Bakenranef. In fact, the chronology given here from Tefnakht to Shebitku is in some measure minimal. The only major foreseeable change is the possibility that the Ramesseum bandage read as Year 33 under Osorkon I were to be Year 13, giving him 15 years (Manetho). He would then reign 924–909 B.C., and the 20 years' balance be split up among several of his successors down to Shoshenq V, with slightly raised dates in each case. In the possible event of some further king being added to the main line of rulers, such 'spare' years would be attributable to him, in whole or in part.

401. *BASOR* 130 (1953), 5, n. 7a; *CPO*, 89, § 130.

However, all such changes remain at present in the realm of pure hypothesis and conjecture; the foregoing observations serve merely to indicate possible lines of adjustment, should they be needed. The writer offers the chronology of this book not as absolute truth, but in the conviction that this scheme is about as near as possible on the existing published evidence. Unpublished data can be its touchstone. One methodological point may be worth making. Namely, that any proposed changes must be compatible with *all* lines of evidence here used: regnal dates, use of titles, royal and otherwise, and not least the genealogical and other data. Mere conjuring with a few reigns and year-dates, or with but one dynasty is simply not good enough – nor is the invention of co-regencies or of ante-dating in the teeth of other evidence.

The total chronology for the 21st–26th Dynasties will be found in Part VI, Tables 1–4, diagrams of years of contemporaneous *régimes* in Tables 5–6, genealogies of the royal families in Tables 7–11, and lists of other principal people in Tables 12–24. In Parts III and V are set out important complementary data for I and II, essential to the scheme of dates worked out above.

PART THREE

Chronology
Officials of the Realm

CHAPTER 12

Dignitaries at Memphis

§ 151* 1. HIGH PRIESTS OF PTAH IN MEMPHIS,
21st DYNASTY

Two major genealogical documents form the core of our knowledge of
Memphite pontiffs for this period, and (combined with contemporary
data) have an important and direct bearing on 21st-Dynasty chronology.
These are the remarkable genealogies of Memphite priests, one of which is
in Berlin (23673) and the other is a partial parallel from the Serapeum,
which is now in the Louvre ('96'; *Cat.* 52).[1] They provide the following
sequence:

Kings	*Priests (Berlin)*	*Priests (Louvre)*
2:1 . . .	HPM,[2] Ptah-em-akhet	—
1:15 Amenemnisu	HPM, Asha-khet A	—
1:14 Akheperre Setepena[mun] }	HPM, P(i)p(i) A	7: HPM, Pipi A
1:13 Psusennes	HPM, ⟨Har⟩siese J	6–7: HPM, Harsiese J
1:12 Psusennes	Pr,[3] P(i)p(i) B	5–6: HPM, Pipi B[4]
1:11	CS-Pr,[5] Asha-khet B	5: HPM, Asha-khet B

1. Berlin 23673 published by L. Borchardt, *Die Mittel zur zeitlichen Festlegung*
von Punkten der ägyptischen Geschichte und ihre Anwendung, 1935, 96–112, pls. 2–2a;
earlier, cf. Borchardt, *Sitzungsberichte Berlin Akademie der Wissenschaft (Phil.-hist.*
Kl.), 1932, Heft XXIV. Louvre 96: E. Chassinat, *RT* 22 (1900), 16–17, No. 54;
Lieblein, *Dictionnaire de Noms*, No. 1027; *PM*, III, 210; now, Malinine, Posener,
Vercoutter, *Catalogue des stèles du Sérapéum de Memphis*, I, 1968, No. 52, pp. 48–9.
pl. 16. On both documents, cf. Kees, *ZÄS* 87 (1962), 146–9.
2. Abbreviation used here for High Priest of Ptah in Memphis, i.e. *wr-ḫrp-ḥm(wt)*.
3. Abbreviation used here for 'prophet' (*ḥm-nṯr*).
4. Written KNIFE plus BOW, probably a sportive writing.
5. Abbreviation here for Chief of Secrets of the Great Seat and Prophet, *ḥry-*
sštꜣ (n) st-wrt, ḥm-nṯr.

| 1:10 | Pr, Ankhefensekhmet A | 4: HPM, Ankhefen-sekhmet A |
| 1:9 | CS-Pr, Shedsunefertem A | 3–4: HPM, Shedsunef-ertem A |

After this point, the two genealogies continue in two separate lines, stemming from two sons of Shedsunefertem. As seen by Borchardt, Kees and others, it is clear that these two lines coincide precisely and show the same line of priests, even though the last four are not cited by their highest titles in the Berlin document.

§ **152** Thanks to Grdseloff's observation, which has been confirmed by Anthes and Kees,[6] there can be no doubt that the king who is named as contemporary of Ashakhet A is Amenemnisu. The prenomen that follows it in the next generation is that of Psusennes I, while the Psusennes named twice with the two subsequent generations could also simply be Psusennes I. We would thus have Psusennes (I) named as contemporary of three successive generations of High Priests of Ptah, which would desiderate quite a long reign for that king. On the basis of a long reign of Psusennes I of 46 years (Manetho) and up to 48/49 years (attributable dates from Thebes), Asha-khet A would have served under Amenemnisu and have died in the initial decades of the reign of Psusennes I. His lineal descendants Pipi A and Harsiese J would then have officiated during the main part of the reign of Psusennes (say, years 5/10 to 40/45, some 30/40 years between them). Thereafter, Pipi B would have been inducted in the last years of Psusennes I, and have served under his immediate successors, Amenemope, Osochor and the first years of Siamun. The last three high priests would then have served under the last kings of the 21st Dynasty (Siamun, Psusennes II) and into the early 22nd Dynasty. The one question one may ask is, why was Psusennes I cited once by his prenomen and then twice by his nomen? Did the excerptor of the Berlin genealogy think that these were two different kings, or did he merely reproduce the forms of royal name found in the documents that he drew upon? The latter is perhaps the more satisfying explanation. The phenomenon *could* be used to raise a doubt on the scheme which has just been outlined (cf. § 153, below), but not with any great conviction.

However, some first-hand confirmation of this genealogy and its dates of dignitaries is available. Happily, the high priest Shedsunefertem is securely attested in office under Shoshenq I, in the early 22nd Dynasty. He named

6. Grdseloff, *ASAE* 47 (1947), 207–11, esp. 210; Kees, *Pr., Nachträge*, 1958, 17.

his own son (who succeeded him in office) Shoshenq after his royal patron and relative-by-marriage; his own father is likewise confirmed as the high priest Ankhefensekhmet (A).[7]

Two generations before Ankhefensekhmet and Shedsunefertem, the high priest Pipi B is attested under Siamun on temple buildings at Memphis, where the well-sculptured gateways included a lintel of the high priest 'Neterkheperre Meryptah who is called Piupiu'. He attends on Siamun in whose honour he adopted this loyalist name which is based on the king's prenomen.[8]

These finds fully confirm the picture drawn from the genealogy: there was one generation under Amenemnisu and early Psusennes I, two in the long reign of Psusennes I, and a fourth which was appointed late under Psusennes which continued through his ephemeral successors to the time of Siamun. Then Asha-khet B will have served both under Siamun and early under Psusennes II, Ankhefensekhmet A under Psusennes II and perhaps in the first years of Shoshenq I, and Shedsunefertem for most of the reign of Shoshenq I.

§ 153   Before leaving the Berlin genealogy which has been so neatly confirmed in this later part of its long series of names, and has been acknowledged to be probably a reflection of facts in still earlier periods,[9] it may be well to note that it does seem to betray some omissions or dislocations, even though its *sequences* of generations and kings can be taken as correct.

Thus, for roughly 150 years or more from the death of Ramesses II to the early 21st Dynasty,[10] the Berlin document has only *one* generation (Ptah-em-akhet B) between Ramesses II and Amenemnisu. It is theoretically possible to argue a simple omission of six or seven names (a haplography?) or even that further names in the top row are lost on some slab that was once contiguous with it.[11] But no such explanation will hold for the

---

7. Embalming-table of the Apis-bull at Memphis, made by the high priest Shedsunefertem son of the high priest Ankhefensekhmet, with cartouches of Shoshenq I; cf. Brugsch, *ZÄS* 16 (1878), 37 f., and *Thesaurus*, 817, 949. Statue Cairo Cat. 741, naming Shedsunefertem, four sons, two daughters, father, and female forebears, Borchardt, *Statuen u. Statuetten*, III, 68–9, and Daressy, *RT* 18 (1896), 46–49; cf. Kees, *ZÄS* 87 (1962), 140–2. Statue, Cairo JdE 86758, cf. Kees, *op. cit.*, 142–5.

8. Texts, Petrie, *Memphis II: Palace of Apries*, 1909, pl. 24, top. For another mention of Neterkheperre-Meryptah Pipi, on the statue of a descendant (now in Paris), cf. Kees, *op. cit.*, 147, n. 2.

9. Cf. (e.g.) remarks of Wente, *JNES* 26 (1967), 156, and nn. 7, 8. One may note, for example, its realistic attribution of four successive priests to the long reign of Ramesses II, among other sequences.

10. In round figures, *c.* 1230 to *c.* 1180/1160 B.C., between 150–70 years.

11. Cf. (e.g.) Wente, *op. cit.*, 156, n. 8.

remarkable figure of six whole generations between Ptahemhab under Mentuhotep Nebhepetre and Neteryhotep under Amenemhat I.[12] Here, one has to assume that a king's name has 'slipped' either forward (Mentuhotep) to too early a point in the list, or backward (Amenemhat I) by a generation or two, to too late a point in the series, if biological reality is to be securely restored.

This approach *might* be held to be applicable to the top rows of the Berlin genealogy, if a different interpretation of its 'Psusennes' cartouches be preferred. This would be yet another way to relieve the gap between Ramesses II and the 21st Dynasty.[13] Noting the distinction in use of the prenomen Akheperre in 1:14 and the nomen Psusennes in 1:13, 1:12, some scholars have suggested that the former refers to Psusennes I, and the latter to Psusennes II.[14] But, as others have rightly pointed out,[15] this view leaves no room for Amenemope (especially if he had reigned 49 years) and his two successors between Psusennes I and II.

There is, however, yet another way of regarding these cartouches. Akheperre conceivably might not be Psusennes I at all, but the little known Osochor who also used this prenomen.[16] On this interpretation, we would have Amenemnisu, then Osochor, then Psusennes II twice. The most important result of this interpretation is that the Berlin genealogy (i) would not actually mention Psusennes I at all, and (ii) would offer no evidence on the order of Psusennes I and Amenemnisu, and so would no longer be in contradiction with Manetho. But if this identification of the cartouches were in itself acceptable, they could not easily stand correctly where they stand now. For we would have two generations of high priests

12. Thus, at the optimum, one might argue that the vizier Neteryhotep might be attributed to the very last year or so of Amenemhat I, that his father Sokaremhab and grandfather Nebneferu had flourished in the middle and beginning (respectively) of that 30-year reign, and at the very end of the 11th Dynasty. Before them, Ptahhotep would belong under Mentuhotep Sankhkare and the last years of Nebhepetre, leaving three preceding generations to be fitted into his long reign – but, in fact, all within its last 30 years, if the later-type cartouche (with oar) Nebhepetre be taken *au pied de la lettre*, as reflecting their appointments under this king following his conquest of all Egypt. This is barely likely, so it would be easier to postulate that his cartouche really belongs to a generation or two later in the series.

13. On the possible limitations of the Berlin genealogy – drawn up in the 22nd Dynasty about 300 years after Psusennes I – and the question of the real significance of the bow-caps of Psusennes I with Amenemnisu in the former's tomb, one should not overlook the observations of E. Young, *JARCE* 2 (1963), 109, n. 50.

14. E.g., Černý, *CAH*[2], II: 35 (1965), 44.

15. Refutation is implicit in the discussion, Hornung, *OLZ* 61 (1966), 439–40, where the intervening reigns are considered.

16. King discussed by Young, *JARCE* 2 (1963), 99–101. The variation between Setepenre and Setepenamun might speak against identifying Osochor in the Berlin genealogy, but this variation is fully permissible in the following dynasty and thus would be of little weight here.

between Shedsunefertem (attested under Shoshenq I) and Pipi B as *second* high priest under Psusennes II (a situation contradicted by first-hand evidence of his serving Siamun). In this case, it would be necessary to assume here – precisely as with the 11th Dynasty – a shift of cartouches in relation to generations of high priests, and so to bring the cartouches Akheperre, Psusennes, and Psusennes down two places, to correspond with Pipi B (who 1 : 12 would then have served Osochor and Siamun), Asha-khet B (1 : 11, Psusennes II) and Ankhefensekhmet (1 : 10, under Psusennes II and Shoshenq I). This would mean that Pipi B could have begun his pontificate late under Amenemope, have served Osochor, and have ended it under Siamun (with surname, Neterkheperre Meryptah). Asha-khet B would then have served Siamun, and Psusennes II, and so on, as required by the first-hand data. Before them, Harsiese J and Pipi A would have been contemporary *either* with a long reign of Amenemope *or* with a long reign of Psusennes I (depending on the hypothesis preferred), since neither king is named. On the former hypothesis, Asha-khet A would have served Psusennes I, Amenemnisu, and perhaps during the early years of Amenemope; on the latter hypothesis, under Amenemnisu (if not Smendes I) and in the early years of Psusennes I. The order of the two kings, Amenemnisu and Psusennes I, would depend on the view adopted.

Once this has been said, the best view of the Berlin genealogy is still, most probably, the straightforward one, and *not* the view which has just been hypothetically outlined. Against the straightforward view, only one objection can be urged: this view entails reversing the order of two kings (Psusennes I, Amenemnisu) in Manetho. But, in view of the unevenly corrupt state of *extant* Manetho (as opposed to the original), this one divergence is not of great weight. This straightforward view necessarily entails accepting a long reign for Psusennes I, instead of Amenemope (which agrees with Manetho); a view which is most likely on quite other grounds.

By contrast, the alternative to the straightforward view has various disadvantages. It requires gratuitous emendation of the data of the Berlin genealogy, not at some earlier point where defects might conceivably be expected (cf. 11th Dynasty), but precisely in its later part where partial *confirmation* (on Pipi B, Ankhefensekhmet, Shedsunefertem) is available from first-hand sources. And a likely explanation for the assumed 'slip' of two generations in the cartouches has yet to be found in this case. Yet, to maintain the theory of a long reign for Amenemope, some such thesis would be needed. As this theory is already beset with difficulties on other grounds, its validity is not enhanced by invoking emendation of the Berlin document in its best section.

In conclusion, the thesis of a long reign for Psusennes I goes perfectly with the data of the Berlin and Louvre genealogies, and is confirmed in part by first-hand documents; one change in Manetho apart, it offers no problems. The contrary is true of the long-reigned Amenemope thesis. The gap in generations between Ramesses II and Amenemnisu *can* be readily explained as a simple haplography (with omission of six or seven names between two similar ones) by the compiler, and as a less likely hypothesis by a supposed incompleteness of the slab. Therefore, the 'straightforward' view is adopted in this work, not least in the light of the difficulties which are attendant upon any alternative.

§ 154   2. HIGH PRIESTS OF PTAH IN MEMPHIS, 22nd DYNASTY

After Shedsunefertem A, who is securely attested under Shoshenq I, the history of his office can be followed throughout most of the Libyan dynasty, and from his family to theirs.

Shedsunefertem's lineal successors are recorded on the Louvre Serapeum stela which has already been utilized above (§ 151) and which was erected by a man his descendant by six generations, and are in part known from other monuments.[17] This stela (1. 1–4) gives the series Shedsunefertem A, Shoshenq C, Osorkon A, all high priests (*wr-ḥrp-ḥmwt*), then Takeloth who remained se(te)m-priest of Ptah. Neither he nor his three descendants (ending with Asha-khet C, who made the stela) ever attained to the pontificate.

The sequence of names – Shoshenq, Osorkon, Takeloth, and his son Osorkon – parallels remarkably that of the early kings of the 22nd Dynasty as known to us from the Pasenhor stela and other historical evidence.[18] So it seems that, in turn, Shedsunefertem – who has already been linked to this royal family – named his son 'Shoshenq' after his friend, relative, and royal

High Priest		King
Louvre '96': Shedsunefertem A	—	Shoshenq I: Pasenhor
|		|
Shoshenq C	—	Osorkon I
|		|
Osorkon A	—	Takeloth I
|		|
Sem-priest, Takeloth A	—	Osorkon II
|		|
God's Father, Osorkon, etc.	—	(etc.)

17. Cf. the studies by J. Vandier, *JEA* 35 (1949), 135–8, and H. Kees, *ZÄS* 87 (1962), 140–9.

18. A point already discerned a century ago by Brugsch, *ZÄS* 16 (1878), 42.

master, and this Shoshenq did likewise, naming his son Osorkon after Osorkon I. In turn, the high priest Osorkon as a contemporary of Takeloth I named his son 'Takeloth', and the latter named his son Osorkon after either his own father, or Osorkon II, or after them both. We have thus the series given above.

§ 155 The sudden cessation of high-priestly office in the family of Shedsunefertem, after so many generations, was no accident, but the direct result of a deliberate emphasis in royal policy under the second Osorkon of the Pasenhor stela, the historical Osorkon II.[19]

This same king installed his eldest son, the Crown Prince Shoshenq (D), as high priest in Memphis – and thus ousted the family of Shedsunefertem from the post it had so long held. Hence, neither Takeloth A nor his descendants ever attained that post.

The Crown Prince Shoshenq D never became king, but died while still high priest, shortly before his father. His tomb has been found in Memphis.[20] In turn, his own descendants established in some measure a new 'dynasty' of high priests in Memphis. The affiliations of the pontiff Merenptah[21] under Takeloth II are unknown; but, either before or after this Merenptah, the high-priesthood of Ptah devolved upon the son of Shoshenq D, the Great Chief of the Mā, Takeloth B, and then upon the latter's son by the princess Tjesbastperu. The Apis bull 'found' in Year 28 of Shoshenq III (and buried in Year 2 of Pimay) was inducted in Year 28 under Pediese.[22] On the stelae of the same Year 28, which commemorated the burial of the previous Apis, our Pediese duly appears – but entitled simply Great Chief of the Mā, while his son Pef-tjau-awy-Bast (by the lady Tairy)[23] bears the high-priestly title.[24] This conjunction suggests that

19. Cf. already, Kees, *Pr.*, 183–5. That the Osorkon concerned is Osorkon II is clear from their both having the same son Nimlot who was born by the lady Mut-udj-ankhes (Pasenhor's version of names such as Djed-Mut-es-ankh) and became high priest of Arsaphes in Heracleopolis, attested by Cairo stela JdE 45327 (Daressy, *ASAE* 15 (1915), 41; Iversen, *Two Inscriptions concerning Private Donations to Temples*, 1941, 3 ff.).

20. Badawi, *ASAE* 54 (1957), 154–77 and pls.

21. Named on block with cartouches of Takeloth II, Malinine, Posener, Vercoutter, *Catalogue des stèles du Sérapéum de Memphis*, I, 1968, No. 19.

22. This according to the titles accorded to Takeloth B, Pediese, and Tjesbastperu on the Serapeum stela, new *Catalogue* No. 22 (IM. 3697) of Year 2 of Pimay. This document also states clearly that the bull buried in this year was inducted as Apis 26 years earlier in Year 28 of Shoshenq III by the high priest, sem-priest, great chief of the Mā, Pediese, son of (the same titles) Takeloth (B) and the princess Tjesbast-peru. For this lady, cf. above, Part II, § 81.

23. As Tairy was daughter of Takeloth B, she was sister (or half-sister) of her husband Pediese; so also, Černý, *JEA* 40 (1954), 23–4.

24. Serapeum stela, new *Catalogue*, No. 21 (IM. 3749), Year 28 of Shoshenq III.

Pediese (attested from Year 28 of Shoshenq III to Year 2 of Pimay) had installed his son in office with himself, perhaps to relieve him of priestly duties and to secure the family claim to the office. A second son of Pediese, by another wife, one Takeloth D, became a sem-priest, but not high priest.[25] But 26 years later, in the 2nd year of Pimay, there appears alongside Pediese a third son (by a third wife), Harsiese H, on the Serapeum stelae, not only as sem-priest but also in turn as high priest.[26] In those functions, he had evidently replaced Pef-tjau-awy-Bast who was presumably dead.

§ 156   Regrettably, the Serapeum stelae henceforth seemingly cease to include dedications by the higher clergy after Pimay's reign. However, another document[27] indicates that Harsiese's successor as pontiff was his own son, Ankhefensekhmet B. As Pimay's reign probably lasted little more than its attested 6 years, while that of Shoshenq V his son lasted just over 37 years, one may place the pontificate of Ankhefensekhmet B squarely within the long reign of Shoshenq V. Beyond this point in time, records of high priests of Memphis virtually cease until about the Persian period.[28] Thus, the later series of Memphite high priests in the Libyan era can be listed (with relationships) as follows:

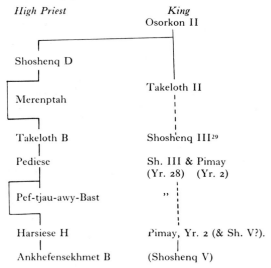

High Priest	King
	Osorkon II
Shoshenq D	
Merenptah	Takeloth II
Takeloth B	Shoshenq III[29]
Pediese	Sh. III & Pimay (Yr. 28) (Yr. 2)
Pef-tjau-awy-Bast	,,
Harsiese H	Pimay, Yr. 2 (& Sh. V?).
Ankhefensekhmet B	(Shoshenq V)

25. Same stela as preceding note.
26. Serapeum stelae, *Catalogue*, Nos. 22, 23, respectively (IM. 3697, 3736).
27. Statue, Cairo Cat. 1212 (Borchardt, *Statuen u. Statuetten*, ad loc.; Kees, *Pr.*, 185).
28. Cf. *RT* 21 (1899), 6; *RT* 23 (1901), 84.
29. For contemporaneity of Takeloth B and Shoshenq III, cf. above, in Part II, § 81 end and references.

CHAPTER 13

Dignitaries at Thebes

§ **157** 1. HIGH PRIESTS OF AMUN, 22nd–25th
DYNASTIES

The known Theban pontiffs of the period may be set out in their approximate order as follows, with dating-evidence as available.

1. *Iuput A*, son of Shoshenq I (Hedjkheperre) is attested in that
monarch's Year 10 on bandages of Djed-Ptah-ef-ankh A,[30] Year 21 on the
stela Gebel Silsila 100,[31] and on sundry other monuments.[32]

2. *Shoshenq ('II')*, son of Osorkon I (Sekhemkheperre) by Maatkare B,
the daughter of Psusennes II and heiress of the 21st Dynasty, who
eventually enclosed his name in a cartouche;[33] he was father of a later
pontiff, Harsiese A (No. 5, just below), and probably was briefly co-regent
with Osorkon I as Shoshenq II (Heqakheperre).[34]

3. *Iuwelot*, son of Osorkon I, was a youth in the 10th year of Osorkon I
(*stèle de l'apanage*).[35] Thus, as a successor of his elder brother Shoshenq II
in a Year 5 (Nile-level text No. 16)[36] he would be pontiff in Year 5 of
Takeloth I (cf. already, § 96, Pt. II, above).

4. *Smendes ('III')*, son of Osorkon (I) is attested by Nile-level texts Nos.
17–19, of Years 8, 14, [x], of an unnamed king,[37] precisely as with No. 16 of
Iuwelot in a 5th year. This peculiarity makes it probable that the un-

30. *G3*, 308–9, VI–VIII.
31. Caminos, *JEA* 38 (1952), 46 ff.
32. E.g. Karnak reliefs of Shoshenq I, *RIK*, III, pls. 10–11.
33. Nile statue, British Museum; *G3*, 299, 330–1.
34. See above, Part II, §§ 93–4.
35. Legrain and Erman, *ZÄS* 35 (1897), 13 ff., 19 ff. Iuwelot also is fixed by
reference to the Djed-Thut-ef-ankh/Nakhtefmut genealogy, § 184.
36. Cf. text, von Beckerath, *JARCE* 5 (1966), 50.
37. *Ibid.*, 51.

attributed Years 8–14 are of the same reign as Year 5 – and hence that this Smendes succeeded his brother Iuwelot as pontiff during the middle and second half of Takeloth I's reign. All these years are much less likely to pertain to Osorkon II, because there are already three, if not four, pontiffs in his time (cf. below).

5. *Harsiese A*, son of Shoshenq II, and thus grandson of Osorkon I.[38] As high priest, he is attested under Osorkon II.[39] He is undoubtedly identical with the *king* Hedjkheperre Setepenamun Harsiese who is equally attested under Osorkon II.[40] He was father of another pontiff, whose name is now lost.

6. [. . . *du/ʿawti?* . . .], son of Harsiese, named on a monument from Coptos.[41]

7. *Nimlot C*, son of Osorkon II, was high priest of Arsaphes in Heracleopolis and Great Chief of (Pi-)Sekhemkheperre until at least Year 16 of his father;[42] therefore, he became Theban pontiff after this date.[43] He was father of a further pontiff, Takeloth, see No. 10a below.

8. *Osorkon B*, son of Takeloth II (Hedjkheperre) by a daughter of Nimlot C,[44] was Crown Prince. He is first attested from Year 11 of his father to Year 29 of Shoshenq III in his 'chronicle' texts,[45] and last in Year 39 of that king.[46]

9. *Harsiese B*, whose antecedents are not known for certain, is attested in Year 6 of Shoshenq III,[47] in Year 12 same as Year 5 of Pedubast I,[48] and in the Years 8, 18, 19 of Pedubast I.[49] He was rival to Prince Osorkon B.

10a. *Takeloth F*, was son of the high priest Nimlot C, and grandson of Osorkon II.[50]

10b. *Takeloth E*, for whom no antecedent is given, is attested in Year 23 of Pedubast I and Year 6 of Shoshenq IV.[51]

These two Takeloths may be one and the same (cf. discussion below).

38. The Alnwick Bes-statue, Legrain, *RT* 30 (1908), 160; *G3*, 331, n. 2, *b*.
39. On statue Cairo Cat. 42225, cf. § 177 below.
40. As on statue Cairo Cat. 42208, cf. § 184 below.
41. Legrain, *ASAE* 6 (1905), 123–4; Daressy, *RT* 35 (1913), 143.
42. Stela Cairo JdE 45327, Iversen, *Two Inscriptions concerning Private Donations to Temples*, 1941; Daressy, *ASAE* 15 (1915), 141.
43. Named as such by his son Takeloth (cf. just below), and nephew-cum-grandson Prince Osorkon, *RIK*, III, pl. 16.
44. *Ibid., loc cit.*
45. *RIK*, III, pls. 16 ff., and *CPO*.
46. Karnak Priestly Annals, fragment 7, Legrain, *RT* 22 (1900), 55; *G3*, 365, XVIII. Nile-level No. 22, von Beckerath, *JARCE* 5 (1966), 51.
47. Nile-level No. 23, von Beckerath, *op. cit.*, 51.
48. Nile-level No. 24, *ibid.*
49. Karnak Priestly Annals, fragment 2 (*RT* 22 (1900), 52) and Nile-levels Nos. 27, 28 (von Beckerath, *op. cit.*, 52).
50. Cf. Kees, *Hhp.*, 113 and n. 1, and references.
51. Nile-levels Nos. 29 and 25 (von Beckerath, *op. cit.*, 52).

11. *Takeloth G,* son of Osorkon II and Tentsai,[52] later was king as Takeloth III.

[12/13. No high priest of Amun is so far attested from the accession of Takeloth III until the reign of Shabako at the earliest – an interval of at least 40 years. This would be long enough for two pontificates, so far unattested. It is conceivable that the office was vacant, and that the cult of Amun was conducted in the interval by the 2nd, 3rd and 4th Prophets of Amun and the God's Wife of Amun, who was now prominent.]

14. *Haremakhet* was the son of king Shabako by Tabaktenamun(?),[53] and is known to have been contemporary with Taharqa and Tantamani.[54]

15. *Harkhebi,* son of his predecessor Haremakhet,[55] is attested in office in Years 9 (Nitocris stela)[56] and 14 (oracle papyrus)[57] of Psammetichus I.

'16'. *Wasakawasa,* son of Iuwelot (No. 3, above), is known from an electrum pectoral.[58] As pointed out by Jacquet-Gordon,[59] this man is simply the *son* of a high priest, and was *not* himself a pontiff. He therefore requires no further consideration here.

§ **158** The relative order of most pontiffs in the foregoing list is sufficiently clear, from the data cited, to need no extended comment beyond the handful of points gathered up in the paragraphs that follow. The first four high priests clearly exemplify *the non-hereditary principle* applied by the early kings of the 22nd Dynasty, in contrast to the long family succession from Piankh to Psusennes 'III' in the 21st Dynasty. Under Shoshenq I and Osorkon I, the sons of the reigning king, and under Takeloth I his brothers, were successively appointed to the office of Theban pontiff.

§ **159** After the death of Smendes III, an important change occurred. The next pontiff was Harsiese, son of the former high priest Shoshenq II. With this appointment, the non-hereditary rule was broken and a dangerous precedent set. The person responsible for this lapse remains unknown. It could have been Takeloth I, in his last year or so, or the new king Osorkon II. If Takeloth I was the veritable nonentity that the present writer in-

52. Cf. block published by Gauthier, *ASAE* 37 (1937), 16–24 and pl.; stela, Loat, *Gurob* (with *Saqqara Mastabas I*), 8, pls. 18–19; as king, Nile-level No. 4 (von Beckerath, *op. cit.,* 49).

53. Lefebvre, *ASAE* 25 (1925), 25–33.

54. Statue, Cairo Cat. 42204.

55. Cf. Parker, *A Saite Oracle Papyrus from Thebes,* 1962, 5, 29, No. 50.

56. Caminos, *JEA* 50 (1964), 75, 90, line 22, pl. 10.

57. Parker, *op. cit.* (last note but one).

58. Petrie, *A History of Egypt,* III, 1905, 265, fig. 108.

59. *JEA* 53 (1967), 67, n. 3.

clines to suppose, so grave a political error may well be in keeping with his weak character – an ambitious Harsiese was perhaps able to press his claims on a weak and ailing king. However, it must also be borne in mind that such an event would have to fall very close indeed to the end of Take-loth's reign (since Smendes III was in office up to Year 14), and therefore it is wiser provisionally to assign Harsiese's appointment to the first years of Osorkon II. Once installed, Harsiese seemingly lost little time in pressing his claims still further – for kingship. While his total monuments are few enough, it may be significant that he is far more attested as 'king' than simply as pontiff.[60] Therefore, one may suppose, for example, that Harsiese might have been high priest for about 5 years and then 'king' for 10 or 15 years. His claim to kingship would seem difficult to account for, were he an ordinary commoner (even if of rank). But as son of an almost-king (the co-regent Shoshenq II), he may have pressed his claim to royal style on this and other grounds which are now unknown to us. He had full royal style, but no known regnal years. His position vis-à-vis Osorkon II has been aptly compared[61] with that of the high priest Pinudjem I who was 'king' under Smendes I and Psusennes I in the 21st Dynasty.

§ **160**   On one monument, a pink granite sarcophagus or receptacle[62] from Coptos, Harsiese as 'king' has associated with him his son, whose name is all but totally lost, as pontiff. It is possible, maybe even probable,[63] that Harsiese as 'king' took steps in turn to have his own son appointed high priest of Amun under himself, during his own lifetime. Thereby, the germ of a single hereditary succession would be planted, and the path lie open for a sub-dynasty of pontiffs as in the 21st Dynasty. However, Osorkon II sooner or later saw the dangers, and sought to re-establish his dynasty's principle of non-hereditary succession to the principal high-priesthoods. Before his reign ended, his son Nimlot C was probably already in power at Thebes, which suggests that the pontificate of Harsiese's son was ended as soon as possible (forced retirement?) after his ambitious father's death. The lack of monuments would also favour a relatively brief tenure of office.

§ **161**   However, when Osorkon II did act he was thoroughgoing. Not only was his son Nimlot C appointed to Thebes, but the Crown Prince

60. As pontiff, only on the Bes-statue (G3. 331, n. 2) and on statue Cairo Cat. 42225 (G3, 348, 5, II).

61. e.g. by Kees, Hhp., 109.

62. Legrain, ASAE 6 (1905), 123–4, 'cuve'; Jacquet-Gordon, JEA 53 (1967), 67, a libation-basin.

63. As with 'king' Pinudjem I, who appointed successive sons (Masaharta, Djed-Khons-ef-ankh, Menkheperre) to be high priest under him.

Shoshenq D supplanted a very long-established family in the pontificate of Ptah at Memphis (above, Ch. 12, § 155). Here, however, a new priestly sub-dynasty was founded and was not removed by any of Osorkon II's lineal successors; but it remained loyal to the main dynasty, as the Serapeum stelae show. But in Thebes, after the reign of Osorkon II, the two incompatible principles – of hereditary family succession versus appointments of sons of successive pharaohs afresh each reign – led to the major clash that shook Egypt for most of the reign of Takeloth II.

§ 162 There is no record of open conflict so long as Nimlot C was high priest. There is also practically no contemporary record of his tenure of that office. This may suggest that he held it only in the very last years of his father's reign and perhaps died even before Year 11 of Takeloth II, by which date the latter's son Prince Osorkon had been appointed to that office. Takeloth II thus sought in turn to apply the non-hereditary principle. However that may be, Osorkon was evidently a young man. If his high-priesthood is reckoned, say, from the 10th year of Takeloth II, and it is known to have lasted (on and off) to Year 39 of Shoshenq III, his activities as pontiff and would-be pontiff would have covered at least 55 years.

Moreover, Osorkon had his opponents, and in particular a rival for the dignity of high priest. In his chronicle, he himself alludes plainly to '. . . the enemy who will take hold of the office of First Prophet of Amun'. Naturally, he does not name a specific opponent. By far the likeliest candidate for that role is the pontiff Harsiese B, who was attested in Year 6 of Shoshenq III which was very soon after the major eclipse of Osorkon in Year 25 of Takeloth II and up to the latter's death.[64] Who was this Harsiese? Considering the wide prevalence of papponymy in this age – grandsons named after grandfathers[65] – it would seem most likely that he was son of the nameless high priest of the Coptos monument, and thus none other than a grandson of the first pontiff and 'king', Harsiese. If so, the bitterness and long persistence of this particular rivalry – Harsiese B and Osorkon alternating in Shoshenq III's middle years – is readily comprehensible. As we have no monuments so far of Harsiese B as pontiff as early as Takeloth II, it is perhaps best to assume provisionally that he first formally obtained both the rank and the powers of Theban pontiff from the accession of Shoshenq III, when the personal misfortunes of his rival Prince Osorkon were at their darkest. He then remained in office up to Year 19 of Pedubast

64. Kees (*Hhp.*, 120, end) envisaged Takeloth son of Nimlot as a possible rival of Osorkon, but reads (119–20) far too much into a chance reference by Osorkon to Heracleopolis. This Takeloth, § 163 below.

65. i.e. a man named his son after his own father, hence the term.

I (Year 26 of Shoshenq III), but had been replaced by a pontiff Takeloth by Year 23 of Pedubast I (Year 30, Shoshenq III), 4 years later. Therefore, from not later than Year 6 of Shoshenq III, perhaps from his accession, Harsiese probably held office, not without irruptions by Prince Osorkon, for at least 25 years and probably for just over 30 years.

§ 163 This brings us in turn to the pontiffs Takeloth son of Nimlot C, and Takeloth successor of Harsiese B. If the former Takeloth were the eldest son of Nimlot C, who was a man old enough for Prince Osorkon to be his grandson[66] and not easily younger than his early 20s at his appointment to the pontificate by Takeloth II's 10th or 11th year, then Nimlot could not well have died at less than 60–65 or any later than that 10th year. In which case, an eldest son Takeloth would very likely be 45 or so by then – and most unlikely to succeed Harsiese B as pontiff 42 years later (aged 87!), in or after the 19th year of Pedubast I. In this case,[67] one must assume (i) that the pontificate of Nimlot was very brief indeed, (ii) that he was immediately succeeded by his own son Takeloth, in the very last years of Osorkon II or at the very beginning of the reign of Takeloth II, and (iii) that he in turn was succeeded by Prince Osorkon by Year 10 or 11 of Takeloth II. This is all perfectly feasible, and may in fact be the truth. In that case, the Takeloth of Year 23 of Pedubast I is an entirely distinct high priest of whose origins, career and other history we know absolutely nothing.

However, there is not the slightest proof either that Takeloth was Nimlot C's eldest son or that he was his immediate successor. It *is* equally possible that he was, in fact, the youngest son of Nimlot, and only a child when Nimlot C died – perhaps 10 years old by the 10th year of Takeloth II. He would, therefore, have no immediate and effective claim on the very adult responsibilities of being pontiff, governor of Upper Egypt and army-commander of the south, as a child. But in later years, in his maturity, matters might have been very different. By the 19th year of Pedubast I, he would have been in his late prime, at about 50–52, and well able to become the next pontiff from (say) Year 20 of Pedubast I to at least Year 6 of Shoshenq IV, a minimum span of some 23 years, and say 25 years if he died aged about 75–77 in the first years of Osorkon III. In favour of this hypothesis,[68] one may offer two inconclusive observations. First, we have an economy of assumptions: no more Takeloths than are already attested

66. Prince Osorkon being son of Takeloth II by Karomama, daughter of Nimlot C (*RIK*, III, pl. 16).
67. Favoured by Kees, *MIO* 2 (1954), 361; also by M. L. Bierbrier.
68. Provisionally preferred in this book.

otherwise. Second, quite often in the Libyan period, younger sons attain to power: so, Takeloth I and II as successors to Osorkon I and II, and probably Shoshenq III as successor to Takeloth II. The same may perhaps apply here.

§ 164   How long the future Takeloth III was high priest of Amun under his father Osorkon III, before becoming co-regent, is entirely unknown. As king, he survived his father for a further 15 years (Wadi Gasus and co-regency data); hence, it is perhaps unlikely that he was pontiff for the whole of the 23 years of his father's reign prior to the co-regency. If he were, however, his total span of high office could be as high as 43 years – say, 40 years (aged 25/30 to 65/70?), if the previous Takeloth ceased to be pontiff in the first few years of Osorkon III. This assumption underlies the list of high priests given in § 157 above and in Part VI below – but it is perfectly possible that some yet-unknown pontiff may have to be intercalated for 15/20 years (at most) between the former Takeloth and Takeloth son of Osorkon III.

What happened to the high-priesthood of Amun of Thebes *after* the accession of Takeloth III remains a total mystery. While perhaps some record of a couple of incumbents for the 40 years down into the reign of Shabako remains to be found, yet the simplest explanation may well be that the office was actually left in abeyance – no pontiff appears to greet Piankhy at Karnak in the narration of his great stela. This gap certainly coincides very closely with the renewed prominence of the office of God's Wife of Amun from Shepenupet I into the Nubian and Saite periods. And, significantly, when we next meet high priests of Amun in the Nubian period, they are shorn of all political and military pretensions, being neither governors of Upper Egypt nor army-commanders; even in the cult, they can hardly be said to appear prominently in our surviving documents.

§ 165   Finally, there are a few obscurer references. A citation by Lieblein from Brugsch[69] mentions a high priest Osorkon son of a king Takeloth and the *iry-pʿtt*, ⌈*ḥrp-Ḥr*⌉, *Ḥnt-t3wy*. If Hent-tawy were the queen's name, one might assume that here we had a 'new' pontiff, perhaps son of, and serving under, Takeloth III. But *Ḥnt-t3wy* has no personal determinative, and hence is probably nothing more than the epithet 'Mistress of the Two Lands' belonging to a queen left unnamed. In that case, we merely have a further mention of Prince Osorkon, son of Takeloth II.

Other possible high priests of Amun are sometimes cited, e.g. the child Harnakht, son of Osorkon II, who was buried in his father's tomb at

69. *Dictionnaire/Namenbuch*, No. 1010.

Tanis, a Pimay son of Shoshenq, and perhaps others. There is no evidence that any of these were Theban pontiffs – but every probability that they belonged to the 22nd Dynasty royal family, appropriately holding the benefice of high priest of Amun *in Tanis*. (See Excursus D, Pt. V, below.)

§ 166   2. THE NESERAMUN FAMILY*

Together, the two statues Cairo Cat. 42221 and 42224 give the following genealogy,[70] supplemented by other documents as cited.[71]

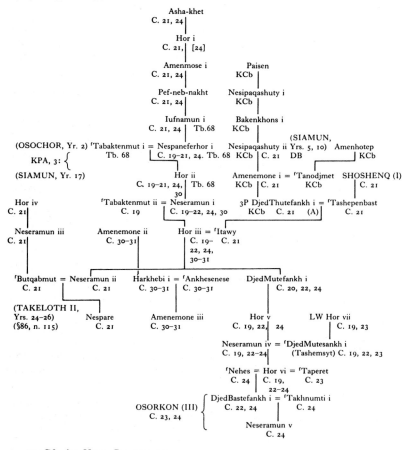

70. Cf. also Kees, *Pr.*, 230–45.

71. For all Cairo Catalogue statues numbered 42201 ff., see Legrain, *Statues, passim*. References under names in the genealogy are as follows. All figures C. 19–31 are for C(airo Cat. 422)19–31, in Legrain, *op. cit.*; KCb is the Karnak

§ **167** The genealogy just given (basically from Cairo Cat. 42221/4) receives support from several other sources.

(i) From Nespaneferhor i down to Djed-Mut-ef-ankh i, from a statue of the latter (Cairo Cat. 42220; cited on genealogy as C. 20).

(ii) From Neseramun i (grandson of Nespaneferhor i, and grandfather of Djed-Mut-er-ankh i) down to Djed-Bast-ef-ankh i, from a statue dedicated by this latter to his father Hor vi (Cairo Cat. 42222; here, C. 22), the mother of Hor vi being Djed-Mut-es-ankh i (text *f* of this statue).

(iii) The series Iufnamun i, Nespaneferhor i (with wife, Tabaktenmut i), and Hor ii receives confirmation from their inscriptions in the Theban Tomb 68 which was usurped by this family[72] and from the Karnak Priestly Annals, fragment 3B, on which see just below.[73]

(iv) The fact that a king Shoshenq (father-in-law of Djed-Thut-ef-ankh i) occurs in the 7th and 8th generations respectively before Djed-Bast-ef-ankh i and his son Neseramun v who dedicated the statue, Cairo Cat. 42224, under an Usimare Osorkon indicates that we have here an *early* Shoshenq and a *late* Osorkon, to be so many generations apart. This of itself automatically rules out Osorkon I (first generation after Shoshenq I) and Osorkon II (3rd after Shoshenq I), leaving only Osorkon III or IV in view. The prenomen Usimare and late-Theban allegiance to the 23rd Dynasty would point clearly to Osorkon III. Again, the Shoshenq involved cannot well be Shoshenq III or IV or V, as neither Osorkon III or IV came seven or eight generations after any of these.[74] Hence, this king must be Shoshenq I.[75]

(v) Support for this dating comes from two sources: (*a*) Fragment 3B of the Karnak Priestly Annals (already cited) records the induction of our Nespaneferhor i, son of Iufnamun i, in a Year 2 of a king Akheperre who is now known to be Osochor of the 21st Dynasty (§ 4, above). It then gives the subsequent induction of Nespaneferhor's son Hor ii, a generation later, in the 17th year of Siamun. This Hor ii obviously served during the

column-base, Varille, *ASAE* 50 (1950), 249–55; KPA, 3*b* is fragment 3B of Karnak Priestly Annals; Tb 68 is Tomb 68 in W. Thebes, cf. n. 72 below; DB is the graffiti in the pit of the great cache near Deir el Bahri, cf. n. 77 below. As titles, 3P is for 3rd Prophet of Amun, and LW for Letter-writer (of Pharaoh). As in all genealogies in this book, women are prefixed by ⌐ and the names of kings are given in capitals.

72. *PM²*, I: 1, *ad loc.*, and especially Černý, *ASAE* 40 (1940), 235 ff.

73. Lines 1–5; Legrain, *RT* 22 (1900), 53–4.

74. Osorkon III was at most in 3rd generation after Pedubast I, and so after the latter's contemporary Shoshenq III; he was direct successor of Shoshenq IV, and senior to Shoshenq V. Osorkon IV was probably son of Shoshenq V (certainly his successor), and not more than 3 generations from Shoshenq III. For his part, Shoshenq II was never cited for dating *as king* in later times (having been only co-regent).

75. As was long ago perceived by Legrain, *RT* 30 (1908), 84.

immediately-following reign of Psusennes II, if not into that of Shoshenq I,[76] who was his approximate contemporary-by-generation in this genealogy; any later Shoshenq is excluded. (*b*) Nesipaqashuty ii, son of Bakenkhons i, features in dockets which were added to the coffins of Ramesses I and II and Sethos I in Year 10 of Siamun, and in graffiti (without his father's name) in the well-shaft of the great cache near Deir el Bahri in Years 5 and 10 of Siamun.[77] In our genealogy, attested also by Cairo Cat. 42221 and a Karnak column-base, Nesipaqashuty ii is a man of approximately the same generation as Nespaneferhor i (under Osochor, Siamun), just before Psusennes II and Shoshenq I, so that the Deir el Bahri data agree perfectly with the other evidence bearing on the genealogy.

§ **168**   A further document belonging to this family is the statue, Cairo Cat. 42219. This gives the series from Nespaneferhor i down to Hor iii (son of Neseramun i and Tabaktenmut ii), it being dedicated to Hor iii by 'his son' a Hor son of a Neseramun! Obviously, this latter Hor cannot be the real son of Hor iii – unless the latter were also called Neseramun[78] – and may better be taken as some more distant descendant of Hor iii. Such a descendant exists: Hor vi, son of Neseramun iv and the lady Djed-Mutes-ankh i who *does* bear the second name Tashemsyt (Cairo Cat. 42223, cf. § 170 below). Thus, the statue Cat. 42219 need be no problem; particularly as its style would agree with a period close to Osorkon III, like other statues of the age, as Kees noted in passing.[79] It is a 'late' statue (by Hor vi) in honour of an 'early' ancestor (Hor iii, grandson of Shoshenq I).

§ **169**   However, Kees had doubts about this genealogy,[80] which were inspired by an apparent complication in its relations with a vizier Nesipaqashuty. Because this vizier was son of the 3rd Prophet of Amun, Djed-Thut-ef-ankh i (son-in-law of Shoshenq I) and also had a statue[81] bearing the names of Shoshenq III who reigned about a century later, Kees considered that the genealogy which is set out here would have to be shortened, to fit the father–son relationship of Djed-Thut-ef-ankh and this vizier. Of the various points of doubt he raises against the genealogy as set forth in §§ 166–168 above, not one can be justified at all.

76. The next entry in the Annals is to a 'Year 13', perhaps of either Psusennes II or possibly Shoshenq I, and conceivably the occasion of the induction of a son of Hor ii.

77. *MMR*, 557–8; 521, 522; *BAR*, IV, §§ 665–8; for Year 10 not 16, see Černý, *JEA* 32 (1946), 26–8, esp. 28.

78. But there is no other evidence to suggest this.

79. Kees, *Pr.*, 237.

80. Kees, *Pr.*, 237–8.

81. Cairo Cat. 42232, cf. §§ 170–1, below.

(i) Despite Kees, the titles of Neseramun i on Cat. 42221 *cannot* differ from those on Cat. 42224, as the latter quotes them only as *mitt*, 'ditto'![82]

(ii) The considerable correspondence between the titles held by Neseramun i and those of his grandfather Nespaneferhor i shows only that the family aspired to retain some or all of offices held by its members over several generations – a commonplace in this period.

(iii) The grandfather Nespaneferhor is not *'nicht genannt'* (so, Kees) nor does the text in Cat. 42221e suddenly 'spring back' to Nespaneferhor i. In fact (although reaching the same result), Kees failed to note that, just as text *d* continues *c*, so *e* merely continues *d*. Nespaneferhor is the 'missing' grandfather, and his titles run straight on from *d* to *e*.

(iv) Again, on the statue, Cairo Cat. 42222, the name of the great-grandfather of Hor vi son of Nes(er)amun iv is not missing: the text *f* is to be read *retrograde* (as Legrain noted, *ad loc.*), still preserves the traces of Djed-Mut-[ef-ankh], and so corresponds exactly with Cat. 42224. The Hor of Cat. 42221 who is great-grandson of Nespaneferhor is the Hor iii of Cat. 42224 and father of Djed-Mut-ef-ankh; he is *not* to be identified with Hor vi son of Neseramun iv (and great-grandson of Djed-Mut-ef-ankh!) as Kees had suggested. The repeated titles prove nothing more than the success of various members of the family in holding down various posts and dignities in succeeding generations, as has already been remarked, and cannot prove identity of *persons* in the absence of corroborative evidence. As shown above in §§ 167–168, all the available sources mutually support each other and the resultant genealogy set out in § 166. Within that genealogy and its sources, therefore, there is no basis for Kees's scepticism. But this does not resolve the initial cause of his doubts – the paternity of the vizier Nesipaqashuty A, to which we must now turn.

§ **170**   The Karnak statue Cairo Cat. 42223 was presented by Osorkon Si-Ese, god, Ruler of Thebes, i.e. Osorkon III, and its inscriptions offer the following genealogy:

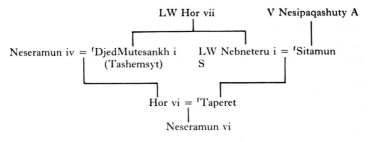

82. As Kees ultimately admits, *Pr.*, 238.

As Legrain noted[83] long ago, it is natural to assume that the 'letter-writer of Pharaoh', Hor, father of Djed-Mut-es-ankh is the same man as the identically-titled Hor, father of Neb-neteru i, in the same region and generation; they are here treated as one, as Hor vii.

The occurrence of the lady Djed-Mut-es-ankh alias Tashemsyt enables us to identify her husband and her son as Neseramun iv and Hor vi of the main genealogy of § 166 above. The statue was dedicated to Hor vi by his son Neseramun vi, by his wife Taperet, who is quite distinct from his like-named son Neseramun v by the lady Nehes.

Taperet's antecedents are the ones that matter most; through her mother Sitamun, she was the granddaughter of a man Nesipaqashuty who is accorded all the titles of a vizier except that of $t\beta ty$, 'Vizier', itself.[84] Fortunately, this omission is repaired on other monuments, showing clearly that Sitamun's father really had been a vizier: the set of four canopic jars of Sitamun in the Fitzwilliam Museum at Cambridge.[85] Is this vizier to be identified with the vizier Nesipaqashuty whose statue (Cairo Cat. 42232) is double-dated by the names of Shoshenq III and the Theban pontiff Harsiese B? This identification would fit well into the genealogy so far: Shoshenq III is fifth full king after Shoshenq I, which would on generation-count put him about Hor vii and Neseramun iv in the genealogy – which coincides very well with Nesipaqashuty as about contemporary with Hor vii on Cat. 42223 and Hor v on the main genealogy. Therefore, on this ground, the identification seems acceptable.

§ **171** But it is precisely the vizier Nesipaqashuty of Cat. 42232 who is given as son of a 3rd Prophet of Amun with many titles, Chief Inspector and General, Djed-Thut-ef-ankh, and grandson of 'ditto', Amenemone (text *j*). Scholars have not unnaturally identified[86] these two forebears with the like-named son-in-law of Shoshenq I and his father Amenemone of Cat. 42221 and the Karnak column-bases. It is this which appears to make the vizier Nesipaqashuty officiate under Shoshenq III some 80 years or more after the time that his father was a younger contemporary of Shoshenq I. Hence the difficulties which were felt by Kees, even if his solution has to be rejected.

83. *RT* 30 (1908), 81, Document 3; in genealogy above, LW, S stands for the 'Letter-writer (of Pharaoh) for the Southern region.'

84. He is called: 'Prophet of Amenresonter, Count and Hereditary Noble, He of the Curtain ($t\beta ty$), Dignitary ($s\beta b$), Man of Nekhen, Prophet of Maat' (with *kheru* erroneously added).

85. Budge, *Catalogue of the Egyptian Collection in the Fitzwilliam Museum, Cambridge*, 64; Weil, *Veziere des Pharaonenreiches*, 155, § 35*a*.

86. e.g. Gauthier (*G3*, 368, XLI, with n. 4, contrast 324, LIX!), Varille, *ASAE* 50 (1950), 255, and Kees, *Pr.*, 238, 240.

Originally, a different approach seemed possible to me. Namely, to intercalate the Amenemone and Djed-Thut-ef-ankh (direct forebears of the
vizier Nesipaqashuty on Cat. 42232) as son and grandson of the well-
known Djed-Thut-ef-ankh, son-in-law of Shoshenq I, thus putting two
whole generations between the latter dignitary and the vizier.
This simple solution would solve the problem very neatly, but for the
contrary evidence offered by Liverpool City Museum stela M. 13916.[87]
This document had the following genealogy:

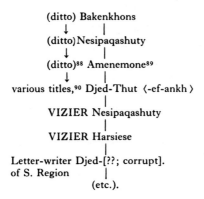

(ditto) Bakenkhons

(ditto) Nesipaqashuty

(ditto)[88] Amenemone[89]

various titles,[90] Djed-Thut ⟨-ef-ankh⟩

VIZIER Nesipaqashuty

VIZIER Harsiese

Letter-writer Djed-[??; corrupt].
of S. Region

(etc.).

Here, the four predecessors of the vizier Nesipaqashuty are transparently
identical in sequence with the Bakenkhons i, Nesipaqashuty ii, Amenemone
i, and Djed-Thut-ef-ankh i of our main genealogy. Therefore, the suggestion which I made just above (to intercalate two additional generations
before the vizier) must be rejected – unless one assumes an erroneous
omission in the genealogy of the Liverpool stela. This is *just* possible;
because, in fact, not only is this text badly written (with four blanks left in
it), but also the name Djed-Thut⟨-ef-ankh⟩ occurs right at the end of line 6
as simply Djed-Thut. At the start of the next line, the scribe carelessly
omitted ⟨-ef-ankh, justified⟩ before going on with 'son of'. Now, by the
process of *homoioteleuton*, it is possible that this avowedly careless scribe
has omitted not just 'ef-ankh, justified', but the whole of 'ef-ankh, justified,
son of *ditto*, Amenemone, justified, son of *ditto* Djed-Thut-ef-ankh,

87. Now destroyed. For opportunity to utilize a copy of its texts, I am indebted to
the kindness of Professor H. W. Fairman.
88. Written *ii-im* – blunder for *mi-nn*.
89. The end of the name is written *-iwnt*, not *int*; this quirk recurs on other
monuments of the general period, e.g. Cairo Cat. 42230–1.
90. e.g. 2nd (elsewhere, 3rd) Prophet of Khons-in-Thebes, Neferhotep; scribe
of the Temple of Osiris lord of Abydos; army-scribe; *wr-diw*.

justified', before going on with 'son of *ditto*, Amenemone', his eye having lighted upon a second *and earlier* Amenemone of two in his *Vorlage*.

§ **171** However, while this is possible, it is bad method to assume error for the sake of a theory. Therefore, one must finally ask instead whether the solution first rejected by Kees is really as impossible as he thought. With all due reserve, I would suggest that the vizier Nesipaqashuty A could still be the direct son of the well-known Djed-Thut-ef-ankh i/A, on the following bases and assumptions.

Point I: the vizier Nesipaqashuty's statue is double-dated to the reign of Shoshenq III and the pontificate of Harsiese B. This very strongly suggests a date at the *beginning* of the reign of Shoshenq III, as his rule was later discarded for dating by the Thebans in favour of the 23rd Dynasty, and as we have this very pontiff Harsiese explicitly attested in office in the 6th year of Shoshenq III.[91]

Assumption 1: Nesipaqashuty was probably a man of mature years when he was first appointed vizier – say, 40 or 50 – and might have been 70 by the 10th year of Shoshenq III. On this basis, the bulk of his career during the age-span of, say, 20–60, would have fallen within the reigns of Osorkon II and Takeloth II (24 and 25 years, nearly 50 years in total); he could thus have been born early in the reign of Takeloth I, and conceivably a little earlier still.

Point II: Nesipaqashuty and his father Djed-Thut-ef-ankh were no mere *parvenus* as no less than five generations of their forebears had served in distinguished military office already. Their distinction and importance are both illustrated and enhanced by the fact that Shoshenq I deemed it politic to give a daughter (Tashepenbast) in marriage to Djed-Thut-ef-ankh i/A.

Assumption 2: as Amenemone i was the approximate contemporary of Shoshenq I by generation, one may suggest that it was later in Shoshenq's reign that the latter honoured Amenemone and bound the family fortunes to the throne by giving his daughter in marriage to Amenemone's son, and further that this son Djed-Thut-ef-ankh was himself still young at that time (in his 20s?), in say about Year 20 of Shoshenq I.

Point III: the latter calculation (plus that under Assumption 1) would leave some 38–42 years, say 40 years, between this marriage of Djed-Thut-ef-ankh and the birth of Nesipaqashuty; the latter, therefore, was not born of Tashepenbast.

Assumption 3: there seems no reason why Nesipaqashuty should not, in fact, have been a son of Djed-Thut-ef-ankh's old age (at about 60

91. Nile-level text No. 23, Karnak quay; von Beckerath, *JARCE* 5 (1966), 51.

or even older)[92] by a later, much younger wife, perhaps long after Tashepen-bast's death. By the latter, he had probably had other sons much earlier in life who may have attained to some of the appointments which were traditional in this family (Royal Scribe of Ta-set-Mery-Thoth; General; Chief Inspector, etc.). It is especially noteworthy that Nesipaqashuty did *not* follow in the family tradition of six generations before him, but struck out at a tangent, followed an entirely different career, and ended up as Upper-Egyptian Vizier. In that dignity, he was followed by a son Harsiese, whose son Djed-[???] became royal Letter-writer for the South. So Nesipaqashuty, who was born late in his father's lifetime, represents not a continuation of his family's main tradition, but a breakaway segment.

§ **172** In the light of the foregoing, then, I would be so bold as to suggest that it is possible that Nesipaqashuty A was alive as vizier or retired vizier in the first years of Shoshenq III, and that he was the son of the old age of Djed-Thut-ef-ankh i/A who had earlier in life married a daughter of Shoshenq I. Should this solution – requiring no emendations or other adjustments – not be acceptable, then the best alternative is my initial suggestion § 171, above, to intercalate two additional generations after Djed-Thut-ef-ankh, and assume a large but feasible haplography in the badly-written stela Liverpool M. 13916. But it is certain that no other text or genealogy should be tampered with, least of all the main genealogy in § 166, which is buttressed by so many interlocking documents.[93]

§ **173** To round off the main genealogy, the statues Cairo Cat. 42230/31 require brief consideration. They show the following relationships:

Cat. 42230   Cat. 42231

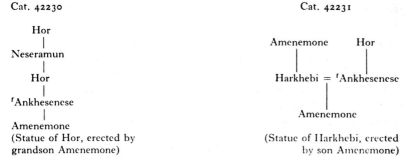

Hor
|
Neseramun
|
Hor
|
ʿAnkhesenese
|
Amenemone
(Statue of Hor, erected by
grandson Amenemone)

Amenemone   Hor
| |
Harkhebi = ʿAnkhesenese
|
Amenemone
(Statue of Harkhebi, erected
by son Amenemone)

92. This is far from unparalleled in the Near East (sheikhs or an Ibn Saud still begetting children in their 70's). The longevity of Djed-Thut-ef-ankh would not be remarkable; cf. the 96 years claimed by Nebneteru iii (Cairo Cat. 42225c), the 80 years of Amenhotep son of Hapu in the 18th Dynasty (*Urkunden IV*, 1828), the 60 or 70 years' career of Bakenkhons in the 19th Dynasty (cf. Bierbrier, *JEA* 58 (1972)), and not least the very long careers of Prince Osorkon and Shoshenq III.
93. Thus, if Djed-Bast-ef-ankh i was indeed a brother (or related contemporary)

If one may assume that Ankhesenese is the same lady in both cases, since the graphic variants of Amenemone are known in other instances, then the following combined genealogy results:

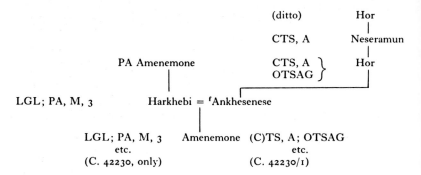

§ **174**   As can be seen clearly from the distribution of relevant ciphers,[94] the younger Amenemone sooner or later inherited offices from *both* sides of the family – scribal on his mother's side, and dealing with linen and a place in the 3rd phyle on his father's side, the former series being of course derived from his grandfather. He thus very fittingly erected one statue each to the two men to whom he owed these benefices. The 'gap' of one generation (between the later Hor and the later Amenemone) in tenure of the scribal offices may combine neatly with the possible link between these statues and our main genealogy.

§ **175**   In that main genealogy, either Hor iii or Hor vi could be the father of Ankhesenese, as both were sons of Neseramuns and grandsons of Hors. In favour of Hor iii, one may note that his titles on Cairo Cat. 42220 include Temple Scribe of the [Estate] of Amun, and of all gods of South and North; and on Cat. 42219, his title Chief Temple Scribe of the Estate of Amun, which was borne also by his father Neseramun i, and which was precisely the same as that of Ankhesenese's grandfather Neseramun. Furthermore, between Hor iii (if he was father of Ankhesenese) and his possible grandson Amenemone, the scribal functions were held precisely

of Djed-Mut-ef-ankh (as suggested by Kees, *Pr.*, 241 top), then surely it is quite incredible that on Cat. 42224 he should make him into a distant ancestor (great-great-grandfather)! Confusion in a long genealogy is a possibility, but *not* between one's own brother or contemporary and so distant an ancestor!

94. CTS, A is 'Chief Temple-scribe, Estate of Amun'; OTSAG is 'Overseer of Temple-scribes of all gods of south & north'. LGL is 'Chief of Secrets of the Linen of the god's limbs'; PA,M,3 covers 'Prophet of Amun, Montu, on third phyle'. Non-recurrent titles are omitted.

by the *son* of Hor iii, Neseramun ii, which gives a straight series of incumbents through these three generations. Later, Neseramun iv would take over from our later Amenemone.

By contrast, Hor vi did *not* hold these offices, even though his father did. Instead, he was a Scribe of Mut (not Amun), and *imy-st-ʿ* of the Estate of Amun, and *sš sḏȝyt-nṯr* of that god.

§ 176 Therefore, one may suggest that Harkhebi of Cat. 42231 was in about the third generation after Shoshenq I, i.e. flourishing about the time of Osorkon II; the statue which was erected by his son could have been set up under Takeloth II (by c. 830 B.C.). Such a date would doubtless also take care of Cat. 42230.

§ 177 3. THE NEBNETERU FAMILY*

The combined data on statues Cairo Cat. 42226/7, 42225, a Cairo block,[95] and the figure Berlin 17272[96] give the following genealogy.[97]

```
              LW Nebneteru ii
              C. 25, BLN |
                         |
              3P, V Neseramun vii = ʿMuthetepti i
              C. 25-27, Cb, Q, BLN |    C. 25
                                   |
                   LW Nebneteru iii = ʿDjedMutesankh ii ┐   HPA
                   C. 25-27, Cb, Q, BLN |        C. 25   │ Harsiese A
                       ┌────────────────┘─────────┐       │   C. 25
DjedMutesankh iii = LW Neseramun viii  LW Nebneteru v  LW Hor viii ┘ OSORKON II
   BLN        |    S   C. 26-27, Cb, BLN   Cb |      C. 25; Q?        C. 25
     ┌────────┘──────────────────────────────┘
PEDUBAST I    ~   LW Hor ix = ʿMerutamun   ~   SHOSHENQ (III/IV)[98]
   C. 26           C. 26-27,  |       Cb
               Cb, BLN, LD 34 |
OSORKON III[99]  ~  LW, 3P Nebneteru iv
   BLN, LD 34       S   Cb, BLN, LD 34
```

95. This, Legrain, *RT* 30 (1908), 161–2, Document 10.

96. *Aegyptische Inschriften, Berlin*, II, 73–4.

97. Cf. already, Kees, *Pr.*, 223–9. Ciphers used: titles, V is vizier, HPA is High Priest of Amun, and 3P Third Prophet of Amun. LW (S) is 'Letter-writer (of S. region)'. Sources: BLN is Berlin 17272; Cb is the Cairo block (n. 95, above); C. 25–7 are Cat. 42225–27. LD34 is the Louvre vase, D34; Q is Quibell, *The Ramesseum*, pl. 25: 5.

98. Funerary cones of Hor, Davies-Macadam, *A Corpus of Inscribed Egyptian Funerary Cones*, 1957, Nos. 25, 26.

99. Whose cartouches date the Louvre vase D34 of Nebneteru son of Hor, Legrain, *RT* 30 (1908), 171, Document 18.

This genealogy is chronologically important because the 3rd and 4th generations were contemporary with Osorkon II, while the 5th generation coincided with Pedubast I and a Shoshenq (III, probably) and the 6th with an Osorkon who in this sequence can only be Osorkon III. The most important figures here are Hor viii and his nephew Hor ix who eventually succeeded him in office as a Letter-writer of Pharaoh (or royal secretary). They are both reminiscent of Hor vii in the Neseramun genealogy dealt with above, and of such a Hor in yet other documents.

§ **178**   A further genealogy is provided by the combined data of the coffins Berlin 20132–36,[100] the statues Cairo Cat. 717 (Borchardt) and 42228/9 (Legrain), and some other coffins, which are mainly in Cairo.[101] The full genealogy is dealt with in § 180, below. We look first at that of Cat. 42228/9.

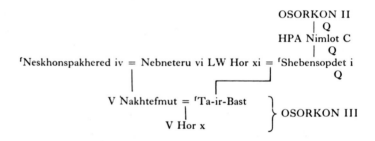

Here, we have an Usimare Osorkon (III) Si-Ese contemporary with the 3rd and 4th generations after an Usimare Osorkon, known to be II; his son, the pontiff Nimlot C, is attested elsewhere. These are the same two kings in the genealogy, § 177 above, where Osorkon III is in the 2nd and 3rd generation after Osorkon II. As Osorkon II reigned for at least 22 years and Osorkon III for nearly 30 years, this range of 2/3 to 3/4 generations is feasible: the documents concerned are not dated to specific years in these reigns, and can obviously vary in date within a reign, either in the early or late part. 'Generation-count' is not a rigid, but a flexible tool.[102]

The question arises over the possible relationships between the various

100. See Anthes, *MDIK* 12 (1943), 45–50.
101. Lieblein, *Dictionnaire*, Nos. 1113, 1347, 2309 (Berlin, 8239). Q is Quibell, *The Ramesseum*, pl. 27: 8.
102. Particularly if one bears in mind that the genealogy of Cairo Cat. 42226/7 includes a man like Nebneteru iii who lived 96 years. We do not know whether either of his named sons (Hor viii, Neseramun viii) was his eldest, or how early or late in his life they were born.

'letter-writers' Hor: xi here, vii and ix in § 177 above, and vii in the Neseramun genealogy (§ 166 ff.). In the first place, it seems legitimate to identify Hor vii of the Neseramun family with Hor ix of Nebneteru's line. Each has a son Nebneteru (i, iv) as letter-writer of the South region, who would then be one and the same. The general date would agree: Hor vii is about the time of Takeloth II, while Hor ix approximates to Pedubast I who began to reign about 8 years after Takeloth's death. This would leave two men – Hor viii or Hor vii/ix – to relate to Hor xi. Either would seem theoretically a possible candidate for identification with Hor xi.

Hor viii is a contemporary of Osorkon II and the high priest Harsiese (A), not yet 'king' (statue, Cairo Cat. 42225). Hor xi was married to a *granddaughter* of Osorkon II (Shebensopdet, Cat. 42229). If one assumed the identity of Hor viii and xi, Osorkon would be giving his granddaughter to a man of his own generation. This is possible, but somewhat unlikely. However, Hor vii/ix who was active during the reign of Osorkon's son and successor Takeloth II, and is attested on a monument dated early in the next-generation reign of Pedubast, might very well have married a granddaughter of Osorkon II, a lady who would be only slightly younger than himself. This solution has already been adopted by Kees.[103]

§ **179** However, Kees did not stop there. Following Legrain, Kees took Hor *son* of Nebneteru on Cat. 42225 to stand for Hor *grandson* of Nebneteru,[104] thus identifying Hor viii with our Hor vii/ix/xi. This on principle is possible – Hor vi once called himself 'son' of Hor iii (meaning 'descendant'), on Cat. 42219 (cf. § 168, above).

But this suggestion leads into difficulties. If Hor viii is none other than Hor vii/ix/xi, who was active under Takeloth II, Shoshenq III and Pedubast I, what becomes of the cartouches Usimare Osorkon and the mention of a pontiff Harsiese on statue Cairo Cat. 42225? As we have just seen, the late date of Hor vii does not favour him being also in active service as early as the first years of Osorkon II; he would perhaps have been 'letter-writer' for nearly 40 years, and have married Osorkon II's granddaughter when in his 60s. This is possible, but not too likely. The dateline can hardly be Osorkon III, or his activity might be over-long the other way – and one would have to invent a new pontiff Harsiese (III). Again, this is all possible, but is hardly likely on the evidence that is available at present. Therefore, it is better at present to assume a succession-in-office of Nebneteru iii, Hor viii, Neseramun viii, Hor vii/ix/xi.

103. Kees, *Pr.*, 223, 226.
104. *ZÄS* 74 (1938), 74–5; presupposed in *Pr.* and *Hhp.*

§ 180   4. THE VIZIER NAKHTEFMUT AND RELATIVES ANKHPAKHERED*

The statue Cairo Cat. 42229 of a vizier Nakhtefmut C was erected by his son, the vizier Hor x, under Osorkon III, and traces back their ancestry to Osorkon II (cf. §§ 178–179).[105] It is possible, but not proven, that he is the same vizier Nakhtefmut of Cat. 42217 and Lieblein[106] 1113, and very likely is the same Nakhtefmut of several other documents.[107] These all combine to give the following genealogy:

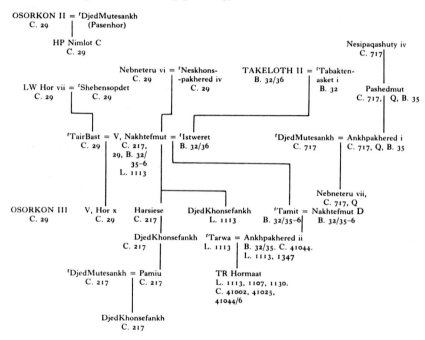

With Kees,[108] one may identify the Ankhpakhered of Lieblein 1347 (with his genealogy, plus Lieblein 2309 = Berlin 8239) with the Ankhpakhered of Lieblein 1113 and Berlin 21032/35, on account of the rather

105. Cf. Anthes, *MDIK* 12 (1943), 45–7, and Kees, *Pr.*, 228, 256–60.
106. Here and hereinafter, all references to Lieblein are to his *Dictionnaire* or *Namenwörterbuch*.
107. Again, C. 29, 217, are Cat. 42229 and 42217. C. 717 is Cat. 717 in Borchardt's *Statuen und Statuetten*. Q is Quibell, *Ramesseum*, pl. 25: 23. L is Lieblein; B. 32–6 are the coffins Berlin 20132–6. C. 41002–46 are Cairo coffins in Moret and Gauthier, cf. n. 109.
108. Kees, *Pr.*, 259 and n. 3.

special titles (concerning Khons-the-Child) which are characteristic of Ankhpakhered and his family. Then, Hormaat the Treasurer of Pharaoh (var., of Estate of Amun) who was son of an Ankhpakhered and father of a lady Neskhons, recurs in the extensive Besenmut genealogy (cf. § 190 below), and on various coffins and perhaps two stelae.[109] One may thus add the following relationships to the bottom right of those set out above.

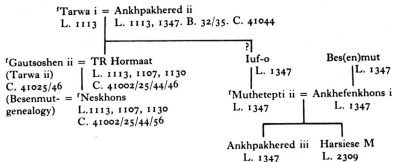

'Tarwa i = Ankhpakhered ii
L. 1113 | L. 1113, 1347. B. 32/35. C. 41044

'Gautsoshen ii = TR Hormaat
(Tarwa ii) | L. 1113, 1107, 1130
C. 41025/46 | C. 41002/25/44/46
(Besenmut- = 'Neskhons
genealogy) L.1113, 1107, 1130
C. 41002/25/44/56

Iuf-o
L. 1347

Bes(en)mut
L. 1347

'Muthetepti ii = Ankhefenkhons i
L. 1347 | L. 1347

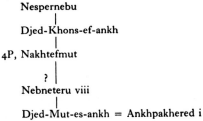

Ankhpakhered iii   Harsiese M
L. 1347   L. 2309

Further back in history, the top line on the right side of the statue Cairo Cat. 717 is continued by the vertical line on the right edge of its dorsal pillar, giving Nakhtefmut, son of Djed-Khons-ef-ankh, son of Nespernebu. But this latter line is not directly connected with the ancestry of the lady Djed-Mut-es-ankh by the surviving texts, as was assumed by Kees.[110] It is conceivable that her father Nebneteru (viii) was a *son* of Nakhtefmut (not his brother), which puts the latter in roughly the same generation as Osorkon II, and agrees with his own fuller genealogy (§§ 183 ff., below). We thus might have:

Nespernebu
|
Djed-Khons-ef-ankh
|
4P, Nakhtefmut
? |
Nebneteru viii
|
Djed-Mut-es-ankh = Ankhpakhered i

109. The stelae, Lieblein, Nos. 1107, 1130. The coffins, Cairo Cat. 41002, possibly 41025 (both, in Moret, *Sarcophages de l'Époque Bubastite à l'Époque Saïte*, 1912–13), and on Cat. 41044/46 (in Gauthier, *Cercueils anthropoïdes des Prêtres de Montou*, 1912–13), being Lieblein 1096+2314. The one assumption is that Hormaat's wife Gaut-soshen bore the second name Tarwa, that of her husband's mother. Such double names are otherwise attested; cf. Tashemsyt/Djed-Mut-es-ankh, or Tasherenmut/Shepenese (§ 183), or various people in the Besenmut genealogy, § 190 below.

110. *Pr.*, 257, table; he had erroneously treated the text on the right edge of the dorsal pillar as the continuation of the text on the rearmost flat surface of the pillar.

§ **181**   As it stands, the main genealogy presents no inherent problems. No evidence so far exists to contradict the assumption that the *same* vizier Nakhtefmut is mentioned in all the documents used above. Likewise, the second assumption is so far uncontradicted by data, i.e. that Iuf-o was the son of that Ankhpakhered (ii) who was a grandson of that same vizier Nakhtefmut.

So constructed, this genealogy further supports the sequence of kings of the 22nd/23rd Dynasties which can be observed in the Neseramun and Nebneteru genealogies and is equally derivable from other monumental sources (Serapeum stelae; Nile-level texts; high priests of Amun):

Osorkon (II)

Takeloth (II)

Osorkon (III)

The two cases of a generation-gap, before and after Takeloth II, illustrate two points. Between him and Osorkon III, one gap fits in well with the presence there of Pedubast I and Shoshenq III (contemporaries). The other is only an apparent gap (there being no king between Osorkon II and Takeloth II), which shows the possible one-generation variation in flexible entities such as genealogies that we have seen already.[111]

§ **182**   Finally, there is the possibility of linking up the genealogy of this vizier Nakhtefmut with the notable family of that other Nakhtefmut, who was 4th Prophet of Amun, surnamed Djed-Thut-ef-ankh (§§ 183 ff.).

One such link has been noted above, § 180 end, provided by the statue Cairo Cat. 717. A second contact is through the *younger* 4th prophet, Nakhtefmut (great-grandson of his famous namesake), and contemporary of Osorkon III and Takeloth III (Cairo Cat. 42211). This date agrees with his presence in the Besenmut genealogy in about the same generation as the treasurer Hormaat (§ 180, above). The latter was both a grandson (via his mother) of a brother of the vizier Hor x, (early?) contemporary of Osorkon III, and an approximate contemporary by generation of Neseramun v, a (late?) contemporary of Osorkon III. This spread is a further indication that the reign of Osorkon III was relatively *long*, not short – a view which fits well with the 29 years allowed him in Part II, above; a reign of but 9 years is grossly inadequate. Thus we have a triple corres-

---

111. Thus, one whole generation would easily be contained entirely within the almost 50 years of the combined reigns of Osorkon II and Takeloth II. One may also recall the fact that the chief queen of Takeloth II was Karomama, at once his own niece (daughter of his brother Nimlot C) and granddaughter of his father Osorkon II, precisely as was Shebensopdet the wife of Hor vii/ix/xi.

pondence[112] which would establish an approximate link between the large Besenmut genealogy and the Libyan Dynasties, so that it goes far back into the 22nd, and down into the 25th Dynasty.

§ 183 5. THE FAMILY OF 4th PROPHET DJED-THUT-EF-ANKH CALLED NAKHTEFMUT*

Four statues from Karnak[113] and a stela from the Ramesseum[114] combine to give the following genealogy of the 4th Prophet of Amun, Nakhtefmut.[115]

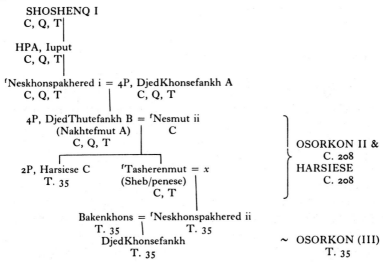

```
SHOSHENQ I
C, Q, T|
       |
HPA, Iuput
C, Q, T|
       |
ʿNeskhonspakhered i = 4P, DjedKhonsefankh A
C, Q, T              |   C, Q, T
                     |
   4P, DjedThutefankh B = ʿNesmut ii
      (Nakhtefmut A)    |   C
         C, Q, T        |
    ┌──────────┴──────────┐
   2P, Harsiese C    ʿTasherenmut = x
     T. 35           (Sheb/penese)
                       C, T
                        |
    Bakenkhons = ʿNeskhonspakhered ii
       T. 35   |      T. 35
            DjedKhonsefankh
               T. 35
```

OSORKON II &
C. 208
HARSIESE
C. 208

~ OSORKON (III)
T. 35

It will be seen that this presentation of statue T. 35 (and in one point, of Cairo Cat. 42206/7) does not agree with the genealogy as given by Kees.[116] Scrutiny of the data from Cat. 42206/7 provides *no* evidence that Nesmut ii was a daughter of the high priest Iuput as Kees had asserted[117] – and in fact, provides no evidence for her parentage at all. In fig. 142 of *Karnak-Nord*

112. Hormaat in the Besenmut clan, and vizier Nakhtefmut; 4th Prophet Nakhtefmut B in Besenmut clan, and vizier Nakhtefmut; 4th Prophet Nakhtefmut A in his own genealogy and in that of Besenmut.

113. Cairo Cat. 42206–8; and T. 35 from Temple of Montu, Barguet and Leclant, *Karnak-Nord IV*, 1954, figs. 140–5 and pls. 123–7.

114. Quibell, *The Ramesseum*, pl. 30A, No. 3.

115. Cf. already, Kees, *Pr.*, 205–23 and n. 21, end; 246–7. Ciphers: Q is Quibell, *op. cit.* (n. 114); T, T. 35, is the statue T. 35 (n. 113). C is for Cat. 42206–8 (208 is Cat. 42208 alone). HPA is high priest of Amun, while 2P, 4P, are for the 2nd and 4th prophets respectively.

116. *Pr.*, table to p. 206; *Hhp.*, 98.

117. *Pr.*, 204, No. 2; 214.

IV, Kees had identified our Nes-Khons-pakhered ii with the daughter of Iuput by that name (i, above). The simple prophet of Amun, the youngest Djed-Khons-ef-ankh, would then have been a half-brother of Nakhtefmut A. Only by this means can the high priest Iuput be credited with a wife Shepenese, as no other evidence for the name of a wife of Iuput has yet come to light. By this means also, Kees sought to identify the 4th prophet Nakhtefmut of *Karnak-Nord IV*, fig. 142, as a great-grandfather (on his mother's side) of the famous Nakhtefmut A. He called them I and II.

But is this justified? All this construction rests ultimately *and solely* upon the assumption that there was only *one* lady called Nes-Khons-pakhered in the main genealogy. This assumption in turn requires another: that this lady married two husbands in succession, both a Bakenkhons (giving him a son Djed-Khons-ef-ankh) and the 4th prophet of Amun Djed-Khons-ef-ankh (bearing him our Nakhtefmut A). This is all *theoretically* possible, but totally unnecessary. It is perhaps curious that Kees's 'Nakhtefmut I' and early Shepenese are never mentioned or commemorated elsewhere on family monuments. In fact, it is simpler by far to identify the 4th prophet Nakhtefmut and his daughter Shepenese with the two people we already know, and to assume two ladies called Nes-Khons-pakhered,[118] rather than to extrapolate a new 4th prophet, a new wife of a high priest, and two marriages for a supposedly unitary Nes-Khons-pakhered. Finally, in *Karnak-Nord IV*, fig. 142, Nakhtefmut's words actually express good wishes for his descendants – he is made to say: 'May his (N's) young people (*ḏꜣmw*) succeed him, (namely) the prophet of Amun, Djed-Khons-ef-ankh, son of the prophet of Amenresonter, Bakenkhons', etc. Surely, this is the *same* famous Nakhtefmut (A) who is commemorated everywhere else on statue T. 35, and the aspirations of his descendants are put into *his* mouth, not that of some more distant ancestor who is otherwise unmentioned and is virtually forgotten.[119] In fact, the aspirations of this Djed-Khons-ef-ankh probably came to nought. The 4th prophetship never came to him, but remained in the line of

118. A third lady of this name is a daughter of an Ankhefenkhons in a genealogy that may link up with this present one (cf. § 188, below); and there are at least three Nesmuts in the full Nakhtefmut tree.

119. The sole point of doubt that affects the statue T. 35 is its actual date; the cartouche upon it could be either Osorkon II or III. By the time of its erection, Harsiese had evidently not only succeeded his father Nakhtefmut (as 4th prophet) but had been appointed as 2nd prophet. Furthermore, his relatives on the statue come down to a great-nephew. This all hardly seems likely as early as the reign of Osorkon II when Harsiese's own father Nakhtefmut A was alive, and not really conceivable before very late under Takeloth II. In fact, it seems much better to consider the statue as a late dedication in honour of Nakhtefmut A by another branch of the family with some aspiration to his former offices (but never fulfilled).

Harsiese C and *his* sons (including further and different Djed-Khons-ef-ankhs!), as we shall see below (§§ 184, 187, 189).

§ **184** The main genealogy so far, then, shows a father-to-son succession of the 4th prophet Djed-Khons-ef-ankh A, the 4th prophet Djed-Thut-ef-ankh B (called Nakhtefmut A), and the 2nd prophet Harsiese C.[120] To this genealogy may immediately be fitted those of the Karnak statues Cairo Cat. 42210 and 42211. The latter names Nespernebu as father of the 4th prophet Djed-Khons-ef-ankh A[121] – which ties in the further statue Cairo Cat. 559 (Borchardt) which names Nesmut i as wife and mother of these two men. Cat. 42211 enumerates ten lineal ancestors of Nespernebu. Combined with Cat. 42210, it shows that Harsiese C[122] was variously both 4th and 2nd prophet of Amun, that he married Istweret, daughter of 'king' Harsiese, and that his son[123] Djed-Khons-ef-ankh C became 4th prophet, married Shepensopdet ii (daughter of Takeloth II) and in turn had a son Nakhtefmut B.[124] Furthermore, Cairo Cat. 42211 is dated by the double cartouches Osorkon (III) Si-Ese and Takeloth (III) Si-Ese, both Meryamun. Cairo Cat. 559, on the other hand, bears the cartouche Sekh-emkheperre – Osorkon I – which fits in well with the fact that this statue commemorates the son-in-law of the high priest Iuput, brother of Osorkon I. Finally, one may here add the statues Cairo Cat. 42214/5. Both have as ancestor a vizier Padimut. His grandson Harkhebi married a Nesmut (iii), sister of the famous 4th prophet Nakhtefmut A. The other man commemorated, the 3rd prophet Padimut ii called Patjenfy, who was the great-grandson of the vizier, had married a daughter of the high priest Iuwelot, known otherwise (above, § 157, 3) as a son of a king Osorkon. Like Har-khebi, Iuwelot was of about the same generation as Nesmut iii and her brother the 4th prophet Nakhtefmut A. Thus, Iuwelot's father king Osorkon is approximately contemporary with Nakhtefmut's father, the 4th prophet Djed-Khons-ef-ankh A who was the son of Nespernebu. But Nakhtef-mut's father is already linked (by the statue Cat. 559) with the reign of

120. For the series Nespe(r)nebu, Djed-Khons-ef-ankh, Nakhtefmut A, Harsiese C, see Quibell, *The Ramesseum*, pl. 23: 5 & 8. There, pl. 24: 2 may mention Nakhtef-mut (A) son of Djed-Khons-ef-ankh, while pl. 22 records a Djed-Mut-es-ankh perhaps daughter of the 4th prophet Nakhtefmut A (so, Kees, *Pr.*, 214, n. 1).

121. The title 3rd prophet here is probably a simple graphic error for the usual 4th prophet (omission of one stroke).

122. Just once, his name is erroneously confused with that of his father, Nakhtef-mut (Cat. 42211*d*).

123. The fragments Quibell, *Ramesseum*, pls. 24: 4 and 25: 3, give two daughters of Harsiese C and Istweret, namely Takhnumti (names of grand-parents preserved, but not of parents), cf. Kees, *Pr.*, 216, n. 1; and a Djed-Mut-es-ankh.

124. For Nehem-sy-Bast, daughter of Djed-Khons-ef-ankh C, cf. Quibell, *Ramesseum*, pl. 27: 7 with 26: 6.

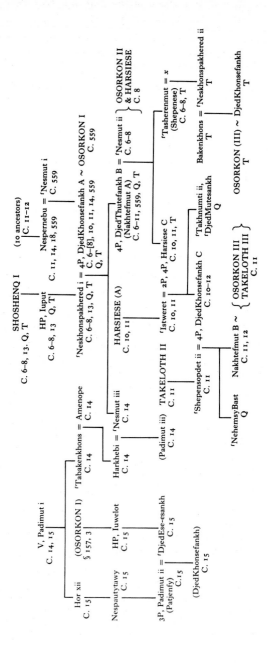

Sekhemkheperre Osorkon I, as noted above, and therefore the high priest Iuwelot is indubitably a son of Osorkon I, and not of any later Osorkon. Least of all was he a son of Osorkon III as Meyer had thought.[125] The main skeleton of the genealogy may be set out as shown on page 220.

§ **185**   For the 22nd/23rd Dynasties, we thus have a clear succession by generations:

(Dynasty 22):
1st generation, Shoshenq I, Hedjkheperre.[126]
2nd generation.
3rd generation, Osorkon I, Sekhemkheperre.
4th generation, Harsiese.
4th/5th generation, Osorkon II, Usimare.
5th generation, Takeloth II.
6th generation.

(Dynasty 23):
7th generation, Osorkon III and Takeloth III.

This agrees perfectly with the succession and relative chronology of the Libyan kings as obtained from the Serapeum stelae, the other genealogies reviewed in this chapter, and various other monuments (dealt with in Pt. II). Osorkon I overlaps the 3rd generation (as well as the 2nd, probably) because he reigned so long – 35 years on the view adopted here (cf. Pt. II, § 89, above); and no statue of this family (or of any other!) happens to be dated to Takeloth I. Thereafter, Osorkon II (plus Harsiese) and Takeloth II follow in regular order. The 6th generation was that of Pedubast I and the first part of the reign of Shoshenq III, plus the brief sole reigns of Iuput I and Shoshenq IV. Then, the 7th generation brings us to Osorkon III and Takeloth III (who would thus be contemporaries of Pimay and Shoshenq V, as in Pt. II, above. For their prenomens in a similar genealogical series, cf. the Neseramun genealogy above.)

§ **186**   To the middle part of the main genealogy given in § 184 above, further sources add other relatives, which confirm its arrangement and time-scale; Cairo Cat. 42213 and 42216 give us the following:

125. Meyer, *Gottesstaat*, 27; *BAR*, IV, § 795. Rightly rejected by Kees, *Pr.*, 195–7 (less clearly, 246), and *Hhp.*, 98, and by Drioton and Vandier, *L'Égypte*[4], 1962, 674. Non-mention of the king in the Nile-level date-lines merely reflects the insignificance of Takeloth I. Sources in genealogy here: C. 6–15 are Cat. 42206–42215; C. 559 is in Borchardt; Q is Quibell, *op. cit.*; T is T. 35 in *Karnak-Nord IV*. V, HP, 2P, 4P, are vizier, high priest of Amun, and 2nd and 4th prophet.
126. Prenomen from Cat. 42213.

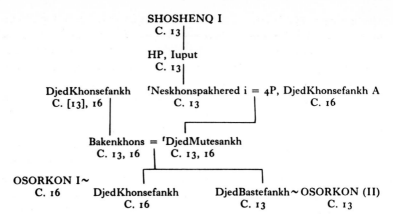

SHOSHENQ I
C. 13

HP, Iuput
C. 13

DjedKhonsefankh   'Neskhonspakhered i = 4P, DjedKhonsefankh A
C. [13], 16   C. 13   C. 16

Bakenkhons = 'DjedMutesankh
C. 13, 16 | C. 13, 16

OSORKON I~
C. 16   DjedKhonsefankh   DjedBastefankh ~ OSORKON (II)
              C. 16   C. 13   C. 13

If Djed-Khons-ef-ankh A was in full service earlier in the long reign of
Osorkon I (cf. § 184, above), then doubtless his like-named grandson could
have become active in the priesthood in the latter years of the same reign.[127]
Otherwise, one would have to dissociate the 4th prophets Djed-Khons-ef-
ankh of Cairo Cat. 42213 and 42216 (with identically named daughters,
sons-in-law and grandsons) from each other, as two separate and unrelated
individuals. In view of the correspondences of names not only of the 4th
prophet in each case but also of their equivalent relatives, such a distinction seems very unlikely.

§ 187 Other documents carry the family downward in time. The statue
Cairo 42212 from Karnak bears the cartouches of Neferkheperre-Khakhau,
Thutemhat, beloved of Thoth and the gods of Hermopolis, includes an
address to the temple-staff of Hermopolis in its texts, and gives the following genealogy:

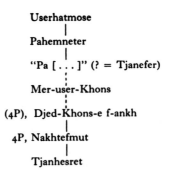

Userhatmose
|
Pahemneter
|
"Pa [. . .]" (? = Tjanefer)
|
Mer-user-Khons
|
(4P), Djed-Khons-e f-ankh
|
4P, Nakhtefmut
|
Tjanhesret

127. Kees (Pr., 220) erroneously marries off Djed-Mut-es-ankh to her son (whose
name is lost in Cat. 42216, c, ii, but must there be supplied). With Kees, Pr., 221,

At first sight, Tjanhesret's father and grandfather appear to be the Nakht-efmut A and Djed-Khons-ef-ankh A of the main genealogy of § 184 above.[128] But the latter was son of a Nespernebu, not of a Mer-user-Khons. However, Tjanhesret's genealogy is in fact a defective one. The text is broken away from Djed-Khons-ef-ankh to the latter's fourth lineal ancestor Mer-user-Khons who was recorded on Cairo Cat. 42211, then three more generations are lost before reaching (counting backwards) Tja[nefer],[129] Pahemneter and Userhatmose, precisely like Cat. 42211.

Nakhtefmut A was a contemporary of Osorkon II and Harsiese A. If Tjanhesret were his son, he would be a contemporary of Osorkon II and Takeloth II as well as of Thutemhat. But what warrant have we to postulate a local *king* in Hermopolis as early as Osorkon II and Takeloth II? The former king took good care to put his sons into the leading offices of the land – including, for example, Nimlot C in Heracleopolis. A generation or so later, the country came under the dual rule of two dynasties in the Delta (Shoshenq III, Pedubast I), and within a century it was split between four lines of kings, including a Nimlot at Hermopolis. In 730 B.C., a king at Hermopolis such as Nimlot or Thutemhat makes sense – but *not* in 850 B.C. which was long before even the main ruling house had split.

Therefore, with Kees,[130] it seems mandatory to suggest a larger interval between Tjanhesret's grandfather Djed-Khons-ef-ankh and his precursors. And in fact, to identify Tjanhesret's grandfather *not* with the 4th prophet Djed-Khons-ef-ankh A, but with the latter's great-grandson, the 4th prophet Djed-Khons-ef-ankh C (son of Harsiese C).[131]

If this is so, then the second Nakhtefmut (B, who dedicated Cairo Cat. 42211) must in due course have obtained the long-standing family benefice of 4th prophet of Amun. The two statues 42211, 42212 (which alone share most elements of a very long genealogy) would be quite close in date. Besides, the 4th prophet Djed-Khons-ef-ankh C was the first of his family also to hold a benefice in Hermopolis.[132] See further § 189.

the younger Djed-Khons-ef-ankh and Djed-Bast-ef-ankh (Cat. 42213) were brothers. Cat. 42216 might have been dedicated by the (elder ?) brother about the end of Osorkon I's reign, while Cat. 42213 would have been dedicated perhaps 16 to 20 years later by the other (younger ?) brother at the beginning of Osorkon II's reign.

128. It is just possible that the Tjanhesret named as father of the lady Tadit-nebhenen on a fragment (Quibell, *Ramesseum*, pl. 21 : 10) may be the man discussed here.

129. Legrain, *Statues, ad. loc.*, prints the *pꜣ* bird. Whether by him or by the ancient sculptor, this must be a slip (very easy) for the *tꜣ* bird.

130. *Pr.*, 218, 219.

131. This gives an omission of 6, not 4, lineal ancestors back to Mer-user-Khons.

132. So, with Kees, *Pr.*, 217–18.

§ **188**   The statue Cairo Cat. 42218 would by contrast provide us with an
early but important side-branch of Nakhtefmut A's remarkable family,
if the Nespernebu named thereon were his grandfather:[133]

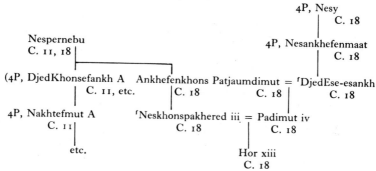

As the son who erected the statue of Padimut (hoping for blessings
thereby), the position of Hor xiii in his family seems clear from text *f*
of Cat. 42218. As Kees saw, it is significant that Nesy and his son would
(by generation) be direct predecessors of Djed-Khons-ef-ankh A in the
office of 4th prophet – and that Nesy was a Libyan chief (*wr ꜥ n Mhswn*)
and by generation a contemporary of Shoshenq I. The latter probably
installed, thus, a fellow Libyan chief as 4th prophet alongside his own son
Iuput as high priest.

§ **189**   Finally come the 4th prophets, father and son, Nakhtefmut and
Djed-Khons-ef-ankh, of the Besenmut genealogy[134] (see next section).
These two must be Nakhtefmut B and his son Djed-Khons-ef-ankh D,
and *not* here Nakhtefmut A, as the latter was succeeded in office by Harsiese
C, not a Djed-Khons-ef-ankh. As his father was contemporary with
Osorkon III, Djed-Khons-ef-ankh D would be a brother of Tjanhesret,[135]
the last-known of his series of 4th prophets, and a contemporary of (at
the earliest) Takeloth III, Rudamun, Thutemhat and Piankhy.

§ **190**   6. NOTABLES OF THE BESENMUT FAMILY*

The following basic genealogy comes from the sarcophagi of Ankhefenkhons i and various of his relatives, as follows:[136]

133. With Kees, *Pr.*, 220, and table to p. 206 (Ankhefenkhons).
134. On coffins Cat. 41003, 41004, in Moret, *Sarcophages*.
135. So also, Kees, *Pr.*, 219.
136. C. 1–47 refer to Cat. 41001 to 41047, published in Moret, *Sarcophages* and
Gauthier, *Cercueils*, works cited n. 109 above.

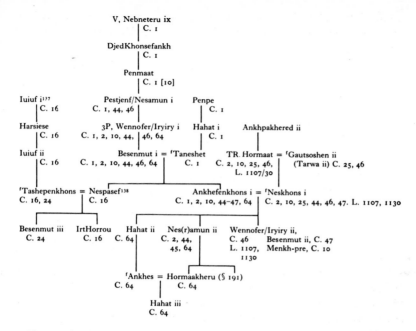

Few points require much comment; the texts on coffin Cat. 41046 make it perfectly clear that both Wennofers were each surnamed Iryiry.[139] These double names make it very likely that its Nesamun i is similarly a second name of Pes-tjenf. The prominence of Wennofer i as 3rd prophet of Amun and of Hormaat as Chief Treasurer of Pharaoh are useful points of reference.

§ 191   At this juncture, the sarcophagi and coffins of an Ankhefenkhons ii and his mother Neskhons ii[140] extend the basic genealogy further, and enable us to link up with that of that notable 4th prophet of Amun, Djed-Thut-ef-ankh B (called Nakhtefmut A), dealt with above (§§ 183 ff.). These documents yield the following genealogy (p. 226).[141]

As noticed above (§ 189), this 4th prophet Djed-Khons-ef-ankh cannot be either the first or second incumbent (A, C) of this name, as their fathers' names are in each case different. As there is no reason to make of this man a

137. So, Moret, *op. cit.*, 173–4, as opposed to his table.
138. Despite Moret, table (160/1), there is no evidence that Nespasef was Besenmut's son by the lady Ta-in.
139. Likewise, Tarwa was a surname for Gaut-soshen i (Cat. 41025).
140. Cat. 41001 (lid only), 41004, 41048–9; Neskhons, Cat. 41003.
141. Except for the bracketed names, here included for orientation, from the previous genealogy.

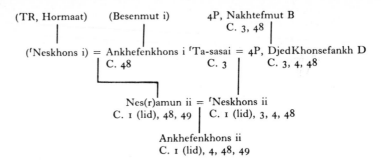

son of Nakhtefmut A who is otherwise unattested,[142] the proper place for him would, again, be as son and successor-in-office of Nakhtefmut B. The latter was a contemporary of the co-regents Osorkon III and Takeloth III, and his other son – Tjanhesret – of Thutemhat in Hermopolis. Hence, the 4th prophet Djed-Khons-ef-ankh D would be a brother of Tjanhesret, and may well have been a witness of Piankhy's invasion of Egypt.

If this is so, the same approximate dating applies to Ankhefenkhons i. The latter's father Besenmut i and the treasurer Hormaat were then contemporaries of Osorkon III and possibly of Takeloth III. This eliminates the difficulties felt by Kees[143] who had dated Besenmut i too late, by as much as 30–50 years. Accordingly, Nes(r)amun ii must have flourished in the early to middle of the 25th Dynasty, Ankhefenkhons ii in the middle to late 25th Dynasty, and the next generation (e.g. Hahat iii) on the eve of the 26th Dynasty.

§ 192   To the other side of the family – that of Besenmut's son Nespasef – may be added some members who are all too easily confused with later personalities. Nespasef's son Irt-Hor-rou married a Gaut-soshen iii and had a son, Hor xvi. The sarcophagi and coffins of Gaut-soshen iii[144] and her son Hor xvi[145] name her forebears as follows (genealogy, p. 227).

As the 3rd prophet of Amun, Pediamen-neb-nesttawy B, is of the same generation as Besenmut i (and Hormaat), he likewise will have belonged to about the time of Osorkon III and Takeloth III (say c. 750 B.C.?). This

142. Who was in fact succeeded by his son Harsiese as 4th prophet.
143. *Pr.*, 282–3, in relation to the 4th Prophet Djed-Khons-ef-ankh D.
144. Cairo Cat. 41018, 41063; Copenhagen 1522; stela, Seattle, 32. 1. For the last two items, cf. De Meulenaere in Parker, *Saite Oracle Papyrus*, 22, 23 and fig. 5. Cat. 41017 wrongly dittographs Irt-Horrou's own name for that of his father Nespasef.
145. Cat. 41017, 41062. Ciphers used are: Cp for Copenhagen 1522; St for Seattle 32. 1; C. 17–63 for Cat. 41017–63.

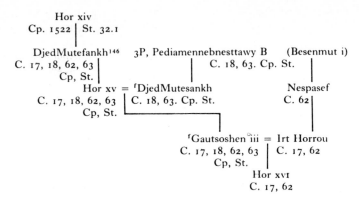

virtually excludes any real possibility of identifying him with a later 3rd Prophet of this name who was in office almost a century later in the 9th year of Psammetichus I (656 B.C.),[147] as has sometimes been done.[148] This much later Pediamen-neb-nesttawy C was succeeded by his son Hor (xvii) as 3rd prophet by Year 14 of Psammetichus I.[149] No trace of such a son appears in the genealogy of the earlier Pediamen-neb-nesttawy (B) as given above.

§ **193** In fact, it seems that no less than *four* datable Pediamen-neb-nesttawys have to be clearly distinguished from each other, while some who feature on yet other monuments still cannot be identified beyond doubt with their dated namesakes.

Pediamen-neb-nesttawy A as 3rd prophet was (by marriage of their children) brother-in-law of Djed-Ptah-ef-ankh D, 2nd prophet and 'King's Son of (King) Takeloth', by the following genealogy:[150]

2P, DjedPtahefankh D ʿAnkh-Karoma = 3P, Pediamennebnesttawy A

ʿTa-miut = Mentuhotep

146. Var., Djed-Mont-ef-ankh.

147. Nitrocris adoption stela, line 23; Caminos, *JEA* 50 (1964), 75, pl. 10.

148. e.g. by Kees, *Pr.*, 281, who had erroneously down-dated Besenmut i (but perhaps contrast his *Nachträge*, 24 end, if I understand him aright). Also, De Meulenaere, in Parker, *Saite Oracle Papyrus*, 22, 23, fig. 5.

149. Parker, *Saite Oracle Papyrus*, ad loc. Offering-table, J. C. Goyon, *BIFAO* 70 (1971), 57–9, 73, n. 1, §3, Fig. 4, pls. 15–17.

150. On a statue-fragment (formerly Amherst collection); cf. Sharpe, *Egyptian Inscriptions*, I, pl. 35, see Kees, *Pr.*, *Nachträge*, 20–1, after De Meulenaere. The dating of the prince as son of Takeloth II is probably to be confirmed by the Stockholm fragment published by Peterson, *ZÄS* 94 (1967), 128–9; also, De Meulenaere, *CdE* 41 (1966), 112.

Kees suggested that the Takeloth concerned was perhaps Takeloth II; one may suggest in support that Ankh-Karoma was named from either the wife or daughter of Osorkon II or the wife of Takeloth II (all called Karoma or something similar).

Pediamen-neb-nesttawy B as 3rd prophet and chief lector-priest belonged to the generation of Besenmut i, of the time of Osorkon III and Takeloth III (see § 192, above).

Pediamen-neb-nesttawy C served as 3rd prophet some 70/100 years later, until shortly after the 9th year of Psammetichus I (cf. end of § 192 above). By Year 14, his son Hor had succeeded him. This incipient genealogy can be extended a step further to Hor's son and successor-in-office, *Pediamen-neb-nesttawy D*, by the statue[151] Cairo JdE 36664, and probably by the statue[152] Louvre A. 83 (both, regrettably, unpublished), and can be set out thus:

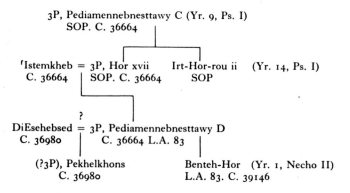

3P, Pediamennebnesttawy C (Yr. 9, Ps. I)
SOP. C. 36664

ˊIstemkheb = 3P, Hor xvii   Irt-Hor-rou ii   (Yr. 14, Ps. I)
C. 36664 | SOP. C. 36664   SOP

?
DiEsehebsed = 3P, Pediamennebnesttawy D
C. 36980 | C. 36664 L.A. 83

(?3P), Pekhelkhons   Benteh-Hor   (Yr. 1, Necho II)
C. 36980   L.A. 83. C. 39146

§ **194**   To one of these two latter Pediamen-neb-nesttawys (C or D) must probably be attributed another unpublished Cairo statue (JdE˙86908),[153] which names him Scribe of the Temple of Mut, and Superintendent of Cattle of the Roof-temple of Re in the Temple of Amun, with a benefice in Shas-hotep, like Hor xvii, son of the one, and father of the other, Pediamen-neb-nesttawy.

151. On which statue, cf. Kees, *Pr.*, 285 and n. 1, and *Orientalia* 18 (1949), 437, n. 4; citations, cf. De Meulenaere, fig. 5, in Parker, *op. cit.*, 23.

152. *PM²*, I: 2, 793, attribute the statue to Benteh-Hor (cf. Yoyotte, *Supplément au Dictionnaire de la Bible*, VI, 368, fig. 609), while De Meulenaere, *BiOr* 11 (1954), 169 top, attributes it to 'a descendant of Pediamen-neb-nesttawy'– who, one assumes, is Benteh-Hor.

153. Cf. Kees, *Pr.*, 286 and n. 1. One may add here the bronze box-case No. 64365 of the Pushkin State Museum of Fine Arts, Moscow, published by M. E. Matthieu, *Palestinskii Sbornik* 13/76 (1965), 3–14.

Still another such statue (Cairo JdE 36980)[154] names a 3rd prophet Pediamen-neb-nesttawy as father of one Pekhelkhons by a 'King's Daughter', Di-Ese-hebsed. As this statue on typological grounds[155] may be assigned to the later years of Psammetichus I, it would best belong to our Pediamen-neb-nesttawy D, with Pekhelkhons as a brother or half-brother of Benteh-Hor (Year 1 of Necho II). If so, then the Saite kings may initially have followed the example of their Libyan and Nubian predecessors in allying leading Thebans by marriage to the royal house.[156] One may then further ask whether the 3rd prophet Pekhelkhons cited by De Meulenaere[157] is not the same man as the son of Pediamen-neb-nesttawy D – particularly as the (other?) son Benteh-Hor inherited various of his father's titles and offices (e.g. chief lector-priest),[158] but *not* that of 3rd prophet of Amun so far as is known. For the correct identification of a 3rd prophet Pediamen-neb-nesttawy who is mentioned on a column-base in eastern Karnak,[159] there is no adequate indication.

§ 195   Similarly, two other Pediamen-neb-nesttawys (having different mothers, Karut and Djed-Mut-es-ankh) cannot yet be safely identified with any of the four dated ones discussed above. One of these has a noteworthy family, which is attested by six or seven monuments,[160] as follows:

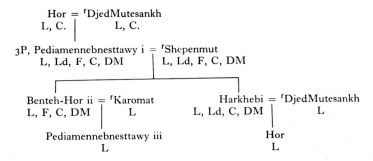

Hor = ꞋDjedMutesankh
L, C. | L, C.

3P, Pediamennebnesttawy i = ꞋShepenmut
L, Ld, F, C, DM | L, Ld, F, C, DM

Benteh-Hor ii = ꞋKaromat   Harkhebi = ꞋDjedMutesankh
L, F, C, DM | L   L, Ld, C, DM | L

Pediamennebnesttawy iii   Hor
L   L

154. Formerly Karnak No. 301; cf. Legrain, *RT* 34 (1912), 172 middle; De Meulenaere, *OLZ* 55 (1960), 129; Kees, *ZÄS* 87 (1962), 65.
155. So Kees, after De Meulenaere.   156. As noted by Kees, *loc. cit.*
157. *OLZ* 55 (1960), 130 (Leningrad situla).
158. Thoueris-statue from Karnak, Cairo Cat. 39146 (Daressy, *RT* 24 (1902), 162, CXCV, and *Statues des divinités*, sub no.).
159. Varille, *ASAE* 50 (1950), 160–1; cf. Kees, *Pr.*, 286, n. 1, and *ZÄS* 87 (1962), 65–6, n. 5 end.
160. Four statues, Louvre A. 117 (Pierret *Recueil, Inscriptions ined. du Louvre*, I, 35 ff.); Florence 7245 (Pellegrini, *RT* 20 (1898), 97–9); Cairo JdE 34710, 34714, both unpublished (cf. De Meulenaere, fig. 5 in Parker, *Saite Oracle Papyrus*, 23). A scarab, Leiden O.87 (De Meulenaere, *OLZ* 55 (1960), 129 end) and one or both of the cones, Davies and Macadam, *Corpus, Egyptian Inscribed Funerary Cones*, Nos. 20, 401.

The other is also the son of a Hori (entitled *mi-nn*, hence presumably also a 3rd prophet), on British Museum stela 8462:[161]

Hori = ʿKarut

|

3P, Pediamen-neb-nesttawy ii

The basic difficulty here is that as long as the parents of the three dated Pediamen-neb-nesttawys A, B, C remain unknown, then the two Pediamen-neb-nesttawys whose parents *are* known can neither be certainly identified with any of those who are dated (A, B or C) nor therefore can they be dated either. Neither can be identified with D, because he has a different mother (Istemkheb). The document WAG. 166 can at present be set aside, as its father-to-son sequence of Padimut–Hor–Djed-Mut-ef-ankh–Hor–Pediamen-neb-nesttawy (not a 3rd prophet) has no proven link with any of the foregoing genealogies.[162]

§ 196   7. NOTABLES OF THE FAMILY OF
MONTEMHAT*

Fortunately, the ancestry and family of the famous Montemhat has long been clearly established[163] from a multitude of documents, with only the most minor queries, much as follows (p. 231).

Nothing in Montemhat's genealogy requires special comment, being adequately covered by the documentation cited, and by the studies of Legrain and Leclant. As Leclant has indicated,[164] there is no evidence for a further Istemkheb as fourth wife of Montemhat.

§ 197   More delicate is the problem of possible links between Montemhat's family and the other great Theban families. In about the same generation as Montemhat is a Besenmut son of an Ankhefenkhons, who were both prophets of Montu. This is a link with the great Besenmut family,

161. Mentioned in the British Museum *Guide to 3rd & 4th Egyptian Rooms*, 85–6, No. 140.

162. Published by Steindorff, *Catalogue of Walters Art Gallery*, 56–7. One might assume (with De Meulenaere, in Parker, *loc. cit.*) that this Pediamen-neb-nesttawy was an otherwise unattested brother of Gautsoshen iii, and that Pedimut was the father of her grandfather Hor.

163. Above all by Legrain, *RT* 33 (1911), 180–92; *RT* 34 (1912), 97–104, 168–75; *RT* 35 (1913), 207–16; *RT* 36 (1914), 57–68, 145–52; cf. latterly, Leclant, *Montouemhat*, 1961, ix ff., 261 ff. Baboon of vizier Khamhor, dedicated by his son, J. C. Goyon, *BIFAO* 70 (1971), 71–2, § 16, Fig. 25, pl. 25B.

164. *Montouemhat*, 163: 6.

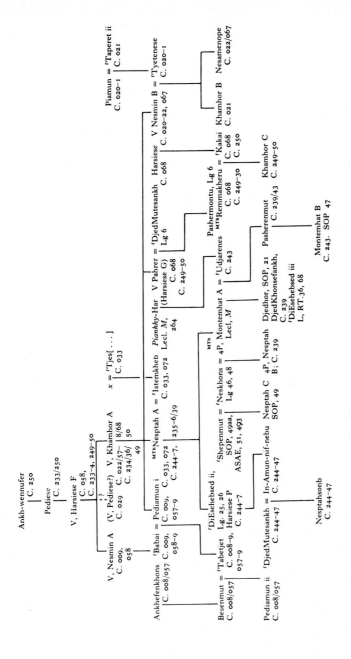

but with which one of at least four Besenmuts? One may rule out Besenmut i (§ 190, above), son of Wenennufer, and his grandson Besenmut iii, son of Nespasef. This leaves principally another grandson, Besenmut ii son of Ankhefenkhons i by Neskhons, daughter of the treasurer Hormaat. His only rival is a so far unplaced Besenmut iv (also grandson of a Besenmut!), son of an Ankhefenkhons by a lady Ta-at. He and his parents cannot be identified with Besenmut ii and his family (even by treating Ta-at as a surname of Neskhons), because his mother Ta-at was daughter of a God's Father of Amun, Pen-nest-tawy,[165] and not of the Treasurer Hormaat.

However, we have no justification at present to prefer an identification of Montemhat's Besenmut with this unplaced and undatable Besenmut iv, rather than with the more usually adduced[166] Besenmut ii. There are slight hints that confirm that Besenmut ii is quite late enough, on a generation-count, to be approximately the contemporary of Montemhat. A steatite plaque of Montemhat in the Ashmolean Museum at Oxford[167] also names a steward of Montemhat's funerary estate as 'the Prophet of Montu, Scribe of divine offerings of the House of Amun, Hor-⌈maat⌉, son of the same, Irt-Hor-rou, son of the Beloved of the God, the Overseer of the Seal, the Heqa-Bat, Hor-maat-kheru'. This latter man, two generations before Montemhat and his steward, is remarkably reminiscent of the treasurer Hormaat (var., Hormaatkheru) who similarly occurs in the Besenmut family tree just two generations before Besenmut ii, who was probably Montemhat's contemporary. As Hormaat's activity was roughly contemporary with Takeloth III (say, c. 750–720 B.C.) and that of Montemhat with Taharqa and Psammetichus I (say, c. 700–650 B.C.), then the activity of the generation between these two would easily embrace the period c. 720–700 B.C.) leaving some margin on either side. Certainly, if one equated Montemhat with any generation later than Besenmut ii, then there would be no question of equating the two Hormaat(kheru)s. Likewise, it is unrealistic to try moving Montemhat's generation any earlier in time beyond that of Besenmut ii. Therefore, while the equation of Besenmut ii with the Besenmut of Montemhat's family tree still lacks (as Kees noted) any clinching proof, it certainly remains the most attractive solution and the only serious one at present.

165. For Besenmut iv and his relatives, cf. Cairo Cat. 41069 (in Gauthier, *Cercueils*). It is conceivable that Besenmut iv was a grandson of either Besenmut ii or iii, but all evidence is lacking wherewith to support such hypotheses at present.

166. So, by Legrain, table to *RT* 36 (1914), 150; Moret, *Sarcophages*, table to 160/1. Kees, *Pr.*, 282, had agreed to either this solution, or else to an identification with Besenmut iii (perhaps forgetting that this latter idea, making Besenmut iii son of Ankhefenkhons instead of his known father Nespasef, is not practicable).

167. Legrain, *RT* 35 (1913), 210, Document 34; Leclant, *Montouemhat*, 154, pl. 51A, Document 35.

Less easy to place is the vizier Pediese son of 'the same' (i.e. vizier) Harsiese by Babai (Cairo Cat. 41029): was he son of Harsiese F, or of Harsiese G (Pahrer), or of some other vizier Harsiese? There is at present no decisive evidence. Moret[168] considered him a son of Harsiese F, so that three brothers would then have been successively viziers: Nesmin A, Pediese, and Khamhor A. Even if this is unusual, it is not impossible. Pediese would then have been named after his grandfather, which was an extremely common practice in the Late Period. Also, Babai the daughter of the vizier Nesmin A would have been named after his mother, Babai, the wife of Harsiese F and mother also of our Pediese. For the moment, this is all conjecture, but it is at least worthy of consideration.

168. *Sarcophages*, 160/1, table.

CHAPTER 14

Dignitaries in Middle Egypt: Heracleopolis

§ **198**   In the 20th year of Piankhy (*c.* 728 B.C.), a 'king' Pef-tjau-awy-Bast was ruling at Heracleopolis, and was allied with the Nubian power in opposition to Tefnakht. His 10th year is attested (cf. §§ 108, 319). How long this kinglet reigned, and whether he did so much beyond, say, 720 B.C., is currently impossible to determine. During the first half of the 25th Dynasty, the local history of Heracleopolis remains at present a blank.

§ **199**   We do not know who directly followed Pef-tjau-awy-Bast in the rule of Heracleopolis. But during the second half of the 25th Dynasty, one Pediese (who was already an old man by the 4th year of Psammetichus I)[169] was Chief of Shipping and (High) Priest of Arsaphes. He was son of an Ankh-Shoshenq who was a priest of Amenresonter of Thebes.[170] Such an appointment would fit in well with the Nubian period when Thebes enjoyed the royal favour, as opposed to the 26th Dynasty when Delta men were increasingly favoured for leading posts. Thus Pediese may have become shipmaster and chief of harbours based on Heracleopolis sometime early in the reign of Taharqa. If this were so, then at least one other local ruler (and just possibly two) may be surmised to have served there between him and king Pef-tjau-awy-Bast.

§ **200**   As shipmaster of Heracleopolis, Pediese was effectively succeeded by his son Somtutefnakht. It was this worthy who, in his capacity as shipmaster, brought Nitocris, daughter of Psammetichus I, to Thebes as the future God's Wife of Amun, in that king's 9th year. According to

169. So, Papyrus Rylands IX, 5: 15–19.
170. Statue Stockholm 81, Lieblein, No. 1026; Papyrus Rylands IX.

234

Papyrus Rylands IX, Somtutefnakht's father Pediese had already received a nephew (Pediese son of Ieturou) as assistant, in Year 4 of Psammetichus I. In practice, doubtless, he became assistant to Somtutefnakht, as Pediese senior had virtually 'retired' in Heracleopolis. But Papyrus Rylands IX makes no mention at all of Somtutefnakht, until his father's death in Year 18 of Psammetichus I. At the worst, Papyrus Rylands IX (written about 140 years after these events)[171] must be dismissed as wrong, and at the best can only be described as very one-sided in its emphasis on the two Pedieses at the expense of Somtutefnakht (who had been shipmaster of Heracleopolis for at least 9 years before his father's death). Therefore, the king's offer to the younger Pediese to make *him* shipmaster (as reported in Papyrus Rylands IX) must be treated with some reserve, unless it were rhetorical and Pediese were expected to refuse it. The text of Papyrus Rylands IX (10: 3–6) implies that, far from Somtutefnakht having been already 9 years the shipmaster, the pharaoh hardly knew of him and now first appointed him to this office at this juncture (Year 18) – which is definitely mistaken, on unimpeachable monumental evidence, for example the Nitocris stela already alluded to.[172]

Combining the Nitocris stela and Papyrus Rylands IX, one may suggest that, in Year 4 of Psammetichus I, Somtutefnakht was appointed shipmaster at Heracleopolis, with his cousin Pediese son of Ieturou as his assistant; his father Pediese lived on (in semi-retirement?) with his priestly stipends at Heracleopolis until Year 14 (first 'stela' of Papyrus Rylands IX), and perhaps until Year 18 when he died. At that time, his son and nephew were confirmed in their posts (*not* first appointed). Papyrus Rylands IX would make Somtutefnakht still active in Year 31 of Psammetichus I; nothing more is attested of him beyond that date.

§ 201   While Pediese as son of a Theban priest may have owed his appointment to a Nubian pharaoh, he apparently owed his continuance in that post to his links with the rising Saite house. On no less than three statues, Somtutefnakht claims a royal princess (*s3t-nsw n ḥt.f*) as his mother, one of which names her as Ta-khered-en-ta-iht-[weret].[173] Thus it seems that

---

171. For which see the edition by F. Ll. Griffith, *Catalogue of the Demotic Papyri, Rylands Library*, III, and esp. pp. 62, 71 ff., 84, n. 7, 108, n. 8.

172. Cf. also W. Wessetsky, *ZÄS* 88 (1962), 69–73 (esp. 72), who would stress a shrewd division of power between pairs of officials by Psammetichus I (with the two Pedieses and Somtutefnakht, in turn).

173. A statue in Cairo (trade), cf. Spiegelberg, *RT* 33 (1911), 176: 74, and Otto, *Biographische Inschriften, Äg. Spätzeit*, 10 and n. 6; Ehnasya statue now in Cairo (museum), cf. Daressy, *ASAE* 18 (1918), 29; and especially a statue seen at Luxor, for which see Otto, *op. cit.*, 10, No. 21.

Necho I, king of Sais, Memphis and the West, had earlier made a marriage-alliance with Pediese of Heracleopolis, and had ultimately bound the ruler of northern Middle Egypt to the Saite cause. Psammetichus I thus had a ready-made alliance with northern Middle Egypt, right from the time of his accession to local power in the West Delta. The honours enjoyed by Somtutefnakht are further illustrated by the texts on two of his statues from the East Delta.[174]

§ **202** The probable fixing of the tenure-of-office of Somtutefnakht in Years 4 to $31+x$ of Psammetichus I helps in turn to settle an intriguing little problem of long standing: the interpretation of the so-called 'Piankhy blocks' from the temple of Mut at Karnak.[175] The Misses Benson and Gourlay[176] attributed these scenes of ships to an expedition supposedly sent into Nubia (like Hatshepsut's to Punt) by Piankhy, with Tefnakht of Sais as second-in-command. They speak (p. 258) of the ships as 'departing' for Nubia – which is contradicted by the presence of heavy cargoes which they are surely bringing to the quay. While agreeing with Benson and Gourlay that the scenes represented a peaceful expedition (but shown returning to Thebes), Griffith correctly pointed out[177] that Somtutefnakht (master of shipping on block 2) could hardly be other than the well-known person of that name and title who is firmly dated to the reign of Psammetichus I (Years 4, 9, 18, up to 31).[178] Somtutefnakht cannot be identified with Tefnakht of Sais who died 60 years before, and the mention of a 'ship of Piankhy' does not necessarily imply contemporaneity with that king. Griffith suggested that the Saite king had sent Somtutefnakht on a friendly visit to the king of Nubia (e.g. Tantamani), which resulted in an alliance and exchange of presents. In support of this theory, Griffith noted that the ships were being rowed, not sailed[179] and inferred that they were therefore coming downstream from Nubia to Thebes. But the inference does not necessarily follow. None of these vessels has a mast, and all of them seem to be powered exclusively by oars. Therefore we have no clue here to the direction of movement of the ships.

174. For which see H. S. K. Bakry, *Kêmi* 20 (1970/71), 19–36.
175. Latest bibliographies, Leclant, *Recherches*, 1965, 115, and *PM²*, II, 257–8: 9 (misattributed to Piankhy and Tefnakht the later king).
176. *The Temple of Mut in Asher*, 1899, 257–8.
177. *Catalogue, Demotic Papyri, Rylands Library*, III, 73.
178. This one fact of itself sufficiently disposes of the theories of Breasted, *BAR*, IV, pp. 414–15, § 811 (and his *History*, 546), and others, as noted by Yoyotte, *RdE* 8 (1951), 233 and n. 3. It must be stressed that Somtutefnakht and his father Pediese were a new 'dynasty' in Heracleopolis, stemming from a Theban priest, and had nothing to do with earlier rulers in the north.
179. *Op. cit.*, 73, n. 2.

§ **203** Studying the barque of Amun in relation to the Theban Valley Festival, but here devoting his attention exclusively to block 5 (with quay and a ship's prow), Foucart disputed[180] the general assumption that this block depicted the quay at Thebes, and specifically at Karnak. He preferred to refer it (and the other blocks, not discussed by him) to Piankhy's pious gifts at the solar sanctuary of Heliopolis. But this view fails in many particulars. His objections to interpreting block 5 as showing the quay at Karnak are insubstantial. The height of the quay is compatible with its full known height; the obelisk shown may easily stand for the pair erected by Sethos II; the statue and human-headed sphinx are probably lesser features that have long since perished from the top of the quay.[181] More positively Foucart failed to explain what two ships of Amun (block 5 + 1; block 2, text, lower right) and a vessel of the *Harim* of Amun (block 2, text, lower left) are doing at the dedication of gifts in Heliopolis. And in any case, Foucart's whole explanation in terms of Piankhy is ruled out irrevocably on date – on the presence of Somtutefnakht on block 1. The presence of that worthy was entirely ignored by Foucart, who was too exclusively concerned with block 5.

§ **204** It was Daressy who made the far more realistic suggestion[182] that these blocks in fact illustrate the arrival in Thebes of Nitocris, the daughter of Psammetichus I, as future God's Wife of Amun. They would thus be a pictorial complement to the great stela of the adoption of Nitocris of Year 9. On this thesis, they would depict the moment of arrival at Karnak. After the vessel of Amun[183] comes Somtutefnakht, appropriately playing a leading role precisely as in the text of the great stela. Daressy would connect the 'vessel of Piankhy' with the fact that the reigning God's Wife, Shepenupet II, was a daughter of Piankhy. It may have been some venerable vessel dating from his time (and her installation?), or simply be a ship named in his (and her) honour for this occasion. Daressy's view was adopted by Kienitz[184] and seemingly was considered the more likely hypothesis by Yoyotte.[185] It was adopted also by Stevenson Smith.[186]

Daressy's view fits very well with the date of the blocks under Psam-

180. *BIFAO* 24 (1924), 118–20, and pl. 9B.

181. The human-headed sphinx in particular should not be confused with the *ram*-headed sphinxes inland from the quay – which disposes of one of Foucart's objections.

182. *ASAE* 18 (1918), 31–2.

183. Which might have gone forth to meet the northern fleet; but a better interpretation, cf. § 205 below.

184. *Politische Geschichte Ägyptens, 7. bis zum 4. Jahrhundert.*, 1953, 16 and n. 1.

185. *RdE* 8 (1951), 233, n. 4 end.

186. *Interconnections*, 1965, 178.

metichus I as required by the presence of Somtutefnakht; his explanation of the boat of Piankhy in relation to Shepenupet II is also feasible. Still other points can be adduced in favour of Daressy's view, and others be integrated with it.

§ **205**   One piece of favourable evidence so far ignored in almost all earlier discussions is the presence on block 2 (text, lower left) of a 'barge of the Harim of Amun'. The word 'harim' is unambiguous, being determined by the sign for a woman and that of three plural strokes. Such a vessel has no role that is readily explicable in any expedition for war or peace in Nubia. But if these blocks indeed commemorate the arrival of Nitocris as future head of the Harim of Amun, then the prominence of a barge of that harim in the scenes makes sense. Likewise, the presence of other vessels of Amun, besides the ship of Sais, then fits into the picture. The God's Wife of Amun was chief of his harim which included the daughters of Delta princelings as well as of Theban families.[187] The harim-vessel either brought such ladies to Thebes in company with young Nitocris, or perhaps brought gifts for those who were already in Thebes. No doubt full negotiations took place between the powers of Sais and Thebes before Nitocris ever sailed south. The priestly figure (name damaged) in the first boat of Amun may represent the head of a Theban delegation to Sais, which was now returning home alongside the great Saite flotilla headed by Somtutefnakht and bringing Nitocris. The cargoes of the vessels would be gifts for Thebes, as is hinted on the stela (l. 8).[188] One may further notice the figure standing on the quay, with arms raised, who faces the ships (block 5). On the photograph,[189] and especially on Foucart's drawing,[190] the figure appears to be that of a woman wearing a short wig and flowing linen robes. If this is so, perhaps it is the God's Wife Shepenupet II greeting the argosy from Sais that brings her new adoptive daughter Nitocris.

It should be noted that blocks 5 and 1 adjoin each other in that order, with an inscription (*p3 d3y n Imn*) running straight across both. These two blocks belong to the top of the scene, directly under the moulding of the screen-wall of which they once formed part. Unfortunately, one cannot now be sure that any further scene of the landfall had existed to the right of block 5. No further joins can be proved absolutely between either these two blocks and any of Nos. 2, 3 or 4, or among the blocks Nos. 2, 3 and 4.

187. As 'Chantresses of the Abode of Amun', cf. Yoyotte, *CRAIBL: 1961*, 1962, 43–52.
188. Cf. in this regard, the custom of Prince Osorkon, 150 years before; *CPO*, *passim*.
189. Benson & Gourlay, *Temple of Mut*, pl. 22: 5.
190. Foucart, *BIFAO* 24 (1924), pl. 9B.

If they had all belonged to one top row of blocks, a minimum of thirteen vessels were once depicted, five being on a lower row of lost blocks with only traces on the surviving ones. However, if some of these blocks Nos. 2, 3, 4, were to belong to a second row underneath that of blocks 5 and 1, which is very likely, then the lower texts on these would pertain to a *third* and otherwise lost row of ships still lower down. In such a case, thirteen or fourteen ships would represent only a part of a once larger array, perhaps of twenty ships or so. Benson and Gourlay[191] speak of fragmentary religious scenes on the reverse of three blocks, which were regrettably never published. They included kneeling priests and the date 4th month of Shomu, Day 19 on the reverse of block 1. Nitocris reached Thebes on 2nd month of Akhet, Day 14; hence, these traces may relate to some ceremony or festival which took place some 9 months at the earliest after her arrival in Thebes.[192]

191. *Op. cit.*, 46, 258, 379.
192. No festival on this date appears (e.g.) in Schott, *Altägyptische Festdaten*, 1950.

PART FOUR

Outline Historical Survey
(c. 1100–650 B.C.)[*]

CHAPTER 15

The Fall of the Ramessides

§ 206   1. THE HISTORICAL SETTING*

For one golden century (*c.* 1300–1200 B.C.), the Ramesside kings of the
19th Dynasty governed a prosperous realm with much show of outward
magnificence at home and prestige abroad. Sethos I and Ramesses II
restored a respectable part of Egypt's empire in Syria and sought to develop
Nubia. Spectacular temples lined the Nile all the way from the new Delta
capital of Pi-Ramessē southward for well over a thousand miles past the
gem-like fanes of Abydos and the marvels of Thebes to the theatrical rock-
temples of Abu Simbel and the far frontiers beyond distant Napata and its
'Holy Mountain' (Gebel Barkal).

Two details within this magnificent kingdom alone need be noted, precisely because their significance was initially minimal in that brief golden
age but grew increasingly as that glory faded. From of old, the broad
Delta of Lower Egypt and the long narrow valley of Upper Egypt had,
for administrative convenience, each been governed by a separate vizier
responsible to the king in civil affairs (as was Nubia by a viceroy); the
military machine of empire was a separate command.[1] Under the able and
confident rulers of the 18th and early 19th Dynasties, these practical
divisions of geography and of powers meant a strong, balanced state.
Under weaker rulers, less loyal executives, and the union of civil and military powers in the same hands, these same 'convenient' geographical

1. For division of the vizierate during the Middle Kingdom and throughout
the New Kingdom, see W. Helck, *Zur Verwaltung des Mittleren und Neuen Reichs*,
1958, 19–28. Viceroys of Nubia and its administration, see G. A. Reisner, *JEA* 6
(1920), 28–55, 73–88; H. Gauthier, *RT* 39 (1921), 179–238; T. Säve-Söderbergh,
Ägypten und Nubien, 1941, 175 ff.; L. Habachi, *Kush* 5 (1957), 13–36, and *Kush*
7 (1959), 45–62; J. Černý, *Kush* 7 (1959), 71–5. On the military, cf. *inter alia* R. O.
Faulkner, *JEA* 39 (1953), 32–47; L. Christophe, *Revue du Caire* 39 (1957), 387–405,
and A. R. Schulman, *Military Rank, Title and Organization in the Egyptian New
Kingdom*, 1964.

divisions could spell the break-up of the realm. The other detail became apparent earlier. Sethos I had to defeat the Libyans in at least one campaign,[2] while Ramesses II built a chain of temple-forts out to Alamein and the Mediterranean[3] to prevent any further threat, and in Nubia the viceroy Setau raided the southern Libyans.[4] Thus, the western borders seemed once again secure. But pressure from this quarter could threaten Egypt on a very long front.

In his 67 years, Ramesses II had reigned for seemingly endless length of days, and his successors were dwarfed in comparison. However, his first successor Merenptah was no mere shadow. He successfully fended-off a great combined invasion of Libyans and Sea Peoples from the northlands, sent grain to the Hittites, kept his name in the Levant from Gezer to Ugarit, broke a rebellion in Nubia,[5] and so maintained Egypt's renown as a great power; but his advancing years and limited length of reign allowed of no vast enterprises of peace. With his death, the power of the throne swiftly declined under the ephemeral princes Amenmesses, Sethos II, and Siptah with Queen Tewosret backed by the Chancellor Bay. Fortunately the victories of Merenptah abroad and administrators at home who were initially loyal cushioned the decline, until ambitious and grasping local officials and administrators made themselves felt by the dynasty's end.[6]

The second Ramesside century (c. 1200–1100 B.C.) and the 20th Dynasty began with Setnakht whose relation to his predecessors (if any) remains unknown. His son Ramesses III renewed Egypt's martial vigour in time to repel three successive waves of invaders – Libyans and their allies on the west, the Sea Peoples (including the Philistines)[7] on the

2. Great hypostyle hall, Karnak (N. wall, W. half, middle); scenes, cf. W. Wreszinski, *Atlas zur altägyptischen Kulturgeschichte*, II, pls. 50–2, and texts latterly in *KRI*, I/1 (1969), 20–4, § 7.

3. At Zawiyet Umm el-Rakham, Alamein, and traces at El-Gharbaniyeh, cf. *PM*, VII, 368–9, plus L. Habachi, *Les grandes découvertes archéologiques de 1954*, Éditions *Revue du Caire*, 1955, 62–5. For the oases at this epoch, cf. *PM*, VII, 295 (Dakhla), 301 (Bahriya).

4. Cf. J. Yoyotte, *BSFÉ* 6 (1951), 9–14, pls. I, II.

5. Relevant texts and finds of Merenptah, cf. *KRI*, IV/1 (1968), 1–24, and *KRI*, IV/2 (forthcoming), 33 ff.

6. Such is probably the historical reality behind the remarks of Ramesses III/IV in Great Papyrus Harris I, 75, 2 ff. (W. Erichsen, *Papyrus Harris I*, 1933, 91–2; *BAR*, IV, § 398, Wilson in *ANET*, 260). On this text, it should be noted that Arsu is merely an epithet ('he who made himself'), most likely referring to the 'king-maker', the Chancellor Bay (cf. A. H. Gardiner and J. Černý, *JEA* 44 (1958), 17–22 esp. 21), and that there was no interregnum between the 19th and 20th Dynasties, cf. W. Helck, *ZDMG* 105 (1955), 44–52, and internal chronological data to be dealt with elsewhere.

7. On which peoples, cf. survey, K. A. Kitchen, 'The Philistines' in D. J. Wiseman (ed.), *Peoples of Old Testament Times*, 1972.

north-east, and the Libyans again in the west, in the 5th, 8th and 11th years of his reign.[8] Thousands of captured Libyans and others were settled in Egyptian territory;[9] Ramesses III caused 'them to cross the River (Nile), being brought into Egypt. They were put into military settlements of the Victorious King. . . .'[10] This followed the practice of Ramesses II who transplanted northerners and southerners, easterners and westerners – 'the Libyans on the (Delta) gezirehs,[11] filling the military settlements of his building with the captures of his valiant sword.'[12] Thus, no doubt, there came into being under Ramesses II and III those Libyan groups, in the south-east Delta, around Bubastis, who were of such importance a little later in this history. Ramesses III's great funerary temple in Western Thebes (Medinet Habu) epitomized the outward grandeur of his reign as a second Ramesses II. But, significantly, it was the sole vast building enterprise of the reign. The country did not lack wealth[13] – or in Ramesses III's earlier years, prosperity – but the growing failure alike in the integrity and efficiency of the nation's administrators[14] had set in well before the old king's death.

§ **207** A line of kings followed Ramesses III, all Ramesses (IV–XI) so prestigious was the name, and most for but brief reigns. Ramesses IV began vigorously, exploiting the Hammamat quarries of the Eastern desert;

8. Scenes and texts, Chicago Epigraphic Survey, *Medinet Habu*, I–II, and *RIK*, II; texts, *KRI*, V/1 (1970) and V/2 (1972); translations, W. F. Edgerton and J. A. Wilson, *Historical Records of Ramses III*, 1936.

9. Cf. settlements of Sherden (Sea Peoples) and Tjuku (Libyans, Biblical Sukkiim, cf. below, Chapter 18, § 253) a generation or so later attested in the great Wilbour Papyrus cadastral survey, cf. A. H. Gardiner, *The Wilbour Papyrus, II, Commentary*, 1948, 80–1, and Bernadette Menu, *Le régime juridique des terres et du personnel attaché à la terre dans le Papyrus Wilbour*, 1970, 109–10.

10. Deir el Medineh Stela, in *KRI*, V/2 (1972), 91: 5–7. Cf. also Year 5 text, Medinet Habu (Chicago ed., I, pl. 28: 40; *KRI*, V/1 (1970), 24: 2 ff.), and the Great Papyrus Harris I, 76, 8 and 77, 5 (Erichsen, *Papyrus Harris I*, 93–4; *BAR*, IV, §§ 403, 405).

11. The sandy land-spits or 'islands' amid the cultivation, on which the Egyptians often built their Delta settlements to avoid using agricultural land which was also subject to the Nile flood.

12. Scene, Abu Simbel, Wreszinski, *Atlas . . .*, II, pl. 182; text, *KRI*, II/4 (forthcoming), 206: 14–16; cf. also *BAR*, III, § 457.

13. As attested by the wealth of the temples, especially that of Amun of Karnak in the Great Harris Papyrus (Erichsen, *Papyrus Harris I, passim*; *BAR*, IV, §§ 151 ff., *passim*; Helck, *Materialen zur Wirtschaftsgeschichte des Neuen Reiches*, III, 1963, 415–41.

14. e.g. inefficiency in paying rations to the workmen of the royal tomb leading to strikes, from Year 29 of Ramesses III, in Turin Strike Papyrus, cf. A. H. Gardiner, *Ramesside Administrative Documents*, 1948, 49–58 *passim* (text), and W. F. Edgerton, *JNES* 10 (1951), 137–45 (translation and comments). On graft, see next note but one.

his prayer for more than the 67 years of Ramesses II went unheeded, since his reign lasted for only 6 years. Four years later, his young son and successor Ramesses V was cut off, possibly by smallpox. The latter's uncle Ramesses VI sought (like Sethos II) to leave a monumental mark in tradition (on others' works) but he and his son Ramesses VII at 7 years each achieved little. Still less is to show for his ephemeral brother Ramesses VIII.[15] During this period, the growing corruption of sections of the administration (and inadequate oversight by the kings) is graphically illustrated by the 10 years' pilfering of grain from temple-revenues by a ship's captain and his accomplices.[16] In the same period, grain prices rose steeply from the 29th year of Ramesses III into the reign of Ramesses IV, then dipped under his son, then soared again under Ramesses VII–IX, and did not return to a lower level until late in the reign of Ramesses XI.[17] Doubtless this brought much hardship to the poorer classes and to the workmen of the royal tombs. Others, such as the remarkable family of Merybast, achieved careers so brilliant and well-rewarded as to be safely cushioned against such troubles.[18] Merybast was Chief Taxing Master and High Steward of Ramesses III; his son, Ramesses-nakht I, became High Priest of Amun by Year 1 of Ramesses IV[19] and kept that dignity through to at least Year 2 of Ramesses IX.[20]

Under the longer reign of Ramesses IX (18 years), the family maintained its hold on the high-priesthood (Nesamun, Amenhotep succeeding their father) and on other lucrative offices.[21] Security along the west side of

15. For the succession and relationships of the Twentieth Dynasty, see Kitchen, *JEA* 58 (1972).

16. Turin Indictment Papyrus; text, Gardiner, *op. cit.*, 73–82; translated, T. E. Peet, *JEA* 10 (1924), 116–27, esp. 120 ff.; Gardiner, *JEA* 27 (1941), 60–2; and graphically excerpted by J. A. Wilson, *The Culture of Ancient Egypt*, 1956, 279–80. In 10 years, this wholesale peculation included over 6,000 sacks of grain.

17. For the fluctuations, see J. Černý, *Archiv Orientalni* 6 (1933), 173–8, esp. 176–7, and W. Helck, *Materialen zur Wirtschaftsgeschichte des Neuen Reiches*, IV, 1963, 616–20, esp. 618 f.; other commodities, cf. Černý, *Journal of World History* 1 (1954), 903–21.

18. Cf. Helck, *Zur Verwaltung des Mittleren und Neuen Reiches*, 1958, 381–3, 493–4, §§ 36–7. On the power of this family in state finance and Theban priesthoods, cf. H. Kees, *Pr.*, 123–30 and briefly Gardiner, *Wilbour Papyrus*, II, 1948, 204. Cf. also G. Lefebvre, *Histoire des grands prêtres d'Amon*, 1929, 177–204, 263–72, and K. C. Seele, *The Tomb of Tjanefer at Thebes*, 1959, *passim*, in the light of Kees, *OLZ* 56 (1961), 5–10.

19. Cf. Černý, *CAH²*, II: 35 (1965), 23 and n. 4.

20. Cairo Papyrus published by Helck, *JARCE* 6 (1967), 135 ff.; for its earlier history (found with Papyrus Wilbour ?), perhaps cf. Gardiner, *Wilbour Papyrus, II*, 2.

21. Amenhotep's brother Usimare-nakht was high steward, and another brother Merybarset perhaps was attached to a West Theban temple; cf. line 30 of a Karnak text edited by E. F. Wente, *JNES* 25 (1966), 79, 81, n. 30a, and fig. 3.

Egypt was slackening. In Years 10–15 the environs of Thebes itself were haunted by roaming Libyans and desert tribesfolk, to the fear of some.[22] In Years 13–17 broke the scandal of robberies in the royal tombs, real and alleged. Economic conditions (famines, high price of food), graft and corruption, loss of respect for the kings whether dead or reigning were all factors that transformed the sporadic violation of a royal tomb into a flood of pillage in the ensuing decades.

§ 208   Ramesses X reigned briefly (whether 3 years or 9) and left no mark. But fresh crises persisted into the early years of Ramesses XI. In one of these reigns, disturbances arose in both Thebes and the North; in Thebes, the High Priest of Amun, Amenhotep, was 'suppressed' for 8 or 9 months. He may have survived this experience for a time at least.[23] The 'war of the High Priest' was long remembered.[24] Most prominent was the Viceroy of Nubia, Panehsy, who – assuming control of his own province's militia (unlike his predecessors-in-office) – suppressed the troubles in Thebes and as far north as Hardai (Cynopolis) in northern Upper Egypt. He it was who may have reinstated Amenhotep on behalf of the king.[25] In those times, famine still afflicted Egypt; this is reflected by a year being dubbed the 'year of the Hyenas'.[26] Amenhotep's successor in the Theban pontificate would seem to have been Ramesses-nakht II (his son?) under either Ramesses X or XI.[27] Meantime, Panehsy continued long as Viceroy of Nubia; he dealt with grain-supplies and Nubian products in the 12th and

22. Cf. Černý, *CAH²*, II: Chapter 35 (1965), 14–16 and references.

23. Cf. Karnak text, Wente, *JNES* 25 (1966), 73–87, figs. 1–3, pls. 8–10.

24. Cf. Peet, *JEA* 12 (1926), 254–7; Černý, *CAH²*, II: 35 (1965), 27–8; Wente, *op. cit.*, 81–7. One may perhaps refer to this period Papyrus Moscow 127 – just conceivably a cryptic effusion from the 'suppressed' Amenhotep himself, as suggested by G. Fecht, *ZÄS* 87 (1962), 12–31, based only on the summary presentation by M. A. Korostovtsev, *An Unpublished Ancient Egyptian Literary Text*, Moscow, 1960 (XXV Congress of Orientalists). Full publication by Korostovtsev, *Ieraticheskii Papirus 127* . . . , 1961, affects Fecht's thesis at just one fatal point: the 'hero' is not Huy (= Amenhotep) but 'Urmai' son of Huy. To save Fecht's idea one could, of course, assume an archaic use of Middle-Kingdom inverted filiation (Urmai's son Huy) or else assume a transposition and understand 'son of the Chief of Seers (Ur-mai), Huy'. Others may not, perhaps, consider the thesis worth saving. If it were the son of Huy (= Amenhotep) who was author, one might suggest that it came from Ramesses-nakht II – but in what context is beyond conjecture at present.

25. So, with J. von Beckerath, *Tanis und Theben*, 1951, 93, and Wente, *JNES* 25 (1966), 84–5; cf. Kees, *Herihor und die Aufrichtung des thebanischen Gottesstaates* (*NAWG*, NF, II/1), 1936, 2–6 (except for restoring Amenhotep).

26. Cf. retrospective remark, Papyrus BM 10052, 11, 8, T. E. Peet, *The Great Tomb-Robberies of the Twentieth Egyptian Dynasty*, I, 1930, 153.

27. For this 'new' High Priest of Amun, see M. L. Bierbrier, *JEA* 58 (1972).

17th years of Ramesses XI.[28] Thereafter, both Ramesses-nakht II and Panehsy disappear from the Theban scene, and the political picture changes abruptly.

§ 209 2. RAMESSES XI AND THE 'RENAISSANCE ERA'

In this epoch, the weakness of the central government allowed the natural geographic regions of south and north to change from areas of mere administrative convenience into distinct political entities. The self-sufficient pride of the Theban hierarchy and weakness of the kings, who lived almost entirely in the northern capitals, helped to accentuate the practical cleavage between south and north which was now to be formalized politically.

Panehsy's virtual sole rule of Upper and Middle Egypt as well as Nubia was irregular. By Year 19, he had fallen into disgrace, at least in Thebes.[29] Instead, from that year on, a new *régime* ruled, termed 'the Renaissance' (*wḥm-mswt*, lit. 'the repeating of birth'), and in datelines one meets 'Year 1 . . ., corresponding to Year 19'.[30] The anomalous union of Upper Egypt and Nubia was now regularized to adapt the administration to the new *status quo*. A new man, one Herihor, now appeared as High Priest of Amun, as Generalissimo and Army-leader (*ḥȝwty*) – more specifically 'Captain at the Head of the Army of All Egypt'– and also as Viceroy of Nubia to replace Panehsy who was now himself a rebel in Nubia. Thus, for the first time ever, this man united in himself wide military powers, the Theban high-priesthood, and the rule of Nubia. To these he for a time added the office of (southern) Vizier. This was the situation in Year 6 of the 'Renaissance Era'.[31] Northwards, Herihor's rule probably extended to El Hibeh[32]

28. Year 12, cf. Gardiner, *Ramesside Administrative Documents*, 1948, 36; Helck, *Zur Verwaltung*, 1958, 341. Year 17, Papyrus Turin Pleyte and Rossi 66–7, now in A. M. Bakir, *Egyptian Epistolography*, 1970, pl. 24–5, XXXI (Pap. Turin Cat. 1896); translated, *BAR*, IV, §§ 595–600, cf. also Helck, *op. cit.*, 342.

29. Cf. references given by Černý, *CAH*², II: 35 (1965), 31, n. 4.

30. Abbott Dockets, cf. Peet, *Great Tomb-Robberies . . .*, I, 128–9, 131 ff.; cf. also Part I, Chapter 2, § 14, above.

31. Year 6 docket, *G3*, 233, § 1, I, confirmed by Wente, *Late Ramesside Letters*, 1967, 3, n. 13; also Karnak statue of Herihor, Cairo Cat. 42190. Herihor thus acquired the title of vizier after the vizier Nebmarē'-nakht who officiated in Years 1 and 2 of the 'Renaissance' (Helck, *Zur Verwaltung*, 342–4, cf. 341).

32. This fortress was situated at a strategic point on the Nile, able to control traffic passing southwards, cf. G. A. Wainwright, *ASAE* 27 (1927), 79–93 *passim*; however, his attribution of the origins of the 22nd Dynasty to the Heracleopolis region is mistaken (cf. Chapter 17, § 239, below). The discovery of the Wenamun papyrus at El Hibeh (W. Golénischeff, *RT* 21 (1899), 74) suggests that some fort or centre had been established there by Piankh or even Herihor before the buildings of 21st-Dynasty date.

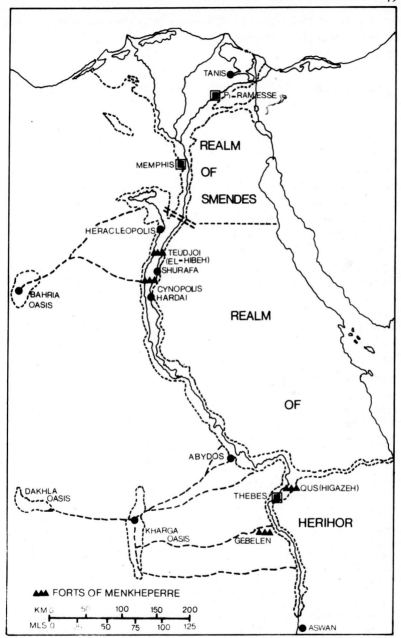

FORTS OF MENKHEPERRE

Fig. 1. Egypt in the 'Renaissance Era' and 21st Dynasty.

to the north of Hardai (raided by Panehsy) and some 20 miles south of Heracleopolis and the approaches to the Fayum. In Thebes itself, Herihor's accession to power was seemingly endorsed by oracles of the Theban deities, who promised him 20 years of power as their protagonist.[33]

In the northern half of Egypt, from Heracleopolis to the Delta shores, Smendes – a younger man[34] – was similarly appointed there as supreme executive under the king, in parallel with Herihor. His authority in the north is clearly evident from the narrative of Wenamun (§ 210 below). He calls Smendes and his wife Tentamun 'the foundations whom Amun has given to the North of his land',[35] and reports to Smendes before proceeding to Syria, is dispatched by them, and continues to rely on their help even in Byblos. It is hard to believe that, endowed with such powers in the north, Smendes would hold any lesser rank than Herihor;[36] at the very least, he may have been northern Vizier[37] and army-commander for the north of the land. Of the origins of both Herihor and Smendes, we still know absolutely nothing. But Herihor is always General(issimo) as well as High Priest of Amun – a combination hitherto unknown; and his entire line of direct successors always retained their military title. Thus, he may well have been by profession a soldier called upon by the king to replace Panehsy's irregular and *ad hoc régime*. Of Smendes, not even this much is known; but whether or not he was actually Herihor's son,[38] he quickly became real ruler in Pi-Ramessē and its new suburb and port of Djarnet or Tanis a dozen miles to the north.

§ 210   So, from the 19th year of Ramesses XI (c. 1080 B.C.), all of Egypt and Nubia were divided into two great provinces, each under a chief whose common link and sole superior was the pharaoh. The boundary-point was

33. If one may so interpret the indecisive remnants of a stela engraved for Herihor under Ramesses XI in the temple of Khons, Karnak (*PM*, II, 80 (39)). Meyer, *Gottesstaat*, 495/6, and von Beckerath, *Tanis und Theben*, 1951, 95, would refer this stela to the introduction of the 'Renaissance Era'; cf. Černý, *CAH²*, II: 35 (1965), 38. Sethe, *ZÄS* 66 (1931), 6, n. 2, and Kees, *Herihor*, 1936, 12, both expressed scepticism of this view. The fact is that the text is too fragmentary to say more than that it records oracles in favour of Herihor – his induction would be the obvious occasion.

34. Because Herihor died within 7 years of his appointment (Chapter 2, above, §§ 15 ff.), whereas Smendes survived his appointment for over a decade to become king for a further 26 years. If with Wente (*JNES* 26 (1967), 174) Smendes be taken as a son of Herihor, this would not be surprising; cf. Chapter 5, § 64 above.

35. Following the rendering of Černý, *CAH²*, II: 35 (1965), 39 and n. 4.

36. Unfortunately, neither Herihor nor Smendes are accorded any titles by the laconic Wenamun who took such matters for granted.

37. A suggestion also made by Kees, *Herihor*, 13, 14, n. 3.

38. As Wente suggests (*JNES* 26 (1967), 174), noting 'Queen' Nodjmet's epithet *mst kꜣ nḫt*, 'she who bore the Strong Bull' (a king's designation).

at El Hibeh which became the northern base of the Theban ruler. Thus, under the last Ramesses a basic political pattern was established that was to last for over three centuries, through the 21st Dynasty and down to Prince Osorkon and the final collapse of the fractured unity of post-imperial Egypt.

In the south, Herihor's sole major monument was his work on the Temple of Khons, the Theban moon-god, in the Karnak precinct.[39] Here, the hypostyle hall is in the name of Ramesses XI as king, with Herihor as high priest. In the forecourt, all is inscribed in the name of Herihor as 'king', with five-fold titulary and cartouches.* But the appearance was more impressive than the reality. Herihor's prenomen was nothing more than his real office: 'High Priest of Amun'. His other titles reflected his actual horizon, the Karnak precinct and the worship of its gods.[40] For Herihor's 'kingship' appears only in the halls of Karnak (Temple of Khons; great hypostyle hall of the Temple of Amun), and on the funerary equipment of his family – e.g. of Nodjmet his wife or 'queen'.[41] In ordinary administrative documents, he remained as ever High Priest of Amun, military leader and Viceroy, even Vizier, but never king.[42] It may be that, in his exalted position of effective royal deputy over vast tracts far from the king's presence, Herihor felt entitled to adopt royal style as a virtual 'co-regent' whose regnal years were those of the 'Renaissance Era'.[43]

In the 5th year of that Era (c. 1076 B.C.), Herihor sent forth his emissary Wenamun* to Byblos in Phoenicia, to procure timber for a new state barge of Amun, a trip endorsed by Smendes who assigned Wenamun to a ship outward bound from Tanis. His subsequent adventures lasted more than a

39. Cf. the accounts of that work as given by Lefebvre, *ASAE* 26 (1926), 139–47, and Černý, *CAH²*, II: 35 (1965), 34–5.

40. As Horus, Herihor was 'Strong Bull, Son of Amun', plus 'Rich in Benefactions in Karnak'; 'Son of Amun' appears also in his nomen. As Nebty, he was 'Contenting the Gods . . .' and 'Purifying the Benenet (temple of Khons), filling it with monuments . . .'. As Golden Horus, he was 'Performing benefactions in Karnak for his father Amun', etc. Cf. *G3*, 234–5, XII/XIV.

41. For whose titles, cf. *G3*, 236–7, and above, Chapter 4, §§ 37 ff.

42. So, besides the dockets on royal reburials, Ostracon Cairo Cat. 25744 (draft letter), Černý, *Ostraca hiératiques, Musée du Caire*, 90*, and *CAH²*, II: 35 (1965), 32. Likewise his statue, Leiden stela, and two graffiti in Karnak, but one with epithet 'Son of Amun' (P. Barguet, *Temple d'Amon-rê à Karnak*, 1962, 257).

43. On the thesis that Herihor was not related to Smendes, one might suppose that Herihor had hoped to 'get his oar in first' by claiming royal style even before Ramesses XI had died; if so, his aim was defeated by his own prior death.

But, on the proposition that Herihor was perhaps father of Smendes, and Smendes established a claim by marriage with the princess Henttawy *Q*, one may alternatively argue that Herihor claimed seniority in order of intended royal succession before his own son – but, again, death removed him during Ramesses XI's continued reign from that aim's fulfilment.

year,[44] so that the timbers could not have reached Egypt until well into the 6th year. In the meantime, with lively anticipation, Herihor had had scenes of the Festival of Opet engraved in the Temple of Khons, showing the (new?) barge of Amun which was decorated in his name.[45] During that same 6th year, he had also to renew the burials of Sethos I and Ramesses II, as the dockets on their substitute coffins bear witness. Shortly thereafter, in the 7th year at the latest, and probably in his 70s, Herihor died and was succeeded by his son Piankh in all offices except the vizierate and the shadow 'kingship'.

Apart from Wenamun's chequered career as envoy of Amun in Phoenicia, knowledge of Egypt's foreign relations in the 'Renaissance Era' is of the scantiest. Near its end, 'the king of Muṣri' – i.e. Ramesses XI – sent a gift of a crocodile and a large ape to Assur-bel-kala, king of Assyria (then campaigning in the Levant) not later than c. 1070 B.C.[46]

§ 211   During Herihor's 6 or 7 years of rule, Piankh also had held benefices both civil and military. In the latter he was Commander of Horse, while in the former he was not only a prophet of both Mut and Khons (wife and son of the god Amun) but – much more important – was also High Steward of Amun, with oversight, therefore, of Amun's vast temporal wealth.[47] Another son, Prēʿ-Amun-en-Amun, was 4th Prophet [of Amun?] and Prophet of Onuris and [another god].[48] A third son, Ankhefenmut A, took over from Piankh as High Steward of Amun.[49] The other sons and daughters of Herihor are of little moment historically, some bore

44. Wenamun started out in Year 5, 4th (or earlier?) month of Shomu, spent five months from leaving Thebes to gaining his interview with Zakarbaal, prince of Byblos, and in 1st month of Peret obtained fresh credit from Smendes. It was by the 3rd month of *next* Shomu that the timber was ready, while Wenamun noted the migratory birds in flight 'for the second time' (cf. G. Lefebvre, *Romans et contes égyptiens*, 1949, 208 with nn. 2, 6; 212 with n. 30; 216, 216, 219 and n. 75, respectively).

45. This suggestion (that the Opet-scenes were carved in anticipation of building the new barge) would allow up to almost 2 years for execution of the scenes; otherwise, cf. Wente, *Late Ramesside Letters*, 1967, 4, n. 13, latter part.

46. The 'Broken Obelisk', *LAR*, I, § 392. For its attribution, see latterly R. Borger, *Einleitung in die assyrischen Königsinschriften*, I, 1961, 135 ff. (year 3 of Assur-bel-kala for gift of 'king of Muṣri', p. 140), and A. R. Millard, *Iraq* 32 (1970), 168–9. On the ape and crocodile, see E. F. Weidner, *Archiv für Orientforschung* 18 (1958/59), 354 on Z. 27, and references given by W. von Soden, *Akkadisches Handwörterbuch*, Lieferung 8, 729, (*namsuḫu*, 'crocodile'), 809 (*pagû*, 'ape').

47. Temple of Khons, cf. *G3*, 237, XIX, § 1, A, after Champollion, *Notices Déscriptives*, II, 228, and *LD*, III, 247a, etc. Cf. also Kees, *Hhp.*, 13.

48. Temple of Khons, *G3*, 238, § 2 (*LD*, III, 247a); cf. Kees, *Hhp.*, 16.

49. Unless one conceded that his title *sꜣ-nsw* is for 'King's (grand)son', which would make him identical with the like-named and titled son of Piankh noted just below. Cf. Kees, *Hhp.*, 19–20, and Wente, *JNES* 26 (1967), 174, n. 151.

ordinary Egyptian names (often those used by Ramesside princes),[50] others had 'group-written' names possibly of Libyan stamp.[51] Thus, Herihor had quickly obtained entry for members of his family to one or two important posts within the ambit of the Theban hierarchy, but certainly did not monopolize or dominate all its major offices.

By the 7th year Piankh was in full command of Upper Egypt as High Priest of Amun and military commander. That year, for example, we find him soliciting the oracle of Amun in the presence of the 2nd Prophet of Amun, Nesamun(re?),[52] about the appointment of another, humbler Nesamun to the post of Scribe of the Stores of the Estate of Amun, which was held by the claimant's father Asha-khet.[53] During the pontificate of Piankh (or early in that of his successor), three of his sons obtained important posts in the Theban hierarchy – Heqanefer as 2nd Prophet of Amun (doubtless as successor to Nesamun(re)), Heqamaat as Sem-priest of the great temple of Ramesses III (Medinet Habu), and Ankhefenmut B as High Steward of Amun.[54] Thus did the new dynasty of military high priests begin to develop its hold on the major benefices in the Thebaid and eventually beyond it.[55] On the military front, Piankh's efforts were directed southward – in Nubia, as late as Year 10 of the 'Renaissance' (c. 1071 B.C., Year 28 of Ramesses XI), he was still endeavouring to eliminate Panehsy.[56] Other records of Piankh's régime are very few,[57] and he also probably died before Ramesses XI (Year 29, Year 11 of the 'Renaissance'?), leaving his offices to his own eldest son Pinudjem (I). Elsewhere during this period, some of the king's subjects preferred to reckon by his continuing regnal

50. e.g. *G3*, 258–9, Nos. 4 (It-Amun, cf. Ramesses VII), 5 (Amen-hir-wenmef). More ordinary-type names, cf. Nos. 9 (Pashedkhons), 14 (Bik-nuteri) and 17.

51. e.g. Nos. 7 (Masaharta, three generations before the high priest of that name), 8 (a Masaqaharta), and perhaps 15, 16 and 19.

52. The Rēᶜ is uncertain, cf. Nims (next note), 159, n. *a*. He is most likely *not* the same man as the 2nd Prophet of Amun Nesamun of Year 16 of Ramesses IX (Papyrus Leopold-Amherst), or any earlier homonym.

53. The oracle published by C. F. Nims, *JNES* 7 (1948), 157–62, and pl. 8.

54. Graffito, temple of Luxor, under Pinudjem I (Daressy, *RT* 14 (1892), 32).

55. So, with Kees, *Hhp.*, 18–19 (his Heqa-ao should be read Heqa-maat).

56. Panehsy as probable opponent is named in *Late Ramesside Letters*, No. 4 (Černý, text, 7: 16; Wente, translation, 24, 25 n. *g*). The bulk of these letters concerns the Necropolis-Scribes Butehamun and his father Thutmose (Tjuroy) and their master Piankh. These letters even include plans for the liquidation of undesirables at Thebes itself (letters Nos. 28, 34, 35), cf. references, Wente, 8, n. 28.

57. Stela from Abydos, in Cairo (*G3*, 241, V), Petrie, *History of Egypt*, III, 1905, 203, fig. 80 after Mariette. Draft for a letter, Western Thebes (Ostracon Cairo Cat. 25745, Černý, *Ostraca hiératiques*, sub no.). A daughter of Piankh, *G3*, 243, X, and above, Chapter 4, § 54. The hypothesis of a long reign for Amenemope would require assumption of a long pontificate of Piankh (most of Smendes' reign); the dire shortage of documents from Piankh's incumbency would not support this double hypothesis (cf. Chapter 3, above) – unless nothing much really happened!

years rather than by the new-fangled 'Renaissance Era'. Thus, one votive stela at Abydos was dated to Year 27 of Ramesses XI, rather than to the corresponding Year 9 of the Era (*c.* 1072 B.C.).[58]

§ **212*** In the north during all this decade, we have no light on the status and activities of Smendes and Tentamun beyond their mention by Wenamun. Nevertheless, when Ramesses XI died it was Smendes who succeeded him and not a Theban or any other grandee. As already suggested,[59] Smendes perhaps married a younger daughter of Ramesses XI, Henttawy Q. This alliance, his supreme rule in the North,[60] and closeness to the seats of kingship in Memphis and Pi-Ramessē would all favour his becoming heir-apparent to an ageing king without surviving sons. If in due course Smendes I were to have officiated over the burial of Ramesses XI, then as Horus caring for Osiris he would indeed become the last Ramesside's legal successor.[61]

58. Mariette, *Abydos*, II, pl. 62a; *G3*, 221, VI. There is no warrant whatever for believing that the 'Renaissance Era' reckoning was given up until the death of Ramesses XI brought its triumvirate rule to a natural end – thus, Year 10 of the Era (*Late Ramesside Letters*, No. 9) is that king's Year 28, which is later than the Abydos stela of Year 27.

59. Above, Chapter 4, § 41, for the otherwise totally anomalous use of the name 'Ramesses' by Psusennes I and Ankhefenmut C, son and grandson of Smendes I.

60. Even though he was emissary of Amun and of Herihor, Wenamun still had to present his credentials to Smendes in the north (and to Smendes rather than to the pharaoh, even though the journey was for materials for the great state barge of Amun).

61. Cf. on this matter, the observations by H. W. Fairman in S. H. Hooke (ed.), *Myth, Ritual and Kingship*, 1958, 99–100, 104, on succession.

CHAPTER 16

The Twenty-first Dynasty: the Founders*

§ 213   1. SMENDES I, AMENEMNISU AND
PINUDJEM I

A. THE REIGN OF SMENDES I (*c*. 1069–1043 B.C.)
The new king adopted a titulary in the imperial style of his predecessors
the Ramessides – a Horus-name beginning with 'Strong Bull';[62] long
Nebty (and Golden Horus?) names;[63] prenomen (Hedjkheperre) with
complement (Setepenre); and Meryamun, 'Beloved of Amun' in the
second cartouche with his personal name Nesu-ba-neb-djed, or 'Smendes'
to use the convenient Greek form. This style, which gradually became
more fossilized and jejune in expression, was to be followed by Egypt's
kings for some three further centuries (*c*. 1070–770 B.C.) during what one
may, perhaps, call the 'post-imperial' epoch of her history.

From this reign of a quarter of a century, hardly any monuments have
so far been recovered that explicitly name the new pharaoh himself in their
datelines. At Thebes, however, a long series of year-dates without royal
name – from burials and graffiti in the necropolis – from Years 1 to 21 can
be attributed to this reign; likewise the 'Banishment Stela' (Louvre C. 256)
from Year 25 of this king and an early year of his successor. Thus, all but a
year of Manetho's figure of 26 years for the reign of Smendes seems
assured.

Significantly, the only two real 'monuments' of the reign link Smendes I

62. In this case, 'beloved of Rēꜥ (like Sethos II), plus further special epithets,
'whose arm Amun strengthens in order to exalt Truth' (*maꜥat*). The initial term
'Strong Bull' had been imperial style ever since Tuthmosis I.
63. Nebty name, Dibabieh stela, quoted below, § 241. Golden Horus name, not
yet recovered.

255

with Thebes. A stela inscribed in the quarry at Dibabieh near Gebelen describes how the king, while residing in Memphis, heard of danger to the temple of Luxor from flooding, gave orders for repairs (hence the quarry-works), and received news of the success of the mission.[64] Thus, as once Memphis and Pi-Ramessē had been Egypt's northern capitals, so now it was to be Memphis and Tanis. At Karnak itself, acknowledgement of Smendes is evidenced by the graffito-like insertion of his name and figure in a scene of Sethos I on the gateway of Tuthmosis I in the precinct of Montu.[65] A lapis bead offers only his names.[66]

§ 214   The Dibabieh stela and the Karnak figure at least show clearly that Smendes I was undisputed pharaoh of *all* Egypt, whatever the pretensions of Herihor had been and those of Pinudjem I were to be. If Smendes and Herihor were entirely unrelated, then they had evidently quickly reached an understanding on their respective spheres of power. If they were in fact related (father and son?), then the two wings of the family as represented by Smendes I and (his nephew?) Pinudjem I at Ramesses XI's death must in any case have agreed on their respective spheres and roles. The essential content of such a *concordat* (regardless of degree of family relationship) is easily postulated even in the absence of any available document. Smendes and his line were to be recognized by the Theban pontiffs as indeed the legitimate kings of Egypt, so long as they in turn confirmed the line of Herihor and Piankh in the military command of Upper Egypt and the high-priesthood of Amun at Thebes. The east-Delta estates of Amun would serve the temples of Amun (and their royal incumbents!) in the Delta residence of Tanis, while the Theban line held undisputed sway over the benefices of the Thebaid. The pact was strengthened by inter-marriages; these perhaps had already begun in the 'Renaissance Era'. Pinudjem I married Henttawy A, the daughter of Smendes and Tentamun, and a daughter of Pinudjem I may have married Smendes I or Amenemnisu who was probably his son. Total failure to produce an heir in either line might allow the throne or the pontificate to pass to the nearest scion in the other line (so, if Psusennes 'III' really were also Psusennes II, following Siamun). One might well say that one half of Egypt (Tanis) ruled the whole realm only by kind permission of the other half (Thebes). Under such a *régime*, the nation might well live in relative unity and

64. Regrettably, the text has no year-date; published by G. Daressy, *RT* 10 (1888), 133–9.

65. Published by A. Varille, *Karnak* [-*Nord*] *I*, 1943, p. 36, fig. 26, pl. 98: 71, and in C. Robichon, L. Christophe, *Karnak-Nord III*, 1951, 77. No doubt exists over reading of the prenomen; of the nomen, final *dd* is clear.

66. Newberry, *PSBA* 24 (1902), 248, § 32*b* (MacGregor collection), cf. *G3*, 288.

amity, but its rulers would rarely be tempted into ambitious ventures abroad or great projects at home.

Manetho calls the 21st Dynasty 'Tanite'. This reflects the fact that its founder hailed from there. Smendes lived and worked in Djaʿnet or Tanis when it was but the port for Pi-Ramessē. Now it probably became his Delta residence, replacing Pi-Ramessē, and the discovery of one of his canopic jars from near Tanis[67] would suggest that he was eventually buried in his native residence. Tanis was henceforth a capital, and both a major seaport for trade in the Levant[68] and a fortress against alien incursions from that quarter.[69]

B. PINUDJEM I AS HIGH PRIEST OF AMUN

§ **215**[*] In Thebes, Smendes' contemporary for the first 15 years was Pinudjem I, who was possibly his nephew, a younger man, and more ambitious than his father Piankh. Very early in the reign Pinudjem had to bury his grandmother, Herihor's 'queen' Nodjmet.[70] Otherwise, year by year, Pinudjem's major concern in Western Thebes was the conservation in their lonely valley tombs of the mummies of the great pharaohs of the bygone Empire. So, in Year 6 (c. 1064 B.C.) he renewed the burials of Tuthmosis II and Amenophis I. In Years 10 and 11 (c. 1060/59 B.C.), the graffiti of the Necropolis Scribe Butehamun attest Pinudjem I in Western Thebes;[71] in Years 12, 13 and 15 (c. 1058/57, 1055 B.C.), his care was lavished on Amenophis III, Ramesses III and Ramesses II.[72]

But the pontiff's activities were by no means limited to rewrapping the venerable royal dead. As High Priest and military commander, his name appears as far south as Sehel island at the First Cataract,[73] and as far north as the fortress of El Hibeh, northernmost bastion of his temporal power. Here, he began the walls which are still extant, in the name of himself and his senior(?) wife, Istemkheb A.[74] In the temples of Thebes, his memorials vary from mere graffiti to a royal colossus. The earliest is perhaps the hieroglyphic graffito at the Luxor temple[75] in which he and his

67. W. C. Hayes, *BMMA* NS 5 (June 1947), 261–3.
68. Cf. the Wenamun narrative.
69. Cf. Kees, *Tanis* (*NAWG*), 1944, 168 ff.
70. A bandage on her foot, made under Pinudjem I in 'Year 1'; see Excursus B, III, 6.
71. W. Spiegelberg, *Theb. Graffiti*, 1921, Nos. 1001, 1021a–e (Year 11, not 21), Excursus B, III, 15, 17.
72. See Excursus B, III, 22, 25, 26, respectively.
73. *G3*, 245, VII; theoretically, it could belong to Pinudjem II, but this is inherently less likely as Pinudjem II is otherwise not attested beyond Thebes itself.
74. See above, Chapter 4, § 50.
75. Forecourt of Ramesses II, E. side, S. wall, E. end; Daressy, *RT* 14 (1892), 32, *G3*, 245, IX; used after own copy.

three brothers 'perpetuate the name' of the deceased pontiff Piankh and honour Amun 'that he may grant a [long] lifespan within Thebes' to their grandmother Nodjmet – a wish not long fulfilled, as seen above. Some time later two more Luxor graffiti were carved, one on a column[76] and one just west of the early graffito, naming three daughters of Pinudjem I including Maatkare A in the dignity of God's Wife of Amun.[77] At Medinet Habu, Pinudjem added long, pompous dedications to the old temple of Amun and renovated doorways and brick subsidiary buildings in the vast precinct and temple of Ramesses III, headquarters of the Theban necropolis.[78] At Karnak, Pinudjem usurped and reinscribed the avenue of sphinxes laid down by Ramesses II from the quay to the second pylon of the vast temple of Amun. He boasted already of his works for Amun and (exaggeratedly) of doing what no king had done.[79]

By the 15th year of his uncle(?)'s reign, Pinudjem I was openly aiming at royal status and style. A statuette bearing his normal titles shows him as a kneeling king making offering, while before Pylon II he erected a kingly colossus still with ordinary titles.[80] Finally, in the temple of Khons, he completed the decoration of its pylon and the gateway thereof, openly adopting a Horus name, 'Strong Bull, beloved of Amun', plus the titles 'King of Upper and Lower Egypt, pacifying the gods', while Khons in the inscriptions addresses him as 'my son'.[81]

C. PINUDJEM I AS KING – EARLIER YEARS

§ 216* In Year 16 of Smendes, the datelines changed dramatically in the dockets which recorded the renewal of the burials of bygone pharaohs. That year it was 'the High Priest of Amun, Masaharta, son of King Pinudjem I' [in cartouche] who then renewed Amenophis I,[82] which care he extended to Queen Merytamun in Year 19 (*c.* 1051 B.C.).[83] Thus

76. The much-discussed graffito that once named Pinudjem I's mother; cf. Wente, *JNES* 26 (1967), 160 and nn. 41, 44, with references.

77. Daressy, *RT* 14 (1892), 32; *G3*, 245, VIII; following own copy. Although Pinudjem I is but high priest, the three women are called *sȝt-nsw*, 'princess' in each case.

78. *G3*, 247, XIII, refs., and U. Hölscher, *The Excavation of Medinet Habu*, V, 1954, 3–5 and refs. Cf. also lintel fragment there of a high priest Pinudjem and a Henttawy, Daressy, *RT* 19 (1897), 20; *G3*, 247, XIV.

79. Cf. conveniently, P. Barguet, *Le temple d'Amon-rê à Karnak*, 1962, 44.

80.* The statuette, Legrain, *Statues et statuettes de rois et de particuliers*, II, Cat. 42191 (p. 60, pl. 53), *G3*, 248, XVI. Colossus, cf. refs. in Barguet, *Temple d'Amon-rê à Karnak*, 55 and n. 2. While, as Dr. Bernard V. Bothmer has impressed on me, the workmanship of this statue is genuinely of the Late Period (with special reference to the queen's figure), the block utilized must originally have been quarried by the Ramessides whose cartouche(s) it bears under the present base.

81. Cf. conveniently, *G3*, 246, XI, esp. D, A; F, G.

82. Cf. Excursus B, IV, 27, 28.   83. Excursus B, IV, 29, 30.

Pinudjem I came to enjoy the full titles, style and status of a pharaoh for the final decade of Smendes' reign, the brief rule of Amenemnisu, and the opening years of Psusennes I. He now affected a regular prenomen (Kheperkhare Setepenamun) and called himself Pinudjem (I) Beloved of Amun in the regular fashion.

His 'kingship' was widely recognized, both on the monuments and in administrative practice which was in sharp contrast to that of Herihor. Within Karnak, his cartouches appear on the west exterior wall of the temple of Khons,[84] on a lintel of a minor Osiris-chapel,[85] and – at the instance of his 'Queen' Henttawy A – on one of the innumerable statues of Sekhmet in the temple of Mut when Pinudjem I 'brought ram-headed sphinxes to the House of Amun'.[86] Beyond Thebes, an altar from Abydos shows his cartouches[87] as does a private stela from Coptos depicting the 'royal' pair.[88] Tanis, too, accepted his rank (see § 219 below). The activity of Masaharta (as, later, of Menkheperre) in the Thebaid[89] suggests that Pinudjem as 'king' had his seat elsewhere – at least in El Hibeh, if not as co-pharaoh in Tanis itself.

It is, however, less easy to discover how and why Pinudjem I successfully obtained royal status precisely in Years 15/16 of Smendes I, rather than, for example, at the deaths of either Ramesses XI or Smendes himself when he might have claimed kingly status as the price of his support for a new northern ruler. Doubtless some particular circumstance or occasion still unknown to us led to his recognition in Tanis as titular co-king. Pinudjem's one indubitable link with Tanis was his second(?) wife, Henttawy A, daughter of Smendes and Tentamun, and hence now a 'princess'; but his long-standing status of royal son-in-law would hardly justify his elevation to kingship.[90]

§ 217* Perhaps after an illness at El Hibeh,[91] Masaharta died before his 'royal' father. It is possible that Pinudjem first appointed a second son,

---

84. *G3*, 250, XXII.
85. *Ibid.*, 250, XXIV, where he uses the old Tuthmosid Horus-name, 'Strong Bull appearing in Thebes'.
86. *Ibid.*, 250, XXIII, wrongly described as a sphinx.
87. Illustrated by Petrie, *History of Egypt*, III, 1905, 206–7, fig. 83.
88.* Cairo JdE 71902, to be published elsewhere.
89. Masaharta left a small scene at Karnak (*G3*, 261, II; Barguet, *Karnak*, 251), and a small doorway east of pylon IX (Barguet, *op. cit.*, 18, 257); a falcon is in Brussels (*G3*, 261, III). For his daughter's catafalque, see above, Chapter 4, § 50.
90. Neither, surely, would the marriage of a daughter of Pinudjem I and Henttawy to either Smendes I, his heir Amenemnisu, or his second son Psusennes (making 'Queen' Henttawy a 'King's Mother(-in-law)', cf. her title *mwt-nsw*).
91. If one may so interpret a fragmentary letter from El Hibeh, cf. W. Spiegelberg, *ZÄS* 53 (1917), 4, 13–14.

Djed-Khons-ef-ankh, to the command of Thebes and the south, but he as quickly vanishes from view.[92] For, in Year 25 of Smendes, a younger son Menkheperre travelled south to Thebes and was installed as High Priest of Amun and generalissimo.[93] Menkheperre was summoned to Thebes by Amun himself to 'come South in valour and victory to pacify the land and suppress its (his?) foe' – a person unnamed,[94] perhaps some Theban pretender to the high-priesthood of Amun who had arisen as focus of local opposition in a hiatus period following the death of Menkheperre's predecessor. Such opposition was quickly beaten down and the ringleaders exiled to the western oases (cf. § 218, below).

Thus, behind the proud façade of Pinudjem's pose as nominal[95] co-pharaoh in Tanis with his sons as successive military commanders of the south and high priests in Thebes, there lurked outright opposition, even rebellion, against the ruling house in Thebes itself. With its talk of exiles in the oases and stays of execution, the Banishment stela of Menkheperre casts a lurid light on a sombre pattern of tension between priestly military commanders based in the north and local opposition parties in Thebes itself. This pattern of dissension was to be repeated on a far more menacing scale in succeeding centuries,[96] doubtless for much the same reasons. Those reasons included rivalry over the tenure of the more important and lucrative benefices in Thebes and Upper Egypt. Already, we have seen three brothers of Pinudjem serving as 2nd Prophet of Amun, Sem-priest at Medinet Habu, and high steward of Amun (§ 211, above). Maatkare A, a favoured younger daughter of Pinudjem I, was early installed as God's Wife of Amun, i.e. chief votaress of the god, with the special prenomen Mutemhat.[97] 'Queen' Henttawy A was endowed with a plurality of livings. Besides being a prophetess of Mut and Khons and God's Mother of Khons-the-Child, she more significantly was steward of the estates ($r3(t)$-n-pr) of both Mut and Khons. Beyond Thebes, she was also prophetess of Onuris-Shu of Thinis.[98] These were so many perquisites for the ruling family – and correspondingly fewer 'livings' for leading repre-

92. Cf. above, Chapter 4, § 55, and below, Excursus C. That Djed-Khons-ef-ankh may even have been murdered was envisaged by J. von Beckerath, *RdÉ* 20 (1968), 32, n. 3.

93. Louvre C. 256, the Maunier or 'Banishment Stela', now fully edited by von Beckerath, *RdÉ* 20 (1968), 7–36, pl. 1; here, line 8.

94. Line 6 of this stela.

95. Nominal, because he had no regnal years other than those of the Tanite kings.

96. So particularly with Prince Osorkon under Takeloth II and Shoshenq III, but also long before and after.

97. A new usage which became customary from the Twenty-third Dynasty. A son of Pinudjem I, Nespaneferhor, was a God's Father of Amun, *G3*, 259, XXXVI, 2.

98. For all these titles, cf. *G3*, 257, G, 258, I.

sentatives of other Theban priestly families, including those descended from the notables of the outgoing Ramesside era.[99] In particular, the stewardships of the temples and estates of Mut and Khons (even if delegated to subordinates in practice) must have been offices of some worth. However, whatever reconciliation was eventually effected in Thebes by Menkheperre, it certainly did *not* take the form of restricting his family's hold on the range of Upper-Egyptian benefices – quite the contrary, as will appear.

D. KING NEFERKARE AMENEMNISU (*c.* 1043–1039 B.C.)

§ 218   When at length Smendes I died full of years, his direct successor was probably Amenemnisu, who was destined to reign for only 4. This figure, if true,[100] suggests that Amenemnisu was eldest son of Smendes and so in turn an elderly man at his accession, perhaps not even in good health.[101] His prenomen – Neferkare – was of ancient stamp, hardly used in Egypt since the late Old Kingdom except by Ramesses IX; by it, he appears in Manetho as Nephercheres.

Of the events of the reign, our knowledge is minimal. Asha-khet A was High Priest of Ptah in Memphis at this time,[102] a dignity retained by his lineal descendants for over a century to come. Also in this brief reign,[103] and now firmly in the saddle at Thebes as well as El Hibeh, Menkheperre now deemed it politic to seek fuller reconciliation with local interests at Thebes. Encouraged by a favourable oracle of Amun during his procession in Karnak a day before New Year's Eve, Menkheperre recalled the exiles from the oases and set aside the death-penalty except for such as might in future seek to use it.[104] These concessions seem to have secured him peace.

99. A theme well developed by Kees (though with some confusion of the Hent-tawys); cf. his *Pr.*, 163–4, and his *Hhp.*, 34.

100. Four years in all main texts of Manetho, corresponding well with the nearly total lack of known memorials of the reign.

101. As predecessor of Psusennes son of Smendes, Amenemnisu evidently left no heir of his own. One might postulate that an ailing, elderly and childless Amenemnisu appointed his young half-brother Psusennes co-regent and died very soon afterwards. For such hypotheses, our sole evidence would be their joint cartouches on the gold bow-caps from the tomb of Psusennes I. They require explanation, whether or not that just offered is anywhere near correct. Cf. Chapter 4, § 56, above.

102. On the evidence of the 'Berlin genealogy', Chapter 12 above.

103. Accepting von Beckerath's point that, most probably, there is only space for a quite small number (1 to 5) lost at the end of line 8 on the 'Banishment stela' (*RdÉ* 20 (1968), 17, 8*d*, and 33, n. 2). This low regnal figure would, perforce, belong to a successor of Smendes I – and preferably to a date as soon as possible after his 25th year. This consideration would favour Amenemnisu rather than Psusennes I, as the king in whose reign the final oracle was given and the stela erected.

104. Cf. von Beckerath, *op. cit.*, 34–5, cf. 26, n. 23*b*. Von Beckerath interprets the

E. PINUDJEM I AS KING – UNDER PSUSENNES I

§ 219* The new pharaoh probably ascended the throne in the prime of life,[105] becoming perhaps the greatest and most active ruler of his line. He inherited from his father and half-brother the ageing Pinudjem I, as co-ruler, while the commander and Theban high priest Menkheperre was probably a man more his own age. Early in the new reign, the royal burials in Western Thebes required attention. Princess Ahmose-Sitkamose and Sethos I were reburied in Year 7 (bandages of Year 6), while in Year 8 'King' Pinudjem I commanded the '(re)osirification'[106] of Ahmose I and prince Siamun.[107] At Tanis, it is probable that the new king and his aged 'shadow' jointly constructed some edifice, as their respective cartouches occur on a group of reused blocks from a well at Tanis itself.[108]

Thereafter, no more is heard of Pinudjem I; he was duly buried in Western Thebes with the pomp of a king in the adapted coffin of Tuthmosis I, with the more essential equipment.[109] Henceforth, Psusennes had only to cope with Menkheperre as his southern counterpart. But Menkheperre made no very serious claim to kingship, merely using the isolated title 'King of Upper and Lower Egypt' on some brick stamps upon the bricks for his buildings at El Hibeh,[110] and hardly ever a cartouche.

§ 220   2. PSUSENNES I (*c.* 1039–991 B.C.) AND THE COURT AT TANIS

A. THE KING, ROYAL FAMILY AND COURT

(i) *The King*

The discoveries at Tanis and elsewhere permit at least a glimpse of the personalities and works of this long reign, which were centred on that metropolis.

The new pharaoh followed the imperial style in his titulary, but with a strongly 'Amunist', even Theban, tone. As Horus, he was 'Strong Bull of Amun's giving, rich in splendour, who is manifested in Thebes', and as

phrase 'not slaying the living' as a figurative reference to exiling people, and hence that it is the practice of exile that was to be banned.

105. Aged perhaps about 40; cf. above Chapter 5, § 64.

106. On the phrase *rdit Wsir n*, perhaps meaning 'restore (the status of) Osiris to' a deceased person, cf. discussion by Elisabeth Thomas, *RNT*, 257 and n. 109.

107. These datelines, cf. below, Excursus B, VII, 37–41.

108. Sole report, P. Montet, *BSFÉ* 6 (1951), 30, unfortunately without illustration.

109. References, *G3*, 251–2.

110. *G3*, 268, XIX.

Nebty (*protégé* of the goddesses of north and south) 'Great of Monuments in Karnak'.[111] This fashion is not unduly surprising – Amun had been outwardly chief deity of the empire for over four centuries, Thebes was his city above all others, and almost all kings of that era had included some link with either Amun or Thebes somewhere in their official titularies (even if only Meryamun, 'Beloved of Amun'), regardless of whether they were by origin Thebans (as was the 18th Dynasty) or outright northerners like the Ramessides. Furthermore, the former Delta residence Pi-Ramessē lay upon, or included, domains of Amun and had a temple or temples of Amun.[112] Thus, at the new capital of Tanis little more than a dozen miles to the north, it was Theban Amun with his consort Mut and son Khons who headed the pantheon.[113]

However, a major new departure was the adoption by Psusennes I of the title 'High Priest of Amun' – not only after the title 'King of Upper and Lower Egypt', but also as a variant prenomen within a cartouche (replacing Akheperre Setepenamun) or alongside Psusennes' name.[114] That the former Theban high priest Herihor did this as mere 'shadow king' meant little. But here, the real Pharaoh himself boasted of his headship of a particular priesthood, that of Amun – and in the nature of the case, at Tanis – which implied something more than being in principle the high priest of all the gods of Egypt.

Psusennes also sought to maintain a proper continuity with the past. Twice, his nomen appears in the form 'Ramesses-Psusennes, Beloved of Amun', while his son, prince Ankhefenmut C, was more fully styled 'Ramesses-Ankhefenmut'.[115] This fact suggests that, by their mother Henttawy Q (if a Ramesside princess), Psusennes I and his sister-queen Mutnodjmet had some Ramesside blood in their veins, which reinforced the legitimacy of the dynasty.

§ 221 (ii) *The Royal Family*
Chief consort of Psusennes I was the 'King's Daughter, King's Sister, King's Wife, Chief Great Queen of His Majesty', Mutnodjmet, for whom

111. For full titulary, cf. remarks of Montet, *Psus*, 177 and fig. 66, cf. fig. 51.
112. Cf. already Kees, *Tanis* (*NAWG*), 1944, 154 and nn. 1–2, 177; further, Excursus D, below.
113. See Excursus D, below.
114. Outside cartouche, cf. *Psus*, figs. 4 (bottom right and left), 5, 39 (top, twice), 51, 54 (middle and bottom), and corresponding plates. Inside cartouche, cf. *Psus*, figs. 4 (top left), 39 (bottom left), 40 (402), 41 (401), 42 (middle left), 44 (bottom left), 52, 54 (top right), 57 (right), 63 (right), pp. 177–8, and corresponding plates. Also, in Montet, *Le lac sacré de Tanis*, 1966, 41, pl. IV: 14, outside cartouche.
115. Cf. above, Chapter 4, § 41; documents, *Psus*, pp. 12, 58–9, 74, and figs. 1, 21, 27. The title 'King's Son of Ramesses' is distinct and later.

he provided a burial-chamber the twin of his own in his tomb within the precinct of the temple of Amun at Tanis. By her titles,[116] she was probably Psusennes' full sister. The prince Ramesses-Ankhefenmut was very likely their son, if not in fact their eldest son;[117] he too was provided with a chamber in the tomb of his father whom he probably predeceased.

Queen Mutnodjmet, significantly, held priestly benefices, as did her Theban counterparts. As her husband, the king, was high priest – First Prophet of Amun – she was his female counterpart as 'First Chief of the Harim of Amenresonter' (as were wives of high priests in Thebes) *and* his 'lieutenant' as *2nd Prophet* of Amenresonter. Again, like her Theban opposite numbers, she was prophetess of Mut and Khons and God's Mother of Khons-the-Child. As final perquisite, she had also the office of steward of the goddess Mut. This constellation of benefices, based on the cult, temple(s) and estates of Amun, Mut and Khons *at Tanis*,[118] served the same purpose of providing a befitting income for members of the new dynasty as did such 'plural livings' for the family of Herihor's successors in Thebes.

Prince Ramesses-Ankhefenmut boasted titles both military and religious.[119] Whatever the powers of Herihor's line in Upper Egypt, in the north it was Psusennes' son who was 'First Generalissimo of His Majesty' and (like many a Ramesside princeling), 'First Charioteer of His Majesty' besides 'Companion (*iry-rdwy*) of the Lord of the Two Lands'. At court he was 'Pre-eminent (*wr*) in his offices, great in his dignity before the nobles of the King'.

In the realm of the official cults, he too was well-established, as high steward of Amenresonter and 'Chief Steward of the Cattle[120] of Amenresonter', in charge of the temporal wealth[121] of the Tanite Amun of whose cult his parents were the chief celebrants.

We know nothing of any other sons of Psusennes I but may postulate that his successor Amenemope was to be found among them. One daughter is known, Istemkheb C, who was entitled at Tanis 'God's Mother of Khons-the-Child', as was Queen Mutnodjmet, and 'King's Daughter'.[122] It was

116. Which are all recorded on the foot of her sarcophagus, see *Psus*, 164, fig. 60.

117. Cf. traces of the titles of an heir(?), *iry-p'̒t ḥry-tp tꜣwy*, visible on the tomb walls, *Psus*, pls. 37, 38 (top right).

118. Not in Thebes, where the corresponding benefices were firmly in the hands of the Thebans. Cf. also Excursus D.

119. For what follows, cf. sarcophagus-inscription of Ankhefenmut, *Psus*, pl. 39 (below). Other fragments belonging to this prince, *Psus*, pp. 58–9, fig. 21, No. 408 (pl. 71), pp. 98, 104.

120. Rather than the 'horses' read by Montet, *Psus*, pp. 65, 68.

121. As were his namesakes (sons of Herihor and Piankh) earlier, for Theban Amun.

122. *Psus*, No. 403, pp. 101, 103, fig. 42, pl. 69.

perhaps she who became wife of the Theban high priest Menkheperre and mother of Pinudjem II who ever after was pleased to call himself 'son' (grandson) of king Psusennes as well as more exactly son of Menkheperre. If so, her mother Wiay will have been a lesser wife in the harim of Psusennes I.

§ **222*** (iii) *The Court and Officials*

The court of Tanis had its great men of the day. Of special pre-eminence was Wen-djeba-en-Djed who was eventually favoured with a richly-appointed burial in an outer room of the tomb of Psusennes I at Tanis.[123] He was probably chief courtier, with a title perhaps to be read 'Superintendent of the Sole Friend(s)'[124] plus such honorifics as 'Hereditary prince and count', 'Seal-bearer of the King of Lower Egypt' and 'God's Father, beloved of the god'.

More illuminating are Wen-djeba-en-Djed's military and religious appointments. Under the king's son, he was 'General and Army-leader of Pharaoh, L(ife), P(rosperity), H(ealth)', and alongside the royal family he was high steward of Khons besides being a prophet of Khons-re.[125] The office of 'Prophet of Osiris, Lord of Djedet' may stamp him as a native of Mendes (Djedet).[126] Finally, as 'Superintendent of the Prophets of all the Gods', he bore a dignity more appropriate to the high priest of Amun in Tanis.[127] Perhaps, therefore, he may have functioned as the king's deputy in the day-to-day conduct of Amun's cult in Tanis.

At Tanis, one other family attained highest distinction in the service of this pharaoh and probably his two predecessors.[128] One Nesy-en-Amun,

123. *Psus*, Chapter 6.

124. *Psus*, pl. 41; reading the title as *imy-r (s)mr(w) wꜥ(w)*, not *ḥs* with Montet.

125. *Psus*, pls. 41, 45, for these titles.

126. Cf. also the name of Smendes himself, meaning 'He who pertains to the Ram, Lord of Mendes'.

127. *Psus*, pls. 41 top left, 45. In New Kingdom Thebes, this title had been a common abbreviation for 'Superintendent of Prophets of all the Gods *of Thebes*' (cf. Kees, *Pr.*, 18, etc.), entirely distinct from the much wider title for 'all Gods of South and North'. The limited title was always borne by the Theban high priest of Amun; the latter, by whichever dignitary the king favoured with it (often these high priests). Hence, on the Theban model, Wen-djeba-en-Djed's title should similarly stand for 'Superintendent of Prophets of all Gods *of Tanis*'.

128. Commemorated on a competently-executed figure of Osiris, probably from a niche in a mud-brick tomb-chapel from a tomb in or near Tanis itself (cf. note 131 below), and bearing remarkable inscriptions. Published by Labib Habachi, *ASAE* 47 (1947), 261–82, pls. (32), 33. As Psusennes I is called 'the great god', and that in relation to a *ḵny*, 'palladium' (portable image in carrying-chair), typical of funerary cults of kings, this monument was most likely made soon after the death of Psusennes I – say, under Amenemope. As both father and daughter are mentioned in matching texts by her husband, one may suggest that they died about the same time, being jointly commemorated on the one monument.

who was possibly a Theban by origin,[129] served as Superintendent of the Chamberlains[130] of Pharaoh, L.P.H. – most likely under Smendes I, Amenemnisu and the early years of Psusennes I. In the service of Psusennes he was followed by his son Ankhefenamun who died aged 72 years, 5 months and 14 days, perhaps in the next reign (Amenemope), and so would be close to Psusennes I for probably the last three decades or more of that king's reign. Ankhefenamun once had a finely-sculptured tomb-chapel of his own at Tanis, but the merest fragments have been recovered, reused in later edifices.[131]

Besides being Chief of Chamberlains, Ankhefenamun was 'Scribe of Pharaoh' and 'of Documents of Pharaoh', and probably Superintendent of the Granary and of the Treasury. Finally his attachment to the cult of Psusennes I (still alive) is denoted by the title 'Sem-priest of Pharaoh before Amun . . .'.[132] In relation to the gods of Tanis, Ankhefenamun was priest (wᶜb) and prophet of Amun, God's Father of Mut and of Khons, besides being 'Scribe of the Temple of Khons-the-Child, First and Very Great One of Amun'.[133] Beyond Tanis, he was in addition 'Prophet of the House of Amun of Khapu' (location unknown).[134]

His daughter Ir-Mut-panufer illustrates the intimate links of this family with the Tanite dynasty, for she had been 'King's Nurse' (mnᶜ(t)-nsw).[135] She died aged only 43 years, 9 months and 26 days. She also was attached to the metropolitan cults: Chantress of Amun, Chief of the Chantresses of Khons, and Singer of the Choir(?) of Mut. Her husband

129. As he is the only person on the monument termed 'justified before all the gods of Thebes' (Habachi, op. cit., 269). Additional titles of Nesy-en-Amun, as father of Ankhefenamun, include Chief of Craftsmen of Pharaoh, L.P.H., and Superintendent of Granaries (?), on Tanite blocks of the son, next note but one below.

130. So, and not mortuary priests (as Habachi and Montet); cf. Ramesside viziers as imy-ẖnt, 'chamberlain', or imy-r imyw-ẖnt, 'superintendent of chamberlains', Helck, Zur Verwaltung des Mittleren und Neuen Reichs, 1958, 312, 449, 454.

131. Principally in the tomb of Shoshenq III; blocks published by Montet, Chéchanq III, 1960, 87–93, pls. 53–61.

132. Cf. blocks Nos. 8, 9, 10, 11 in Montet, op. cit., 88 and pl. 54. Note that his 'first prophet of Amun' (p. 87) is a misinterpretation of the stroke following ordinary ḥm-nṯr 'prophet', not from a proper writing of tpy.

133. This epithet of Khons (ᶜȝ wr tpy n 'Imn) is also applied to him in the titles of Queen Mutnodjmet of Tanis, and is attested at Thebes.

134. Cf. Habachi, op. cit., 269, for a 'district of Khepu', possibly the same. Perhaps the Chantress of Amun, Ankhes-en-[Amun?] was his wife (Montet, Chéchanq III, block No. 12).

135. Hardly to Psusennes I, already king before she was born, especially if she and her father died at much the same time, after the death of Psusennes I. Hence, she was perhaps formerly royal nurse to Amenemope, most probably king at the time of erection of this monument.

Sia was an important man of state in his own right,[136] as Granary-Superintendent of the Granaries of Pharaoh (as successor to Ankhefenamun?). In the cult, he was a God's Father of both Amun and Khons. More interesting by far is his function as a funerary priest, eventually, of the 'late, great' Psusennes – 'Controller of the Palladium of King Psusennes (I), the great god', which gave him a further bond with the reigning house.

§ **223** (iv) *Foreign Relations*

By its extreme northerly position as a citadel dominating the flat lands and marches to the Mediterranean coast, Tanis could not well serve as a central administrative capital for all Egypt.[137] For that function, Memphis doubtless retained its long-standing role.[138] Rather, Tanis was Egypt's northeast bulwark toward the Levant and had replaced Pi-Ramessē as a port highly convenient for trade with the Near East, as was reflected in the narrative of Wenamun.

That the armies of Psusennes I ever marched or sailed to foreign wars beyond Egypt's borders may be doubted. They probably served mainly as security forces to police the coasts and desert-borders against pirates and petty marauders. Contacts with more distant powers of the Near East remain veiled from us except for one intriguing detail. One of the collars placed on the mummy of Psusennes I included a large lapis-lazuli bead inscribed in cuneiform for a lady who had been the eldest daughter of the grand vizier Ibashshi-ilu of Assyria.[139] How this bauble found its way from the court of Assur to that of Egypt (and when) remains unknown. At the most, it could reflect diplomatic relations between the courts of Assur and Egypt,[140] but more modestly it may be the result of indirect contact, a second-hand piece traded across the Levant to Egypt. Perhaps it was inherited from Smendes if he got it in some return by Assur-bel-kala to Ramesses XI when the latter sent his exotic gift of crocodile and ape to the Assyrian king.[141]

136. Unless, of course, marriage to a royal nurse and daughter of Pharaoh's chief chamberlain had gained him his high office!

137. On Tanis geographically, cf. Kees, *Tanis*, 1944, 168 ff.; Kees, *Ancient Egypt, A Cultural Topography*, 1961, 196; J. van Seters, *The Hyksos*, 1966, 139–40; E. Uphill, *JNES* 27 (1968), 305, 308.

138. Cf. Smendes I being at Memphis when he decreed the opening of the Gebelen quarries for repair-work at Luxor, and the buildings of Psusennes I, Amenemope, and Siamun at Memphis and Giza.

139. See E. Dhorme in Montet, *Psus*, 139–43 (and pl. 112), with previous literature and esp. R. Borger, *Einleitung in die assyrichen Königsinschriften*, I, 1961, 20–2 (§ *b*) who eliminates the name Napalte.

140. Cf. the ingenious suggestions of Dhorme, *op. cit.*, 143, who even envisaged Napalte as having entered the harim of Psusennes and dedicating this gold and lapis-adorned collar to her deceased Egyptian husband. Contrast Borger, *op. cit.*, 21–2.

141. See above, § 210, end.

B. PSUSENNES I, THE BUILDER KING

§ 224 (i) *The Builder of Tanis*

Of the royal palaces of Tanis, the town and seaport of this age, nothing is yet known. But the temple precincts are still impressive, even in their utter ruin. Psusennes I erected a vast mud-brick enclosing wall, of irregular plan, to protect the temples of Amun and his fellow-deities – and the royal tomb. Within that massive enclosure, its walls up to 60 feet thick and the bricks stamped in their thousands with the royal name, Psusennes constructed the temple or temples of Amun, Mut and Khons upon an east–west axis with the main temple façade facing west. Apart from one foundation-deposit recovered *in situ*,[142] little has survived except the merest fragments of reliefs and of an architrave with dedicatory text for 'a temple of fine white Tura limestone',[143] principally for Amun.[144] Otherwise, we know only that Psusennes took over various earlier sculptures – sphinxes and the like – and reinscribed them to adorn his new buildings.[145]

In the south-west corner of the precinct the king built his tomb of limestone and granite, reusing older stonework throughout. Besides the twin chambers for the king and queen, it comprised an ante-hall and side-rooms eventually occupied by the burials of other Tanite royalty and grandees. One may speculate whether, perhaps, the brickwork foundations east of the tomb may have belonged to a funerary chapel of the king; but his cult may have been integrated with that of the main temple of Amun.

§ 225 (ii) *Works Elsewhere*

Beyond the residence at Tanis, no works of Psusennes are recorded in the Delta beyond a statue-base from Tennis near Lake Menzaleh.[146] At Memphis, three High Priests of Ptah served in this reign, from father to son[147] – Pipi A, Harsiese and Pipi B, of whom the last-named saw out the final years of Psusennes and officiated under three of his successors.[148] Among their subordinates the priest of Ptah and of the House of Osiris Lord of Restau, Ptah-kha, erected for his like-titled father Asha-khet

142. See *Psus*, 15 and pl. 1, No. 7.
143. Cf. Montet, *Psus*, 17, fig. 5, and *Le lac sacré de Tanis*, 1966, 41: 14, pl. 4.
144. Who is the deity principally named on the fragments so far published by Montet, *Psus*, 16, fig. 4; for a goddess Shahadet, cf. *ibid.*, 12, fig. 1. Other fragments of Psusennes I come from the South ('Anta') temple, *Psus*, 17, and are associated with Khons.
145. *Psus*, 18; *Le lac sacré*, 42, No. 16 (not illustrated and cited as No. 15); *PM*, IV, 16, 17, 20.
146. Cairo, JdE 41644; *G3*, 290, VII, and *PM*, IV, 13.
147. 'Berlin genealogy', Louvre 96; cf. above, Chapter 12.
148. See below, under Siamun, § 234.

a chapel(?) with a stone doorway.[149] Out at Giza, perhaps late in his reign, Psusennes I began a small temple to 'Isis, Mistress of the Pyramids' at the third queen's pyramid by the Great Pyramid of Kheops.[150]

Elsewhere (so far), the name of Psusennes occurs on hardly any contemporary monument anywhere south of the area of Memphis. His authority certainly reached south-westward into the oases, where a later stela from Dakhla refers back to land-registers of Year 19 of Pharaoh Psusennes (i.e. *c.* 1021 B.C.).[151] No works of this king bear his name in Thebes (despite his Nebty-name!).[152] The cult of a king Psusennes (I or II?) was honoured in Thebes still, in the 22nd Dynasty.[153] Other traces of this king's name are minimal.[154]

C. THE PONTIFICATE OF MENKHEPERRE

§ 226 (i) *As Builder and Administrator*

At his northern fastness of El Hibeh, Menkheperre continued the building of its walls, the bricks being stamped in the name of his wife Istemkheb C and himself. These endeavours gave rise to an ancient nickname for the fort, Teudjoi 'their walls'. At the south end of this strategic stretch of the Nile, Menkheperre built an additional fort near Shurafa; thereby, effective control of river traffic could be exercised in northern Middle Egypt.[155] Just north of the Thebaid proper, at Higazeh near Qus, a building yielded a brick of Istemkheb, 'mother of the God's Wife of Amun' – perhaps the wife of Menkheperre and mother of a successor to Maatkare A.[156] Such a fort could check traffic in and out of Thebes via the north and Wadi Hammamat. Still further south, at Gebelen,[157] the names of Menkheperre

149. R. Anthes *et al.*, *Mitrahineh 1956*, 1965, 92–6, fig. 12, pl. 31.

150. *PM*, III, 5, end; *G3*, 289, 2, II. A further block, seen by Petrie, was destroyed by local people, Petrie, *History of Egypt*, III, 1905, 222.

151. Published first by Spiegelberg, *RT* 21 (1899), 12–21, and definitively by Gardiner, *JEA* 19 (1933), 19 ff., esp. 22, 23, pl. 6.

152. The burial of the chantresses Istemkheb and Isty was attributed to this reign, as their mummy-braces were said to be stamped with the cartouche of a Psusennes (Daressy, *ASAE* 8 (1907), 26, No. 58, 27/28, No. 66), but the true reading of the half-obliterated cartouches may be Amenemope (ref., courtesy M. L. Bierbrier, after Černý). Other such corrections, cf. Černý, *CAH²*, II: 35 (1965), 45, n. 9, 49, n. 1.

153. Mentioned on Cairo Cat. 42224; cf. Helck, *Materialen zur Wirtschaftsgeschichte des Neuen Reiches*, I, 1961, 121, § 7, and Kees, *Pr.*, 243 (misquoted as Pinudjem).

154. Cf. (e.g.) small bronze capital, clay sealing, etc., *Psus*, 18, n. 2 (after Yoyotte); Petrie, *History*, III, 221–3; *G3*, 290/1, VI, VIII, IX.

155. Bricks from these places, *G3*, 266, XI, 268, XVII (Shurafa), XIX, 269–70, B/C. Cf. Wainwright, *ASAE* 27 (1927), 79–93, *passim*.

156. *G3*, 269, XXIII, A (Cairo, JdE 44670, unpublished).

157. *G3*, 267, XV and n. 4, after Fraser, *PSBA* 15 (1893), 498, pl. V: XXI.

and Istemkheb occur yet again on bricks, completing their chain of forts and check-points with oversight of the southernmost reach of the Nile of Egypt, between Thebes and Aswan.

In Thebes itself, Menkheperre carried out a variety of works in and around the great temples in the later years of Psusennes and himself. One fragment of the Karnak Priestly Annals (No. 3A) records an inspection of Theban temples conducted in his name by the 4th Prophet of Amun, Tjanefer in Year 40 (*c.* 1000 B.C.):[158] the temples of Amun at Karnak and Luxor, and of Mut, Khons, Ptah, Montu and Maat (all known to us today) all feature. A Karnak stela of Year 48 (*c.* 992 B.C.) records more serious measures of conservation: building 'a very great wall' on the north of the temple of Amun, to exclude the encroaching houses of the population from Amun's sacred domain.[159] At Luxor, yet more bricks of Menkheperre attest similar works there,[160] which were perhaps commemorated by a short line of text by Menkheperre that adjoins the small west doorway from the south part of the colonnades of Amenophis III.[161] An oracle inscribed in the temple of Khons appears to record a property settlement.[162]

§ 227 (ii) *The family of Menkheperre*

During this long pontificate, not a few of Menkheperre's lesser priestly contemporaries passed to rest in the Theban mountain. Some seven such burials are known.[163] His own mother Henttawy A was buried in a full set of coffins with fullest titles.[164] Little is known of his wife Istemkheb C. Neither his burial nor hers has yet been discovered.[165] The lady Henttawy C was probably their daughter and possibly also the eventual wife of Smendes II, their eldest son.[166] Two sons, Smendes II and Pinudjem II, were to succeed Menkheperre in office. A third son, Psusennes,[167] was

158. *G3*, 265, IV, and references.
159. *G3*, 265, V; Barguet, *Le temple d'Amon-rê à Karnak*, 1962, 36–8, pl. 32*b*.
160. Seen by Lepsius; *G3*, 267, XVI; *LD*, III, 251*k*, *LDT*, III, 88.
161. *PM*, II, 109 (132); II², 334 (208).
162. Published *LDT*, III, 62–3, cf. *PM*, II, 80, 1st column (attributed to Pinudjem I); II², 232, 1.
163. Nos. 11, 13, 14, 64, 96, 109, 115, in Daressy, *ASAE* 8 (1907), 22 ff., and in *RArch*³ 28 (1896–I), 76, etc.
164. In the time of Menkheperre, because of the leather braces in his name found on her mummy, *MMR*, 576–7. For her titles, cf. above. Chapter 4, § 43.
165. The account of her titles given by Kees, *Hhp.*, 48 (and more briefly, *Pr.*, 164) is mistaken, because based on a set of coffins that belonged *not* to Istemkheb C (wife of Menkheperre) but to Istemkheb D (daughter of Menkheperre) – for this attribution, see above, Chapter 4, §§ 51 f. We need not doubt that Istemkheb C was duly endowed with appropriate benefices, but direct evidence is lacking at present.
166. Her burial was found by Winlock; cf. above, Chapter 4, §§ 46 (ii), 52.
167. Stela, Maciver and Mace, *El Amrah and Abydos*, 1902, 94, pls. 31, 34: 8; *G3*, 272, 3. Discussed by Kees, *Hhp.*, 76–8.

District-Officer and army-leader, doubtless for the region from Abydos to Coptos, as he held priesthoods of Min, Horus and Isis of Coptos and of Amun of Thinis and the 'Storehouse',[168] besides being a God's Father of Amenresonter. As well as Henttawy C, Menkheperre produced a brood of daughters – Istemkheb D, wife of Pinudjem II (see § 232 below), Gautsoshen and Merytamun.[169] Gautsoshen's husband was that Tjanefer active as 4th Prophet in Year 40, who before his death became 3rd Prophet of Amun.[170]

D. PSUSENNES I, AMENEMOPE, AND SMENDES II

§ 228* There is no reason to believe that Menkheperre survived much beyond Year 48 of Psusennes I, if at all. The latter, now very old, perhaps had Amenemope as co-regent from his 47th year and died in Year 49 or soon after. Menkheperre's successor in Thebes was his eldest son Smendes II, who was himself no youngster. For the funeral of Psusennes, Smendes II gave bracelets in the name of Psusennes which were dedicated by himself.[171] The wealth of the Tanite Dynasty may be gauged from the treasure of fine gold and silver vessels, the solid silver coffin and the solid gold mask and collar with which the old pharaoh was interred, while the burial of Wen-djeba-en-Djed indicates the quite lavish scale of provision probably made for Queen Mutnodjmet and Prince Ankhefenmut. The glories of empire had long gone, but the rulers of Tanis were men of substance and were far from being impoverished squatters in their northern citadel.

Of the joint *régime* of Amenemope and the high priest Smendes II, few traces survive other than their names together, on braces and pendants respectively, from a mummy in Western Thebes.[172] Smendes II himself quickly passed from the scene and was followed in office by his brother Pinudjem II. No sons are known, but they probably had two daughters, Istemkheb E and Nesikhons A.[173]

168. On 'the storehouses of This', see Černý, *Studi . . . Ippolito Rosellini*, II, 1955, 27–31.
169. For these daughters, cf. above, Chapter 4, § 54, D, E.
170. Kees, *Hhp.*, 69 and n. 1.
171. *Psus*, 149, fig. 54.
172. Mummy No. 135; Excursus B, X, 49, below.
173. Pylon X text at Karnak, Chapter 4, §§ 46 (ii), 52 E, above.

CHAPTER 17

The Twenty-first Dynasty: the Later Kings

§ 229   1. AMENEMOPE AND OSOCHOR

A. AMENEMOPE (c. 993–984 B.C.)

On the view preferred here, the reign of Amenemope lasted barely a decade, leaving but few traces.

At Tanis the new king's main monument was a small tomb ('IV') of only one chamber. The whole structure was barely 20 feet long by 12–15 feet wide, a mere cell compared with the tomb of Psusennes I.[174] Elsewhere, his only known original works were to continue the decoration of the little temple of Isis Mistress of the Pyramids at Giza,[175] and to add to one of the temples in Memphis itself.[176] In Tanis, Amenemope was not only king but also High Priest of Amun like his predecessor.[177] In Thebes, his authority as king was undisputed – no less than nine burials of the Theban clergy had braces, pendants or bandages inscribed in the name of Amenemope as pharaoh and of Pinudjem II as pontiff.[178] Pen-nest-tawy, captain of the barge of Amun in Thebes, possessed a Book of the Dead dated to Year 5 of this reign.[179]

In his own burial, Amenemope was indeed equipped as a king, but with far less opulence than Psusennes I: his wooden coffins were covered with

174. See Lezine in Montet, *Psus*, 173–5, pls. 138–9.
175. *PM*, III, 5; relief in Cairo, jamb in Berlin, *G3*, 293, V, VI.
176. *PM*, III, 220, references.
177. Attested on a faience seal or signet-ring (Groff collection), *G3*, 292, I, after Daressy (unpublished).
178. Nos. 24, 38, 42, 81, 82, 85, 113, 121, 130, cf. Daressy, *ASAE* 8 (1907), 23 ff.
179. Papyrus BM. 10064, cf. A. W. Shorter, *Catalogue of Egyptian Religious Papyri in the British Museum*, I, 1938, 7.

gold leaf instead of being of solid silver; he wore a gilt mask rather than one of solid gold, and there were more vessels of bronze than of silver or gold. Nor was he destined to occupy his modest tomb for very long.

§ 230*   B. OSOCHOR (c. 984–978 B.C.)

Of the new king, only his prenomen is known – Akheperre Setepenre – and not even his personal name. To this brief reign of 6 years, only two and a half lines of one damaged inscription can so far be attributed with certainty.[180] From this, we learn only that in his 2nd year (c. 983 B.C.), on the 20th day of the 1st month of Shomu, the priest Nespaneferhor son of Iufnamun was inducted into office at Karnak. He was a God's father of Amenresonter, Temple Scribe of Mut, and Chief of Scribes of the Offering-table of the House (or, Estate) of Amun.

In Thebes, Pinudjem II continued as high priest of Amun. Of the various datelines from Years 1 to 7 attested during his pontificate, it is possible that some belong to the reign of Osochor (or even to that of Amenemope); but most are here classed with others that belong indubitably to the reign of Siamun. Neither a tomb nor any vestige at Tanis can so far be assigned to Osochor.

§ 231   C. FOREIGN AFFAIRS UNDER AMENEMOPE AND
                                      OSOCHOR

From Egyptian sources, nothing is known – not surprisingly, when even the kings themselves are so ill-attested. But some gleams of light come from external sources. By c. 1040 B.C., about the time of Psusennes I, the political situation in Palestine had finally begun to crystallize: the Philistines and Zikkalu ruled the coastal cities and ports, while inland the new Hebrew kingdom under Saul struggled to survive against the opposition of the Philistines and remnants of the Canaanite city-states. By c. 1000 B.C., David (c. 1010–970 B.C.)[181] had become ruler of all the Hebrew tribes and seized Jerusalem to make it his capital. In a series of campaigns, he fended-off and restricted the Philistines and made Israel the principal state in Palestine and South Syria.

During the first half of David's reign, his forces conquered Edom, whose infant crown-prince Hadad was spirited away by faithful retainers who sought refuge for him in Egypt (1 Kings 11: 14–22). There, the reigning pharaoh gave him 'a house, food-allowance and land' (verse 18).[182] As he

180. Karnak Priestly Annals, fragment 3B, lines 1–3; G3, 289, I (put under Psusennes I); cf. E. Young, JARCE 2 (1963), 99–101.
181. For dates of Hebrew and other Near-Eastern kings given in this work, cf. Kitchen, HHAHT, Tables and Commentaries.
182. For house and food-allowance, cf. Sinuhe B 286–307 (e.g. J. A. Wilson in ANET, 22a), almost a thousand years before. The land assigned to Hadad would

grew up, young Hadad found favour at court and was given in marriage the sister of the Egyptian queen (Tahpenes).[183] Their son Genubath was probably weaned at about 3 years old[184] and placed 'among the sons of Pharaoh' (verse 20).[185] But at David's death, Hadad and his entourage returned to Edom with the aim of opposing the Israelite rule. If Genubath was about 5 years old then (*c.* 970 B.C.) – a minimum – and was born when Hadad was about 18, and if Hadad himself had been brought to Egypt aged at the most 2 or 3 years (as an infant), then his arrival in Egypt would fall somewhere about 991 or 990 B.C.;[186] Amenemope would be the pharaoh

provide an income (from its yield) and be his 'estate' (*pr*). Cf. estates of members of the royal family or for support of officials (e.g. of the treasury), Helck, *Materialen zur Wirtschaftsgeschichte des Neuen Reiches*, II, 1960, 211–15, and doubtless the estates of Henttawy C and Maatkare B under this Dynasty (Gardiner, *JEA* 48 (1962), 57–69), of the high priest Iuwelot under the next (cf. Legrain & Erman, *ZÄS* 35 (1897), 13 ff., 19 ff.), and for Nitocris in the Twenty-sixth (Caminos, *JEA* 50 (1964), 71–101). Emendations of the Hebrew text to eliminate such features as the land-grant or court-upbringing, as suggested by some (e.g. J. Gray, *I, II Kings*, 1963, 263, *a*, *d*) is wholly gratuitous, given the known Egyptian usages here illustrated.

183. The Egyptian original of this term remains undecided. By far the most attractive view is to take it as a slightly-syncopated Hebrew transcription of the Egyptian phrase *tꜣ-ḥ(mt)-pꜣ-nsw*, 'wife of the king', i.e. 'queen'. In this, the fem. ending *t* of *ḥmt* had long since ceased to be pronounced, and the *m* may be assimilated to following *p*. This view (without changes just suggested) was offered by B. Grdseloff, *RHJÉ* 1 (1947), 88–90. In its support, one may cite the closely similar transcription of *tꜣ-ḥm(t)-nsw*, 'the king's wife', 'queen', into slightly Hurrianized Hittite cuneiform as *daḫamunzu* in the 14th century B.C., see W. Federn, *JCS* 14 (1960), 33. Alternatively, Albright considered it a proper name beginning with *Tꜣ-ḥ(nt)-*, *BASOR* 140 (1955), 32. One may compare Ta-hent-Thuty, mother-in-law of Pinudjem II. More precisely, if a proper name must be found, I would prefer to take the Hebrew form as transcribing a **Ta-hep(et)-en-Ese (*Tꜣ-ḥp(t)-n-ꜣst)*, cf. a name like Hor-em-hepet-Ese (*Ḥr-m-ḥpt-ꜣst*), J. Černý and A. A. Sadek, *Graffiti de la Montagne Thébaine*, IV, 1970, 42, No. 2138: 2.

184. So both in Egypt (*Instruction of Aniy*, 7, 19; *ANET*, 420, end), and among the Hebrews (cf. A. Bertholet, *A History of Hebrew Civilization*, 1926, 162 and n. 8, on 1 Samuel 1: 23, 2 Maccabees 7: 27, and Josephus, *Antiquities*, II, ix, 6). Therefore, this custom may well have applied to Hadad's son also.

185. A court upbringing for Genubath belonged to a very old and longstanding Egyptian tradition, embracing notables, commoners and foreigners. In the Old Kingdom, Ptahshepses (Fifth Dynasty) was 'brought up among the king's children within the palace' (Sethe, *Urkunden I*, 51; H. Brunner, *Altägyptische Erziehung*, 1957, 153, Qu. II), similarly Kar of Edfu (cf. *Urk. I*, 253 f., Brunner, *op. cit.*, 154, Qu. IV). In Middle Kingdom, cf. Khety of Siut (Brunner, *op. cit.*, 157, Qu. VII), Ikhernofret (*ANET*, 329, Brunner, 161, Qu. XVI). In New Kingdom terms, Genubath would have been a 'page' or *ḥrd-n-kꜣp* (cf. Helck, *Zur Verwaltung des Mittleren und Neuen Reiches*, 1958, 254, 270, etc.). For foreigners at court, including foreign princes, cf. *ANET*, 239a (Year 30, Tuthmosis III), and series of references, Kitchen in *NBD*, 343b, 844–5. For Late Period officials as confidants of the palace, cf. E. Otto, *Die Biographischen Inschriften der Ägyptischen Spätzeit*, 1954, 105, 106, 111, 115, 147–8.

186. i.e. *c.* 970 + 5 + 18 (−2 or 3) years = *c.* 991 or 990 B.C. This date, not later

who assigned him and his people home and maintenance, while Hadad probably acquired his wife and son early in the reign of Siamun. Thus, we catch a fleeting glimpse of friendly relations between the court at Tanis and those of other, smaller nations in the Levant. In particular, such relations between Egypt and Edom were not wholly new, to judge from one obscure document under Ramesses X or XI.[187]

§ 232   2. THE REIGN OF SIAMUN (c. 978–959 B.C.)

Siamun must at present rank as virtually the most active and best-attested king of the dynasty, easily rivalling Psusennes I.[188] Both in Thebes and in the north, we gain glimpses of personalities and events.

A. PINUDJEM II AND HIS FAMILY IN THE SOUTH

The reigning pontiff had two principal wives[189] – his sister, Istemkheb D, and his niece, Nesikhons A. The titles of Istemkheb in particular [190] show how widely the ruling Theban house had spread its net, to assure its leading members of benefices that would provide an adequate income. As wife of the high priest she was, of course, Leading Lady and First Chief of the Harim of Amenresonter, plus a prophetess of Mut and Khons and God's Mother of Khons-the-Child. Like Henttawy A two generations back, she was steward of both Mut and Khons. Much more striking is her impressive number of benefices outside Thebes[191] – prophetess of Amun of Iu-rud (16th Upper Egyptian nome), of Hathor of Cusae, of Horus of Djufy, of Min, Horus and Isis in Akhmim, of Osiris, Horus and Isis in Abydos, and of Onuris-Shu in Thinis, all north of Thebes, plus that of Nekhbet of El Kab to the south. Thus the Theban ruling house drew revenues from almost a third of all the provinces ('nomes') of Upper Egypt. A similar if less extensive 'plurality of livings' was bestowed upon the other wife, Nesikhons A, who was also a First Chief of the Harim of Amun. She was prophetess of

than about the 20th year of David, would well fit the overall picture of events in his reign; cf. Kitchen, *HHAHT*, Table IV, Commentary, § 4, latter part.

187. The 'literary letter', Papyrus Moscow 127, 5, 4–7, whose hero seems to seek help from 'those of Se'ir', i.e. Edomites; for this text, cf. above, § 208, note 24.

188. We have, perhaps, more monuments of consequence from the barely 20 years of Siamun's reign than for the nearly 50 years of Psusennes I. The new king adopted the old Horus-name of Ramesses II, 'Strong Bull, beloved of Maat' (plus 'son of . . .', *G3*, 297, XIV), but a highly original prenomen, Neterkheperre plus Setepenamun.

189. And probably others, cf. Kees, *Hhp.*, 68, top, with Maspero.

190. Recorded on her two sets of coffins; refs., cf. above, Chapter 4, § 52.

191. See already, Kees, *Pr.*, 164–5, and *Hhp.*, 67.

Nebet-hetepet, lady of Sered (location unknown, Northern Nubia?) and of Khnum lord of the First Cataract,[192] as well as of Amun of Khnem-Waset (Temple of Ramesses III, Medinet Habu) in Western Thebes. Her southern connections were rounded off with two remarkable titles: Superintendent of Southern Foreign (or, Desert) Lands, and Viceroy of Nubia! That Nesikhons actually served in either capacity is extremely unlikely, but these titles may indicate her rights to revenue from wealth obtained in Northern Nubia or dues levied on trade passing thence.[193] Possibly later still, Pinudjem II's daughter Nesitanebtashru inherited several benefices from her stepmother Istemkheb D, i.e. prophetess of the deities in Iu-rud, Akhmim, Abydos, Thinis and El Kab of those listed above, to which she added those of Pakhet lady of Sro (Speos Artemidos) and Anty of Hieracon.[194]

One remarkable fact, however, is that the ruling family of the high priests from Menkheperre onwards seemingly did *not* lay claim to the Theban key-posts of 2nd, 3rd, and 4th Prophet of Amun. This is in clear contrast to their position under Piankh and Pinudjem I, when, for example, the latter's brother was 2nd prophet of Amun. Instead, these offices were now held by men of *other* Theban families, whose links with the ruling house were by marriage, not by descent. This changed situation most probably resulted from the clearing-up of Theban grievances by Menkheperre in the years shortly following his appointment in Year 25 of Smendes I. Under an agreement to 'live and let live', in return for a proper share in the priestly and administrative positions in Thebes, the local Theban notable families would not oppose the acquisition of 'livings' by Menkheperre's family in provinces beyond Thebes.[195] Thus, that Tjanefer who was active as 4th Prophet of Amun in Year 40 of Psusennes I and attained to 3rd Prophet, was himself son of a previous 4th Prophet, Nespaherenmut.[196] He married Gautsoshen, daughter of Menkheperre,[197]

192. Cf. Kees, *Pr.*, 165 f., and *Hhp.*, 66, who adds also benefices from Khnum of *Gḥsti*, and Hathor lady of ʿAgni (N. of El Kab).

193. Cf. also the remarks of Maspero, *MMR*, 715, top. Reisner (*JEA* 6 (1920), 53) a little ungallantly opined that these titles were bestowed on Nesikhons 'to satisfy the vanity of a woman'!

194. Cf. Kees, *Hhp.*, 72–3, from Papyrus Greenfield. Her daughter Nesikhons B was a Chantress and Chief of Harim of Amun (*G3*, 284, 2).

195. This important development seems (unusually) not to have been perceived by Kees, partly because of confusion over the identities of the different Tjanefers of this epoch.

196. Karnak Priestly Annals, fragment 3A, lines 4–6 (Legrain, *RT* 22 (1900), 53). The mother of this Tjanefer and wife of Nespaherenmut was an otherwise unknown Istemkheb (so also Kees, *Hhp.*, 69, 70).

197. Cf. above, Chapter 4, § 54, D; this Tjanefer (from his papyrus) was also Superintendent of Cattle of the Roof-Temple of Rēʿ in the Temple of Amun, and

and served under Pinudjem II in Years 2–5 (of Siamun?).[198] The office of
3rd Prophet went to his son, another Menkheperre, and that of 4th
Prophet to his other son Pinudjem.[199] Thus, Menkheperre, Smendes II and
Pinudjem II maintained a *modus vivendi* and developed family ties with the
local Theban families. Of the sons of Pinudjem II, nothing is known
beyond their names, and that the eldest(?), Psusennes, eventually succeeded his father in office.

§ **233** During Years 2, 3 and 5 of an unnamed king (Siamun?), the breath
of scandal hung over the administrative staff of the estates of Amun in
Thebes, with charges of fraud. This apparently centred on the steward and
granary-archivist Thutmose, son of Su-awy-Amun, who was eventually
cleared of all charges and then left a major inscription about it near Pylon X
at Karnak.[200]

In Year 5 of Siamun (*c.* 974 B.C.), Nesikhons A, younger wife of
Pinudjem II, died and was buried in the remote tomb of an early queen
Inhapi, beyond Deir el Bahri in Western Thebes.[201] In Years 5, 6 and 8,
sundry arrangements were made concerning the property of the lady
Henttawy C, widow of Smendes II, and their daughter Istemkheb E,
guaranteeing their rights to property inherited and purchased. The 3rd
prophet of Amun, Tjanefer, was involved, possibly once in the role of 2nd
prophet.[202]

Finally, Year 10 of Siamun (*c.* 969 B.C.) was a year of drastic upheaval in
the necropolis of Western Thebes. In that year, Pinudjem II died and was
succeeded by his son, Psusennes 'III'. For over a century, the new man's
predecessors had striven vainly to check the plundering of the noble dead,
the pharaohs and great families of the empire. Here and there, groups of
mummies had been collected in one tomb or another for greater safety.[203]
Now at last it was decided to guard the ancestral dead in the same way as
had been used by the priests themselves to secure the burials of their own
company: by interment in one or two large groups in secret hiding-places.

prophet of Khnum lord of the (First) Cataract, besides being a prophet of Theban
Montu (Kees, *Hhp.*, 68–9).
    198. Text of judgment of Amun, Pylon X, E. end (Naville, in next note but one);
Kees, *Hhp.*, 64, 69.
    199. Kees, *Hhp.*, 71, for these two.
    200. E. Naville, *Inscription historique de Pinodjem III* [sic], 1883; *BAR*, IV, §§
671–3 (extracts only). The 3rd Prophet of Amun, Tjanefer, is depicted in the relief,
cf. Kees, *Pr.*, 26 and n. 2 (after Sethe).
    201. See Černý, *JEA* 32 (1946), 25–6, 30, 1.
    202. See Gardiner, *JEA* 48 (1962), 57–64, and references.
    203. e.g. Ramesses I, Sethos I and Ramesses II in the tomb of Sethos I, cf.
Černý, *JEA* 32 (1946), 30, 3.

So the bodies of the revered Amenophis I, and of Ramesses I, Sethos I and Ramesses II were lodged in the secret tomb of Pinudjem II and his wife. Psusennes 'III' then proceeded to inter almost forty mummies of empire pharaohs and their relatives and of his own line,[204] together with the battered remains of their funerary equipment.[205]

Of other activities of Psusennes 'III' and his contemporaries for the last decade of Siamun's reign, very little is yet known; mummy-linen of Year 12 is attested, and a destroyed entry for Year 14 in the Karnak Priestly Annals follows an equally destroyed back-reference to Pinudjem II who was already dead.[206] In Year 17 of Siamun, the priest Hori was inducted as successor to his father Nespaneferhor of a generation earlier (Year 2 of Osochor) and his grandfather Iufnamun.[207]

§ 234   B. SIAMUN: OTHER HOME AFFAIRS

Siamun probably rivalled Psusennes I in the amount and quality of building-work he achieved in Egypt – not that either was outstanding in terms of earlier and palmier days.

In Tanis, Siamun undoubtedly extended the main temple of Amun – two massive column-bases of his were found still *in situ*, west and in front of the area that produced the foundation-deposits of Psusennes I.[208] One may, therefore, suggest that Siamun added a pillared forecourt[209] before the main temple of Psusennes I. To a shrine somewhere east of the tomb of Psusennes I, he added a modest façade with small triumph-scenes of the king smiting his foes (§ 235, below). He also built at the South Temple of Khons(?), the so-called 'Anta temple'.[210] At Tanis, it was probably Siamun who transferred the burial of his grandfather(?) Amenemope to the tomb of Psusennes I (evicting Queen Mutnodjmet in the process), to judge from

204. Perhaps about this same time, other groups were finally hidden away, e.g. nine more pharaohs in the tomb of Amenophis II, and further groups of Theban priests (including some still hidden today).

205. For Year 10 as date of the main *cache*, and its dockets in the tomb-shaft and on coffins of Ramesses I, Sethos I and Ramesses II, see Černý, *JEA* 32 (1946), 28 ff. Original publication of the find is *MMR*.

206. Karnak Priestly Annals, fragment 33, line 2 (Legrain, *RT* 22 (1900), 61). Year 12, mummy No. 65 of priest Pi-Amun, *G3*, 285, II.

207. Karnak Priestly Annals, fragment 3B (Legrain, *RT* 22 (1900), 53–4, and *RT* 30 (1908), 87); *G3*, 296, VIII.

208. *Psus*, 14 ff.; earlier, *G3*, 297, XIV–XV (base and deposit of Siamun).

209. Conceivably a hypostyle hall; but in that case, one might expect to find more traces of columns and bases, even allowing for later destruction. For a frieze block of Siamun, of good cutting in granite, see photo in Petrie, *History of Egypt*, III, 1905, 224, fig. 91.

210. *Psus*, 17; Montet, *Tanis*, 1942, 187–8, figs. 53–5, *Les énigmes de Tanis*, 1952, 135–6, fig. 30, p. 143; cf. *Nouvelles Fouilles de Tanis*, 1933, 89 f.

a scarab found in the flooring of tomb IV of Amenemope.[211] Siamun's cartouches on a block from Khataanah may indicate some minor work in the old Delta residence of Pi-Ramessē [212] At Heliopolis, Siamun added a line of text to the obelisk of Tuthmosis III,[213]

More important was a building at Memphis which included over half-a-dozen stone doorways[214] and limestone pillars[215] and was possibly a small temple to a minor form of Amun, 'Amun, Lord of Lapis-lazuli'.[216] It is of excellent, if conventional, workmanship. The structure was erected by the veteran High Priest of Ptah, Pipi B, who now boasted the loyalist surname Neterkheperre-Meryptah which was based on the King's prenomen, and by his adjutant, the prophet of Amun of the lapis-lazuli, Ankhefenmut D, who was the son of Khamwese called Hatiay. As Pipi B had already served under three previous kings, this work may date from early in Siamun's reign, and Pipi B will have later been succeeded in office by his son Asha-khet B.[217] Across the river, in the eastern part of the Memphite province, a stela of Year 16 of Siamun (c. 963 B.C.) receipted a land-sale between some lesser clergy of Ptah.[218]

South of the Memphite region, typically of this dynasty, Siamun's works are thin on the ground. At Abydos a graffito dates from the 17th year,[219] as does an entry in the Karnak Priestly Annals (§ 233 end, above). At Thebes, this king's name appears in datelines perhaps more frequently than was the case with his predecessors. Minor works of the reign call for little comment beyond mention of a fine bronze sphinx in the Louvre.[220] Of the royal family, nothing certain is known, and not even whether his successor was his son or from Thebes.

§ 235 *   C. SIAMUN: FOREIGN AFFAIRS

For this reign, a combination of meagre internal and external sources per-mit a tantalizing glimpse of Siamun's dealings with his neighbours.

---

211. *Psus*, 55 f., 186; Montet, *Les énigmes de Tanis*, 1952, 113.
212. Naville, *Goshen & Shrine of Saft el Henneh*, 1888, 21, pl. 9E.
213. *G3*, 296/7, XIII.
214. Six lintels and various jambs, found by Petrie, *Memphis I*, 1908, 12, pl. 31, and *Memphis II*, 1909, pls. 19, 23, 24. Plan, *Memphis I*, pl. 30. Other refs., *PM*, III, 225. Further lintel and jamb, Anthes *et al.*, *Mitrahineh 1956*, 1965, 90, 92, fig. 11: 24, 25, pls. 32b, 33a. Naos of Siamun from Memphis, *PM*, III, 227.
215. A pillar, *PM*, III, 223; *G3*, 296, IX.
216. So, on the doorways, last note but one.
217. On evidence of Berlin genealogy and its Louvre parallel, Chapter 12 above.
218. Stela, Munier, *Recueil Champollion*, 1922, 361–6.
219. *G3*, 295, VII.
220. *G3*, 298, n. 4; usurpations at Tanis, *ibid.*, 297 n. 2; scarabs, 298.

(i) *Edom*

As noted above (§ 231), Haded the crown-prince of Edom had been made welcome in Egypt, had grown up under Siamun's predecessors and was given a sister-in-law of the pharaoh as wife, by whom he had a son. But about 970 B.C., David of Israel died, so Hadad and his entourage went back to try and regain his kingdom. He seems to have been popular at Tanis, as the pharaoh was loth to see him go (1 Kings 11: 21–22).

(ii) *Philistia, South-West Canaan, and Israel*

Two pieces of evidence, taken together, suggest that Siamun launched his armies into South-West Palestine against his nearest neighbours, the Philistines, and reached as far as Gezer, a late-Canaanite enclave on the borders of Philistia and Israel. In 1 Kings 9:16, a pharaoh of Egypt had captured, destroyed and depopulated Gezer, before giving it as dowry with his daughter's hand in marriage to Solomon. This latter event pretty certainly occurred very early in Solomon's reign, and the fall of Gezer must have occurred at the latest just before the gift: in fact, within the first decade of Solomon's reign (i.e. *c.* 970–960 B.C.), and most probably within his first 4 years (*c.* 970–966 B.C.).[221] This puts both the Egyptian conquest of Gezer (and Philistia) and the link with Solomon squarely into the last decade of the reign of Siamun (*c.* 978–959 B.C.), and makes him the conqueror in question.

At this point, it is apposite to cite (as others have done)[222] a fragmentary relief of Siamun from a thoroughly-destroyed building which had been erected by Psusennes I and Siamun, east of the royal tombs and just south

---

221. The pharaoh's daughter that Solomon married lived in the city of David 'until he (= Solomon) had finished building his own house *and the house of the Lord*, and the wall of Jerusalem' (1 Kings 3: 1). From the words italicized, it is clear that she was already married to Solomon and living in 'the city of David' while the Temple there was still being built, a task that took the 4th to 11th years of Solomon, i.e. *c.* 966–959 B.C. However, as Grdseloff has noted, the timbers for the Temple brought by the sailors of Hiram I of Tyre landed at Joppa (2 Chronicles 2: 16) and so would be brought up to Jerusalem via Gezer (*RHJÉ* 1 (1947), 91), and so the gift of Gezer to Solomon as dowry should (with the Egyptian conquest of Gezer) fall before the timber agreement with Tyre for the Temple building, i.e. before the 4th year, 966 B.C. One may note also, that mention of the marriage comes after the early 'security' measures of Solomon's first three years (1 Kings 2, cf. 2: 39) before the rest of his history; so too, Malamat, *JNES* 22 (1963), 11.

222. e.g. Montet, *Le drame d'Avaris*, 1941, 196, fig. 58; *Osorkon II*, 1947, 36, pl. 9A; *L'Égypte et la Bible*, 1959, 40, fig. 5; B. Grdseloff, *RHJÉ* 1 (1947), 92–3; A. Malamat, *BA* 21 (1958), 99 (= *BA Reader*, II, 1964, 93), and *JNES* 22 (1963), 12; J. Černý, *CAH²*, II: 35 (1965), 53–4; O. Eissfeldt, *CAH²*, II: 34 (1965), 52 (indirectly); S. H. Horn, *Biblical Research* 12 (1968), 3–17; W. Helck, *Geschichte des alten Ägypten*, 1968, 220 and n. 7.

of the main temple of Amun in the great precinct of Tanis.[223] This relief shows Siamun in the pose of smiting with uplifted mace a group of prisoners who grasp a double axe of a type reminiscent of the Aegean and West Anatolian world.[224] A merely conventional temple-scene of this kind would of itself prove nothing, and least of all that the pharaoh had ever actually gone to war. But such reliefs were commonly carved under kings who did, and here the detail of the very special form of axe-head suggests that this relief was a commemoration, in traditional 'theological' form, of a real campaign against the Philistine and Sea-peoples population in South-West Canaan.

§ 236* The political importance of Siamun's activities – the war in Philistia and the alliance with Israel – was probably two-fold. The campaigns of David had weakened the Philistines militarily, and so Siamun would feel less compunction in acting against them. His reasons were perhaps more commercial than political; since the time of Smendes and the 'Renaissance Era', Tanis had been a merchant-city, linked with the ports of the Levant (Wenamun). Siamun's campaign, therefore, may have been a 'police-action' intended to crush Philistine commercial rivalry[225] which was already facing rising Phoenician competition. Gezer was simply the furthest north-east bastion of Philistia – but right on its border with Israel.[226] The arrival of a pharaonic army on his borders may have led to a near-confrontation between the forces of Solomon – a powerful war-machine, newly inherited from David – and the armies of Siamun. But both kings evidently found it in their mutual interest to become allies rather than to fight;[227] by such an alliance, both militarily and com-

223. Location of relief, Montet, *Osorkon II*, 36 and pl. 1, point 11 on plan. Drawings of this relief, Montet, works cited in last note, photo in *Osorkon II*, pl. 9A.

224. Cf. Kitchen, 'The Philistines' in D. J. Wiseman (ed.), *Peoples of Old Testament Times*, 1972, *ad loc.*; also, S. H. Horn, *Biblical Research*, 12 (1968), 14–15 and references.

225. On the coast, Ashdod was destroyed at this time (or at least its Tell Mor suburb), cf. D. N. Freedman, *BA* 26 (1963), 137, and Malamat, *JNES* 22 (1963), 12 and n. 49. Inland, a scarab of Siamun comes from Tell Farʿah South (perhaps ancient Sharuhen), Petrie, *Beth Pelet I*, 1930, pl. 29: 259, cf. Malamat, *op. cit.*, 12 and n. 48. For traces of destruction at Gezer at this time, cf. Y. Yadin, *IEJ* 8 (1958), 80–6, and esp. W. G. Dever *et al.*, *BA* 34 (1971), 110–11, 114, n. 27, and 130.

226. For non-occupation of most of Philistia by David, cf. Malamat, *op. cit.*, 14–16.

227. Malamat's hypothesis (*op. cit.*, 13, 16 f.) that Siamun intended to conquer Israel but was overawed by Solomon's might (and even transferred large areas of Philistia to Solomon) is theoretically possible, but is entirely unsupported and quite needless. We need not even assume that Siamun intended a permanent occupation of Philistia by Egypt, rather than a punitive raid; the alliance with Solomon was also very advantageous.

mercially, Philistia was now caught as in a vice between Egypt and Israel. Gezer on its north-east periphery was of no special consequence to Siamun but was of vital importance to Solomon; hence its inclusion in the dowry that came to Solomon with the hand of Siamun's daughter. Thus, by his campaign and alliance, by c. 967 B.C., Siamun had probably crushed Philistia as a commercial rival, and gained security and possibly commercial advantages in Palestine–Syria. Solomon for his part now had a secure south-west frontier with Egypt, and dominance over the long-standing Philistine foe.

The marriage-alliance by which Solomon gained a pharaoh's daughter to wife was in itself quite remarkable. As often noted, such a marriage of an Egyptian princess to a foreign potentate was unthinkable in the New Kingdom or Empire period, a few centuries earlier.[228] It is also true that princesses were not too readily married-off to commoners then, either.[229]

However, what was true of the great kings of the Empire had ceased to apply in the humbler days of the post-imperial epoch of the 21st and 22nd Dynasties.[230] Thus, in the late 21st Dynasty itself, for example, daughters of a pharaoh *were* given in marriage to commoners, including non-Egyptians. The lady Tentsepeh B was a princess (daughter of Psusennes II?) who married the High Priest of Ptah in Memphis, Shedsunefertem A, probably before his accession to that dignity. As for foreigners, either Siamun or Psusennes II married the daughter of Shoshenq A, Libyan Great Chief of the Mā, and it is indubitable that Maatkare B, daughter of Psusennes II, married the young Libyan Osorkon (the future Osorkon I), son of Shoshenq (I).[231] In turn, the Libyan pharaohs of the 22nd Dynasty not infrequently gave their daughters in marriage to non-royal dignitaries of the realm.[232] Therefore, particularly in the 21st/22nd Dynasties, there is no *a priori* reason why Siamun should not have granted one daughter to the court favourite, Hadad of Edom, and another to Solomon of Israel which was the nearest thing to a 'great power' of the day. That the latter alliance was nevertheless a notable event (at least for Israel) is evident from the

---

228. So (e.g.) Malamat, *BA* 21 (1958), 96–9 (= *BA Reader*, II, 1964, 91–3), with *BA* 22 (1959), 51; *JNES* 22 (1963), 9 ff.

229. Cf. the widowed Ankhsenamun's request to the Hittites after Tutankhamun's death (Güterbock, *JCS* 10 (1956), 94–8, 107), to avoid marrying a commoner ('servant'). However, a sister of Ramesses II, Tjeia, was married to the treasurer Tjeia (a commoner), cf. L. Habachi, *RdÉ* 21 (1969), 41–7; but this marriage could have occurred while this whole family were still commoners, i.e. before accession of Ramesses I.

230. A point already made by Spiegelberg, *Ägyptologische Randglossen zum Alten Testament*, 1904, 28, n. 1.

231. For the foregoing relationships, see Chapter 7, §§ 90–1.

232. See Table 12, Part VI, below.

relative frequency of the allusions to 'the daughter of Pharaoh' in the narrative of 1 Kings.[233]

Thus, so far as Siamun is concerned, we see the 21st Dynasty pursuing a policy of limited 'police action' across its north-east border in Philistia, to protect its immediate interests, and of alliance (and so, of mutual security) with more distant peoples and states such as Edom and the powerful realm of Solomon.

§ 237 3. PSUSENNES II AND THE END OF THE DYNASTY (c. 959–945 B.C.)

A. THE IDENTITY OF PSUSENNES II

It remains uncertain precisely who it was that succeeded Siamun. If the High Priest of Amun Psusennes 'III' is distinct and a different person from the king Psusennes II, then the latter may well have been a son of Siamun, succeeding him in the ordinary way. Otherwise, one must assume that Siamun died without a surviving, direct (or effective) heir, and that Psusennes the high priest succeeded him as principal member of the collateral line, being himself (through Pinudjem II's mother) a great-grandson of the redoubtable Psusennes I whose name he bore.

Either way, Psusennes II took the throne as Tyetkheperure Setepenre,[234] Har-Psusennes (II), Beloved of Amun, and was to reign for some 14 years.

§ 238 B. GENERAL HISTORY

Of these 14 years, very little record has survived, and practically nothing of the acts of the king himself who was the merest shadow upon the stage of history. No building-work or even decoration of existing temples is known.

At Abydos, a graffito names this king in the sanctuary of Ptah in the great temple of Sethos I,[235] as does likewise a pot from the Archaic Cemetery, found at the supposed tomb of Osiris.[236] His most powerful subject established a funerary endowment at Abydos (see § 239, below).

At Thebes, a statuette of Tuthmosis III at Karnak was usurped in his name, to be 'restored' by his successor;[237] otherwise, with one possible

233. Cf. 1 Kings 3: 1; 7: 8; 9: 16, 24; 11: 1; a fact also noted by Malamat, *BA* 21 (1958), 98, n. 13, and *JNES* 22 (1963), 9–10.

234. As noted above, Chapter 2, § 8, n. 50, the isolated prenomen Hedjheqa- . . . -re given for a Psusennes by Wilkinson from 'a tomb at Thebes' remains unsubstantiated and unexplained. Unless Psusennes II and III really are distinct, and III briefly took this cartouche ? Speculation remains profitless pending verification of the datum.

235. *G3*, 301, 6, I; Daressy, *RT* 21 (1899), 9–10.

236. *G3*, 302, III, and references.

237. *G3*, 301, II; Cairo Cat. 42192.

exception, he is named merely as grandfather or ancestor of the later high priest Shoshenq (II).[238] The one possible exception is an inscription on the north face of Pylon VII at Karnak (west end of the west wing) – a decree designed to protect the ownership of land bought in the Thebaid by 'Maatkare (B), daughter of King Psusennes (II) Beloved of Amun'.[239] If she was truly a Tanite princess, her purchase of land in Thebes during her father's reign would be remarkable evidence of Tanite interests there. But two other possibilities exist. If she were the daughter of a Psusennes II who was none other than the former high priest Psusennes ('III'), then her Theban acquisitions in his time would be in no way surprising. Or if she acquired the property in later life when her son Shoshenq (II) was high priest in Thebes, then again (regardless of her ancestry) her interests there would not be unexpected. An entry in the Karnak Priestly Annals[240] and some linen prepared by an Istemkheb, Chief of the Harim of Amun,[241] may be dated to the 13th year of Psusennes II (i.e. *c.* 947 B.C.), if not in fact to the 13th year of his successor.[242] Hardly any other definite traces of this reign are known.[243]

§ 239   C. LEADING PERSONALITIES OF THE REIGN

If Psusennes II and 'III' were distinct individuals, then the latter as high priest of Amun left in effect no real mark on the history of the time. If they were but one person, the high priest having become king, then we know virtually nothing of his deputies in Thebes and the south – Tjanefer's sons and successors as 2nd and 3rd prophets of Amun probably led the cult in Karnak, whoever may have governed Upper Egypt.

In Memphis, the long-established line of High Priests of Ptah continued to hold sway, Asha-khet B being succeeded by his son Ankhefensekhmet. Relations between Tanis and Memphis were so close that Psusennes II

238. *G3*, 300, V, A/B; cf. records concerning a priest Nespautytawy son of a Harkhebi, Karnak Priestly Annals, fragments 17 + 34 + 37 (Legrain, *RT* 22 (1900), 58, 62).
239. Gardiner, *JEA* 48 (1962), 64–9, and refs.; *G3*, 300, V, C.
240. Fragment 3B, line 6, after the entry for Year 17 of Siamun; everything after the date is lost.
241. *G3*, 283, C; from mummy of Nesi-tanebt-ashru, daughter of Pinudjem II.
242. The linen shroud from burial No. 117, the lady Tent-pahau-nefer, of the 'second find' at Deir el Bahri is dated to Year 5(?) with Psusennes 'III' as high priest of Amun (Daressy, *RArch³* 28 (1896–I), 77; *G3*, 285, 7, I; *PM²*, I: 2, 633). That year – if correctly read – can only date to the reign of Psusennes II (as a separate person), unless one assumed that Psusennes 'III' lasted as pontiff to Year 5 of Shoshenq I in the next dynasty.
243. The ivory knob mentioned by *G3*, 302, IV, could as easily belong to Psusennes I's reign; so also, the rings in the Petrie (UC) and Berlin collections, etc.; refs. in *G3*, 290, VIII, and n. 5, 291, n. 2, end.

seemingly gave his daughter Tentsepeh B in marriage to Shedsunefertem A, son of the high priest Ankhefensekhmet; outside of Tanis itself, the main building-works of the Dynasty had been almost entirely at Memphis. But midway between Memphis and Tanis was the city of Bubastis where a line of Libyan chiefs had by this time been settled for up to five or six generations, each bearing the title 'Great Chief of the Mā(shwash)',[244] and so reaching back to the end of the Ramesside period.[245] That Libyan tribesfolk should be found in the east Delta from that epoch onward is the natural result of the settlement of Libyan captives there by Ramesses III after his victories (c. 1180 B.C.), a century earlier still.[246] These chiefs at Bubastis also developed relations with the sovereigns of Tanis which were such that Shoshenq A and his wife Mehtenweskhet A gave a daughter in marriage to a pharaoh (Siamun or probably Psusennes II) and that Mehtenweskhet could later be termed 'God's Mother(-in-law)'.[247] Shoshenq's successor at Bubastis was the Great Chief of the Mā, Chief of Chiefs, Nimlot A. By his wife Tentsepeh A, Nimlot had at least two children. One, their daughter Mehtenweskhet B, they married off to Shedsunefertem, son of Ankhefensekhmet the High Priest of Ptah; thus, that influential Memphite family had close ties with both the Tanite kings and the Libyan chiefs. The other was their son, Shoshenq B, who succeeded his father Nimlot as chief.

The full power and influence of Shoshenq B later, as the leading personality in the reign of Psusennes II, can be seen from the great dedicatory stela for his father's memorial foundation at the sacred city of Abydos.[248] Here, Shoshenq petitioned Amun of Thebes, probably during the great annual Festival of Opet,[249] in the presence of the king himself, requesting

244. Pasenhor stela from the Serapeum: ancestor, 'the Libyan' (*ṯḥn*) Buyuwawa, followed by five lineal descendants, Mawasen, Nabnashi, Paihut, Shoshenq A, and Nimlot A (father of Shoshenq I), all *mi-nn*, 'like-titled' from the Great Chief Nimlot.

245. Six generations before Psusennes II (c. 959–945 B.C.) at but 20 years each would put Buyuwawa c. 120 years minimally before that king, say c. 1080 B.C. and thus contemporary with Ramesses XI and the 'Renaissance Era'.

246. A point well made by Yoyotte (*YMM*, 148, §§ 40, 41), and citing the great Papyrus Harris I, 77, 4–6, and stela *LD*, III, 218c, 2–4 (now, *KRI*, V/2 (1972), 91, 5–7). Cf. also § 206 above.

247. Cf. above, Chapter 7, §§ 90, 91 and table; her title, Pasenhor stela.

248. A. M. Blackman, JEA 27 (1941), 83–95, pls. 10–12. Note that the word spelt with triangle plus chair-like 'stand' (rendered by Blackman as 'altar', then as 'statue(?)' at Gardiner's suggestion, pp. 94–5) is none other than the word *ḳny(t)*, *ḳ* plus chair-sign, for 'portable image' or 'palladium'; on this, cf. Helck, *Materialen zur Wirtschaftsgeschichte des Neuen Reiches*, I, 1960, 119–22; add *KRI*, V/1, 6, line 7.

249. One notes (lines 6, 8) that, with the petitions granted, the king sent Nimlot's image *northwards* to Abydos (i.e. from Thebes), to be installed with due ceremony there.

to be associated with the king in the great festivals of 'victory'. He bore the title 'Great Chief of Chiefs', a whole fleet of vessels took Nimlot's statue north to Abydos by the king's orders, and Shoshenq had not only his 'adherents' but also an 'army' (l. 6) at his command. The gifts for the endowment included a handsome contribution from the king himself (l. 11).

§ 240   D. THE PASSING OF THE KINGSHIP

At his death, Psusennes II left no male heir; some time either before or after his death, his daughter Maatkare B was married to the young Osorkon, son of Shoshenq B, the leading man in the kingdom.

It was this man who now ascended the throne as Shoshenq I. The new ruler was no brazen usurper or mere *parvenu* especially if the marriage of Maatkare had preceded Psusennes' death. Politically Shoshenq's eminence was seemingly unmatched. By marriage, both his family and the late Tanite dynasty were indirectly linked, through their ties with the line of the High Priests of Ptah in Memphis. At Thebes and Abydos, Shoshenq had appeared as the chief and army-commander uniquely in the favour of the king, even aspiring to share in the formal royal feasts of victory. Doubtless it was he who, at Tanis, conducted the burial of Psusennes II, which has never yet been discovered, and so sealed his claim to the king ship, *de jure* as well as *de facto*.

CHAPTER 18*

The Twenty-second Dynasty: I, The Era of Power (Shoshenq I to Takeloth I)

§ **241** 1. SHOSHENQ I (*c*. 945–924 B.C.)

A. INTERNAL AFFAIRS

(i) *Accession*

The new king and dynast was undoubtedly one of the most shrewd and astute personalities to ascend the Egyptian throne in many a long year; nor did he lack ambition, tempered with realism. While Bubastis had been his inherited fief,[250] Tanis became his Delta capital where his successors (if not also himself?) were eventually buried.

His very titulary exemplifies his qualities and policies. By taking the pre-nomen Hedjkheperre Setepenre, that of Smendes I, founder of the pre-vious dynasty, Shoshenq proclaimed at one stroke both his continuity with the past – i.e. that he was, so to speak, 'another Smendes' – and a new beginning. Like Smendes, he now opened a new era. Nor is the concept of a 'new Smendes' limited to Shoshenq's prenomen. He also adopted Horus, Nebty, and Golden Horus names reminiscent of those of Smendes I.[251] Just as the latter had been Horus 'Strong Bull, beloved of Re' plus epithets (whose arm Amun strengthened to exalt Truth),[252] so now Shoshenq I was

250. Whence Manetho derives the dynasty. The statue cited for Shoshenq as Great Chief of the Mā, supposedly from Bubastis, by Maspero (*Z ÄS* 22 (1884), 93, § LX) – now Cairo JdE 25572 – belongs in fact to a much later chief, Shoshenq (F), prince of Busiris *c*. 670 B.C., whence it probably came; cf. Yoyotte, *YMM*, 169–70, Document V, §§ 76–7, and pl. II, 2, 5.

251. Contrast (e.g.) those of Psusennes I, given by Montet, *Psus*, 177, fig. 66, except perhaps for the end part of his Golden-Horus name.

252. Dibabieh stela, *G3*, 287, II; Daressy, *RT* 10 (1888), 135.

Horus, 'Strong Bull, beloved of Re' plus epithets (whom he (= Re) caused to appear as King to unite the Two Lands).[253] The reference in Smendes' Horus name to 'exalting Truth' (*Maᶜat*) is re-echoed in Shoshenq's Nebty name, 'Appearing in the Double Crown like Horus-son-of-Isis, contenting the Gods with Truth'.[254] In turn, Smendes' Nebty name beginning with 'Powerful of strength, smiting (*ḥw*) those rebellious (against) him . . .', was taken up in the Golden Horus name of Shoshenq, 'Powerful of strength, smiting (*ḥw*) the Nine Bows, Great of Victory in all lands'.[255]

§ 242   However promptly and willingly the accession of Shoshenq I was recognized in the old northern capitals of Tanis and Memphis, thanks to his ties with the late dynasty and with the High Priests of Ptah in Memphis, the Thebans in the far south were perhaps less ready initially to recognize the new ruler as truly Pharaoh. In the Karnak Priestly Annals fragment No. 4, a new paragraph began:[256] 'Regnal Year 2, 3rd month of Akhet, day 17, of the Great Chief of the Mā, Shoshe(n)q, justified' – with the throw-stick determinative-sign added to his name as for an alien, and no cartouches or pharaonic titles. By Year 2, his titles were surely known already. But from Year 5 onwards, even reluctant Thebes acknowledged him officially as full pharaoh,[257] from recognition of whose authority there could be no retreat.

§ 243   (ii) *Internal Reunification*
The intention 'to unite the Two Lands' expressed in Shoshenq's titulary was no idle epithet. Hitherto the Thebaid (and with it, much of Upper Egypt) had been virtually a state-within-the-state, headed by the dynasty of army-commanders as high priests of Amun in an unbroken hereditary succession. This was no longer permitted. Henceforth, the Thebaid was to be bound to the royal house by two related methods: the appointment of members of the royal family and its allies to leading offices in the Theban hierarchy, and marriage-alliances with notable Theban families.

§ 244*   *Thebes.* Thus, Shoshenq I quickly took over all four leading posts in Amun's hierarchy at Thebes. He appointed his second son Iuput as High

253. Examples, *G3*, 309–11.
254. e.g. *G3*, 309, 311.
255. *G3*, 309, 311; the Golden Horus name of Smendes is still unknown.
256. Legrain, *RT* 22 (1900), 54, No. 4, line 3 after space following lines 1–2; *G3*, 318, C and n. 2.
257. So, on bandage-epigraphs of Years 5, 10, 11 on mummy of Djed-Ptah-ef-ankh from the great cache (*G3*, 307–9); Year 13, text, previous note. Years 5 and 6 recur in Nile-level texts Nos. 1 and 3 on Karnak quay, Legrain, *ZÄS* 34 (1896), 111: 1, 3 *G3*, 308, III–IV; von Beckerath, *JARCE* 5 (1966), 44, 49: 1, 3.

Priest of Amun ('First Prophet') – a mark of honour for the Thebaid, doubtless, but this son was naturally also a royal representative in personal charge at Thebes. He was entitled Generalissimo and Army-leader ($ḥȝwty$) besides high priest;[258] later monuments add the title Governor of Upper Egypt.[259] Nor was he alone. It is highly probable that the 2nd and 3rd prophet of Amun Djed-Ptah-ef-ankh A, called the 'King's Son of Ramesses and King's Son of the Lord of the Two Lands', was also a northerner, related to either the last dynasty or this one. He was buried in the 11th year of Shoshenq I (c. 935 B.C.) or very soon after, during the pontificate of Iuput, in the great royal cache beyond Deir el Bahri – the last time that cavern of wonders, of Egypt's most glorious royal dead, was to be opened for nearly three millennia. A much clearer case of royal allies being appointed to Theban posts and benefices is afforded by Nesy, a chief of the Mahasun (Libyan tribe), who appears as 4th prophet of Amun, to be followed by his own son Nes-ankhef-maʿat.[260] Thus, the Libyan and royal element were put firmly in the saddle by the new king.

§ 245* However, the subtler measure of marriage-alliance featured also in Shoshenq's politics. Thus, probably late in his reign, he gave his daughter Tashep-en-Bast in marriage to one Djed-Thut-ef-ankh A, who had been duly appointed as 3rd prophet of Amun,[261] as (a) successor to Djed-Ptah-ef-ankh A. The 'new' man came of a distinguished military family, reaching back five generations. [262] Probably also well on in the reign of Shoshenq, his son the high priest Iuput married-off his own daughter Nesi-Khons-pakhered to one Djed-Khons-ef-ankh A, who was the young scion of a Theban family of very long lineage.[263] This alliance in turn was to benefit him in the next reign (Osorkon I, cf. § 266 below), when he became in turn 4th prophet of Amun, and in fact the first of a long hereditary line of such under less strict kings.

Finally, it was perhaps quite early in his reign that at Thebes Shoshenq

---

258. Cf. *G3*, 321–2.

259. On monuments of his descendants, *G3*, 322–3.

260. Probably both contemporary with Shoshenq I; the first, perhaps early in the reign, pensioned off as 4th prophet as a loyal senior supporter and his son as successor later in the reign. Cf. Pt. III, § 188, above.

261. See Part III, § 166, above.

262. Djed-Thut-ef-ankh's grandfather, a Nesipaqashuty, was functioning in Years 5 and 10 of Siamun, being mentioned in texts of the great cache near Deir el Bahri; cf. Černý, *JEA* 32 (1946), 26, 27, on these graffiti. Pillar-bases of Djed-Thut-ef-ankh at Karnak, cf. A. Varille, *ASAE* 50 (1950), 249–58. The identification of Tashep-en-Bast's father as Shoshenq III (as by Kees) is erroneous.

263. Eleven earlier generations are recorded (statues, Cairo Cat. 42211–12); cf. above, Part III, §§ 166 ff., for the family and sources.

had an old statue of Tuthmosis III[264] rededicated (if not totally reinscribed) for the late Psusennes II, his immediate predecessor. Doubtless this act of rather economical piety was intended to stress his attachment to the late king and his own legitimate succession before Amun of Karnak and his priests.[265]

§ 246* *Middle Egypt.* Shoshenq took care not to leave *all* effective power south of Memphis in the hands of one man, even though it was to his own son. At Heracleopolis, centre of a broad, fertile region in the north part of Upper Egypt and near the entry to the Fayum province, he stationed as 'Leader of the entire Army' (*ḥ3wty n mšʿ (r) ḏrw*) his third son Nimlot B, born to him by the lady Pen-resh-nes,[266] herself daughter of an unnamed Libyan chief.[267] Nimlot's known titles are simple and basically military. His military powers were perhaps wider than those of Iuput, though in civil affairs he perhaps ranked after him as well as his father.

§ 247* (iii) *Personalities and Activities of the Reign*
Few events are known for most of the 21 years of this king. Wayheset – son of a Chief of the Mā subordinate to the king – was sent out by Shoshenq to restore order in the oasis of Dakhla, and to adjudicate in local land and water disputes in Year 5 (*c*. 941 B.C.), appeal being made to land-registers of the 19th year of Psusennes I, of some 80 years previously.[268]

At Heracleopolis, the army-commander Nimlot occasioned the reinstatement of the daily offering of a bull to Arsaphes, restoring customs that had lapsed. The 365 animals per annum were to be levied from the principal officers and settlements of the province,[269] varying from sixty bulls (2 months' supply) from Nimlot himself to one each from many lesser persons. As the text elegantly puts it (ll. 2–6): 'Now, His Majesty sought any occasion for benefactions to be made for his father (the god) Arsaphes, (a matter) that had been on his mind (all the) while he had been king. So, when Prince Nimlot came before His Majesty . . .' (to report on lapse of

264. The name Menkheperre is visible on the belt-buckle of the statue, cf. Legrain, *Statues et statuettes de rois et de particuliers*, III, 1914, Cat. 42192, p. 1 and pl. 1.
265. Publication, cf. previous note; workmanship, probably basically Tuthmoside; attribution of name-list, less certain.
266.* Name perhaps meaning 'Our joy (pertains) to her'.
267. For Nimlot B, cf. Gauthier, *ASAE* 18 (1919), 246–50, and for the Heracleopolis 'altar', add Tresson, *Mélanges Maspero*, I, 1938, 817–40.
268. Larger Dakhla stela, Spiegelberg, *RT* 21 (1899), 12–21, fully re-edited by Gardiner, *JEA* 19 (1933), 19–30, pls. 5–7.
269.* Text of the decree, fully treated by P. Tresson, *Mélanges Maspero*, I, 1938, 817–40, and plate, improving on Kamal and Daressy.

the offering and ask for its restitution), the king replied 'Congratulations, my son . . ., your heart is like that of your begetter, it's myself young again.' Shoshenq's own expression for 'a chip off the old block'!

§ **248**   Just north of Heracleopolis, at Memphis, Shoshenq's brother-in-law the new High Priest of Ptah, Shedsunefertem, prepared a new embalming-table for the sacred Apis bulls;[270] however, the burials of such bulls for the entire 21st and first half of the 22nd Dynasties remain unknown to us.

South of Heracleopolis, at Teudjoi (El Hibeh), which had been the old northern bastion of the Theban high priests and army-commanders from Herihor's days long past, up to his own time, Shoshenq I built a temple to Amun, which is now regrettably nearly all destroyed.[271]

Apart from this temple and the major works which were undertaken at Thebes at the end of his reign, Shoshenq I is not known to have built any more extensively in Egypt than his 21st Dynasty predecessors; but a few works survive. The Delta was the main theatre of operations. At Tanis itself, he built on to the great temple,[272] and adorned it with old sphinxes which he had usurped.[273] Fragments attest his efforts at the family seat of Bubastis, at Tell el-Maskhuta, and possibly elsewhere in the Delta.[274] At Memphis, scattered blocks bear his name.[275] South of El Hibeh, there is practically nothing before the end of the reign. At Abydos, his son Iuput built himself a tomb or memorial chapel in the holy precincts of Osiris.[276]

§ **249***   During the 22nd Dynasty, in the West Delta, there emerged a line of Great Chiefs of the Libu (whence modern 'Libya'), who ruled over further Libyan tribes along that border of Egypt.[277] One such chief, Niumateped A, dedicated a donation-stela in a Year 10 probably to be attributed to Shoshenq I,[278] and is to be set alongside other tribal rulers of the Mahasun or the long-established Mā(shwash).

270. Brugsch, *ZÄS* 16 (1878), 38–41; Brugsch, *Thesaurus*, 817, 948–9.
271. *PM*, IV, 124.
272. Cf. Montet, *Tanis, Douze années* . . . , 1942, 230; Montet, *Les énigmes de Tanis*, 1952, 35; blocks, otherwise unpublished.
273. *PM*, IV, 15 (Louvre, A. 23, Cairo).
274. *PM*, IV, 31 (Bubastis), 39 (Tell Balala, uncertain), 53 (Tell el Maskhuta).
275. *PM*, III, 220, 222 top, 227.
276. *PM*, V, 75.
277. Cf. excellent treatment of these chiefs by Yoyotte, *YMM*, 142–51, also my summary tables, *JARCE* 8 (1970/71), 66, and Part VI, below.
278. Stela Hermitage 5630, Leningrad; Yoyotte, *YMM*, 142, § 29, Document A. While the prenomen Hedjkheperre would point to Shoshenq I, Yoyotte observed that the epithet 'god, Ruler of Heliopolis' might rather indicate Shoshenq III, the scribe having retained the prenomen of Takeloth II (identical with that of Shoshenq

Besides Libyan chiefs and Theban priests, little is yet known of the major civil officials of the day. The Theban vizier Padimut A perhaps held office later in Shoshenq's reign and under his successor.[279] Besides the three princes Osorkon, Iuput and Nimlot and their sister Tashep-en-Bast, little is known of the royal family. The Queen, Kar-am-at A, is so far known as wife of Shoshenq I and mother of Osorkon I only from the much later stela of Pasenhor.[280]

§ **250 B. FOREIGN AFFAIRS: BYBLOS, NUBIA AND ISRAEL**
The main effort of Shoshenq's reign probably went into achieving a renewed unity of the realm centred on the kingship of his dynasty. As ruler of an Egypt more united and internally at peace than it had been for generations, his eyes turned abroad, both to the north and to the south.

(i) *Byblos*
Throughout the Old, Middle and New Kingdoms, for seventeen centuries,[281] Egypt's rulers had maintained close links with Byblos, the seaport on the Levant coast for 'cedar of Lebanon'. The trade had continued even under Ramesses XI ('Renaissance Era') in the time of Egypt's eclipse abroad; for the 21st Dynasty, no record of contact has so far been found.

Shoshenq I certainly renewed the link with Byblos. In due course, he presented a seated statue of himself, probably to the temple of its patron deity Baalat-Gebal ('Lady of Byblos'). By this, he probably set the seal on a political and commercial alliance[282] with Abibaal, king of Byblos, who proudly added his own dedication down the side of the throne of the statue: '[Statue ? which] Abibaal, King [of Byblos, son of x . . ., King of] Byblos, had brought from Egypt for Baal[at-Gebal, his lady. May Baalat-Gebal lengthen the lifespan ('days') of Abibaal and his (regnal) years] over Byblos!'[283]

I) by mistake. However, a date in Year 10 seems rather late for such a slip, and in fact Shoshenq I sometimes did have such additional epithets – cf. *G3*, 312, XVIII, XIX, and esp. 314, XXXIII, 316, XLVII, for 'god, Ruler of Heliopolis' used by Shoshenq I.

279. Named as an ancestor on the statues Cairo Cat. 42214–15 (Legrain, *Statues*, III, *ad loc.*), and in the same generation as Iuput, son of Shoshenq I, cf. above, Part III, § 184.

280. The references given by *G3*, 320, B–E, to an Adoratrix or God's Wife of Amun, Kar-am-at, pertain to a different and later individual officiating in Thebes.

281. Cf. Montet, *Byblos et l'Égypte*, 1928, 270 ff.; M. Chehab and J. Leclant in W. A. Ward (ed.), *The Role of the Phoenicians in the Interaction of Mediterranean Civilizations*, 1968, 1–8, 9–31, respectively.

282. There seems to be no warrant at all for assuming either an Egyptian overlordship at Byblos, or any hostility of Byblos towards Egypt; simply the alliance of two independent powers. Cf. and contrast W. Herrmann, *MIO* 6 (1958), 27–31.

283. Statue from Byblos, refs. in *PM*, VII, 388, esp. R. Dussaud, *Syria* 5 (1924),

§ 251* (ii) *Nubia*

In the south, Shoshenq seemingly inaugurated a policy very different from that of his Byblite alliance. For nearly 150 years, starting with the rebellion of the viceroy Panehsy from about the 19th year of Ramesses XI (*c.* 1080 B.C.), Nubia south from Aswan had been independent. Shoshenq now opened the way south, to obtain from 'the land of Nubia' (*p(3)*) *t3 n Nḥs*) all manner of products for Amun of Karnak. That he did so by marching his armies into Nubia is not absolutely certain, but extremely probable,[284] and this undertaking was perhaps followed by the opening of trade relations further southward. In some Karnak texts which are now all too fragmentary,[285] the king says: (D, 5) 'Oh Amun, what I have done to the land of Nubia, grant(?) . . .'; (E, 7) '. . . Nubia; lo, I have brought it for thee from the land of Nubia . . .', (E, 8) '. . . all the things which come to thee from the land of Nubia – thy *k*[. . .], . . .' (E, 9) '. . . thy *dôm*-nuts, thy yellow-red ochre, thy pure (= ritual) sand, thy [. . .]s', (E, 10) '[. . .]s, basket(fuls?) for thy offerings . . .'. (F, 1) 'I have brought for thee thy things . . .' (F, 2) '. . . the Nubian. Oh Amun, lo [I] (have) made(?) . . .' (F, 3) '[thy] red bulls, thy prime(?) bulls, . . .' (F, 4) '. . . the high branches of the *dôm*-palms . . .'.

§ 252 (iii) *Israel*

So long as a strong, united, well-armed Hebrew kingdom straddled Syria– Palestine under the rule of Solomon (*c.* 971/70–931/30 B.C.), Shoshenq I tried no conclusions with his outwardly powerful northern neighbour. However (unlike Siamun), he viewed that neighbour as a rival or hindrance

145–7 (§ 5) with pl. 42 and fig. 5. On Phoenician text of Abibaal and its interpretation, see W. F. Albright, *JAOS* 67 (1947), 157–8; W. Herrmann, *MIO* 6 (1958), 15–17, 31; H. Donner and W. Röllig, *Kanaanäische und Aramäische Inschriften*, I (1962), 1, No. 5, II (1964), 7–8, No. 5; further refs., Leclant, in Ward (ed.), *op. cit.*, 12. Chronology, cf. Albright, Herrmann, Donner & Röllig, *op. cit.*, and Kitchen, *HHAHT*.

284. The phrase 'thou hast trodden down the natives of Nubia' (*iw ptpt.n.k 'Iwntyw-Sty*) in line 2 of the rhetorical text of the great triumph-scene at Karnak (*RIK*, III, pls. 3/5, line 6) is reminiscent of that of Merenptah's scene in the *Cour de la cachette* at Karnak (*KRI*, IV/1, 1968, 24: 13), but occurs in a broader context sufficiently original in its manipulation of set phrases to merit Breasted's inference (*BAR*, IV, § 723) that Shoshenq I controlled and had conquered Lower Nubia. Of all the triumph-scenes at Karnak, the texts of that of Shoshenq I are certainly the most unusual and original in a very traditional *genre*.

285. Karnak blocks (north-west of barque-sanctuary of Philip Arrhidaeus), published by W. M. Müller, *Egyptological Researches*, II, 1910, 143–53 and figs. 50–6, blocks B to H only. Müller's block A (figs. 48, 49, pl. 43) is probably of the 25th Dynasty (cf. Barguet, *Temple d'Amon-rê à Karnak*, 1962, 122–3, pls. 18, 19), while his blocks I, J (figs. 57, 58) are of Osorkon II (cf. also Legrain, *ASAE* 5 (1904), 282: 3). Shoshenq's blocks, cf. also *BAR*, IV, §§ 723–4.

to his own pretensions, commercial, political or both – not as an ally – and bided his time to act when a favourable opportunity arose.

Soon after the 24th year of Solomon (i.e. soon after 945 B.C.),[286] the young corvée-chief Jeroboam son of Nebat was hailed as future king of most of Israel, and fled from Solomon's wrath into Egypt (1 Kings 11:26–40). Shoshenq gave sanctuary to Jeroboam, and thereby harboured a potential 'government in exile' to await future opportunity.

With Solomon's death (*c.* 931/30 B.C.) that opportunity at last came. Jeroboam was quickly summoned back to Palestine by his partisans who were challenging Rehoboam son of Solomon, and in no time at all the former Hebrew 'empire' split asunder – into two rump-kingdoms mutually hostile, Judah centred on Jerusalem, and 'Israel' whose first capital was at Shechem (1 Kings 12).

§ **253*** Now at last, Shoshenq could launch the second phase of his aggressive policy of *divide et impera*, dispatching his forces (fresh from a Nubian victory?) into Palestine. The formal *casus belli* was probably a border-incident – incursions across Egypt's East-Delta boundaries by Semitic tribesmen whom it pleased Shoshenq to consider as Judean subjects committing hostile acts. The signal for war was apparently one such skirmish at the Bitter Lakes, directly followed by an all-out Egyptian attack. So much may be deduced from the fragments of a victory-stela from Karnak:[287] 'Now, My [Maj]esty found that . . . [they] were killing . . . [my soldiers?, and] my army-leaders. His Majesty was troubled about them, . . . [and acted? as] they desired. Then said His Majesty to his courtiers [in the following]: "[See . . .] these vile deeds that they have committed!" Then they replied [to His Majesty, ". . ."]. [Then His Majesty went forth . . .], his chariotry accompanying him, without their (i.e. the enemy's) knowing (it). Lo, . . . His Majesty wrought great slaughter among them . . . he [slew] them on the shore, the edge of the Bitter Lakes (*Km-wr*). It was his father [?Amun who decreed the victory for him . . .].'

286. A figure obtained by noting that 7 years to build the temple at Jerusalem (1 Kings 6: 38), from the 4th to 11th years of Solomon (1 Kings 6: 1, 38) plus 13 years building the palace-complex there (1 Kings 7: 1) was totalled as '20 years' (1 Kings 9: 10), a 20 years that would end in the 24th year (20 years after 4th year). It would probably be after these major undertakings that Solomon proceeded to further projects in Jerusalem and elsewhere (1 Kings 11: 27, cf. 9: 15, 17–19) and appointed Jeroboam son of Nebat as northern overseer of works (1 Kings 11: 28). For this chronological sequence, cf. already, B. Grdseloff, *RHJÉ* 1 (1947), 90–91. Thereafter, Jeroboam was proclaimed a future king by the prophet Ahijah and fled to Egypt, 'to Shishak' (1 Kings 11: 28–40), an event that could not well precede the latter's accession in 945 B.C., Solomon's 25th year, and could well be a few years later.

287. Legrain, *ASAE* 5 (1904), 38–9, § 21; Grdseloff, *RHJÉ* 1 (1947), 95–7; *BAR*, IV, § 724A.

Once over the border, Shoshenq and his forces swept through and around both Judah and Israel with impunity in the spring and summer of 925 B.C., so that 'in the 5th year of king Rehoboam, . . . Shishak king of Egypt came up against Jerusalem; he took away the treasures of the House of the Lord (YHWH) and the treasures of the king's house – he took all. He took all the golden shields that Solomon had made' (1 Kings 14: 25–26). He came (2 Chronicles 12: 3–4) 'with 1,200 chariots,[288] with 60,000 (or, 60 *'eleph*, divisions?) 'horsemen' (*pārašīm*),[289] and innumerable people came with him from Egypt: Libyans,[290] Sukki,[291] and Nubians.[292] He captured

288. A large but very reasonable chariot-force. Cf. the 2,500 chariots attributed to the Hittites at the Battle of Qadesh by Ramesses II ('Poem', §§ 84, 132; Reliefs, § 19: *KRI*, II/1, 1969, 31, 45; II/3, 1970, 135; Sir A. H. Gardiner, *The Kadesh Inscriptions of Ramesses II*, 1960, 9, 10, 39); in Canaan, the 924 chariots captured by Tuthmosis III (cf. *ANET*, 237b) and 730 and over 1,034 chariots captured by Amenophis II (*ANET*, 246b, 247b). Like Shishak, Benhadad II ('Adadidri') of Damascus could muster 1,200 chariots (Qarqar, 853 B.C.), while Ahab of Israel furnished some 2,000 chariots on that occasion (*ANET*, 278/9).

289. A large figure, but not totally impossible when compared with the possibly 90,000 men fielded by Teos and the 100,000 deployed by Nectanebo II to defend Egypt in the fourth century B.C. (cf. F. K. Kienitz, *Die politische Geschichte Ägyptens vom 7. bis zum 4. Jahrhundert vor der Zeitwende*, 1953, 96 n. 2, 105). However, it could be argued that the '60,000' (*šišim 'elep*) of 2 Chronicles 12: 3 might be a later scribal error for '6,000' (*šeš 'ălapīm*) – cf. 1 Kings 4: 26 (Hb. 5: 6), '40,000' (*'arba'im 'elep*) for the correct '4,000' (*'arba'at 'ălapīm*) of 2 Chronicles 9: 25. For Shoshenq I one would then have a force of 1,200 chariots, 6,000 *pārašīm*, and a large number (up to 10,000 ?) of Libyans, Tjukten and Nubians. That *pārašīm* is actually 'horsemen', i.e. calvalry is perhaps possible, but both the meaning of this word and the early history of cavalry (as opposed to chariotry) require urgent reconsideration. The first-hand nature of such details as reference to the Sukkiim (Tjukten) and Nubians and realistic number of chariots forbid a purely cavalier treatment of the data of this passage in 2 Chronicles. On varying sizes of Egyptian expeditions noted by S. Herrmann, *ZDPV* 80 (1964), 70–2, one should, of course, add G. Goyon, *Nouvelles inscriptions du Wadi Hammamat*, 1957, No. 61, pp. 17–20, 81–5, figure, pls. 23–4 – a rock-inscription of Year 38 of Sesostris I (*c.* 1945 B.C.) commemorating a huge expedition of about 18,000 people (17,000 workmen, and other personnel given in detail) to Hammamat. Herrmann's assertion (*ZDPV* 80, p. 72) that Shoshenq I's army must have been smaller than that of Ramesses II rests on no particle of evidence; for Late Period armies in Egypt, cf. on Teos and Nectanebo II earlier in this note.

290. *Lubim*, Semitic equivalent of Egyptian *Rbw*, 'Libu', our 'Libya'.

291. *Sukkiyim*, equivalent of Egyptian *Ṯk(tn)* as long since set out by W. Spiegelberg, *Aegyptologische Randglossen zum alten Testament*, 1904, 30–1, and further remarked by Sir A. H. Gardiner, *The Wilbour Papyrus, II: Commentary*, 1948, 81, n. 1; W. F. Albright in H. H. Rowley (ed.), *Old Testament & Modern Study*, 1951, 18; R. A. Caminos, *Late-Egyptian Miscellanies*, 1954, 176–7, 180. From the Egyptian data of the thirteenth–twelfth centuries B.C., it is clear that, in part at least, the Tjuk(ten) were Libyan forces from the oases of the western desert – perhaps auxiliaries.

292. *Kušim*, 'Nubians', Egyptian *Kš*; the classical term 'Ethiopian' is too misleading to use today, in view of its use for the modern empire of Ethiopia far away south-east of any area remotely 'Kush' or 'Nubia'.

the fortified towns of Judah and came up to Jerusalem.' That Libyans should be included in the forces of Shoshenq is to be expected. The inclusion of the Sukki or Tjuk(ten) is an especially interesting detail, while the presence of Nubians would find ready explanation in the presence of Nubian militia under Egyptian arms at several epochs, and in Shoshenq's forces very likely as conscripts or slave-troops in the wake of his Nubian campaign.

§ 254   The course of Shoshenq's campaign is not certain in detail; from the combined biblical and archaeological/epigraphic evidence, it embraced both Judah and Israel.[293] These data may be interpreted to yield a picture possibly somewhat as follows.[294]

At Gaza, Shoshenq dispatched a considerable 'task-force' via Yurza (IX: 133)[295] and Sharuhen (IX: 125?) into the Negeb region on the south of Judah-with-Simeon. The precise routes taken by these forces cannot yet be fully recovered. Beyond Sharuhen, the main force probably split into three or four 'flying columns'. One perhaps went via Photeis fort (VI: 68–69) and then east and north into the Hebron district of south Judah and Simeon, striking at El-gad fort (VII: 97, if = Hazer Gaddah), Tappua[h] (VI: 82), Beth-Anath (IX: 124), and Ashna (VII: 88?). A second column probably struck east past Beersheba to 'the forts' (VIII : 107) of 'Greater Arad' (VIII: 108–109) and 'Arad-of-the-House-of-Jeroham' (VIII: 110–112), and the east Negeb lands of the Kenites and Shuhathites (VII: 93). This force or a third cadre also raided Ezem (VI: 66) and perhaps a southern Jeroham (X: 139 – ? Bir Rakhma). How much further the Negeb task-forces may have penetrated is very uncertain – just possibly to the SSW (if VIII: 100 were Hazar-'Addar), or even to Ezion-Geber about 100 miles south of the Dead Sea on the Gulf of Aqaba,[296] although the great distance plus rough country makes this rather unlikely.

293. The truth of this fact was well stressed long ago by M. Noth, *ZDPV* 61 (1938), 278–80, plus the primary interest of the *Kings* historian (and *a fortiori*, of the Chronicler) in what befell Judah more than Israel, this accounting for the emphasis on Shishak's campaign in Judah rather than on its Israelite phase.

294. For an analysis of Shoshenq I's great topographical list, a review of previous major interpretations, and reasons for adopting the view set forth here, the reader should consult Excursus E, Part V below.

295. Numbers in brackets inserted after names give the row (top to bottom, then at right) and individual number for the names in Shoshenq's great list, esp. as set forth in Excursus E below.

296. Glueck attributed the destruction of Ezion-Geber level I to Shishak (*The Other Side of the Jordan*, 1940, 105; and cautiously, in D. W. Thomas (ed.), *Archaeology & Old Testament Study*, 1967, 440), a view followed by many others, e.g. B. Mazar, *VTS* IV, 1957, 65, and Aharoni, *LB*, 288, n. 18 (cf. J. R. Bartlett, *PEQ* 104 (1972), 30). But their tentative identification of Ezion-Geber with VI: 73–4 (*Šbrt n gbry*) of the list has nothing to commend it, esp. philologically.

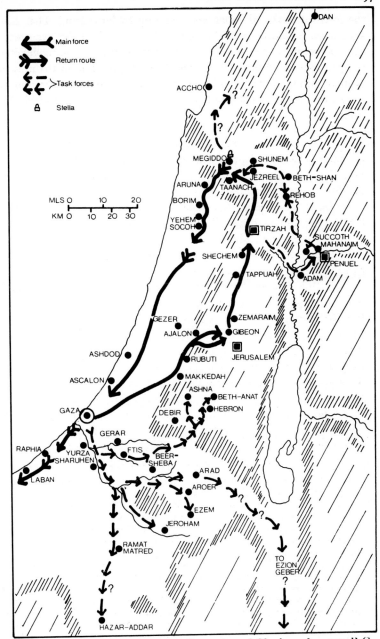

Fig. 2. Course of the Palestinian Campaign of *Shoshenq I, c.* 925 B.C.

§ 255   Meanwhile, Shoshenq and the main army continued north-east along the borderlands of Philistia and Judah, and inland to the north end of the Shephelah, perhaps first reaching Makkedah (I: 12?) and Rubuti (I:13 - Beth-Shemesh??),[297] thus beginning his assault on 'the fortified towns of Judah'. Thence he went up by a well-worn route through the hills by Ajalon (II: 26) and the Beth-Horons (II: 24) to Gibeon (II: 23). There, with his vast force, Shoshenq awaited Rehoboam's decision in nearby Jerusalem to submit or fight. Within that citadel, Rehoboam and his princes pondered in contrition while the prophet Shemaiah counselled submission - those who had spurned God's service would not in their contrition be destroyed, but be disciplined by experiencing vassaldom, 'service', under a foreign, worldly ruler (2 Chronicles 12: 5-8); thus stood Shemaiah at the head of a line that culminated in Isaiah and Jeremiah. So, Rehoboam paid his massive tribute - the rich treasures of the Davidic-Solomonic treasuries of temple and palace in Jerusalem, even the gold ceremonial shields - and Shoshenq retired north with his booty. Jerusalem was cowed; but, unconquered. It does not appear in Shoshenq's great list.[298]

§ 256   From this success, Shoshenq moved north into Israel, via Zemaraim (V: 57) to Shechem (and its Migdol? - V: 58) and to Tirzah (V: 59?) - but this time, the bird had flown. Far from presenting personally a handsome tribute to his former host in Egypt, the wily Jeroboam had probably fled east down Wadi el Farʿa, slipped across the Jordan, and gone up the vale of the Jabbok to the holds of Penuel and Mahanaim.[299] The pharaoh probably did not deign personally to pursue his erring protégé, but moved on north and north-west, sending out instead a second sizeable 'task-force' which in turn sped down Wadi el Farʿa, crossed Jordan by the ford at Adam(ah) (V: 56) and travelled on past Succoth (V: 55?) to catch up with Jeroboam at Penuel (V: 53) and Mahanaim (II: 22). Mission accomplished, this division then probably returned to the Jordan (V: 53-56?) or cut across east Manasseh and then up the Jordan,[300] to Rehob (II: 17), Hapharaim

297. Cf. Excursus E, below, for Makkedah rather than Gezer, and for Rubuti (for which cf. Aharoni, *LB*, 286-7). Recent work at Gezer does *not* indicate a major destruction there by Shoshenq, cf. W. G. Dever *et al.*, *BA* 34 (1971), 111, 117, attesting limited destruction (e.g. gateway) and ongoing occupation by the local populace.

298. The only probable gaps that might once have contained Jerusalem are in row IV – II: 20 was probably in the Jordan valley or eastern Palestine, and V: 61-3 between Zemaraim and Jezreel (i.e. in Israel). And if row IV represented some foray by a task-force going off from the main army, then it is unlikely that Jerusalem even featured in this row. The other rows with lacunae (VIII–XI) were all occupied by place-names in the south and south-west, far from north-central Judah.

299. A move possibly reflected in 1 Kings 12: 25, but cf. § 258 below.

300. From Mahanaim north to Rehob/Hapharaim/Beth-Shan, we have II:

(II: 18), and especially Beth-Shan (II: 16), and were perhaps joined there by other troops of Shoshenq that had meantime subdued Taanach (II: 14) and Shunem (II: 15), while Shoshenq himself directed further operations from Megiddo (III: 27).

§ 257 From Tirzah, Shoshenq had probably proceeded directly NNW through northern Israel to the vale of Jezreel, 'the valley', *pa-ʿemeq* (V: 65) *par excellence*, to reach Megiddo. There, he awaited the victorious return of the East Jordan task-force, possibly sending a force via Taanach and Shunem to meet it, as suggested above. While at Megiddo, he may also have sent out contingents into the plain of Accho and into Galilee (?III: 28–31, and possibly IV: 40–[52]??).[301] At Megiddo itself, Shoshenq erected a massive commemorative stela,[302] originally about 10 feet high, of which only one top corner bearing his cartouches has been recovered.[303]

At last, Shoshenq moved south, via the shortest pass over Carmel, to Aruna (III: 32), Borim (III: 33), Giti-Padalla (III: 34), Yehem (III: 35) and others (III: 36, 37, 39) by Socoh (III: 38) and on towards Gaza (?XI: lost names down to 1*bis*). Here, he was doubtless rejoined by the Negeb task-force, and the entire host returned via Raphia (XI: 2*bis*), Libna (XI: 3*bis*) and other staging-posts (XI: 4*bis*, 5*bis*), back to Egypt along the Mediterranean road across the Sinai isthmus, to celebrate their triumph in Tanis.[304]

21–20–19. From these it may perhaps be rather daring to suggest that II: 21, *šwd*, is *Shuṭ(t)a for Beth-Shiṭṭah (Judges 7: 22) in the north-central Jordan valley (on which, cf. Abel, *Géographie de la Palestine*, II, 273 end, Tell Slihat). As II: 20 is totally lost, any identification (as with Zaphon by Mazor and Aharoni) can only be purest guesswork. No. II: 19, *šdrn*, is also unidentifiable at present.

301. See below, Excursus E for details.

302. Presumably made of local limestone from the nearby Carmel ridges; regrettably, the publications fail to state the material. The relatively rough carving of the surviving fragment suggests a job done locally and quite rapidly, quickly erected to emphasize Shoshenq's claim to suzerainty and to impress the locals. The statue-base referred-to by Gray, *I–II Kings*, 1964, 313, ²1970, 345, belongs *not* to Shoshenq I but to Ramesses VI of two centuries earlier.

303. Published by C. S. Fisher, *The Excavation of Armageddon* (*OIC*, 4), 1929, 12–16 and figs. 7–9; A. T. Olmstead, *History of Palestine and Syria*, 1931, 355, fig. 142; R. S. Lamon and G. M. Shipton, *Megiddo I*, 1939, 60–1, fig. 70. For scale of fragment and size of stela, cf. Fisher, p. 16.

304.* Apart from the official records (cf. § 260, just below), few of Shoshenq's contemporaries allude to his campaign. The Theban priest Hori appears on his cartonnage mummy-casing to attribute to his father the vizier Iaʿo the titles and epithets (written in retrograde groups!): '[Prophet of] the Temple of Amun, King of the Gods, real Royal Scribe accompanying (*r-gs* ??) the King at his incursions (*nmtwt.ʿfʾ*) in the foreign lands of Retenu' (= Syria-Palestine). Text, J. E. Quibell and W. Spiegelberg, *The Ramesseum*, 1898, pl. XXXA, 1 (first transverse band), noted by W. M. Muller, *OLZ* 4 (1901), 280–2, and Breasted, *BAR*, IV, p. 348, *b*.

§ **258**   Shoshenq I probably left behind him two very much sobered (and impoverished!) petty kings in Judah and Israel, and not a few burnt or damaged townships – destruction-levels at various Palestinian sites have been attributed to Shoshenq's campaign, including those at Tell Beit Mirsim (Debir?),[305] perhaps Beth-Shemesh,[306] Yurza (Tell Yemmeh),[307] and others[308] besides just possibly Ezion-Geber (cf. above). At Sharuhen (Tell el Farʿa South), a fort found there has been attributed to Shoshenq's work,[309] rightly or otherwise. If so, it may have been intended as an advance-base for future raids.[310] It was perhaps in the wake of Shoshenq's invasion that the twin kingdoms took counter-measures against possible future raids. In Israel, Jeroboam I is reported as not only residing in Tirzah (cf. 1 Kings 14: 17 in full context) and (re)building Shechem (1 Kings 12: 25), but also going 'thence and (he) built Penuel' (1 Kings 12: 25) – evidently, again, as a bolt-hole against future invasions.[311] In Judah, Rehoboam fortified a whole series of towns – possibly before Shoshenq's invasion, but more likely afterwards; none but Ajalon appeared in Shoshenq's list (cf. 2 Chronicles 11: 5–12).[312]

§ **259**   C. END OF THE REIGN: LAST WORKS OF SHOSHENQ I
In Egypt, no doubt, appropriate gifts were made to the gods of the realm – Amun of Tanis, Bast of Bubastis, Ptah of Memphis, perhaps Arsaphes of Heracleopolis and Amun of Teudjoi, and above all to Amun of Thebes; no direct record survives. One notable fact about Shoshenq's campaign is that, seemingly, he did *not* seek to go any further north than Palestine on this first expedition – no unrealistic 'prestige' thrusts, inadequately supported, into Syria or Phoenicia by *this* shrewd politician. However,

305. W. F. Albright, *Excavation of Tell Beit Mirsim*, III (= *AASOR*, 21–2), 1943, 38, and in D. W. Thomas (ed.), *Archaeology & Old Testament Study*, 1967, 216; G. E. Wright, *Biblical Archaeology*, 1957, 149.
306. So Albright, *The Biblical Period from Abraham to Ezra*, 1963, 59; G. E. Wright, *Journal of Biblical Literature* 75 (1956), 216, but who now prefers to attribute this destruction to Siamun (so, Malamat, *JNES* 22 (1963), 13, n. 50).
307. Wright, *Biblical Archaeology*, 1957, 148–9.
308. e.g. Megiddo itself (IVB; Albright, *Tell Beit Mirsim*, III, 29, n. 10; J. N. Schofield in D. W. Thomas, *op. cit.*, 323); Tell Abu Hawam, mid-stratum III (cf. S. Yeivin, *JEA* 48 (1962), 79); Shechem, stratum X (G. E. Wright in D. W. Thomas, *op. cit.*, 366), and others.
309. Wright, *Biblical Archaeology*, 1957, 148–9; Petrie, Starkey, Harding, *Beth Pelet*, I, II.
310. So J. Bright, *History of Israel*, 1960, 214, ²1972, 230, n. 17.
311. Cf. § 256 above, for a possible alternative view of this verse relating it to Shoshenq's invasion; cf. further, U. Jochims, *ZDPV* 76 (1960), 73–96, who suggests that Jeroboam fortified Penuel before Shoshenq's invasion.
312. Cf. Aharoni, *LB*, 290–3, Map 25; Aharoni and Avi-Yonah, *Macmillan Bible Atlas*, 1968, 76, Map 119.

there is no knowing whether, as overlord of Palestine, he then planned any further expeditions to extend Egyptian arms and rule still further north.

§ **260*** In the meantime, flushed with success and increased wealth, the pharaoh immediately undertook an ambitious building-programme, especially at Thebes and Memphis. Of the latter, practically nothing is known.313 But the Theban works are famed. Perhaps only months after the triumphal return, late in Year 21 by the 2nd month of Shomu, probably Day ⟨1⟩ – January of 924 B.C. – work began in the sandstone quarries at Gebel Silsila, which was commemorated by a splendid rock-stela so dated.314 It features the high priest Iuput, the chief of works, Haremsaf, and his son Paheqanufer. We learn that the pharaoh planned for 'a very great pylon ... (with) ... its doors, (and) ... to make a festival hall for the House of ... Amenre, ... and to surround it with statues and a colonnade'. The great project was named 'the Mansion of Hedjkheperre Setepenre in Thebes'. So, at Karnak, before Pylon II of the great temple of Amun, a vast court with lateral colonnades was duly built, which was probably to be enclosed by a pylon-gateway where that of Nectanebo now stands (Pylon I).315 By the south exit from the court, along the south face of Pylon II, was engraven the huge formal triumph-scene of the king smiting his Palestinian foes before Amun who offers the sword of victory, and a woman personifying 'Victorious Thebes' as of old, leading the captive 'name-rings' of Israel and Judah. Above all this, a long rhetorical text (largely modelled on New Kingdom texts proper to such scenes) vaunted the king's prowess in appropriately traditional terms – but Amun also compliments Shoshenq on his great building project:316 'My beloved son Shoshenq, you came forth from me to be my protector. I have seen that your plan(s) are effective, for you have prepared [?benefaction]s for my House. You have adorned(?) my [city] of Thebes, the Great Place wherein my heart is.

313. Except the official name 'Mansion of [Millions of Years of the King of Upper & Lower Egypt], Hedjkheperre Setepenre, Son of Re, Shoshenq I Beloved of Amun, which is in Memphis' (*Ḥwt-kꜣ-Ptḥ*), mentioned on Karnak block D, part *c*, lines 1–2, in Müller, *Egyptological Researches*, II, 1910, 148, fig. 53. At Memphis, only a few traces of Shoshenq's works have survived, cf. above, § 248.

314. Latest publication, R. A. Caminos, *JEA* 38 (1952), 46–61 and pls. 10–13. Decree of the King then residing in 'Pi-Ese ('Estate of Isis'), the Great Soul of Pre-Harakhte' (line 40). The latter phrase links this 'residence' with the old Pi-Ramessē which had this epithet from the latter years of Ramesses II (Gardiner, *Anc. Egyptian Onomastica*, II, 1947, 171* ff., 278* f.; *JEA* 5 (1918), 136). Hence, I would suggest that Pi-Ese was a new country residence south of Tanis proper and on the north side of old Pi-Ramessē, bounded by the Estate of (the goddess) Edjo (Caminos, *Late-Egyptian Miscellanies*, 37, 154), Edjo being replaced by Isis.

315. On date of the existing Pylon I, see Caminos, *JEA* 38 (1952), 60–1, and Barguet, *Temple d'Amon-rê à Karnak*, 1962, 45–7.

316. Lines 12–17 in *RIK*, III, pl. 4.

You have undertaken the making of monuments in Southern On (= Thebes) and Northern On (= Heliopolis), and every city likewise for each god within his province. You have made my Temple of Millions of Years,[317] its doorways(?) [adorned?] with electrum for my [image?] therein.' Next to this famed scene and list, the great gateway now known as the 'Bubastite Gate' was built and its side-pilasters decorated on the north side with three scenes each of Shoshenq I, Iuput and the gods, while the architraves were adorned with the imperially-luxuriant titles of the pharaoh, engraved in large-scale and highly-competent work.[318] So, for a brief moment in time, a breath of the past greatness of empire enlivened Thebes – no pharaoh had wrought in Karnak on this vast scale for almost four centuries, when Sethos I and Ramesses II had built the great hypostyle hall. Within the old temple – fittingly, just north of the hall of Syrian annals of Tuthmosis III – Shoshenq carried out works whose dedicatory texts for Amun included reference to his Nubian undertakings (already quoted, § 251, above), and to dues 'when I made it as thy tribute (i.e. Amun's) of the land of Palestine (*Khuru*) which had turned away from thee'.[319] In this temple he also erected the victory-stela (cf. § 253 above), and had engraved a further triumphal relief (now lost) in the temple of Amun at El Hibeh.[320]

Then, suddenly, Shoshenq died. His works were left practically all unfinished,[321] his wishes for jubilee-festivals unfulfilled,[322] and all his grandiose schemes died with him.

§ 261   2. OSORKON I (*c.* 924–889 B.C.) AND
         SHOSHENQ II (*c.* 890 B.C.)

A. INTERNAL AFFAIRS

(i) *Accession of Osorkon I*

The heir of Shoshenq I took official titles much in the style of his father.

317. Mentioned again, inner temple block D, *c*, line 4, after the Memphis temple as 'the Temple of Millions of Years', (etc.) of Shoshenq I, 'which is [in Thebes/ Estate of Amun]'.

318. Scenes and architrave, *RIK*, III, pls. 1, 10–12; great triumph-scene, *ibid.*, pls. 2–9. In the Temple of Mut, Shoshenq I added further Sekhmet statues, *G3*, 311, XVI and n. 2.

319. Block D, *a*, line 6 (Müller, *Egyptol. Researches*, II, 147, fig. 52 top). For these works, cf. Barguet, *Temple d'Amon-rê à Karnak*, 1962, 122–3.

320. *PM*, IV, 124.

321. Under Osorkon I, only three further formal scenes were added to the Bubastite gateway (W. face, E. pilaster), *RIK*, III, pls. 13–15, and all other work was abandoned.

322. Cf. the base-line (13) of bottom scene, W. pilaster (*RIK*, III, pl. 10, bottom left) – 'first occasion of repeating the jubilee-festival; may there be made for him many more, like Rē forever'; also on the architrave (*ibid.*, pl. 12).

He also was Horus, 'Strong Bull, beloved of Re', augmented with epithets – in this case, 'whom Atum placed on his throne to provide for the Two Lands'.[323] More original was his Nebty name, 'magnifying Forms, rich in marvels',[324] while his Golden Horus name was closer to those of his father and of Psusennes I: 'Strong in might, subduing the Nine Bows, Sovereign who conquers all lands.'[325] His prenomen, Sekhemkheperre Setepenre, combined originality with formation on his father's pattern.

§ 262* (ii) *Delta Activities*

During the first 4 years of his reign,[326] Osorkon I bestowed handsome gifts of gold and silver vessels and furnishings upon the temples of the major deities of Egypt[327] – to Re-Harakhte, Hathor-Nebethetepet, Mut, Arsaphes, all(?) of Heliopolis; to Thoth at Hermopolis and elsewhere, to Bast of Bubastis, and to Amenre, King of the Gods. For the Heliopolitan deities, the total weight of gold, silver and lapis-lazuli was 594,300 *deben*,[328] while for Amun some fragmentary figures record over 2,000,000 *deben* of silver and over 2,300,000 *deben* of gold and silver – in each case, very roughly 500,000 lb troy weight of precious metal. None of this glittering wealth has survived to modern times, of course; but the possible quality of workmanship may be illustrated from the fine bronze statuette of this pharaoh, its details and inscriptions inlaid in gold, found near Tell el Yahudieh (northern dependency of Heliopolis), now in Brooklyn.[329] The sources of such wealth are unknown to us – doubtless general taxation from a unified, better-run and relatively more prosperous country, crown revenues from trade abroad,[330] and doubtless something still from the spoils of Solomonic treasure so recently obtained during his father's campaign in Palestine.

323. Epithets given by a fragment from Bubastis, Naville, *Bubastis*, 1891, pl. 41D (omitted by *G3*!), and the MMA stela of note 334 below: *Kʒ-nḫt mry-Rᶜ*, *rdit.n s(w) 'Itm ḥr nst.f r grg-tʒwy*.
324. *Sᶜʒ-ḫprw, wr-biʒwt*, attested only by the MMA stela. Cf. the *Smʒ-ḫprw* of Psusennes I, beginning his Golden Horus name (*Psus*, Fig. 66).
325. *Nḫt-ḫpš, dr pḏt 9, ity iṯi tʒw nbw* – first two segments from the MMA stela, and second and third from Naville, *Bubastis*, pl. 51, fragment C1 (again, not in *G3*). Cf. Golden Horus name of Psusennes I, 'Uniting Forms, subduing the Nine Bows, seizing all lands by his power' (*Smʒ-ḫprw, dr pḏt 9, iṯi m šḥm.f m tʒw nbw*), Montet, *Psus*, Fig. 66.
326. 'Three years, three months and sixteen days' as the text more precisely puts it (Naville, *Bubastis*, pl. 51, C2, line 3).
327. Naville, *Bubastis*, pls. 51–2; cf. *BAR*, IV, §§ 729–37.
328. The *deben* was about 91 grammes, cf. Gardiner, *Egyptian Grammar*, § 266,4.
329. From Shibin el-Kanatir, cf. refs., *PM*, IV, 58; now Brooklyn Museum 57. 92, cf. B. V. Bothmer, *JEA* 46 (1960), 6, n. 2.
330. Probably thanks to the link with Byblos, the subdued state of Philistia, and inability of the Hebrew kingdoms to compete.

The fragmentary record of this munificence was engraved on a pillar in a small temple of the sun-god Atum, probably built entirely by Osorkon, well beyond the main precinct at Bubastis[331] his home town. In the main temple of the cat-goddess Bast, Osorkon I probably built extensively – a whole series of reliefs (in three registers of scenes) adorned the outermost of two eastern forecourts, behind which courts he probably built a hypostyle hall that included Hathor-headed pillars with lotus-bud and palm-leaf capitalled columns (reused).[332]

Elsewhere, Lower Egypt saw little such activity except at Heliopolis and Memphis. Near the former, a plot of ground (3 *arourae*)[333] was accorded to Hory, mayor of Heliopolis, through the agency of the Heliopolitan high priest of Re-Atum and General, Djed-Ptah-ef-ankh B son of the lady Tasherit-en-Ese, in Year 6 of Osorkon I.[334] From Memphis comes half of a massive lintel from a once considerable shrine of Bast.[335] On it appears the dignitary probably locally responsible for the work: the Count and dignitary (*iry-pʿt ḥȝty-ʿ*), Superintendent of Cattle of the Estate of Ptah, prophet and priest who opens the doors of the Eternal Horizon (= naos of the deity), Chief of Secrets of Horus master of the Two Lands (etc.), Djed-Ptah-ef-ankh C.[336]

§ 263 (iii) *Middle and Upper Egypt*

Osorkon added to the temple of Isis at Atfih,[337] and continued to work on his father's temple at El Hibeh.[338] Much more significantly, he founded a new strongpoint and domain named after himself – Pi-Sekhemkheperre, 'Estate of Osorkon I' – near the entry to the Fayum, probably north of Heracleopolis.[339] It most likely served as a military base separate from the

331. Naville, *Bubastis*, 60–2, pls. 50–2; an architrave of Ramesses II was perhaps merely reused by Osorkon I. See further, L. Habachi, *Tell Basta*, 1957, 119–20, for the identification as a temple of Atum.

332. Naville, *Bubastis*, *passim*, and esp. L. Habachi, *Tell Basta*, 55–70.

333. The *aroura* (Egyptian *stȝt*) was about two-thirds of an acre, cf. Gardiner, *Egyptian Grammar*, § 266, 3.

334. Stela MMA, 10.176.42, details of which I owe to the kindness of Mostafa El-Alfi (studying this monument); its true date is Year 6, not Year 5 as reported in *RdÉ* 20 (1968), 137, n. 8.

335. As the present fragment is 1.65 metres long, the whole lintel must have been at least 3 metres (10 feet) long. *PM*, III, 227, to which now add H. W. Müller (ed.), *Die ägyptische Sammlung des Bayerischen Staates* (*Ausstellung . . .*), 1966, § 64 (Gl. 78), and photo, 64, Gl. 78.

336. Titles from the two ends of the existing block.

337. Slab, cf. Petrie *et al.*, *Heliopolis, Kafr Ammar & Shurafa*, 1915, pl. 40.

338. *PM*, IV, 124.

339. On Pi-Sekhemkheperre, cf. Yoyotte, *YMM*, 135, n. 1, and A. R. Schulman, *JARCE* 5 (1966), 35, n. *e*, both with further references.

metropolis of Heracleopolis and as a stronghold to guard the passage between Middle Egypt and the Fayum.[340]

In the far south, this Osorkon (or less likely, another) added his name to a doorway of Tuthmosis III at Coptos;[341] his name recurs on an ostracon from the supposed 'tomb of Osiris' at Abydos.[342] Abydos was venerated by the house of Shoshenq I – the latter had endowed a chapel there for his father Nimlot A (§ 239 above), and his son Iuput had a shrine there (above, § 248 end). Under Osorkon I, a Libyan 4th prophet of Amun of Thebes, Pashedbast A, visiting Abydos, found an ancient stela, restored it and endowed it with offerings for Osiris, leaving his own stela as witness.[343]

§ 264   (iv) Thebes

The High-priestly Succession. In Thebes, Osorkon's brother Iuput may initially have continued to function as pontiff and even have completed three panels of scenes on the east buttress of the Bubastite Gate at Karnak for the new pharaoh.[344] There is possibly evidence, however, that he very soon died or retired from office. The Karnak Priestly Annals include four fragments[345] pertaining to the reign of Osorkon I. No. 17 barely preserves some 'day [of induction into office?]' for a God's Father of Amun, Nespautytawy son of Harkhebi, including reference to [a relative or relic?] 'of king Psusennes . . .', in possibly Year 1 of a king Osorkon.[346] No. 34 may explain the connection: it appears to mention induction or promotion of the same '[Nespau]tytawy son of Harkhebi, son of Iufenkhons' to 'the goodly places of Amun, by the agency of the High Priest of Amun, Shoshenq [. . .]'.[347] If not in Year 1, then certainly but a few years thereafter, we here first meet the successor of Iuput. Following his own father's example and precept, Osorkon I allowed no dynastic succession in the

340. No governors of Pi-Sekhemkheperre are yet known before Nimlot under Osorkon II; both then and later, it was closely linked with the rulers of Heracleopolis and Thebes.

341. Petrie, *Koptos*, pl. 13.

342. *PM*, V, 90.

343. Stela, University College, London, published by H. Jacquet-Gordon, *JEA* 53 (1967), 63–8 and pl. 11, eliminating the false reading of 'Year 36' from this stela (but not necessarily from the history of the dynasty, see above, Part II, § 89).

344. *RIK*, III, pls. 13–15. The king appears alone in these scenes, without either Iuput or Shoshenq as high priest. Here also the wish for jubilees is expressed (pl. 13).

345. Nos. 17, 34, 35, 37, in Legrain *RT* 22 (1900), 58, 62.

346. Doubtless of Osorkon I (himself son-in-law of Psusennes II), as no other Osorkon had any direct connection with kings of the 21st Dynasty.

347. No. 37 records only 'ᵣDayᴸ of Induction [of . . . some son?] of Nespautytawy, son of the prophet of Amun, Har[khebi . . .]', mentioning also a man Padimut. (The Nespautytawy of Fragment No. 14 is of a different family and undated.) No. 35 is dated to Sekhemkheperre, i.e. Osorkon I, and dealt with prophets of Mut, Khons and Montu, their names now lost.

offices of high priest of Amun and military ruler of Upper Egypt. He now appointed a son of his own to the vacancy, not a son of Iuput. He chose to send to Thebes his eldest son Shoshenq, born to him by Queen Maatkare B, daughter of Psusennes II. Thus, the Thebans now received as pontiff a man who was not only their intending future king and leading representative of the reigning dynasty but who also was a scion of the previous Tanite dynasty with whom their former line of pontiffs had had the closest links.[348]

§ 265* *The High Priest Shoshenq.* The new incumbent probably held office for most of his father's reign. In Karnak itself, he left four fine statues, and at Luxor a graffito.[349] Two of the statuettes name him simply as high priest and son of King Osorkon. The finer one[350] gives also the titles of his royal mother – 'Prophet(ess) of Hathor Lady of Dendera and God's Mother of Harsomtus, Maatkare, royal daughter of King [Psusennes]'. Thus this Tanite princess and Libyan queen held benefices in Dendera not far north of Thebes.[351] In Thebes itself the remains of a long text on Pylon VII at Karnak indicate that she had acquired land in Thebes, which would yield her an income.[352] Nor was she alone in so doing. One of Shoshenq's brothers, prince Iuwelot who was but a young man in Year 10 of Osorkon I, eventually built up a holding of some 556 *arourae* of arable land on the north-west of Thebes – an estate that he passed on to one of his sons years later.[353]

The fourth Karnak statue – of the Nile-god[354] – dedicated by Shoshenq (perhaps much later) shows us most clearly his hopes and pretensions, for on this he used a cartouche – 'High Priest of Amenresonter (Shoshenq, Beloved of Amun)', also preceded by 'Lord of the South and North,

348. If (as some think) Psusennes II, king, were the same man as Psusennes 'III', high priest, then, of course, Shoshenq was himself grandson of the last-but-one Theban pontiff, an even closer relationship.
349. Graffito, Daressy, *RT* 35 (1913), 133; *G3*, 330, XXVIII, 1A. Statue-base, Habachi, *ASAE* 51 (1951), 455–6, pl. 3.
350. Cairo Cat. 42194 (of green brecchia ?), Legrain, *Statues*, II, 3–4, pls. 3–4; *G3*, 329, XXVII, 1B. The second statue, Cat. 42193, Legrain, 3, pl. 2, is of black granite and less refined. But the 'brecchia' one may have been usurped from a previous owner. Third, Cairo JdE. 37881, *PM*, II², 148 top, (*c*).
351. Again, not surprising for a member of the former Theban high priestly family, if Psusennes II and 'III' be identical.
352. Last translated by Gardiner, *JEA* 48 (1962), 65–9. While this text could have been inscribed as early as the reigns of either Psusennes II or Shoshenq I, yet one could equally well argue that it was inscribed as late as the pontificate of Shoshenq and reign of Osorkon I, in which the new high priest sought to guarantee the integrity of his maternal inheritance in Thebes.
353. So-called *stèle de l'apanage*, cf. Legrain and Erman, *ZÄS* 35 (1897), 13–16, 19–24; *BAR*, IV, § 795 (wrongly dated under Osorkon III).
354. British Museum No. 8, over 7 feet high; references, *G3*, 299, II; 331, D.

Leader' (Shoshenq) 'who is leader of the great army of all Egypt, son of King Osorkon'. As heir, he here anticipated his future kingship. More ostraca from Abydos, naming him, show he shared the Dynasty's interest in that sacred site.[355]

Other works of Osorkon's reign at Karnak are limited in scope. But blocks from the north-west part of Amun's precinct belonged to the frieze of some large building;[356] the Temple of Khons has but a line of text.[357] In Year 12, the height of the inundation was commemorated by a 'Nile level' text on the Karnak quay before Amun's temple.[358] None of these works name anyone but the king. A much later monument[359] names two of Shoshenq's wives: Nesi-taudjat-akhet,[360] mother of an Osorkon (ordinary prophet of Amun), and Nesi-tanebt-ashru B, mother of Harsiese, a later high priest (cf. § 272, below).

§ 266* *Other Theban Dignitaries*. It is still not known who served as 2nd prophet of Amun under Osorkon I. A steady succession of *protégés* of the Libyan dynasty held the offices of 3rd and 4th prophet. As 3rd prophet, Djed-Thut-ef-ankh A – son-in-law of Shoshenq I himself – probably continued well into the reign of Osorkon (cf. § 245 above).[361] He certainly had followed Djed-Ptah-ef-ankh A, and perhaps directly after another incumbent (of briefer tenure?), the southern vizier Neser-Amun A. This worthy was the son of a Royal Secretary (lit., 'Letter-writer of Pharaoh') and high priest of Montu, Nebneteru ii, and in turn fathered another Nebneteru (iii) who became Royal Secretary and reached the age of 96 years.[362] The Thebans thus retained a hold on this post, although in part through having royal connections (marriage, secretariat). A whole series of men were successive 4th prophets under Osorkon I. After his father, the chief of the Mahasun, Nesy, his son Nes-ankhef-maat served probably into the early years of Osorkon I (cf. § 244 above). Thereafter, this office

355. *PM*, V, 80.
356. *ASAE* 22 (1922), 64.
357. *PM*, II, 80, column 27; II², 1972, 232, No. 20; Bouriant, *RT* 11 (1889), 153.
358. Text No. 2, Legrain, *ZÄS* 34 (1896), 111; von Beckerath, *JARCE* 5 (1966), 44, 49.
359. The Bes statue formerly in the Alnwick Castle collection; *G3*, 331, E, and n. 2, Legrain, *RT* 30 (1908), 160.
360. Who also occurs in one of two funerary papyri naming the high priest Shoshenq, *G3*, 331, n. 2, references.
361. His daughter Itawy married a priest Hor (iii) whose many offices included that of keeper of the cults of kings past and present – Chief of the Portable Image (*kny*) of ⟨Ramesses III⟩, Ruler of Heliopolis, ... [man]ifestor(?) of the gods of Pinudjem, and *wˁb*-priest of the image (*ibib*) of King Osorkon (I), cf. statue Cairo Cat. 42221 in Legrain, *Statues*, III, 49, *c*, d.
362. See above, Part III, §§ 177 ff.

passed to Pashedbast A (cf. § 263 above), yet another chief of the Mahasun – perhaps in turn a son of his predecessor.[363] After him, Osorkon I broke with this incipient hereditary series by next awarding the 4th prophetship to a Theban notable of his acquaintance – to Djed-Khons-ef-ankh A, son-in-law of Iuput and descendant of a very old Theban family.[364] On his statue (Cairo 559) dated to Osorkon I, and perhaps dedicated by his own son, Djed-Khons-ef-ankh is further entitled the (civil) Governor of Upper Egypt and portrays himself as a 'king's man' in picturesque phrases: 'The good god, Osorkon I, favoured me, and his heirs more so. . . . . The grandees of the land desired to emulate me, so great was my favour with the King. I did not approach too (familiarly?) near to the King in his palace, and he excluded me not from his royal barque. His drink was pleasant – I ate with him and drank wine with him. . . . I reached Thebes at an advanced age, and did what was praiseworthy in Karnak.'[365] A grandson of the aged Djed-Khons-ef-ankh A, one Djed-Khons-ef-ankh B, set up his own statue in Karnak in this reign,[366] as did the seal-bearer of the god, Ankhefenkhons for his father Nespaherenhat.[367] Near the end of the reign a lesser priest Nakhtefmut was buried at the Ramesseum, his mummy being adorned with leather tabs and pendant emblazoned in the name of Osorkon I, and wrapped in bandages marked Year 33 and Year 3 of unnamed kings.[368]

§ 267   B. FOREIGN AFFAIRS: BYBLOS AND JUDAH

Here, Osorkon I followed-out the policies of his father: friendship and alliance with the commercial port of Byblos, and assertion of political power over (or at least, against) near neighbours.

(i) *Byblos*

Like his father, Osorkon presented a statue of himself to the ruler and deities of Byblos; the upper portion, which is of good workmanship, still survives.[369] Upon it, collar-like around the neck, Elibaal the ruler of Byblos

363. No parentage recorded. For gem of a 'King's Son of Ramesses Pashedbast' from the burial of Harnakht at Tanis, cf. Montet, *Osorkon II*, 66, fig. 21: 87, and pl. 58.

364. See above, Part III, §§ 183 ff.

365. Cairo Cat. 559, Borchardt, *Statuen und Statuetten*, II, 105–8, pl. 94; other references, *PM*, II², 337 end. Cf. further, E. Otto, *Biographische Inschriften der ägyptischen Spätzeit*, 1954, No. 2, pp. 132–3. As Otto and Kees remark, the 4th-prophetship was a pensioning appointment.

366. Cairo Cat. 42216 (Legrain, *Statues*, III, *ad loc.*); cf. above, Part III, § 186.

367. Cairo Cat. 42189, Legrain, *Statues*, II, *ad loc.*

368. Quibell, *The Ramesseum*, 10–11, pls. 16–18. The Year 33 should be attributed to Osorkon I; could the Year 3 be that of his co-regent, Shoshenq II?

369. Pictured, Dussaud, *Syria* 6 (1925), pl. 25 and often since.

added his own independent dedication: '[Statu]e which Elibaal, King of Byblos, son of Yehi[milk, King of Byblos,] made [for Ba]alat-Gebal, his lady. May [Baalat-Gebal] lengthen [the days of E]libaal and his (regnal) years over Byblos!'[370]

§ 268 (ii) *Judah*

In 2 Chronicles 14: 9–15 (Hebrew, 8–14), the Old Testament records how 'there came forth Zerah the Nubian ("Kushite") with an army of myriads and 300 chariots, and he came to Mareshah'. There, king Asa of Judah gave battle, defeated the intruders, and pursued them as far as Gerar near the southern borders of Judah and Philistia. The event can be dated to about the 14th year of Asa, i.e. *c.* 897 B.C.[371] This date would fall into the 28th year of Osorkon I. There is no question of identifying Osorkon with Zerah as is sometimes done: the names differ entirely,[372] Osorkon is a king and of Libyan origin, whereas Zerah is not called a king and is a Nubian. By 897 B.C., Osorkon I was already an old man, and so he may well have sent a general of Nubian extraction[373] to lead a force into Palestine, to emulate his father's exploit, bring home some fresh booty, and dismantle the military build-up of king Asa. However, Zerah proved no match for the Judean king, and so we have no trace of a triumphal relief of Osorkon to adorn anew the temple walls of Egypt.

§ 269   C. SHOSHENQ II AS CO-REGENT, AND THE
                    END OF THE REIGN

Near the end of his reign, the ageing Osorkon apparently deemed it politic to make his eldest son, the high priest Shoshenq, co-regent. This forceful man in his 50s[374]– heir in his person to both the 21st and 22nd

370. Text of statue, Dussaud, *op. cit.*, 101–17; and better, Albright, *JAOS* 67 (1947), 158; W. Herrmann, *MIO* 6 (1958), 17–18, 32; H. Donner and W. Röllig, *Kanaanäische und Aramäische Inschriften*, I (1962), 1, No. 6, II (1964), 8, No. 6; other, general references, cf. *PM*, VII, 388, and J. Leclant in W. A. Ward (ed.), *The Role of the Phoenicians in the Interaction of Mediterranean Civilizations*, 1968, 12–13 and n. 27.

371. The victory of Asa was followed by a call for reforms from the prophet Azariah, and this in turn by reforms in the 15th year of Asa (2 Chronicles 15: 1–10); also, the 35th/36th years 'of Asa' (2 Chronicles 15: 19; 16: 1) are most probably, in fact, those of the Divided Monarchy, and so about Year 14 of Asa himself; for discussion, cf. particularly, Thiele, *MN*, 1951, 58–60, ²1965, 59–60.

372. Hebrew *z* is not equivalent to Egyptian *s*, nor is Hebrew *ḥ* a suitable equivalent of Egyptian *k*; only *r* is common to these two names. The error of equating Zerah and Osorkon was remarked long ago by (e.g.) Albright, *JPOS* 4 (1924), 147.

373. Recalling the Nubian campaign of Shoshenq I, which probably brought a considerable Nubian contingent into the Egyptian forces then and afterwards; cf. already 2 Chronicles 12: 3.

374. Cf. Derry, *ASAE* 39 (1939), 549–51; *Psus*, 40.

Dynasties – now at last shared his father's throne as King Heqakheperre Setepenre, Son of Re, Shoshenq II Beloved of Amun.[375] His prenomen was original but on the pattern of his father and grandfather. Meantime, a younger brother Iuwelot was probably sent to Thebes as the next high priest of Amun.

Thus, the future must have seemed full of promise – when suddenly the new co-regent died. His father bestowed on him a splendid burial – a gold mask of noblest style, solid silver coffin (falcon-headed, as befitted the young Horus), richly-adorned pectorals upon his mummy, matching silver coffinettes for his inner organs in a hastily-assembled set of canopic vases, and a full array of amulets.[376] Also included were family heirlooms – a fine pectoral of his grandfather Shoshenq I made when the latter was still 'Great Chief of the Mā, son of . . . Nimlot', and a pair of attractive bracelets of Shoshenq I as king.[377] A more outlandish memento from far away in space and time was a Mesopotamian cylinder-seal of the third millennium B.C. – already a venerable antiquity when buried with Shoshenq II.[378] Thus adorned, this ephemeral king was ultimately laid to rest in the vestibule of the tomb of his mother's ancestor Psusennes I within the great precinct at Tanis along with other 'guests' – whether originally, or as a reburial is not known.

In all probability, the death of the heir, his eldest son by the great heiress Queen Maatkare, was a mortal blow to the aged Osorkon I; probably within a year or so, he too passed to the other world to join his son, leaving the throne to his second son Takeloth.

§ **270** 3. TAKELOTH I (*c.* 889–874 B.C.)

The new pharaoh is the least-known king of the entire Libyan epoch – and *not one* single, contemporary monument can yet be cited bearing cartouches that are *definitely* his beyond all question.[379] That his personal name as Son of Re was Takeloth is guaranteed by the genealogical stela of Pasenhor, many generations later. Even his prenomen remains unknown, with all other titles. To Pasenhor we owe knowledge of the facts that Take-

375. His Horus, Nebty and Golden Horus names remain unknown.
376. For this burial, see Montet, *Psus*, 37–50, fig. 28 right, second coloured plate, and pls. 17–36.
377. Cf. colour-plate, Montet, *Psus*.
378. P. Amiet in Montet, *Psus*, 46–8, fig. 13, pl. 30.
379. The entire series of monuments bearing cartouches of Usimare (± Setepen-amun), Takeloth (± Beloved of Amun, Son of Isis) can be referred without diffi-culty to Takeloth III, whose cartouches these are. The supposed Florence stela of Takeloth belongs in fact to Pedubast I; see under the latter.

loth's mother was Tashedkhons[380] (second queen of Osorkon I), and that
Takeloth's wife was Kapes, mother of prince Osorkon (II) his eventual
successor.[381] A heart-scarab from the burial of Osorkon II in Tanis,
belonging to a Takeloth Beloved of Amun *may* have been left from Takeloth I;[382] but this and the attribution to him of a broken limestone stela
with the same cartouche – in the Grant collection in 1881 – is wholly
beyond proof.[383]

This virtually total failure of contemporary sources to name the new
king clearly in the normal manner seems not entirely accidental. To this
period and reign may be attributed the Theban pontificates of two younger
brothers of Takeloth I – Iuwelot who left three Nile-level graffiti at the
Karnak quay of Year 5 (No. 16) and years lost (Nos. 20, 21), and Smendes
III who left three more, year lost (No. 19), Year 8 (No. 17) and Year 13
or 14 (No. 18).[384] From the entire series of forty-five Nile level epigraphs
spanning almost three centuries, it is remarkable and surely significant that
these and these alone fail to name the king to whose years they are dated –
such an utter nonentity was Takeloth I that his own brothers as Theban
high priests used his reign as dating-era but ignored the king himself.
Before his own death, Iuwelot made over his Theban properties to his son
Khamweset whom his wife, the royal granddaughter Tadenitenbast had
long since borne him. The will is engraved on a superb granite stela in his
own name and omits all mention of the reigning king, referring only to his
father Osorkon I.[385] On it we learn also of the northward limit of Iuwelot's
rule as military commander of the south 'to the province of Siut' (Middle
Egypt). Evidently, military responsibility north of this region lay with the
ruler of Heracleopolis and the fort of Pi-Sekhemkheperre. In connection
with the founding of the latter, it is tempting to assume that this division of
military responsibility was introduced by Osorkon I and subsisted under

380. She, at least, is attested by a stray ushabti-figure found in the burial of
Takeloth II at Tanis, cf. Montet, *Osorkon II*, 84, Inv. 42, p. 80, fig. 25 (centre
left), pl. 56.

381. A fact confirmed by her occurrence as mourner on a panel by the entry to the
tomb of her son Osorkon II; see Montet, *op. cit.*, 71–3, pls. 22–3.

382. Published by Montet, *op. cit.*, 59, 65 fig. 20 (Inv. 58), pl. 58.

383. See A. Wiedemann, *PSBA* 13 (1890/91), 36, for this text.

384. Legrain, *ZÄS* 34 (1896), 113; von Beckerath, *JARCE* 5 (1966), 46, 48,
50–1.

385. 'Stèle de l'apanage', Legrain and Erman, *ZÄS* 35 (1897), 13–16, 19–24. The
stela British Museum 1224 shows Iuwelot and his 'sister' (wife) T(a)denit(enbast)
worshipping Re-Harakhte (Budge, *Br. Mus. Guide, Sculpture*, 1909, 215 and pl.
28). One Wasakawasa, son of the high priest Iuwelot, is attested by an electrum
pectoral (Petrie, *History*, III, 1905, 265, fig. 108; Petrie, *Scarabs & Cylinders*,
1917, pl. 51, K). As correctly pointed out by H. Jacquet-Gordon, *JEA* 53 (1967),
67, n. 3, Wasakawasa was *not* himself a high priest.

Takeloth I. Iuwelot's daughter Djed-Ese-es-ankh married the priest Padimut who became a 3rd prophet of Amun and whose great-grandfather (an elder Padimut) had been southern vizier, probably under Shoshenq I.[386] The younger Padimut was probably only a simple prophet under Takeloth I and became 3rd prophet under Osorkon II.

Of Smendes III, next to nothing is known.[387] Of other affairs at home and abroad, nothing whatever is known;[388] this shadow-king passes from the scene without further trace of name or tomb.

386. Statue, Cairo Cat. 42215 (Legrain, *Statues*, III, 37–9, pl. 24), dedicated to Padimut by his son Djed-Khons-ef-ankh.
387. For a writing-palette that probably belonged to Smendes III (now MMA. 47. 123, A-H), see W. C. Hayes, *JEA* 34 (1948), 47–50, pls. 13–14.
388. e.g. no statue at Byblos like his two predecessors and successor.

CHAPTER 19

The Twenty-second Dynasty: II, An Age of Crisis (Osorkon II, Harsiese, Takeloth II)

§ 271 I. OSORKON II (*c.* 874–850 B.C.) AND HARSIESE (*c.* 870–860 B.C.?)

A. INTERNAL AFFAIRS

(i) *Accession*

Osorkon II was as forceful as his father is elusive. His titles proclaim him as an adherent to the styles both of his own dynasty and of the Ramessides of Egypt's imperial past. Thus, as his principal Horus name, Osorkon II took that of Ramesses II: 'Strong Bull, beloved of Truth' (*maʿat*),[389] expanded (as was now usual) with variable epithets linking king, sun-god and the kingship – 'He whom Re caused to appear, to be King (var., Ruler) of the Two Lands'.[390] His Nebty name closely echoed that of Sho-shenq I[391] – 'Uniter of the Two Portions (*sc.* of Egypt) like the Son of Isis, contenting the gods by performing Truth', a resemblance heightened by

389. The variant *Kȝ-nḫt ḥʿ-m-Wȝst*, '. . . appearing in Thebes' occurs on one Theban priestly statue (*G3*, 338, XIIA).
390. Comparing the traces for *Kȝ-nḫt mry-mȝʿt, sḫʿ sw Rʿ r nsw* (var., *ḥkȝ*) *tȝwy*, to be deduced from the Karnak blocks (Legrain, *ASAE* 5 (1904), 282; *G3*, 337, X; Müller, *Egyptol. Researches*, II, 151, figs. 57, 58) and Bubastis naos (Daressy, *RT* 23 (1901), 132; *G3*, 339, XXI). A further variant of the epithets is probably offered us by the statue of Harmose from Leontopolis [Horus, *Kȝ-nḫt mry-mȝʿt, sḫʿ*]? *sw* DEITY? *r spd tȝwy*, '. . . to refurbish the Two Lands' (Naville, *Ahnas*, pl. 4C, 1; not in *G3*).
391. For which see § 241 above; cf. allusions to (Horus) son of Isis, and contenting the gods with 'truth'; Nebty name of Osorkon II, cf. *G3*, 340, XXIII, Montet, *Osorkon II*, 12.

the further epithets 'and has conjoined the Double Crown(s) in peace'.[392]
As Golden Horus, Osorkon II was: 'Great of strength, smiting the Mentyu
(Asiatics; var., Enemies), Rich in splendour.'[393] For prenomen, Osorkon II
chose one early discarded by Ramesses IV but reminiscent of many kings
from Ramesses II to Amenemope – Usimare Setepenamun; to his personal
name he often added at will the epithet 'Son of (the goddess) Bast' alongside the invariable 'beloved of Amun'.

§ **272**   (ii) *Families and Pretenders in Thebes*
Probably early in the new reign,[394] it was necessary once more to appoint a
new high priest to govern in Thebes and Upper Egypt. Osorkon either could
or would not appoint a son of his own, to succeed his uncles Iuwelot and
Smendes III. Instead, Harsiese, son of the long-deceased Shoshenq II and
a cousin of Osorkon II himself, made good his claim to be pontiff in
Thebes. In so far as Shoshenq II had been (previous to his momentary
co-regency) high priest of Amun, the new appointment constituted an
ominous breach of fundamental principle – namely, that *no* 'inner-
dynastic' father-to-son succession should be allowed from one Theban
high priest to another; instead, the post should be occupied by a son,
brother or other relative of the reigning king, so avoiding a collateral
dynasty that would weaken the unity of the realm. Osorkon II's breach of
this rule by appointing Harsiese set an explosive precedent that in little
more than a generation or so was destined to plunge Egypt into civil war
and a 'divided kingship'. What compounded the error still further was the
fact of Harsiese's own descent not only from kings of the ruling Dynasty
but also – through his father and grandmother – from the late 21st
Dynasty, itself linked by marriage and descent with the former dynastic
succession of high priests in Thebes. Harsiese, therefore, was an all-too-
tempting focus for the growing aspirations of the Thebans to control their
own destinies in effective independence of the kings in distant Tanis.
Harsiese lost no time in commemorating his high-priestly ancestry.[395]

392. i.e. *dmḏ.n.f sḥmty m ḥtp* (*G3*, 338, XIIB, XVB; Theban priests' statues),
and additional *dhn* . . . , 'promoted . . . ', Karnak blocks, last note but one.
393. *Wr* (var. *sḥm*) *pḥty, ḥw Mntyw* (var. *ḥftyw*); *G3*, 337, X; 338, XIIB with
varr. 340, XXIII. With these epithets, cf. Golden Horus names of Shoshenq I
and Osorkon I, §§ 241, 261, above. At Leontopolis, Osorkon II added to his Golden
Horus name the further epithets, *dr pḏtyw, ity sḥm m tꜣw nbw*, 'Subduer of bar-
barians, sovereign who conquers all lands' (Naville, *Ahnas*, pl. 4C, 1), reminiscent of
the expanded Golden Horus names of Osorkon I and even Psusennes I (§ 261 above).
On titulary of Osorkon II, cf. also H. Jacquet-Gordon, *JEA* 46 (1960), 13–15.
394. If not already in the last year or so of Takeloth I, depending on whether
Smendes III died under Takeloth I or Osorkon II.
395. By setting up the Bes statue (former Alnwick collection), naming himself as

§ 273* The hereditary principle in major Theban priesthoods not tied to political power had long been allowed in some measure;[396] it was probably under Takeloth I that the aged Djed-Khons-ef-ankh A was succeeded as 4th prophet of Amun by his notable son Djed-Thut-ef-ankh B, called Nakhtefmut (A). This worthy was a sufficiently close friend of Harsiese to name his own son and later successor after the latter, and this younger Harsiese C married Istweret A, daughter of the high priest.

Other Theban families yet kept the balance of loyalty to both the pharaoh and his ambitious high-priestly cousin. The royal secretary for Upper Egypt, Hori viii, dedicated a statue to his (grand?)father and predecessor-in-office, Nebneteru iii, dating it by the cartouches of Osorkon II and the name and title of the pontiff Harsiese.[397] Nebneteru iii himself, who died at 96 or more, would have witnessed the accession of the Libyan Dynasty in his youth, and his own father the southern vizier Neser-Amun A was probably in office at that time.[398]

§ 274* However, Harsiese did not stop at remaining high priest. He further pressed to become a king, and titular co-ruler with Osorkon II himself, with full pharaonic style and titles, precisely like Pinudjem I of Thebes with Psusennes I of Tanis almost two centuries earlier. Harsiese's Horus name, 'Strong Bull, appearing in Thebes', was precisely that of Pinudjem I as full 'king';[399] his prenomen Hedjkheperre Setepenamun combined the main element of that of the *two* dynastic founders Smendes I and Shoshenq I (both, Harsiese's distant ancestors) with the complement common to that of his cousin Osorkon II and to several kings of the previous dynasty (including, again, Pinudjem I).

As 'king', Harsiese probably enjoyed no more real power (pontiff, military chief of Upper Egypt) than before, but his role would foster a sense of independence in the Thebaid. As he was now a 'king', he most likely at this time bestowed the effective high-priesthood of Amun upon his *own* son, . . . *di*/ʿ. . ., name otherwise lost,[400] so still further eroding the non-hereditary principle already broken at his own appointment. The close

high priest son of Shoshenq (II) as high priest, plus also his mother, stepmother, and half-brother; Legrain, *RT* 30 (1908), 160.

396. Cf. the sequence of 4th prophets from Nesy, above, §§ 244, 266.

397. Statue Cairo Cat. 42225 (Legrain, III, *ad loc.*); on Nebneteru's 'outlook', see Kees, *ZÄS* 88 (1962), 24–6, correcting and completing Kees, *ZÄS* 74 (1938), 73–87.

398. If not to be identified with the 3rd prophet and vizier Neser-Amun of time of Shoshenq I/Osorkon I, § 266 above.

399. *G3*, 250, XXIV, from Karnak; used also by Osorkon II in Thebes.

400. Hereinafter NL (name lost). After Year 16 of Osorkon II, no other high priest of Amun is known before Nimlot C.

links between Harsiese and the Nakhtefmut family probably helped Nakht-efmut's son Harsiese C to become not only 4th prophet of Amun, but even 2nd prophet (adjutant to his father-in-law) by the end of Osorkon II's reign.[401] Such personal ties certainly explain the dedication of three or four statues 'by royal favour' (of Harsiese as 'king') to Nakhtefmut by the agency of his daughter Tasheritenmut called Shepenese.[402]

§ 275 (iii) *Dynastic Policy Reaffirmed*
Whether the appointment of Harsiese in Thebes was his own error or his father's, Osorkon II was not prepared to see local power in Thebes, Memphis or anywhere else being indefinitely appropriated by local, hereditary 'sub-dynasties'. By Year 16 (c. 859 B.C.), his third son Nimlot C was well-established in Heracleopolis as high priest of Arsaphes, great chief of Pi-Sekhemkheperre, general and army-leader.[403] Still later, when Harsiese was dead and buried in Western Thebes,[404] Osorkon II replaced the latter's son as high priest of Amun by appointing Nimlot to this post over and above his existing command at Heracleopolis.[405]

Osorkon meantime had gone still further in Memphis itself by appoint-ing his own eldest son, the Crown Prince Shoshenq D, next High Priest of Ptah, thus supplanting the long-established family that had hitherto re-tained that post for nearly two centuries. Shedsunefertem A had had close links with Shoshenq I whom he served in office. He was succeeded in turn by his son Shoshenq C, probably under Osorkon I, and his grand-son Osorkon A who then doubtless saw out the closing years of Osorkon I, lived through Takeloth I's reign, and died under Osorkon II. His son

401. Statue dedicated by him and his sister's children to Nakhtefmut A in the temple of Montu, Karnak, T. 35 (Leclant, *Karnak-Nord IV*, figs. 140–5, pls. 123–7). As Kees noted, Harsiese had probably been brought up at the royal court in Tanis (*Pr.*, 214 and n. 4), and his family were Treasurers (*Pr.*, 212, 213, 215).
402. Statues Cairo Cat. 42206–42209 from Karnak (Legrain, *Statues*, III, 15 ff.), all but one probably dedicated to Nakhtefmut as deceased. Another daughter of Harsiese, name broken and obscure, is known from an Abydos coffin-fragment (*G3*, 349, IX, 350, XI, 2) and the Karnak Priestly Annals, fragment 23, line 1 (Legrain, *RT* 22 (1900), 59).
403. Cairo donation-stela, JdE 45327 (TN 27/1/21/2), last published by E. Iversen, *Two Inscriptions concerning Private Donations to Temples.* 1941.
404.* Tomb and burial in the precinct of Medinet Habu, U. Hölscher, *Excavation of Medinet Habu*, V, 1954, 8–10, pls. 8–10. The condition of Harsiese's trephined and partly-healed skull suggests that he had suffered some severe illness for some while before his death. For the Coptos monument of Harsiese and his son, cf. Part III, §§ 157, 160, above. A cult of Harsiese as 'king' was kept up in Thebes until the 26th Dynasty (cf. *G3*, 349, V, references).
405. For Nimlot as high priest of Amun, cf. above, Part III, §§ 157, 161 f; he is so entitled by his daughter Shebensopdet, and his successor Prince Osorkon, *G3*, 345–6.

Takeloth A never rose beyond the office of Sem-priest, and his descendants in turn remained at yet lower levels of the Memphite hierarchy.[406] No doubt, the appointment of the Crown Prince himself to the high-priesthood of Ptah was represented as a signal royal recognition of the cult of Ptah,[407] but it was in reality simply an assertion of the dynastic principle of the ruling house over that of local inheritance.

§ 276   Osorkon II gave clear expression to his family hopes and ambitions in the inscription on a stela held by a superb statue of himself, erected in the temple of Amun at Tanis.[408] Here, he petitioned Amun,[409] first to gain the favour of the gods of Egypt (ll. 1–6), then for family matters: (7) [You will fashio]n my issue, the seed that comes forth from my limbs, [to be] (8) great [rulers] of Egypt, princes, high priests of Amenresonter, great chiefs of the Mā, [great chiefs of] (9) foreigners, and prophets of Arsaphes. . . . (10) You will turn their hearts towards the Son of Re, Osorkon II, you will cause them [to walk] on (11) my path. You will establish my children in the [posts] (12) [which] I have given them, so that brother is not jealous(?) of brothe[r. As for] (13) [the Great Royal Wife . . .] Karoama, you will cause her to stand before me in all my jubilee festivals. . . . (14) You will cause her children, male and [female], to live.' These lines illustrate clearly Osorkon's concern to have offspring and to establish his sons in the leading positions in Egypt and in harmony with each other. In the closing lines (15–21) of the inscription, he looked for military success against foes – including the Pyudu, ironically Libyans in Libya, not Egyptianized like the Māshwash from whom he himself was descended.

§ 277   (iv) *The Builder King*
Delta. At the capital, Tanis, Osorkon II built what was probably a vast forecourt and gateway, in front of that placed by Siamun before the temple proper which was erected by Psusennes I. In that court, he placed the

---

406. See above, Part III, §§ 151 ff., esp. § 155.

407. In line with venerable precedent, exemplified in the appointment of Prince Tuthmosis by his father Amenophis III (cf. Kees, *Pr.*, 66, 81, 298), and especially of Prince Khamweset by his father Ramesses II (*Pr.*, 67, 93–4, 104, 112, 298; *Nachträge*, 13), whose fame in the Demotic tales of Setne-Khamwas even outlasted the pharaonic period.

408. For the statue, Cairo Cat. 1040 (Borchardt, *Statuen und Statuetten*, IV, 34–6, pl. 161) plus head in Philadelphia University Museum, E.16199 (Bothmer, *JEA* 46 (1960), 3–11, pls. 1–6), see Bothmer, *loc. cit.*, and Helen K. Jacquet-Gordon, *JEA* 46 (1960), 12–23, pls. 7–8.

409. A masculine person is addressed, admitted to be a deity; deposition of the statue in the great Amun-temple at Tanis suggests that Amun is the deity intended. The translation given here closely follows that of Jacquet-Gordon.

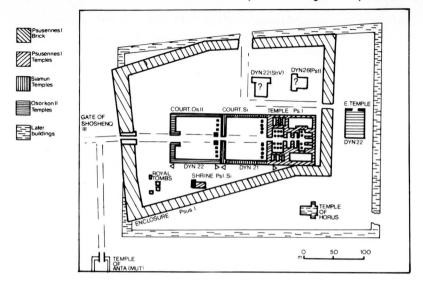

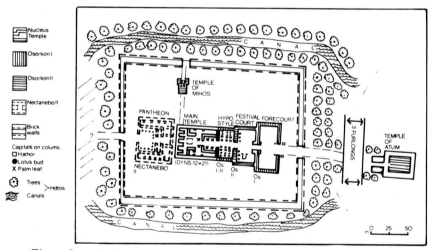

Fig. 3. Imaginative reconstructions of Temple precincts, *Tanis* and *Bubastis*. (a) Tanis; (b) Bubastis.

statue with the inscription just quoted.[410] The scheme of the court and its gateway was probably closely similar to that which he later built at Bubastis.[411] East of the main temple of Amun in Tanis, Osorkon II apparently built a columned edifice, using fine, early columns which had already once been reused by Ramesses II.[412] Within the main precinct, he took over a ruined tomb hard by that of Psusennes I, and made of it a capacious tomb for himself.[413] At the dynastic home town of Bubastis, he completed the works of his grandfather Osorkon I in the new hypostyle hall, and built a small colonnaded temple for the god Mihos to the north of the main temple of Bast.[414] He eventually added to the latter, a festival court and gateway like that at Tanis in commemoration of his jubilee-festival in Year 22 (cf. § 279, below).[415] Throughout, he ruthlessly used up as building-material, old monuments of Ramesses II derived from the temples of both Pi-Ramessē and Bubastis.

At Leontopolis, one of two statues of Sesostris III was reinscribed for Osorkon by the royal official Harmose,[416] perhaps in connection with a chapel or temple whence we have a block naming the king and his officer.[417] Harmose was 'God's Father of Amenresonter, Superintendent of the Seal of the Lord of the Gods of the Two Lands, Deputy of the Mansion of Millions ⟨of Years?⟩ of Osorkon II, Superintendent of Domains (ḥwwt), adorning the temples of the Two Lands, Chief Inspector, and Secretary of the Great House and of the Estate of Queen Karoama.' A donation-stela names the gods of Horbeit or Shedenu.[418] Further south-east at Tell el Maskhuta (Pithom?), Ankhrenpnefer, Deputy of Pharaoh and of the Temple of Atum, erected his statue; a royal statue there may belong to Osorkon II.[419] A block from Memphis suggests minor building-works there.[420]

410. Foundation-deposit found by Montet, cf. Montet, *Osorkon II*, 25–6, fig. 2. For probable extent of Osorkon II's court, cf. *ibid.*, pl. 1, with deposits marked at points 2 and 3 and statue at 4.

411. In agreement with Montet and Lezine, *Osorkon II*, 27–8, fig. 3, right.

412. Cf. Montet, *op. cit.*, 29–33, his *Tanis, douze années* . . ., 1942, 178–85, and *Les énigmes de Tanis*, 1952, 45–6.

413. Cf. Lezine and Montet, *Osorkon II*, 41–7, esp. 46.

414. On which, see L. Habachi, *Tell Basta*, 1957, 46–55, figs. 14–15, and pls. 11–12, 13A.

415. Cf. E. Naville, *Bubastis*, 47–52 *passim*; Naville, *Festival Hall of Osorkon II*, 2–3; and esp. Habachi, *Tell Basta*, 55–70.

416. British Museum 1146; Naville, *Ahnas*, 29–31, pls. 4C, 2–3, 12C.

417. Reused in a later tomb, cf. Gauthier and Edgar, *ASAE* 21 (1921), 23, 26–7; this block preserves clearly the same particular titles of Harmose, although his name is lost.

418. Daressy, *ASAE* 22 (1922), 77; found at Mit-Yaish, south of Leontopolis.

419. References, *PM*, IV, 51, 52.

420. *PM*, III, 219, end; for Apis bull, see below § 286.

§ 278* *Upper Egypt.* Away from the Delta capitals, Osorkon II's activities were confined to Thebes almost exclusively.[421] There, he erected one small chapel in the great Karnak precinct,[422] and left inscriptions in the 'Bubastite room' of Shoshenq I, north of the barque-sanctuary of Amun as built by Tuthmosis III.[423] Only tantalizing fragments of this text survive: (I, 4) 'His Majesty decreed to (I, 5) protect all the temples of Thebes', and (J, 2) '. . . in the majesty of the Palace, to the House of Amenre, Lord of the Thrones of the Two Lands . . .', (J, 4) '. . . hearing . . ., (J, 5) . . . present in the temple of Amun, (J, 6) . . . in the 1st month of Shomu . . ., (J, 7) His Majesty . . . d that the Governor of the South, Pa . . . had made . . . (J, 8) . . . in protecting . . .'. Thus, one may guess (rather than read, here) that we have a record of decrees and actions of Osorkon II in relation to the privileges of the priesthoods and temples of Karnak.

§ 279 (v) *The Jubilee of Osorkon II*
In Year 22, 4th month of Akhet (early summer, *c.* 853 B.C.), Osorkon celebrated a *sed*-festival or royal 'jubilee' for the renewal of his kingship, probably at Bubastis.[424] As in the days of the Empire, high officials were probably sent out to the main cities throughout the length and breadth of Egypt to proclaim the festival.[425] One such was probably the priest of Amun and chief of the guard of the temple of Amun, Bakenkhons, who says on a Karnak statue erected to him by his son:[426] 'The Falcon (= the king) promoted me because of my service(s), and he appointed me to

421. Elsewhere, only vase-fragments from Abydos, *PM*, V, 80, end.
422. For Osiris Wep-Ished, *PM*, II², 203–4, J. Scenes with queen, in Chapel 'e', precinct of Montu, cf. PM, II², 15, *e* (56).
423. Published by Müller, *Egyptological Researches*, II, 1910, 151, figs. 57, 58; other references, cf. *PM*, II², 92 (264).
424. Publication, Naville, *Festival Hall of Osorkon II*, 1892; recent studies, cf. E. P. Uphill, *JNES* 24 (1965), 365–83, and 26 (1967), 61–2 (has useful outlines on festival but erroneous general chronology), also C. J. Bleeker, *Egyptian Festivals*, 1967, 96–123 (is now outdated). In favour of Bubastis as venue is the fact that Osorkon's court and festival gateway were built there (Naville, *Festival Hall*, pl. 6: 8, lines 1–2 – king comes from shrine of Amun into festival hall). But the principal deity involved is Amun, not Bast – however, the image of Amun may have travelled to Bubastis for the occasion, and it is also true that Osorkon's festival ritual was based largely on an original of ultimately Theban origin, *temp.* Amenophis III (see below). The possible 'tomb' in the rites may not prove that the festival was held in Tanis (cf. Uphill, *JNES* 24 (1965), 378, n. 56), as a 'ritual tomb' could have been made and used with other 'stage-props' at Bubastis. After all, New Kingdom pharaohs often celebrated jubilees in Memphis, but never in the Valley of the Kings.
425. Cf. most recently, L. Habachi, *ZÄS* 97 (1971), 64–72, for officials proclaiming the jubilees of Ramesses II and Amenophis III.
426. Cairo Cat. 42213, cf. Legrain, *Statues*, III, 35, *d*, lines 10 ff.; see E. Otto, *Biographische Inschriften, ägyptischen Spätzeit*, 1954, 134, No. 3.

travel into Upper Egypt and proclaim(?) the Jubilee for the House of Eternity.'

From the jubilee-reliefs, the dateline text runs:[427] (1) 'Year 22 (etc.), arising in the [Shri]ne of Amun, whi[ch] is (2) in the Hall of the Jubilee,[428] resting on the portable throne, (under)taking the exemption(?)[429] of the Two Lands by the King(?), (3) exempting the Harim of the House of Amun and exempting all the women of (4) his city who have been servants since the time of the (fore)fathers, (5) they being servants in every estate ("house"), assessed for their dues (6) annually. Lo, His Majesty sought great occasions for benefactions (7) for his father Amenre when he (= Amenre) proclaimed the first jubilee for his son who abides (8) on his throne – may he proclaim many more, in Thebes, Mistress of (9) the Nine Bows! Then said the King in presence of his father Amun, "I have exempted Thebes (10) in her height and her width, pure and given over to her lord. The Inspectors of the King's House shall not interfere (11) with her – her ("their") people are exempted enduringly[430] (in) the great name of the good god!" '

§ **280** This text has been widely interpreted[431] to mean that the Tanite pharaoh was hereby granting tax-exemption to Thebes as the holy city of Amun. However, this very text is nothing more than a *word-for-word* copy of just such a text as also occurs over the king carried in procession for a jubilee of Amenophis III depicted at Soleb temple in far-away Nubia.[432] Therefore, it may indicate *only* that Osorkon II used for his jubilee a basically 18*th Dynasty, Theban recension* of the jubilee-ritual and texts, which was doubtless that observed for Amun of Tanis who – via Amun of Pi-Ramessē – most likely had his rites from New Kingdom, Theban sources. At most, one may concede that Osorkon II, in using this version of the jubilee-rites, *may* have granted an exemption to Thebes – as to the Two Lands – for the period of the year of the festival.[433]

427. Naville, *Festival Hall*, pl. 6: 8–9, and (first part) Naville, *Bubastis*, pl. 42, B; *BAR*, IV, §§ 750–1.

428. *Hwt ḥb-sd* – i.e. a shrine of Amun within the great festival court (second court if at Bubastis; first court if at Tanis).

429. *Ḥwi*, lit. 'protect(ion)', but here and throughout this text best rendered as 'exempt(ion)'.

430. *Ḥr ḥnty.*

431. e.g. by Breasted, *BAR*, IV, § 750; Meyer, *Gottesstaat*, 513; Kees, *Pr.*, 181, and *Hhp.*, 101; Uphill, *JNES* 24 (1965), 374, etc.

432. First noted by Naville, *Festival Hall*, 4; Soleb, cf. LD, III, 86*b*. This point was further discussed by me, *BiOr* 23 (1966), 277 – the detailed correspondence is beyond any doubt. Much better contemporary evidence for Osorkon II's attitude to, and treatment of, Thebes would have been furnished by his Karnak blocks, § 278 above, if better-preserved.

433. Depending on the real value of the phrase *ḥr ḥnty*, as *ḥnty* can be 'forever', 'duration', or else merely a limited 'span' of time.

Perhaps a little more closely related to Osorkon's own deeds are the words over the [portable barque] of Amun in the scene below.[434] (1) 'Arising by the Majesty of this august god [Amenresonter] (2) upon the (processional) way in order to repose in the Hall of Jubi[lee]s (3) which His Majesty made anew for [his fathe]r, [adorning] (4) all its walls with electrum and [its] colonnades [with gold, silver??].' This, at least, was appropriate to Osorkon II's great court and its splendid granite gateway, adorned with the Jubilee reliefs.

§ 281 (vi) *The Royal Family*

Osorkon II's principal consort was the Queen and Royal Daughter Karoama B by whom he had at least two sons – the Crown Prince Shoshenq[435] and young Harnakht[436] – and three daughters, Tasha-kheper, another Karoama, and [Ta?]-iir-mer, who accompany their mother in the jubilee reliefs.[437] A third son, Takeloth by a lesser spouse, is hardly attested during the reign.[438] The fourth known son, Nimlot C, high priest in Heracleopolis, thereafter also in Thebes, was born to Osorkon by the lady Djed-Mut-es-ankh.[439] By the lady Istemkheb G, Osorkon II had a daughter Tjesbastperu A.[440] If she was very much a younger daughter, born in Osorkon's later years, she may possibly even be the princess Tjesbastperu who married Takeloth, son of the Crown Prince Shoshenq, who eventually succeeded his father as high priest in Memphis.[441]

§ 282* The institution of the God's Wife of Amun continued throughout the Libyan epoch, although few incumbents of the period are known before

434. Naville, *Festival Hall*, pl. 6: 10; cf. *BAR*, IV, § 748.

435. References, *G3*, 344, XXXI; Tait, *JEA* 49 (1963), 124; § 286, below.

436. Cf. § 282, end, below. Of doubtful date is Djed-Ptah-ef-ankh son of an Osorkon (*CdE* 41 (1966), 112).

437. Naville, *Festival Hall*, pl. 4; *G3*, 346.

438. Unless Daressy's red wax impression of a text reproduces a text of this prince after his elder brother's death (*G3*, 344, XXX, C, 2). If the damaged name of the mother were Daressy's [Ist]n[kheb], the identification might stand, but if one read [Te]n[tsa], the text would belong to Takeloth III as crown-prince under Osorkon III.

439. Cairo stela, JdE 45327, lines 5–6 (Iversen, *Two Inscriptions concerning Private Donations to Temples*, 1941); her name is spelt Udj-Mut-es-ankh, meaning virtually identical, by Pasenhor.

440. Canopic jars, *G3*, 343, 2, A (B and C are doubtful).

441. Named on the Serapeum stelae of Year 28 of Shoshenq III and Year 2 of Pimay, as wife of Takeloth and mother of his son the high priest and chief of Mā, Pediese – Nos. 21, 22 (IM. 3749, 3697, respectively) in Malinine, Posener, Vercoutter, *Catalogue des Stèles du Sérapéum de Memphis*, I, 19–22 with pls.; called 'princess' (*sȝt-nsw*) on No. 22, p. 22, lines 10–11. A vase-fragment from Heliopolis might belong to the same lady (cf. Petrie, *Heliopolis, Kafr Ammar & Shurafa*, 1915, pl. 8: 9).

its end. However, two such seem to belong to the middle years of this dynasty. The more important was 'the God's Wife, Lady of the Two Lands, Sitamun Mutemhat, Daughter of Re, Lady of Epiphanies, Karomama Merytmut I', also 'Adoratrix of Amun, of pure hands'.[442] In Thebes, a stela makes her contemporary with Harsiese as 'king', hence also with Osorkon II.[443] She continued to officiate in the reign of Takeloth II, as she appears with him in a Karnak chapel in the precinct of Montu.[444] That she was the daughter of a queen (merely termed 'Mistress of the Two Lands'?) seems certain – hence, she will have been a king's daughter – of Osorkon II, or perhaps more likely of Harsiese as 'king'.[445] The other possible Adoratrix is Ta-sha-kheper B. Despite the identity of name with that of Osorkon II's first daughter, she may rather belong to the earlier years of Osorkon III than II.[446]

Very early in life, Osorkon II's youngest son by his chief queen, Harnakht, was appointed titular high priest of Amun, obviously to the royal benefice in Tanis itself;[447] he died while yet a boy of but 8 or 9 years old, and was buried with full pomp by his parents in the rear part of his father's tomb within Tanis.[448]

§ **283**   B. FOREIGN AFFAIRS: BYBLOS, ISRAEL AND
                         ASSYRIA

Of the nonentity Takeloth I, no foreign policy is known; Osorkon II in part continued the earlier policies of this Dynasty, and in part reverted to those of the 21st Dynasty.

442. For the titles, monuments and date of this lady, see H. Jacquet-Gordon, *ZÄS* 94 (1967), 86–93 and pl. V; to her belongs the famous Louvre statuette of 'Karomama'.

443. Berlin Museum 14995 from Luxor (*Aegyptische Inschriften, Berlin*, II, 210).

444. Mariette, *Karnak*, 10; Jacquet-Gordon, *ZÄS* 94 (1967), 91, 92 (Document 3); *PM*, II, 7 (2/e); *PM*, II², 15, Chapel 'e', Room II (57).

445.* Statue of a man Basa, on side-panel (*LD*, III, 256*h*), Berlin Museum 2278 (*Aeg. Inschriften, Berlin*, II, 206); this should be added as Document No. 7 to Jacquet-Gordon's list, and shows that the lady was a royal daughter; *ḥent-tawy* could be her mother's epithet or name.

446. Mentioned as forebear(?) of the author of a graffito, Year 7 of Takeloth III, formerly at the Temple of Khons, Karnak, and described as 'God's Wife of the Pharaoh Osorkon' (i.e. his daughter??); published by Daressy, *RT* 18 (1896), 51, and assigned to an earlier date by *PM*, II², 242–3.

447. Harnakht as a mere child could not possibly have been appointed to the pontificate of Amun in Thebes – essentially a military post involving responsibility for the rule of Upper Egypt from El Hibeh to Thebes and beyond, besides sacerdotal duties – work for an adult. His sole title was that of high priest, without military or other attribute. The priesthoods of Tanis, on the other hand, were probably perquisites for the royal family much as they certainly were in the 21st Dynasty (Excursus D, below).

448. See Montet, *Kêmi* 9 (1942), 22–50, and *Osorkon II*, 43, 59–70, pls. 48–61.

(i) *Byblos*

Following the examples of Shoshenq I and Osorkon I, Osorkon II maintained the friendship and alliance with Byblos in the now customary way, of presenting a statue of himself to that city. Regrettably, no trace of the name of his contemporary as ruler of Byblos survives on the extant remains of this statue.[449]

§ 284* (ii) *Israel*

It is in Palestine that a major change of 22nd Dynasty policy suddenly appears. From the palaces of Omri and Ahab at Samaria come remains of a large alabaster vase bearing traces of the cartouches of Osorkon II, and the notation of capacity, '81 *hin*'.[450] From a position of relative strength, Osorkon II's forebears had sought to subdue their immediate neighbours in Palestine, with success (Shoshenq I) then failure (Osorkon I). But within Egypt, Osorkon II was already much less of an absolute ruler than they – Upper Egypt and the Thebaid had moved towards greater independence from his effective rule, focused on Harsiese and his son while they lasted. Hence, major military adventures abroad were beyond the king's prudence or Egypt's capacity, except for defence, or a 'police-action' like Siamun's brief raid. And far beyond Egypt and Palestine, the lesser kingdoms of Western Asia were now falling prey to a new conqueror: Assyria.

Thus, a *rapprochement* between Egypt and her Palestinian neighbours, to pool resources against common foes both local (as ever, the Philistines?) and upon the northern horizon (Assyria) would well explain the presence of such objects as an alabaster presentation vase[451] (once filled with valuable ointment?) in the palace at Samaria – part of the gifts of an Egyptian embassy to the court of Ahab and Jezebel. The Egypto-Israelite alliance was soon called into effect, and was to last for well over a century.

449. Published by Dunand, *Fouilles de Byblos*, I, 115–16, No. 1741, pl. 43.
450. Published by G. A. Reisner, C. S. Fisher, D. G. Lyon, *Harvard Excavations at Samaria*, 1924, I, pp. 132 (room 741), 243 (fig. a, b, c, bottom rt.), 247 (c, 1, Reg. 4106, S-7-742), 334, fig. 205 (cf. other alabasters, 333, fig. 204); II, pls. 54*b* (locus), 56*g* (fragments).
451. One may compare, e.g., the occurrence of such vases of Akhenaten, Haremhab and Ramesses II in the palace of the kings of Ugarit in the 14th–13th centuries B.C.; cf. C. F. A. Schaeffer, *Syria* 31 (1954), 41; Kitchen, *Suppiluliuma & the Amarna Pharaohs*, 1962, 36–7 (on Haremhab); Schaeffer *et al.*, *Ugaritica III*, 1956, 167, figs. 120–1. For alabasters found in Phoenician contexts in Spain of the kings Osorkon II, Takeloth II and Shoshenq III, cf. Leclant in Ward (ed.), *The Role of the Phoenicians in the Interaction of Mediterranean Civilizations*, 1968, 13 and n. 31, and J. M. Blazquez, *Tartessos y los origenes de la colonización fenicia en Occidente*, 1968, pl., 76B, 77A, 81–3, 85.

§ **285*** (iii) *Assyria*

Under the energetic rulers Assurnasirpal II (*c.* 884–859 B.C.) and Shalmaneser III (*c.* 859–824 B.C.), Assyrian armies began the reduction of the petty kingdoms of Syria and the Levant to vassaldom and then to the rank of mere provinces.[452] In 853 B.C., the rulers of south Syria, Phoenicia and Palestine united to resist the Assyrian invader – military forces were gathered by the kings of Hamath, Damascus, Israel (under Ahab), plus '500 soldiers from By⟨bl⟩os,[453] 1,000 soldiers from Egypt',[454] and contingents from six other petty rulers. In a pitched battle at Qarqar that year, the allies staved-off the Assyrian war-machine, but at the cost of heavy losses.[455] Here, in line with Egypt's long-standing alliance with Byblos and her new alignment with Israel, we see a division of 1,000 troops contributed by Osorkon II to the cause of fending-off a dangerous common foe of the most menacing kind.[456] Henceforth, Egypt stood discreetly behind the states of Syria–Palestine, using them as a shield and diversion against Assyrian penetration of her own territory, sometimes sharing their resistance to Assyria, sometimes temporizing with diplomacy and gifts.

§ **286**   C. END OF THE REIGN

(i) *Burial of Apis*

In Year 23 of Osorkon II (*c.* 852 B.C.), so soon after the excitements of the jubilee at home and international warfare abroad, the Apis bull of Memphis died and was buried under the auspices of the Crown Prince Shoshenq as High Priest of Ptah, the Mayor Huy and others, and doubtless its successor was inaugurated.[457] This is our first glimpse of Apis since Shedsunefertem installed an embalming-table for Shoshenq I.

452. For the Levant during *c.* 1200–600 B.C., in parallel with this present work, cf. Kitchen, *HHAHT*.

453. For the suggested emendation *Gu⟨bal⟩a*, 'Byblos', on the Kurkh monolith, see H. Tadmor, *IEJ* 11 (1961), 144–5, 149–50 (PS, 1). Translation of the text (without this correction), cf. Oppenheim, *ANET*, 278–9.

454. For Musri as 'Egypt' in Assyrian texts from the tenth century B.C. onwards, and not some imaginary realm in either Arabia or Anatolia (or, in this case, the trans-Tigris area of Musur), see Tadmor, *op. cit.*, 145–7.

455. One may note with amusement, that on the monolith Shalmaneser III puts the enemy dead at 14,000, and ups the figure to 25,000 (var. 20,500) in later 'editions' such as the Calah bull texts and the Black Obelisk (*ANET*, 279; 6th year). So his rhetoric must be treated with some reserve. But the lower figure may simply record the initial body of deportees, and the larger number reflect the final count; they would then illustrate accounting, not rhetoric.

456. The text of 'all lands, . . . Upper and Lower Retenu . . . being under the feet' of Osorkon II on a jubilee-relief at Bubastis (Naville, *Festival Hall*, pl. 6) should not hastily be correlated with this occasion, as it is traditional terminology (cf. Soleb).

457. Stela of Year 23, set up by the royal scribe, Amenemope; Malinine, Posener,

(ii) *The Succession*

Soon after Apis, the Crown Prince Shoshenq himself died, before his father, and was buried in a stone tomb close to the temple of Ptah.[458] The shadowy prince Takeloth now took the throne when Osorkon II himself died and was interred in his great tomb at Tanis.[459] Again, an Osorkon was succeeded by a lesser son Takeloth.

§ **287** 2. TAKELOTH II (*c.* 850–825 B.C.)

A. THE INITIAL DECADE

(i) *Accession*

The new pharaoh took as Horus-name that of Harsiese, occasionally used by his own father –'Strong Bull, appearing in Thebes', a name ironically inappropriate in the light of the rising tide of Theban opposition to his family's rule there! His other ceremonial names remain unknown. For prenomen, Takeloth II took that of Shoshenq I, founder of the dynasty,[460] and added the epithet 'Son of Isis' alongside 'Beloved of Amun' to his personal name. All told, an uninspiring *pastiche* of his predecessors' styles.

§ **288** (ii) *Foreign Affairs*

During the period *c.* 850–840 B.C., the Levant states continued both to quarrel among themselves and to unite in fleeting coalitions against the incursions of Shalmaneser III of Assyria, or to pay him tribute when resistance seemed futile or had failed. Egypt may have continued to send her very modest contingents to aid the foes of Assyria; all direct evidence is lacking. In this period, a king of Damascus warring with Israel could be pictured as fearing the impact of either North Syrian ('Hittite') or Egyptian forces which had been called out as allies against him (2 Kings 7: 6).[461]

Vercoutter, *Catalogue des stèles du Sérapéum de Memphis*, I, No. 18, pp. 17–18 and pl.; older literature, see *G3*, 336, n. 3 end, *PM*, III, 207 end (Shoshenq and Huy).

458. Preliminary report, A. Badawi, *ASAE* 54 (1956), 153–77 and 16 pls. A further Memphite statue perhaps of this prince, see H. Jaquet-Gordon, *Brooklyn Museum Annual* 6 (1964–65), 43–9. As this particular prince Shoshenq *never* became either king or co-regent, and never bore any royal titles or cartouche, the occasional habit of calling him Shoshenq II is erroneous and should be finally dropped.

459. Tomb and burial, see Montet, *Osorkon II*; magical text of this king, cf. Jaquet-Gordon, *Brooklyn Museum Annual* 7 (1965–66), 54, 57 f., figs. 3, 4, 7.

460. Hedjkheperre Setepenre, to which Takeloth II occasionally added the epithet 'god, Ruler of Thebes' (*G3*, 354, XV, 10 to 355, XVII).

461. So, Benhadad II of Damascus (*c.* 860–843 B.C.), attacking J(eh)oram of Israel (*c.* 852–841 B.C.), cf. 2 Kings 3: 1 and 6: 24 for the kings involved down to

However, by *c.* 841–838 B.C., the Westlands were in some measure cowed. After his accession in Israel in 841 B.C., Jehu paid tribute – with others – to Shalmaneser III, as shown on the latter's 'Black Obelisk' and thus within *c.* 841–838 B.C. On that same monument, the Great King records also 'the tribute of the land of Muṣri' (Egypt) – twin-humped camels, a hippopotamus, a rhinoceros, an antelope, elephants and two sorts of monkeys, nearly all exotic African fauna.[462] Thus, Takeloth II was content to play along with his neighbours in buying-off further Assyrian irruptions. Thereafter, for a century, Egypt needed to pay no further *Danegeld*.

§ **289** (iii) *Official Works*

Unlike his energetic father, Takeloth II was no builder. At Tanis itself, he probably owed even his tomb (inside that of his father) to his successor's self-interest. From Bubastic come one donation-stela of Year 9 (*c.* 842 B.C.) and two others probably of this reign.[463] At Memphis, the Apis bull installed at the end of his father's reign died soon after Year 10 probably in Year 14 (*c.* 837 B.C.) and had to be buried and replaced – perhaps under the auspices of the little-known high priest Merenptah, who was a successor of Shoshenq D.[464] At Thebes, the titles of Takeloth II occur in the little chapel erected by the God's Wife of Amun, Karomama Merytmut I in Montu's precinct,[465] while the restoration-text in the sixth gateway of the temple of Ptah nearby may as well be of Takeloth III as

and beyond 2 Kings 7: 6; on chronology, see *HHAHT*. The reference to 'kings of Egypt' in the plural alongside 'kings of the Hittites' in 2 Kings 7: 6 may be interpreted in one of at least three ways: either (i) a rhetorical plural, balancing the two elements, Egypt and the Hittites, or (ii) a graphic error for singular, 'king' (cf. LXX), or (iii) a reflection of the *then* recent twin reigns of Osorkon II and Harsiese, or (iv) to the *primus inter pares* status of the pharaoh among the other effective rulers in Egypt (chiefs of Mā, high priests of Amun, etc.), rather as the Assyrians called these *šarru*, 'king'. At 850/840 B.C., the reference is too early to reflect the joint rule of the 22nd/23rd Dynasties.

462. Except for the two-humped camel, perhaps itself an exotic curiosity in Egypt; not everything offered by a country as tribute or gift is necessarily native to it or produced there. Otherwise, cf. also *ANET*, 281, and Tadmor, *IEJ* 11 (1961), 146–8. For Ramesses XI's gifts to an Assyrian king, cf. above, § 210 end.

463. Year 9 stela, Daressy, *RT* 18 (1896), 52–3; the others, one, former Grant collection, Wiedemann, *PSBA* 13 (1890/91), 36, the other, Berlin 8437, cf. Brugsch, *Thesaurus*, 808B. Cf. *G3*, 352, II, 334, IV, 354, XIII.

464. Stela No. 20, of Ptah-djed-ef-ankh, of Year 10+*x* (? 14, with Mariette), Malinine, Posener, Vercoutter, *Catalogue, stèles, Sérapéum*, I, 18–19 and pl., and cf. block of Takeloth II, *ibid.*, No. 19, p. 18 and pl., naming the high priest Merenptah.

465. References, cf. § 282 above.

II.[466] Great works could not be expected later in the reign; lack of works earlier suggests an indolent and unambitious king.

§ **290*** (iv) *Royal Family and Personal Alliances in Thebes*
Initially, the key figure was Nimlot, High Priest of Amun, governor of both Thebes and Heracleopolis (and so, all Upper Egypt), the king's half-brother. While they were but princes, Takeloth had early on married Karoama (Nimlot's daughter), his niece; thus, the two brothers had close ties. When Takeloth II became king, his wife became Queen as Karoama D Merytmut II, and their young son Prince Osorkon became heir to the throne.[467]

So long as Nimlot continued as high priest, he seems to have been accepted by the Thebans, and thus formed a vital link between them and their distant Tanite sovereign. So much so, that Nimlot's daughter Shebensopdet A married a Royal Secretary of the south, Hori vii, son of Neser-Amun viii (a predecessor-in-office), grandson of the long-lived Nebneteru iii (same employ) and great-grandson of the old vizier Neser-Amun A. In turn, Hori and Shebensopdet had a daughter Tairbast who married the future vizier Nakhtefmut C.[468]

It was perhaps during almost a decade of relative peace that Takeloth II established further personal links with the south. Thus, several of his daughters went to Thebes, most as wives of Theban dignitaries. His daughter Shebensopdet B was married-off to Djed-Khons-ef-ankh C, son of the 2nd and 4th prophet Harsiese C,[469] who eventually succeeded the latter as 4th, but not as 2nd, prophet.[470] A second daughter Istweret B was married-off to that same younger Theban (later a vizier) Nakhtefmut C,[471] who (later?) married Nimlot's granddaughter Tairbast, noted just above. It is further possible that Takeloth II married-off two more daughters – Ir-Bast-udja-tjau and Di-Ese-nesyt – to a brother Pakhuru, and a nephew Nesipaqashuty B, of the vizier Pediamonet (son of a vizier Pamiu). Both of these 'in-laws' of the pharaoh also became viziers eventually. However,

466. *Urkunden IV*, 880, 11.
467. See especially the scenes above the texts of the 'Chronicle' of Prince Osorkon at the Bubastite Gate, Karnak (*RIK*, III, pls. 16–17, 20; *G3*, 358). It is possible (even probable) that Shoshenq III and Pedubast I were younger, later sons of Takeloth II, but no evidence is available on this point.
468.* For these relationships, see above, Part III, §§ 177 ff.; documents include the statues Cairo Cat. 42228/29, plus 42226/27, and Berlin 17272.
469. By Istweret A, daughter of 'king' Harsiese, cf. § 273 above.
470. On statue Cairo Cat. 42211 of later date (under Osorkon III–Takeloth III), by Nakhtefmut B, son of Djed-Khons-ef-ankh C.
471. Berlin coffins 20132, 20136; see Part III, § 180 above.

the Takeloth concerned could possibly be III, not II.[472] Finally, a fifth daughter[473] Karoama was consecrated to Amun of Karnak as a Singer of the Abode of Amun, now or later.[474]

So far, so good. Most of the posts of the hierarchy remained in Theban hands. As 3rd prophet of Amun, Padimut B (son-in-law of Iuwelot)[475] perhaps officiated under Takeloth I and Osorkon II. Very little is known of the 3rd prophet Wenennufer called Iryiry except his Theban origin and his date as roughly this epoch as a younger(?) contemporary of Takeloth II.[476] The post of 4th prophet continued regularly in the one family, from Harsiese C to his son Djed-Khons-ef-ankh C.[477]

But into this picture, Takeloth II eventually thrust an alien element, appointing his *own* younger son,[478] Djed-Ptah-ef-ankh D, to the post of 2nd prophet, succeeding Harsiese C. This was probably not welcomed by the possessive and independent Thebans.

In Heracleopolis, Nimlot's son Ptah-udj-ankhef[479] probably deputed for his father while the latter was high priest in Thebes and effective governor of Upper Egypt, and perhaps was allowed to succeed him directly in Heracleopolis.

§ 291*   B. YEARS OF CATACLYSM

(i) *The Advent of Prince Osorkon*
How long Nimlot remained at the helm in Upper Egypt is not exactly known – probably for almost the entire first decade of his brother's reign.

472. For attribution of this family to Takeloth II's time, cf. (e.g.) Kees, *Pr.*, 229 (cf. 204), and *Nachträge*, 22, to *Pr.*, 229–30; H. De Meulenaere, *CdÉ* 33/66 (1958), 195–6.
473. Or third, if the 'third' and 'fourth' were really those of Takeloth III, of course.
474. Stela granting her 35 *arourae* of land, Year 25 of Takeloth (II) in the time of Prince Osorkon as high priest (*ASAE* 4 (1903), 183, 185–6). On the ḥst nt ḥnw n 'Imn as a class of virgins dedicated to Amun and under the God's Wife of Amun, see provisionally J. Yoyotte, *CRAIBL: 1961* (1962), 43–52.
475. Statute erected by his son, Cairo Cat. 42215; cf. Part III above, § 184.
476. Descended from him by a Besenmut and an Ankhefenkhons (cf. coffins Cairo Cat. 41001/02/44, etc., in Moret, *Sarcophages de l'époque bubastite à l'époque saïte*, 1912–13), his grandson Neser-Amun married the lady Nesikhons, a great-great-granddaughter of Takeloth II via the Nakhtefmut family of 4th prophets of Amun, cf. Cairo coffins, 41001 (lid), 41003/04/48 (in Moret); cf. Part III, above, §§ 190 f.
477. See Part III, §§ 183 ff., above.
478. For imperfect but plausible evidence for the date of this man, see H. De Meulenaere, *CdÉ* 41/81 (1966), 112, and esp. B. Peterson, *ZÄS* 94 (1967), 128–9; the Stockholm slab definitely dates to Takeloth II, but its attribution to [Djed-Ptah]-ef-ankh depends directly on the correctness of this restoration.
479. Form of name given by Pasenhor; perhaps really a Djed-Ptah-ef-ankh?

Certainly by Year 11 (perhaps slightly earlier), his successor was in office. When Nimlot died, there were several theoretical candidates for the pontificate in Thebes. Nimlot himself left at least two sons: Ptah-udj-ankhef, probably the elder, and a Takeloth who was probably a mere youth.[480] More to the point in Theban eyes was a pretender called Harsiese (B) – a young man very probably the grandson of that Harsiese who had been both pontiff and 'king' not long before Nimlot was high priest. Finally, on Tanite dynastic principle, a son of the reigning king might be appointed.

This, Takeloth II did. He appointed the Crown Prince Osorkon, an energetic, probably impatient, perhaps precocious, young man in his 20s,[481] to be high priest of Amun, general of the whole land, army-leader, and Governor of the South. He probably now confirmed Ptah-udj-ankhef in the rule of Heracleopolis, marrying-off to him yet another princess, Tentsepeh D,[482] to reinforce his allegiance to Tanis. The youth Takeloth could be disregarded for the moment, but Harsiese B, of the same age-group as Prince Osorkon, had claims that were passed-over brusquely and completely. Even the role of 2nd prophet was denied him, it being assigned to Prince Djed-Ptah-ef-ankh D. The embittered Harsiese now became the focus of resurgent Theban discontent.

§ 292* (ii) *The Storm Breaks*

In Year 11 (*c.* 840 B.C.), from his headquarters at El Hibeh, Prince Osorkon sailed south for Thebes, perhaps to ensure his acceptance there as high priest, foreseeing some 'enemy who will take hold of the office of high priest of Amun'.[483] The god Arsaphes of Heracleopolis encouraged Osorkon to go forth 'that he might suppress wrong-doing'.[484] At Hermopolis and beyond, Osorkon promoted works of restoration, and 'suppressed were his opponents within the interior of the land, which had fallen into

480. Eventually, this Takeloth seems to have succeeded to the high-priesthood (cf. § 299, below), but I do not believe (with Kees, *MIO* 2 (1954), 360–1) that he directly succeeded his father Nimlot, to be supplanted by Prince Osorkon. It seems simpler to consider him a much younger son of Nimlot who, when grown up, followed Harsiese (B) as 'counter-pope' to the ageing Prince Osorkon.

481. He appears certainly from Years 11 to 25 of Takeloth II and up to Years 29 and 39 of Shoshenq III – a total of about 54 years. Hence, by Year 39 of Shoshenq III, he would be in his 70's or approaching a lively 80; cf. already, Caminos, *CPO*, 174.

482. Data, Pasenhor stela. Unlike Kees, *MIO* 2 (1954), 360, I do not believe that Prince Osorkon got his brother Bakenptah installed in Heracleopolis this early, to last there till Year 39 of Shoshenq III; again, it seems better to make Bakenptah a much younger brother of Osorkon, perhaps in his 40's by Year 39 of Shoshenq III, and appointed much nearer that date.

483. Chronicle text, Year 11, line 20 (*RIK*, III, pls. 16/17: 20; *CPO*, §§ 32, 242; Kees, *MIO* 2 (1954), 354, 357, n. 2).

484. The same, line 23.

turmoil in his time' (l. 24). Having beaten-down opposition *en route*, Osorkon landed at Thebes and presented handsome offerings to Amun. The priests denounced 'irregularities' in administration and cult, asking Osorkon to act. The guilty were arraigned, executed, and their corpses burnt.[485] Having outwardly crushed opposition by main force, Osorkon made new appointments and issued no less than six decrees to confirm the administration and revenues of the main temples of the Theban gods. Four months later, at a festival on 1st Shomu Day 11, a priest Hori successfully petitioned Prince Osorkon to obtain his father's place in temple services, when the prince was again in Thebes.[486] Year 12 saw Osorkon making his thrice-yearly visits to Thebes from El Hibeh for the great festivals, bringing rich oblations, in a situation of outward but deceptive calm.[487]

§ **293**   (iii) *The Cataclysm*

Then suddenly in Year 15, *c.* 836 B.C., without any omens or warning signals of disaster,[488] Egypt erupted into civil war – 'a ⌈great⌉ convulsion broke out in this land . . . the children of rebellion, they stirred up strife in (both) South and North . . .'. For his part, Osorkon 'did not weary of fighting in their midst like Horus following his father'. The Egyptian kingdom was shaken to its foundations – 'years passed by, when one could not repel the depredations of one's fellow',[488] as Osorkon put it.

The conflict probably dragged on for nearly a decade, towards the 24th year of Takeloth II. Then, at last, feelers of peace went forth; even Prince Osorkon admitted to his fellows, 'I am worn and afflicted', and at last

485. Destruction of the body was inimical to a proper immortality, cf. the burning of Webaoner's adulterous wife in Papyrus Westcar.

486. Block with graffito of Year 11, from Akh-menu temple, Karnak (now Louvre E. 3336), Daressy, *RT* 35 (1913), 130; cf. S. Schott, *Altägyptische Festdaten*, 1950, 105, No. 144. Also, Karnak Priestly Annals, fragments 26+27 for 1st Shomu, 25 (Legrain, *RT* 22 (1900), 60).

487. Second Chronicle inscription, line 6 (*RIK*, III, pl. 20: 6; *CPO*, §§ 128, 260 end).

488. The disaster came 'even though the sky did not swallow the moon'; so great an upheaval demanded a suitable omen, such as a lunar eclipse, to give warning to the wise – but none was vouchsafed. The plain meaning of this text, with *n sḏm.f* (Perfective, past), is that no eclipse occurred. The rendering of Albright (*BASOR* 130 (1953), 4–5) as 'the sky not having swallowed the moon (completely)' reads into the text what is *not* there, is totally devoid of foundation, and must resolutely be dismissed. As pointed out by Parker (*ibid.*, 5, n. 7a) and Caminos (*CPO*, pp. 88–9) with others, an eclipse interpretation of this passage would require a (*n*) *sḏmt.f*, a form which was still current in the New Kingdom and Late Period (cf. for forms, Erman, *Neuägyptische Grammatik*², 1933, §§ 442–5). This passage, therefore, cannot be used for establishing an absolute chronology.

489. These citations, from line 7 of second Chronicle text.

decided on a policy of conciliation, repression having so obviously failed. Loaded with gifts for Amun, a vast fleet thus set sail for the south und' Osorkon. After a tumultuous welcome, he made rich offerings to Amun a virtually reproached him over the long conflict, receiving an oracular answer.[490] In his 'Chronicle', he listed his gifts to Amun for Year 24, and those appointed 'for every year'.[491] Again, peace seemed assured, as in Year 11.

§ 294   C. THE SUCCESSION

(i) *The Eclipse of Prince Osorkon*
From that brief calm, a stela of Year 25 (*c.* 826 B.C.) dated by Takeloth II and the high priest Osorkon records a land-grant for the latter's sister, the priestess Karoama,[492] and a bandage-epigraph probably dates to Year 26.[493] But then, again, Thebes and the southland erupted into opposition ('those who rebelled against him'), and again all was lost for Osorkon. Seemingly lacking support from 'the grandees within this land', his 'Chronicle' says of Osorkon, '. . . he was there quite alone, such that there was not one friend [with him(?)]'.[494] So, the Theban opposition triumphed, and Osorkon lost both the pontificate in Thebes and most probably the rule of the south entirely.

(ii) *The Succession*
Amid this trouble came the final blow. Takeloth II died at Tanis, almost certainly in the absence of the harrassed Prince Osorkon. For, the next pharaoh was not Osorkon but a Shoshenq (III), under whom Osorkon was later to serve once more – even though Osorkon was Crown Prince with every expectation of succeeding his father.[495] What happened? The facts remain unknown, except that the well-equipped mummy of Takeloth II was buried in a second-hand sarcophagus of Middle-Kingdom date in an anteroom of the tomb of his own father Osorkon II at Tanis.[496] But a

490. Text, lines B, 7, to C, 1.
491. Text C, 7–11.
492. Cf. § 290, above, for references.
493. Bandages published by Capart, *BMRAH*³ 13 (1941), 26 ff. (who dated them to the 21st Dynasty).
494. Text, C, 2, for these citations.
495. In what Caminos justly calls 'a reference . . . unparalleled', Osorkon actually looked forward to pleasing Amun for the benefit of Takeloth II '*until I am upon his throne*' (Text, B, 53; *CPO*, §§ 101, 102, note *c*, p. 71; §§ 257, 289), was called '(royal) youth' (*CPO*, § 117, *d*, p. 80), and 'one whom his lord taught, that he might become the Horus strong-armed for the whole populace' (Text, B, 5; *CPO*, §§ 114, 260, 289).
496. See Montet, *Osorkon II*, 42 (Tomb I, room 3), 77 (with pls. 37–8, cartouches

probable hypothesis can be offered. Shoshenq may be presumed to have been a much younger brother of Osorkon,[497] and had been in Tanis when Takeloth II died and Prince Osorkon was far away. This ambitious princeling saw his chance, conducted his father's burial adequately, but in minimum time, and so (like Horus burying Osiris) became the next legitimate king in accord with ancient precedent.[498] All was *fait accompli* by the time Prince Osorkon ever reached Tanis from his *débacle* in the south.

add_d to N. and E. walls), 81–5 (cartouches merely painted in a Middle Kingdom sarcophagus, quickly inserted via roof of room).

497. In view of the fact that, once enthroned, Shoshenq III reigned for 52 years (cf. Part II, above).

498. One may note the representation of Ay *as king* performing the rites on the mummy of Tutankhamun in the latter's tomb (e.g. E. Otto and M. Hirmer, *Osiris und Amun*, pl. IV); the succession of property 'by the law of Pharaoh' to him who conducts the burial, as at Deir el Medineh (cf. Papyrus Bulaq 10; e.g. as cited by W. Helck, *Materialen zur Wirtschaftsgeschichte des Neuen Reiches*, III, 1963, 346–7); and the reports of Amasis II burying Apries whom he had supplanted (stela, Daressy, *RT* 22 (1900), 1–9; Herodotus, ii, 169). On the general principle, cf. H. W. Fairman in S. H. Hooke (ed.), *Myth, Ritual and Kingship*, 1958, 99–100, 104.

CHAPTER 20

The Twenty-second and Twenty-third Dynasties: III, The Libyan Decline (Shoshenq III and Early Twenty-third Dynasty)

§ 295 1. SHOSHENQ III (*c.* 825–773 B.C.) AND DIVISION OF THE KINGSHIP

A. BEGINNINGS

(i) *Accession*

Shoshenq III adopted the prenomen of Ramesses II – Usimare Setepenre (but with variant, Setepenamun); to his name, besides 'Beloved of Amun', he added the sobriquets 'Son of Bast' and 'god, Ruler of Heliopolis', the latter being of New Kingdom stamp. In Horus-names, he showed a truly Ramesside love of variety. On the walls of his tomb at Tanis, he flaunts the unusual formulation 'Strong Bull, Offspring of Re',[499] but on other monuments the more usual 'Strong Bull, beloved of Re', once with added epithets 'whom [Re?] caused to appear [as King, etc. . . .?]'– quite in the regular style of his own forebears.[500] Finally, a small donation stela has 'Strong Bull, beloved of Maʿat' (Truth), the Horus-name most favoured by Ramesses II.[501] Neither Nebty nor Golden Horus names have yet been recovered.[502] Whatever his pretensions, Shoshenq III certainly rivalled

---

499. *Kȝ-nḫt mswt(y) (n) Rʿ*, e.g. Montet, *Chéchanq III*, pls. 29, 30.
500. *G3*, 366, XXII, XXIII.
501. *G3*, 364, XV, of Year 30; Spiegelberg, *RT* 25 (1903), 197 and plate.
502. A possible trace of Nebty-name, . . . *p* . . ., Montet, *Chéchanq III*, pl. 29, lower right.

Ramesses II in no respect other than mere length of reign (52 years to Ramesses' 66 years), the longest since Ramesses II until Psammetichus I.

§ 296 * (ii) *First Years*

With the political eclipse of Prince Osorkon, Shoshenq III apparently accepted the preferences of the Thebans for a pontiff and southern governor of their own choosing, and in turn was initially recognized by the Thebans as their legitimate king. Thus the vizier Nesipaqashuty A placed on his statue in Karnak the cartouche of Shoshenq III and the name and title of Harsiese B as high priest,[503] while a 'Nile level' text on the Karnak quay is dated to Year 6 of Shoshenq III, naming again Harsiese as pontiff.[504] Several fragments of the Karnak Priestly Annals reflect new priestly appointments, etc., under Shoshenq III,[505] including an Amenemonet or his son,[506] and a Mentuhotep, perhaps the son of the 3rd prophet of Amun, Pediamen-neb-nesttawy A, and grandson-in-law of the late Takeloth II, as well as Harkhebi.[507] From the Delta, a donation-stela of Year 3 attests Shoshenq's rule;[508] outwardly, Egypt had hardly seemed so united for decades.

§ 297   B. DIVISION OF THE KINGSHIP

By the 8th year (*c.* 818 B.C.) however, some kind of crisis over the kingship had arisen in Tanis itself. From that year on, as a later document indicates,[509] Shoshenq III now had to share the throne with a king Pedubast

503. Cairo Cat. 42232 (Legrain, *Statues*, III, 78–80, pls. 40, 41); Karnak Priestly Annals, fragment 5 (*RT* 22 (1900), 54), top line probably was for an induction under Osorkon II, while lines 2–3 (vertical) mention the appointment of someone as southern vizier under Shoshenq III – a successor to Nesipaqashuty A?
504. No. 23; Legrain, *ZÄS* 34 (1896), 114; von Beckerath, *JARCE* 5 (1966), 46, 48, 51.
505. Including fragments Nos. 11 (a Pediamun), 19 (mention of a Patjenef); Legrain, *RT* 22 (1900), 52, 58. And Fitzwilliam Museum, Cambridge, No. 391 (Daressy, *RT* 35 (1913), 131–2).
506. Fragment No. 32 (cf. No. 9), Legrain, *RT* 22 (1900), 61 (and 56); possibly compare the Amenemonet son of Harkhebi, who dedicated the two statues Cairo Cat. 42230–31, and who probably lived under Takeloth II and early Shoshenq III, cf. above, Part III, §§ 173 f.
507. Karnak Priestly Annals, fragment 44 (Legrain, *op. cit.*, 63), lines 1, 3; note also a Nebneteru, [. . .] of the S. Region (?), in line 4, perhaps the same man as on Berlin 17272 (Part III, § 177, above) who became 3rd prophet of Amun, perhaps after Pediamen-neb-nesttawy A. For the latter's son Mentuhotep, cf. the Amherst fragment, Sharpe, *Egyptian Inscriptions*, I, pl. 35; Kees, *Pr., Nachträge*, 20–21, after De Meulenaere.
508. Chicago, Oriental Institute collection, 10511, unpublished; cf. *YMM*, 144, n. 7.
509. Nile-level text No. 24 (Legrain, *ZÄS* 34 (1896), 114; von Beckerath, *JARCE* 5 (1966), 46–7, 48, 51).

(I) who is known to subsequent history as the founder of the 23rd Dynasty. In the first instance, this perhaps appears as little more than a nominal joint rule of a kind seen already under the reigning Dynasty and its predecessor – like Pinudjem I with Psusennes I, or Harsiese with Osorkon II.[510]

However, three fundamental differences were to distinguish the rule of Pedubast I from those of his shadow-precursors. First and foremost, unlike any of them, he counted *his own regnal years*[511] – he was, therefore, not a mere 'courtesy'-king, but at least a full co-pharaoh or co-regent with Shoshenq III. Secondly, he (or his successors) adopted *a separate Delta capital or residence* from which their rule was recognized throughout Egypt – Leontopolis (Tell Moqdam) – outside, but neighbouring on, the ancestral 22nd Dynasty territory of Bubastis with Tanis.[512] Hence, the new (23rd) Dynasty was indeed Tanite by origin (as Manetho notes),[513] but posed and lived as a separate line of kings with Leontopolis as capital. Thirdly, in the 15th year of his reign, Pedubast appointed a co-regent of his own, Iuput I, and acted thus as a wholly independent pharaoh (without reference to Shoshenq III), being senior partner in a co-regency of his own instituting.[514]

Thus, with the accession of Pedubast I, there came a real division of the kingship between two contemporary and independent pharaohs reigning side-by-side in Tanis and Leontopolis respectively, and in principle both recognized officially throughout Egypt. The pharaonic kingship was brought to this sorry pass by the precedents of earlier nominal co-rulers (especially Harsiese), the civil wars under Takeloth II (which undermined Tanite authority), and the sharp practice of Shoshenq III himself in seizing the throne by supplanting the known heir. Why Shoshenq III had in the sequel to concede equality to Pedubast, we do not know. Perhaps he, too, as a third son of that king, had shared significantly in the prompt formal interment of Takeloth II, and came to consider himself as having an equal claim to the crown that Shoshenq could not effectively deny. A precedent was now set for other aspirants.

510. Not to mention Herihor's very localized 'kingship' during the 'Renaissance Era' under Ramesses XI.
511. Years 5, 6, 7, 8, 16, 18, 19, 23, 25, are known for Pedubast I; cf. below.
512. On this question of location, cf. above, Part II, § 102.
513. A datum rightly stressed by Schulman, *JARCE* 5 (1966), 88, n. 13, but he mistakenly confuses Manethonic place of *origin* of the Dynasty (offspring of Dyn. 22 in Tanis) with its seat of rule, *not* given by Manetho.
514. Nile-level text No. 26 (Legrain, *ZÄS* 34. 114; von Beckerath, *JARCE* 5, 47, 48, 52).

§ **298**   2. SHOSHENQ III'S CONTEMPORARIES:
PEDUBAST I, IUPUT I, SHOSHENQ IV[515]

A. PEDUBAST I (*c.* 818–793 B.C.)

The counter-king was perniciously unoriginal in his style of titulary[516] –
prenomen, Usimare Setepenamun, and nomen accompanied by 'Beloved
of Amun' and usually 'Son of Bast'[517]– and merely copied Osorkon II
and Shoshenq III. In his banality, Pedubast was (regrettably) to be followed by almost his entire dynasty.[518]

(i) *Thebes*

The authority of Pedubast was promptly recognized throughout Egypt
and nowhere more keenly than in Thebes which was glad of the opportunity to discard all further allegiance to the Tanite kings by ostentatiously
supporting their colleagues instead. In Nile level No. 24, Shoshenq III is
not even named – just 'Year 12' by itself, followed by the equivalent of
Year 5[519] of Pedubast I (named) and the name of the high priest Harsiese B.
Thereafter, in the known inscriptions of the Thebans, the name and datelines of Shoshenq III (and his lineal successors) *never appear again* – with
the solitary exception of documents of Prince Osorkon, the king's brother.
Elsewhere in the south, lesser people were less antipathetic towards the
senior king,[520] but the independent Theban notables dated by the 23rd
Dynasty until new powers crossed their horizon. By way of contrast to
their outright opposition to Prince Osorkon, they did not object to representatives of the new dynasty being installed in Thebes. Thus, the Karnak
Priestly Annals[521] record for Year 7 of Pedubast [Year 14 of Shoshenq
III],[522] the day of induction (1st Shomu, ⟨1⟩) of 'his son, the God's Father

515. For correlations of reigns of the 22nd, 23rd Dynasties and high priests of
Amun, cf. Part VI, Table 6, below.
516. So far as preserved; Horus, Nebty and Golden Horus names are lacking.
517. So (e.g.) in Nile-level texts Nos. 26–9; 'Son of Isis' just once in No. 24.
518. The prenomen Usimare Setepenamun was thus used by Iuput I, Osorkon
III, Takeloth III and Rudamun; Shoshenq IV was forced to use the epithet
Meryamun, as Shoshenq III had pre-empted Setepenamun, while that of Iuput II
remains unknown.
519. So read by von Beckerath, *JARCE* 5 (1966), 51 and 48: 26, n.*a*, and not
Year 6 as Legrain had done.
520. As is probably shown by Papyrus Brooklyn 16.205, recording oracles over
disputes about fields at Hefat, some 22 miles south of Thebes, with dates of Year 49
and Year 4 – hardly other than of Shoshenq III and Pimay; cf. R. A. Parker, *Saite
Oracle Papyrus*, 1962, 49–52.
521. Fragment No. 1, line 1, Legrain, *RT* 22 (1900), 51.
522. i.e. *c.* 812 B.C.; hereafter, I generally add in brackets corresponding year-
date of the other ruling line, for ready comparison; cf. also, Part VI, Table 6.

Pediamonet, justified, into the places of Mut and Khons [. . .]'– i.e. of a
lesser son of the new king into priestly service for Amun's fellow-deities in
Thebes. In 'Year 8 of this King', 'favours [were repeated]', on the day of
induction of another Pediamonet of long lineage into the ranks of the
bearers of Amun's processional images, and this Pediamonet's 'inaugural
speech' is partly preserved.[523] Also in Year 8[524] (1st Shomu, 19) fell the
induction-day of the much-betitled vizier Pentyef-ankh, son of a former
vizier Hori;[525] a great shrine for Amun was made by the high priest Harsiese B, also entitled Governor of the South. The events of Year 14
[Shoshenq III, Year 21; 805 B.C.] are lost.[526]

§ **299**   Thereafter, the Thebaid witnessed both tension and compromise.
In Year 15, *c.* 804 B.C. [Shoshenq III, Year 22], Pedubast I appointed as
co-regent a king Iuput I who was perhaps a son.[527] That very same year,
Prince Osorkon reappeared in Thebes as high priest after 20 years'
absence. Overtures between Thebes and Tanis permitted the restless
Osorkon to resume his ministrations in the south, sealed by presentation of
rich oblations to Theban and other southern deities[528]– notes and lists for
Years 22, 24, 25, 28, 29 of Shoshenq III and so named [Pedubast I,
Years 15, 17, 18, 21, 22] survive in his 'Chronicle' texts.[529] During Years
22–25 [Years 15–18 of Pedubast], correspondingly little is heard of Osor-
kon's rival, Harsiese – then, suddenly, he recurs for 2 years, Years 18–19 of
Pedubast [Years 25, 26, Shoshenq III], hard on the heels of Osorkon.[530]
By Year 29 of Shoshenq III [Year 22 of Pedubast], when Prince Osorkon

523. Fragment No. 1, lines 2 ff., Legrain, *op. cit.*, 51–2.
524. Fragment No. 2, Legrain, *op. cit.*, 52–3, plus corrigendum, *RT* 26 (1904), 88.
525. Just conceivably the vizier Hor[y] of Papyrus Berlin 3048, verso 5 (G. Moller,
Zwei ägyptische Eheverträge aus vorsaïtischer Zeit, 1918, 4, 6 n. *f*), in marriage-
contract records dated to Year 14 of a 'Pharaoh Takeloth, Son of Isis, Beloved of
Amun', if the king concerned were Takeloth II. But, as Mr. M. L. Bierbrier points
out to me, this document could possibly date to Takeloth I, if the Harsiese son of
Merkhons son of O-ef-en-Mut (lines 16 ff.) be compared with Quibell, *The
Ramesseum*, 1898, pl. 21: 9, the stela of a daughter of Harsiese son of Merkhons,
from among burials largely dated to Osorkon I (cf. Quibell, pp. 11, 17), although
some of later date (*temp.* Osorkon II, Takeloth II) are attested. E. Lüddeckens,
Ägyptische Eheverträge, 1960, 184, n. 3, also favours Takeloth I.
526. Annals, fragment 5, line 4 (2nd horizontal line), the Year 14, 1st Shomu, ⟨1⟩,
of Usimare Setepenamun is more probably Pedubast I than Shoshenq III (called . . .
Setepenre in an earlier line).
527. Nile-level text No. 26, 'Year 16 of Pedubast which is Year 2 of Iuput'.
528. *RIK*, III, pl. 22; *CPO*, §§ 177, 271, text C, 2–7.
529. *RIK*, III, pl. 22; *CPO*, §§ 188/273 end, 211/275, 222/276, 234/278.
530. Nile-level texts Nos. 28 and 27 respectively, mentioning Harsiese; for
reading of dates, cf. von Beckerath, *JARCE* 5 (1966), 47, 48, 52. For a Year 18
possibly also of Pedubast, cf. Fitzwilliam Museum fragment No. 392, published by
Daressy, *RT* 35 (1913), 132.

made his last appearance in Thebes for a further decade,[531] Harsiese B was perhaps already dead and gone. For, in Year 23 of Pedubast, *c.* 796 B.C. [Shoshenq III, Year 30], a new man – Takeloth – appears as high priest in Thebes.[532] The newcomer may have been the youngest son of Nimlot C, uncle and predecessor-in-office of Prince Osorkon, and have been in his 50s when he claimed his father's office. If so, he was author of a small chapel in the precinct of Amun at Karnak.[533] He served for at least another 15 years, and replaced Harsiese B in opposition to Prince Osorkon.

But, most probably during Osorkon's second spell of intermittent activity in Thebes in Years 22–29 of Shoshenq III, the latter's rule was represented by his own son, [the General]issimo and Army-leader, Pashedbast (B), king's Son of Shoshenq (III)', who built a vestibule door to Pylon X at Karnak, and in one and the same commemorative text there-on named his father as Shoshenq (III) but dated his record by his father's colleague, Pedubast I.[534]

§ **300** (ii) *Middle Egypt*
As in Thebes, so at Heracleopolis, the rival claims to local power showed themselves. Nimlot's son and successor, Ptah-udj-ankhef, probably died by about the accession of Shoshenq III. His son, Hem-Ptah A, probably did *not* immediately succeed him – instead, two adherents of Pedubast I appeared in Heracleopolis and Pi-Sekhemkheperre, respectively. A crudely-carved donation-stela of Year 6 of Pedubast [Year 13, Shoshenq III] was dedicated at Memphis by Ewelhon A, [Great Chief(?) of Pi-]Sekhemkhe-perre, Commander of *Tuhir*-troops, Army-leader, and Prophet of Amun Lord of Per-Khenu,[535] while a rather better-quality stela[536] was dedicated (probably also at Memphis) by his superior, the '[Count and Chief of Heracleopol]is,[537] High Priest of Arsaphes, Lord of Heracleopolis, *Mek-*

531. Besides the Chronicle, he occurs in Nile-level text No. 22, duly dated to Shoshenq III, Year 29 (von Beckerath, 51); No. 14 hardly seems likely to date to the same year (despite von Beckerath, 45), but may rather belong to Osorkon III.
532. Nile-level text, No. 29 (Legrain, *ZÄS* 34 (1896), 115; von Beckerath, 52). Perhaps also cf. a Year 23 (Pedubast I??) in Karnak Priestly Annals, fragment 5 (horizontal lines), followed by a Year 11 (Iuput I??).
533. On which, cf. Kees, *Hhp.*, 113 and n. 1, references; *PM*, II², 203–4.
534. The date itself is lost with the tops of the lines; Legrain, *ASAE* 14 (1914), 14, 39. This text of itself suffices to illustrate the official and outwardly 'peacefully-agreed' nature of the condominium by the 22nd and 23rd Dynasties.
535. Cairo JdE 45530, published by Schulman, *JARCE* 5 (1966), 33–41, pl. 13: 2.
536. Copenhagen, Glyptotek Ny Carlsberg, Inv. 917, cf. Erichsen, *Bibliotheca Aegyptiaca*, VI, 1936, pl. 5.
537. Probably restore something like [*ḥȝty-ꜥ, imy-r ḥmw-nṯr Nni-nsw*]; of the last word, slight traces are visible, of seated child, a horizontal line, *t*-sign, and city

chief of Kahtan, Pimai', also in the reign of Pedubast (date lost). Probably these men held office during the 20s of Shoshenq III's reign, as long as Pedubast I held sway;[538] thereafter, Hem-Ptah A, grandson of Nimlot C, was perhaps granted the latter's (and his father's) old post until the late 30s of Shoshenq III.

Then in turn, by Year 39 (*c.* 787 B.C.), the redoubtable if aged Prince Osorkon had succeeded in getting a younger brother of his own, Bakenptah, appointed as General of Heracleopolis and Army-leader. In that year, Prince Osorkon in his old posts 'was within Thebes, celebrating the festival of Amun, in one accord with his brother, the General (etc.) Bakenptah, all [. . .] resting/at peace in [. . .]. Then they overthrew everyone who fought against them. On this day, induction of the vizier (etc.), Har[sies]e (E), [son of *x*[539] and Ta-]hent-Ese, into the great, noble, festal shrine of Amun (etc.). He said . . .' (inaugural address).[540] By then, still incurably forceful, Osorkon must have been approximately 80 years old, and even his younger brother Bakenptah have been in his 40s or 50s at least. Henceforth, nothing more is heard of either again.[541] At Heracleopolis, in the 40s of Shoshenq III's reign, one may assume that Bakenptah was succeeded by Pasenhor A, who was the son of Hem-Ptah A and great-grandson of Nimlot C.[542] So, in Middle Egypt also, the key post of Heracleopolis passed back and forth between representatives of both Dynasties, among three families (Pimai; Bakenptah, son of Takeloth II; Hem-Ptah A and Pasenhor A, descendants of Nimlot C and Osorkon II).

§ 301   (iii) *Memphis*

In Memphis proper, the High Priests of Ptah were close cousins of the 22nd Dynasty, and dated by its kings to the very end, in stark contrast to Thebes. In Year 28 of Shoshenq III (*c.* 798 B.C.), one Apis bull died and another was installed. Previously, following on Merenptah, Takeloth B

sign. One may remark the mention of 'the House of Eternity of King Shoshenq in the district of Ta-ʿat-Tjilu', perhaps near Tanis; cf. Schulman, *op. cit.*, 38.

538. For a further stela-fragment naming Pedubast I, actually found at Heracleopolis, cf. Daressy, *ASAE* 21 (1921), 140, § 3.

539. Just possibly the same as the vizier Harsiese son of a vizier Harkhebi, of the statue MMA. 35. 9. 1? On which statue, see L. Bull, *BMMA* 30 (1935), 142–4 and fig. 3.

540. Karnak Priestly Annals, fragment No. 7 (Legrain, *RT* 22 (1900), 55–6). In line 1, the month-number is missing; at line-end, restore [*sȝ-nsw nb-tȝwy*]. In lines 2–3, after *m* and one lost group, I suggest restoring [*wn.in*].*sn ḥr sḫr* . . .

541. For a stela-fragment of Bakenptah from Heracleopolis itself, see Daressy, *ASAE* 21 (1921), 139, § 2.

542. Hem-Ptah A, Pasenhor A, and later Hem-Ptah B, all from stela of the priest Pasenhor B, Year 37 of Shoshenq V.

the grandson of Osorkon II had served as High Priest of Ptah, but his son Pediese now ruled in Memphis. The latter's elder son, Pef-tjau-awy-Bast – entitled high priest – undertook the conduct of religious affairs, including the care of the Apis bulls.[543] However, Pediese lived on at least another quarter-century, surviving his elder son into the next reign.

(iv) *The Delta*

Here, again, Pedubast I is remarkably little attested, whereas a stream of stelae attest year-dates of Shoshenq III, and various blocks attest his building-activities (§ 304, below). A bronze statuette of Pedubast I has been said to derive from Tanis, but this provenance is doubtful.[544] From Bubastis, the ancestral territory of both dynasties, comes a donation-stela of Year 23 of Pedubast I, which was erected by a priest Harkhebi.[545]

§ 302 *   B. IUPUT I (*c.* 804–783 B.C.)

Of Pedubast's co-regent and successor, little is known. After the Theban notation of his Year 2 being the Year 16 of Pedubast, we have few other dated records before a donation-stela of Smendes, Chief of the Mā in Mendes, dated 'Year 21 of Pharaoh Iuput'[546]– a date corresponding to Year 42 of Shoshenq III, *c.* 784 B.C. Embarrassingly, several monuments can be attributed to a king Iuput with the prenomen Usimare Setepen-amun – but it is not absolutely certain that this prenomen (and the monuments) does belong to Iuput I rather than II.[547] They include a barque-stand from Tell el Yahudieh (dependency of Heliopolis),[548] a bronze door-fitment from Leontopolis (Tell Moqdam) itself, naming also his Queen

---

543. See above, Part III, §§ 155–6. Takeloth's tomb at Memphis was next to his father's, cf. Badawy, *ASAE* 44 (1944), 181, n. 2, and *ASAE* 54 (1956), 197–8. Fragments of a chapel of Sekhmet by Takeloth and Shoshenq III at Memphis, cf. Daressy, *ASAE* 20 (1920), 169–70; the lady Djed-Bast-es-ankh was probably a wife of Takeloth.

544. Cf. above, Part II, § 102.

545. See Caminos, *Centaurus* 14 (1969), 42–6, pls. 1–2; this monument was formerly misattributed to Takeloth I.

546. This stela, cf. Yoyotte, *YMM*, 125, § 10, also *BSFÉ* 25 (1958), 21, fig. 3; doorjamb, induction of Smendes, earlier, Daressy, *RT* 35 (1913), 124–6, and *YMM*, 125, Document 11. Years 9 and 12 of a Iuput occur in graffiti of a priest of Khons at the temple of Khons, Karnak; for this information, I am grateful to Mme H. K. Jacquet.

547. The long reign of a king (21 years) early in the Dynasty may favour attribution of these monuments to him, rather than to the powerless kinglet of Piankhy's time; the style of the Brooklyn relief, however, would not exclude a later date than Iuput I.

548. Naville, *Mound of the Jew & City of Onias (Tell el Yahudiyeh)*, 1890, p. 1.

Tent-kat [. . .],[549] and a glazed relief of the king formerly in the Hood collection and now in the Brooklyn Museum.[550]

§ 303   C. SHOSHENQ IV (c. 783–777 B.C.)

Iuput's successor, Usimare Meryamun, Shoshenq IV, Beloved of Amun, was short-lived; his highest-known year-date is Year 6, and his monuments are minimal in number. But he was accepted in Thebes, and the Nile level text of Year 6, c. 778 B.C. [Year 48, Shoshenq III] attests also the continuing pontificate of Takeloth there,[551] 18 years after his last-known date under Pedubast (Year 23). This king's cult perhaps survived in Thebes, to judge from a reference in fragment 18 of the Karnak Priestly Annals to [some official of the shrine?] 'of Usimare Meryamun, justified', but it may rather refer to Ramesses III.[552] Also more probably of Ramesses III than Shoshenq IV is a stray block at the later temple of Osiris-Ruler-of-Eternity in Karnak.[553] A scarab of 'Usimare Meryamun Shoshenq' could commemorate either this king or his contemporary Shoshenq III, depending on whether one attributes the 'Meryamun' to prenomen or nomen, respectively.[554] Exactly the same total ambiguity haunts the same compound cartouche on the funerary cones of Hori, a count, prophet of Amun and Montu, and Secretary of Pharaoh.[555]

Nothing else is known of Shoshenq IV unless his successor was also his son. If so, then Osorkon III's mother, Queen Kamama Merytmut III, would have been Shoshenq IV's queen.[556] In the 3rd year of Osorkon III [Year 51 of Shoshenq III], an unusually high inundation of the Nile flooded the temples of Thebes.[557]

549. Daressy, *RT* 30 (1908), 202, and *BIFAO* 30 (1930), 626 f., now Cairo JdE 38261; cf. Yoyotte, *BIFAO* 52 (1953), 190, n. 1.

550. Brooklyn Museum, 59. 17; sale of Hood collection, cf. Sotheby's *Catalogue* of 1924, plate. The prenomen here reads [*Wsr*]*mˁtrˁtrˁrˁStp*ˀ. [*n.*]*rˁ* (instead of *Stp.n.'Imn*), but the nomen is the usual one.

551. No. 25 (Legrain, *ZÄS* 34 (1896), 114; von Beckerath, *JARCE* 5 (1966), 52). A graffito of one Djed-Ioh is dated to 'Year 4 . . . of Pharaoh Shoshenq' (IV?), at the Khons temple, and another (same man?, -KAK) in 'Year 5 . . . of Pharaoh X, Son of Isis Beloved of Amun'; X may be read in several ways ('*In-bb*; '*In-rdwy*; *Si-y*; alternative combinations of these). I am tempted to refer the second graffito to Osorkon III (keeping the two close in time), if *Si-y* were possible (cf. 'So' for Osorkon, §§ 333–4, below). For knowledge and details about these two graffiti, I am greatly indebted to the kindness of Mme Jacquet (personal communications, 4 June, 20 November, 1965).

552. Legrain, *RT* 22 (1900), 58; *G3*, 369, III.

553. Legrain, *op. cit.*, 148; *G3*, 370, IV.

554. *G3*, 370, VI, with references.

555. Cf. above, Part II, § 99, and Part III, § 177 f.

556. An alternative, less likely relationship is to make Shoshenq IV and Osorkon III brothers, in which case the latter's mother would have been a queen of Iuput I.

557. *G3*, 382–3, I, with references, esp. Daressy, *RT* 18 (1896), 181–4, and 20

§ 304   D. SHOSHENQ III: OFFICIAL WORKS,
             ROYAL FAMILY, DELTA PRINCEDOMS

(i) *Monumental Projects*
In Tanis itself, Shoshenq III built a massive pylon-gateway of granite
through the great enclosure-wall, on the main processional way into the
great temple of Amun.[558] His source of supply was 'cannibalized' colossi
and architraves of Ramesses II from the ruins of nearby Pi-Ramessē. Several
registers of scenes once showed Shoshenq III before Amun, Mut and
Khons plus other deities, and the processional barque of Amun; part still
stands today. Since he reigned so long, Shoshenq III may well have celebrated a jubilee in the 30th year of his reign. But no record has come to
light, and one can hardly attribute his gateway to the commemoration of
such an event (as with Osorkon II at Bubastis), as the surviving scenes show
no trace of jubilee-rites. Elsewhere in Tanis, Shoshenq III was content to
build himself a tomb near the rest;[559] he also buried other royalties in the
antechambers of the tomb of Osorkon II,[560] close to his own predecessor,
Takeloth II.

Across the Delta, Shoshenq III built a little in several centres; his long
reign enabled him to do as much as any ruler of the dynasty, and more than
most. At Mendes, well west from Tanis, he built a chapel.[561] At Tell
Umm Harb (Mostai by Quesna) – ancient Mosdai – he built a further
chapel (reusing Ramesside works),[562] and a block of his was found further
west at Bindaria in the Central Delta.[563] Across the west branch of the
Nile at Kom el Hisn, Shoshenq III apparently added a gateway to the
temple there.[564] At Memphis, remains of a chapel of Sekhmet are known.[565]

§ 305[*] (ii) *The Royal Family*
Shoshenq III's queen was the 'Royal Wife' or 'Great Chief Queen of His
Majesty', Tentamenopet, by whom he had a daughter Ankhes-en-Shoshenq
whose son in turn married a daughter of Pediese, son of Takeloth B,

(1898), 80; *BAR*, IV, § 743. Cf. also Nile-level text No. 5, Legrain, *ZÄS* 34 (1896),
111, von Beckerath, *JARCE* 5 (1966), 49.
    558. Published by Goyon in Montet, *Chéchanq III*, 13–50, pls. 1–24.
    559. Montet, *op. cit.*, 53 ff., pls. 1, 25 ff. (Tomb V).
    560. Montet, *Osorkon II*, 76, 79–81, pl. 30; cf. *Chéchanq III*, 52.
    561. Blocks, Daressy, *ASAE* 13 (1913), 86; Cairo JdE 38272.
    562. Edgar, *ASAE* 11 (1911), 165, 167–9.
    563. Daressy, *ASAE* 12 (1913), 206.
    564. Daressy, *ASAE* 4 (1903), 283–5; it is regrettable that more blocks of this
gateway have not been excavated.
    565. Cf. above, § 301, note 543.

who were both High Priests of Ptah of Memphis.[566] This queen's household steward and 'Keeper of [. . .] of Pharaoh Shoshenq' was a certain Amenemhat.[567]

At least three sons are known. The heir to the throne was the 'Great Prince, Chief of the Two Lands, Eldest King's Son of the Lord of the Two Lands, Army-leader', Bakennefi A,[568] who is known by a stela from near Heliopolis and mentioning the settlement 'Wall of Shoshenq'.[569] From later evidence it is most probable that Shoshenq III had placed the provinces of Athribis and Heliopolis in the charge of the Crown Prince Bakennefi A;[570] henceforth, this double province remained the fief of a titular 'regent' or 'crown prince'[571] until the dawn of Saite rule, when it remained a double province even then.

Shoshenq's second son, Pashedbast B, was active in the Thebaid (§ 299, end, above), and likewise predeceased his father. A third son, Pimay, was 'Great Chief of the Mā, son of the Lord of the Two Lands, Shoshenq (III)'[572] – possibly the Pimay who eventually succeeded Shoshenq, despite differing orthographies of name. It is uncertain where his fief was, but it may possibly have been Sais whence came the monument cited here. A fourth son was a 'King's Son of Ramesses, Commander of All Troops, Great Chief of [. . .],[573] Takeloth (C), son of the Lord of the Two Lands, his mother being Djed-Bast-es-ankh', whose activity at Busiris is denoted by a donation-stela of Year 18, most likely of Shoshenq III.[574] A fifth possible prince was the 'High Priest of Amenresonter, King's Son of Ramesses, *Mek*-prince of Pawer . . ., Army-leader, Padebehenbast', on a donation-stela of Year 28 of Shoshenq III, probably from Kom el Hisn.[575] Like Harnakht under Osorkon II, Padebehenbast was doubtless High Priest of Amun in Tanis,[576] a royal benefice, rather than ruler of some

566. Genealogical monument of their descendant, the Memphite priest Ankh-Shoshenq, see Legrain, *RT* 29 (1907), 174–8; *G3*, 368, XXXVI–XXXVII.
567. Cf Petrie, *History of Egypt*, III, 1905, 257.
568. Possibly '[son of] [Ta]dibast (ii), whose mother was Tadibast (i)'.
569. Daressy, *ASAE* 16 (1916), 61–2.
570. On links between these two places, cf. Yoyotte, *YMM*, 176–8.
571. A stela of Year 15 of Shoshenq III is of this Bakennefi A, and appears to mention his son(?) Pediese (also entitled 'Great First Hereditary Prince of His Majesty'), perhaps his successor in Athribis.
572. Cairo 9430 (Daressy, *RT* 35 (1913), 137, n. 3; *ASAE* 16 (1916), 62). It should be noted that the orthography of the name of the prince Pimay differs from that used by king Pimay, which may not favour their identity.
573. Either [of Foreigners] or [of Pi-Sekhemkheperrēᶜ], cf. *YMM*, 131–2 and n. 1.
574. Stela, Louvre 20. 905 (Guimet, C. 73), cf. Spiegelberg, *RT* 35 (1913), 41–3, and *YMM*, 131–2.
575. Stela Berlin 7344, Spiegelberg, *op. cit.*, 43–5, *Aeg. Inschriften, Berlin*, II, 209; cf. *YMM*, 150–1, and *BIFAO* 58 (1959), 50–1.
576. A point made by Yoyotte, *YMM*, 151, n. 1.

fief away from the capital. A further high priest of Amun attributable to Tanis is perhaps a high priest of Amenresonter, Shoshenq son of Pimay who was perhaps a grandson of Shoshenq III and the future Shoshenq V, and may have officiated late in Shoshenq III's reign.[577]

§ 306* (iii) *The Delta Princedoms*

A whole series of local dynasties, especially of Chiefs of the Mā, took root and flourished principally in the Delta during the last century or so of the Libyan dominion.[578]

At *Mendes*, a hereditary line of Great Chiefs of the Mā and Army-leaders was represented by Harnakht A (son and successor of a Nes-khebit(?)), in Year 22 of Shoshenq III (*c.* 804 B.C.) on one donation-stela,[579] while his son and successor Smendes switched allegiance to Iuput I in whose 21st year, *c.* 784 B.C. [Year 42 of Shoshenq III] his donation-stela is dated (cf. § 302 above). This local dynasty probably continued right through to the rise of Sais, *c.* 670/660 B.C. A lesser Mendesian stela is of Year 30 of Shoshenq III.[580]

Further south, at *Pharbaithos* (Horbeit), a great chief of the Mā, Iuf[er]ᶜo A, ruled under Shoshenq III, by a donation-stela from Tukh el Garamus,[581] while to another such chief, Pawarma A, his two sons dedicated a faience vase (also found there) in a 'Year 33' – probably of Shoshenq III (unless V).[582] Here, too, a minor dynasty was begun, but did not retain its hold.[583]

Across in *the west*, there had arisen a series of Great Chiefs of the Libu, a line of rulers to whom local lords in centres such as Kom Firin, Kom el Hisn and Kom abu Billo owed their immediate allegiance. Such a Great Chief was In-Amun-nif-nebu, known from a donation-stela of Year 31 of Shoshenq III;[584] these chiefs laid the foundations of a consolidated

577. Scarab, Cairo JdE 26378, quoted with great reserve by Gauthier (*G3*, 373, n. 1, after *MMR*, 742–3).
578. For a brilliant exposé of the distribution and history of these local dynasts, see the detailed survey by Yoyotte, *YMM*, 121–81.
579. Details, cf. Kitchen, *JARCE* 8 (1969–70), 59–63, figs. A, 1–3; Brooklyn Museum 67. 118.
580. Stela, Strasbourg 1379, cf. Spiegelberg, *RT* 25 (1903), 197, III, and pl.; cf. also *YMM*, 140, n. 1.
581. Daressy, *RT* 20 (1898), 85, § CLXIV; *YMM*, 124, Document 1. Rulers of Pharbaithos, *YMM*, 132–3, § 11.
582. Published by Naville, *Mound of the Jew & City of Onias*, 1890, 30, pl. 8A; cf. Spiegelberg, *RT* 23 (1901), 100–1, and *YMM*, 127, Document 29.
583. e.g. replaced by the eldest son of Bakennefi B of Athribis, by Piankhy's time.
584. Stela Moscow 5647 (*YMM*, 143, Document 31*c*). On these chiefs, see especially Yoyotte, *YMM*, 149–50.

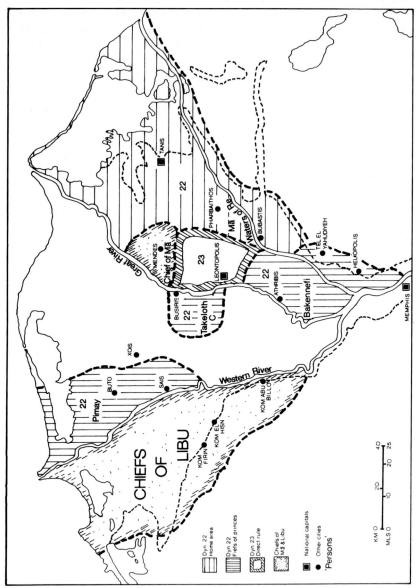

Fig. 4. Distribution of Delta Fiefs under *Shoshenq III, c.* 800 B.C.

kingdom of their own. A stela of Year 32 belongs to an Ankhpakhered who was probably a lesser chief at Kom el Hisn.[585]

Doubtless other centres, such as Sais, Busiris and Sebennytos, already likewise had their lines of local rulers, but they are not yet attested as early as Shoshenq III. Sais and Busiris were possibly fiefs for royal princes under Shoshenq III (cf. § 305 above, Pimay and Takeloth C). But already, within the half-century reign of Shoshenq III in Tanis, one may perceive not only the outward division of the monarchy between two lines of kings in Tanis and Leontopolis, but also the emergent dissipation of real authority locally among the Libyan chiefs of the Mā right across the Delta, and their compeers (even, superiors) the Great Chiefs of the Libu along its western edge, all of whom tended to form closed, hereditary dynasties of their own. Meantime, scions of the royal house held rule in Athribis-with-Heliopolis, Sais, and Busiris, at least initially.

585. Stela, Cairo no number; Spiegelberg, *RT* 25 (1903), 196–7, II, and pl.; cf. *YMM*, 150 and n. 2, and *BIFAO* 58 (1959), 51.

CHAPTER 21

The Twenty-second and Twenty-third Dynasties: IV, The Libyan Collapse (Late Twenty-second and Twenty-third Dynasties)

§ 308   1. PIMAY (c. 773–767 B.C.)

A. ACCESSION

When at last Shoshenq III was finally laid to rest in his tomb in Tanis, his successor was the short-lived king Pimay. Typically of the age, this worthy showed no originality whatever in his known titles – e.g., prenomen Usimare Setepenamun (var., Setepenre) precisely like Osorkon II, Shoshenq III, Pedubast I, Iuput and Osorkon III. Two Nile levels of Years 5 and 6 of Osorkon III correspond to Years 1 and 2 of Pimay.

B. REIGN

In Pimay's 2nd year, there died the Apis bull inducted in Year 28 of Shoshenq III, it being aged 26 years; a successor was duly installed. At least four stelae commemorate the burial. Two major stelae are in the name of Pediese, ruling in Memphis still, and a younger son of his, the effective high priest of Ptah, Harsiese H,[586] and two others in the name of lesser clergy.[587] South of Thebes, at Hefat (now Moalla), fields in dispute since Year 49 of Shoshenq III were confirmed to their purchaser by oracle in Year 4, probably of Pimay.[588]

586. Malinine, Posener, Vercoutter, *Catalogue, stèles, Sérapéum*, I, 21–23 and pls., Nos. 22, 23; IM. 3697, 3736.
587. *Ibid.*, Nos. 24, 25 (IM. 4205, 3441), pp. 24–5, pls.
588. Parker, *Saite Oracle Papyrus*, 1962, 49–52, pls. 17–19; Pap. Brooklyn 16. 205.

In the capital, Tanis, Pimay did some building-work in the temples, of which the merest traces have been recovered;[589] from Bubastis, a rather poor donation-stela seemingly bears his name.[590] One other stela, in the Louvre, dates to Year 6 of the reign.[591] Some highly dubious scarabs apart,[592] Pimay then passes from the scene, leaving the throne in Tanis to his son[593] Shoshenq V.

§**309** 2. SHOSHENQ V (*c.* 767–730 B.C.), EARLY
YEARS, AND OSORKON III (*c.* 777–749 B.C.)

A. ACCESSIONS AND TITLES

When he ascended the Leontopolitan throne about a decade ahead of Shoshenq V in Tanis, Osorkon III showed – as ever in the 23rd Dynasty – absolutely no originality in his cartouche-names: Usimare Setepenamun, Osorkon III, Beloved of Amun and Son of Isis. But he did begin a new trend towards a greater simplicity, of archaizing tone, in his other official titles.[594] His Horus-name followed the old imperial and post-imperial style, being the now totally banal 'Strong Bull, appearing in Thebes', following Osorkon II, Harsiese and Takeloth II. But his Nebty name, 'Favourite of the Two Lands' (*St-ib t3wy*), and Golden Horus name, 'Born of the Gods' (*Ms-ntrw*) bear a simpler and far older stamp.[595]

This trend was carried to its logical conclusion by Shoshenq V, who was marginally a little more original in his cartouche-names, and abandoned the imperial style completely in his other official names – at least, until his last years.[596] As Usimare had been pre-empted as a prenomen by two previous Shoshenqs (III, IV), the new king adopted another old 21st Dynasty prenomen: Akheperre, often without further complement, balancing the simple nomen Shoshenq. To these 'nuclear' forms, Setepenre was sometimes added to Akheperre, and 'Beloved of Amun, Son of Bast, and god, ruler of Thebes' to Shoshenq;[597] but the simpler style is by far

589. Cf. Montet, *Le lac sacré de Tanis*, 1966, 44, pls. 5, 6, 48 (fragmentary blocks Nos. 23, 24, 25, the latter in fine relief-work).
590. Daressy, *ASAE* 15 (1915), 145–7.
591. *G3*, 372, VI, and references.
592. Cf. *G3*, 372, VII–IX; none are very convincing.
593. So, on Serapeum stela (IM. 3049, *Catalogue*, No. 26) of Year 11 of Shoshenq V, called 'son of Pimay' (latter name in cartouche).
594. Preserved mainly in the Karnak temple of Osiris-Ruler-of-Eternity (from late in the reign), cf. *G3*, 384, V.
595. For *St-ib t3wy*, cf. Neuserrēʿ in the Old Kingdom (*G1*, 127–8), and with *ms-ntrw*, cf. ḥtp-ntrw of Sesostris II (*G1*, 296, III) and *nfr-ntrw* of Awibrēʿ Hor (*G1*, 317) in Middle Kingdom.
596. For which cf. below on his jubilee-chapel at Tanis. § 315.
597. So on jubilee-chapel, § 315 below.

the commoner.[598] Shoshenq V's other formal names followed the severely simple, repetitive style seen previously far back in the Old and Middle Kingdoms – Horus, Nebty and Golden Horus names all 'Great of Strength' (*Wsr-pḥty*).[599] While the Saite period (26th Dynasty) has long been recognized as the age of archaism *par excellence*, and the trend is visible under the Nubian dominion (25th Dynasty), we see here already the officially backed genesis of that movement emerging in germ in the late 22nd and 23rd Dynasties, a century or so before the Saites.

§ 310   B. SHOSHENQ V, EARLY YEARS (1–22): THE NORTH

(i) *Memphis*

In the 11th year of Shoshenq V (*c.* 757 B.C.), the Apis bull inducted by Pimay died and was buried; there were some five stelae commemorating the event,[600] but none by the high priest (perhaps still Harsiese). In the course of time both Pediese and his son Harsiese, as successive chiefs of the Mā and high priests of Ptah, were themselves buried in tombs adjoining those of their predecessors, Shoshenq and Takeloth.[601] By the middle of Shoshenq V's reign, the next high priest was doubtless Ankhefensekhmet B, son of Harsiese H.[602] Further south from Memphis, at Atfih, the local priest of Hathor dedicated a stela in Year 22 of Shoshenq V.[603]

§ 311* (ii) *The Delta Dynasts*

In Year 11 of a pharaoh left unnamed, but most probably Osorkon III[604] (equal to Year 1 of Shoshenq V, 767 B.C.), a new chief of the Mā, Harnakht B, succeeded his father Smendes as ruler in Mendes – so little did he regard his royal overlord, that the latter's cartouches were simply left blank in the inscription.[605] A decade or so later,[606] much further west, Sais had become the seat of another chief of the Mā and army-leader, Osorkon (C), who steadily extended his rule in the West Delta, northwards to include

598. So in all examples in *G3*, 373–5, and most monuments published since.
599. Stela Cairo JdE 45779, Daressy, *ASAE* 15 (1915), 144.
600. Malinine, Posener, Vercoutter, *Catalogue, stèles, Sérapéum*, I, Nos. 26–30, pp. 25–9 and pls. (IM. 3049, 3719, 3061, 2702, 3110).
601. Cf. Badawy, *ASAE* 44 (1944), 181, and *ASAE* 54 (1956), 157–8.
602. Statue, Cairo 1212 (Borchardt, *Statuen und Statuetten*, IV, *ad loc.*); cf. above, Part III, §§ 155–6.
603. Published by Peet, *JEA* 6 (1920), 56–7 and pl. 7.
604. See Kitchen, *JARCE* 8 (1969–70), 62, 63 and n. 18; as Harnakht's father Smendes had already switched to dating by the 23rd Dynasty, there is no reason to assume that the son did any differently.
605. Text added to doorjamb of Smendes, Cairo JdE 43339, Daressy, *RT* 35 (1913), 126–7.
606. For approximate date of this Osorkon, cf. above, Part II, § 113.

Buto and south-westwards to Kom el Hisn – he boasted eventually the titles of Prophet of Neith (at Sais), of Edjo (at Buto), and of the Lady of Imau (at Kom el Hisn, Hathor-cult).[607] Thus was formed a Princedom of the West, alongside the chiefs of the Libu. Among the latter, one chief succeeded another with some rapidity. After In-Amun-nif-nebu of Year 31 of Shoshenq III (*c.* 795 B.C.), there ruled Niu-mateped B, known from a donation-stela of Year 8 of Shoshenq V[608] (*c.* 760 B.C., Year 18, Osorkon III). He must very soon afterwards have been replaced by the next Libu chief, Titaru son of Didi, who was attested on another donation-stela in Year 15 (or 17) of Shoshenq V,[609] *c.* 753 (or 751) B.C. His rule was brief – by Year 19 (*c.* 749 B.C.), a third chief, Ker, is honoured on another such stela by a 'shield-bearer of Pharaoh' Weshtihet.[610] Ker had probably only just come to power by then, and may have held office into the 30s of Shoshenq V's reign.

By contrast, in his home territory of Bubastis, Shoshenq V dedicated endowments for minor offerings to the goddess Bast through no intermediaries other than the serving priests, as is shown by an undated stela probably from Bubastis;[611] here, at least, his rule was direct and absolute.

§ 312* C. THE REIGN OF OSORKON III (*c.* 777–749 B.C.)

(i) *The North*

As already seen, Osorkon III was recognized as pharaoh, albeit perfunctorily, by the rulers of Mendes. In the Theban Nile level texts of Years [3], 5, 6, of his reign, Osorkon III is termed son of Queen Kamama (Merytmut III).[612] In due time, this queen-mother was probably entombed at the dynastic capital of Leontopolis – the burial of Queen Kama⟨ma⟩ found at Tell Moqdam contained a fine set of goldwork and jewellery as befitted her station.[613] Otherwise, Osorkon III is far less

607. Cf. the 'Talisman of Osorkon' and his ushabtis, published and identified respectively by Yoyotte, *BSFÉ* 31 (1960), 13–22, figs. 1–4.

608. Published by Spiegelberg, *ZÄS* 56 (1920), 57–8, pl. 5; cf. *YMM*, 143, § 30, Document B.

609. *YMM*, 144, § 32, Document D; published, Kitchen, *JARCE* 8 (1969–70), 64–6, figs. B, 4; formerly Michaelides collection, now Brooklyn Museum 67. 119. This and the stela of previous note both probably came trom Kom Firin, likewise that published by Bakir, *ASAE* 43 (1943), 75–81.

610.* *YMM*, 144, § 33, Document E; Maspero, *RT* 15 (1893), 84–6, and Müller, *Egyptological Researches*, I, 1906, pl. 88; *BAR*, IV, §§ 782–4.

611. Daressy, *ASAE* 15 (1915), 143–5.

612. Legrain, *ZÄS* 34 (1896), 111; von Beckerath, *JARCE* 5 (1966), 49, Nos. 5, 6, 7; name of queen lost in No. 5.

613. Cf. Edgar and Gauthier, *ASAE* 21 (1921), 22–7, and esp. pl. 1; a reused block of Harmose, a known official of Osorkon II, indicates a date for this queen's tomb clearly *after* the reign of Osorkon II.

attested in the north than his Tanite colleague. From Memphis, a small bronze plaque names Osorkon (III) Son-of-Isis,[614] and a statue-base of an Usimare Setepenamun from there could belong to him or (alas!) to one of seven other Libyan pharaohs with this prenomen.[615]

Other members of the royal family included the principal queen, Karo-atjet, by whom Osorkon III had a daughter Shepenupet (I), and a lesser wife Tentsa who bore him one son, Takeloth (III), if not his other son, Rudamun.

§ 313* (ii) *Middle Egypt*

At Heracleopolis, Pasenhor A (great-great-grandson of Osorkon II) was probably followed in office there by his own son, Hem-Ptah B, during the reign of Pimay and the early years of Shoshenq V. Thereafter, this subsidiary line of the 22nd Dynasty disappeared from Heracleopolis, never to rule there again.[616] Instead, Osorkon III for the 23rd Dynasty managed to install his own son Takeloth as High Priest of Arsaphes, Governor of the South, General and Army-leader, and Chief of Pi-Sekhemkheperre[617] – much as did Osorkon II for his son Nimlot C about a century before.

Furthermore, when the Nubian Piankhy raided Egypt, he found another Nimlot (D) as 'king' in Hermopolis; the name is Libyan and proper to the Libyan royal house. Hence it is quite possible (if hypothetical at present) that Nimlot was installed at Hermopolis by Osorkon III, and possible that (even more hypothetically) he was a further son of Osorkon III who sought thus to provide him with a fief elsewhere than in the 'overcrowded' Delta, which was already well-peopled with petty princedoms.

§ 314* (iii) *Thebes*

In due course, again as Osorkon II had done for Nimlot C, Osorkon III appointed his son Takeloth (already ruling in Heracleopolis) as High Priest of Amun in Thebes.[618] Two monuments attest the new pontiff: one in his honour with figures of Amun and Arsaphes by a priest and artisan Nes-Ptah,[619] and a donation-stela in Gurob by his subordinates in Heracleopolis.[620] Thus in Middle and Upper Egypt, at the main centres of Thebes,

614. *G3*, 386, XV, after Daressy, *ASAE* 3 (1902), 140.
615. *G3*, 393, V, after Petrie, *A Season in Egypt*, 26, pl. 21: 11 (who had, without clear justification, dated it to Rudamun).
616. Pasenhor B (son of Hem-Ptah B), to whose Serapeum stela we owe so much for the Libyan period, was himself but a *Sameref* and Prophet of Neit.
617. See second and third notes following.
618. We do not yet know whether the new incumbent directly followed in office that Takeloth functioning from Year 23 of Pedubast I to Year 6 of Shoshenq IV, or some intervening pontiff so far unattested.
619. Gauthier, *ASAE* 37 (1937), 16–24 with plate, esp. 18 ff.
620. See Loat, *Gurob*, 8, pls. 18–19 (bound with Murray, *Saqqara Mastabas I*).

probably Hermopolis, and certainly Heracleopolis, the 23rd Dynasty suc-
ceeded in totally supplanting the senior Dynasty's representatives, gaining
formal local allegiance almost everywhere south of Memphis and the Delta.
Turning to the rest of the Theban hierarchy, practically nothing is
known of the 2nd prophets of Amun until the end of Libyan rule.[621]
However, the office of 3rd prophet passed via Padimut B, the vizier
Pakhuru and a Pediamen-neb-nesttawy A (cf. §§ 290, 296, above) to
Wenennufer called Iryiry (§ 290), for the reigns of Osorkon II, Takeloth
II, and Shoshenq III with Pedubast I and Iuput I his contemporaries.
Then in line probably came the Royal Secretary Nebneteru iv[622] (great-
grandson of iii) as 3rd prophet under Shoshenq IV and early Osorkon
III, and Pediamen-neb-nesttawy B under Osorkon III if not later.
Nearly all these men belonged to large, often interrelated Theban priestly
families.[623] More consistently, the office of 4th prophet of Amun stayed
firmly in the hands of the descendants of Nakhtefmut A and Harsiese C.
From the latter's son Djed-Khons-ef-ankh C (perhaps under Pedubast I
and Iuput I), it passed to the grandson Nakhtefmut B, contemporary of
Osorkon III and Takeloth III.[624] Among civil officials, a whole series of
southern viziers followed one another in what must have been a quite
rapid succession.[625]

Dated records at Thebes continued to be reckoned solely in terms of
reigns of the 23rd Dynasty. These would include the further Nile level texts
of Years 12 (twice), 13(??), 21, 22, if belonging to Osorkon III rather than
II.[626] Finally come one such text dated to Year 28 of Osorkon III (c. 750 B.C.)
'which is Year 5 of his son' Takeloth III, with the latter as co-regent, no
longer simply pontiff; and a last text of Year 29 of the end of the reign.[627]
Jambs of a chapel from Karnak must date from earlier under Osorkon III.[628]

621. When we have Nes-hor-behdet and Patjenfy, under Piankhy and Shabako.
Of uncertain date, and perhaps from a rather later epoch, are the Ankhefenkhons
and son Nespautytawy (Spiegelberg, RT 35 (1913), 40) cited by H. De Meulenaere,
BiOr 11 (1954), 169, and the Ihats cited by him, OLZ 55 (1960), 130.
622. Husband of Sitamun, daughter of the Vizier Nesipaqashuty A; cf. above,
Part III, §§ 170, 177.
623. See Part III, Chapter 13, above.
624. See above, Part III, § 184, etc.
625. See Table of southern viziers in Part VI, below.
626. Nile-level texts Nos. 8–12, Legrain, ZÄS 34 (1896), 112; von Beckerath,
JARCE 5 (1966), 49–51, cf. 45, 48.
627. Nile-level texts Nos. 13, 14 (Legrain, 112; von Beckerath, 51, cf. 45, 48).
That of Year 29 may better be attributed to Osorkon III than Shoshenq III
(favoured by von Beckerath), because Shoshenq III is qualified as Setepenre in one
such text of Year 29 already clearly dated to him (No. 22), whereas the king of No.
14 is Setepenamun, the invariable epithet of Osorkon III. Such considerations are
not to be overpressed, of course, but should also be borne in mind.
628. G3, 385, VI; PM, II, 71, N (called Os. II), PM, II², 223, U.

§ 315 3. SHOSHENQ V, LATER YEARS, AND LATE 23rd DYNASTY

A. LATER YEARS OF SHOSHENQ V

(i) *Jubilee and Delta Monuments*
In the great precinct of Amun, Mut and Khons at Tanis, Shoshenq V built a temple to that triad, perhaps in the north-east quarter (which was turned into a sacred lake at a much later date), from whose walls and colonnades some 200 reused fragments survive.[629] It was probably to this same temple that he added a Jubilee gateway or chapel of which less than twenty fragments have been recovered.[630] On the fragmentary reliefs of these structures, Shoshenq V affected a florid new titulary of imperial style like that of many of his predecessors, rather than his customary simpler usage. This included: Horus, 'Strong Bull, appearing in Thebes'[631] plus epithets 'Whom R caused to appear [. . .];[632] Nebty, probably 'Magnifying forms, great (??) [of . . .] ';[633] and Golden Horus, 'Great of marvels (like [. . . some deity?])'.[634] His cartouches likewise appear in their fuller forms (§ 309, above). From the remains of dedicatory texts and other fragments, it is probable that the temple was dedicated to Khons in particular.[635] The date of the Jubilee is unknown, but Year 30 would be an obvious choice in so long a reign. A donation-stela may have recorded an endowment for the temple.[636]

Elsewhere, Shoshenq V is but little attested as a builder – some fragments of granite from Tell el Yahudiyeh show his simpler Horus name and prenomen.[637] A stela doubtfully attributable to his reign is known in Bahriya Oasis.[638] Supposed scarabs of this king from Palestine are probably not explicitly his.[639]

629. Published by Montet, *Le lac sacré de Tanis*, 1966, 44–56, Nos. 27–211, pls. 7–27 and photos; on columns, cf. Lezine in Montet, *op. cit.*, 30–1 and figs. 1–5.
630. *Ibid.*, 57–61, Nos. 212–29, pls. 28–9 and photos.
631. Used already by Osorkon II, Takeloth II and Osorkon III; here, on Montet's blocks Nos. 30–4, 36, 39(?), 205(??).
632. *Sḥˁ s(w) Rˁ*[. . .], block No. 48.
633. *Sˁꜣ-ḫprw, [w]r?* [. . .], block No. 62; cf. Nebty-name of Osorkon I.
634. *Wr-biꜣwt*, twice with *m[i* . . .]; blocks Nos. 35, 38, 39.
635. Cf. the mentions of Khons, Montet, *Le lac sacré*, 47 (Nos. 42 ff.), 48–9, 51, *passim*.
636. Montet, *op. cit.*, No. 26, p. 45 and pls. 5, 46.
637. Birch, *ZÄS* 10 (1872), 122 (British Museum fragment), true identity seen by Daressy, *ASAE* 15 (1915), 145. Fragment of a 'Shoshenq', cf. Petrie, *History of Egypt*, III, 1905, 253 (under his imaginary Shoshenq II, identity already doubted by him).
638. Cf. *PM*, VII, 310, after Fakhry.
639. A. Rowe, *Catalogue of Egyptian Scarabs in the Palestine Archaeological*

§ 316* (ii) *Memphis and the Princedom of the West*

In year 37 (*c.* 731 B.C.) the Apis bull of Year 11 died at 26 years old (like its predecessor-but-one) and a new sacred bull was installed. A whole series of stelae commemorate the burial of Year 37, mainly by the lesser clergy of Ptah.[640] But one (though dated by the Tanite king) was offered to Apis by the priest Pasherenptah not only for himself but also on behalf of 'the Great Chief of the Libu, Ankh-Hor (and) his son Harbes'.[641] Thus, by the 37th year of Shoshenq V, a man who had become long since the successor of Ker (of Year 19, § 311, above) had attracted his adherents in Memphis – the chiefs of the west were extending their power southwards to the old capital.[642]

This was not, however, without tensions. In Year 36 Tefnakht of Sais – successor there of Osorkon C – was already himself claiming the title of great chief of the Libu on a donation-stela of that year.[643] By Year 38, Ankh-Hor was gone, and Tefnakht ruled alone over the entire princedom of the west, both of Sais and of the Libu.[644] Thus, in Year 37, Ankh-Hor may have been in Memphis in retreat before Tefnakht; the erased stela of a Libyan chief under Shoshenq V may even be witness to the *coup* of Tefnakht.[645] By now, the Prince of the West ruled in practice a larger and more unified realm than any of his chieftain compeers or his theoretical overlords, the pharaohs of Tanis–Bubastis and of Leontopolis.

(iii) *The Succession: Osorkon IV*

Very soon after Tefnakht's success, Shoshenq V died and was succeeded on the throne of Tanis by the last king of the 22nd Dynasty proper: Osorkon IV, with the now unoriginal prenomen Akheperre Setepenamun,[646] being son of a queen Tadibast.[647] The new king's effective realm was simply the 'home territories' of Bubastis and Tanis.

Museum, 1936, p. xxxviii, attributes 'Kheperre' scarabs to this king, and some winged-scarab seals. The latter have nothing to do with Shoshenq V, and the former probably likewise.

640. Malinine, Posener, Vercoutter, *Catalogue, stèles, Sérapéum*, I, Nos. 31–44, pp. 29–43; other stelae attributable to Shoshenq V and the late 22nd Dynasty are Nos. 45–90 (*ibid.*, pp. 43–75).

641. *Ibid.*, No. 37 (IM. 3078); cf. *YMM*, 144–45, § 34, Document F.

642. Like many others, Ankh-Hor also presented a daughter to Amun in Thebes, to be a chantress of the abode of Amun; cf. *YMM*, 145, § 34: G.

643. The 'Abemayor' stela; *YMM*, 153, § 48.

644. Buto stela of Tefnakht, *YMM*, 151–3, §§ 46–7, pl. I: 1. The cartouches of the king were left blank, but could hardly be other than for Shoshenq V.

645. Cairo JdE 85647 (Bakir, *ASAE* 43 (1943), 75–81); cf. *YMM*, 153, n. 2, also 146, § 37.

646. Glazed ring, Leiden, *G3*, 399; cf. Petrie, *History of Egypt*, III, 1905, 264, fig. 107.

647. Cf. *G3*, 399–400.

§ 317*   B. LATE 23RD DYNASTY: TAKELOTH III
(*c.* 754–734 B.C.)

(i) *Accession*

In *c.* 754 B.C., his 24th year, Osorkon III took further measures to bolster up his dynasty and its relations with the south. His son became co-regent as Takeloth III, and his daughter Shepenupet was made God's Wife of Amun in Thebes. The new king's cartouches were as banal as ever: Usimare (Setepenamun), Takeloth (III) Beloved of Amun, Son of Isis, and sometimes 'god, Ruler of Thebes'. Like his father, he (in Shoshenq V's style) often omitted the epithets to be just Usimare Takeloth. But his other formal titles – like those of his senior contemporary, Shoshenq V – further illustrate the new trend towards an archaic simplicity: as Horus, Nebty and Golden Horus, he was simply 'Blessing of the Two Lands' (*Wꜣḏ-tꜣwy*).[648]

§ 318* (ii) *Arrangements in Upper Egypt*

With the elevation of Takeloth to kingship in Leontopolis in the distant Delta, his former posts as southern ruler and high priest in both Heracleopolis and Thebes became vacant. Nimlot D was retained at Hermopolis, while at Heracleopolis, a certain Pef-tjau-awy-Bast was perhaps installed when Takeloth III became his father's co-regent. He was linked to the 23rd Dynasty at least by marriage, his wife being Ir-Bast-udja-nefu, daughter of Rudamun,[649] who was Takeloth's brother. Thus, control was retained in Middle and Upper Egypt. With Shepenupet I as God's Wife of Amun in Thebes, perhaps no high priest of Amun was appointed– she would be her father's principal representative, while daily and festal rites would come under the 2nd, 3rd and 4th prophets of Amun. She was given full cartouches as Lady of the Two Lands, United with the Heart of Amun (*Ḥnm-ib-'Imn*), Lady of Epiphanies, Shepenupet I, Merytmut IV, God's Wife of Amun and Adoratrix of the God. Of her establishment in Thebes, next to nothing is known; doubtless she was appropriately endowed with lands for income, and with a high steward to look after her estates.[650]

648. Co-regent, Nile-level text No. 13; titles, *G3*, 390 – *Wꜣḏ-tꜣwy* follows Unas of the 5th Dynasty.
649. Cf. *G3*, 392–4, and in Part II, above.
650. Sander-Hansen, *Das Gottesweib des Amun*, 1940, 39, § 10, mentions a high steward Thut-nefer (Borchardt, *Statuen und Statuetten*, IV, Cairo Cat. 1286), attributed to the Libyan period. If this date be acceptable, then Thut-nefer may have served either Shepenupet I, or a predecessor of hers such as Karomama-Merytmut I or Ta-sha-kheper B (cf. §§ 282, 289, above).

The trio – Osorkon III, Takeloth III, Shepenupet I – built and decorated in Karnak, at the east end of Amun's precinct, the little temple of Osiris-Ruler-of-Eternity;[651] few other traces have been found of their joint activity or of works of Shepenupet I.

§ **319*** (iii) *Takeloth III as Sole Ruler (c. 749–734 B.C.)*
As sole king, Takeloth III continued to be accepted in Thebes. In the year of his father's decease (Year 29), the new king's reign was marked by a corresponding Nile level text of his Year 6, which is the only one of his reign.[652] To Year 7 of Takeloth III probably belong two badly-damaged genealogies which were formerly on the roof-terrace of the temple of Khons at Karnak.[653] From Abydos come a glazed statuette of the king, and a private stela.[654] Other traces could belong to this king, or to Takeloth I or II.[655] Within the Thebaid, the office of 2nd prophet of Amun probably passed to Nes-hor-behdet,[656] whereas the immediate successor of Pediamen-neb-nesttawy B as 3rd prophet of Amun remains unknown to us. As 4th prophet, Nakhtefmut B was duly succeeded (probably under Takeloth III) by his elder son, Djed-Khons-ef-ankh D,[657] who thus retained this benefice in the family for a sixth generation.

In Middle and Upper Egypt, Takeloth III's contemporaries continued to rule. Perhaps it was at the death of Osorkon III and with the 'sole' rule of Takeloth III that they in turn claimed royal status (perhaps as the price of their nominal allegiance). Certain it is, that both Nimlot of Hermopolis and Pef-tjau-awy-Bast of Heracleopolis adopted full royal style as local 'pharaohs' – with cartouches, regnal years and suchlike trappings.[658] Nimlot's royal style is known so far only from Piankhy's stela, but first-hand records attest that of Pef-tjau-awy-Bast. Two donation-stelae of his own Year 10 (c. 740 B.C., on the view here adopted), giving his prenomen Neferkare, record endowments for either one or two daughters consecrated

651. Publications, cf. *PM*, II, 69: I, and II², 204–6: K. A new publication of the whole is in preparation by a Canadian expedition under Dr. D. B. Redford.
652. Text No. 4 (Legrain, *ZÄS* 34, 111; von Beckerath, *JARCE* 5, 49).
653. *G3*, 333, I; Daressy, *RT* 18 (1896), 51; *PM*, II, 83 end, II², 242–3.
654. *G3*, 333, II, III, for references.
655. Such items include the Grant stela, *G3*, 334, IV, a Karnak sphinx (*G3*, 334, n. 1; *PM*, II², 143), and other indefinite Takeloths (*G3*, loc. cit.). It remains uncertain whether a priest Osorkon 'son of king Takeloth' and the princess and queen Irty-Bast was a son of Takeloth I, II or III (predeceasing the latter); cf. R. Anthes, *MDIK* 12 (1943), 33–4, Tomb 27. Likewise the prophet of Amun, Djed-Ptah-ef-ankh, son of the principal(?) King's Son, Ankh-Takeloth (Cairo Cat. 42196; cf. *G3*, 391, VIII, 3; Kees, *Pr.*, 202), and so perhaps grandson of Takeloth I, II or III.
656. Cf. Kees, *Pr.*, *Nachträge*, 25 to 286.
657. See above, Part III, §§ 187, 189, 191.
658. Piankhy names Nimlot's 'queen' as Nes-tent-meh on his great stela.

to Theban Amun,[659] by his 'Queen' Tasheritenese.[660] A gold statuette of Arsaphes from Heracleopolis itself also bears his name.[661]

§ 320* (iv) *Emergence of the Kingdom of Napata*

Far to the south of Thebes and its jockeying families, a more significant power had arisen. In the distant region of the 4th-cataract stretch of the Nile a local kingdom had come into existence in the late 10th or early 9th century B.C., whose chiefs were buried in relatively simple graves at El Kurru.[662] After almost half a millennium of Egyptian occupation, and subjection to Egyptian cultural norms and forms, the Nubians on the Nile from its 1st to 4th cataracts had doubtless become considerably Egyptianized in their culture, and their leaders, bilingual (Nubian, Egyptian). Contacts between Egypt and Nubia in the 21st Dynasty remain obscure,[663] but barely 150 years after the end of Ramesside rule, Shoshenq I probably warred in Nubia, securing its products and tribute for Amun.[664] Barely a century later, a kingdom had been formed; its seventh ruler was probably the Alara of later inscriptions.[665] Then Kashta became king and he expanded Nubian rule northwards. He occupied the whole of Lower Nubia, adopted pharaonic style as 'King of Upper and Lower Egypt', Maatre (?), Son of Re, Kashta, and erected a stela in the temple of Khnum on Elephantine Island at Aswan.[666] Thus, in the time of Osorkon III, Thebes found itself with a vigorous new neighbour to the south whose rule effectively reached Aswan, if it did not, in fact, even penetrate north beyond it.

Kashta may already have opened up relations with Thebes, but we have no direct evidence for this. His adoption of Egyptian style and Theban religion (Amun being also god of Napata) is further evidenced by an aegis of Mut inscribed in his name,[667] and possibly by a scarab.[668] From later sources we learn that Kashta had by a queen Pebatma two daughters

659. As 'chantress of the inner abode of Amun', on which cf. Yoyotte, *CRAIBL: 1961*, 1962, 43–52.

660. The two stelae are Cairo JdE 45348 (Daressy, *ASAE* 17 (1917), 43–5) and TN 11/9/21/4 (Daressy, *ASAE* 21 (1921), 138–9).

661. Cf. *G3*, 400, references.

662. Cf. tombs cited under generations A to E by D. Dunham, *El Kurru*, 1950, 2–3, and their descriptions in that work.

663. Sole explicit datum is the title 'Viceroy of Nubia' accorded to Nesikhons A, wife of Pinudjem II, § 232 above. Theories on the supposed origins of the Nubian kingdom are too speculative to waste time on, here.

664. Cf. § 251, above.

665. References, Dunham and Macadam, *JEA* 35 (1949), 141, No 5.

666.* See Leclant, *ZÄS* 90 (1963), 74–81, esp. 74–8 and fig. 1. Interpretation of Kashta's prenomen remains doubtful.

667. Published by Leclant, *op. cit.*, 77 (figs. 2–5), 78–80.

668. Cf. Leclant, *op. cit.*, 81.

(Peksater and Amenirdis), plus a son Piankhy and daughter Abar, mother(s) unknown.[669] At his death in *c*. 747 B.C., Kashta was buried in a tomb at El Kurru (1).[670]

§ **321*** (v) *Napata and Thebes under Takeloth III*
So, Nubia had a new king in 747 B.C., 8th year of Takeloth III. This new prince Piankhy certainly extended his influence as far north as Thebes, and in fact within the first decade of his reign (*c*. 747–737 B.C.) laid claim to being the protector and in effect ruler of Thebes. He probably established garrisons in southern Upper Egypt and an army-force;[671] he probably also sought the allegiance of local rulers at least as far north as Middle Egypt – Nimlot of Hermopolis was later considered to have defected from Piankhy to Tefnakht.[672] The ambitions of the young Nubian king to rule Egypt as well as Nubia perhaps find expression at this period on a sandstone stela which he erected in the temple of Amun at Napata (Gebel Barkal).[673] Amun of Napata grants him rule of every land and power to make or unmake chiefs, and Amun of Thebes likewise grants him the rule of Egypt with similar powers (ll. 17–24). Doubtless inspired by the high deeds and style of Tuthmosis III on his Gebel Barkal (Napata) stela, Piankhy adopted the Horus-name 'Strong Bull, appearing in Napata',[674] Nebty, 'Enduring of kingship like Re in heaven',[675] and Golden Horus, 'Holy of epiphanies, powerful of might',[676] plus the epithets 'by seeing him, everyone lives, like (Har)akhte'. The crude style of the hieroglyphs would suit a date in the earlier years of Piankhy.

At Thebes, he installed his sister (or half-sister) Amenirdis I as God's Wife of Amun elect, and had her 'adopted' by Shepenupet I, the daughter of Osorkon III. She took the prenomen Kha-neferu-Mut, 'the beauty of Mut appears'. So, in Wadi Gasus, near the Red Sea, a graffito reads: 'Year 12 – Adoratrix of the God, Amenirdis (I)' and 'Year 19 – God's Wife,

669. Relationships, cf. Dunham & Macadam, *JEA* 35 (1949), 149; above, Part II, § 121.
670. Generation (1), mastaba(?)-tomb Kurru 8, in Dunham, *El Kurru*, 3, 46 f.
671. One notes the garrisons and forces of Piankhy *already* in southern Egypt *before* his campaign, at the time of Tefnakht's drive south (cf. great stela, lines 6, 8).
672. Cf. great stela, line 7.
673. Published by Reisner, *ZÄS* 66 (1931), 89–94 and pls. 5–6 (No. 26). On possible relative dating of Piankhy's titles and monuments, cf. Reisner, *ibid.*, 94–100, *passim*.
674. *Kȝ-nḫt ḫʿ-m-Npt*, based directly on the Horus name of Tuthmosis III, *Kȝ-nḫt ḫʿ-m-Wȝst*, 'Strong Bull, appearing in Thebes'.
675. Taken directly from the Nebty-name of Tuthmosis III.
676. Again, copied directly from Tuthmosis III, with elements in the same inverted order as on the Gebel Barkal stela of that king.

Shepenupet (I)'.[677] These dates can be referred to the reigns of Piankhy and Takeloth III, respectively, *c.* 736 B.C.[678] This document, so interpreted, would indicate that Shepenupet I had already had to adopt Amenirdis I before the end of the reign of Takeloth III, and that Piankhy had clearly established by then a practical ascendancy at Thebes. The Thebans, therefore, cheerfully dated by both *régimes.* Less than a decade later, they were to see more of Piankhy.

§ 322   C. THE REIGN OF RUDAMUN (*c.* 734–731 B.C.)

Takeloth III was succeeded not by a son, but by a younger brother, Rudamun, of whose reign, which was probably brief, the merest traces are known. In his name, slight work was done at the temple of Osiris-Ruler-of-Eternity at Karnak,[679] and perhaps at Medinet Habu;[680] a vase bears his names,[681] and a descendant of his was buried in Western Thebes.[682] The temple of Osiris shows most of his titulary: Horus, 'Lord of truth' (*Nb-mȝˁt*), and Nebty, 'Rejoicing in truth' (*Ḥkn-m-mȝˁt*), which were both ancient names.[683] As ever in this dynasty, his cartouches were the inevitable Usimare Setepenamun, and 'Beloved of Amun' with the personal name. The Medinet Habu block gives the name of Rudamun's queen as Tadi[amun?], and of his daughter by her, Nesit-er-pauty; for his son-in-law, Pef-tjau-awy-Bast, king of Heracleopolis, cf. above, § 318.

§ 323*   D. IUPUT II (*c.* 731–720? B.C.)

At Leontopolis, Rudamun was succeeded by the last king of this dynasty who is known for certain – Iuput II, of whom no original monument is definitely known as yet;[684] only the mention of him on the great stela of Piankhy. Of his relation to his predecessors, nothing is known, although one might assume him to have been a son of Rudamun. Like Osorkon IV of the senior dynasty in Tanis and Bubastis, Iuput II probably had only local

677. See Christophe, *BIE* 35 (1953/54), 141–52; Leclant, *Recherches,* 1965, 382–3 and n. 1 (where read '12' for '13', as the author kindly informs me).
678. See above, Part II, §§ 143–5, for discussion.
679. *G3,* 392, II, 394, 6; Legrain, *RT* 22 (1900), 130, 132, 134.
680. *G3,* 392, I; Daressy, *RT* 19 (1897), 20–1.
681. In the Louvre; *G3,* 392, III, references.
682. *G3,* 392–3, IV, and 393, n. 1.
683. The Horus name of Snofru and Nebty-name of Amenemhat II of the Old and Middle Kingdoms, respectively. Golden-Horus name, not given. By their occurrence in this temple (built by Osorkon III and Takeloth III), these names must belong to a successor of Takeloth III, Rudamun being the natural choice.
684. Unless one attributed to him, the monuments and prenomen Usimare Setepenamun of a king Iuput usually assigned to Iuput I (*q.v.*), who probably reigned longer and more effectively than Iuput II, and to whom they therefore seem more likely to belong.

effective rule; in his case, at and around the dynastic seat of Leontopolis.

With the division of powers between two senior pharaohs in the Delta (22nd Dynasty, Tanis–Bubastis; 23rd, Leontopolis) and two lesser pharaohs in Middle Egypt (Heracleopolis, Hermopolis), an 'Hereditary Prince' of the senior line in Athribis-with-Heliopolis, a whole series of local chiefs of the Mā in the Delta cities, plus a Princedom of the West covering the west Delta, and Nubia ruling from Thebes southwards, the whole former pharaonic dominion in the Nile Valley lay in fragments by the year 730 B.C. Only two of these were of substance – Nubia and the Princedom of the West – and from their contest, a new Egypt was gradually to be born.

CHAPTER 22

The Twenty-fourth Dynasty and Napata: Nubian Dawn and Libyan Eclipse

§ 324   1. FIRST CONFLICT OF SAIS AND NAPATA (*c.* 728 B.C.)

A. EXPANSION BY TEFNAKHT, PRINCE OF THE WEST

Already by Year 36 of Shoshenq V, *c.* 732 B.C., Tefnakht of Sais was Great Chief of the Mā, Army-leader, and claimed to be Great Chief of the Libu,[685] thus challenging Ankh-Hor who still claimed this title in Year 37.[686] To those same titles, Tefnakht's donation-stela of Year 38 of ⟨Shoshenq V⟩,[687] *c.* 730 B.C., adds not only the boastful epithet 'Great Chief of the entire land' but also the religious titles of prophet of Neith, Edjo and the Lady of Imau, which reflected his rule in Sais, Buto to the north, and Kom el Hisn to the south-west. Apart from that of the Libu, most of these chief-ships were inherited from his precursor, Osorkon C. The specially Libyan titles of Tefnakht, *Mek*-prince of Pehut, and of Kahtan, help us little, but his final title of Prince of the Western Provinces ('Nomes') aptly sums up Tefnakht's control of the western half of the Delta.

These facts 'confirm most objectively'[688] the rule of Tefnakht as out-lined by Piankhy on his great stela very soon afterwards, naming Tefnakht

685. Date from 'Abemayor' stela, *YMM*, 153, § 48.
686. Serapeum stela, § 316 above.
687. At Buto, *YMM*, 152–3, § 47, Pl. I: 1.
688. As effectively set out by Yoyotte, *YMM*, 154–6, §§ 49–53. The speculations by Goedicke (*BASOR* 171 (1963), 65) that the non-royal titles given by Piankhy to Tefnakht 'are thus either indignities inflicted by the victorious Ethiopian or the result of misinformation supplied by Tefnakht's rivals' could not possibly be further from the truth, along with much else in his paper on 'So' (e.g. confusion of Tefnakht with the much later ruler of Heracleopolis, Somtutefnakht

as ruler 'in the ⟨Harpoon?⟩[689] Nome, in the ⟨Xo⟩ite Nome,[690] in Haᶜpy.[691] in [. . .],[692] in A(y)n,[693] in Per-Nūb,[694] in the Memphite Nome[695] – he had taken the entire West(land) from the (coastal) marshes as far (south) as Ithet-tawy'. Thus, Piankhy found him in complete control of the West Delta from Ithet-tawy and Memphis to the Mediterranean; in Memphis, Tefnakht was even a Sem-priest of Ptah, supplanting Ankh-Hor. The further title accorded him by Piankhy, 'Count, Grandee in Netjer' (l. 2) was a distinction associated with Buto.[696]

Tefnakht welded this wide region into virtually a kingdom wherein he was the undisputed chief – no other great chiefs of the Mā or Libu ever arise to dispute the rule of any of its towns or territories with him, even when he is cowed by Piankhy.[697] This solid bloc was to be a power-base for the future. From this West-Delta realm, Tefnakht turned his eyes south, by-passing the chiefs and 'pharaohs' of the East Delta (who bowed to his authority),[698] and began to subdue the local princes of Upper Egypt, besieging Heracleopolis, and securing the adhesion of the rest southward towards Hermopolis. Penetration towards Abydos, then Thebes, could only be a matter of time.

§ 325*   B. THE CAMPAIGN OF PIANKHY IN EGYPT

(c. 728 B.C.)

Reports of Tefnakht's southward advance reached Piankhy in distant

(p. 65, n. 11), uncritically taken from *G3*, 408, IV). On the contrary, Piankhy's statement is closely accurate; and he even *adds* to Tefnakht further rule and dignities (e.g. in Memphis) that other sources (including Tefnakht's own texts) do not yet report to us! The fact remains that Tefnakht did not become king until *after* Piankhy's notable campaign – and shipwreck attends any chronology that would ignore this fact.

689. In the text (line 3), a nome-standard with emblem omitted; Yoyotte (*YMM*, 154) appositely suggests that the complex emblem of the Harpoon province was left to be added later, and was forgotten.

690. Bull upon standard, for kꜣ⟨ḥꜣst⟩, the Xoite province, *YMM*, 154, esp. as the other provinces with bull-standards were ruled by other known chiefs.

691. Haᶜpy, the territory (ww) of the later provinces of Sais and Prosopis (*YMM*, 155, with Gauthier, *Dictionnaire géographique*, IV, 17–18); cf. Tefnakht's title of prophet of Neith.

692. Name totally lost in lacuna.

693. The marshlands of the western province of Imau (*YMM*, 156); cf. Tefnakht's title of prophet of the Lady of Imau.

694. An uncertain location in the West Delta, cf. *YMM*, 156 and n. 4.

695. Doubtless under the purely nominal kingship of Shoshenq V and Osorkon IV; cf. also his title of Sem-priest of Ptah, Piankhy stela, 20.

696. See *YMM*, 154–5, esp. § 51; cf. Tefnakht's title of prophet of Edjo and stela found there.

697. As is well pointed out by Yoyotte (*YMM*, 157).

698. As is evident from Piankhy's listing of Tefnakht's allies on the latter's drive southwards, cf. Piankhy's stela, lines 3, 19.

Napata,[699] but at first he dismissed them disdainfully. Only the defection of Nimlot of Hermopolis stirred him to order his Egyptian-based forces into action to recover Hermopolis, and to send north a further force in support. These latter were given instructions both to let the foe concentrate his forces[700] and to submit themselves to Amun in Thebes while *en route* for the north. One battle on the river was quickly followed by two more near Heracleopolis where Tefnakht's troops were still besieging the faithful Pef-tjau-awy-Bast. Nimlot returned south to Hermopolis to stiffen his town's resistance to Piankhy's soldiers. So, Tefnakht's drive was halted but not decisively worsted.

This merely partial success left Tefnakht in control of strong forces, displeased Piankhy and made him decide to go north and conduct the campaign himself, visiting Thebes *en route*. The army's capture of three townships did not mollify him. When the New Year rites were over at Napata, Piankhy sailed north to Thebes where he celebrated the Opet Festival of Amun (2nd Akhet to 3rd Akhet, day 2), and went on to Hermopolis to press home the siege. Nimlot sought clemency; in a memorable aside, we learn of Piankhy's anger at Nimlot allowing his horses to starve in the siege.

So, at last, Heracleopolis could be relieved in the north, where Pef-tjau-awy-Bast greeted Piankhy with joy. Piankhy struck north for Memphis,[701] key city of Egypt, and obtained the surrender of Pi-Sekhemkheperre, Medum and Ithet-tawy on the way. Only Memphis itself shut fast its gates against the invader and offered resistance. Tefnakht had left there a garrison of 8,000 men, amply supplied, and went off to raise reinforcements in the Delta. The great walled city seemed impregnable. But at length, Piankhy sent his warships to capture every boat at the Memphite harbour-walls and sent the entire armada right up to the walls, so that – using masts and rigging, perhaps, as scaling-ladders – his troops went straight onto these walls and down into the city. Despite this tactical success, stiff hand-to-hand fighting resulted in considerable bloodshed. At last victory came, Piankhy proclaimed protection for the temple of Ptah, where he appeared,

699. All that follows on this topic derives, of course, principally from Piankhy's great granite stela from Gebel Barkal temple, now in Cairo. For text, see H. Schäfer, *Urkunden III*, 1–56, translated by Breasted, *BAR*, IV, §§ 814–83. Further fragments of the stela, see Loukianoff, *Ancient Egypt*, 1926 (III), 86–9, plus Dunham, *The Barkal Temples*, 1970, 12, 48 (fig. 36: 20-3-87), 77–8 (fig. 49: 16-3-336), 79–81 (figs. 50–1: 20-1-41, and 20-1-185); other bits seem to belong to other stelae.

700. On this passage, cf. Gardiner, *JEA* 21 (1935), 219 ff. Piankhy's explicit aim seems to have been to show the foe that his own arms had the confidence of Amun's support behind them; he may also have intended to achieve a 'knockout' blow by defeating a maximal enemy force in one pitched battle.

701. By-passing on his way, the Fayum and places like Atfih on the side.

then occupied the royal palace. Thereupon, other local Memphite garrisons capitulated immediately.

§ **326** The fall of Memphis was the turning-point. Piankhy held the south and Memphis, and could reduce the Delta as and when he pleased. Its rulers made their submission in five phases. First came king Iuput II of Leontopolis (23rd Dynasty), Akunosh Chief of Mā in Sebennytos, and Pediese, Hereditary Prince of Athribis-with-Heliopolis[702] to acknowledge Piankhy. He then went to the Kher-aha and Heliopolis temples to worship, and received there king Osorkon IV of Tanis and Bubastis (22nd Dynasty).

Thereafter, Piankhy made camp in the eastern part of the nome of Athribis, receiving Pediese's hospitality, when the third group came to make submission: 'those kings and rulers of the Delta, all the chiefs who wear the plume, every vizier, all dignitaries, and every "royal acquaintance", from (both) west and east, and the isles in the midst,[703] to see the beauty of His Majesty' (l. 107). Fifteen local rulers, from pharaohs to local mayors, are listed in due order.

Meantime, Tefnakht endeavoured to raise insurrection at Mosdai on the northern edge of Pediese's realm.[704] The attempt was quickly crushed, and the district added by Piankhy to Pediese's domains. Thus, at last, Tefnakht had to admit defeat, and sent a messenger to announce his submission. In sharp contrast to all the rest, he did not come and submit to Piankhy in person, but stayed proudly aloof in his own capital Sais, treating by envoy.[705] Piankhy was content to indulge him in this independent stance, and was content to send his officers to Sais to take Tefnakht's oath of allegiance and his gifts or tribute. This agreement of terms led finally to the fifth capitulation, of the last small pockets of resistance, in the Fayum (Per-Sobek) and at Atfih, which had been by-passed in Piankhy's main thrust north. The four 'pharaohs' finally did obeisance to Piankhy as supreme, but all except Nimlot were excluded from his palace on grounds of ritual impurity (eating fish) – a final humiliation for their discredited kingship for the excluded three.

702. Pediese having probably just succeeded Bakennefi (mentioned in the first list of Tefnakht's allies, Piankhy's stela, line 19). Pediese seems to have smartly taken over the main principality of Athribis, leaving his elder brother Nesnaisu ruling the fief of Heseb-ka; he therefore probably valued Piankhy's support as ruler of Athribis, against the possible jealousy of a (dispossessed?) elder brother.

703. i.e. the settlements on the *gezirehs* or 'sand islands' on which the Delta *tells* or city-mounds arose, from amid the cultivation and marsh.

704. A shrewd move by Tefnakht (close to Heseb-ka), perhaps to stir up insurrection in the adjacent realm of Pediese, probably hardly as yet fully accepted as new ruler of his domain, and to rally Nesnaisu to his own side (cf. last note but one).

705. Cf. already, the perceptive remarks of Yoyotte (*YMM*, 157–8).

§ **327**   Then at last, covered in glory, loaded with booty for Amun of Thebes and of Napata, besides the king himself, and to the outward cheers of the populace, the victorious Piankhy sailed back south, on past Thebes, on to Napata – and was never to be seen in Egypt again, or to be challenged in the Thebaid, so far as we know. At the next New Year, in Year 21 (*c.* 727 B.C.), he set up his massive stela of victory at Napata. Nor was it the sole record of his triumph. Leaving aside the sandstone stela probably belonging to his earlier years (above, § 321), there remains the court (B 501) of the great temple of Amun at Napata on the walls of which Piankhy had sculpted incidents from his campaign, including a procession of Libyan chiefs leading out horses for Piankhy.[706] Traces of label-texts from these scenes once named '[Great Chief of the Mā, Djed-Amen-ef-ankh] in Mendes and the Granary of Re', then various traces (*s[ḥ]tp*, 'pacifying . . .'), then 'from the choicest of its ruler, to pacify [. . . His Majesty??]'.[707] A third stela perhaps also recounted Piankhy's achievement.[708] A fragment of silver naming king Nimlot found its way from his treasury (at Hermopolis) to that of the temple of Ṣanam in Nubia as part of Piankhy's loot.[709]

§ **328**   C. POLITICAL GEOGRAPHY AND HIERARCHY OF EGYPT
(*c.* 728 B.C.)

The picture of Late Libyan Egypt portrayed by Piankhy is both clear and remarkable. In the East Delta, alongside the pharaohs Osorkon IV of the Tanis district[710] and Bubastis and Iuput II of Leontopolis,[711] there sat the

706. Cf. Nimlot of Hermopolis shown leading a horse to Piankhy on the great stela (Mariette, *Monuments Divers,* pl. 1; conveniently reproduced by Petrie, *History of Egypt,* III, 1905, 269, fig. 109); photo of detail, W. Stevenson Smith, *Art & Architecture of Ancient Egypt,* 1958, pl. 174B.

707. On these ruined reliefs (now, regrettably, lost), cf. Smith, *op. cit.,* 238–9 and pl. 174A (who notes a loose block, naming the ruler of Heracleopolis), and now Dunham, *The Barkal Temples,* 1970, pl. 50 (from which I quote the inscriptions and traces in the sequence of their proper order, C–B–A).

708. Cf. Loukianoff, *Ancient Egypt,* 1926 (III), 88, fragment F (now, Dunham, *The Barkal Temples,* 79–80 (fig. 50: 20-1-77)); Dunham, *op. cit.,* 58–9 (fig. 42: 16-4-247b), naming king Nimlot. Possibly also the Berlin fragment, Loukianoff, *op. cit.,* G on plate (*Urkunden III,* 78–9).

709. *PM,* VII, 202; Griffith, *LAAA* 9 (1922), 117, 119, pl. 55: 1.

710. Given as 'the district of Ro-nefer'; for location of a settlement Ro-nefer at Tell Balala (varr. Tebilla, Billi), cf. Daressy, *ASAE* 30 (1930), 78–90; G. Lefebvre, *RdE* 1 (1933), 87–94; Montet, *Kêmi* 8 (1946), 88–9; Yoyotte, *BIFAO* 52 (1953), 180, n. 3; Montet, *Geographie de l'Égypte ancienne,* I, 1957, 140–1 (p. 141, § 2, to be corrected by *RdE* 1, 88, n. 1); Yoyotte, *YMM,* 1961, 129, n. 2, who would extend the district (as opposed to the settlement or city) to the east to include the plain of Tanis, towards Sile. For the Piankhy reference, this would fit well. One should note that this means that the north half of the later XVth province ('Ibis nome') belonged to Osorkon IV, while the south half belonged to Ankh-Hor, son of the Prince of

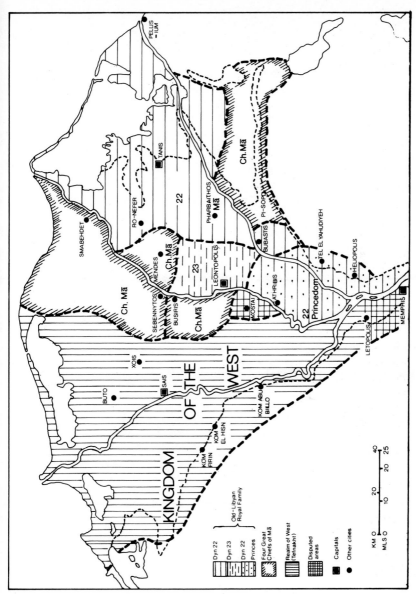

Fig. 5. Late Libyan Egypt *c*. 730 B.C., Time of Piankhy.

'Hereditary Princes' their relatives (Bakennefi, Pediese) in Athribis-with-Heliopolis, plus a junior fief in Ka-heseb (Nesnaisu).[712] These formed one 'bloc' of senior and royal rulers. In Middle and Upper Egypt, two other pharaohs sat at Heracleopolis (Pef-tjau-awy-Bast) and Hermopolis (Nimlot), and ranked with the northern two. This top rank of the hierarchy of four kings and a prince is clearly set out in both the scene and the text of Piankhy's great stela.[713] Second rank is occupied by the Prince of the West – Tefnakht – with the other and western half of the Delta. Third come the four main Great Chiefs of the Mā. Three of these occupied a narrow wedge of territory in the Central Delta, between the domain of Tefnakht and the northern pharaohs. From south to north, Pamiu son of Shoshenq ruled Busiris; Djed-Amen-ef-ankh ruled in Mendes (with his son Ankh-Hor in an adjoining fief);[714] and Akunosh ruled a large, swampy domain from Sebennytos to Sma-behdet and the sea.[715] The fourth chief ruled the southeast route into the Delta (Wadi Tumilat), from Pi-Sopd[716]– at this time, Patjenfy. Fourth and last in the hierarchy came the lesser, very local chiefs and city-mayors of the second and third class.[717]

This four-fold division, so clearly etched by Piankhy's great inscription, underlay the political geography of Egypt not only in Piankhy's time but for almost another century, being but thinly veiled behind the purely superficial unity of rule presented by the Nubian or 25th Dynasty.

Mendes. These two halves could, of course, have been brought together at some later date.

711. Taremu, now Tell Moqdam, Yoyotte, *BIFAO* 52 (1953), 179–92. Ta'an is still utterly obscure; Yoyotte (*YMM*, 129, n. 2 end) rejected Gauthier's suggested equation with a ⌐Ta'ant¬ (*Dictionnaire géographique*, VI, 6) on a Pharbaithos donation-stela of Year 8 of Psammetichus I (*PSBA* 14 (1892), 238), but if this plot of land was S.S.W. of Pharbaithos, then Ta'ant(?) could be east of Leontopolis.

712. i.e. Nesnaisu ruled in what later became the XIth Lower Egyptian province; in *c.* 730 B.C., it must in fact have been the territory north of Athribis (and contiguous with it, to be an apanage thereof), and south of Leontopolis – if Heseb were separate from Tell Moqdam, then it is far likelier to be in *this* area than near to Pharbaithos (for which location there is no good evidence) or north of Leontopolis.

713. Cf. *YMM*, 128–9.

714. In Per-Thoth-Wep-Rehwy (Baqlia), to W.S.W. – i.e. in the southern half of the later XVth province.

715. A very large realm on the map, but largely undeveloped then.

716. Saft el-Henneh, and doubtless Wadi Tumilat; the 'Granary of Memphis' remains obscure (cf. *YMM*, 133, n. 1).

717. Such were the local chiefs of the Mā at Pharbaithos (not even mentioned by Piankhy), in Per-Gerur (? east end of Wadi Tumilat, perhaps subject to Pi-Sopd), and Taweret and Tabekhnet (unknown, cf. *YMM*, 126, n. 1), and mayors and prophets in Letopolis and Rehes, in Khent-nefer, and over at Kher-Aha/Per-Hapi.

§ 329 2. THE LULL BETWEEN THE STORMS
(c. 728–715 B.C.)

A. PIANKHY AND THE SOUTH

(i) *Piankhy in Nubia*

At Napata his capital, below the towering cliffs of the 'Holy Mountain' (Gebel Barkal), Piankhy vastly enlarged the modest temple of Amun (B 500), founded in New Kingdom times, over half a millennium earlier. He first cased-round the older temple with new walls,[718] and fronted it with a pylon (II) and a large bipartite[719] columned hall; later, he built before these a great colonnaded forecourt and another pylon (I).[720] Nearby, he built a chapel and a paved and walled processional roadway.[721] In the great temple, he erected his stelae. Thus, Napata was already becoming architecturally the Karnak of Upper Nubia. In Amun's halls he installed a barque-stand,[722] and before the pylons granite rams of Amenophis III from Soleb.[723]

At Ṣanam, Piankhy left a usurped statue, and in the Letti area a granite obelisk.[724] On his monuments, Piankhy preferred to use his name plus 'Beloved of Amun', sometimes also 'Son of Bast'. The prenomen Usimare he later varied with Seneferre, and took the Horus names 'Pacifying his Two Lands', 'Strong Bull, appearing in Thebes', 'Bull of his Two Lands',[725] plus the Nebty names 'The Bull' and 'Ruler of Egypt'.[726]

At El Kurru, Piankhy erected a pyramid for himself,[727] and tombs for five of his queens and two of his daughters.[728] None of these ladies feature in Egypt proper except Queen Peksater for whom a chapel was built on the sacred territory of Abydos.[729]

718. Cf. Reisner, *JEA* 4 (1917), 225, for red sandstone casing and its date; lintels and architraves of Piankhy, *ibid.*, 224.

719. Main hall, 4 rows of 7 columns, rear part, 6 rows of 3 columns; cf. plans, Reisner, *ZÄS* 69 (1933), opposite p. 76, Dunham, *The Barkal Temples*, 1970, plan V.

720. Columned hall (B. 502), 'early Piankhy', forecourt (B. 501), 'later Piankhy', Dunham, plan V; abaci of columns of B. 502, cf. Dunham, 55, fig. 40.

721. Chapel, first phase (B. 900, first) and contemporary roadway of Piankhy, cf. Reisner, *JEA* 6 (1920), 261, 264. He and Kashta probably built early shrine at B. 800 (*PM*, VII, 212).

722. *PM*, VII, 220–1 (47); a second altar or stand from Old Merowe, *ibid.*, 198.

723. Cf. *PM*, VII, 216 (1–6), 219 (22–5).

724. *PM*, VII, 192; cf. Reisner, *ZÄS* 66 (1931), 94–7, for the titles.

725. First, from Barkal 'altar', latter two, Letti obelisk (Reisner, *loc. cit.*).

726. From Letti obelisk (*ibid.*).

727. *PM*, VII, 197, No. 17; Dunham, *El Kurru*, 1950, 64–6.

728. Cf. *PM*, VII, 195, No. 3; 196, No. 6; 197–8, Nos. 51–5; Dunham, *ad locc.*

729. Cf. *PM*, V, 70, references.

§ 330* (ii) *Life at Thebes*

In Thebes, with the old Libyan dynasties now discredited and the Nubian conqueror a devotee of Amun, datelines henceforth were written in the name of 'Pharaoh P(iankh)y,[730] Son of Isis, Beloved of Amun'– so in papyri which were doubtless of Theban origin, recording the sale of 'northern' slaves in Years 21 and 22 of that king[731] (immediately after his campaign), a chief steward of Amun, Djed-Bast-ef-ankh featuring in the latter year. A bandage-fragment from Western Thebes has a date something over Year 20 of Piankhy.[732]

As nominal heads of the Theban theocracy, the two God's Wives of Amun, Shepenupet I and Amenirdis I, functioned throughout. High steward or major-domo of Amenirdis was the affluent and portly Harwa, of whom at least eight statues are known, and a splendid tomb in Western Thebes.[733]

Among the rest of the Theban hierarchy, few personalities stand out from the crowd of priests of Amun and Montu who found their last resting places in Western Thebes. As 2nd prophet of Amun, Nes-hor-behdet was succeeded by his son-in-law Patjenfy,[734] while probably Djed-Khons-ef-ankh D (last of a long line) still officiated as 4th prophet. His family had developed ties with Hermopolis, and his younger brother bore the Hermopolitan name Tjanhesret, on whose Theban statue[735] – along with words addressed to Hermopolitan priests – appear the cartouches of a new local pharaoh of Hermopolis, Thutemhat (§ 331, below). In the meantime a new family of southern viziers had appeared;

730. Py is possibly an abbreviated form of P(iankh)y – or (more likely?) actually the true reading of his name, if it is a Nubian word in which the ʿ*ankh*-sign is merely an ideogram or complement; cf. Leclant, *OLZ* 61 (1966), 552.

731. See Parker, *ZÄS* 93 (1966), 111–14, whose identification of Py with Piankhy was cautious but is hardly open to serious doubt. Year 21 is in Papyrus Leiden (Belzoni), and Year 22 in Papyrus Vatican 10574. The epithets given P(iankh)y, Son of Isis, Beloved of Amun, are those typical for later 22nd/23rd Dynasties.

732. British Museum 6640; I am indebted to Mr. T. G. H. James (communication of 27 February 1968) for notes on this fragment and a drawing of the date. This clearly shows *ḥȝt-sp* plus patch with trace, plus '20' and a flat sign that could be a *t*. The trace could well be a further '10' (with nothing lost below it), and the final sign, merely the otiose *t* that follows the numeral in many Late Period datelines (e.g. the 21 of Year 21 of Piankhy on his stela). Thus, the BM date is not less than '20' and most probably '30' – which fits well into a 32-year reign of Piankhy.

733. Gunn and Engelbach, *BIFAO* 30 (1931), 791–815 and pls., for the statues; Tomb 37, *PM*², I: 1, 68–9.

734. Whose son the prophet of Amun, Amenemhat, offers on an Edfu stela of Shabako's reign (Engelbach, *ASAE* 21 (1921), 190–2, fig. 2). On Patjenfy, etc., cf. Kees, *Pr.*, 286, corrected by *Nachträge*, 25.

735. Cairo Cat. 42212; cf. above, Part III, §§ 187–8.

Harsiese F and his sons Nesmin A and Khamhor A probably served under Osorkon III, Takeloth III, and Piankhy.[736]

§ 331* (iii) *Middle Egypt*

Oases. Piankhy's writ ran well beyond Thebes alone. Out in the Oasis of Dakhla, the local Great Chief of the Sha(m)iun, Nes-Ṯḥuty, was guarantor for an endowment set up by a local official Harentbia for his father, commemorated by a stela dated to Year 24 of 'Pharaoh Py, Son of Isis, beloved of Amun'[737] – i.e. in the 24th year of Piankhy.

Hermopolis. In Middle Egypt, Nimlot may have been succeeded locally by a new man very soon after Piankhy's great campaign: the Horus, 'Atum is truly Lord' (*Nb- 'Itm-m-mȝ't*), 'king of Upper and Lower Egypt' (!), Neferkheperre Kha-khau, Son of Re, Thutemhat. Besides the Theban statue of Tjanhesret already cited (§ 330, above), this kinglet is known from a bronze shrine in the British Museum.[738] Whether he was in fact the predecessor or the actual successor of Nimlot remains uncertain. Thereafter, by the end of Piankhy's reign (or still later), it is possible that the local throne of Hermopolis passed to yet a third kinglet, Menkheperre ⌈Khmun⌉ y, whose ambitious formal titles were: Horus, 'Uniter of the Two Lands' (!), Nebty, 'Creator of Crafts(?)', and Golden Horus, 'Multiplier of Warriors' (respectively, *Smȝ-tȝwy*; *Ms-ḥmt*; *S'šȝ-ḳnw*). In Thebes, on a stela dedicated for his daughter, he called himself 'Son of Amun, born of Mut' and – in a snatch of charming lyric poetry – vaunted the charms of his daughter, Mutirdis, prophetess of Mut and Hathor.[739] Here again, as with Thutemhat, one sees a bond between Hermopolis and Nubian-ruled Thebes.

Heracleopolis. Further north, the succession after 'king' Pef-tjau-awy-Bast remains totally veiled from us until well into the 25th Dynasty; that kinglet may have been succeeded by a son of his own until a new line was installed later by the 25th Dynasty or its Saite rivals.

§ 332   B. THE 24TH DYNASTY AND LAST BUBASTITES
IN THE NORTH

(i) *Tefnakht as King* (c. *728/7–720 B.C.*)

Once Piankhy had gone straight back south, left no new administration,

736. Khamhor A being grandfather of the famous Montemhat, 4th prophet and Mayor of Thebes, Part III, § 196, above.

737. Smaller Dakhla stela, first published by Spiegelberg, *RT* 25 (1903), 194 ff., and now more fully and correctly by J. J. Janssen, *JEA* 54 (1968), 165–72, and pls. 25–25A.

738. BM 11005; cf. S. Morenz, *Der Gott auf der Blume*, 1954, 28 and n. 36.

739. Stela, Louvre C. 100; Prisse, *Monuments*, 4, more conveniently Petrie, *History of Egypt*, 1905, 293, fig. 121. Khmuny may be Piankhy, cf. §79, n. 71 end.

clearly had no intention of reigning as king of Egypt in Memphis, and then made no further move to return north, the existence of a power-vacuum in Egypt, especially in the north, must have been almost immediately evident to all in the Delta. The older dynasties of Tanis and Leontopolis had ceased to count as anything more than the local petty chiefs they in fact had become; they, their Middle-Egyptian colleagues and the chiefs of the Mā had all bowed in subservience to Piankhy. Tefnakht alone had stood aloof, and stood his ground, in Sais, retaining the whole of his considerable kingdom intact. And he alone ruled not only a large, but a united kingdom.

Without any serious rival, therefore, Tefnakht in all probability lost little time in filling the gap, becoming Pharaoh in the north, from Memphis northward. He took the formal titulary of Horus, Nebty and Golden Horus, with the cartouches Shepsesre Tefnakht.[740] As pharaoh of the west, Tefnakht made no attempt to challenge or evict Osorkon IV or Iuput II in the east, whether he claimed any overlordship or not. Nor, seemingly, did he risk any renewed Nubian reaction by moving south again. Of two stelae bearing his royal style, only one is dated, to his 8th year (*c.* 720 B.C.).[741] Thereafter, Bakenranef ruled from Sais, and was officially accepted as king throughout the north.

§ **333*** (ii) *The Last Bubastites: Osorkon IV* (*c. 730–715 B.C.*)

This powerless shadow-pharaoh continued to reign over the large north-eastern principality of Ro-nefer, Tanis and Bubastis until after 716 B.C., and so was contemporary with the entire 24th Dynasty of Tefnakht and Bakenranef. Being the north-easternmost of Egypt's quintet of pharaohs, he was most immediately exposed to contacts with Western Asia across the Sinai isthmus.

Thus, in 726/725 B.C., Hoshea king of Israel conspired to throw off the yoke of Assyria under Shalmaneser V, ceasing to pay tribute and sending envoys to 'So, king of Egypt' (2 Kings 17: 4); his embassy thither availed him nought and he lost his throne. Israel was now incorporated into the Assyrian provincial system and its population was mainly carried into exile. The identity of So has long been debated, but can now be closely narrowed down. On title and name, he was certainly *not* the supposed

---

740. So, on his Athens stela (see next note). On this stela, 'Horus' is followed by *Siȝ-ib*, 'Discerning of mind'; Nebty by a lacuna; and 'Golden Horus', merely by his first cartouche.

741. Year 8, Athens stela, *G3*, 409, V; Spiegelberg, *RT* 25 (1903), 190–3, photo in J. Capart, *Recueil de monuments égyptiens*, II, 1905, pl. 92. An undated stela is in the Michaelides collection, cf. R. Sayed, *VT* 17 (1967), 118, to be published by Yoyotte.

'Sib'e', *turtan* (army-commander) of Egypt, mentioned by Sargon II of Assyria in 720 B.C.[742] An army-commander is *not* a pharaoh, and in fact the name of this commander is to be read as Re'e, not Sib'e.[743] Equally, on date and name, So was not the later pharaoh Shabako: the latter did not rule Egypt until *c.* 715 B.C. onwards, a whole decade later, and the names do not correspond, where Re'e is concerned.[744] Nor should the Hebrew text be read as 'vizier of the king of Egypt';[745] nor is Iuput II a likely candidate. Tefnakht has been suggested on two grounds, and his dates as king (*c.* 728/7–720 B.C.) would fit. One suggestion[746] which is to take Hebrew *Sōʾ* as *Seweʾ*, interpreted as a transcription of Tefnakht's Horus-name (*Siʾ-ib*) is highly ingenious but totally unlikely – foreign rulers and scribes *never* referred to Egyptian pharaohs by any name other than their cartouche-names, and in the Late Period (22nd–26th Dynasties) only by their *personal names*;[747] so, 'So' is not *Siʾ-ib*. The other suggestion is to read 2 Kings 17: 4 as 'he sent envoys to Sais, ⟨to⟩ the king of Egypt'– i.e. to Tefnakht left unnamed.[748] That Tefnakht was potentially a stronger ruler than Osorkon IV or Iuput II may well have been true; but terri-torially, his large Princedom of the West was not unduly greater than the areas ruled directly by Osorkon IV as heir of the 22nd Dynasty. Tempting as the equation with Sais and Tefnakht may seem at first sight, a whole series of objections militate against it. First, he was geographically too far distant in Sais to be of immediate aid to a king in Palestine. Secondly, the reading of 'So' as Sais in 2 Kings 17: 4 requires a gratuitous emendation to the text after it, quite needless if So is a personal, not a place, name. Thirdly, there was a long-standing alliance (from Osorkon II and Takeloth II onwards) with the 22nd Dynasty kings and Israel – and no kingdom

742. e.g. *LAR*, II, § 55; *ANET*, 285.

743. See R. Borger, *JNES* 19 (1960), 49–53, for this reading. Egyptian Raia (Ranke, *Ägyptischen Personennamen*, I, 216: 23) or Raʿia (*ibid.*, I, 220: 7–10) would be equally good originals for the Akkadian Re'e. This man may well have been the army-commander for Osorkon IV in 720 B.C.

744. In the Late Period, in any case, Eg. *š* is rendered by Heb. *ś*, not by Heb. *s* (cf. Shoshenq, Shishak).

745. As suggested by S. Yeivin, *VT* 2 (1952), 164–8 (taking Heb. *sōʾ* as trans-literating Eg. *tʾ*); on vocalic grounds, this is ruled out by Vergote (to whom I am indebted for a personal communication).

746. Cf. Ramadan Sayed, *VT* 17 (1967), 116–18; his appeal to 'Sib'e' is also to be discarded, seeing that this name is to be read Re'e.

747. e.g. Shishak (Shoshenq I), Tirhakah (Taharqa), Necho (Necho II), and Hophra (Wahibre, Greek Apries). Back in the late 2nd millennium B.C., the prenomen was used abroad (so, for Amenophis III and IV and Tutankhamun, in the Amarna letters), but never any other name such as a Horus-name.

748. See H. Goedicke, *BASOR* 171 (1963), 64–6, with postscript by Albright, *ibid.*, 66. The suggestion that So may be for Sais is the only really valuable point in this paper, its chronology (after Albright) being much too low.

of Sais was hitherto known to the Hebrew court. Fourthly, the Hebrew prophets of the day inveigh against envoys going not to distant Sais, but to the *East Delta*: Isaiah denounced 'the princes of Zoan' (Tanis) as 'utterly foolish', they being 'the wisest counsellors of Pharaoh' (Isaiah 19: 11), for 'the princes of Zoan are become fools' (*ibid.* 19: 13). He further denounced such Hebrew rulers as would 'strengthen themselves with the might of Pharaoh' (*ibid.* 30: 2), as 'his princes are at Zoan and his envoys reach Hanes'[749] (30: 4). Throughout, the 8th-century Hebrew prophet firmly condemned false alliances with 'Pharaoh'– and for him, the pharaoh and his counsellors were to be found at *Tanis* – which was the Delta capital of Egypt throughout the 21st–25th Dynasties (but never of Tefnakht) – never at Sais, and rarely elsewhere.[750] Fifthly, there is a far better candidate who fits the part of So perfectly – Osorkon IV, king in Tanis and Bubastis.

§ **334*** In favour of Osorkon IV are many points. First, one may treat 'So' as simply an abbreviated form of his name, (O)so(rkon);[751] all the rest then fits into place. Secondly, this identification dispenses with needless emendation (or strained interpretation) of the Hebrew text. Thirdly,

749. Hebrew Hanes is commonly equated with *Ḥ(wt-nni)-nsw*, 'Heracleopolis' – philologically impeccable, but geographically highly improbable, as long since pointed out by Spiegelberg, *Ägyptologische Randglossen zum Alten Testament*, 1904, 36–8. The geographical problem, as he has seen, can be neatly solved by referring Hebrew Hanes to the Lower-Egyptian Heracleopolis in the East Delta. This would be the *Anysis* of Herodotus (II, 137, 166) east of Tanis, perhaps the *Herakleous mikra polis* (ancient Sethroe?) possibly midway between Tanis and Pelusium cited by Gardiner, *Ancient Egyptian Onomastica*, II, 1947, 176*; see further the notes of Caminos, *JEA* 50 (1964), 94. This would be geographically excellent. The only alternative would be to take Hanes as a transliteration for Eg. *Ḥ(wt)-nsw*, 'Mansion (or, Domain) of the King'. In parallel with Zoan or Tanis in Isaiah 30: 4, it would then refer to the palace in Tanis itself (cf. already, Kitchen, *NBD*, 504). Philologically, this equation is as good as the other; the main objection to this idea is that *ḥwt-nsw* is not the usual term for a palace, and is too *recherché* to suit the prophet's straightforward reproofs to a Hebrew audience.

750. Memphis occurs but once in Isaiah (19: 13), where its princes are put in parallel with those of Tanis; it will be recalled that Memphis recognized the Tanite kings throughout and was their administrative capital – so this 'parallelism' well fits the conditions.

751. Cf. in the New Kingdom, 'Sesse' as a well-known abbreviation for Ramesses II (*ANET*, 477, 478; Gardiner, *JEA* 6 (1920), 103), 'Mose' in Papyrus Salt 124 is an abbreviation for King Amenmesses (cf. Černý, *JEA* 15 (1929), 255), while in the Late Period Shoshenq can be abbreviated to Shosh (cf. on scarabs, *G3*, 314–15), possibly Py for Piankhy (unless, as probable, Py is the real form), sundry shortenings of Osorkon and Takeloth, and Shilkanni for (U)shilkanni, below. Abbreviations of private names are common from the New Kingdom onwards, e.g. Huy for Amenhotep, Mahu for Amenemhab, Aniy for Amenemonet, Apiy for Amenemope, etc. (Gardiner, *Eg. Grammar*, Appendix B with references).

Osorkon IV ruled in Tanis as senior pharaoh, precisely where the Hebrew prophets condemned their rulers' envoys treating with Egypt. Fourthly, his territorial domain in the East Delta was, if smaller, still comparable with that of Tefnakht in the far west, and with a little outward show, his court in the great metropolis of Tanis, with his ancestors' palaces and temples, would impress a Hebrew envoy far more than the *ménage* of the upstart Tefnakht in Sais which was still rural. Fifthly, Osorkon IV in the East Delta was directly adjacent to Palestine, to give speedy help if called upon and able to do so. Sixthly, there was the long-standing alliance between the 22nd Dynasty (from Osorkon II onwards) in Tanis and Israel (§§ 283, 288, above) which had been stimulated initially by the campaigns of Shalmaneser III of Assyria; Hoshea may well have invoked it in applying to So (Osorkon IV, perhaps great-great-grandson of Takeloth II) for military aid. Seventhly, the Hebrew annalist records no help given by Osorkon IV – this shadow-ruler, for all the splendid setting of his court bequeathed him by his predecessors, just did not have the resources to muster or launch large armies like Shoshenq I or Osorkon I as of old. He presumably dithered and delayed over sending even a token force (such as Osorkon II sent to Qarqar); while he did so, Hoshea was captured (*c.* 724/723) and in 722 B.C. Samaria and all Israel fell to the Assyrian conquerors.[752]

Thus, in 726/725 B.C., Osorkon IV was called to face the first major challenge to Egyptian action in Western Asia for about a century and probably sidestepped it through sheer lack of resources. The long reign of Shoshenq III, the brief tenure of Pimay and much of the reign of Shoshenq V had been virtually free of any threat from Western Asia – during *c.* 825–750 B.C., the Assyrian grip on the Westlands slackened and the conquering impetus declined.[753] Only with Tiglath-pileser III and his successors did the threat renew itself, and not to Egypt immediately.

§ 335   After the crisis of 725, the Assyrian spectre loomed up again in 720 B.C. – the year of the death of Tefnakht and of the accession of Bakenranef in Sais. That same year, Sargon II crushed a revolt in Syria and subdued Philistia as far as Gaza. On this occasion, the Egyptian king *did* assist the Palestinians – he sent Re'e (a Raia), his army-commander (*tartannu* KUR *Muṣuri*) with a force to assist Hanun, king of Gaza.

752. Cf. H. Tadmor, *JCS* 12 (1958), 35–9.
753. Only Adad-nirari III had intervened decisively in the Westlands, between the last years of Shalmaneser III and the advent of Tiglathpileser III. In that relatively undisturbed century, Egypt doubtless maintained ordinary commercial and other relations with the Levant, but we have no Wenamun to reveal it to us.

But the allies were defeated, Gaza fell, Re'e fled back to Egypt, Raphia fell to the Assyrians, and was looted and sacked.[754]

§ 336* Finally, in 716 B.C., Sargon II struck again at Philistia and towards Egypt. He subdued the local Arabs, and established a vassal sheikh at Laban to regulate affairs at *Naḥal Muṣur*, the biblical 'Brook (Wadi) of Egypt', near El-Arish.[755] The Assyrian cohorts were now but 120 miles away from Tanis itself, less than 100 from the border-fort of Sile. At this juncture, Osorkon IV found it politic to buy off his dangerous new neighbour with a handsome present: 'Shilkanni (Osorkon IV),[756] king of Muṣri (Egypt) – a remote ⌐ region ⌐ – the fear of the effulgence of Assur my lord [over-whelmed him], and he (had) brought to me as his present twelve large horses of Egypt without their equals in the land (of Assyria)', as Sargon put it.

Thereafter, in the fateful year 715 B.C., Osorkon IV disappeared from view, and with him the last vestige of the 22nd Dynasty as a sovereign power; half a century later, his descendants perhaps claimed a narrowly-localized kingship in Tanis under the Nubian dominion (cf. § 357, below). In Leontopolis, the collateral line also disappears into obscurity after Iuput II, unless one concedes the existence of a shadowy and suspect Shoshenq VI (prenomen, *Wasneterre*[757]) whose very historicity is open to doubt.

§ 337   3. BAKENRANEF (24th DYNASTY,
        c. 720–715 B.C.)

In Sais, Tefnakht's successor[758] appears as King Wahkare, Son of Re, Bakenranef, the Bocchoris of Manetho. His acceptance in later tradition as sole 'official' ruler of his dynasty suggests that Bakenranef ruled at Memphis not only *de facto* as Tefnakht had done, but also was recognized *de jure*, following the eclipse of the Bubastite royal line with the invasion of Piankhy. The nature and extent of the rule of Bakenranef is unknown. He

754. Cf. (e.g.) *ANET*, 285; *LAR*, II, §§ 5, 55; Tadmor, *JCS* 12 (1958), 35–9.
755. Cf. *ANET*, 286, § c, amplified by Tadmor, *op. cit.*, 77–8.
756. For the philological equivalence of Shilkanni and (O)sorkon (IV), see Albright, *BASOR* 141 (1956), 24. The chronology there proposed (p. 25) must now, of course, be completely discarded – e.g. there is no truth whatever in the assertion that Piankhy ended the rule of Tefnakht. For Assyrian tribute-officers bringing horses from Egypt at this same epoch, cf. Saggs, *Iraq* 17 (1955), 134–5, 152–3, on ND 2765.
757. For whom, cf. above, Part II, §§ 67, 110.
758. The relationship (if any) of Tefnakht and Bakenranef – father and son? – remains unknown.

evidently did nothing to eliminate the older royal lines who still ruled locally in Tanis–Bubastis and Leontopolis, or chiefs of the Mā outside the Princedom of the West. Nor do we know how far in practice these local rulers actually recognized any overlordship of Bakenranef.

§ **338**   Of the events of Bakenranef's reign, again, nothing is known, at least until its end; later tradition made of him a legal reformer, or at any rate a lawgiver.[759] Monuments of his reign are almost nil – a few scarabs, and a Phoenician vase that reached Italy.[760]

Then, in his 6th year (c. 715 B.C.), there died the Apis which had probably been installed 16 years earlier in the 37th year of Shoshenq V – between ten and twenty humble stelae attest its obsequies.[761] But before the vault was finally closed upon the burial of the embalmed remains of the sacred bull, Bakenranef himself was no more and Egypt had a new pharaoh: Shabako. For on the walls of that same vault was written an epigraph of Year 2 of Shabako[762] who, a year earlier (716), had succeeded his elder brother Piankhy at Napata. Whether Bakenranef had made any attempt to gain real control in Middle and Upper Egypt is unknown. But Shabako supplanted him as effective ruler of all Egypt.[763]

759. Cf. remarks by Yoyotte, *YMM*, 158, § 58. Studies on Bakenranef, cf. A. Moret, *De Bocchori Rege*, 1903, and J. M. A. Janssen, 'Over farao Bocchoris' in *Varia Historica . . . A. W. Byvanck . . .*, 1954, 17–29.

760. *G3*, 411–12, *PM*, VII, 408; W. Stevenson Smith, *Art & Architecture of Ancient Egypt*, 1958, 242 and n. 21 with fig. 76.

761. Cf. Malinine, Posener, Vercoutter, *Catalogue, stèles, Sérapéum*, I, Nos. 91 ff.

762. See Vercoutter, *Kush* 8 (1960), 65–7; cf. above, Part II, § 114.

763. Manetho records that Shabako captured Bocchoris and burnt him alive; for this, there is no independent evidence, and unless it was followed by entombment of the remains, it would have militated against the acceptance of Shabako by Egyptians.

CHAPTER 23

The Twenty-fifth Dynasty: Nubian Rule and Assyrian Impact

§ 339* 1. SHABAKO (c. 716–702 B.C.)

A. ACCESSION IN NUBIA

In 716 B.C., after 31 years' reign, Piankhy died and was buried in his pyramid, having stipulated that a team of horses should be interred nearby to accompany him into the afterworld.[764] His brother and successor Shabako adopted the venerable prenomen Neferkare which had been most popular in Egypt some fifteen centuries before,[765] and uniform Horus, Nebty and Golden Horus names – all Sebaq-tawy (*Sb(ʾ)ḳ-tʾwy*), 'He who blesses the Two Lands'[766] – according to Old and Middle Kingdom style.

§ 340* B. ASSERTION OF RULE IN EGYPT

Precisely why, in his 2nd year (715 B.C.), Shabako marched north to the reconquest of Egypt is unknown. Possibly, like Tefnakht long before him, Bakenranef had finally begun to show some interest in the south, or perhaps Shabako himself simply decided to rule Egypt as a real pharaoh, and not as a make-believe overlord in Napata. However that may be, by Year 2 he was in control of Memphis, and closed the vault on the burial of an Apis bull that had but lately died and been embalmed in what had been the 6th year of Bakenranef (§ 337 above). He certainly eliminated the latter

764. Pyramid, cf. § 329, end, above; Horse-graves, cf. *PM*, VII, 198.
765. In the 3rd(?), 6th, 7th–8th, 9th–10th Dynasties, then only by Ramesses IX and Amenemnisu; on possible alternative prenomen each for Shabako and Shebitku (in the manner of Piankhy), cf. above, Part II, § 124. On Shabako's titulary, cf. Leclant, *Recherches*, 335–6, n. 5.
766. Taking *Sbḳ* as from *Sb(ʾ)ḳ* (*Wörterbuch der Aeg. Sprache*, IV, 86–7); it is written *sbḳ* oftener than *sḳb* ('who refreshes . . . ').

king, if not other royal dynasts, and with firmness and dispatch took effective control of all Egypt right up to the Asiatic frontier. Thus, he issued a commemorative scarab to celebrate his suppression of 'revolt' in Egypt, overawing the foreign foes:[767] '(Titles of:) Shabako, given life, more loved by Amun than any king who has existed since the founding of the land. He has slain those who rebelled against him in both South and North, and in every foreign land. The Sand-dwellers [Asiatic semi-nomads] are faint because of him, falling for (very) fear of him – they come of themselves as captives and each among them seized his fellow – for he (the king) had performed benefactions for ⟨his⟩ father (Amun), so greatly does he love him.' Shabako thus quelled any opposition. In Sais itself, he probably installed a Nubian governor, at least initially.[768] Mention of the Sand-dwellers may be intended for the tribes-folk of Sinai, who were possibly briefly chastized by Shabako's forces to assure border security. But the dissension and offering of captives among the Asiatics may, rather, reflect the tensions in Philistia or beyond which resulted from differing attitudes to Assyrian overlordship. Shabako certainly maintained Piankhy's rule of the oases, since blocks of his have been found in the Bahria oasis.[769]

Within Egypt itself, his assumption of effective rule (at least as generally-recognized overlord) is marked not only by the Apis-burial at Memphis but also by a Nile level text (Year 2) at Karnak,[770] and especially by dona-tion-stelae from the Delta – one of Year 2 from Pharbaithos,[771] one of Year 3 from Bubastis,[772] and one of Year 6 from Buto in the heart of the former domain of Sais.[773] A reflection of Shabako's victory in Egypt is given by his dedicatory-text for work done on the porch and gateway of Pylon IV of the temple of Amun in Karnak – 'he has made for it a plating of good gold which the Majesty of . . . (titles) Shabako, Beloved of Amun,

767. Scarab, Royal Ontario Museum, Toronto, 910. 28.1 (formerly 1718), first published indirectly by Maspero, *ASAE* 7 (1906), 142, and by Müller, *OLZ* 17 (1914), 49–52. It was later dismissed as a fake, then rehabilitated by Yoyotte, *Biblica* 37 (1956), 457–76, and 39 (1958), 206–10.
768. Cf. the entry in Manetho (var. Eusebius) under the (proto-) 26th Dynasty, 'Ammeris the Ethiopian (i.e. Nubian) for 12 (var. 18) years', a figure probably nearer 20 years (*c*. 715–695 B.C.); cf. Part II, §§ 116–18, above.
769. *PM*, VII, 311.
770. No. 30 (Legrain, *ZÄS* 34 (1896), 114–15; von Beckerath, *JARCE* 5 (1966), 52).
771. By a local chief of the Mā, Patjenfy; cf. *G4*, 13, II, and *YMM*, 126: 21.
772. Date read by Yoyotte, *YMM*, 134, n. 2; from description by S. Adam, *ASAE* 55 (1958), 307, it is Shabako himself, not the local chief, who is depicted offering the field to Bast. Thus, the old Tanis-Bubastis domain of the 22nd Dynasty had come under Nubian rule more directly than most principalities, at least for a time.
773. *G4*, 13, III; now, MMA 55. 144. 6, cf. references by Yoyotte, *YMM*, 172, n. 4, and Schulman, *JARCE* 5 (1966), 40, No. 38.

brought from the victories that his father Amun had decreed for him.'[774]

§ 341*   C. FOREIGN AFFAIRS

In 712 B.C., Sargon II sent his army-commander (the *turtanu*)[775] to settle accounts with the Philistine city of Ashdod, where the usurper Iamani sought anew to throw off the Assyrian yoke.[776] Ashdod was captured, a victory stela was erected,[777] and a governor was installed alongside a new king to keep an eye on him. Iamani fled to Egypt. There, Shabako, the 'Pharaoh of Egypt' (*Pir'u* king of *Muṣru*), 'which (land) belongs (now) to Kush' (Nubia),[778] obligingly extradited the fugitive Iamani to the Assyrian's satisfaction. Subsequently, Shabako probably maintained outwardly friendly (or, at least neutral) relations with Assyria, whatever sympathies he may have had for the petty Palestinian states that stood as a buffer between him and Assyrian power. He was shrewd enough to avoid any armed confrontation with the might of Assur. So much seems probable from the discovery at Nineveh of a clay seal-impression or bulla bearing the titles of Shabako over his figure in triumphal pose; associated with an 'Assyrian' seal-impression, it may have been the sealing from some papyrus document of diplomatic import which has long since perished.[779] Thus, Shabako's 14 or 15 years' rule meant external peace for Egypt.

§ 342   D. HOME AFFAIRS
(i) *General Tone*
Within Egypt, Shabako was patron of the gods, their temples and their

774. Dedicatory text, Karnak, see Leclant, *RdE* 8 (1951), 107, 110–11 (cf. pl. 4), 111–12. It was 'restored' in the Ptolemaic period, cf. Leclant, 115–20, and Barguet, *Temple d'Amon-rê à Karnak*, 90, 310.

775. A detail reflected in Isaiah (20: 1), warning his people against trusting in the power of Egypt and Nubia.

776. Texts, cf. *ANET*, 286, 287 (and *LAR*, II, §§ 30, 62, 193–5), but against rendering Iamani as 'the Greek', cf. Tadmor, *JCS* 12 (1958), 80, n. 217. Azuri of Ashdod had rebelled, and was replaced in 713 by the pro-Assyrian Ahimeti whom Iamani and his fellows overthrew.

777. Cf. Tadmor, *BA* 29 (1966), 94–5, figs. 9–11, for the stela and Assyrian reliefs of the capture of nearby Ekron and Gibbethon.

778. This reference to Egypt and Nubia under *one* ruler, a pharaoh, rules out automatically *any* ruler of this period other than a king of the 25th Dynasty (Tefnakht and Bakenranef *never* ruled or claimed to rule in Nubia). And in the 25th Dynasty, no king earlier than Shabako is feasible: he ruled effectively in Egypt, from Memphis, which Piankhy did not – this latter spent a few weeks there only, subduing the Delta chiefs, and promptly sailed straight back to Napata, showing no further interest in Egypt anywhere north of Thebes. These facts alone suffice to exclude all the ultra-low chronologies for this epoch.

779. See A. H. Layard, *Discoveries in Nineveh and Babylon*, 1853, 156 and figure, now BM. 81-2-4, 352; further references, *PM*, VII, 397, plus a duplicate (cf. H. R. Hall, *Catalogue of Egyptian Scarabs, British Museum*, I, Nos. 2775, 2776).

learning. At Memphis, he undertook various modest constructions[780] and caused the remarkable Old Kingdom theology and cosmogony of the god Ptah to be engraved on a durable basalt slab, from a worm-eaten papyrus.[781] In his 14th year (c. 703 B.C.), the Apis installed in his 2nd year probably died and was buried.[782] A fragment from Athribis may be his.[783]

In Upper Egypt, a stela from Dendera commemorated Shabako's gifts to Hathor, which were stimulated by the interest of a locally-born chief architect employed by the king on (re)building the sacred enclosures of Egyptian temples.[784] At Abydos, Istemkheb H, daughter of Shabako, had a tomb or cenotaph, like so many royalties before her.[785] And at Esna a naos was given to the temple.[786] From Edfu came the stela of a son of the 2nd prophet of Amun, Patjenfy.[787]

§ 343   (ii) *Thebes*

Two more Nile-level texts date to Shabako, one of Year 4(?) and one, year lost.[788] Over in Western Thebes, he was the first king to build for centuries, adding a pylon to the now venerable 18th-Dynasty temple of Amun of Djeme at Medinet Habu.[789] At Karnak, besides the work on Pylon IV, he erected a 'treasury' or 'hall of gold' in the north part of Amun's capacious precinct,[790] a gateway for the temple of Ptah,[791] fragments elsewhere,[792] and works in the precinct of Montu.[793] Down at the Luxor temple, he

780. *PM*, III, 220; cf. *YMM*, 131, n. 2, and Leclant and Yoyotte, *BIFAO* 51 (1952), 28, n. 3.

781. The 'Shabaka Stone' or 'Memphite Theology', *PM*, III, 226, *ANET*, 4.

782. See for this Apis, Vercoutter, *Kush* 8 (1960), 69–70; one stela of a Year 14 (king, unnamed), cf. Malinine, Posener, Vercoutter, *Catalogue, stèles, Sérapéum*, I, No. 123, p. 98 and pl. 34.

783. Bearing cartouches Neferkare and Wahibre; attribution is doubtful, cf. above, Part II, § 124, and below, §§ 357, 361.

784. Cairo JdE 44665, stela of the Chief Builder of South and North, Pa-uden-Hor son of Pa-wah-Amun; see Leclant, *Enquêtes sur les sacerdoces et les sanctuaires égyptiens* (*XXVe Dynastie*), 1954, 31–42, pl. 7. For a possible statuette of Shabako or Shebitku from Dendera, cf. *ibid.*, 42, n. 4.

785. *PM*, V, 68.

786. *PM*, VI, 117.

787. Engelbach, *ASAE* 21 (1921), 190–2, fig. 2; F. B. de la Roque, *BIFAO* 25 (1925), 47–8, pl.; *PM*, V, 204.

788. Nos. 31, 32 (Legrain, *ZÄS* 34, 115; von Beckerath, *JARCE* 5, 47, 48, 52–3).

789. *PM*, II, 165 (brick, 171), II², 464–5 (and 474).

790. *PM*, II², 202, G; Barguet, *Temple d'Amon-rê à Karnak*, 17–18 h.

791. Or, rather, two gateways; *PM*, II, 67, II², 197.

792. Colonnade near Pylon III (*PM*, II², 192, A; Barguet, *17g*), statue (*PM*, II², 143), plaque (*ibid.*, 167), blocks (*ibid.*, 221, 223). Cf. also, Leclant, *Recherches*, §§ 16 *bis*, 17 *bis*, 18, 33, 49 (p. 186, B, a).

793. *PM*, II, 7; II², 14, Chapel b (50), 15.

added scenes to the pylon-gateway of Ramesses II and erected a modest colonnade.[794] None of these were vast works, but they heralded a new era of royal building activity both within Thebes and throughout Egypt.

§ 344* The hierarchy of Thebes witnessed both continuity and change. Shabako's sister Amenirdis I continued as God's Wife of Amun; her superb statue in Cairo (from Karnak)[795] probably dates to this time. In Wadi Hammamat a desert graffito of Year 12 of Shabako (715 B.C.) names her,[796] and her name recurs as far north as Memphis.[797] Her funerary chapel and tomb were constructed at Medinet Habu in Western Thebes,[798] near the Djeme temple of her divine master Amun. In civil government, the southern vizier Khamhor A was succeeded by two of his sons, Pahrer (also called Harsiese) and Nesmin B,[799] all of good Theban family.

But the Nubian pharaohs did not hesitate to follow traditional policy in installing their own men in Thebes. Thus, Kelbasken was Mayor of Thebes and 4th prophet of Amun, probably under Piankhy and Shabako – in the latter office, perhaps as successor to the last Djed-Khons-ef-ankh (D) of the Nakhtefmut family.[800] More ambitiously, Shabako eventually installed a son of his own – Haremakhet – as High Priest of Amun,[801] an office which had long been left 'in the shade' and was now shorn of all political and military power, being again wholly a religious benefice. The last shadows of Theban political independence seemed to have faded away. The statue of Iti, attached to the cults of Amun, Khons, and the funerary cult of Piankhy, was dated in the Year 15 of Shabako (702 B.C.), which was probably his last.[802]

(iii) *Nubia and End of the Reign*

Shabako did some work at Kawa,[803] but few other traces of his reign appear

794. Scenes, *PM*, II, 101, II², 305–6 (15). Colonnade, *PM*, II², 302, 321, 332; Leclant, *Recherches*, § 39 and p. 337. Edifice at Medamud, *ibid.*, § 37 and p. 337.

795. *G4*, 20–1, F; *PM*, II, 5/7, II², 14–15; Leclant, *Recherches*, § 27. The activities of Amenirdis I, Leclant, pp. 356–7.

796. Couyat and Montet, *Inscriptions . . . du Ouadi Hammamat*, 96, pl. 35, No. 187.

797. *G4*, 21, G; other minor remains, cf. *G4*, 20–2, etc.

798. *PM*, II, 175–7, II², 476–8.

799. See above, Part III, §§ 196–7.

800. Theban Tomb, 391 (*PM²*, I: 1, 441–2); *LDT*, III, 289; cf. Kees, *Pr.*, 276, 283, n. 3.

801. Cf. above, Part III, §§ 157 ff.

802. BM 24429, studied by Leclant, *Enquêtes sur les sacerdoces . . .*, 1954, 15–27. The cult of Piankhy in the form of a portable image (*kny*) follows a pattern familiar from the New Kingdom and attested for Psusennes I (*q.v.*).

803. On a column of Temple B, *PM*, VII, 184.

in Nubia,[804] other than his pyramid at El Kurru.[805] He too had horses buried for his service hereafter.[806]

§ 345* 2. SHEBITKU (c. 702–690 B.C.)

A. ACCESSION

Being a son of Piankhy, the new pharaoh was a nephew of his predecessor. His cartouches followed the now customary old, simple forms, Djedkaure, Shebitku.[807] His usual Horus name 'Enduring of Epiphanies' (*Dd-ḫꜥw*)[808] was occasionally replaced by the imperial style of the New Kingdom – witness the well-worn 'Strong Bull, appearing in Thebes' of his Nile-level text, Year 3 (c. 700 B.C.) at the Karnak quay[809] – a style which was maintained in his varying Nebty-names[810] and Golden Horus names.[811] This sudden reversion to the imperial style deviated from the usage of his predecessors for over 70 years back, and it was not continued by his immediate successors, either. By it, the ambitious new ruler perhaps indicated his adoption of a new line of policy, more aggressive than that of his predecessor.

§ 346* B. FOREIGN AFFAIRS

Very soon after his accession, the new king summoned his brothers north from Nubia to Thebes and to the Delta, among them Taharqa who was then 20 years old.[812] With the princes there went north an army-force[813] which they had doubtless been commissioned to muster and bring with them.

In Western Asia, Sennacherib of Assyria was engaged in reaffirming

---

804. Letti basin, a bronze stamp (*PM*, VII, 192); seals in temple treasury, Ṣanam (*ibid.*, 202); scarab, Sennar, plaque, Gebel Moya (*ibid.*, 273).

805. *PM*, VII, 196; Dunham, *El Kurru*, 1950, 55–8 (Kurru 15).

806. *PM*, VII, 198.

807. Nomen occasionally expanded with 'Beloved of Amun' or '... of Ptah' (*G4*, 29, IVB, IIIA). Titulary, cf. Leclant, *Recherches*, 340–1, n. 3.

808. Based on that of Djedkare Isesi of the 5th Dynasty, also prenomen.

809. No. 33 (Legrain, *ZÄS* 34, 115; von Beckerath, *JARCE* 5, 48, 53); cf. Leclant, *Recherches*, 5, 243–4, 342.

810. *Dd-ḫꜥw* in Nile-level text cited; but either *ꜥ-šfyt m tꜣw nbw*, 'Great of renown in all lands', or *sḫꜥ mꜣꜥt mry tꜣwy*, 'Manifesting Right, Beloved of the Two Lands', in an Osiris-chapel taken from Karnak to Berlin (*G4*, 29).

811. Either *ꜥ-ḫpš ḥwi pdt 9*, 'Great of strength, smiting the Nine Bows' or *ḥri ḥr nḫt*, 'Satisfied with victory' (same chapel, *G4*, 29).

812. Kawa stelae of Taharqa, IV, 7–10, V, 13, 14, 19. On translation of these texts, see Leclant and Yoyotte, *BIFAO* 51 (1952), 17 ff. On the chronology, see above, part II, §§ 126 ff.

813. Kawa IV, 10.

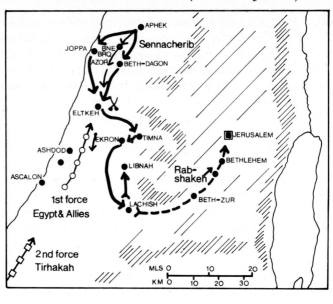

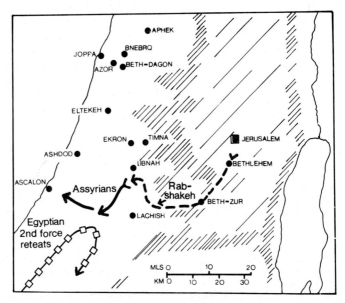

Fig. 6. Battle of Eltekeh, 701 B.C. (a) First phase: Assyrian victory at Eltekeh, conquests and mission to Jerusalem. (b) Second phase: Second Egyptian advance, Assyrian regrouping and Egyptian retreat.

Assyrian rule, and the petty rulers of Palestine in plotting to overthrow that rule. Thus it seems that straightaway, in 702/701 B.C., Hezekiah of Judah and others opened negotiations with the new pharaoh Shebitku to obtain his support against Assyria. Unlike his shrewder predecessor, Shebitku decided on an aggressive policy in Western Asia, and readied his forces to fight in Palestine against the Assyrians. His brother, prince Taharqa (at 20–21) became titular head of the expedition, and was doubtless supported by generals. In 701, Sennacherib struck into Phoenicia,[814] Philistia, and Judah. The local allies, together with the Egypto-Nubian force under Taharqa, prepared for battle at Eltekeh.[815] Having earlier captured Sidqia king of Ascalon, Sennacherib defeated the confederates, besieged and took Eltekeh, Timnah and Ekron,[816] and swung across to Lachish. Thence he sent on his commander with a large army-force[817] to Jerusalem to demand the surrender of Hezekiah of Judah. In the meantime he reduced Lachish[818] and moved on to attack Libnah. Hezekiah had to pay tribute,[819] and gave up Padi of Ekron,[820] but the gates of Jerusalem remained firmly shut and unbreached by the Assyrian forces.[821] However, at this point, Sennacherib recalled his commanders from Jerusalem with their forces – rumour had reached him that Taharqa and the Egyptian army were aiming to attack him, now that his own forces had been divided between Libnah and Jerusalem.[822] Thus, the reunited Assyrian forces returned smartly to Philistia; before this renewed threat, Taharqa and the Egyptian forces swiftly retired homewards to Egypt. In Philistia, the

814. From Sidon to Accho, replacing Luli by Ittobaal II as king of Tyre and Sidon (see *HHAHT*); *ANET*, 287, 288.

815. Possibly Tell es-Shalaf, about 10 miles N.N.E. of Ashdod; cf. B. Mazar, *IEJ* 10 (1960), 72–7; only occurs twice in the Old Testament, in Joshua 19: 44 and 21: 23 (city-lists of Dan); is Altaku in Assyrian.

816. Cf. Assyrian account, *ANET*, 287/8.

817. Isaiah 36: 2; 2 Kings 18: 17; 2 Chronicles 32: 9.

818. Conquest of Lachish, graphically portrayed in Sennacherib's palace reliefs (reproduced *ad nauseam*, e.g. *ANEP*, figs. 371–4); text, *ANET*, 288.

819. Cf. 2 Kings 18: 14–16. For the order of events in Hebrew (and Assyrian) narration as sometimes *retrospective*, cf. W. J. Martin, *VTS* 17 (1969), 179–86.

820. As is mentioned by Sennacherib, *ANET*, 286.

821. As promised by Isaiah, the Assyrian king himself was not destined to besiege and conquer Jerusalem (as he had Lachish, for example); cf. Isaiah 37: 33–5. The initial defeat of Taharqa and the allies at Eltekeh is probably reflected in Isaiah 36: 6–7 (2 Kings 18: 21), wherein the Assyrian spokesman dismisses the pharaoh as 'a broken reed'.

822. Cf. Isaiah 37: 8–9 (2 Kings 19: 8–9). The initial defeat of the Egyptian and allied forces at Eltekeh was probably signal but not disastrous. The sequence in Isaiah 36–7 (2 Kings 18–19) would suggest that, while the Assyrians got themselves involved within Judah with their forces divided, the Egyptians and their allies had possibly regrouped their own forces at a safe distance and now saw their chance to strike back at Sennacherib while his army was thus dispersed in at least two bodies.

Assyrians reaffirmed their political hold, but an epidemic or similar mis-
fortune probably dictated an early return to Assyria and to Nineveh.[823]
  On their return to Egypt, Taharqa and his generals and army could
hardly be said to have covered themselves with glory by feat of arms such as
Shebitku's imperial-style titles desiderated. But at length the Assyrian had
had to retreat, even if through other than military factors. No more
foreign adventures are recorded for Shebitku's reign, nor is there any
explicit evidence that Sennacherib campaigned again in Palestine.[824]

§ 347   C. HOME AFFAIRS

Within Egypt, the remaining decade of Shebitku's reign apparently
passed off peacefully. Like his predecessor, he promoted work on the
temples of Egypt. From Memphis come a statue and a block from structures of his. [825] At Thebes, Shebitku continued the policies of Shabako.
Within Amun's precinct at Karnak he erected a chapel,[826] and with the
God's Wife of Amun, Amenirdis I, added a court and a gateway to the
little temple of Osiris-Ruler-of-Eternity at the east end of the area.[827] In
Luxor, Shebitku added two scenes of his own at the south end of the

823. Cf. Isaiah 37: 36 (2 Kings 19: 35–6). The verses that follow to complete the
Hebrew narrative (Isaiah 37: 37–8; 2 Kings 19: 37) narrate the murder of Sennacherib and accession of Esarhaddon – which happened in 681 B.C., a decade
after the accession of Taharqa as king of Egypt and Nubia. Hence, the epithet
'king of Nubia' (*melek Kuš*) applied to Taharqa by the Hebrew prophet, writing *in
or after 681 B.C.*, is in terms of the *time of writing* (c. 680 B.C.), and *not* of the time of
the events described (701 B.C.). Just as today one may say 'Queen Elisabeth II was
born in 1926' – yet, in that year, she was not Queen. *Precisely* the same usage is
exhibited by Taharqa himself on Kawa stela IV, lines 7–8, wherein he refers to
himself as 'His Majesty', proleptically, in relation to a time (in Shebitku's reign)
when he was explicitly only a prince and king's-brother among several others of this
rank and *not king* (as already pointed out by me, *Ancient Orient & Old Testament*,
1966, 82–3, and elsewhere). There is *no* anachronism or contradiction in the Hebrew
text (or any other sources, here), despite the almost pathological mania of some Old
Testament scholars for reading such into these data.
  824. There is no clear, explicit evidence for the assumed second Palestinian
campaign of Sennacherib sometimes conjured up for 690–680 B.C. Attempts to
postulate one find their genesis almost entirely in misinterpretation of the phrase
'king of Nubia' used of Taharqa in Isaiah 37 (2 Kings 19). For the most recent
such attempt, taking as gospel a wholly imaginary co-regency of Shebitku
with Taharqa and evading the full evidence on Egyptian chronology for the
eighth–seventh centuries B.C., see the otherwise excellent work of J. Bright,
A History of Israel[2], 1972, 296–308. As soon as the true explanation of the phrase
'king of Nubia' is apparent (see preceding note, and above, Part II, §§ 126–37),
then there is simply no more need to invent an imaginary second campaign of
Sennacherib. Nor does the Hebrew text require it.
  825.*G4, 29, III; *PM*, III, 220, top.
  826. Taken to Berlin by Lepsius; *G4*, 29, II; *PM*, II, 71, M, II[2], 223, T; cf.
Leclant, *Recherches*, 59–61, § 16, pls. 36–7 (one block in Yale).
  827. *PM*, II, 69; II[2], 204–5, K; to be published by a Canadian expedition.

THE 25TH DYNASTY 387

temple (exterior).[828] The Nile-level text on the Karnak quay notes Shebit-ku's presence in Thebes in Year 3 (*c.* 700 B.C.) and his interest in a good inundation. Other fragments may belong to his works in Thebes.[829] By his time, the aged Shepenupet I was probably dead, his aunt Amenirdis I was chief God's Wife of Amun, and perhaps by now she had at her side as 'heiress-apparent' Shebitku's and her sister Shepenupet II (prenomen, 'Mistress of Beauty, is Mut the Eye of Re', *Ḥnt-nfrw-Mwt, irt-Rˁ*).[830] By this reign, Nesptah A was probably Mayor of Thebes, and Nesipaqashuty C the southern vizier. In the north, at Sais, Stephinates had perhaps taken over as local ruler. He was of local origin, perhaps even of Tefnakht's descent, and ruled *c.* 695–688 B.C.

At El Kurru, Shebitku followed family custom in being interred in a pyramid, with horse-burials in attendance.[831] Other traces of his reign in Nubia are few.[832]

§ 348   3. TAHARQA (*c.* 690–664 B.C.)

A. ACCESSION

In the year 690 B.C., Taharqa 'received the crown in Memphis, *after the Falcon* (= Shebitku) *flew to heaven*' (died), as he himself put it with crystal clarity. Shebitku at his death in Memphis left the throne empty, and it was that empty throne that Taharqa now occupied.[833]

828. *PM*, II², 335–6; cf. Leclant, *Recherches*, 139–40, § 40.
829. e.g. limestone fragment at Cairo, Leclant, *op. cit.*, § 49, *c*, i (cf. *ibid.*, 342, n. 4).
830. Sander-Hansen, *Das Gottesweib des Amun*, 1940, 10.
831. Pyramid, *PM*, VII, 197, and Dunham, *El Kurru*, 67–71. Horses, *PM*, VII, 198. Wives' pyramids, *PM*, VII, 196, 5/6, and Dunham, 38–43. Funerary cult of Shebitku (in Thebes?), cf. stela Edinburgh 444, Leclant, *Recherches*, 188, 269, n. 3.
832. Faience fragment, Kawa temple, *PM*, VII, 183.
833. Kawa V, 15. There is, therefore, absolutely no justification for assuming any co-regency of Taharqa with his predecessor. Macadam's ingenious thesis to the contrary was long ago examined with care and rejected on solid grounds by Leclant and Yoyotte (*BIFAO* 51 (1952), 17–27) and re-examined by me (above, Part II, §§ 132–7, and in a preliminary way elsewhere). Almost throughout, Egyptology has given a very chilly reception to Macadam's hypothesis – the supposed co-regency is essentially rejected not only by such acknowledged experts on this epoch as Leclant and Yoyotte (*op. cit*), and in Part II of this work, but also by J. M. A. Janssen, *Biblica* 34 (1953), 26, 33; by G. Schmidt, *Kush* 6 (1958), 121–30, a study dedicated to this particular topic; by Drioton and Vandier, *L'Égypte*⁴, 1962, 564, 572 (Table), 677; implicitly by Sir A. H. Gardiner, *Egypt of the Pharaohs*, 1961, 342, 344, 450 (Table); by W. Helck, *Geschichte des alten Ägypten*, 1968, 237 and n. 2, among others. Seemingly oblivious of this situation and despite warnings (e.g. by me, *Anc. Orient & OT*, 1966, 82–4, etc.), Old Testament scholars have accepted this purely hypothetical co-regency in highly uncritical fashion, and it is now

The new king, aged about 32, took the unusual prenomen Nefertum-khure,[834] alongside his name Taharqa. As both Horus and Nebty he was 'Exalted of Epiphanies' ($K\bar{3}$-h^cw) and as Golden Horus, 'Protector of the Two Lands' (Hw-$t\bar{3}wy$).[835] The reign of Taharqa, at 26 years, divides with convenient balance into two epochs of some 13 years each – the first, years of peace, and the second, years of conflict with Assyria.

§ 349*   B. THE YEARS OF PEACE

(i) Events

At Medinet Habu in Western Thebes, two stelae of Year 3 (c. 688 B.C.) commemorated the erection there of a precinct-wall to protect the sanctuaries of the gods of Djeme.[836] In his 2nd year, Taharqa manifested his youthful interest in the neglected temple of Kawa in Nubia by presenting rich gifts to its treasury, and likewise annually during Years 3–8.[837] Within Years 2–5, Taharqa had at Memphis to bury one Apis bull and install another.[838]

In his Year 6 (c. 685 B.C.), Egypt suffered a remarkably high inundation of the Nile, exceeding even that of the 3rd year of Osorkon III nearly a century earlier; Nubia, correspondingly, had rain. Two Nile-level texts on the Karnak quay attest its extreme height.[839] However, this apparent disaster of an over-high Nile that flooded the land was followed by blessing, according to Taharqa. Amun gave him 'four wonders', a four-fold blessing, after the great flood, of good cultivation everywhere, the destruction of rodents and vermin, the warding-off of the greed of locusts, and prevention of the south wind blighting the crops – so, in due course,

canonized into their current mythology – so much so, that Egyptologists such as Leclant, Yoyotte and myself have now been, with exquisite effrontery, accused of 'evading' the non-existent co-regency (Bright, *A History of Israel*, 1972, 298, n. 9)!

834. Or possibly better, Khu-nefertum-re, 'whom Nefertem and Re protect'.

835. *G4*, 34, XVI, and Leclant, *Recherches*, 343–4, n. 1, who notes the particularly Memphite flavour of Taharqa's titulary (allusion to Nefertem, epithet Khu-tawy, proper to Nefertem).

836.* First stela, Carter and Maspero, *ASAE* 4 (1903), 178–80, fig. 4; notice of the second, Gauthier, *ASAE* 18 (1918), 190, cf. Leclant, *Recherches*, 154, § 42, F, pp. 346–7. For an abnormal-hieratic document of Year 3 from Thebes, cf. Papyrus Louvre E. 3228*d*, edited by Malinine, *Choix de textes juridiques . . .*, I, 1953, 43–9; other documents, Year 5, cf. Schmidt, *Kush* 6 (1958), 127 and n. 34.

837. Kawa stela III; Macadam, *Temples of Kawa*, I, 4–14, pls. 5, 6. The temple thus favoured is 'Temple T' of the excavations.

838. See Vercoutter, *Kush* 8 (1960), 67–9, pls. 21*a*/*b*.

839.* Nos. 34, 35 (Legrain, *ZÄS* 34 (1896), 115–16; von Beckerath, *JARCE* 5 (1966), 47–8, 53), both of Year 6; and the latter, the highest on the quay, was perhaps an added notation after the floodwaters had overtopped the first one (so, with von Beckerath). Emendation to Year 5 in No. 34 is not justified.

Taharqa and Egypt benefited from a bumper harvest.[840] During the long years that he had been away from Nubia, first at the court of Shebitku and then as king in the north himself (some 18 years all told), Taharqa had not seen his mother, and so rejoiced in Year 6 to have her visit him as king, probably in Memphis.[841]

In that same auspicious Year 6, Taharqa took in hand the (re)building of the Kawa temple, which was commemorated by a special stela.[842] By Year 10 this work was complete – one stela of that year records his further donations to the temple in Years 8, 9, 10, while another celebrated the dedication of the temple.[843] Taharqa records having devoted people of Lower Egypt to the service of the newly-restored temple. One may wonder if these were voluntary services, or whether they were deportees, captives, after the suppression of some Delta revolt against Nubian rule.[844] After the 6th year flood, Nile levels continued to be marked at Karnak in the 7th, 8th and 9th years,[845] when they ceased for another generation.

§ 350* (ii) *Buildings*

While Memphis received some buildings and endowments from Taharqa,[846] and a copy of the great 'wonders' inscription was inscribed at Tanis,[847] elsewhere in Egypt Taharqa's name is rare with one conspicuous exception: Thebes. At Thebes, he was a truly monumental builder. In the vast Bubastite forecourt at Karnak, he erected a noble colonnade whose re-

840.*See Leclant and Yoyotte, *BIFAO* 51 (1952), 22–4, correcting the translations of Macadam, for stela V published by Macadam, *Temples of Kawa*, I, 22–32, Pls. 9–10, with its parallels from Coptos, Mataana and Tanis. Cf. further, V. Vikentiev, *La haute crue du Nil*, 1930; Griffith and Kuentz, *Mélanges Maspero*, I, 423–30, 430–2; Leclant and Yoyotte, *Kêmi* 10 (1949), 28–37, pls. 2–3, and *BIFAO* 51 (1952), 16 ff.

841. Kawa V, lines 16 to the end, prefaced by an account of Taharqa's earlier years with Shebitku by way of 'background' – included in the parallel text from Tanis, but not in those from Coptos and Mataana. For the king in Memphis in Year 6, cf. Kawa IV, line 22.

842. Kawa IV, Macadam, *op. cit.*, I, 14–21, pls. 7, 8. The text mentions Taharqa's youth under Shebitku as 'background' of when he planned to work on the Kawa temple.

843. Kawa stelae VI, VII; Macadam, *op. cit.*, 32–41, 41–4, pls. 11–12, 13–14, respectively.

844. Cf. already, Macadam, 40, n. 64, and Leclant and Yoyotte, *BIFAO* 51 (1952), 27–8. However, just as Delta (and other) chiefs had formerly chosen to send their relations to serve Amun in Thebes, so it is possible that they were encouraged now to do so for Kawa.

845. Nos. 36, 37, 38 (Legrain, *ZÄS* 34, 116; von Beckerath, *JARCE* 5, 48, 53–4).

846.*Stela, fragments of buildings, etc., cf. Leclant and Yoyotte, *op. cit.*, 28, n. 3; *YMM*, 131, n. 2.

847. Cf. above, § 349; a doubtful inscription, Year 20, on a statue of Sesostris III at Tanis, *G4*, 33, XIII.

mains still compel admiration. Likewise, in order to complete the four cardinal points, he built further colonnades at the north entry of the temple of Montu, before the East Temple at Karnak, and in the south before the temple of Khons.[848] Between the main temple of Amun and the sacred lake, Taharqa built a special 'high temple' (with crypts below) having some relation to the lake. He and the God's Wife of Amun, Shepenupet II, added to the long series of Osiris-chapels at Karnak, and statues of the king were set up in Amun's precincts.[849] Across the Nile at Medinet Habu, Taharqa continued the works of Shabako.[850] Activity under Taharqa in Wadi Hammamat to the east is marked by his cartouches,[851] and in the Bahria oasis to the west by remains of a chapel there.[852]

In Nubia, Taharqa built not only at Kawa (cf. above),[853] but also at Buhen,[854] at or near Kasr Ibrim[855] to the north and at Semna[856] to the south, at Old Merowe,[857] and a full temple at Ṣanam.[858] At Napata, the Karnak of Nubia, Taharqa built a new temple (B 300) and worked on the great temple of Amun (B 500), also setting up there a statue and an altar or barque-stand.[859]

§ 351* (iii) *People*

At Thebes, the southern vizierate continued in the hands of the new incumbents, passing from Nesipaqashuty C to his son Nespamedu. Likewise, in due time, Nesptah A passed on the mayoralty of Thebes to his nephew Re-em-makheru and to his own son, the remarkable Montemhat who otherwise was principally 4th prophet of Amun.[860] Above him, in the Theban hierarchy, Haremakhet was eventually succeeded by his own son, Harkhebi (so, grandson of Shabako) as High Priest of Amun,[861] while Taharqa installed his own son Nesishutefnut as 2nd prophet of Amun.[862]

848. On all these, see Leclant, *Recherches*, §§ 3, 14, 21, 22; p. 345, refs.; PM, II², 5, 24–5, 209–11, 227. W. colonnade, J. Lauffray, *Kêmi* 20 (1971), 111–164.

849. A convenient summary of these works, Leclant, *Recherches*, 347 ff.; further detail, PM, II², cf. Index, 557.

850. Leclant, *op. cit.*, 346–7; *PM*, II², 464–5, 474–5, 481.

851. *PM*, VII, 335.

852. *PM*, VII, 311.

853. Macadam, *Temples of Kawa*, I, II, *passim*.

854. *PM*, VII, 136, 137.

855. *PM*, VII, 94.

856. *Ibid.*, 149–50.

857. *Ibid.*, 198, block.

858. *Ibid.*, 198–202.

859. See *ibid.*, 208 ff., 215–22, and Dunham, *The Barkal Temples*, 1970.

860. On whom see the monograph by J. Leclant, *Montouemhat, quatrième prophète d'Amon*, 1961, plus R. A. Parker, *A Saite Oracle Papyrus*, 1962; cf. also Part III, §§ 196–7, and Kees, *ZÄS* 87 (1962), 60–6.

861. See Parker, *op. cit.*, and above, Part III, §§ 157 ff.

862. Cf. Kees, *Pr.*, 276, and *ZÄS* 87 (1962), 63–4.

During much of the reign (for its latter part, certainly) one Pediamen-neb-nesttawy (C) was 3rd prophet.[863] Thus the benefices and the powers in the Thebaïd were shared between members of the great Theban families and the ruling dynasty. The God's Wife of Amun, Shepenupet II, in due time adopted Amenirdis II (daughter of Taharqa) as her designated successor.[864] Her high steward was the famous Akhamenrou, known from a series of statues and other monuments.[865] Doubtless many lesser clergy of Amun, Mut, Khons and Montu flourished in this period.[866]

Elsewhere, local chiefs continued to rule their fiefs, often as series of local dynasties as in the Libyan epoch. In Sais, Stephinates was probably succeeded c. 688 B.C. by Nechepsos, the Nekauba of a few small monuments (c. 688–672 B.C.), and then by Menkheperre Necho I (c. 672–664 B.C.).[867] Local dynasts thus persisted in Tanis, Athribis, and elsewhere as is seen below (§§ 356–358).

§ 352*   C. THE CONFLICT WITH ASSYRIA

(i) *First Blows*

In 677 B.C., Esarhaddon of Assyria vanquished and deposed Abdimilkutte, king of Sidon, and beheaded him the following year.[868] Perhaps not without good reason, Esarhaddon viewed Taharqa of Egypt as the source of unrest among his vassals in Palestine and Phoenicia. So in Taharqa's 17th year (674 B.C.) he attempted to invade Egypt,[869] but was defeated by the forces of Taharqa.[870]

Nothing daunted, Esarhaddon again invaded Egypt in his 10th year,

863. Cf. Parker, *op. cit.*, and above, Part III, §§ 192 ff.

864. See Leclant, *Karnak-Nord IV*, and *Recherches*, 363–7. Her prenomen is unknown unless it be the mysterious Meryt-Tefnut on two monuments of this general age (references, Leclant, *Recherches*, 354, n. 1). For the activities of Shepenu-pet II, cf. Leclant, *op. cit.*, 359–63.

865. Cf. M. Lichtheim, *JNES* 7 (1948), 163–79; Leclant, *JNES* 13 (1954), 154–84; cf. Leclant, *Enquêtes sur les sacerdoces . . .*, 1954, chapter 1, and his chapters 4, 5, for other Thebans of this period.

866. As evidenced by the burials of numerous priests of Montu, etc., in Western Thebes; cf. *PM²*, I: 2, 643 ff., etc.

867. See Part II, § 117, above; Yoyotte, *Supplément au Dictionnaire de la Bible*, VI, 364–5; *YMM*, 131, n. 3.

868. For Year 4 of Esarhaddon, cf. the Babylonian Chronicle (*ANET*, 302, 303) and texts of Esarhaddon (*ANET*, 290–1); R. Borger, *Die Inschriften Asarhaddons Königs von Assyrien*, 1956, 122–3 and 48, 49–50, 111 (B, D), respectively.

869. Esarhaddon boasted of reaching and destroying Arza(ni), El-ʿArish, and of deporting its ruler Asuhili (*ANET*, 290a, b; Borger, *Asarhaddon*, 33, 50–1, 86, 111, B), but it is not clear whether this was in 677 or 674 B.C.

870. As is made clear by the Babylonian Chronicle for that year (the 7th), *ANET*, 302, 303, Borger, *Asarhaddon*, 123. The town 'Sha-awile' mentioned in one version may possibly be Sile, cf. G. Fecht, *MDIK* 16 (1958), 116–19.

671 B.C. (Taharqa's 20th), and this time defeated Taharqa, drove him from Memphis, and even captured members of the royal family.[871] On his triumphal monuments, he showed the 'vanquished' Taharqa of Egypt and Baal of Tyre.[872] When trouble broke out again in his 12th year, 669 B.C., Esarhaddon set out at once for Egypt, but died *en route.*[873]

§ 353 (ii) *Assyrian Rule*

The breathing-space thus gained was brief. In 667/666 B.C.,[874] Assurbanipal then marched to subdue Egypt where Taharqa had naturally re-established his rule since 671 B.C. The Egypto-Nubian forces were defeated in battle and Taharqa fled to Thebes. The Assyrians in turn penetrated south to Thebes, while Taharqa presumably escaped still further south to Napata. Assurbanipal then received the formal submission of all the Delta and Upper Egyptian dynasts, headed by Necho I of Sais, including rulers as far south as Montemhat of Thebes and probably Nespamedu of Aswan.[875] Amid these upheavals, in Taharqa's 24th year, the Apis bull of Memphis died and had to be entombed.[876]

The Assyrian's return to Nineveh was – as usual – the signal for more unrest; the Delta chiefs found Assyrian military rule less congenial than

871. Cf. chronicles, one mentioning three fierce battles and seemingly the capture of the king's son and brother (*ANET*, 302–3, 303; Borger, *Asarhaddon*, 124). Texts of Esarhaddon, cf. *ANET*, 292–4, Borger, *op. cit.*, 65–6, 86, 98–9, 101–2, 112, 113(H, I), 114(K). He claims to have appointed local rulers anew. Three rock-inscriptions in Nubia of Year 19 of Taharqa (672 B.C.) may mark the route north by which he had earlier brought his Nubian levy to Egypt, cf. F. Hintze, *MIO* 7 (1959/60), 330–3.

872. Picture, cf. *ANEP*, No. 447.

873. Babylonian Chronicle, Year 12; *ANET*, 303, Borger, *Asarhaddon*, 124. H. von Zeissl, *Äthiopen und Assyrer in Ägypten*, 1944, 39–40, adduces here oracle-queries edited by Knudtzon and Klauber, but these require re-editing before their relevance is assured.

874. Accession of Assurbanipal in 669, and installation of his brother Shamash-shum-ukin as king of Babylon in the spring of 668; that year, a minor campaign was conducted against Kirbitu in the north-east ('first campaign' of most documents, omitted by others) – cf. E. Ebeling and B. Meissner (eds.), *Reallexikon der Assyriologie*, I, 204, the Babylonian Chronicle (*ANET*, 303a, b), and J.-M. Aynard, *Le prisme du Louvre AO 19.939*, 1957, 17–18. Assurbanipal's 'first' Egyptian campaign (so called in some documents, omitted in others) thus was in 667/666 B.C. Cf. also above, Part II, § 131 near end.

875.* Cf. Assurbanipal's narrative, *ANET*, 294; *LAR*, II, §§ 770–1. For 'Ishpi-matu' (Nespamedu) as possibly ruler in Aswan (Taini for a *Shaini), cf. Fecht, *MDIK* 16 (1958), 114–16; but Thinis near Abybos is cautiously preferred by Helck, *Geschichte des alten Ägypten*, 1968, 243 and n. 2. Details of the other dynasts, see below §§ 356–8.

876. Stelae of Year 24, etc., cf. Malinine, Posener, Vercoutter, *Catalogue, stèles, Sérapéum*, I, Nos. 125–8, 158–60 (pp. 99–103, 122–4); cf. above, Part II, §§ 130–1.

the overlordship of Napata. They intrigued with the distant Taharqa, to share rule with him, the plot was discovered, many of the princes were arrested and sent to Nineveh, while executions were held in Sais, Mendes, Pelusium,[877] and elsewhere as a punishment and a warning to the Egyptian populace against attempting a revolt. Of the princes sent on to Nineveh, Assurbanipal executed all but Necho of Sais and his son. Necho he ceremonially appointed as kinglet and returned him to the rule of Sais and Memphis as a vassal, while his son (Psammetichus) was appointed under the Assyrian name of Nabu-shezibanni to the rule of Athribis.[878] All this probably took place in 665 B.C.

§ 354* (iii) Disaster

Thereafter, in 664 B.C., events moved apace. At Memphis a new Apis was established in one of the intervals amid the unrest.[879] Far south in Thebes and Napata, Taharqa who was now perhaps a sick man, recognized his nephew Tantamani as his intended successor, and died soon afterwards.[880] The small new chapel of Osiris-Ptah at Karnak was dedicated in the names of both kings.

Tantamani now claimed the double kingship of Nubia and Egypt (which had been promised him in a dream). After he had been accepted in Napata, he sailed straight back north to Elephantine, to Thebes, and then stormed Memphis and invaded the Delta.[881] As Assyrian vassal and appointee for Memphis as well as Sais, Necho I was the soul of resistance to Tantamani,[882] and so was slain by the Nubian king.[883] At length the Delta chiefs decided to recognize Tantamani, and – since Necho I was dead – sent a deputation to Tantamani led by Pekrur, ruler of Pi-Sopd.[884]

877. Ṣinu should perhaps be distinguished from Ṣanu 'Tanis'; if so, then the likeliest equivalent is Pelusium (Sin), despite the variation in sibilant (assimilation by the scribe?).

878. ANET, 294, 295; LAR, II, §§ 772–4. Doubtless Bakennefi C of Athribis was one of the conspirators and executed by Assurbanipal; Psammetichus thus replaced him in Athribis during c. 665–664 B.C.

879. Cf. Part II, §§ 130–1, above.

880.* For the possibility of a very brief co-regency, cf. above Part II, § 139. The data of Tantamani's stela are too ambiguous to prove a co-regency, and the scenes of the two kings in the chapel of Osiris-Ptah at Karnak may have been done under Tantamani to stress his link with Taharqa. Taharqa was buried not at Kurru, but at Nuri in a pyramid (No. 1), cf. Dunham, Nuri, 1955, 6 ff.

881.* Cf. narrative of his 'Dream stela', Schäfer, Urkunden III, 57–77; BAR, IV, §§ 922 ff.

882. As was Tefnakht against Piankhy, and perhaps Bakenranef against Shabako.

883. Death of Necho I, cf. Yoyotte, Supplément au Dictionnaire de la Bible, VI, 365, and remarks of Breasted, BAR, IV, p. 468, n. b (but 664, not 663). At his father's death, Psammetichus fled from Egypt to Assyria (cf. corrupted story of Herodotus, II, 152) whence he returned under Assurbanipal's aegis.

884. Stela of Tantamani, line 36; BAR, IV, §§ 932–3. Pekrur, ruling in Pi-Sopd

§ 355   4. TANTAMANI (*c.* 664–656 B.C.)[885]

A. EARLY YEARS

News of Tantamani's succession[886] and reoccupation of Egypt soon reached Assurbanipal. That year, the exasperated 'Great King' dispatched his forces once more to Egypt (664/663).[887] Once more, the Assyrians quickly regained Memphis while Tantamani fled south to Thebes. Thither Assurbanipal's army followed him again, while Tantamani sped on south to 'Kipkipi'[888] and doubtless to Napata. This time, the Assyrians[889] plundered and looted Thebes of its balance of fourteen centuries of treasures,[890] including two solid electrum obelisks.[891] The reverberations of this calamity echoed round the ancient world; a few decades later, the Hebrew prophet Nahum could invoke no more dire fate on Nineveh itself than what had befallen No-Amon, 'city of Amun'.

The disaster of 663 B.C. spelt the end of the Nubian dominion in Egypt. In the north, Psammetichus I of Sais, Memphis and Athribis ruled as vassal of Assyria, and the other Delta chiefs likewise. In Thebes,

from before 667/666 B.C. (mentioned by Assurbanipal then) was evidently not among those hapless princes arrested and executed in Nineveh; presumably, he avoided arrest and resumed his rule after the *putsch*. At Sais, Psammetichus (I) was direct successor to his father Necho I, and so reckoned his own regnal years from the latter's death in 664. Whether, on taking up rule in Sais, he then directly appointed Harwa as his subordinate in Athribis is less certain but probable.

885. Counting here only his years of Egyptian/Theban rule.

886. As Bakarēᶜ Tantamani, Horus *Wȝḥ-mrwt*, 'Enduring of Love'. Also his may be the [Nebty-name] *Sᶜnḫ-tȝwy* and Golden Horus name, *Ḥw-tȝwy*, *ḥkn*[. . .], from Ṣanam (Dunham and Macadam, *JEA* 35 (1949), 147, pl. 16, 76e). Cf. also, Leclant, *Recherches*, 351, n. 1.

887. Later editions of his texts suggest that the king went in person, but earlier records simply attribute the reconquest of Egypt to Assurbanipal's army (cf. Aynard, *Le prisme du Louvre AO 19.939*, 19, 23). Thus, the main campaign was probably conducted by Assurbanipal's generals; he himself may have followed on later, to receive the spoils. Texts, cf. *ANET*, 295; *LAR*, II, §§ 776–8, etc.

888. Obscure geographical term; cf. Aynard, *op. cit.*, 33, n. *a*, for one dubious possibility.

889. One Assyrian, at least, losing his helmet there; dug up by Petrie (cf. his *Six Temples at Thebes in 1896*, 1897, 18 and pl. 21).

890. Reckoning from the 11th Dynasty (twenty-first century B.C.) since when no conquest had stripped Thebes (the Hyksos being more in the north), although tomb and temple robberies, internal corruption and graft would have taken some toll.

891. On this detail, cf. C. Desroches-Noblecourt, *RdE* 8 (1951), 47 ff., and Aynard, *op. cit.*, 23–5 (so, contra Oppenheim, *ANET*, 295, n. 13). For Egyptian loot in Assyria, cf. probably the items given in *PM*, VII, 396, 397 (Taharqa seal, Palmyra; vase, Assur), and by J. Leclant in W. A. Ward (ed.), *The Role of the Phoenicians in the Interaction of Mediterranean Civilizations*, 1968, 13, 15, and notes 34a, 35, 54 (22nd–23rd Dynasty pieces; statues of Taharqa at Nineveh).

the authorities continued to date by the militarily discredited and absent Tantamani, following long custom since Piankhy, owing no allegiance to any of the Delta rulers; in fact, the Thebaid was virtually an independent entity under its mayor, Montemhat, the God's Wife of Amun, Shepenupet II, and their officials. The Assyrian *débacle* had seemingly shattered an outwardly united Egypto-Nubian realm, and left Egypt divided, subdued and prostrate; the prospect of continuing Assyrian rule seemed likely to inhibit any change, at first sight.

§356* B. POLITICAL GEOGRAPHY OF LATE-NUBIAN EGYPT

The prominence of the Nubian pharaohs as seemingly sole kingly rulers of Egypt (especially on Theban monuments) gives the superficial impression that, from the time of the reconquest under Shabako, they had united Egypt firmly under one rule, and that the day of local dynasts was over. In fact, they had simply superimposed a central overlordship (based on Memphis, Thebes and Napata) upon the existing series of Delta and Upper Egyptian chiefs and mayors, as the Assyrian enumeration of local rulers by Assurbanipal (667/666 B.C.) makes abundantly clear – a situation which is well confirmed by surviving traces of the local rulers in Egypt itself at this general period.

It is thus clear that the 'Princedom (in fact, kingdom) of the West' as built up by Tefnakht and Bakenranef continued as a substantial unity[892] *after* Shabako's conquest – at first, perhaps ruled by a Nubian governor ('Ammeris'?), but then reverted under Shebitku and Taharqa to its own line of rulers: Stephinates ('Tefnakht II'?), Nekauba (Nechepsos), and Necho I who adopted pharaonic style with the prenomen Menkheperre.[893] Nekauba already put his name in a cartouche, prefixed with 'King of Upper and Lower Egypt'.[894] Thus, at least in the later 25th Dynasty, claims to full local royalty were tolerated in Sais itself. At Athribis-with-Heliopolis, the titular 'Hereditary Princes' held sway in lineal succession: Bakennefi B, who died in 728 B.C., gave place to Pediese and he to his son (c. 700 B.C.?) Bakennefi C,[895] who was probably slain (665 B.C.) by Assurbanipal who then installed Psammetichus I there.

892. Only Memphis was probably lost to the central Nubian power, until returned by the Assyrians to Necho I as their vassal, c. 671 and c. 667/666 B.C.; he is explicitly called 'king of Memphis and Sais' in Assurbanipal's list of Egyptian local rulers, *ANET*, 294*b*. His cult, De Meulenaere, *BIFAO* 60 (1960), 117ff.

893. Glazed statuette of Horus, Petrie, *Scarabs & Cylinders with Names*, 1917, pl. 54, 25: 5, 1; cf. Yoyotte, *Supplément au Dictionnaire de la Bible*, VI, 365.

894. On a *menat* counterpoise, cf. *G3*, 414; *RT* 8 (1886), 64.

895. Aside from Assurbanipal's mention of him, cf. the Egyptian data collected by L. Habachi, *MDIK* 15 (1957), 68–77, and esp. Yoyotte, *YMM*, 161–5 (§§ 61–9). 173–9 (§§ 89–92).

Elsewhere in the Delta, with one exception, non-royal local chiefs held sway. The four great chiefdoms of the Mā who had been prominent under Piankhy (at Busiris, Mendes, Sebennytos, all central Delta, and Pi-Sopd, east) were now held by Shoshenq, Buiama, Harsiese (K) and Pekrur, respectively. At Busiris, Shoshenq (F) was son and successor of Pimay who had succeeded a previous Shoshenq (E) there at Piankhy's invasion,[896] while at Mendes Buiama[897] was probably the direct successor to a whole line of rulers.[898] In Sebennytos, Harsiese K was probably second successor to the Akunosh of Piankhy's time, and was succeeded in turn by a second Akunosh by the time of Psammetichus I.[899] Less is known of Pi-Sopd and whether Pekrur was in any degree a lineal descendant of the Patjenfy of Piankhy's day.[900]

§ 357   The one exception is Tanis-with-Bubastis. Perhaps a royal fief under Shabako, Tanis was ruled by its own prince, Pedubast, under Assurbanipal (667/666 B.C.). Bubastis was not named by the latter at all. This latter fact suggests that the former realm of Osorkon IV was still an entity down to c. 667 B.C. Finds at Tanis suggest that here also, after but a brief lapse under Shabako, the local line of hereditary rulers had soon re-established themselves – and as ultimate offspring of the old 22nd Dynasty, also took royal titles. Thus, a king Sehetepib(en)re, Pedubast II, is attested from Tanis, Memphis and elsewhere,[901] and he is most likely none other than the Pedubast (*Putubišti*) of Assurbanipal. His statue from Memphis was left unfinished.[902] The work had perhaps been interrupted by the Assyrian invasion, or the arrest of Pedubast in 665 B.C. Before and after Pedubast II, other kinglets may have reigned in Tanis – conceivably, Gemen-ef-Khons-Bak before him,[903] and just possibly a Neferkare after him.[904]

896. See for this local dynasty, *YMM*, 165–73, §§ 70–80, also § 6.

897. On this name, cf. Fecht, *MDIK* 16 (1958), 112–13 (Eg. Pa-yam ?).

898. Djed-Amen-ef-ankh and Ankh-Hor from Piankhy's day, and then probably others in mid-25th Dynasty; cf. Kitchen, *JARCE* 8 (1969–70), 62–3, and Table in Part VI, below.

899. Cf. *YMM*, 159–61, §§ 59–63, and references.

900. Pi-Sopd, cf. *YMM*, 133.

901. See L. Habachi, *ZÄS* 93 (1966), 69–74, pls. 5–6. Blocks from Tanis, *idem* plus Montet, *Le lac sacré de Tanis*, 1966, 63–5, pl. 30 (Nos. 230–8). Memphis statue, Habachi, *ibid*. The Copenhagen blocks are of very uncertain provenience (Fayum seems unlikely); mention of Atum on them suggests either Heliopolis, Bubastis or Tanis.

902. Cf. Habachi, *op. cit.*, 70–4. Full titulary of Pedubast II included Horus name [. . .]-*tȝwy* and Golden Horus name *Sḥtp-nṯrw*, 'Pacifying the Gods', despite Montet's doubts (misreading Sehetepibre as Sehetepibtawyre).

903. On whom, cf. latterly Montet, *Le lac sacré de Tanis*, 70–3, correcting earlier estimates of this ruler's date.

904. Montet, *Le lac sacré de Tanis*, 73–5, and pl. 32, produced a king possibly

Most other Delta rulers named by Assurbanipal were probably little more than local mayors, chiefs of second rank. Such were the Assyrian Sharruludari at Pelusium(?),[905] Pasenhor C and Wenamun as rulers of the two places called Natho,[906] Bakennefi D of 'Ahni', nearby(?),[907] plus the obscurely-located worthies Tefnakht ('III') of Punubu,[908] Bakenranef of 'Pahnuti',[909] Nakhthor-na-shenu of 'Pishabdi'a',[910] and Nefertemirdis[911] of Pi-Hathor-nebt-mefek(?).[912]

§ 358   In Upper Egypt, the structure of local divisions which had been visible 70 years earlier under Piankhy still survived, possibly with further slight subdivision. The 'Heracleopolis' (*Hininsi*) of Assurbanipal which was ruled by one Nah-ke is most likely that of Lower Egypt. If so, Pediese, ruler of Upper Egyptian Heracleopolis (and ultimate successor of king Pef-tjau-awy-Bast) does not appear in the Assyrian record.[913] But in Hermopolis the Akkadian 'Lamentu' is transparently a Nimlot (E), and is the ultimate successor of the Nimlot (D) who opposed Piankhy. Geographically between these two came the second-ranking chiefdom of Siut under a Djedhor ('Siha'); a further new name is Nespamedu of Aswan(?) or Thinis(?).[914]

The principal power in southern Upper Egypt was Montemhat, Mayor of Thebes, whose authority ran at one time[915] from Elephantine–

Horus Neterty-kha‘, King of Upper and Lower Egypt, Neferkare, Son of Re, P [. . .]. These titles seem to indicate Pepi II, but the association (on block No. 254) with the goddess Mut, Lady of Asheru, hardly suggests an Old Kingdom date. If this Neferkare, then, is really a late and local Tanite kinglet, he *may* be the Neferkare whose prenomen alternates with a Wahibre (Psammetichus I ?) on a well-known stone fragment from Athribis. If so, then one might suggest that Neferkare as a local ruler had some hold at Athribis, and was briefly recognized by Psammetichus I in his earliest years. Cf. also *YMM*, 179, n. 1.

905. For this identification, cf. ref., § 353 above.

906. One, perhaps, by Tell el Yahudiyeh, and one by Leontopolis; cf. Gardiner, *Ancient Egyptian Onomastica*, II, 1947, 146*–149*.

907. If 'Ahni' were the Iat-Khenu near Leontopolis, cf. Yoyotte, *RAAO* 46 (1952), 213.

908. Commonly taken as Per-Nub (obscure location), but is possibly a Per-Inbu, cf. Yoyotte, *RAAO* 46 (1952), 212–13, and Caminos, *JEA* 50 (1964), 92.

909. Cf. Yoyotte, *RAAO* 46 (1952), 214 (in the Sebennyte nome ?).

910. Possibly a Per-Sopd-ia(ty), north of Memphis, cf. *ibid.*, 214, and n. 3.

911. For this personal name, cf. Fecht, *MDIK* 16 (1958), 113–14.

912. Commonly identified with Atfih, well south of Memphis, but is perhaps Kom Abu Billo in the West Delta or even a similarly-named place on the eastern borders of Lower Egypt, Yoyotte, *RAAO* 46 (1952), 213–14; also, Caminos, *JEA* 50 (1964), 92.

913. The name Nah-ke recurs as that of a princeling in the late *Cycle of Pedubastis*, see Excursus G, Part V, below. For Pediese, see above, Part III, §§ 199 ff.

914. Cf. above, § 353, references.

915. On statue Berlin 17271, C (cf. Leclant, *Montouemhat*, 1961, Document 9 and p. 268, top).

Aswan in the south to touch Hermopolis in the north – a good area of Upper Egypt. His celebrated inscription in a sideroom or crypt of the Temple of Mut at Karnak is dated to Taharqa's reign,[916] and hence its references[917] to 'the whole land being overthrown', and 'repelling rebels in the southern nomes' (= provinces) could refer to an Assyrian incursion only in the case of Assurbanipal's first raid south in 667/666 B.C. (not 663); otherwise, these allusions can only reflect inner Egyptian tensions of yet earlier date.[918] Thus the basic political divisions of Egypt encountered by Piankhy c. 728 B.C. persisted right through the era of the Nubian dominion, to confront its successor in the early 7th century B.C. – a fact which is also evidenced (for the Delta) alike by the story of the Dodearchy in Herodotus and by the late Demotic tales belonging to the *Cycle of Pedubastis*.[919]

916. By the central scene at rear of the 'niche-room' between the walls bearing Texts A and B (Leclant, *Montouemhat*, 231–2 and pl. 70; Mariette, *Karnak*, pl. 43). For this entire text, see now the edition of Leclant, *op. cit.*, 193–238, and pls. 66–70.

917. Text B, lines 11–14 (Leclant, *op. cit.*, 199, 202–3; *BAR*, IV, § 907). For Breasted's restoration (§ 905) of line 4, there is no textual warrant.

918. Cf. already, Leclant, *op. cit.*, 235–8, 268.

919. Cf. Herodotus, II, 151–2; the *Cycle of Pedubastis*, Excursus G, Part V, below. On the Libyan/Egyptian warrior-classes and their geographical distribution as mirrored in Herodotus and Egyptian sources, cf. E. Meyer, *Gottesstaat*, 1928, 525–6.

CHAPTER 24

The Saite Triumph: Early Twenty-sixth Dynasty

§ 359* 1. THE SHIFT OF POWERS (*c.* 664–656 B.C.)

A. TANTAMANI AND THE SOUTH

In Nubia, Tantamani's rule went on unchallenged. In 663 B.C., not even the Assyrians would pursue him beyond Aswan. While he was still in Memphis in 664 B.C. (ere the storm broke), Tantamani had envisioned proud buildings in Napata.[920] No trace of these has been recovered, but he left two statues there[921] along with his great stela, and another at Sanam.[922] Otherwise, his sole major monument is his pyramid at El-Kurru which was accompanied by horse-burials like his forebears.[923]

In Thebes, Tantamani performed no further works after the little chapel of Osiris-Ptah; there are few other traces of his name there.[924] But in the absence of any other acceptable soveréign, the Thebans continued to date by his reign. In Year 3 (662 B.C.) a text commemorated the induction of two priests at Luxor,[925] while in Year 8 (657 B.C.) a stela recorded the sale of some land involving a chantress of the abode of Amun.[926] In Thebes, the real ruler was still undoubtedly Montemhat, Mayor, 4th Prophet of Amun, 'Governor of the South', and the God's Wife of Amun, Shepenupet II, and their supporters. The relative independence of

---

920. Dream stela, lines 18–24 (*BAR*, IV, § 929).
921. *PM*, VII, 221; Dunham, *The Barkal Temples*, 1970, 17 ff., pls. 9–11.
922. *PM*, VII, 174.
923. *Ibid.*, 196, 198; Dunham, *El Kurru*, 1950, 60–3, etc.
924. Leclant, *Recherches*, 352 f.
925. *G4*, 43, II; Leclant, *Recherches*, 352–3, § 41, B, 1, 2.
926. *G4*, 43, III; Legrain, *ASAE* 7 (1906), 226–7; Leclant, *op. cit.*, 353, § 49, B, C.

Thebes even before Taharqa's death is illustrated by the scope of the inscription of Montuemhat in the Temple of Mut which has already been quoted (§ 358).

§ 360*   B. PSAMMETICHUS I AND THE NORTH
(i) Delta

For the fourth time, history seemed at first to repeat itself.[927] Psammetichus I found himself, as Assyrian vassal, king of the west from the Mediterranean to Memphis, with also the rule of Athribis-with-Heliopolis,[928] where he in due course appointed his own man, Harwa. Here, the most significant change is that the High Priest of Har-Khentekhtai of Athribis and High Priest in Heliopolis was no longer a 'Hereditary Prince' or perpetual 'royal heir', like all his precursors, but was now simply a high priest and local administrator.[929]

Psammetichus succeeded also in imposing his primacy on other districts of the Delta contiguous with the kingdom of the west. In Busiris, another Pimay, successor of Shoshenq F, was 'prince and count' (*iry-pʿt ḥ₃ty-ʿ*) and prophet of Osiris Lord of Busiris – but no longer a great chief of the Mā and army-leader.[930] Likewise in Sebennytos, Akunosh B was 'prince and count', prophet of Onuris-Shu, Son-of-Re, Lord of Sebennytos, and likewise no longer great chief of the Mā and army-leader.[931] Thus, early in the reign of Psammetichus I, two out of four of the great chiefdoms of the Mā, who adjoined his own territories, had already become his subordinates.

§ 361   Elsewhere in the Delta, final recognition of the overlordship of Psammetichus I may not at first have come so readily or quickly. For a while, the kinglets of Tanis, especially Pedubast II and perhaps Neferkare, may have held aloof, considering themselves to be as good 'kings' as Psammeti-

---

927. Tefnakht became principal ruler of Lower Egypt before and after Piankhy's invasion; Bakenranef succeeded him in this, being the 24th Dynasty in himself; Necho I as king of Memphis and Sais (so, Assurbanipal) was leader in the Delta until slain by Tantamani; Psammetichus I now followed in their footsteps.

928. Where Assurbanipal had first installed him in 665 B.C., when Necho I was his principal vassal. The rulers of Tanis had also, perhaps, pretensions to the overlordship of Athribis.

929. For Harwa and his son and successor Harudja, and their role, cf. *YMM*, 177–8, § 91.

930. Cf. again, *YMM*, 165–6, where the titles of the elder and younger Pimays, grandfather and grandson, can be seen in contrast, and for the date of the younger Pimay as contemporary of Psammetichus I. This Pimay on foundation-plaques is a 'great chief', and 'his favoured and beloved' (in relation to the king), but not chief of the Mā or army-leader. On the possible elimination of this Pimay by Psammetichus I (erasures, Florence statue, 1792), cf. *YMM*, 173, n. 1.

931. Cf. *YMM*, 161, § 63.

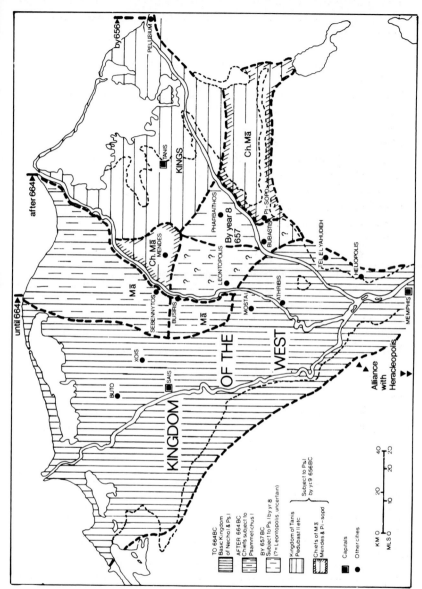

Fig. 7. Eastward expansion of realm of Psammetichus I, prior to 656 B.C.

chus with a far older royal ancestry. However, within their territory, the second-rank chiefdom of the Mā at Pharbaithos had recognized Psammetichus I by his 8th year. On a donation-stela from this place and date, it is Psammetichus I who appears in the scene (not the local chief) and by whose reign it is dated, although it is the local 'prince and count, great chief and army-leader, Pedikhons' who made the donation and set up the stela.[932] Of the Tanite kinglets of the region, we hear no more. Thus it is possible that, by his 8th year, Psammetichus I had effectively made himself overlord of the entire Delta[933] by the voluntary submission or involuntary suppression of potential rivals.

§ 362   The power of Psammetichus may well have resided in two factors – the relatively greater size and inner unity of his realm (and so, of its man-power and resources) compared with those of most of his compeers,[934] and the probability of his having stiffened his forces with a small nucleus of Greek mercenaries, 'the bronze men from the sea' of whom Herodotus spoke. The sequence of the spread of the power of Psammetichus I in the Delta (partly-sketched above) remains hypothetical but probable. After gaining the adhesion of two great chiefdoms, he would thus have isolated that of Mendes with the kingdom of Tanis–Bubastis in the north and that of Pi-Sopd in the east. The defection of Pharbaithos may have been one step in the fall of Tanis–Bubastis into the control of Psammetichus; thereafter, the isolated chiefdoms of Mendes and Pi-Sopd could hardly do other than submit. Early year-dates of Psammetichus I are as yet few and not very informative.[935]

§ 363   (ii) *Middle Egypt*
In the key-post of ruler of Heracleopolis, Psammetichus I probably had an early ally and supporter. In the late 25th Dynasty, a 'prince, count, Chief of Prophets of Arsaphes' named Pediese ruled there.[936] His son

932. Louvre C. 297; *PSBA* 14 (1892), 237–8; *G4*, 67, III; cf. *YMM*, 126: 22, 140.

933. As surmised also by Yoyotte, *YMM*, 173, in relation to the younger Pimay of Busiris and the Pharbaithos stela of Year 8. For the enclaves of Mendes and Pi-Sopd, we have as yet no evidence for their local history following on Assurbanipal's records and Tantamani's 'Dream stela', for after 667–664 B.C.

934. Nearest in size (but not in inner unity ?) was the principality of Tanis-Bubastis. As principal Assyrian vassal, Psammetichus I may have secured the authority of the Assyrian troop-commanders to gain control of the whole Delta as keeping the area 'faithful' to Assyria, besides in fact extending his own real power in their name.

935. *G4*, 66, I, reports a stela of Year 3 (Louvre C.101); a Year 4 occurs on a Florence stela (*G4*, 67, II).

936. Statue, Stockholm No. 81, with erased cartouche which suggests a 25th-

Somtutefnakht was born to him by the princess ('bodily daughter of a king') Ta-khered-en-ta-ihet-[weret].[937] Given the later close association of Psammetichus with Somtutefnakht, to whom he entrusted his daughter Nitocris for safe conveyance to Thebes, it is probable that Pediese had married a daughter of either Nechos I, Nekauba, or Stephinates[938] – the more so, as the Papyrus Rylands IX preserved the tradition that Somtutef-nakht had grown up at the court of Sais,[939] and Pediese on two statues[940] bore the title 'Grandee in Netjer'.[941]

Thus, in Pediese and his son Somtutefnakht, Psammetichus I had powerful allies in Middle Egypt, leaving him a free hand in the Delta. Somtutefnakht succeeded Pediese in the functions of ruler of Heracleopolis and Chief Shipmaster of Egypt there in Year 4 of Psammetichus I (661 B.C.), his father retiring and his own cousin (another Pediese) assisting him.[942] So, in Year 8, with the whole Delta acknowledging his rule and with a strong ally in Middle Egypt, Psammetichus I could now look southwards towards Thebes.

§ 364 2. THE REUNION OF EGYPT (656 B.C.)

In Year 9 of Psammetichus I, doubtless after suitable prior negotiations, occurred the event that gained him the recognition and adherence of Thebes, setting the seal on the full outward reunion of Egypt under his sceptre. Psammetichus decreed that he would present to Amun his daughter Nitocris, who was to be adopted by Shepenupet II and Amenirdis II as the future God's Wife of Amun, under the cognomen of Shepenupet III.[943] Thus, in March 656 B.C., there stood forth from the royal quays

Dynasty date (Lieblein, *Namenwörterbuch*, No. 1026). Cf. for background, H. De Meulenaere, *CdÉ* 31/62 (1956), 251–3; Kees, *Pr.*, 278–9, 294–5, above, Part III, §§ 198 ff. Pediese's father Ankh-Shoshenq was a priest of Amun of Teudjoi (El Hibeh).

937. Cf. E. Otto, *Biographische Inschriften der ägyptischen Spatzeit*, 1954, 10, 127: 21.

938. A Nubian princess hardly seems likely, and Pediese lived too late to have married a daughter of Pef-tjau-awy-Bast, *c.* 730 B.C.

939. Papyrus Rylands IX, col. X has Somtutefnakht leaving the court at Sais to succeed Pediese in Heracleopolis in Year 18 of Psammetichus I; on this, cf. Part III, § 200 above.

940. Stockholm No. 81 (cited above), and in Lichatscheff collection (*ZÄS* 48 (1916), 160).

941. Here, as with Tefnakht (*YMM*, 154–5), to be taken in relation to Sais and Buto, rather than to Sebennytos.

942. So in Papyrus Rylands IX; see above, Part III, §§ 198 ff.

943. In due time, Nitocris took a prenomen, *Nb-nfrw-Mwt*, 'Mut is the possessor of beauty'.

in the north[944] an armada of ships under the command of Somtutefnakht, shipmaster of Heracleopolis, to convey the Princess Nitocris south to Thebes. After her landfall amid a jubilating crowd, the young princess was presented first to Amun and then to the reigning God's Wife Shepenupet II and her heiress-apparent, Amenirdis II, who now both accepted and adopted her as their successor.[945] The details including note of extensive endowments bestowed on Nitocris in the 7th–20th nomes of Upper Egypt and from both east and west sides of the Delta, were recorded on a splendid granite stela erected at Karnak.[946]

The great occasion was also commemorated in a set of reliefs at the Temple of Mut in Karnak, on which a whole series of great ships of Nitocris' fleet and the Karnak quay can still be seen.[947] That occasion brought together the representatives of the principal powers in and of Egypt: Psammetichus I in the person of his daughter Nitocris, with Somtutefnakht of Heracleopolis, together embodying the new *régime* in Lower and Middle Egypt, while Montemhat, Mayor of Thebes, stood out as the last great political–priestly figure of the old Theban hierarchy, and Shepenupet II and Amenirdis II (with the pontiff Harkhebi) symbolized the now vanished power of the Nubian 'pharaohs' of Napata.[948]

Psammetichus I was now undisputed master of all Egypt from Aswan to the Mediterranean; in return, he sagely retained the Thebans Montemhat and colleagues at their posts for their natural terms.

§ 365* 3. CONSOLIDATION AND CONCLUDING PERSPECTIVE

A. CONSOLIDATION OF SAITE RULE

(i) *Egypt*

For some time, little change was probably noticeable in Thebes; most of the same priestly dignitaries of the 9th year there, reappear in an oracle-papyrus of Year 14 of Psammetichus I (651 B.C.). As 3rd prophet of

944. Whether from Sais itself, or from Memphis, is not certain.
945. Cf. Caminos, *JEA* 50 (1964), 78–9, on the important point that Psammetichus I did *not* eject Amenirdis II, but had her adopt his own daughter Nitocris in proper legal form.
946. Published with exemplary care by Caminos, *JEA* 50 (1964), 71–101, and pls. 7–10.
947. On the so-called Piankhy blocks from the Temple of Mut at Karnak; see above, Part III, §§ 202–5.
948. Cf. Kees, *Pr.*, 278–9, and esp. his *Zur Innenpolitik der Saïtendynastie* (*NAWG*), 1935, 96–7.

Amun, Hor had replaced his father Pediamen-neb-nesttawy C.[949] By Year 17 (648 B.C.), however, Montemhat was dead and initially his son Nesptah B succeeded him as 4th prophet and (nominal?) 'Governor of the South' until his own death by the 25th year;[950] thereafter, this family disappeared from the leading offices in Thebes. Similarly, with the death or disappearance of Har-khebi, the pontificate of Amun faded into total insignificance.[951]

Gradually, Psammetichus I and his successors introduced Delta men of their own preference into the South. Nesnaiu became mayor of Edfu and El-Kab,[952] while the God's Wife Nitocris not unnaturally employed high stewards of northern origin, Aba, Pbes, and Pedi-horresnet.[953] Likewise, the shipmasters of Heracleopolis were gradually eliminated as a political power by the Saite kings.[954] In the Memphite area, localized action against Libyan incursions across the desert was crowned in Years 10 and 11 (655–654 B.C.) by defence-works.[955] Certainly by 654 B.C., Psammetichus I could justly regard himself as the effective, and not only the formal, master of all Egypt.

§ 366* (ii) *Nubia*

It is at least possible that Psammetichus I not only installed a garrison at Elephantine opposite Aswan,[956] but had also sent an expedition south into Nubia itself, to Wawat or the north part.[957] This may have been to repel a possible attempt to intervene in Upper Egypt by some successor of Tantamani (e.g. Atlanersa, *c.* 653–643 B.C., or Senkamenisken, *c.* 643–623 B.C.),[958] or merely the suppression of incursions by local tribesmen of the

949. Papyrus Brooklyn 47.218, published by R. A. Parker, *A Saite Oracle Papyrus*, 1962; Hor is witness No. 29. Later in the reign, Hor's son Pediamen-neb-nesttawy D followed him in office; cf. above, Part III, § 193.

950. See Parker, *op. cit.*, 24, No. 33 (after Malinine).

951. Passing during the 26th Dynasty to a woman, Nitocris, a daughter of Amasis, after being borne by the God's Wife of Amun Ankhnesneferibrē (successor of the earlier Nitocris). For the latter, cf. *G4*, 101; for the former, see H. De Meulenaere, *CdE* 41/81 (1966), 113.

952. Cf. Kees, *Innenpolitik der Saïtendynastie*, 1935, 97; Ranke, *ZÄS* 44 (1907/8), 42 ff.

953. In this order of succession, cf. B. V. B., H. De M., H. W. M., in Edna R. Russmann, *An Index to Egyptian Sculpture of the Late Period (700 B.C. to A.D. 100)*, 1971, 5.

954. Kees, *Innenpolitik der Saïtendynastie*, 1935; W. Wessetsky, *ZÄS* 88 (1962), 69–73.

955. Cf. the three stelae (one of Year 11) published by H. Goedicke, *MDIK* 18 (1962), 26–49, very usefully but with an unrealistic chronological scheme.

956. H. De Meulenaere, *Herodotos over de 26ste Dynastie*, 1951, 38–40.

957. Block from Edfu, cf. Sauneron and Yoyotte, *BIFAO* 50 (1951), 201 and n. 3, plus (*ibid.*, 201, n. 4) allusions by Aba.

958. Dates, cf. conveniently, P. L. Shinnie, *Meroe*, 1967, 58.

region. Thus, the southern frontier may not have been free of tension in the first part of Psammetichus I's long reign.

§ 367 (iii) *Western Asia*

The union of Egypt as a solid fact gave the king enough confidence to cease paying tribute to Assyria and to make alliance with Gyges of Lydia by 655 or 654 B.C.[959] However, he may have mollified the Assyrians by remaining their ally (not an opponent) while they struggled with a rising tide of troubles in the east and south-east.[960] The alliance of Egypt and Assyria was certainly in force at the end of the reign of Psammetichus I (610 B.C.) in the momentous years of the fall of Nineveh (612 B.C.).[961]

§ 368 B. CONCLUDING PERSPECTIVE

The further history of the redoubtable Saite dynasty leads beyond the immediate purview of the present work, but a closing glimpse of its acts and policies in Western Asia and Nubia makes an instructive contrast and comparison with these of the preceding Libyan and Nubian dynasties.

(i) *Nubia*

In the later years of Psammetichus I and during the reign of his son Necho II (610–595 B.C.), there was little further trouble in the south; attention was focused in Western Asia. But this apparently changed under Psammetichus II (595–589 B.C.). As the result of some threat by a Nubian ruler (perhaps Anlamani?) to move northwards into Egypt, Psammetichus II dispatched his armies far south into Nubia in Year 3 (593 B.C.) and they quite probably reached Napata itself; while affairs in Western Asia remained menacing, he would brook no trouble from the far south.[962] Out of the bitterness of this clash came his erasure of the names of the former Nubian pharaohs from monuments throughout Egypt.[963] No further threat came from Nubia again while the pharaohs still ruled Egypt.

959. *LAR*, II, § 785; the pharaoh's name appears in the corrupted form Tushamilki. The death of Gyges in *c.* 653 B.C. requires his alliance with the pharaoh to be earlier.

960. Cf. M. F. Gyles, *Pharaonic Policies and Administration, 663 to 323 B.C.*, 1959, 20–3 (not all of her arguments are now valid). Assyria was involved in Elam and Babylon; Psammetichus I besieged Ashdod.

961. See D. J. Wiseman, *Chronicles of Chaldaean Kings (626–556 B.C.) in the British Museum*, 1956, for this (e.g. p. 19) and what follows.

962. For this campaign of Psammetichus II and his generals, see the full study by Sauneron and Yoyotte, *BIFAO* 50 (1951), 157–207. The victorious pharaoh celebrated his triumph with great *élan* (cf. pp. 192–9, 206), and there arose a popular tradition of the rivalry of Egypt and Nubia (pp. 193–4 – to which add, as last representative, the opera *Aïda* by Verdi, incorporating 'Amonasro', a genuine Nubian king, in a libretto inspired by Mariette).

963. See Yoyotte, *RdE* 8 (1951), 215–39.

§ 369* (ii) *Western Asia*

With the shrunken Assyrian kingdom struggling to survive the onslaughts of Babylonians and Medes at Harran, Necho II marched to its aid in 609 B.C.; the suicidal resistance to Necho offered by the anti-Assyrian Josiah of Judah (2 Kings 23: 29, RSV) sealed the fate of Assyria – by 608 B.C., it had passed off the stage of history forever. In sharp contrast to *any* previous pharaoh (even the wily Shoshenq I) for the previous six centuries since the Empire, the Saite king felt confident enough to challenge the new Neo-Babylonian power on the very Euphrates itself, at Carchemish – only to be signally defeated there in 605 B.C., losing all Syria and Palestine to the rule of Nabopolassar and Nebuchedrezzar II of Babylon.[964] But in 601 B.C., the two powers clashed again; both suffered heavy losses and neither won – but Necho II's impact was enough to send the Babylonian army home for a full year's refit.[965] Honour satisfied, Necho II and Psammetichus II prudently declined any further direct confrontations with Babylon, despite the rebellion of Jehoiakim of Judah (2 Kings 24: 1 f.) that resulted in Nebuchadrezzar's capture of Jerusalem in March, 597 B.C.[966] Following his Nubian victory, Psammetichus II was content to show the flag in Philistia and by his Byblos visitation maintain ordinary Egyptian relations with Phoenicia.[967] By contrast, Apries (589–570 B.C.) foolishly abandoned restraint, marched to support Zedekiah of Judah against Babylon in 588/7 B.C., and promptly retreated again, leaving Jerusalem to be sacked by Nebuchadrezzar II in 587 or 586 B.C.[968] Jeremiah had in turn prophesied that the Babylonian would invade Egypt, which he did in 568 B.C., early in the reign of Amasis (570–526 B.C.).[969]

§ 370 (iii) *Finis*

Thereafter, both kingdoms found it wiser to become mutual allies, faced by the growing power of the Medes. And it was this vast new power that finally (as Persia) swallowed up both realms, of Nabonidus in 539 B.C. and of Psammetichus III (526–525 B.C.) in 525 B.C., under the new Great Kings.[970] Significantly, when the last pharaohs struggled to throw-off

964. Cf. Wiseman, *Chronicles*, 23 ff., 66 ff.
965. *Ibid.*, 29–31, 70–1.
966. *Ibid.*, 32–5, 72–3; 2 Kings 24: 10–17, 2 Chronicles 36: 8–10.
967. Yoyotte and Sauneron, *VT* 1 (1951), 140–4; Sauneron and Yoyotte, *VT* 2 (1952), 131–6.
968. Cf. Ezekiel 17: 11–21; Jeremiah 37: 5 ff. On Hophra (Apries), Jer. 44: 30.
969. *ANET*, 308; Wiseman, *Chronicles*, 94–5; Jeremiah 36: 14 ff. No evidence yet shows how far Nebuchadrezzar penetrated; by contrast with Assyria the Babylonian incursion left no mark on Egyptian tradition and was but transient.
970. For this period in Egypt, cf. especially G. Posener, *La première domination perse en Égypte*, 1936.

Persian rule,[971] they did so as rulers of a united, Delta-led kingdom – a clear testimony to the thorough reunification of Egypt by the Saite kings, unlike their predecessors.

971. For the latest pharaonic dynasties, see particularly F. K. Kienitz, *Die politische Geschichte Ägyptens vom 7. bis zum 4. Jahrhundert vor der Zeitwende*, 1953. Also, H. De Meulenaere and Kienitz, in *Fischer Weltgeschichte 4, Die Altorientalischen Reiche III*, 1967, 220 ff. 256 ff., for a recent sketch of Egypt before, during and after the Saite epoch.

PART FIVE

Excursuses

Forms of Bandage-epigraphs in the Twenty-first Dynasty

§ 371 1. INTRODUCTION

One of the key-sources of datelines for the 21st Dynasty is the series of 'linen-marks' found almost a century ago on the bandages of mummies wrapped and rewrapped during this period: linen 'made by' (i.e. under the direction or authority of) a high priest of Amun or other notable person, usually dedicated to a deity, in the year of a king (commonly left unnamed). This body of data is constantly cited but almost never[1] fully studied. Photos and facsimiles of such data are practically non-existent,[2] and most of the known bandages (e.g. those published by Daressy) seem now to be inaccessible or even lost. This present study cannot begin to attempt to remedy this appalling situation. Instead, the basic series of epigraphs is here presented, imperfections and all, from the mainly pioneer publications. Attention is concentrated here on an analysis of the *formulations* used in such epigraphs. This proceeding is useful in itself (showing a basic form, it having periodic variations), and also provides the indispensable background against which one may better appreciate the possible interpretations of the much-discussed fragment, 'King Amenemope; Year 49'.

As the list and analysis below will make clear, that fragment does *not* fit into the series, in its present brief form. In the forms of epigraph so far known, one never finds an epigraph that has the direct sequence King-plus-Date in any part of its formula. Therefore, we must align this fragment with *known* forms of epigraph. This requires that it be restored as

1. Miss Elizabeth Thomas, *The Royal Necropoleis of Thebes*, 1966, Chapter 13, has gathered together most of the available data of this kind.

2. A notable exception is Winlock, *Tomb of Queen Meryetamun*, 1932, 87, 89, Pls. 40, A, B, 41, C, cf. 43, C–D (docket).

[Date of] Amenemope; Date (Yr. 49) [of 2nd King, a co-regent]. Thus, this particular epigraph cannot now be so easily used as evidence for a 49-year (or more) reign of Amenemope; but a co-regency of that king from at least the Year 49 of [Psusennes I] would fit the conditions perfectly.

§ 372 2. LIST OF FORMS

These are here given in the chronological order used in this work. The letters A1–A4, B1–B3, C, denote the type of formula used. The text of the epigraphs is cited in transliteration and English abbreviations.[3]

TYPE A

A1: 1. ⟨ - - - ⟩ HPA, P. I, s. Piankh: *n it.f 'Imn*: *m*. Yr. 9. (Smendes I); *G3*, 244, III, *MMR*, 564.

2. ⟨ - - - ⟩ HPA, P. I, s. Piankh: *n it.f 'Imn*: *m* Yr. 10. *G3*, 244, n. 2.

A2: 3. *mnḫt ir.n*: HPA, P. I, s. Piankh: *n it.f Ḥnsw:m* Yr. 10. *G3*, 244, IV; *MMR*, 555.

4[a]. *mnḫt ir.n*:[4] HPA, Mshrt: *n it.f 'Imn*: *m* Yr. 18. Winlock, *Meryet-amun*, 87, 89.

5. *mnḫt ir.n*: HPA, Mn, s. P. I: *n it.f Ḥnsw:m* Yr. [*x*]. (Psusennes I); *RArch*[3] 28, 76: 2.

6. *mnḫt ir.nn*: Priestess:[5] *n nb.s Mntw, di.f* LPH ... *ASAE* 8, 27: 64.

7. *mnḫt ir.n*: HPA, Mn, *n it.f 'Imn:m* Yr. 6. *G3*, 263 I; *MMR*, 555.

8. [... ...: ...]: *n it.f 'Imn:m* Yr. 30. *G3*, 292, III; *RArch*[3] 28, 78.

§ 373   TYPE B

B1: 9. Yr. 48 *n HPA*, Mn: *ir.n.f mnḫt*: *rntyny n kỉ.f mry*. *G3*, 265, VI; *ASAE* 8, 30: 105.

10. [...] Kg Amenemope; Yr. 49 [...]. Yr. *x*, Amenemope; Yr. 49 of *X*. *G3*, 293, IV; *RArch*[3] 28, 78.

3. Abbreviations used in this list are: HPA, High Priest of Amun; Kg, King; LPH, 'Life, prosperity, health!'; Mn, Menkheperre; Mshrt, Masaharta; P. I, II, Pinudjem I, II; Ps. III, Psusennes 'III'; s., son of; *x*, *X*, year-number, person's name, lost; Yr., year.

4. Var. 4b, has *ir.nn* for *ir.n*.

5. In this case, the Lady of the House, Chantress of Amun, Nesi-tanebtashru, called Qesen(et)(?), for Montu of Tôd (with other epithets): her burial is dated to the pontificate of Menkheperre by the mummy-braces.

Probably to be restored as:

[Yr. 3,] Kg Amenemope; Yr. 49 [, Kg Psus. I: *mnḫt ir.n* HPA X: *n nb. f 'Imn*.] See § 29, above.

B2: 11. Kg Amenemope:[6] *mnḫt ir.n*. HPA, P. II, s. Mn: *n nb. f 'Imn*: *m* Yr. [*x*]. (Amenemope?); *ASAE* 8, 24: 38.

B1: 12. Yr. 1, 4th Akhet 1 [. . .]. (Amenemope?); *ASAE* 8, 30: 105.

B2: 13. Kg Amenemope:[7] *mnḫt ir.n* HPA, P. II, s. Mn: *n nb. f Imn*: *m* Yr. [*x*]+3.

A3: 14. *mnḫt ir.nn*: HPA, P. II, s. Mn: *n nb. f Ḥnsw*: ⟨*m*⟩ Yr. 3. (Amenemope?);[8] *G3*, 275, V; *ASAE* 8, 37: 143.

15. *mnḫt ir.nn*: HPA, P. II, s. Mn: ⟨ . . . sic! . . . ⟩. *ASAE* 8, 33: 124/4.

16. *mnḫt ir.nn*: HPA, P. II, s. Mn: *n nb. f 'Imn*:*m* Yr. 10. *Ibid.*, 124/5.

17. [*mnḫt ir.n*: HPA, P. II, s. Mn]: [*n nb. f 'I*]*mn*: *m* Yr. 1. *G3*, 274, IC.

18. [*mnḫt ir.n*: HPA, P. II, s. Mn]: [*n nb. f*] *'Imn*: ⟨*m*⟩ Yr. 3. *MMR*, 572; *G3*, 275 n. 1.

19. *mnḫt* {*inn*} *ir.n*: HPA, P. II, s. Mn: [. . .]. *MMR*, 572.

20. ⟨*mnḫt ir.n*⟩: HPA, P. II, s. Mn: *n nb. f 'Imn*: ⟨*m*⟩ Yr. 3. *G3*, 275. IV; *MMR*, 579.

21. *in* (<*mnḫt*) *ir.n*: Priestess:[9] . . . : ⟨*m*⟩ Yr. 5. *G3*, 276, X; *MMR*, 567.

22. *mnḫt ir.n*: HPA, P. II, s. Mn: *n* ⟨*nb. f*⟩ *'Imn*: ⟨*m*⟩ Yr. 7. *G3*, 276, XII; *MMR*, 572.

23. *mnḫt ir.n*: HPA, P. II, s. Mn: *n nbf*. *'Imn*: *m* Yr. 7. *G3*, 276, XIII; *ASAE* 8, 33: 124/1, 2.

B3: 24. *mnḫt ir.n:* HPA, P. II, s. Mn: *n*[*nb*]*t. f Mwt*: Yr. 8 *n* Kg Siamun. *G3*, 276, XIV; *ASAE* 8, 35: 133.

25. [*mnḫt ir.n*: HPA, P. II, s. Mn]: [. . .] *Mwt*: Yr. 8 *n* Kg Siamun. *G3*, 276, XV; *ASAE* 8, 33: 124/6.

A3: 26. *mnḫt irt.n*: HPA, P. II ⟨s.⟩ Mn: *n nb*⟨.*f*⟩ *Ḥnsw*: *m* Yr. 9. *G3*, 277, XVI; *MMR*, 572.

27. *mnḫt ir.n*: HPA, Ps. III, s. P. II: *n nbf*. *Ḥnsw*: *m* Yr. 12. *G3*, 285, II; *ASAE* 8, 27: 65.

28. *mnḫt ir.n*: HPA, Ps. III, s. P. II: *n nb. f 'Imn*: ⟨*m*⟩ Yr. 5(?). *G3*, 285, I; *ASAE* 8, 23: 17.

6. The text itself quotes him by his prenomen, Usimare Setepenamun{mery}.
7. King quoted by nomen; *ASAE* 8, 33: 124/3.
8. This date could pertain to either Amenemope, Osochor or Siamun. Much the same ambiguity attaches to the dates of Nos. 14–23.
9. Namely, the Chief of the Harim of Amun, Prophet(ess) of Amun of Medinet Habu (temple R. III), Neskhons.

TYPE C

29. *mnḫt*: *Min-Ḥr-sꜣ-ꜣst*: *ir.nnt*: Priestess:[10] *m* Yr. 13. *G3*, 283, C; *MMR*, 579, 12.

§ **374** *22nd Dynasty*

A4: 30. *mnḫt šps*: *ir.nn* Shoshenq I, *n it.f 'Imn*: *m* Yr. 5. *G3*, 307, II.

31. *mnḫt šps*: *ir.nn* Shoshenq I, *n it.f 'Imn*: ⟨*m*⟩ Yr. 10. *G3*, 308, VII.

32. *mnḫt šps*: *ir.nn* Shoshenq I, *n it.f 'Imn*: ⟨*m*⟩ Yr. 11. *G3*, 309, VIII.

33. *mnḫt šps*: *ir.nn* HPA, Iuput, s. Sh.I, *n it.f 'Imn*: ⟨*m*⟩ Yr. 10. *G3*, 308, VII.

§ **375** 3. ANALYSIS OF TYPES

Type A, the common basic formulation, has four elements:

I. *mnḫt ir.n*, 'bandage' (or, 'linen') made by.
II. Title, personal name, and often filiation, of person in charge.
III. *n it.f/nb.f*, Deity, 'for his father/master, Deity'.
IV. (*m*) Yr. X, '(in) Year X' – king usually left unnamed.

This basic type is attested as early as the pontificate of Pinudjem I near the beginning of the 21st Dynasty, and (with minor variations) persists right down to the early years of the 22nd Dynasty. The variants may be characterized as follows.

A1 shows omission of element I, giving only II–IV, i.e. the identity of the responsible person, the dedication to a deity, and a regnal year. Except for No. 20 above (under Pinudjem II), perhaps an error, the only examples are two early epigraphs, Years 9, 10 (of Smendes) with Pinudjem I (Nos. 1, 2).

A2 is the standard form, with four elements, discussed initially above. It is usual during the first half of the 21st Dynasty (pontificates of Pinudjem I, Masaharta, Menkheperre), Nos. 3–5, 7–8; it is slight modifications of this scheme (A3, A4, below) which predominate down to the early 22nd Dynasty.

A3 is the standard form but slightly modified. It has all four constituent elements of that form (A2), but with one interesting change in III (dedication to Deity). From Pinudjem II onwards, the Theban pontiff no longer dedicates the linen for 'his *father*' Amun or Khons, but *n nb.f*, for 'his *Lord/master*', Amun or Khons – a rather humbler tone! This characterizes

10. Namely, the Leading Lady, Chief of Harim, Istemkheb.

the latter half of the 21st Dynasty.[11] In the A3 series, the verbal form is often written *ir.nn* for *ir.n*, the more usual form; and the preposition *m* before the year-date is often omitted.

A4 is a further modified standard form, introduced by the 22nd Dynasty. The changes are: in I, adding *šps*, 'fine, noble' linen; in II, naming the king; in III, a return to *it.f*, 'his father' as relation to the deity; IV is unchanged. In this set, *ir.nn* is usual, unlike most of the 21st Dynasty.

§ **376**   Type B is characterized by its actually naming the reigning king, either at the beginning or end of a basically standard formulation. *B1* is extant in only fragmentary form; it would appear to be: Date of King (named, except in anomalous No. 9); then, elements I–III – person responsible, after linen 'made', and dedication. This comes in at end of reign of Psusennes I and with Amenemɔpe.

B2 simply names the King, then adds the entire elements I–IV of the standard formulation of type A (A3): linen, person, dedication, date. So far, this is attested only with Amenemope; Nos. 11, 13, above.

B3 shows the basic standard formulation type A (A3), with King's name added to the year-date at the end. So far, this is attested only under Siamun.

§ **377**   Type C covers those examples that are quite unique or totally anomalous, in particular Nos. 6 and 29 (21 is merely corrupt). No. 6 preserves standard form, Type A, for I–III, but instead of a year-date has a wish for divine blessing ('. . . Montu; may he give life, prosperity, health'). The most remarkable is No. 29, where element III (dedication to deity) has been sandwiched between two parts of element I ('linen', 'made by'). It is basically an example of Type A, with the one element (III) drastically misplaced. The text of No. 9 is most likely corrupt, whether in the original or in the copy. Its dedication makes little sense as published; elements I and II have been changed round (hence, *ir.n.f* instead of just *ir.n*); and Year 48 *n* Menkheperre – apparently attributing the year-date to the pontiff - is wholly without parallel. Therefore, in the absence of collation, this particular epigraph must be treated with considerable reserve.[12] As for the year-date, one might suggest that 'Year 48' is followed merely by a hieratic hooked stroke, rather than by a grammatical *n*; the dedication has been tackled elsewhere (cf. no. 12).

11. One may compare, for example, the modestly-placed Chantress of Amun, Nesi-tanebt-ashru (No. 6, above), who made linen *n nb.s*, 'for her lord' (or, 'master'), Montu of Tôd, seeking his blessing.

12. On this particular epigraph, cf. Young, *JARCE* 2 (1963), 102-3, and n. 21.

§ 378   4. CONCLUSIONS

Several points emerge from the foregoing list and analysis. First, there is a basic form of epigraph current, with slight variations, throughout the 21st, and into the 22nd, Dynasty. Second, these variations come and go at specific times in this epoch. Thus, the simplest form of the basic type (A1) occurs in the early 21st Dynasty. The full basic type (A2) predominates during the first half of the 21st Dynasty into the time of Menkheperre. Then, the complementary variations A3, B1–3, operate in the second half of the 21st Dynasty, and A4 in the 22nd Dynasty. Third, the complementary nature of the two series A3, B1–3, gives us a hitherto unnoticed clue to the possible changes of political power and emphasis in the later 21st Dynasty. In the first half of that Dynasty, the kings go unnamed, and the pontiffs in semi-regal style dedicate linen (like all else) to their 'father' the gods Amun, Khons, Montu, etc. This accurately reflects their relatively independent stance as the real rulers of Upper Egypt, would-be-equals of the Tanite pharaohs themselves. But in the second half of the Dynasty, late under Psusennes and Menkheperre, and fully visible under Amenemope and Siamun, with (Smendes II and) Pinudjem II, two parallel changes occur. The pontiffs now dedicate linen more modestly to their 'lord/master' Amun, Khons, etc., and by now it becomes customary to *name* the king whose year-date is quoted (so, with Amenemope and Siamun). The new trend in the latter case is far from universal, but taken together these phenomena may well reflect a clear superiority in the state with the new king Amenemope, climaxed by Siamun, and possibly relaxed again under Psusennes II, while the pontiffs of Thebes (Smendes II, Pinudjem II) had to be content with a more modest role in place of kingly and theological pretensions current earlier. Fourth, the much-disputed epigraph naming Amenemope and a 'Year 49' can now be fitted into the overall scheme of types of epigraphs, as already noted above (§ 371, end). Fifth, the 22nd-Dynasty epigraphs show a renewal of royal power (king is named; the god is termed *it.f*, 'his (the king's) father', not *nb.f*, 'master').

Datelines from Documents of the 'Renaissance Era' and Twenty-first Dynasty

§ 379   I. 'RENAISSANCE ERA' WITH HERIHOR

0. Year 4, see III/7 below.
1. Year 5, 4th Shomu, 16: Wenamun starts for Phoenicia, sent by Herihor and endorsed by Smendes (Gardiner, *Late-Eg. Stories*, 61).
2. Year 6, 2nd Peret, 7: Vizier, General, HPA Herihor commanded to renew burial of Sethos I (*G3*, 232, I; *RNT*, 249, 2a).
3. Year 6, 3rd Peret(?), 15: ... HPA Herihor commanded [to renew burial of Ramesses II] (*G3*, 232, II; *RNT*, 249, 2b).
–. Year 6, see III/8, 11, below.

§ 380   II. 'RENAISSANCE ERA' WITH PIANKH

4. Year 7, Ren. Era, 3rd Shomu, 28, under Ramesses XI: Day of oracle of Amenresonter in Karnak, for General and HPA Piankh (Nims, *JNES* 7 (1948), 158, pl. 8).
5. Year 10, 1st Shomu, 25: Date of letter under Piankh, *LRL* No. 9 (cf. Wente, *LRL*, 11–12; also, Spiegelberg, *Graffiti*, No. 714, of 3rd Shomu, 23, no year, return of General (Piankh) from Nubia).

§ 381   III. REIGN OF SMENDES I: PINUDJEM I AS HPA

6. Year 1: time of Pinudjem I, bandage-epigraph, mummy of Nodjmet (Smith, *Royal Mummies*, 97; *RNT*, 249, 3).

7. Year 4, 3rd Akhet, 22: Graffito, 'army-scribe' (?), Butehamun, in tomb of Haremhab, VTK 57 (*RNT*, 250, 9); here, or in I above?

8. Year 6, 2nd Akhet, 12: Graffito, same tomb (*RNT*, 250, 10); or in I?

9. Year 6, 3rd Peret, 7: HPA Pinudjem I, s(on of) P(iankh), to renew burial of Tuthmosis II (on coffin; *G3*, 243, 3, I; *RNT*, 249, 4*a*).

10. Year 6, 4th Peret, 7: HPA Pinudjem I, dittogr., sP, commanded to renew burial of Amenophis I (coffin; *G3*, 244, II; *RNT*, 249, 4*b*).

11.* Year 6, 3rd Shomu, 11: Graffito, Necropolis Scribe, Butehamun, Chief Workman, Nebnufer, etc. (Černý, *Graffiti*, No. 1358): or in I?

12. Year 9: ⟨linen made by⟩ HPA Pinudjem I, sP; mummy of Ramesses III (*MMR*, 564; *G3*, 244, III; *RNT*, 250, 5*a*).

13. Year 10: (linen by) HPA Pinudjem I, from same (*G3*, 244, n. 2; *RNT*, 250, 5*b*).

14. Year 10: linen made by HPA Pinudjem I, sP; mummy of Sethos I (*G3*, 244, IV; *RNT*, 250, 6).

§ 382

15. Year 10, 1st Akhet, 3 + *x*: Coming to see the mountains by Necropolis Scribe Butehamun, *n* HPA Pinudjem I, sP (Spiegelberg, *Graffiti*, No. 1001).

16. Year 10, 4th Akhet, 28: Subscript (No. 1286) to graffito 1285, Scribe Butehamun perpetuates name of his father Thutmose; other family names (Černý, *Graffiti*, 1956, 17–18).

17. Year 11, 2nd Akhet, 13: Coming to see the mountains, when HPA Pinudjem I sP came; Scribe Butehamun, Chief Workman, Nebnufer, etc., Scribe Ankhefenamun (Spiegelberg, *Graffiti*, No. 1021, *a–e*, misread as Year 21).

18. Year 11, 4th Akhet, 14(??): Scribe Butehamun, ⌈after⌉ coming to see the mountains (Spiegelberg, *Graffiti*, No. 51, misread as Year 31).

19. Year 11, 4th Akhet, 28(?): Day, coming to see the mountains, by the Scribe Butehamun and Chief Workman Nebnufer (Spiegelberg, *Graffiti*, No. 48, misread as Year 31).

20. Year 11, 3rd Shomu, 13: Scribe Butehamun, sons Ankhefenamun, Nebhepet, both scribes (Černý, *Graffiti*, 1956, 20, No. 1311*a*/*b* and date).

21. Year 12, 4th Akhet, 17: Rallying young men (names, incl. Her-Amun-pena-ef); Cerny and Sadek, *Graffiti*, IV, 1970, 42, No. 2137).

22.* Year 12(?), 4th(?) Peret, 6(?): Renewing burial of Amenophis III by HPA Pinudjem I sP (*RNT*, 250, 13*a* and nn. 31–32; Loret, *BIE*³ 9 (1899), 109).

23. Year 12, 1st Shomu, 8–9: Day, coming to see the mountains by Scribe Butehamun, Necropolis Scribe Ankhefenamun (Černý, *Graffiti*, 1956, 27, No. 1393).

24. Year 13, 2nd Akhet, 15: Prayer to Amun by Scribe Butehamun, coming to see the mountains (Spiegelberg, *Graffiti*, No. 914).

25.* Year 13, 2nd Shomu, 27: HPA Pinudjem I sP, commanded to osirify Ramesses III, with Temple-Scribe Djoser-su-Khons and Necropolis-Scribe, Butehamun (shroud, *G3*, 245, V; *RNT*, 250, 7).

26. Year 15, 3rd Peret, 6: Day of bringing R. III by HPA Pinudjem I (*G3*, 245, VI, misread as Year 17, cf. Young, *JARCE* 2 (1963), 102, n. 15; *RNT*, 250, 8).

§ 383   IV. SMENDES I: PINUDJEM I AS 'KING', MASAHARTA AS HPA

27. Year 16, 4th Peret, 11: HPA Masaharta son of King Pinudjem I, commanded to renew burial of (Amenophis I; *G3*, 249, XXI; *RNT*, 251, 14).

28. Year 16: Graffiti, HPA Masaharta, Scribe Ankhefenamun son of Butehamun (Nos. 1570–77; *PM²*, I: 2, 594).

29. Year 18: linen made by HPA Masaharta (Winlock, *Meryetamun*, 87, 89; *RNT*, 251, 15 *a–b–c*).

30. Year 19, 3rd Peret, 28: Day of inspecting Queen Meryetamun (Winlock, *op. cit.*, 51, pl. 41: 8; *RNT*, 251, 16).

31. Year 20, 2nd Shomu, 6: Coming of Scribe Nebhepet son of Butehamun, etc. (Černý, *Graffiti*, 1956, 22, No. 1337).

32. Year 20, 2nd Shomu, [x]: Coming of priest and Chief Workman, Hor-em-hepet-Ese, to start work in valley, with others, including Her-Amun-pena-ef (Černý and Sadek, *Graffiti*, IV, 1970, 42, No. 2138).

33. Year 21, 1st Akhet, 20: Coming of Necropolis-Scribe Nebhepet (and others); (Černý, *Graffiti*, 24, No. 1359; not Year 22 as in *PM²*, I: 2, 594. Relatives of No. 1359*a* may belong with 1359).

§ 384   V. SMENDES I: PINUDJEM I AS 'KING', MENKHEPERRE AS HPA

34. Year 25, 3rd Shomu, 29: Activities in Thebes pending arrival of Menkheperre? (Louvre C. 256; von Beckerath, *RdE* 20 (1968), 7 ff.).

35. Year 25, 1st Akhet, 4/5(?): Induction of Menkheperre at Thebes (*idem*).

§ 385 VI. AMENEMNISU OR PSUSENNES I: PINUDJEM I AS 'KING', MENKHEPERRE AS HPA

36. Year [1–5?], 4th Shomu, Epag. Day 5: HPA Menkheperre seeks oracle of Amun, concerning exiles (*idem*).

§ 386 VII. PSUSENNES I: PINUDJEM I AS 'KING', MENKHEPERRE AS HPA

37. Year 6: linen made by HPA Menkheperre (on Sethos I; *G3*, 263, 5, I; *RNT*, 251, 17).
38. Year 7, 2nd Peret, 16: Day of burying Sethos I (*G3*, 264, II; *RNT*, 251, 18).
39. Year 7, 4th Akhet, 8: Day of osirifying Princess and Queen Ahmose-Sitkamose (shroud; *G3*, 248, XVIII; *RNT*, 250, 11, n. 28; *MMR*, 541, fig. 12).
40. Year 8, 3rd Peret, 29: King Pinudjem I commanded to osirify Ahmose I (mummy; *G3*, 248, XIX; *RNT*, 250, 12*a*).
41. Year 8, 3rd Peret, 29: His Majesty commanded to osirify Prince Siamun (mummy; *G3*, 249, XX; *RNT*, 250, 12*b*).

§ 387 VIII. PSUSENNES I: HPA MENKHEPERRE

42. Year 19: Psusennes (I?), on later Dakhla stela (*JEA* 19 (1933), 22 f.).
43. Year 30: [linen by ?Menkheperre son of Pinudjem I], (end of cartouche) for Amun (*G3*, 292, III; Daressy, *RArch*[3] 28 (1896-I), 78).
44. Year 40, 3rd Shomu, ⟨1?⟩: Inspection of Theban temples by 4th prophet of Amun, Tjanefer A, under HPA Menkheperre (*G3*, 265, IV).
45. Year 48: Karnak stela, works by HPA Menkheperre (*G3*, 265, V).
46. Year 48: *n* HPA Menkheperre, linen bandage (*G3*, 265, VI).

IX. PSUSENNES I: HPA SMENDES II

47. Year 49: [Psusennes I?] with Amenemope, linen bandage-fragment (*G3*, 293, IV; Daressy, *RArch*[3] 28 (1896-I), 78).
48. [Burial of Psusennes I: bracelets of HPA Smendes II, son of Menkheperre (Montet, *Psus*, 149, fig. 54)].

§ 388 X. AMENEMOPE: HPA SMENDES II

49. Amenemope on braces, and Smendes II on pendants, from mummy No. 135, 'second find', Deir el Bahri (*G3*, 271, XXIV, 1, B; *ASAE* 8, 35–6).

XI. AMENEMOPE: HPA PINUDJEM II

50. Amenemope and HPA Pinudjem II: various combinations on braces, pendants and (undated) linen from nine mummies, 'second find' at Deir el Bahri, Nos. 24, 38, 42; 81, 82, 85; 113, 121, 130 (data, Daressy, *ASAE* 8 (1907), and *RArch*[3] 28 (1896-I); Chassinat, *La seconde trouvaille de Deir el Bahairi*; *PM*[2], I: 2. Note that for Smendes II, *RArch*[3] 28, 76, No. 130 is a slip for No. 135.
51. Year 1, 4th Akhet, 1: bandage on mummy No. 105 having also Year 48 *n* Menkheperre and braces of HPA Pinudjem (II); (*ASAE* 8, 30; *RArch*[3] 28, 77; *PM*[2], I: 2, 633).
52. Year 3: linen by HPA Pinudjem II (mummy No. 143; *ASAE* 8, 37; *PM*[2], I: 2, 635). *NB*: this date could equally be of Osochor or Siamun.
53. Year [x]+3: King Amenemope, linen by HPA Pinudjem II (mummy No. 124; *G3*, 292, II (read 124, not 134); *ASAE* 8, 33; cf. No. 55 below).
54. Year 5, 3rd ⟨ . . . ⟩, [x]: Dateline 'under majesty of King Amenemope', Book of Dead of Captain of Amun's Barque, Pen-nest-tawy, 1: 34 (Papyrus BM. 10064, cf. Shorter, *Catalogue*, 1938, 7).
55. Year 10: linen by HPA Pinudjem II (mummy No. 124; *ASAE* 8, 33; *G3*, 277, XVII, read 124 for 134). *NB*: this may just possibly be Year 10 of Siamun.

XII. OSOCHOR: HPA PINUDJEM II

56. Year 2, 1st Shomu, 20: Karnak Priestly Annals, fragment 3B, lines 1–3; induction of Nespaneferhor under Akheperre Setepenre (*G3*, 289, I; see Young, *JARCE* 2 (1963), 99–101).

§ 389 XIII. SIAMUN: HPA PINUDJEM II

NB: Nos. 57–72 could almost equally be attributed to either Amenemope or Osochor, no king being named.

57. Year 1: bandage, mummy of Pinudjem II (*G3*, 274, I; *MMR*, 572; *RNT*, 251, 20).
58. Year 2(?), [*x*] Shomu, 2: ⎫ Judgement of Amun on officials under
59. Year 2, 4th Akhet, [*x*]: ⎬ Pinudjem II, Karnak, Pylon X, E. end
60. Year 3, 1st Shomu, 12: ⎭ (*G3*, 274/5).
61. Year 3: linen by HPA Pinudjem II (mummy of wife Neskhons; *G3*, 275, IV; *MMR*, 579; *RNT*, 251, 22).
62. Year 3: bandage-fragment, mummy of Pinudjem II (*MMR*, 572; *G3*, 275, n. 1; *RNT*, 251, 21).
63. Year 3: bandage by Pinudjem II, mummy No. 143; see XI/52, above.
64. Year 5, 1st Akhet, 1: Decree for Henttawy, Karnak, Pylon X, N. face (*G3*, 275, VI; *JEA* 48, 58). Cf. Years 6, 8 below.
65. Year 5, 2nd Akhet, [*x*]: Judgement of Amun, cf. Nos. 58–60 above.
66. Year 5: linen by Neskhons (mummy of R. IX; *MMR*, 567; *G3*, 276, X; *RNT*, 251, 23).
67. Year 5, 4th Shomu, 8: 'Rogers Tablet', decree for Neskhons (*G3*, 275, VIII; Černý, *BIFAO* 41, 105–133).
68. Year 5, 4th Shomu, 21: Burial text for Neskhons, wall of pit of great *cache* near Deir el Bahri (*G3*, 275, IX; *RNT*, 251, 24; *JEA* 32, 26).
69. Year 6, 3rd Shomu, 19: Henttawy decree, Karnak (No. 64, above).
70. Year 7: linen docket, mummy of Ramesses IX (*RNT*, 251–2, 25, *MMR*, 568).
71. Year 7: linen by Pinudjem II (his mummy; *G3*, 276, XII; *MMR*, 572; *RNT*, 252, 26).
72. Year 7: bandage-fragment, with one of Pinudjem II, mummy No. 124 (*ASAE* 8, 33; *G3*, 276, XIII (read 124 for 134); cf. Year 8.
73. Year 8: 'of King Siamun', linen by HPA Pinudjem II (*G3*, 276, XIV).
74. Year 8: 'of King Siamun', mummy No. 124 (cf. No. 72, above).

75. Year 8, 4th Akhet, [x]: Henttawy Decree, Karnak (Nos. 64, 69, above).

76. Year 9: linen by Pinudjem II (his mummy; *G3*, 277, XVI; *MMR*, 572; *RNT*, 252, 27).

77. Year 10, 4th Peret, 17: 1st series of dockets under Siamun, on coffins of R. I, S. I, R. II, removing them for eventual burial (*G3*, 295, IV–VI; *RNT*, 252, 28*a*–*b*–*c*; *JEA* 32, 27 f., A. 1–3).

78. Year 10, 4th Peret, 20: 2nd series of dockets, same coffins, at burial in Deir el Bahri *cache* (*RNT*, 252–3, 29*a*–*b*–*c*; *JEA*, 32, 28, B. 1–3).

79. Year 10, 4th Peret, 20: twin texts, burial of HPA Pinudjem II, on walls of pit, Deir el Bahri *cache* (*G3*, 277, XIX; *JEA* 32, 26–7; *RNT*, 253, 30*a*, *b*).

—. (Year 10: linen by Pinudjem II, see under Amenemope, No. 55).

§ 390 XIV. SIAMUN: HPA PSUSENNES 'III'

80. Year 12: linen by HPA Psusennes 'III', mummy No. 65 (*G3*, 285, II; *ASAE* 8, 27). If Psusennes II and III are distinct, this could be Year 12 of Psusennes II as easily as Siamun.

81. Year 14, 4th Shomu, 5: Karnak Priestly Annals, fragment 33, line 2; dateline *subsequent* to entry mentioning Pinudjem II (*G3*, 277, XVIII, 294, III).

82. Year 16: stela under Siamun (Munier, *Rec. Champollion*, 361–366).

83. Year 17, 1st Shomu, ⟨1?⟩: Karnak Priestly Annals, fragment 3B, lines 3–5, under Siamun; induction of Hori son of Nespaneferhor, No. 56 above (*G3*, 296, VIII).

84. Year 17, 1st Shomu, 10 + [x?]: Graffito under Siamun, Abydos (*G3*, 295, VII).

§ 391 XV. PSUSENNES II: HPA PSUSENNES 'III'

85. Year 5(?): linen by HPA Psusennes 'III', mummy No. 17 (*G3*, 285, I; *ASAE* 8, 23).

—. (Year 12, see above under Siamun).

86. Year 13, 3rd Peret, 10 + [x]: Karnak Priestly Annals, fragment 3B, line 6 – later than Siamun (l. 3), so can only be Psusennes II or possibly Shoshenq I (*RT* 22, 53–54; not in *G3*).

87. Year 13: linen by a Chief of Harim, Istemkheb, from mummy of a Nesitanebtashru (not of Neskhons, *RNT*, 251, 19; *G3*, 283, C). *NB*: This Year 13 could be of Siamun, Psusennes II, or Shoshenq I.

Torr on the High Priest of Amun, Djed-Khons-ef-ankh

§ 392   Some 80 years ago, Cecil Torr reported on a mention of a high priest of Amun, Djed-Khons-ef-ankh, in *The Academy*. He had cause in *RArch*[3] 28 (1896-I), 297–8, to remark: 'S'il faut rayer un nom . . . de la liste des grands-prêtres . . ., il convient d'en ajouter un autre, Djot-khonsou-au-f-ankh. Je l'ai (p. 298) signalé dans l'*Academy* du 24 septembre 1892, mais ma notice est restée presque inaperçue. Dans l'inscription d'un cercueil le mort s'appelle "fils du grand-prêtre Djot-khonsou-au-f-ankh, fils du roi Pinedjem". Malheureusement, le cercueil a disparu, mais la copie de l'inscription est digne de confiance.'

Torr's reproach is still true; his *Academy* paper is rarely cited, and the pontiff concerned is equally rarely dealt with. Therefore, we reprint here Torr's original account as given in *The Academy* (Vol. 42/No. 1064 (24 September 1892), p. 270, middle column), so that both his paper and the pontiff Djed-Khons-ef-ankh may not be totally lost to oblivion:

'C. Torr, *Aegean pottery in Egypt.*   London; Sept. 22, 1892.

'In reply to Mr. Petrie's request for further information about the false-necked vase, numbered 22,821, in the Fourth Egyptian Room at the British Museum, I beg to state that I have made inquiries in the proper quarter, and received assurances that the vase really came from the tomb of a grandson of Pinetchem, as stated on the label.

'In the inscription on the coffin in the tomb its owner's name was partly effaced; and, consequently, his name could not be given on the label. The inscription described him as - - - Rā, son of the first priest of Amen, Tchet-Chensu-af-ānkh, son of the lord of the two lands, Pa-netchem-Amen-meri, first priest of Amen. The name Pa-netchem-Amen-meri was enclosed in a cartouche.

424

'The following are the other objects from this tomb which have come to the British Museum. Nos. 22,872, large scarab of opaque blue glass, without inscription or device; 22,822, pilgrim-bottle of white-glazed terra-cotta; 22,826, four-handled vase (with lid) of blue glazed Egyptian faience; 22,825, wooden box (without lid) in form of a hippopotamus. These are all in the Fourth Egyptian Room, and in Table-case A, and Wall-cases 110, 114, 149 respectively.

'In his letter Mr. Petrie makes a statement which needs some explanation. Speaking of false-necked vases, he says: "It may, perhaps, be proved that one vase was buried at a date four centuries later than the dating found with hundreds of others." In the first place, he ignores the fact that false-necked vases are represented in the tomb of Ramessu III, and must therefore have been in use within about two centuries of the date when this particular vase was buried. In the second place he has hitherto spoken of less than a dozen vases of this class, and has not assigned all these to so early a period as four centuries before the date in question. Perhaps he will be good enough to tell us something more about those hundreds of others, and the "dating" found with them.

CECIL TORR.'

Notes on the Cults of Tanis and Thebes

§ 393   1. AMUN, MUT AND KHONS AS THE GODS OF
TANIS

Already by the Ramesside age, the cult of Amun was firmly established in
the East Delta, and not least at the new Delta residence of Pi-Ramessē,
which is to be located in the vicinity of modern Qantir-Khataana,[13]
about a dozen miles south of Tanis (San).

On the stela from Manshiyet es-Sadr[14] as early as his Year 8, Ramesses
II mentions '. . . statues . . . for the House of Amun of Ramesses Meryamun, and for the House of Ptah of Ramesses Meryamun, in Pi-Ramessē
Great-of-Victories'. Amun and Ptah, both 'of Ramesses',[15] thus had temples in that city for which statues were ordered. Likewise, in Year 21,
the preamble to the Hittite Treaty envisages Ramesses II in Pi-Ramessē
'doing the pleasure of his father Amen-re, Harakhti, Atum Lord of the
Two Lands, Heliopolitan, of Amun of Ramesses Meryamun, of Ptah of

13. See latterly J. van Seters, *The Hyksos, A New Investigation*, 1966, 128–37,
137 ff., and E. Uphill, *JNES* 27 (1968), 314 f. For earlier studies, cf. references in
Kitchen, *Ancient Orient & Old Testament*, 1966, 57–8, n. 4, particularly L. Habachi,
ASAE 52 (1954), 443 ff., 510 ff., 545 ff. The essential points are: (i) Real, *in situ*
foundations of buildings of the Ramesside period *are* attested at Qantir and environs,
but *not* at Tanis which has only re-used stonework of that age; (ii) geographically,
Pi-Ramessē on the 'Waters of Re' makes sense in the vicinity of Qantir on a branch
of the Nile now no longer extant (cf. Ali Shafei Bey, *Bull., société royale géogr.
d'Égypte* 21 (1946), 231 ff.), but is impossible to apply to Tanis; (iii) both locations –
Pi-Ramessē and Tanis (as Sekhet-Dja(net)) – are mentioned separately, under
Ramesses II (Memphis geogr. list) and *c.* 1100 B.C. (Onomasticon of Amenemope,
Gardiner, *Anc. Eg. Onomastica*, II, 1947, 200*). On these and other grounds, Pi-
Ramessē and its northern neighbour Tanis are to be regarded as separate entities.
14. Hamada, *ASAE* 38 (1938), 217 ff., esp. 220, 226, line 7; *KRI*, II/7, 361, 10 f.
15. On which epithet, cf. Montet, *Griffith Studies*, 1932, 406–11; Couroyer, *Revue
Biblique* 61 (1954), 108–17; Yoyotte, *Ann. EPHE* 79 (1971/72), 172.

Ramesses Meryamun, and of Seth the great-of-valour, son of Nut'.[16] As Gardiner remarks,[17] the latter three gods were at home in Pi-Ramessē, the others being basically the great state deities of Thebes and Heliopolis.

In the 'miscellanies' from the reigns of Ramesses II, Merenptah and Sethos II, this picture is confirmed. In Papyrus Anastasi II, 1: 1–2: 1 (= Papyrus Anastasi IV, 6: 2–6), mention is made of the House of Amun on the west and the House of Seth to the south, besides Astarte and Edjo (on east and north), and the city is compared to 'Upper Egyptian On', i.e. Thebes,[18] as in Papyrus Anastasi III, 1: 12, 2: 1. We find Sethos II 'doing the pleasure of Amun of Ramesses, and Ptah . . .', in Papyrus Anastasi VI, 1–6. In a miscellany ostensibly penned in Pi-Ramessē (Papyrus Sallier I, 3: 4–5), one Amenemone is over the cattle-stall there which belongs to the temple of Re-Harakhti (*ibid.*, 4: 3–4). Greatings in a letter in Papyrus Bologna 1094 (8: 1–10) are in the names of Amenresonter, Pre-Harakhti, Seth, and 'the gods, the lords of Pi-Ramessē'.[19]

§ **394**   Under Ramesses III, the primacy of Amun is briefly but more clearly manifest. In the great Papyrus Harris I, 8: 2–12, it is in the section addressed to Amun of Thebes that Ramesses III speaks of making Pi-Ramessē[20] a residence, of building a temple for that god, and of setting up

16. *KRI*, II/5, 1971, 226, 4–5; *BAR*, III, § 371.

17. *JEA* 5 (1918), 181 *sub* (5); cf. Yoyotte, *loc. cit.*

18. And *not* Hermonthis as still often assumed (e.g. Caminos, *Late-Egyptian Miscellanies*, 1954, 38; E. Otto, *Topographie des Thebanischen Gaues*, 1952, 35–6, 88), except perhaps in rare cases. See Kees, *Orientalia* 18 (1949), 417 ff. The alternation of Thebes and Southern On, and of Karnak and Southern On, in titles cited by Otto himself as well as by Kees should have made this perfectly clear. In the great festival text of Tuthmosis III (*JEA* 38 (1952), 13 and n. 12), cf. mention of On of both Upper and Lower Egypt, surely none other than Thebes and Heliopolis. Note the references of Kees, *Pr.*, 26–7 ('Dachtempel' of Re in Karnak), 36, 38 (the Colossi of Memnon were brought to Thebes, not Hermonthis!), esp. 97–9; 131, n. 7. Cf. also the cautious statement of Nims, *JNES* 14 (1955), 120.

19. For the miscellanies, see Gardiner, Caminos, *Late-Egyptian Miscellanies*, 1937, 1954, *ad locc*. Other papyri, cf. Gardiner, *JEA* 5 (1918), 196: 30.

20. Here, Pi-Ramesses III Great-of-Victories, *not* incorporating the name of Ramesses II, who had given up the latter epithet in favour of 'the Great Soul of Re-Harakhti'. Hence, Yoyotte (*Ann. EPHE* 79 (1971/72), 171) would refuse to identify the references of Papyrus Harris I as relating to the Delta residence Pi-Ramessē, attributing them to Diospolis Inferior (Tell Balamoun). But in Pap Harris I, 10: 12, one should note that this foundation of Ramesses III is assigned 7,872 people, far more than any other Theban-controlled foundation except for the vast wealth lavished on his funerary temple. And in 8: 2, the king tells Amun that he made him an 'august quarter/estate' (*spꜣt/dꜣt špst*) 'in the city of the Delta'. This does *not* favour Yoyotte's identification with a very minor town and temple in the northernmost backwaters of the Delta; yet, the nomenclature is not identical with Pi-Ramessē. I would suggest that Ramesses III established his *own* foundations at Pi-Ramessē, rejuvenating that city, but named after himself in a manner reminis-

there an image called 'Amun of Ramesses'.[21] In all this, he simply renewed the tradition of Ramesses II. Thus, Pi-Ramessē came to be in the territory assigned to Amun of Thebes; in Papyrus Harris I, 10: 12, Pi-Ramessē is clearly situated in the Northern Region under the administration (*ḥr sdf*)[22] of the estate of Amenresonter,[23] i.e. of the great Theban god. Thus, at the beginning of the 21st Dynasty, Pi-Ramessē lay upon East-Delta territory that had belonged in no small measure to the estate of Amun of Thebes, and that had boasted a temple of that god for nearly 200 years.[24]

§ 395 During the end of the Ramesside period, Tanis itself emerges as a northern outlier of Pi-Ramessē; as such it served as the seat of Smendes in the 'Renaissance Era' under Ramesses XI: thence, Egyptian and Syrian ships traded with the Levant (cf. Wenamun). Like nearby Pi-Ramessē, Tanis most probably stood in territory which was already part of the far-flung domains of the estate of Amun. It can, therefore, be no surprise to find that Amun retained all his imperial prominence during the 21st Dynasty, and the Tanite kings were (ostensibly, at least) his devoted supporters. After all, he was the chief deity of their own region. Smendes I's patronage of Amun is seen in his repairs at the Luxor temple which were commemorated by his Gebelen (Dibabieh) stela, and in his practical support for Wenamun, envoy of Theban Amun.

From Psusennes I onwards, the explicit evidence for established cults of Amun, Mut and Khons at Tanis steadily grows. Besides the adoption by Psusennes I of the title 'high priest of Amun' (not only before his cartouche, but even as a variant prenomen),[25] there is the more concrete evidence of his building-works in Tanis itself. Within his vast precinct enclosed by massive curtain-walls of mud-brick, Psusennes built a temple attested not

cent of Ramesses II. Hence, Pi-Ramessē III Great-of-Victories and perhaps Pi-Ramessē Rich-in-Provision (*KRI*, II/5, 1971, 269, 15) were in fact new foundations of this king in or adjacent to Pi-Ramessē proper.

21. Cf. Gardiner, *JEA* 5 (1918), 194–5.

22. On *ḥr sdf*, see Gardiner, *The Wilbour Papyrus II* (*Commentary*), 1948, 116, and especially Helck, *Materialen zur Wirtschaftsgeschichte des Neuen Reiches*, I, 8–9.

23. For other temples in Pi-Ramessē, see Helck, *op. cit.*, II, 188–9, No. 143, *b–j*. Cf. also Kees, *Tanis*, 1944, 151–2, and *Pr.*, 163.

24. That temple must have had a staff, doubtless headed by a high priest or 'First Prophet'. Possible members of that staff might include (i) the Chantress of Amun of 'Great-of-Victories', the King's Sister Tia, under Ramesses II (Florence *Cat.* No. 1598; Helck, *op. cit.*, II, 188, No. 143, *a*, end; now, L. Habachi, *RdE* 21 (1969), 43 f., fig. 14); (ii) the God's Father of Amenresonter, Khons-hab (20th Dynasty?), who held other offices linking him with the court (Montet, *Chéchanq III*, 81–5, pls. 46–53).

25. References, Part IV, above, n. 114.

only by foundation-deposits but also by fragments of stonework, etc.[26] His queen, Mutnodjmet, was both the First Chief of the Harim of Amen-resonter and also 2nd Prophet of Amun. For Amun's consort, she was prophetess and high steward of Mut; for the third member of the triad, she was prophetess and God's Mother of Khons-the-Child – a title which was borne also by Istemkheb C, daughter of Psusennes I. Prince Ramesses-Ankhefenmut was high steward of Amenresonter, and specifically of the god's cattle. Similarly, the great dignitary Wen-djeba-en-Djed was high steward of Khons and prophet of Khonsu-re.[27] All of these perquisites may be referred to the cult and temples of the *Tanite* Amun, Mut and Khons.[28] In turn, even so poorly-attested a king as Amenemope is known to have followed the example of Psusennes I, and called himself 'High Priest of Amenresonter, Amenemope Meryamun'.[29] The main temple of Amun was extended by Siamun, whose column-bases were found *in situ*.[30]

§ 396   In the Libyan epoch, the attestation of Amun, Mut and Khons in Tanis is still clearer. Shoshenq I is beloved of [A]men-re, Mut and Khons.[31] Osorkon II further extended the great temple,[32] and possibly built or added to another shrine at the east end of the great precinct.[33] More clearly still, the monumental gateway of Shoshenq III shows pre-eminently Amun, Mut and Khons, especially Amun,[34] while Shoshenq V seems to have built a whole chapel or temple for Khons.[35] In the Saite period, Psammetichus I continued to honour Amen-re;[36] other late rulers also

26. References, Part IV, above, nn. 142–4.
27. References for all these titles, Part IV, above, nn. 116, 119–25.
28. Not of Amun in Thebes, because all these offices in Thebes were already held by the Thebans.
29. Glazed ring, Groff collection (1898), *G3*, 292, I. Second example, cf. Montet, *Kêmi* 9 (1942), 30–1 and fig. 21; cf. also Černý, *CAH²*, II: 35 (1965) 46 and n. 2.
30. References, Part IV, above, n. 208.
31. Block and column(?), re-used by Shoshenq III, cf. Montet, *Chéchanq III*, 49, fig. 20, pl. 16 below.
32. Cf. foundation-deposits, Montet, *Osorkon II*, 24–6, figs. 1–2, pl. 1: 2 & 3. Probably a forecourt was intended, cf. *ibid.*, 26–8. Other blocks, cf. (e.g.) Montet, *Le lac sacré de Tanis*, 1966, 43, No. 21.
33. Cf. Montet, *Osorkon II*, 32–3, figs. 4–5; Osorkon II reused columns of Ramesses II, inserting 'Amun', etc., over Seth.
34. For this gateway, see Montet, *Chéchanq III*, 13 ff., esp. 19–22, and pls. 9–11 and following.
35. Cf. especially the blocks recuperated from the later sacred lake at Tanis, Montet, *Le lac sacré de Tanis*, Nos. 27–102 and probably most of Nos. 103–211 (pp. 45–56, pls. 5–27 and photos). Jubilee-chapel, *ibid.*, Nos. 212–29. Donation-stela for Mut and Khons-the-Child, *ibid.*, No. 26 (p. 45, pls. 5, 46).
36. *Ibid.*, Nos. 290, 307, 309; 310, 316, 319, 321, 322–3.

honoured the Theban-cum-Tanite deities.[37] Finally, the Ptolemaic epoch is equally clear: on his foundation-deposits, Ptolemy IV honours Mut and Khons-the-Child,[38] while the Ptolemaic *strategoi* of Tanis in turn commemorate Amun and Khons-the-Child, one even being First Prophet of Amun.[39] Thus, for nearly 1,000 years, there is little doubt of the identity of Amun, Mut and Khons as the principal deities worshipped in the temples of Tanis from the time of Smendes to that of the Ptolemies.

One may here append a brief list of the known 'pontiffs' of Amun in Tanis during the Tanite and Libyan Dynasties; doubtless, future work will augment it in due course.

21ST DYNASTY

1039–991 B.C.: Psusennes I, HPA; Queen Mutnodjmet, 2PA.

(Deputy: ? Wen-djeba-en-Djed – cf. § 222, n. 127, above).

993–984: Amenemope, HPA.

22ND DYNASTY

c. 860: Harnakht, son of Osorkon II; died young (§ 282 end).

798: Padebehenbast, son of Shoshenq III, Year 28 (§ 305 end).

c. 775: Shoshenq son of Pimay (later, Shoshenq V?; § 305 end).

§ 397   2. ON THE CHIEFS OF THE HARIM OF AMUN IN THEBES

During the 21st Dynasty, some slight development is visible in the office of the Chief of the Harim of Amenresonter (*wrt ḥnrt* (*nt*) *'Imnrꜥ nsw-nṯrw*), an office which was usually held by a wife or daughter of the high priest of Amun.[40]

(i) Like their Empire-period predecessors, Nodjmet (wife of Herihor). Hrēre B (wife of Piankh), and Henttawy A and Istemkheb A (who were both wives of Pinudjem I) bear the usual basic form of title just quoted above,[41] to which they could prefix or affix such epithets as *ḥryt*, 'leading lady', and *ḥryt špsyt*, 'chief noblewoman' (*passim*). This simple form and

---

37. One notes role of Khons with Gemenef-Khons-Bak, and perhaps Horus Sankh-tawy (*ibid.*, 68, 70); undated, No. 325. Cf. also the great baboon of Khons, Montet, *Kêmi* 12 (1952), 59–68, pls. 3–4.

38. Montet, *Les énigmes de Tanis*, 1952, 140–1, fig. 33.

39. Montet, *Kêmi* 7 (1938), 123 ff.; cf. Kees, *Tanis*, 1944, 173, 173/4.

40. For the New Kingdom, cf. G. Lefebvre, *Histoire des grands prêtres d'Amon de Karnak*, 1929, 34 f., n. 5, 225 ff., *passim*.

41. *G3*, 236–7 (Nodjmet); *LRL*, No. 38, beginning and end (Hrēre B); *G3*, 255, A (Henttawy A).

its complements remained in use well into the Dynasty, e.g. with Henttawy C (daughter of Menkheperre) and Tayu-heret (linked with Masaharta?).[42]

(ii) Under Pinudjem I at Thebes and Psusennes I at Tanis, the chief wives of these respective pontiffs in south and north – Henttawy A and Queen Mutnodjmet – appear with the more distinctive title *First* Chief of the Harim of Amenresonter (*wrt ḥnrt tpyt* (*nt*) *'Imn-rꜥ nsw-nṯw*).[43] This form of title presupposes that, under the 'First' Chief, other ladies of these sacerdotal families served as 'ordinary' Chiefs of Harim (with the simple title) for Amun of Thebes and Amun of Tanis. This may reflect an expansion of the office to provide livings (or, at least a role in the cult, with stipends) for daughters of these families. The obscure lady Djed-Mut-es-ankh was a 'First' Chief of Amun's Harim,[44] so also were Istemkheb D and Neskhons A, the wives of Pinudjem II.[45]

(iii) In due course, the functioning of the 'subordinates' of the First Chiefs of the Harim was regularized, on the *phyle* system (perhaps by analogy with other priestly service where this applied). Thus, Menkheperre's daughter Gaut-soshen was entitled 'Chief of the Harim of Amenresonter *on the 3rd phyle*',[46] while a little later Pinudjem II's daughter, the lady Har-weben, held such office '*on the 4th phyle*'.[47] It is probable that the same development occurred at Tanis among the female clergy there, but total lack of evidence precludes proof of this suggestion at present.

42. § 46 (ii), above (Henttawy C); *G3*, 262–3, VII (Tayu-heret).
43. *G3*, 256, F; 257, Fc, G; 258, I (Henttawy A); Montet, *Psus*, 164, fig. 60 (Queen Mutnodjmet).
44. Winlock, *BMMA* 21 (1926), March 1926, *Part II*, 18–19, figs. 17–18.
45. *G3*, 270, 272 (Istemkheb D); *G3*, 281, E (Neskhons A).
46. Cf. above, § 54, D.
47. Cf. above, § 52 (v).

The Palestinian Campaign and Topographical List of Shoshenq I

§ 398   That the great topographical list of Shoshenq I at Karnak[48] is a document of the greatest possible value for the history and nature of his campaign against Judah and Israel is now clearly established beyond all dispute,[49] thanks to the labours expended on that list by a series of scholars.[50] However, the composition and interpretation of the list still require further examination and clarification.

1. SURVEY OF THE DATA IN THE LIST

The list falls into three main sections:[51] (i) Name-rows I–V; (ii) name-

48. Definitive publication of the scene and its texts, *RIK*, III, pls. 2–9; older bibliography, see *PM²*, II, 35 (124).

49. Discredited and gone forever are the foolish strictures of the arrogant Wellhausen (*Israelitische und jüdische Geschichte*⁷, 1914, 68, n. 4): 'Er kann einfach eine ältere Liste eines seiner Vorgänger reproduziert haben', 'he (= Shishak) could merely have reproduced an older list of one of his predecessors' – a view servilely followed by Spiegelberg (*Aegyptologische Randglossen zum Alten Testament*, 1904, 27–8) who ought to have known better. In point of fact, Shoshenq's list is *the* most original and non-derivative list in the whole corpus of 40 or 50 assorted lists, having runs of names attested nowhere else in these and rivalled in this respect only by the great list of Tuthmosis III and the exotic Kom el-Hetan lists of Amenophis III. The orthography of Shoshenq's list also distinguishes it sharply from all its predecessors – the kind of inconvenient fact over which a Wellhausen just rides roughshod, with methodology that is slipshod.

50. Among others, one may note the fruitful contributions by (e.g.) J. Simons, *Handbook of Egyptian Topographical Lists* . . ., 1937, 95–102 (esp. 101, on originality of Shoshenq's list); M. Noth, *ZDPV* 61 (1938), 277–304; W. F. Albright, *Archiv für Orientforschung* 12 (1937/39), 385–6; B. Mazar, *VTS* 4 (1957), 57–66; Y. Aharoni, *The Land of the Bible*, 1966, 283–90 and his Map 24; S. Herrmann, *ZDPV* 80 (1964), 55–79.

51. Reading from top to bottom.

rows VI–X (all behind and below Amun and 'Victorious Thebes'); and (iii) name-row XI (nearly all lost) extending along the base of the right half of the whole scene, from centre to right end. Various parts of Palestine may be graphically distinguished in these rows by the following diagram:52

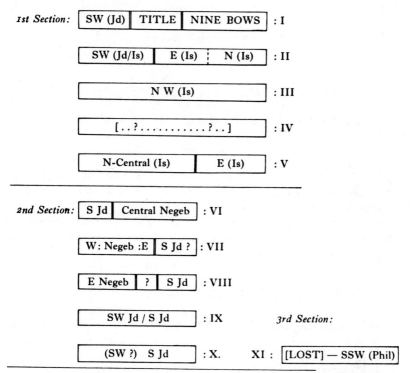

Fig. 8. Diagram of distribution of Geographical areas, List of Shoshenq I.

§ 399   *1st Section: Row I:* As is universally recognized, the first nine names are those of the 'Nine Bows',53 traditional territories and foes of Egypt, a mere literary device to introduce the list.54 The 10th 'name',

52. Direction of hieroglyphs indicates reading from right to left. In the figure, besides N, S, E, W, and compounds for cardinal points, etc., the following abbreviations are used: Is = Israel, Jd = Judah, Phil = Philistia. Only row XI reads from left to right on the original.

53. Namely Upper Egypt (1), Lower Egypt (2), Natives of Nubia (3), Libya (4), Sekhet-Iam (5; Oases?), Beduin of Asia (6), Eastern desert-dwellers (7), Upper Nubia (8), and the Northerners (9). On the Nine Bows, cf. latterly E. Uphill, *JEOL* 19 (1965–66/67), 393–420.

54. A feature found in minor Ramesside lists (e.g. Simons, No. XV, *Orientalia* 34 (1965), 6, 8; now in *KRI*, I/2 (1972), 33–4, and II/3, 1970, 184–6), but not fully in major lists (where the Nine Bows can be grouped-in with other names, cf. Simons,

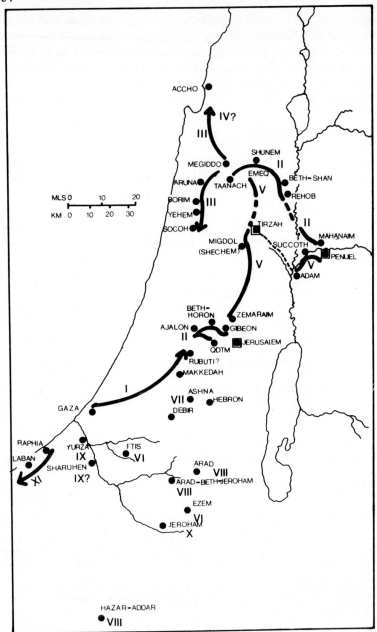

Fig. 9. Route-segments in List of Shoshenq I.

incomplete, has most satisfactorily been interpreted as *mitt* ⸢[*ʒmw*], 'Copy of A[siatic (name)s]',[55] introducing the list proper, Nos. 11 ff. Of the three names that end the first row and begin the list proper, the first (No. 11) as *g* . . . may well be for G[aza], G[*dt*],[56] the key town first reached after crossing the Sinai isthmus. The next (No. 12) is wide open to question; the new copy clearly shows tails of two *differing* birds – probably *m* and *ʒ* – which would rule out 'Gezer', ([*g*]*ʒ*[*d*]*ʒ*[*r*]), as over-confidently advocated by Mazar, Aharoni and others.[57] On the other hand, one may restore M-[*k*]*ʒ*[*d*], Makked(ah), which would come just south of Rubuti (No. 13) as interpreted by Mazar and Aharoni.[58] This, in turn, would then come in nicely before Ajalon, which is named in Row II.

§ **400** *Row II:* This, for prudence, may first be divided into three groups of names: (A) 14–18, (B) 19–22, and (C) 23–26. In reverse order, group (C) is agreed to be Ajalon (26), *Kdtm* (25),[59] Beth-Horon (24), and Gibeon (23), which are all on a well-attested route up into the hills on the northern borders of Judah, to within easy striking-distance of Jerusalem – a self-evident segment from a route-of-march. Likewise, group (A) gives the clearly-agreed names Taanach (14), Shunem (15), Beth-Shan (16), Rehob

Nos. XIII–XIV, *KRI*, I/1, 1969, 27–8, 31). Presence of the Nine Bows has no bearing on the historicity of either Shoshenq's list or any other; that must be decided on contents.

55. So already by Maspero, *Études de Mythologie et d'archéologie égyptiennes*, V, 1911, 88; Müller, *Egyptological Researches*, I, 53; Simons, *Handbook, Egyptian Lists*, 180: 10; and followed by Noth, *ZDPV* 61 (1938), 282. This feature is unique to Shoshenq's list. The reference to Mitanni (*BAR*, IV, § 710, cf. § 722: 19, now *RIK*, III, pl. 4: 23) is *not* in the list itself, but is in the rhetorical text that occupies the upper part of the scene. In this text, much use is made of New Kingdom 'triumphal' phraseology – not surprising, when one considers how many such New Kingdom triumph-scenes (often with lists) at Karnak surround Shoshenq's own relief on every hand. This, again, does not bear on the originality of the list; and Shoshenq's rhetorical text itself makes original use of its traditional elements in combining some account of his buildings with warlike rhetoric.

56. Permissible on the *RIK*, III, copy and plate, despite Müller, *Egyptological Researches*, *I*, *ad loc.*

57. Mazar, *VTS* 4 (1957), 60; Aharoni, *Land of the Bible*, 285, 286; hereinafter cited as Mazar and *LB*, respectively. While they depend on Grdseloff's copies of the list, it must be stressed that the intensive and sustained epigraphic work of the Chicago team is to be preferred in methods and results to the individual readings of an occasional visiting scholar (even of a Grdseloff); it is regrettable that neither Mazar nor Aharoni (appearing in print as late as 1957, 1966) has seemingly made any use of the definitive edition in *RIK*, III, already published in 1954.

58. Which they ingeniously take as possibly identical with Beth-Shemesh; cf. esp. *LB*, 286–7.

59. Identification highly questionable. Very attractive is the suggestion derived from Grdseloff by Mazar, 61, and Aharoni, *LB*, 287, n. 13, that the Egyptian scribe has here misread hieratic *r* as a *d* (very possible), giving an original **Krtm*, **Qirya-thaim*, for Kiriath-Yearim/Baalath.

(17) and Hapharaim (18), all in or close to the Vale of Esdraelon/Jezreel. Here too, a segment of itinerary is self-evident. Between Hapharaim (18) of Group (A) and Gibeon (23) of group (C), one finds the four names which are here called group (B): *Šdrm* (19), [LOST] (20), *Šwd* (21), and Mahanaim (22); only the interpretation of this last name (in East Palestine) is generally agreed. However, the presence of this last name (at the furthest geographical reach from Taanach, 14) could suggest that groups (A) and (B) should be taken together as one long segment,[60] from Taanach to Mahanaim, or Mahanaim to Taanach. Thus, the IInd Row consists of North + East + West name-groups; or, of a North-cum-East and West group respectively.

§ 401 *Row III:* Practically this whole row (27–39) is commonly taken as one series, from Megiddo (27) south to Socoh (38) and possibly a Beth-Tappu[ah] (39). Thus, *ʿAruna* (32) is the place mentioned by Tuthmosis III,[61] now Khirbet ʿĀrā;[62] *Brm* (33), 'Borim', is probably Khirbet Burim;[63] *Ḏt-pṭr* (34) would be the Giti-padalla of North Sharon in the Amarna letters No. 250, now Jett;[64] *Yeḥem* (35) is also named by Tuthmosis III, and is now probably Khirbet Yemmā (Tell Yaham).[65] Two obscure names follow,[66] then Socoh (38),[67] then a very doubtful Beth-Tappu[ah?] (39).[68] Apart from Nos. 36, 37, 39, the main route given is clear, from Megiddo through Carmel ridge, and south across Sharon towards Philistia and Egypt.

There alone remain to be considered the four names 28–31 between Megiddo and Aruna. As these two settlements were only some 8 miles

---

60. Cf. also Noth, *ZDPV* 61 (1938), 283, and Herrmann, *ibid.*, 80 (1964), 57.

61. His Annals, line 32 (*Urk. IV*, 650: 6), *ANET*, 235.

62. Cf. (e.g.) Noth, *op. cit.*, 285; Aharoni, *LB*, 46, etc.

63. Noth, *loc. cit.*; *LB*, 46, 288.

64. *LB*, 163; cf. Albright, *BASOR* 104 (1946), 25 f., and Yeivin, *JEA* 36 (1950), 58 ff.

65. Noth, *op. cit.*, 285; *LB*, 141; J. Garstang, *Joshua-Judges*, 1931, 85 and pl. 9.

66. *Bt-ʿrm* (36), a *Beth-ʿOlam or *Beth-ʿAruma, unknown elsewhere, and *Kqry* (37), totally obscure.

67. Now Khirbet Shuweiket er-Ras, Abel, *Géographie de la Palestine*, II, 1938, 467, 3; *LB*, 45–6 (cf. Noth, 285); not to be confused with the other two Socohs in the Shephelah and S Judah districts (discussed by Abel, *op. cit.*, II, 467, 1–2).

68. No. 39. If it were Beth-Tappuah, then geographically one might just possibly assume a parting sally by some of Shoshenq's troops against Ephraim, striking up by Ain Taffuh (about 10 km NW of Shiloh), at Sheikh Abu Zarad. However, Noth's alternative suggestion (*ZDPV* 61 (1938), 286, n. 5) may be more attractive. This is to restore *Bt-Tp* [*t*], the tall pestle-sign *t* fitting the narrow lacuna even better than *ḥ*. Such a toponym he would identify with Ain Tuba, close to the 'Via Maris', which is probably more realistic than assuming a last-minute 'strike' 18 miles eastwards up to Ephraimite Beth-Tappuah.

(or about 11–12 km) apart – most of the distance being a narrow pass through the Carmel ridge – one would not expect four more settlements of any importance to be situated on that short and limited segment of route. Therefore, with Yeivin,[69] one may suggest that these represent locations lying off the direct main route, possibly even reflect some local Egyptian 'strike' against settlements of North-west Palestine which was launched from Megiddo by Shoshenq I. However, Yeivin's detailed suggestions for identifying these names 'on the ground' are much less satisfactory. No. 28 is *šdr*, not *Ydšr* as his identification with the Idalah of Joshua 19: 15 would require (Hebrew *Yidšălā*). No. 29, *Yad-ha(m)melek*, is still best understood as 'King's Monument', of yet-unknown location.[70] No. 30 may be restorable[71] as [*Ḥb*]*rt*, possibly the Ḥebel of Joshua 19: 29 (cf. Ḥelbah of Judges 1: 31), location uncertain.[72] No. 31, *Ḥnm*, also remains totally obscure. Thus, the most that one may suggest is that, while staying at Megiddo, Shoshenq I had sent a flying-column Northwest to the coast-lands and area north into Asher.[73]

§ **402** *Row IV:* Here, regrettably, nothing certain can be said. No. 40, *šbr*, is doubtless one of ancient Palestine's many Abels, while *Bt-Ḏbi*[. . .] (45) could be an otherwise unknown *Beth-ṣaba . . ./ṣoba . . . .*[74] Apart from the problematic *Ssḏ*[. . .] at No. 51, all else is now lost.

Row V: Rather like the IInd Row, the Vth divides into two main parts:

69. *JEA* 48 (1962), 75–80.
70. A name perhaps applied to some settlement near a (now-perished?) rock-relief on the N. flanks of Carmel; or, a cairn and watchpost on the mountain-part of Wadi ʿÂrā? Cf. later references to a relief at Carmel left by Shalmaneser III (*LB*, 310). On *yad*, 'monument', cf. long since, Brown, Briggs and Driver, *A Hebrew & English Lexicon of the Old Testament*, 390, § 4*a*, esp. 1 Samuel 15: 12, 2 Samuel 18: 18.
71. This is a conjectural restoration, not a textual reading; cf. my note (*Orientalia* 34 (1965), 9) on Yeivin, *op. cit.*, 77–8.
72. Yeivin (*JEA* 48 (1962), 78–9) would set [*Ḥb*]*lt* at Tell Abu Hawam, a minor harbour-settlement (Hamilton, *QDAP* 4 (1934), 1–69), a site hesitatingly identified as (Shihor-)Libnath by Aharoni (*LB*, 139, 238 and n. 160).
73. Yeivin's view (*op. cit.*, 79, map; cf. 76, top) that Shoshenq I may have returned south from Megiddo by going around the Carmel headland (the beach-route) is highly unrealistic; cf. already, Aharoni, *IEJ* 9 (1959), 112, n. 13 end. A local raid conducted from Megiddo (cf. also Yeivin, *op. cit.*, 75/76) is a much more likely explanation.
74. After *ḏbi*, there is room for a low, horizontal sign or group, whether flat *m*, ʿ, *t*, or the like, over a determinative now lost. An *ʿayin* or *ʿm* might permit a link with *Šeboʿim* of Nehemiah 11: 34, compared by Abel (*Géographie*, II, 452) with the Ṣabuma of Amarna Letter 274. Any relation (other than a linguistic parallel) with the Zeboiim of Genesis 10: 19, 14: 2, 8 (cf. Deuteronomy 29: 22; Hosea 11: 8) is chronologically excluded by the long-past destruction of the cities of the Dead Sea plain.

here, (A) Nos. 53–56 relating to East Palestine, and (B) Nos. 57–65, almost certainly in West Palestine. Thus, group (A) clearly ends (No. 56) with *ȝdm*, Adam(ah), the present Khirbet Tell ed-Damieh[75] near the confluence of Jordan and Jabbok. It begins (No. 53) almost equally clearly with [P]enuel: the restoration [*p*] is practically guaranteed by the pseudo-determinative of the animal-skin sign (Gardiner's list, F 27/28) in its late form (lacking only the tail) after the sign *nw*. This determinative was added here because the Egyptian scribe was thinking of the Egyptian word *pnw*, 'mouse', when writing *Pnw-ȝr*.[76] Penuel was on the course of the Jabbok, not far from Mahanaim.[77] Hence, Nos. 54 and 55 listed between Adam(ah) and Penuel should probably lie between these geographically. No. 54 should be read *Ḥdšt*, 'New (town)',[78] and is otherwise unknown. No. 55 is more difficult to interpret. After *pȝ* is written the sparrow-bird (Gardiner list, G 37), then *ktt* (probably for *kt*). The sparrow-sign reads *nḏs* in Egyptian. If one took it for *n* plus Semitic *z/s*, one might read (daringly!) *Pȝ-n-Skt* – 'the one of Succoth'.[79] So, to sum up, group (A) could be taken as reflecting part of a route from Adam(ah) to Penuel via Succoth, and so joining up with the two segments of Row II, (A), (B), Taanach to Hapharaim, and *ȝdrm* to Mahanaim.

§ 403   Group (B) of Row V, Nos. 57–65, is far less well-preserved. No. 57 can definitely be read *ḏmrm*, and be identified as Zemaraim (Joshua 18: 22), in the territory of Benjamin not far from Bethel, and so on the Egyptians' route when moving northwards from the Jerusalem district into the kingdom of Israel. No. 58 is generally admitted to have been a [*Mi*]*gdol* and would be further north still, followed by [. . .]*rḏ*, possibly [*Ti*]*rza*.[80] Thus

75. Bibliography, Abel, *Géographie*, II, 238; cf. Garstang, *Joshua-Judges*, 1931, 136–7, 355, pls. 3, 25.

76. The *nw*, pseudo-determinative and *ir* are all given absolutely clearly in *RIK*, III, pl. 4, and supported by their photo, pl. 7. The wrongly-lit photo of Müller, *Egyptological Researches*, I, pl. 86, agrees, while Müller himself (pl. 80: 53 and n. *c*) did not understand the significance of the determinative-sign; neither did Herrmann, *ZDPV* 80 (1964), 61, n. 22 (whose treatment of Müller's photo is unjustified).

77. The Tulul edh-Dhahab have been identified with either of these two sites. For Penuel, cf. Abel, *Géographie*, II, 406, and on Mahanaim, *ibid.*, 373–4. For both settlements as each having been on one of the two mounds here, cf. Aharoni, *LB*, 381, 382 (lists); on general geographical requirements for Mahanaim, cf. Kitchen in J. D. Douglas *et alii*, eds., *New Bible Dictionary*, 1962, 772–3.

78. So *RIK*, III, pls. 4 and 7, and certainly *not* the *Ḳds*(*t*) alleged by Mazar, 61, and Aharoni, *LB*, 285, list. For a homonym, cf. Joshua 15: 37, in Judah.

79. Agreeing with Mazar, 61, and Aharoni, *LB*, 285; but they fail to justify epigraphically their adoption of the reading 'Succoth' for No. 55. The use of a multi-consonantal sign (*nḏs*) with reduced value (*n-ḏ/s* or just *ḏ/s*) is partly paralleled in No. 85, below, where the sign *ns* probably stands for *n* in *ʿdnt*.

80. Cf. Mazar, 62, and *LB*, 287.

far, we have a direct route from south to north, through the heart of the kingdom of Israel. The next five names are lost (61–63) or broken (60: [. . .]*nr*; 64: *H*[. . .]*pn*),[81] but the last name of this row, No. 65, is clearly *Pa-remeq*, 'the vale': perhaps 'the Vale' *par excellence*, and hence is the valley and plain of Esdraelon/Jezreel. Running from north of Jerusalem to Tirzah and into Jezreel, Group (B) would then be part of a south-to-north route straight through Israel (Ephraim and West Manasseh). Thus, the two parts of Row V are complementary to the two main parts (A, B), (C), of Row II.

§ 404 *2nd Section: Row VI:* Here, we reach the large section of the list devoted to the Negeb regions and southern marches of Judah. No. 66 can be identified as ʿEṣem (Joshua 15: 29 and 19: 3), now Umm el-ʿAzam some 10 km south of Aroer.[82] Three names are compounded with *ḥkr* or *ḥgr*, a word identical with Arabic *ḥiğr*, 'fort'.[83] Hagr *Ftis* (68–69) is probably Photeis, Khirbet Futeis (with ancient site at Tell el ʿUseifir), about 15 km north-west of Beersheba.[84] No. 70, *ʾr-ḥrr*, is well interpreted as an El-hallal and compared with Jehallel, in 1 Chronicles 4: 16, a clan-name in South Judah.[85] More problematical are the two names (73–74) Shibboleth-of (*n*)-*Gbry* and (75–76) Shibboleth-*Wrkyt*.[86] There seems to be no adequate reason to connect the former in any way with Ezion-Geber on the Gulf of Aqaba.[87] No. 80, *Ḏpk*, is possibly the Sapek of 1 Samuel 30: 28

81. The clear traces of base of *ḥʾ* in *RIK*, III, pls. 4 and 7, rule out the Gophna of *LB*, 287. The consequent low position of the *ʾ*-bird in relation to the almost-lost *ḥʾ*-sign would indicate total loss of a further sign at the top left above the bird. As for No. 58, one may wonder whether its Migdol, 'tower', is not a successor to that Migdol, 'tower', of Shechem of the days of the Judges (Judges 9: 46–9).

82. Albright, *JPOS* 4 (1924), 146, 154; Abel, *Géographie*, II, 254; Aharoni, *LB*, 288, and *IEJ* 8 (1958), 27, 29, fig. 1: 40.

83. As set out by M. Burchardt, *Altkanaanäische Fremdwörte im Aegyptischen*, I, 191c, 51–2, § 156: 2, and further by Noth, *ZDPV* 61 (1938), 295–300.

84. *Ftis*, cf. Albright, *op. cit.*, 146; *LB*, 288 and n. 17; Nos. 71–2 and 77–8 remain unidentified.

85. Albright, *op. cit.*, 146; *LB*, 289.

86. In biblical Hebrew, there is no reason to refuse the meaning 'flowing stream' to *šblt*; cf. Brown, Briggs and Driver, *Hebrew . . . Lexicon*, 987 (a choice of good examples, Psalm 69: 2, 15 (Heb. 3, 16), and Isaiah 27: 12), cf. *šbil/šbul*, 'way, path' (*ibid.*, with references). In some special nuance, this word probably underlies the two occurrences here. *Wrkyt* is remarkable in beginning (more like Arabic than Hebrew) with a *w*, rather than *y*; from root *yrk*?

87. As was done by Mazar, 65, and Aharoni, *LB*, 289, n. 18, both of them failing to account for final -*y* and the non-equivalence of Ezion and *šblt*. In this part of the list, Nos. 67 ff., most of Noth's suggestions are either inherently dubious (*ZDPV* 61, 301–3, like Albright's Edomite theory) or vitiated by errors of reading now eliminated by the edition in *RIK*, III, pls. 4, 7; it seems needless to refute these individually.

(LXX), in the Negeb area of Judah.[88] Otherwise, the remaining traces of Nos. 79–82 are still obscure.[89]

§ 405 *Row VII:* No. 83 could be any *Gath/Ginti*, and other single names are unidentified.[90] Three further names are *Hagrs*, and three more are *Negebs*. Of the latter, Nos. 84–85 *Ngb-ᶜdnt* recall the ᶜEznite of 2 Samuel 23: 8,[91] while Nos. 92–93 *Ngb-ᵌšḥt* may compare with the Kenite clan of the Shuḫ(ath)ites (1 Chronicles 4: 11).[92] Of the 'forts', Hagr-*Šny* (87–88) can be compared (at least philologically) with the two Judaean places called Ashna (Joshua 15: 33, 43), both just possibly rather too northerly to fit Shoshenq's list at this point.[93] Nos. 96–97 are probably a Hagr-El-gad, comparable with Hazer-Gaddah in Judah or Simeon, in the 'West Negeb' (Joshua 15: 27),[44] while Hagr-Ḥanan (94–95) compares both with *Ḥnny* (No. 99) and with the clan-name Ben-Ḥanan of 1 Chronicles 4: 20 – there associated with Tilon, comparable in turn with Nos. 101–102, Hagr-*Trwn* ('Fort of Tilon') in Row VIII.[95]

§ 406 *Row VIII:* For Nos. 101–102, see just above. No. 100, *ᵌdr*, could be an 'Adar'.[96] Nos. 103–106 are obscure, and Nos. 113–116 largely lost. However, Nos. 107–112 have been very attractively interpreted as: (107) *Ḥgrm*, 'Forts', (108–109) 'Arad-Rabbath' or 'Great(er) Arad', and (110–112) 'Arad of the House (*Bt*) of Jeroham'.[97] The former is Arad proper (Tell Arad), and the latter was perhaps nearby Tell el-Milh.[98]

Thus far, Rows VI–VIII fall squarely in the East, West, and Central Negeb, skirting Simeon and Judah and touching South Judah.

§ 407 *Row IX:* Here, the entire series of names is far less susceptible of ready interpretation; many are damaged, and some are commonplace

88. So Abel in *Mélanges Maspero*, I: 1 (1935), 28; Noth, *op. cit.*, 301; Mazar, 65.

89. No. 82 is doubtfully read as *Tᶠpᵓ*[. . .] for a Tappu[ah], cf. the Beth-Tappuah near Hebron (1 Chronicles 2: 43), Aharoni, *LB*, 289.

90. Nos. 86 (*Tšdn*), 89 (*Ḥḳ*), 98 (*ᵌdm*); 99, see below.

91. Reading the horizontal sign over *ṭ* as the tongue *ns*, value *n* (cf. *RIK*, III, pls. 4, 7). For Eznites, cf. *LB*, 289, and *IEJ* 8 (1958), 28.

92. So, Mazar, 64; Aharoni, *LB*, 289, and *IEJ* 8 (1958), 28. But appeal to 1 Chronicles 2: 55 is erroneous, because the Shuchathites have *k*, not *ḥ*, in their name, unlike Egyptian *ᵌšḥt*. Nos. 90–91 show a *W*-name, like Nos. 75–6, n. 86 above.

93. The reading *Šny* of No. 88 is perfectly clear in *RIK*, III, pls. 4, 7; the doubtful readings *šnt/šnm* offered by Aharoni, *LB*, 289, must be discarded.

94. Mazar, 65.

95. Mazar, 64–5; *LB*, 289.

96. Cf. possibly Hazar-addar, perhaps located at Ain Qadeis (Aharoni, *LB*, 65, following on B. Rothenberg and Y. Aharoni, *God's Wilderness*, 1961, 138).

97. See Mazar, 64–5; Aharoni, *LB*, 185, 289, and *IEJ* 8 (1958), 30.

98. *LB*, 289, cf. 185.

(Nos. 117: Adar; 122: Abel; 127: Goren; 128: Adam). However, No. 121, *Frtm*, may be related to a clan Pelet (1 Chronicles 2: 33).[99] No. 125 may (with doubts) be identifiable with Sharuhen (Joshua 19: 6) rather than Shilhim (Joshua 15: 32),[100] while No. 133 is certainly Yurza south of Gaza.[101] No. 132, *šrr*[...], is perhaps to be restored as El-ra[m] (cf. 1 Chronicles 2: 9, 27), rather than as El-ro[ʿi],[102] while *Bt-ʿnt* (124) may be the Beth-Anath near Hebron (Joshua 15: 59). No. 126, El-mat(t)an, is unidentified, but compare El-mattan in Ephraim,[103] and a possibly related name Mattanah (Numbers 21: 18, 19). Here again, the limited view obtainable is consistent with South Judah.

§ 408   *Row X:* No. 139, *Yrḥm*, is related to No. 112 above (VIII), and is comparable with Jerahme(el) of 1 Chronicles 2: 9,[104] while No. 140, *šnn*, has been compared with Onam in 1 Chronicles 2: 26.[105] That No. 145 was a *Mʿk[t]*, Maacah, is just possible but very doubtful.[106] No. 150, *Yrdn*, looks at first like 'Jordan'; but the South Judaean/Negeb location of such names as *Yrḥm* suggests that in fact we have here a South-West Palestinian name like Yordā.[107] This row concludes the long series of names in South Judah and the Negeb.

3rd Section: Row XI: These are entirely lost but for the last five names, of which only No. 2 *bis*, *Rph*, Raphia, is certain. No. 3 *bis*, *Rbn*, is Laban south of Raphia.[108] No. 4 *bis*, *ʿngrn*, is almost certainly not Ekron (despite variant *Amqarruna*) but rather some place west of the previous two.[109] This section evidently led homewards to Egypt from south-west of Gaza.

In the VIth to Xth rows, no clear segments of march-routes can be mapped; too many names are unknown, and even of those that are known

99. So, Mazar, 65; and *LB*, 289.

100. The last three horizontal strokes may be for three *n*'s, i.e. *m(w)*, giving Sharuhem for Sharuhen. Noth's interpretation (*ZDPV* 61, 290, n. 1) is not beyond reproach (*tšw* for *t* is improbable), and his restoration of No. 129 as [*š*]*rḥt* is possible but by no means certain.

101. Annals of Tuthmosis III, line 12 (*Urk. IV*, 648: 6), *ANET*, 235. Probably at Tell Jemmeh (*LB*, 140–1, and n. 48).

102. As suggested by Mazar, 65.

103. In the Samaria ostraca, cf. *LB*, 319, 322, 325.

104. *LB*, 289; *IEJ* 8 (1958), 30. Is sometimes compared with Bir Rakhma in the Negeb.

105. Mazar, 65; *LB*, 289.

106. Suggested by Aharoni, *LB*, 289 (invoking 1 Chronicles 2: 48).

107. Mazar, 66; cf. also Noth, *ZDPV* 61, 303.

108. Cf. *LB*, 290, and nn. 23, 24.

109. Cf. already Noth, *ZDPV* 61, 304, n. 1. Unfortunately, we have no direct comparison with the New Kingdom sources for the Sile-Gaza road as studied by Gardiner, *JEA* 6 (1920), 99–116 (cf. particularly his list, p. 113), a study not taken into account by Abel, *Mélanges Maspero*, I: 1 (1935), 27–34.

but few can be firmly located. Row XI is so incomplete that its geographical contribution is nearly negligible.

§ 409   2. PREVIOUS INTERPRETATIONS OF THE LIST

A. NOTH

In 1938, Noth took the view that the pharaoh went north from Gaza up the 'Via Maris' and on to Megiddo which he would have used as his base of operations. Meantime, the king would have sent various contingents into the Negeb, and a force down the vale of Jezreel to Beth-Shan and south down the Jordan to Adamah, Succoth, Penuel and Mahanaim (rows II, V). Perhaps this latter force then came back up westward over the West Palestinian hills to Gibeon, then down to Ajalon and the 'Via Maris' to rejoin the main force (row II) which had come south from Megiddo (row III). Row V would reflect the East Palestinian campaign and the return through the West Palestinian hills. The whole undertaking would have been a warlike demonstration up the 'Via Maris' to Megiddo, plus a series of plundering-raids into and round Israel and into the Negeb (leaving Judah proper almost untouched).[110]

This view has the great merit of simplicity in its view of the list as a whole. Thus, from Row I (Gaza? . . . Rubuti), one passes straight up to the Taanach/Megiddo area, with also a line Taanach via Beth-Shan to Mahanaim, then up through the western hills to Gibeon, and over to Ajalon, straight through row II. Then row III would give the return-route southwards and homewards, from Megiddo via Aruna and Socoh. Row IV is lost; V supplements the data of II. Then, VI–X are Negeb operations, and XI the return through Raphia to Egypt. The use of a main force plus 'flying-columns' fits known pharaonic usage, cf. below, §§ 412, 415.

§ 410   On the debit side, this reconstruction of Shoshenq's campaign clashes with biblical data, and encounters geographical difficulties. 1 Kings 14: 25 f. merely states in general terms that 'Shishak came up against Jerusalem and took away . . . all'. One might well understand this simply to mean that Shishak's forces extracted tribute for him from Jerusalem while the pharaoh in person was elsewhere (in line with Noth's view). But this does not square with the fuller narrative of 2 Chronicles 12. Here,

110. See M. Noth, *ZDPV* 61 (1938), 283–9 (esp. 283–4, 289), and 293 ff. (on Negeb section).

after the general statement (vv. 2–3), verse 4 says explicitly that 'he (Shishak/Shoshenq) took the fortified towns that belonged to Judah and he came (*wayyabō*) to Jerusalem'. This indicates clearly that Shishak himself came at least to the near vicinity of the city of Jerusalem. Perhaps he made his main camp at Gibeon only a short distance away and demanded tribute from there, if he did not actually camp at a bowshot from Jerusalem's walls. At any rate, this passage would require an Egyptian invasion of the northern border of Judah and Benjamin with Israel, up to the vicinity of Jerusalem. Furthermore, in this day and age, the accounts of Chronicles cannot be disregarded as they often contain authentic supplementary data of considerable value (cf., e.g., the Sukki, Tjukten, Pt. IV, § 253, above).

The geographical objection to Noth's reconstruction was posed by Herrmann:[111] the seeming gap between Gibeon and Mahanaim in the supposed itinerary, and especially the lack of a suitable direct road-of-access from the middle Jordan valley south-west up into the western hills directly to Gibeon. After surveying the eastern Ephraimite region, Herrmann found no suitable route to fit this supposed segment, as most tracks between the Wadi Farah in the north and the direct Jericho–Jerusalem route in the south are not suitable for the transit of even an ancient army's strike-force.[112] Therefore, Noth's view would require some serious modifications.

B. MAZAR

§ 411   In 1956/57, Mazar read and published a paper in which he propounded a quite different view, both of the list and of the campaign of Shoshenq.[113] To the first section of the list (I–V) he applied the principle of *boustrophedon*, and so obtained a sequence (I) Gaza, 'Gezer', Rubuti (right to left), (II) Ajalon to Gibeon, then down through the hills and over the Jordan to Mahanaim, and thereafter northward up to Rehob and Beth-Shan (via Tirzah, row V), and west to Taanach (all, left to right). Then (III) from Megiddo southwards via Aruna and homewards to Egypt (right to left). As before, row IV could not be utilized. Mazar simply added-in the two parts of V within his sequence of names from I–III (esp. with names in II), but (as Herrmann has noted)[114] not in *boustrophedon* order. As with Noth, so with Mazar, rows VI–X represented a separate branch-expedition into the Negeb; perhaps, even to Ezion-Geber. With Mazar's view – giving Shishak a 'circular tour' of Palestine – may be grouped that of Aharoni.[115]

111. See Herrmann, *ZDPV* 80 (1964), 58–79, esp. 60, 62 ff.
112. Cf. Herrmann, *locc. citt.*, plus p. 64 and his map.
113. See Mazar, *VTS* 4 (1957), 57–66, with map, p. 58.
114. *ZDPV* 80, 60, n. 16.
115. *LB*, 283–90, with map 24, p. 284; for Yeivin's unlikely minor variation, cf. above, § 401 end, n. 73.

His main change from Mazar's scheme is to take Shoshenq straight north from Gibeon into Israel and up to Tirzah, and *then* down to the Jordan and over to Penuel and Mahanaim before coming back up to Beth-Shan and across to Megiddo.

§ **412** At first sight, this scheme likewise seems attractive, but it too is open to objections. Thus, as Herrmann correctly stressed,[116] Mazar failed to explain by what route Shishak's forces went from Gibeon down into the Jordan valley to reach Adamah and the Jabbok; the topography is clearly against him on this score. This flaw in Mazar's view was avoided by Aharoni, by taking Shishak up to Tirzah, then down the ample Wadi Farah to East Palestine, before returning him to West Palestine and to Megiddo. Moreover, the *boustrophedon* principle cannot be carried through. Besides Mazar's own intentional break with this principle in row V (cf. § 411, above), there is the fact that row V cannot be incorporated into an overall scheme for rows I–V as it stands – it has to be 'cannibalized' by the exegete and fitted hither and thither into the data of row II. And finally, the *boustrophedon* principle as such is not used in other Egyptian topographical lists (or even in Shoshenq's rows VI–XI), not to mention any other Egyptian texts, and so is not a principle of reading to be expected in the upper part of Shoshenq's list either.

A further objection to Mazar's scheme (and Aharoni's) is that it contradicts normal pharaonic tactics in Syria–Palestine. One never normally finds a campaigning pharaoh doing a circular 'Cook's tour', but rather he led the main thrust and sent out strike-forces or 'flying-columns' to deal with particular strategic problems. Besides incidental examples of such 'sideshows' under Tuthmosis III[117] and Amenophis II,[118] the classic example is that of Sethos I. His Karnak reliefs of Year 1 take him straight through Palestine, possibly up to Lebanon, while the larger Beth-Shan stela of that same Year 1 makes explicit how that pharaoh dispatched three 'flying-columns' against Hammath, Beth-Shan and Yenoam.[119] And a

116. *Op. cit.*, 60, 76–7, 78, etc.

117. Reflected (e.g.) in the story of Thuty's capture of Joppa (*ANET*, 22–3), possibly related to a real incident seeing that Thuty was rewarded with a gold bowl, now in the Louvre (*Urk. IV*, 999–1002). The raid in the Negeb, probably as part of the campaign of Year 33 (in which Amenemhab starred) would similarly have been a separate venture (details, cf. *ANET*, 240/1; Gardiner, *Anc. Eg. Onomastica*, I, 153* ff.).

118. e.g. this king's exploits near Hasbeya(?), Year 7, and in Sharon, Year 9 (*ANET*, 246a, 247a).

119. *KRI*, I/1 (1969), 11–12 (esp. 12), *ANET*, 253. Likewise, on the second Beth-Shan stela (*KRI*, I/1 (1969), 16; *ANET*, 255), Sethos I again sends off a task-force to deal with the unrest in 'Djahi', specifically in Yarumtu.

generation later, while Ramesses II himself led a main Egyptian force of four divisions to Qadesh, an auxiliary force (naʿarin) met him there, coming in from the west.[120] Ramesses III defeated the Sea Peoples virtually simultaneously by land and sea.[121] Therefore, one would prefer the general approach of Noth – main force plus 'flying-columns' – to that of Mazar and Aharoni, not least on the grounds of known pharaonic tactics and strategy.

C. HERRMANN

§ 413   In 1964, Herrmann not only offered some critique of the details of the views of Mazar and Noth, but also set forth his own outline view.[122] Like Noth, he favoured a main thrust by Shoshenq up the 'Via Maris' to Megiddo, while several strike-forces were sent out to tackle various objectives – one force went via Ajalon up to Gibeon (to collect tribute from Rehoboam at Jerusalem), and another probably went through Jezreel and Beth-Shan down to Mahanaim by the Jabbok in East Palestine. This latter force could have returned up Wadi Farah to Tirzah, other routes being possible but less easy. It is then conceivable that the Gibeon force could have come north and joined up with the Jordan-to-Tirzah force, whereupon they together rejoined Shishak at Megiddo before the whole expedition returned south to Egypt. As before, a further strike-force raided in the Negeb (not dealt with by Herrmann).

While being essentially a variant of Noth's view (as is Aharoni's of Mazar's), that of Herrmann has (like Noth's) the advantage of taking into account the mode of multiple operations to which the pharaohs were accustomed, while (like Aharoni) he avoids the difficulties that beset Noth and Mazar over the 'gap' between Gibeon and Mahanaim in Row II of the list. He needs no special 'boustrophedon' principle (as invoked by Mazar), but (like Noth) simply takes the list as being made up of groups of connected names, but sometimes more than one group to a row. He is prepared to take some of these groups in a geographical direction opposite to that obtained by reading the hieroglyphic order as it stands (e.g. row II, 23–26), as were Mazar and Aharoni on a larger scale, but not Noth.

§ 414   Possible objections to Herrmann's view are less than those affecting

120. Battle of Qadesh, KRI, II/1–3 (1969–70), 1 ff., Gardiner, The Kadesh Inscriptions of Ramesses II, 1960.
121. Edgerton and Wilson, Historical Records of Ramses III, 1936, 54–6, cf. ANET, 262/3. Already a thousand years before, we see Uni (6th Dynasty) using two separate army-forces – one by land, one by sea – to crush his foe in a 'pincer-movement' (ANET, 228).
122. ZDPV 80 (1964), 72–7.

earlier views here considered, but they cannot be wholly overlooked. In the first place, along with Noth, Herrmann's sending Shishak directly to Megiddo, and only a task-force up to Gibeon and Jerusalem, again falls foul of 2 Chronicles 12: 4.[123] Secondly, if Shishak only sent out his 'flying-columns' (or at least the Jezreel–Mahanaim one) *after* he had first installed himself at Megiddo, he would have had to spend an unnaturally-long time just waiting in Megiddo for his contingents to arrive back there; this is not a fatal objection, but should be considered.

§ **415** 3. SUGGESTED INTERPRETATION OF THE LIST

With Noth and Herrmann, and in line with attested Egyptian practice, it seems essential to hold to the concept of a main force under the pharaoh, from which he detached and sent out at need several task-forces to conquer and despoil various objectives. The Negeb part of the list and campaign certainly demand this form of explanation. With Mazar and Aharoni, in line with the clear implication of 2 Chronicles 12: 4, it seems justified to consider that Shoshenq himself with the main force went up a well-worn route by Ajalon and Gibeon, to secure the submission and tribute of Rehoboam in nearby Jerusalem. From there, he could either have returned direct to the 'Via Maris' and have gone north to Megiddo (cf. Noth and Herrmann), or else simply have moved directly north from Jerusalem/Gibeon through Israel (via Tirzah) to Jezreel and so to Megiddo. At some point in time, he dispatched a force down to the Jordan, and over to the Jabbok and East Palestine. After all this, Shoshenq and his forces would set out from Megiddo via Aruna for Raphia and Egypt.

So much seems reasonably certain. But one may, in turn, suggest a more complete picture. The end of Row I (§ 399, above) would probably take Shoshenq from Gaza(?) to Rubuti (whether it be Beth-Shemesh or not). At the same time, he could have sent a good-sized force to the Negeb via Yurza and Sharuhen. This force probably split into three or more contingents which set off along roughly parallel routes to knock out the Judaean strongpoints in South Judaea and throughout the Negeb (whether or not any force ever reached Ezion-Geber). From Rubuti, Shoshenq and the main army will have gone up by Ajalon and Beth-Horon to Gibeon,[124]

123. On this point, therefore, he is mistaken in claiming biblical support for his view (*op. cit.*, 73).

124. With possibly one contingent going up by Kiriath-jearim, if the emendation of Grdseloff for No. 25 adopted by Mazar and Aharoni is correct.

and have exacted the submission of Rehoboam in Jerusalem, who saved his capital from molestation by paying a heavy tribute (2 Kings, 2 Chronicles). Then, as a supplement to row II, 26–23, one may invoke row V, 57–65, suggesting that thereafter Shoshenq marched north into Israel (via Zemaraim and a Migdol – that of Shechem?) to Tirzah. This time, however, he probably found that the bird had flown – that his intended vassal Jeroboam had already escaped across the Jordan to Penuel and Mahanaim (cf. 1 Kings 12: 25). At this juncture, Shoshenq continued northwards into Jezreel, 'the vale' (*Pa-remeq*), and made his headquarters at Megiddo. But as he left Tirzah going north, he would have sent out a second task-force, down the Wadi Farah and across the Jordan to chase up Jeroboam at Penuel and Mahanaim. As others have noted, there is no inherent reason to suppose that this contingent should have returned to the western territories and to Shoshenq by the very same route. Hence, one may suggest (combining V, 53–56, and II, 22–14) that the East Palestinian force returned north up the Jordan valley via Beth-Shan westward through Jezreel to Megiddo, and joined Shoshenq who had meantime established himself there.[125] From Megiddo, it is possible that Shishak mounted lesser 'strikes' up to the north-west coast (Bay of Acre) and into Galilee (III, 28–31). From Megiddo, in due course, he and the main forces doubtless went south by Aruna, Yehem and Socoh, and crushed any resistance in towns on or flanking the path of their route southwards (III, 27, 32–39). As usual, Row IV cannot be utilized at present.[126] Then, in South-West Palestine, Shoshenq and the main army would be rejoined by his Negeb expeditionaries (cf. rows VI–IX), and the whole expedition return homeward via Raphia (XI) and the Sinai isthmus coast-road.

The reconstitution of the overall campaign suggested here and to which a narrative form has been given in Part IV, §§ 252–258, above, is not 'cast-iron' proof against future modification any more than earlier reconstructions, but it does seek to combine all the available textual and tactical information in a realistic assessment, while avoiding the worst difficulties inherent in previous attempts.

125. It is also possible to suggest that row II, 14–18, represent the path of a small force sent from Megiddo *via* Jezreel to the Jordan by Shoshenq, to link up with the returning E Palestine task-force (cf. II, 22–19) in the vicinity of Beth-Shan.

126. Theoretically, it might reflect a third local 'strike', into Galilee and up to Abel(-beth-maacah) for example. Needless to say, one would not equate *dbi*[. . .] with the too-distant Zobah.

The Data of Manetho for the Twenty-first to Twenty-fifth Dynasties

§ 416   1. INTRODUCTORY

In recent years, the data of Manetho have received more attention than hitherto, in an endeavour to extract from them whatever they may contain of chronological value, and to combine them with the first-hand data of the monuments as an aid towards establishing a firm Egyptian chronology.[127] However, in making any such attempt, it has always to be borne in mind that, however good Manetho's sources and consequent compilation may originally have been, we now possess only very late copies of copies, which have been subjected to centuries not only of straight copying but also at certain periods of tendentious manipulation – and what we have (even in this form) is not Manetho's *History*, but merely an '*Epitome*' of his dynasties and reigns, a few citations (e.g. in Josephus), and largely spurious reminiscences that may ultimately derive in part from his data (e.g. the Book of Sothis).[128] Thus, it is vain to expect total confirmation from the monuments for all our *extant* 'Manetho'; nor should we manipulate the evidence of the monuments merely to fit the extant text of the Epitome of Manetho. However, it is also true that the corruptions in our extant Manetho are very uneven in their distribution: in some parts, most of the data transmitted correspond strikingly well with the first-hand monumental evidence (cf. on the 21st Dynasty), while in other parts – even close by – the Manethonic data are confused and corrupted almost beyond

127. Cf. (e.g.) Rowton, *JEA* 34 (1948), 57–74; Helck, *Untersuchungen zu Manetho und den Ägyptischen Königslisten*, 1956; Hornung, *Untersuchungen zur Chronologie und Geschichte des Neuen Reiches*, 1964, 113–16.
128. Cf. Waddell, *Manetho, Loeb Classical Library*, 1948, xv–xx.

the point of repair in their present state (e.g. chaotic overlaps of late 18th/ early 19th Dynasties), and at our present level of knowledge. The figures for the 26th Dynasty – a securely-attested period – will briefly illustrate this situation. Thus, Africanus rightly gives 54 years to Psammetichus I, but Eusebius and the Armenian version only give him 45 or 44 years, and are therefore a decade short. All three versions give only 6 years, instead of 15 (with a fraction, possibly reckoned 16) to Necho II, and are again 10 years short, while Psammetichus II is correctly given 6 years in Africanus but 17 years in the other versions which are therefore over a decade in excess. Psammetichus III is included by Africanus but omitted by Eusebius. This situation in a dynasty whose lengths of reign and absolute dates B.C. can be closely fixed largely on other grounds,[129] demonstrates in miniature the kind of errors to be expected also in dealing with the 21st–25th Dynasties in Manetho,[130] such as arbitrary lengthenings and shortenings of reigns by decades, etc., omissions of rulers, and so on.

§ 417   2. THE 21st DYNASTY

On this basis, the 21st Dynasty in Manetho can be seen to have been transmitted with a relatively high degree of accuracy. It is very probable that Psusennes I and Amenemnisu (Nephercheres) have been inverted in order, and certainly the figure for Siamun (Psinaches) should be taken as for ⟨1⟩9 years, as 17 years is monumentally attested; otherwise, the figures are unexceptionable.[131] The total of 130 years is perhaps incorrect, as it corresponds neither with the 114 years of Africanus' entries nor with the 124 years which are obtained by combining Manethonic and original data on individual reigns. By one means or another, this 130 years' total does correspond with the totals of Eusebius' figures – but these constituent figures do not match reality, with 5 years short on Psusennes I (excluding co-regency), 10 years short on Siamun, and 20/21 years surplus on Psusennes II. It may be that there has been late cross-contamination in the transmitted total, from the tradition of Eusebius into that of Africanus.

129. See Parker, *MDIK* 15 (1957), 208–12.
130. See more fully, Helck, *Manetho, passim*.
131. See already, Part I, above, esp. § 31; for Manetho and monuments, cf. Smendes 26 and Year 25, Amenemnisu 4 and ephemeral, Psusennes I 46 and 49 (incl. co-regency), Amenemope 9 and 5 or more attested, Osochor 6 and 2 or more attested, Siamun ⟨1⟩9 and 17, and Psusennes II 14 and Year 13.

§ 418   3. THE 22nd DYNASTY

Here, on the contrary, the surviving text of Manetho's Epitome very quickly passes from closest accuracy into a state of corruption and over-abbreviation. The one indisputable datum is the first given: 21 years for Shoshenq I, directly comparable with the Year 21 of his Silsila stela ordering the works at Karnak that were never finished. The total of nine kings (Africanus) is about right, for independent rulers, but does not allow for co-regents like Shoshenq II and Harsiese.[132] The following table sets out the state of the data and possible correlations:

KING	High-est Yr. Date	Prob. Reign	MANETHO		INTERPRETATION
Shoshenq I	21	21 :	Sesonchosis (I), 21	:	(Correct)
Osorkon I	33	35 :	Osorthon (I), 15	: for 25 yrs.?	(If Sh. II had a 10-yr. co-rgncy)
				: for 35 yrs.?	(Omitting all ref. to Shoshenq II)[133]
Shoshenq II	—	—: ⎫			
		(co-rgt)			
Takeloth I	14	15 : ⎬	'3 other kings, ⎫	29 from *49 yrs.? (9 + 15 + 25,
Osorkon II	23?	24 : ⎭	25 (29) years' ⎬ :	or similar combination?)
Takeloth II	25	25 :	Takelothis, 13 :	? shortened by 12 years
Shoshenq III	49	52 : ⎫			
	(52)				
Pimay	6	6 : ⎬	'3 other kings, ⎫	totally corrupt, because irre-
Shoshenq V	38	37 : ⎭	for 42 years' ⎬ :	ducible minimum is 95 years
Osorkon IV	—	15 :	(omitted ?):	(omitted ?)
TOTALS: 224/227		231 :	TOTALS: given, 120 (Afr.), 49 (Eu.); 120/116, counted up		

From the foregoing table, it is clear that (except for Shoshenq I) the surviving text of Manetho does not begin to do justice to the 22nd Dynasty as it is now known to us. One might refer the 'Takelothis, 13 years' to

132. If one wished to include Shoshenq II, one would have to assume omission of Osorkon IV; but, as Shoshenq II was no more of a sole ruler than Harsiese, there seems no warrant at all for this view.

133. One could only accept 15 years for Osorkon I if the Year 33 bandage were in reality to be read Year 13 or otherwise explained away; but on other grounds, this seems unlikely. Perhaps the 15 years of Osorkon and the 35 years of Psusennes II (Eusebius) should be interchanged. Another solution was that of Albright and Helck, assigning the 15 years to Takeloth I (Helck, Manetho, 73).

Takeloth I rather than II, putting after him the 'three other kings for 25 (29) years', and emend to (say) '55 years' (24, Osorkon II, 25, Takeloth II, first 6 or 7 of Shoshenq III before the 23rd Dynasty). The second such entry could be a doublet, and the 120 years' total be an approximation of the length of the 22nd Dynasty prior to the accession of Pedubast I of the 23rd Dynasty – 120 years from 945 B.C. comes down to 825 B.C., the precise year of accession of Shoshenq III adopted here, and barely 7 years before the date (818 B.C.) of accession of the 23rd Dynasty. This is all very well but, at least in the Africanus version, Manetho appears once to have recorded not merely the sole rule of the 22nd Dynasty, but that *entire* Dynasty (nine rulers). In that case, both the totals given (120/49 years) and that gained by addition of Manetho's figures for reigns (120/116 years) are grossly inadequate by at least a century. The possible omission of Osorkon IV would fall into the same category as the omission of Psammetichus III – or, it may be that in fact Osorkon IV *was* included, and it was the co-regent Shoshenq II who was omitted; at present, we cannot know. For other such omissions, see the next section.

§ 419 4. THE 23rd DYNASTY

KING	High-est Yr. Date	Prob. Reign	MANETHO	INTERPRETATION
Pedubast 1	23	25	: Petubates, 40/25 :	25, probably correct
Iuput I	21 (11, co-rgt, 10, alone)	21	: (Omitted— or Psammus, 10) :	40, perhaps from 25 (P.I), plus 10 (Iu. I), plus 5 (Sh. IV) ?[134]
Shoshenq IV	6	6	: (Omitted ?) :	
Osorkon III	29	28	: Osorcho, 8/9 (Osorthon)	: for ⟨2⟩8, ⟨2⟩9, yrs.
Takeloth III	19 (5, co-rgt, 15, alone)	20	: Zet, 31/34	: from *21 or *14 (for 15) yrs. ? Otherwise, is Psammus, 10 (for 20?)
Rudamun	—	3?	: (omitted ? Or Zet, 31/34 ?)	: If Zet, 34 would be for 4
Iuput II	—	—	: (omitted)	: (omitted)
(Shoshenq VI	? 16	?	: (omitted)	: (existence, doubtful)
TOTALS:	—	87 (105).	*TOTALS:* given, 89/44; totals, likewise	

$$(105 = 87 + 16)$$

134. It is to the erroneous datum of 40 years for Pedubast that Africanus adds

Here, the inadequacy of the transmitted data rivals that for the previous Dynasty, but some correlations may be gleaned.

Here, the above table shows the situation clearly. Manetho's 'four kings' is most probably an error for 'five' (Pedubast I to Takeloth III, inclusive), and is still more wrong if we count (as is historically necessary) also Rudamun and Iuput II, if not the highly-questionable Shoshenq VI. But the detailed figures can be seen to have *some* possible relation to what we know from other sources. A point of particular interest to devotees of Manetho will be the close correspondence of the 89 years assigned to this Dynasty in Africanus and the 87 years given here for Pedubast I to Rudamun inclusive. The 44 years of Eusebius is entirely wrong, and this worthless figure is dittographed in the 24th (!) and 25th Dynasties also.

§ 420   5. THE 24th DYNASTY

Here, we may tabulate:

KING	Highest Date	Reign MANETHO	INTERPRETATION
Tefnakht	8	7: (omitted)	: (omitted)
Bakenranef	6	5: Bocchoris, 6/44	: 6 yrs. is virtually correct; 44 yrs. is a worthless error.

The 6th year of Bakenranef was probably incomplete; the 6 years in Manetho probably represents, therefore, a rounding-up of 5 years and a fraction.

§ 421   6. THE 25th DYNASTY

Here, Manetho counts only the three principal kings who indubitably ruled all Egypt, omitting Kashta and Piankhy, and Tantamani who was

the notation that the Olympic festival was celebrated in his reign; this does not appear in the shorter version of Eusebius with the more correct figure of 25 years for Pedubast I. As the date of the festival is traditionally set at 776 B.C., it certainly would not coincide with Pedubast I, nor can he be dated anything like so late, on the *total* evidence considered in this book. However, 776 B.C. falls within a year of 777 B.C., the last year of Shoshenq IV, and the last of 40 years or so that could include the reigns of Pedubast I, Iuput I, and Shoshenq IV, as noted just above. A very slight adjustment of dates would permit direct correlation if desired; but (despite Rowton, *JEA* 34, 61) as the 40 years is not a proper regnal datum, the Olympic notice attached to it is probably equally secondary and should *not* be used to fix Egyptian chronology.

concurrent with the next line, and who ruled principally in the south. The data are less complex, evidently corrupt, but in part explicable:

KING	Highest Date	Reign	MANETHO	INTERPRETATION
Shabako	15	14/15	Sabacon, 8/12	: 8 is wrong; 12, switched for 14, below?
Shebitku	3	12/11	Sebichos, 14/12	: 14 probably excessive, 12 about right; cf. above.
Taharqa	26	26	Tar(a)kos, 18/20	both figures, wrong; 18 yrs. to Necho I, 672? (20 for 2⟨6⟩?).
TOTALS:	—	52 yrs.	*TOTALS:* given, 40/44.	

The table shows the main points. It is certain that Shabako reached his 15th year, and ruled Egypt from his 2nd year; his reign, therefore, was not less than 14 years (15?) in Nubia and 13 (14?) in Egypt. Hence, 8 years is irrevocably wrong, likewise but 12 years. On the other hand, 12 years is very likely to be right for Shebitku; if one may suggest cross-contamination of the traditions of Africanus and Eusebius, and a reversed order of figures, one would have 14 and 12 years respectively for Shabako and Shebitku, which is very close to the probable facts of the case. For Taharqa, the 18 years given may be reckoned from his accession to that of Necho I (672 B.C.),[135] otherwise (like the variant 20 years) the '18 years' is simply wrong. One may note that the suggested revised figures of 14, 12, '18' years for Shabako, Shebitku, Taharqa to 672 B.C. give a total of 44 years (cf. Eusebius version) which would begin in 716/715 B.C. (from 672/671 B.C.) and agree well with the chronology set out in this work. Here, the 44 years may be in place, which it certainly is not, for the 23rd and 24th Dynasties.

A brief word may be added on name-forms. Manetho at least gives us good vocalized forms for the names of this Dynasty's kings. Therefore, along with Dunham and Macadam, I have applied that vocalization to the known consonantal frames, so giving Shabako (not 'Shabaka'), Shebitku (not the inane and colourless 'Shabataka'), and Taharqa.[136] For the latter's

135. Cf. Hornung, *Untersuchungen zur Chronologie und Geschichte des N.R.*, 1964, 114, who dates the event to the Assyrian invasion of 671 B.C.; however, this would give Taharqa not 18, but 19 years from the date of his accession in 690 B.C. (fixed by Dyn. 26 from 664 B.C.), and Manetho surely would date by the accession of an Egyptian king (here, Necho I) even if thereby covering a period of foreign domination.

136. For this last name, the Hebrew version is Tirhaqā. This shows metathesis of *h* and *r* (cf. Aleksandros becoming (Al)iskander in Arabic), and a vocalization perhaps assimilated by the Massoretes to Hebrew imperfective verbal forms (as if *tirhaqa* was from a *rahaq*).

successor, I have adopted the briefer form Tantamani, partly as being briefer than Tanwetamani (Dunham and Macadam's form), partly because there may have been a short (but not full) vowel only after Tan-, or none at all,[137] and partly as more correct than 'Tanutamun'.

§ 422   7. EARLY 26th DYNASTY AND CONCLUSION

The figures for the rulers of Sais from 'Ammeris' to Necho I have been discussed above (Pt. II, §§ 116–118). There, it was seen that the Manethonic figures were basically good, but reading ⟨1⟩6 years for Nechepsos; only that for Ammeris was questionable.

In conclusion, one may say that the survey of Manetho's data for the 21st–25th Dynasties bears out what was said at the outset: that there is much basically-good material, but that it is unevenly transmitted and corrupted, often to the point of being unusable. Some attempt is made above to account for most of the transmitted data in terms of what we otherwise know monumentally (or suspect on overall grounds), but the present writer would stress that he himself is *by no means* totally convinced of the correctness of every harmonizing device set forth above in the attempt to tackle the extant wreckage of Manetho's *Aegyptiaka*. The discovery of an early (Ptolemaic period) and relatively uncorrupt copy of the Epitome (less likely, the great *Aegyptiaka*) from Egypt's tombs or Hellenistic rubbish-mounds would be of far greater value than the endless juggling with the present remains of Manetho's famed work.

137. Cf. already above, Part II, § 120, n. 276.

Notes on the Background of the Story-cycle of Pedubastis

§ **423** Over the years a whole cycle of Demotic stories has come to light, revolving around such figures as King Pedubast of Tanis, Inaros, Pimay, Pedikhons, and other names that are reminiscent of historical figures of the late-Libyan, Nubian, and early-Saite period dealt with in this book. Several of these names can be taken as having derived from historical personages of this general epoch, and were probably incorporated with matter of much later date (Persian age), in stories whose present manuscripts come into the Graeco-Roman period.

§ **424** Of the six or so stories preserved, one may make a vague 'sequence':

A: I. *Inaros and the Griffon*, so far unpublished,[138] tells of Inaros fighting a griffon from the Red Sea, and of the romance of one Bes. Since its heroes include Inaros as still alive, it precedes:

B: II. *Contest for the Benefice of Amun*,[139] in which (during the reign of King Pedubast at Tanis) the high priest of Amun died. Whereupon a benefice of his was claimed by his son, the Priest of Horus of Buto, but instead the King's son Ankh-hor seized it. The consequent strife affects the Festival of the Valley at Thebes (seizure of the barque of Amun).

C: III. *Contest for the Breastplate of Inaros.*[140] This revolves round the death and burial of Inaros, with strife between his son Pemu of Heliopolis and Urtep-Amun-niut of Mendes, under King

138. Texts in Florence and Copenhagen, cf. Bresciani, *MPON*, VIII, 11–12.
139. Papyrus Strasbourg, published by Spiegelberg, *Der Sagenkreis des Königs Petubastis*, 1910.
140. Papyrus Krall, re-edited by Bresciani, *MPON*, VIII, 1964.

Pedubast (whom Pemu had earlier saved from the attacking Assyrians led by *3slstny*). Many other characters appear with either hero, i.e. Pekrur of the East, Pedikhons, Teos (Djed-hor), Montu-Baal.

IV. *Egyptians and Amazons*.[141] This tale concerns Pedikhons, another son of Inaros. He leaves the entourage of Pedubast, going off into Western Asia to look for Serpot, Queen of the Amazons in Assyria. He finds her, they do battle, and then become firm allies. They conquer India and return to Egypt.

V. *Michaelides Fragment*[142] mentions Pemu, Urtep-Amun-niut, Montu-Baal.

D: VI. *Naneferkasokar and the Babylonians*.[143] Here, the action is set in Babylon, after the death of Pedubast.

The most varied elements occur in this cycle of stories: references to a king Pedubast (of whom three such are known) and to chiefs of the Libyan–Nubian periods, also to the Medes and India (known to Egypt in the Persian and Hellenistic periods) and to Ahura-mazda (Persian, but in a form closer to the Greek).[144] Besides these later elements, however, there is also a remarkable fund of reminiscences of the late-Libyan and especially the late-Nubian period, contemporary with the Assyrian threat and invasions.

§ 425   This is seen to best advantage in the two rival alliances in the *Contest for the Breastplate of Inaros* which – remarkably enough – divide well into two geographical regions, consonant with the situation in *c.* 665 B.C., in the time of Pedubast II of Tanis. His allies, who are placeable, are all in the East (and East-Central) Delta, while those of Pemu of Heliopolis include the West and West-Central Delta, and southwards the chief of Medum and the ruler of the Nubian border.

Allowing for limited distortions, this reflects remarkably the period about 665 B.C. plus some earlier and later retouches. Thus, the collocation of Sais plus Busiris and as far as Medum (all on the side of Pemu of Heliopolis) reminds one of the Kingdom of the West under Tefnakht, and the expansion of that nucleus-kingdom under Psammetichus I *before* he took over the realm of Pedubast II of Tanis-with-Bubastis. Here, in the Cycle as in the late 7th century B.C., Bubastis plays *no* role independently

141. Papyrus Dem. Vienna 6165/A, edited by Volten, *MPON*, VI, 1962.

142. Edited by Bresciani, *Testi Demotici nella Collezione Michaelidis*, 1963, 4–8, pls. II–III.

143. Berlin Papyrus Dem. 13640, edited by Spiegelberg, *Festgaben, Büdinger*, 1898, 13 ff.

144. So Bresciani, *MPON*, VIII, 13.

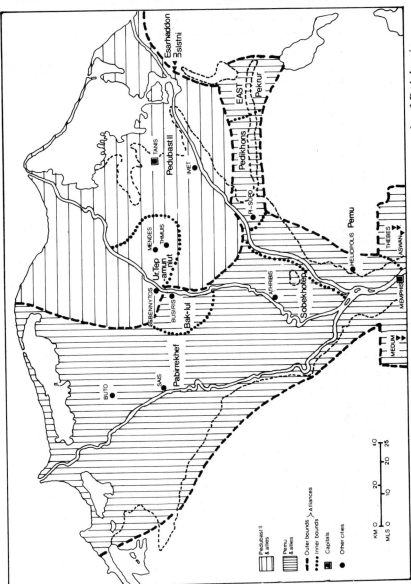

Fig. 10. Reflections of seventh-century political geography in the story-cycle of Pedubastis.

of Tanis (to which it was politically attached), Tanis being the capital of the 22nd Dynasty and its descendants. Similarly, the association of Athribis (plus Heliopolis) with the enlarged Kingdom of the West, including the Memphite region to Medum, recalls the realm of Psammetichus I who, as the son, then successor, of Necho I, was given Athribis by the Assyrians. The other particularly striking comparison in the Cycle is between its Chief of Pi-Sopd, Pekrur, with the Pekrur of Pi-Sopd who was a contemporary of Assurbanipal and Tantamani.

§ 426 However, while the above points concord remarkably well in outline with the days of the Assyrian invasions, other aspects show changes and historical 'refraction' in the transmission of tradition. Thus, in opposition to Tanis and Mendes, it is Pemu of Heliopolis (with Athribis, Sais and Medum behind him) who stands forth so prominently. This contrasts markedly with the late 8th and late 7th centuries B.C., when it was the Kingdom of the West (based on Sais) that stood over against the East and Central nomes of the Delta; also, in earlier times, Athribis and Heliopolis formed one unit politically, and it was Athribis, not Heliopolis, that was the political centre of that unit.

Furthermore, the alliance of Medum with Heliopolis, Athribis and the West-Delta realm might reflect that of Necho I and Psammetichus I with Heracleopolis under its shipmasters Pediese and Somtutefnakht. The alliance with Elephantine and Thebes under Minirami could be a reflex of two periods – either the late 8th century B.C., when Piankhy of Nubia had allies in Heracleopolis (near enough to Medum), Athribis and Sebennytos (the Cycle here has Busiris), or else the 7th–6th centuries B.C. when the 26th Dynasty progressively installed its own men in Edfu, Aswan and the Thebaid (such as Nesmin), allied to itself in the north-west. Inaros, however, is not found among local rulers until the Persian period and the 29th–30th Dynasties.

§ 427 So much may be discerned on the plane of political geography. On that of persons, some comparisons stand out more than others. It seems most probable that the king Pedubast of Tanis in the Cycle is none other than specifically Sehetepibenre Pedubast II of Tanis c. 665 B.C.; Pedubast I did not reign there, and evidence is lacking on Pedubast III. One may see evidence of the 'Assyrian' date of the Cycle's King Pedubast in two allusions which have been preserved in the Cycle. The first is the occasion when Pemu of Heliopolis caused a foe *3slstny*, chief of the land [. . .], to retreat eastwards, after the latter had tried to wrest Egypt from the rule of the pharaoh Pedubast. This name *3slstny*

(*Contest, Breastplate, Inaros*, V, 7) is most probably not only an Assyrian name, but actually a late form of *Esarhaddon*![145] One may compare the role of the 'Asiatics' in the *Contest for Benefice of Amun*, which was taken by Spiegelberg to be a veiled allusion to the Assyrians.[146] Support for this view comes from the second allusion, in the story of the *Egyptians and Amazons*, where one finds broken references (Col. I, $x+6$ to $x+9$) to 'Pharaoh', to someone's 'march before the grandees after his campaign', and 'his march to Nineveh', possibly referring to Pedikhons, the hero of the tale – and he himself is said to have Assyrian troops at his command (cf. Psammetichus I as vassal of Assurbanipal), in Col. III, [4], 27, 39.[147]

§ 428 Besides Pedubast and Pekrur, and Esarhaddon, the first Assyrian conqueror of Egypt, other personalities deserve notice. In the *Breastplate of Inaros*, mention is made of a past ruler of Mendes, Harnakht son of Smendes – doubtless a reminiscence of Harnakht B son of Smendes who is known to have ruled there in 760 B.C. under Osorkon III.[148] Also at Mendes, the *Breastplate* story has a man, a general, Urtep-Amun-niut. This name and title could be a corruption or misunderstanding for 'First Generalissimo of Amun of Nō (Thebes), ⟨Name omitted⟩', son of an Ankh-hor;[149] but, if this is so, the error lies well beyond the scope of the present manuscripts. One Djed-hor (Teos) was Urtep-Amun-niut's brother(?), and an Ankh-khons was adjutant. With this series, one may compare Djed-Amen-ef-ankh,[150] his son Ankh-hor, and the latter's possible successor Djed-hor, all at Mendes, from the time of Piankhy down into the 25th Dynasty.[151]

Another early name is Patjenfy, who is given as the father of Ta-hor, the latter being the wife or the mother of king Pedubast or of his father Ankh-hor. One may compare the Patjenfy of Pi-Sopd under Piankhy and

145. Thus, as Demotic *l* is also for *r* (as throughout pre-Coptic Egyptian), *ꜣsl* is for *ꜣsr*, Assur. Then, *s* can have changed from *š* (as sometimes in Coptic), and the *š* be from *aḫ* (cf. *š/ḫ* as in Hyksos, *Ḥḳꜣw-ḫꜣswt*). Finally, *tni* is from *iddina*. Thus, we have *Assur-aḫ-iddina*, Esarhaddon, becoming *Assur-aš* (*as*)-*itini* here. He is called 'son of *Wsḫ-rnf*', the latter being an Egyptian phrase 'wide is his name'. This could possibly be a *Volksetymologie* for *Si(n)-aḫ-eri⟨n⟩ba*, Sennacherib, the father of Esarhaddon.
146. Cf. his *Sagenkreis, Petubastis*, 8–9.
147. Bresciani, *MPON*, VIII, 11, had referred this to Psammetichus I and the Scyths.
148. See Kitchen, *JARCE* 8 (1970/71), 63, and below, Table 22, Part VI.
149. And so possibly brother of the king Pedubast, also son of an Ankh-hor.
150. One notes the common element Amun in Djed-Amen-ef-ankh and in the name (or title ?) Urtep-Amun-niut; was the former the name possibly lost in the tradition behind our present MSS?
151. See Kitchen, *JARCE* 8, 63, and Part IV, below, Table 22.

the Patjenfy in Pharbaithos in Year 2 of Shabako – both of earlier date than Pedubast II, as befits the Cycle occurrence.[152]

A most striking case is that of 'Ankh-hor the weak', called son of (Pa)Neh-ka, of 'the Isle of Heracleopolis' (*Breastplate*, 17: 25 f., 22: 3). Surely, the latter name is none other than the peculiar *Naḥ-ke*, chief of Ḥininsi (possibly the northern Heracleopolis *mikra*), mentioned by Assurbanipal![153] And Ewelhen at Medum is equally a direct reflex of the Ewelhen of nearby Pi-Sekhemkheperre of the reign of Pedubast I, *c.* 800 B.C., or of others of that name.[154]

§ 429   Further names belong to the Libyan and Nubian periods, or are less closely fixed. The name Pemu (Athribis) compares with the various Pimays, two of whom are attested historically at Busiris, where the Cycle has a mysterious Bak-lul. Helbes father of Ankh-hor[155] may be compared with that Ankh-hor son of Helbes who was last Great Chief of the Libu before Tefnakht. The names 'Tefnakht', 'Bakenranef', 'Pediese', recur in the Cycle, but in no meaningful relation to the known persons of those names who are attested in the Libyan and Nubian periods.[156] Finally, one might compare the Cycle's Pedikhons of Pi-Sopd (East Delta) with the Pedikhons of Pharbaithos in Year 8 of Psammetichus I.[157] Teudjoi (El Hibeh) is perhaps reflected in one ([*Tꜣ*]*ḏꜣy*) of two places ruled by the chief Pasher-en-ta-ihet, 'son of the cow(-goddess)', especially if his name relates to the cult of Hathor of Atfih nearby.[158]

§ 430   Finally, we may note elements which are foreign to, and later than, the Libyan and Nubian periods. These include the Median soldiers serving Montu-Baal from Syria,[159] and the reference to Pedikhons and his Amazon queen Serpot invading India.[160] Combined with a reference to Ahuramazda, these come down to the Persian period, and in the latter case conceivably

---

152. Benefice of Amun text, 13: 23; historical Patjenfys, cf. below, Part VI, Tables 22, D, and 23, A, with references.

153. *ANET*, 294.

154. Cf. Yoyotte, *RdE* 13 (1961), 93–4, and *RdE* 15 (1963), 89–90; Schulman, *JARCE* 5 (1966), 35–6, n. (i).

155. Situated at a Ta-ꜥam-en-pa-mer-ihet (*lḥt*)-en-Sekhme(t); cf. cults of Sekhmet in the Kingdom of the West under the Libu chiefs, e.g. *YMM*, 143 (§ 30, B), 144 (§ 32, D).

156. Pediese father of a Hor-aw, *Breastplate*, 10: 21–2; a Tefnakht, father of Sobk-hotep, *ibid.*, 18: 17; a Bakenranef, *ibid.*, 19: 5.

157. Stela, *PSBA* 14 (1892), 237–8.

158. The name 'Teudjoi', *Breastplate*, 18: 13.

159. Refs., Bresciani, *MPON*, VIII, index.

160. *Egyptians and Amazons, passim*; Bresciani, *MPON*, VIII, 13, thinks here of Alexander's conquests in India.

to the Greek period, if the Egyptian form of the name were really based on the Greek form as Bresciani thought.[161] Reference to Meroe (and not Napata) could reflect conditions from as early as the 6th century B.C., but makes good sense from the 4th century B.C., when Napata finally lost its importance and Meroe became supreme.[162] It has long since been suggested that these narratives owed their stimulus to the enquiries of Ptolemy II into Egyptian history in the early 3rd century B.C.[163] They themselves are not history, but they contain some remarkable reminiscences of historical personages of almost half-a-millennium earlier, amid their tales of heroism, chivalry and romance.

161. *MPON*, VIII, 13.
162. *Breastplate*, 24: 13–14 (*MPON*, 106/107); cf. P. Shinnie, *Meroe*, 1967, 33, 40, 58/59, Table.
163. Spiegelberg, *Sagenkreis, Petubastis*, 10; Bresciani, *MPON*, VIII, 15.

PART SIX

Tables

I. DATES OF KINGS

TABLE I

Preferred Dates: 'Renaissance Era', 21st Dynasty, and Theban Pontiffs

About B.C.:　　　　　　　　I. *'Renaissance Era' (Late 20th Dynasty)*

1098–1069: Ramesses XI (29 y)
　　1080: Beginning of 'Re-
　　　　　naissance Era' (11 y)

North	South (*High Priests*)
1080–1069: Smendes in N (11 y)	1080–1074: Herihor in S (6 y)
	1074–1070: Piankh (4 y)
	(1070 ff.: Pinudjem I)

II. *21st Dynasty Proper*

Kings	High Priests	
1069–1043: Smendes I (26 y)	1070–1055: Pinudjem I, hp (15 y)	⎫ (37 y)
1043–1039: Amenemnisu (4 y)	1054–1032: Pinudjem I, 'kg' (22 y)	⎬
1039–991: Psusennes I (48 y)	1054–1046: Masaharta (8 y)	
993–984: Amenemope (9 y; 2, co-rgt)	1046–1056: Djed-Khons-ef-ankh (1 y?)	
984–978: Osochor (6 y)	1045–992: Menkheperre (53 y)	
978–959: Siamun (19 y)	992–990: Smendes II (2 y?)	
959–945: (Har-)Psusennes II (14 y)	990–969: Pinudjem II (21 y)	
	969–945: Psusennes 'III' (24 y)	

TABLE 2

Alternative Dates: 'Renaissance Era', 21st Dynasty, and Theban Pontiffs

---

I. *'Renaissance Era'*
About B.C.: (*Late 20th Dynasty*)

1118–1089: Ramesses XI (29 y)
  1100: Beginning of 'Re-
    naissance Era' (11 y)

North	*South (High Priests)*
1100–1089: Smendes in N (11 y)	1100–1094: Herihor in S (6 y)
	(1094–1064: Piankh)

II. *21st Dynasty Proper*

Kings	*High Priests*
1089–1063: Smendes I (26 y)	1094–1064: Piankh (30 y)
1063–1059: Amenemnisu (4 y)	1064–1045: Pinudjem I, hp (19 y)
1059–1033: Psusennes I (26 y)	1044–1026: Pinudjem I, 'kg' (18 y) ⎬ (37 y)
1033–981: Amenemope (52 y)	1044–1036: Masaharta (8 y)
984–978: Osochor (6 y; 3, co-rgt)	1036–1035: Djed-Khons-ef-ankh
978–959: Siamun (19 y)	(1 y?)
959–945: (Har-)Psusennes II	1035–986: Menkheperre (49 y)
(14 y)	986–985: Smendes II (1 y?)
	985–969: Pinudjem II (16 y)
	969–945: Psusennes 'III' (24 y)

NB: Certain pontificates could be varied in length from the figures given by a few years on this scheme, likewise Amenemnisu could theoretically follow Psusennes I here.

TABLE 3

The 22nd and 23rd Dynasties*

About B.C.:   *22nd Dynasty*

945–924: Shoshenq I, Hedjkheperre Setepenre (21 y)
924–889: Osorkon I, Sekhemkheperre Setepenre (35 y)
  c. 890: Shoshenq II, Heqakheperre Setepenre (x yrs;
          co-rgt only)
889–874: Takeloth I, [*Prenomen unknown*] (15 y)
874–850: Osorkon II, Usimare Setepenamun (24 y)
c. 870–860: Harsiese, Hedjkheperre Setepenamun (c. 10 y?;
          co-rgt only)
850–825: Takeloth II, Hedjkheperre Setepenre (25 y)
825–773: Shoshenq III, Usimare Setepen-re/amun (52
          y). [*Start of Dyn. 23.*]
773–767: Pimay, Usimare Setepen-re/amun (6 y)
767–730: Shoshenq V, Akheperre (37 y)
730–715: Osorkon IV, Akheperre Setepenamun (15 y)

23rd Dynasty

818–793: Pedubast I, Usimare Setepenamun (25 y)
804–783: Iuput I, Usimare Setepenamun (21 y; 11,
          co-rgt)
783–777: Shoshenq IV, Usimare Meryamun (6 y)
777–749: Osorkon III, Usimare Setepenamun (28 y)
754–734: Takeloth III, Usimare (Setepenamun) (20 y; 5,
          co-rgt)
734–731: Rudamun, Usimare Setepenamun (c. 3 y?)
731–720: Iuput II, [*Prenomen unknown*] (c. 11/16 y)
  (or 715)
(720–715: Shoshenq VI, Wasneterre Setepenre (c. 5 y??);
          existence, doubtful).

TABLE 4
*The 24th–26th Dynasties**

About B.C.:	*Early Saite Princes*

c. 770: Pimay (the later king??)
c. 770–755: Two further governors?
c. 755–740: Chief of Mā, Osorkon (c. 15 y?)
c. 740–727: Chief of Mā, Tefnakht I (c. 13 y; then, kg)

24th Dynasty

727–720: Tefnakht I, Shepsesre (7 or 8 y)
720–715: Bakenranef, Wahkare (5 y)

Proto-Saite Dynasty

715–695: 'Ammeris'– Nubian governor? (20 y?)
695–688: Stephinates – 'Tefnakht II?' (7 y)
688–672: Nekauba – Nechepsos (16 y)
672–664: Necho I, Menkheperre (8 y)

25th (Nubian) Dynasty

c. 780–760: Alara (c. 20 y?)
c. 760–747: Kashta, Maatre (?) (c. 13 y?)
747–716: Piankhy, Usimare, then Sneferre (31 y)
716–702: Shabako, Neferkare (14 y)
702–690: Shebitku, Djedkaure (12 y)
690–664: Taharqa, Nefertumkhure (26 y)
664–656: Tantamani, Bakare (8 y, in S. Egypt)

26th Dynasty

664–610: Psammetichus I (54 y)
610–595: Necho II (15 y)
595–589: Psammetichus II (6 y)
589–570: Apries (19 y)
570–526: Amasis II (44 y)
526–525: Psammetichus III (1 y)

II. READY-RECKONERS FOR CONTEMPORANEOUS REIGNS

TABLE 5

Ready-reckoner: Contemporary Years of Ramesses XI and 'Renaissance Era'

Ramesses XI (Year)	'Renaissance Era' (Year)
19*	1**
20	2**
21	3
22	4
23	5*
24	6*
25	7**
26	8
27*	9
28	10*
29	11
(30	12)

* Denotes year-dates attested in texts.
** Denotes year-dates actually called *whm-mswt* in texts.

TABLE 6

*Ready-reckoner: Contemporary Years of the Twenty-second to Twenty-fifth Dynasties**

Date B.C.:	Dyn. 22: Shosheng III	Dyn. 23: Pedubast I	Dyn. 23: Co-regents
825 —— 1		
824	2		
823	3		
822	4		
821	5		
820 —— 6		
819	7		
818	8 —— 1		
817	9	2	
816	10	3	
815 —— 11	4	
814	12 —— 5	
813	13	6	
812	14	7	
811	15	8	
810 —— 16	9	
809	17 —— 10	
808	18	11	
807	19	12	
806	20	13	
805 —— 21	14	*Iuput I*
804	22 —— 15 —— 1
803	23	16	2
802	24	17	3
801	25	18	4
800 —— 26	19 —— 5
799	27 —— 20	6
798	28	21	7
797	29	22	8
796	30	23	9
795 —— 31	24 —— 10
794	32 —— 25	11
793	33	26	12
		Iuput I, alone.	
792	34	13	
791	35	14	
790 —— 36 —— 15
789	37	16	
788	38	17	
787	39	18	
786	40	19	
785 —— 41 —— 20

Date B.C.:	Dyn. 22: Shoshenq III	Dyn. 23: Osorkon III	Dyn. 23: Co-regents	Dyn. 25 Nubia
784	42	21		
783	43	22		
		Shoshenq IV		
,,	,,	1		
782	44	2		
781	45	3		
780	—— 46	4		
779	47	—— 5		
778	48	6		
777	49	7		
		Osorkon III		
,,	,,	1		
776	50	2		
775	—— 51	3		
774	52	4		
773	53	—— 5		
	Pimay			
,,	1	,,		
772	2	6		
771	3	7		
770	—— 4	8		
769	5	9		
768	6	—— 10		
767	7	11		
	Shoshenq V			
,,	1	,,		
766	2	12		
765	—— 3	13		
764	4	14		
763	5	—— 15		
762	6	16		
761	7	17		
760	—— 8	18		
759	9	19		
758	10	—— 20		
757	11	21		
756	12	22		
755	—— 13	23	*Takeloth III*	
754	14	24	—— 1	
753	15 ——	25	2	
752	16	26	3	
751	17	27	4	
750	—— 18	28 ——	5	
749	19	29	6	
748	20	*Takeloth III*, alone.		*Piankhy*

Date B.C.:	Dyn. 22: Osorkon IV	Dyn. 23: Iuput II	Dyn. 25: Piankhy	Dyn. 24: Tefnakht
,,	,,	7		
747	21	8 ———————		1
746	22	9		2
745 ———	23 ———	10		3
744	24	11		4
743	25	12 ———————		5
742	26	13		6
741	27	14		7
740 ———	28 ———	15		8
739	29	16		9
738	30	17 ———————		10
737	31	18		11
736	32	19		12
735 ———	33 ———	20		13
734	34	21		14
		Rudamun		
,,	,,	1		,,
733	35	2 ———————		15
732	36	3		16
731	37	4		17
		Iuput II		
,,	,,	1		,,
730 ———	38	2		18
	Osorkon IV			
,,	1	,,		,,
729	2	3	19	*Tefnakht I*
728	3	4 ———————	20	
727	4 ———————	5	21 ———	1
726	5	6	22	2
725 ———	6	7	23	3
724	7	8	24	4
723	8	9 ———	25 ———	5
722	9 ———————	10	26	6
721	10	11	27	7
720 ———	11	12	28	8
		(Shoshenq VI?)		*Bakenranef*
,,	,,	(13/1?)	,, ———	1
719	12	(14/2?)	29	2
718	13 ———	(15/3?)———	30	3
717	14	(16/4?)	31	4
716	15	(17/5?)	32	5
			Shabako	
,,	,,	(,,/,,) ———	1	,,
715 ———	16 ———	(,,/,,) ———	2 ———	6

From this year (715 B.C.), Shabako is Pharaoh of all Egypt.

III. ROYAL GENEALOGIES

TABLE 7

The 21st Dynasty:[*]

Summary Genealogy (Kitchen)

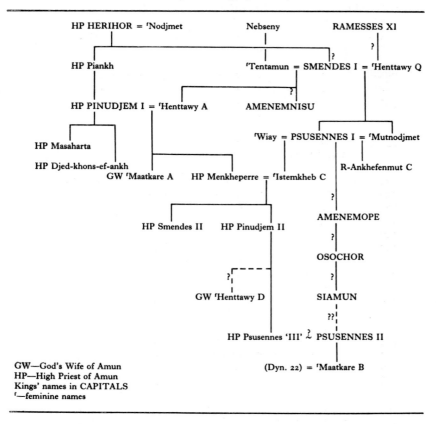

GW—God's Wife of Amun
HP—High Priest of Amun
Kings' names in CAPITALS
'—feminine names

(Dyn. 22) = 'Maatkare B

TABLE 8

The 21st Dynasty:*
Summary Genealogy (Wente)

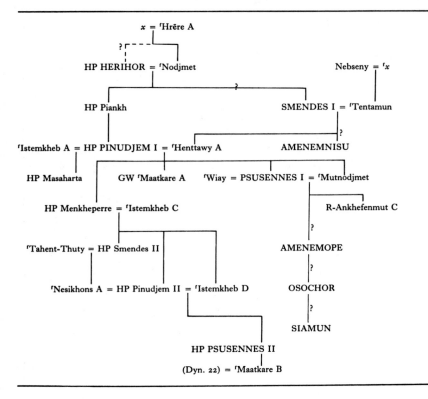

TABLE 9

The 21st Dynasty:
*Fuller Genealogy (Kitchen)**

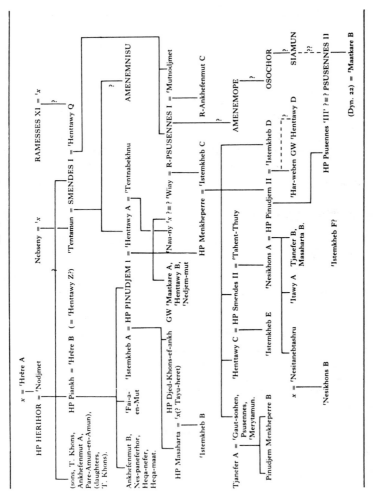

TABLE 10

The 22nd and 23rd Dynasties:
Basic Genealogy

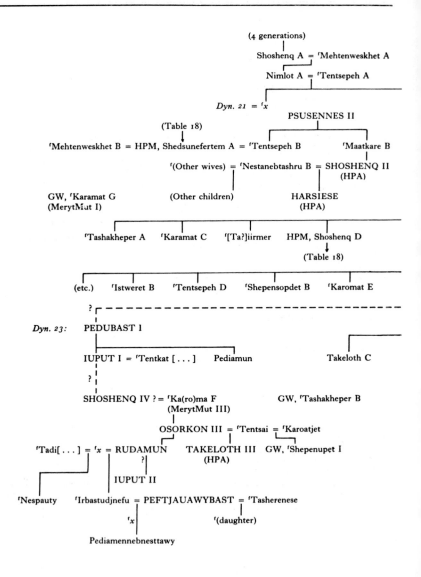

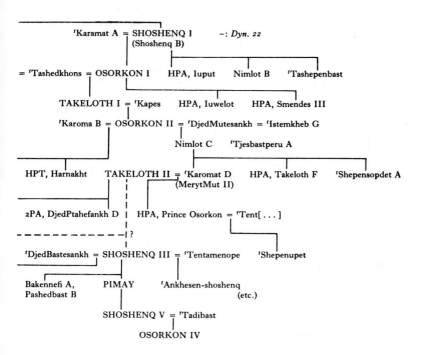

GW —God's Wife of Amun
HPA —High Priest of Amun, Thebes
2PA —2nd Prophet of Amun, Thebes
HPM—High Priest of Ptah, Memphis
HPT —High Priest of Amun, Tanis

NB: All forms Karamat, Karoma, Karomat, etc., are here lettered as if variants of one basic name used by several individuals.

TABLE II
The 25th Dynasty:*
Fuller Genealogy

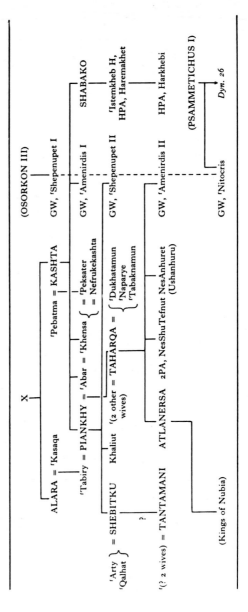

TABLE 12

Marriages of Princesses to Commoners, 21st to Early 26th Dynasties *

21st Dynasty

1. Unnamed, probably d. of Siamun, to Solomon (§§ 235–236)
2. Tentsepeh B, probably d. of Psusennes II, to HPM Shedsunefer-tem A (§§ 90, 91, 236)
3. Maatkare B, d. of Psusennes II, to Osorkon (I), (§§ 5, 49, 91 end, 240)

22nd Dynasty

4. Tashepenbast, d. of Shoshenq I, to 3PA Djed-Thut-ef-ankh A (§§ 166, 245)
5. Istweret A, d. of Harsiese, to 2, 4PA Harsiese C (§ 184)
6. Tjesbastperu, d. of Osorkon II, to HPM Takeloth (§§ 81, 281)
7. Shepensopdet B, d. of Takeloth II, to 4PA Djed-Khons-ef-ankh C (§§ 184, 290)
8. Istweret B, d. of Takeloth II, to vizier Nakhtefmut C (§§ 180, 290)
9. Ir-Bast-udja-tjau, d. of Takeloth II(?), to vizier Pakhuru (§ 290)
10. Di-Ese-nesyt, d. of Takeloth II(?), to vizier Nesipaqashuty B (§ 290)
11. Tentsepeh D, d. of Takeloth II, to Ptah-udj-ankhef (§ 291)
12. Ankh-Karoma, d. of Takeloth II, to 3PA Pediamen-neb-nesttawy A (§ 193)
13. Ankhes-en-Shoshenq, d. of Shoshenq III, to one Iuf-o (§ 305, ii)

23rd Dynasty

14. Ir-Bast-udja-nefu, d. of Rudamun, to Pef-tjau-awy-Bast who became local 'king' in Heracleopolis (§ 318)

Early 26th Dynasty

15. Ta-khered-en-ta-ihet-[weret], d. of Necho I or predecessor, to Pediese of Heracleopolis (§§ 201, 363)

IV. CHIEF DIGNITARIES OF THE REALM

TABLE 13

Theban High Priests of Amun and God's Wives of Amun (22nd–26th Dynasties)

About B.C.:

A. High Priests of Amun (§§ 157 ff.)*

944–924: Iuput, son of Shoshenq I
924–894: Shoshenq (II), son of Osorkon I
894–884: Iuwelot, son of Osorkon I
884–874: Smendes III, son of Osorkon (I)
874–860: Harsiese A, son of Shoshenq II
860–855: [. . . du/ʿawti . . .], son of Harsiese A
855–840: Nimlot C, son of Osorkon II, (OR:
855–845: Nimlot C if directly followed by:
845–840: Takeloth F son of Nimlot C. Otherwise, cf. below)
840–785: Prince Osorkon B, son of Takeloth II; intermittent, 835 ff.
835–800: Harsiese B, ?son of [. . . du/ʿawti . . .]. Intermittent until 825
800–775: Takeloth E – possibly a younger son of Nimlot C
775–765: An unattested pontiff?
765–754: Takeloth, son of Osorkon III, who became king Takeloth III
754–704: Half-century interval: two unattested pontiffs, or office left vacant
704–660: Haremakhet, son of Shabako (max. tenure; could begin later)
660–644: Harkhebi, son of Haremakhet
644–595: Half-century interval: two unattested pontiffs, or vacant
595–560: God's Wife Ankhnes-Neferibre
560–550?: Nitocris B, daughter of Amasis II

B. God's Wives of Amun

870–840: Karomama G, Meryt-Mut I (prenomen, Sitamun Mutemhat)
c. 770?: Tashakheper B, associated with a king Osorkon (III?)
754–714?: Shepenupet I, Meryt-Mut IV (prenomen, Khnumib-amun)
740–700: Amenirdis I (prenomen, Khaneferumut)
710–650: Shepenupet II (prenomen, Hentneferumut Iretre)
670–640: Amenirdis II (prenomen, not Meryt-Tefnut?)
656–586: Nitocris A, Meryt-Mut V (prenomen, Neb(t)neferumut)
595–525: Ankhnes-Neferibre (prenomen, Heqatneferumut)

480

TABLE 14

Theban 2nd, 3rd, and 4th Prophets of Amun (21st–25th Dynasties)

2nd Prophets	3rd Prophets	4th Prophets
'Renaissance Era' and 21st Dynasty		
c. 1074: *Nesamun(re?), §211	—	c. 1075: Pare-Amun-en-Amun, §211
c. 1070: Heqanufer, §211	—	—
c. 1040? Amenhir-pamesha? (Kees, *Pr.*, 318)	c. 1040?: Amenhir-pamesha? (Kees, *Pr.*, 318)	c. 1040?: Amenhir-pamesha? (Kees, *Pr.*, 318)
—		c. 1020: Nespaheren-mut, §232; father of
—	c. 1000: Nesishuenopet (*MMR*, 572–3)	c. 1000: Tjanefer A, §§226–227, and 993; father of
—	c. 991–986: Tjanefer A, §§232–3; father of	c. 990/980: Pinudjem, §232
c. 985?: Tjanefer A?, §233	c. 985: Menkheperre B, §232	
—	c. 950/940?: Neseramun A, §§266, 273 (vizier)	c. 960/: Nesamun (Kees, *Pr.*, 170)
22nd and 23rd Dynasties		
c. 945–935: DjedPtahef-ankh A, §244; Kees, *Pr.*, 168, n. 3	c. 945–935: DjedPtahef-ankh A, §244	c. 945: Nesy, Ch. Mahasun, §§188, 244, 266; father of
—	c. 925 ff.: DjedThutef-ankh A, §§166 ff., 245, 266	c. 930 ff.: Nesankhef-maat, §§188, 244, 266
—	—	c. 920 ff.: Pashedbast A, Ch. Mhsn, §§263, 266
—	—-	c. 900 ff.: Djed-Khonsefankh A, §§183 ff., 245, 266; father of
—	c. 875 ff.: Pedimut B, (Patjenfy), §§184, 270	c. 880 ff.: DjedThutef-ankh B (Nakhtefmut A), §§183 ff., 273; father of
c. 855: Harsiese C, §274 (*pro temp.?*)	c. 850?: Pakhuru, §314 (vizier)	c. 860 ff.: Harsiese C, §§183 ff., 274; father of
c. 835: DjedPtahef-ankh D, §290 (son of T. II)	c. 840 ff.: Pediamenneb-nesttawy A, §§193, 314	c. 830 ff.: Djed Khonsefankh C, §§290, 314; father of

	c. 820/800: Wennufer A, §§ 190, 290, 314	c. 790 ff.: Nakhtefmut B §§ 187, 188, 191, 314; father of
—	c. 775: Nebneteru iv, §§ 177, 314	¦
c. 740 ff.: Neshorbehdet, § 319	c. 750 ff.: Pediamenneb-nesttawy B, §§ 192–193, 314	c. 750 ff.: DjedKhonsef-ankh D, §§ 187, 188, 191, 319

25th/Early 26th Dynasties

c. 720/700: Patjenfy, §§ 330, 342	c. 725 ff.: (?; either of P i, ii, § 195?)	c. 725 ff.: Kelbasken, § 344
c. 680: Nesishutefnut, § 351	c. 695 ff.: DjedAnhuref-ankh (*CdE* 38, 71–77)	c. 705 ff.: (?2 unknown incumbents)
c. 664: Montemhat (*pro temp.?*)	c. 675–653: Pediamen-nebnesttawy C, § 193; father of	c. 680–650: Montem-hat, §§ 196, 351, 365; father of
—	c. 653–630: Hor xvii, §§193, 365; father of	c. 650–640: Nesptah B, §§ 196, 365
—	c. 630–610: Pediamen-nebnesttawy D, § 193; father of	—
—	c. 610–590: Pekhelkhons, § 193	—

---

* Approximate year B.C.

TABLE 15

Southern Viziers, 21st–25th Dynasties*

Vizier	References

'Renaissance Era' and 21st Dynasty

c. 1075:* Herihor,	G3, 232, 1, I
c. 1070: Pinudjem I	G3, 245, IX, 247, XIII
c. 1040?: Amenhirpamesha?	Kees, Pr., 318
c. 960: Neseramun A	§§ 266, 273

22nd and 23rd Dynasties

c. 930: Padimut A	§§ 184, 270
c. 900: Ia-o	§ 257, n. 304
c. 890: Nebneteru ix	§ 190, table
c. 880: Rudpamut	Karnak Priestly Annals, fragment 12 (RT 22, 57, and RT 26, 88 n. 2)
c. 876: Hor[y]	Yr. 14, Takeloth I? (Möller, Zwei äg. Eheverträge, Vorsaïtische Zeit, 1918, 4)
c. 865: Pamiu	§ 290
c. 855: Pakharu, son of Pamiu	§ 290; married daughter of Takeloth II(?)
c. 845: Pediamonet, son of Pamiu	§ 290
c. 840: Nesipaqashuty B, son of Pediamonet	§ 290; married daughter of Takeloth II(?)
c. 835: Nesipaqashuty A	§§ 169–172; prob. 'retired' under Sh. III
c. 825: Harsiese D, son of foregoing	§§ 171 f.
c. 820: Hor xviii, father of next	
c. 815: Pentyefankh	§ 298 (Yr. 8, Pedubast I, 811 B.C.)
c. 800: Harkhebi, father of a v. Harsiese (? next)	Statue, Bull, BMMA 30 (1935), 142–144, fig. 3 (MMA, 35.9.1)
c. 790: Harsiese E (cf. previous?)	§ 300 (Yr. 39, Sh. III, 787 B.C.)
c. 780: Djed-Khons-ef-ankh E	Cf. CdE 33 (1958), 196
c. 770: Nakhtefmut C	§ 290 (twice)
c. 760: Hor x, son of Nakhtefmut C	§ 180 (temp. Os. III); perhaps cf. ASAE 7 (1906), 50–51? (Also, CdE 33, 194–195)
c. 750: Harsiese F	§§ 196, 330
c. 740: Nesmin A, son of previous	§§ 196–197, 330
c. 730: Ankh-hor	YMM, § 60; temp. Piankhy and Akunosh A
c. 720: Pediese, son of Harsiese (F?)	§§ 196–197
c. 715: Khamhor A, son of Harsiese F	§§ 196, 330, 344

c. 700: Pahrer/Harsiese G, son of Khamhor A	§§ 196, 344
c. 690: Nesmin B, son of Khamhor A	§§ 196, 344
c. 680: Nesipaqashuty C	§ 351
c. 670: Nespamedu A, son of previous	§ 351
c. 660: Nesipaqashuty D, son of previous	(Yr. 14, Psam. I, Parker, *Saite Or. Pap.*; 651 B.C.)

---

* Approximate year B.C.

NB: (a) Sequence and dates are both tentative, but probable in many cases.

NB: (b) The large number of viziers attested for the south in this period suggests (i) a rapid succession, and (ii) that this office was held by a series of senior men who did not usually have a long tenure, because of old age.

TABLE 16

Rulers of Middle Egypt, 22nd to Early 26th Dynasties

About B.C.:

A. Heracleopolis

c. 940 ff.: Nimlot B, son of Shoshenq I, § 246

. . .

c. 865–840: Nimlot C, son of Osorkon II, §§ 157 ff., 275, 290
c. 840–820: Ptah-udj-ankhef (a Djed-Ptah-ef-ankh?), son of Nimlot C, §§ 290–291
c. 820–805: Pimai, § 300
c. 805–790: Hem-Ptah A, son of Ptah-udj-ankhef; § 300
c. 790–785: Bakenptah, son of T. II, brother of Prince Osorkon; § 300
c. 785–775: Pasenhor A, son of Hem-Ptah A; § 300
c. 775–765: Hem-Ptah B, son of Pasenhor A; § 313
c. 765–754: Takeloth, later Takeloth III, son of Osorkon III; § 313
c. 754–720: Pef-tjau-awy-Bast, son-in-law of Rudamun; became 'king' (from *c.* 749 ff.?); § 318

. . .

c. 720–685: Either one, or two, unattested local rulers?

. . .

c. 685–661: Pediese –'retired' in 661, died in 647 B.C.; §§ 199 ff., 363
c. 661–630: Somtutefnakht, son of Pediese; §§ 200, 363

B. Hermopolis*

c. 754–725: Nimlot D, became 'king' (from *c.* 749 ff.?); §§ 313, 330–331
c. 725–710: Thutemhat, local 'king', contemporary of 4th prophet of Amun, Djed-Khons-ef-ankh D; §§ 187, 191, 330–331
c. 710–700: Khmuny, local 'king', §§ 331, etc. But see §79, n. 71 end.

. . .

c. 700–680: Perhaps one unattested local ruler?

. . .

c. 680–660: Nimlot E (Akkad. 'Lamintu', 667/666 B.C.); § 358

TABLE 17

*Index of Genealogies of Theban Officials in Part III**

Neseramun Family: §§ 166, 170, 171, 173
Nebneteru Family: §§ 177, 178
Vizier Nakhtefmut C, etc.: § 180 (three parts)
Djed-Thut-ef-ankh B, 4PA: §§ 183, 184 end, 186, 187, 188
Besenmut Family: §§ 190, 191, 192, 193 (two parts), 195 (two parts)
Montemhat Family: § 196

    This outline is intended to facilitate rapid reference to the constituent part-genealogies incorporated in Part III.

TABLE 18

High Priests of Ptah in Memphis, 21st to 25th Dynasties

About B.C.:

'*Dynasty*' *of Asha-khet A*

c. 1040–1025: Asha-khet A, contemporary of Amenemnisu

c. 1025–1005: Pipi A, contemp. Psusennes I

c. 1005–995: Harsiese J, contemp. Psusennes I

c. 995–975: Pipi B (Neterkheperre-Meryptah), contemp. Psusennes I to Siamun

c. 975–960: Asha-khet B

c. 960–940: Ankhefensekhmet A

c. 940–920: Shedsunefertem A, contemp. Shoshenq I

c. 920–895: Shoshenq C, probably contemp. Osorkon I

c. 895–870: Osorkon A, prob. mainly contemp. Takeloth I

'*Dynasty*' *of Crown Prince Shoshenq D*

c. 870–851: Shoshenq D, son of Osorkon II, who died after(?) Year 23 but before his father

c. 851–830: Merenptah, contemp. Takeloth II

c. 830–810: Takeloth B, (younger?) son of Shoshenq D

c. 810–770: Pediese, son of Takeloth B; Yr. 28, Sh. III, Yr. 2, Pimay

(*c.* 790–780: Pef-tjau-awy-Bast, son of Pediese; Yr. 28, Sh. III only)

c. 780–760: Harsiese H, son of Pediese; Yr. 2, Pimay (and later?)

c. 760–740: Ankhefensekhmet B, son of Harsiese H (so, contemp. Sh. V)

For documentation, cf. above, Chapter 12, Part III.

TABLE 19

The Pasenhor Genealogy

Last publication: M. Malinine, G. Posener, J. Vercoutter, *Catalogue des stèles du Sérapéum de Memphis* I, 1968, No. 31, pp. 30–31, pl. 10.

'Libyan' Buyu-wawa
|
(Gt Chief)   Mawasun
|
,,   Neb-neshi
|
,,   Pa-ihut(y)
|
,,   Shoshenq A = 'Mehtenweskhet A
|
God's Father, Gt Ch. Nimlot A = 'Tentsepeh A

                                       :(filiation, *ASAE* 16, 177)
          SHOSHENQ I = 'Karamat A   & *JEA* 27, 84ff)

          OSORKON I = 'Tashedkhons

          TAKELOTH I = 'Kapes

          OSORKON II = 'Mut-udj-ankhes (Djed-Mut-es-ankh)

   Ch., Heracleopolis, Nimlot C = 'Tentsepeh C

        ,,   Ptah-udj-ankhef = 'Tentsepeh D, princess

        ,,   Hem-Ptah A = 'Tjankemit

        ,,   Pasenhor A = 'Petpet-didies

        ,,   Hem-Ptah B = 'Iret-irou

   Memphite priest, Pasenhor B, temp. Yr. 37, Shoshenq V

TABLE 20

The Apis Bulls, 21st to Early 26th Dynasties

About B.C.:

21st Dynasty

1069–945: No burials yet known

22nd Dynasty, First Half

945–870: No burials yet known; embalming-table of Shoshenq I (Brugsch, *Thesaurus*, 817, etc.)

22nd Dynasty, Second Half

?–852: *Apis 22, x + 1* ('1st'; *PM*, III, F, 207): died, Yr. 23, Os. II; *x* yrs. old; § 286, (i)

852–837: *Apis 22, x + 2* ('2nd'; *ib.*, 208): died, Yr. 14 (??), Tak. II; 15(?) yrs. old; § 289

[837–818: *Apis 22, x + 3* (–; –): ?died, early yrs., Sh. III; unattested; *c.* 20 yrs. old?]

818–798: *Apis 22, x + 4* ('3rd'; *ib.*, 208): died, Yr. 28, Sh. III; *c.* 20 yrs. old?

798–772: *Apis 22, x + 5* ('4th'; *ib.*, F', 208): installed, Yr. 28, Sh. III; died, Yr. 2, Pimay; 26 yrs. old; § 126, (iii)

772–757: *Apis 22, x + 6* ('6th'; *ib.*, 208): installed, Yr. 2, Pimay; died, Yr. 11, Sh. V; 15 yrs. old; § 126, (iii)

757–731: *Apis 22, x + 7* ('7th'; *ib.*, F'', 209): installed, Yr. 11, Sh. V; died, Yr. 37, Sh. V; 26 yrs. old; § 126, (iii)

24th Dynasty

731–716: *Apis 24, 1* (24 '1st'/25 '1st'; *ib.*, G, 209–210): installed, Yr. 37, Sh. V; died, Yr. 5, Bakenranef; burial, Yr. 6, Bakenranef/Yr. 2, Shabako; §§ 126, (iii), 340

25th Dynasty

715–703: *Apis 25, 1* (–; –): installed, Yr. 2, Shabako; died, Yr. 14, Shabako; 12 yrs. old; §§ 126, (iii), 342, (i)

703–687: *Apis 25, 2* (–; –): installed, Yr. 14, Shabako; died, *c.* Yr. 4 (?), Taharqa; 16 yrs. old; §§ 126, (iii), 349, (i)

687–667: *Apis 25, 3* ('2nd'; *ib.*, 210): installed, Yr. 4(?), Taharqa; died, Yr. 24, Taharqa; 20 yrs. old; §§ 126, (iii), 353

665–645: *Apis 25, 4* (26 '1st'; *ib.*, H, 210–211): installed, Yr. 26, Taharqa; died and buried, Yrs. 20/21, Psam. I; 21 yrs. old; §§ 130–131, 354

On question of attribution of Apis-burials, cf. observations of Malinine, Posener, Vercoutter, *Catalogue des stèles du Sérapéum de Memphis*, I, 1968, *passim*, and papers by Vercoutter, cited in §§ 126, (iii), 130–131, etc., above. Their work has clarified the evidence for Apis bulls of the 25th Dynasty; also, there seems to be no explicit evidence for an Apis-burial in Year 4 of Shoshenq V – the Year 4 belongs elsewhere (Taharqa?).

TABLE 21

Delta Chiefs: West and South

About B.C.:

A. *The West: Chiefs of Libu* (For Sais, see Table 4)*

c. 936: Niu-mateped A, Yr. 10 of Shoshenq I(?); § 249

. . .

c. 800–790: In-Amun-nif-nebu A, Yr. 31, Sh. III, 795 B.C.; § 306

c. 790–780: ⎫
⎬ Perhaps two rulers, yet unattested?
c. 780–770: ⎭

c. 770–758: Niu-mateped B, Yr. 8, Sh. V, 760 B.C.; § 311

c. 758–750: Titaru son of Didi, Yr. 15/17, Sh. V, 753/1 B.C.; § 311

c. 750–740: Ker, Yr. 19, Sh. V, 749 B.C.; § 311

c. 740–731: Ankh-hor, Yr. 37, Sh. V, 731 B.C.; § 316

c. 732–727: Tefnakht, Yrs. 36, 37, Sh. V, 732/1 B.C.; §§ 316, 324. For Tefnakht in Sais and as king, cf. Table 4 above

B. *The South: Athribis-with-Heliopolis*

c. 815–790: Bakennefi A, son of Sh. III, Yrs. 14, 15, 812/811 B.C. (815–785)* father of Pediese; *ASAE* 16, 61 f.; § 305 and nn. 570, 571

c. 790–770: Pediese F, son of foregoing, § 305, nn. 570–1 (785–760)*

c. 770–750: One unattested ruler?? (Omit?)*

c. 750–728: Bakennefi B, died under Piankhy, 728 B.C.; § 326, n. 702 (760–728)*

c. 728–700: Pediese G, began under Piankhy, 728 B.C.; §§ 326, 356

c. 700–665: Bakennefi C, § 356

c. 665–664: Psammetichus I (Nabushezibanni), § 356

c. 664–650: Harwa, § 360

c. 650–630: Horudja, son of Harwa; *YMM*, § 91

---

* Alternative dates

TABLE 22

Delta Chiefs: Four Great Chiefdoms of the Mā (North-Central; East)

About B.C.:

A. Mendes*

c. 830–810: Nes-khebit(?), father of following

c. 810–790: Harnakht A, Yr. 22, Sh. III, 804 B.C.; § 306; father of following

c. 790–767: Smendes ('IV'), Yr. 21, Iuput I, 784 B.C.; §§ 302, 306; father of

c. 767–750: Harnakht B, Yr. 11, (Os. III), 767 B.C.– induction; § 311

c. 750–735: Djed-hor; cf. *JARCE* 8, 62–63

c. 735–715: Djed-Amen-ef-ankh, under Piankhy, 728 B.C.; § 327; father of

c. 715–690: Ankh-hor

c. 690–665: 'Buiama' (Akkad. form); § 356

(Last two tenures could be shorter, allowing for an additional and still unattested ruler)

B. Sebennytos

c. 740–720: Akunosh A, under Piankhy, 728 B.C.; § 328

c. 720–685: Either one, or two, rulers yet unattested?

c. 685–665: Harsiese K; § 356

c. 665–650: Akunosh B; § 360

C. Busiris

c. 810–790: Takeloth C, son of Sh. III, Yr. 18, 808 B.C.; § 305. Not certain that he actually ruled in Busiris

c. 790–750: Probably two rulers, as yet unattested?

c. 750–728: Shoshenq E, died under Piankhy, 728 B.C.; § 328; father of following

c. 728–700: Pimay iv, began under Piankhy, 728 B.C.; § 356

c. 700–665: Shoshenq F; §§ 360, 356; father of following

c. 665–650: Pimay v; § 360

D. Pi-Sopd

c. 740–720: Patjenfy, under Piankhy, 728 B.C.; § 328

c. 720–680: Probably two rulers, as yet unattested?

c. 680–660: Pekrur, under Assurbanipal and Tantamani, 665, 664 B.C.; §§ 354, 356

TABLE 23
Delta Chiefs: Lesser Rulers in the East

About B.C.:

A. Pharbaithos: Chiefs of the Mā

c. 820–795: Iufero, under Shoshenq III (year lost); § 306
c. 795–770: Pawarma A, Yr. 33 (Sh. III?), 793 B.C.; § 306
c. 770–720: Probably two rulers, as yet unattested?
c. 720–700: Patjenfy, Yr. 2, Shabako, 715 B.C.; § 340, n. 771
c. 700–670: Either one, or two, unattested rulers?
c. 670–655: Pedikhons, Yr. 8, Psam. I, 657 B.C.; § 361

B. Tanis: Local Kings

c. 700–680: Gemenef-Khons-Bak, Shepseskare Irenre; date, wholly uncertain
c. 680–665: Pedubast II, Sehetepibenre; under Assurbanipal
c. 665–657: P(?) . . ., Neferkare; on cornice with Psam. I, Athribis? (Cf. §§ 357, 361, above)

V. THE CONTEMPORARY NEAR EAST

TABLE 24
Near Eastern Rulers Mentioned

About B.C.:

A. Mesopotamia

1. *Assyria:*
1073–1055: Assur-bel-kala
884–859: Assurnasirpal II
859–824: Shalmaneser III
745–727: Tiglath-pileser III
727–722: Shalmaneser V
722–705: Sargon II
705–681: Sennacherib
681–669: Esarhaddon
669–627(?): Assurbanipal
612–608: Assur-uballit II.

2. *Babylon:*
626–605: Nabopolassar
605–562: Nebuchadrezzar II
556–539: Nabonidus

B. The Levant

1. *Byblos:*
c. 930: Abibaal, contemp. Shoshenq I
c. 900: Elibaal, contemp. Osorkon I

2. *Hebrew Monarchy:*

(i) *United Monarchy*
1011/10–971/70: David
971/70–931/30: Solomon

(ii) *Divided Monarchy*

(*Judah*)
931/30–913: Rehoboam

(*Israel*)
931/30–910/09: Jeroboam I

. . .   . . .

493

911/10–870/69: Asa

885/84–874/73: Omri
874/73–853: Ahab

. . .

. . .

841–814/13: Jehu

. . .

732/31–723/22: Hoshea
722: Fall of Samaria

716/15–687/86: Hezekiah (co-rgt from 729)

. . .

640/39–609: Josiah
609: Jehoahaz
609–597: Jehoiakim
597: Jeroiachin
597–587: Zedekiah
587/86: Fall of Jerusalem

All dates in this Table are based on Kitchen, *HHAHT*, forthcoming.

Index

Conventions Used

Users should note that all main numbers are those of *paragraphs*, *not pages*. Thus, 371 & n. 2 stands for § 371 and note 2 (*not* page 371 . . .).

Besides the general abbreviations and conventions already set forth in the main Table of Abbreviations at the head of this work, the following special abbreviations are used in the Index:

(i) *General*. Ch.– Chief of/at; ctp,– contemporary of/with; CycP – mentioned in Story-Cycle of Pedubastis (cf. Excursus G); gn – genealogy (Hori, 235 gn, means that Hori would appear in a genealogy in § 235); kg – king; pl. n – place-name; prn – prenomen, first cartouche; qu – queen (of).

(ii) *Royal*. Ape – Amenemope; Iu. I–II – Iuput I–II; Os. I–IV – Osorkon I–IV; Pd. I–III – Pedubast I–III; Pn. I–II – Pinudjem I–II; Psam. I–III – Psammetichus I–III; Psus. I–III – Psusennes I–III; R. I–XI – Ramesses; Rd – Rudamun; S. I–II – Sethos I–II; Sh. I–VI – Shoshenq I–VI; Si – Siamun; Sm. I–'IV'– Smendes I–'IV'; Tk. I–III – Takeloth I–III.

(iii) *Relations*. s. – son of; d.– daughter of; f.– father of; m.– mother of; br.– brother of; sis.– sister of; -il.– in-law of, *e.g.* s-il.–'son-in-law', br-il –'brother-in-law', etc. Also, gt – great, and grd – grand; hence, gtgrds – great-grandson of, etc.; w.– wife of; h.– husband of.

Other Usages. For simplicity in alphabetic order, Ꝫ ('*aleph*) is treated as equivalent to *a*; ꜥ is ignored, and all other diacritics disregarded, even though printed. Thus, s, ṣ, š, etc., all come together. An occasional (x 2) or (x 3) after a figure indicates that the term occurs that often in the paragraph cited. Sometimes people are cited in the Index by two ciphers (e.g. DjedKhonsefankh C/ii); under adverse work-conditions at present obtaining (cf. Preface), it was not feasible to renumber all the people concerned or to eliminate preliminary double numbers. However, while cumbrous, this should cause no difficulties in practice. Less important numbers are omitted in the genealogies.

1. Principal Texts Quoted or Excerpted in Translation

Bandage-epigraphs (abbr., Exc. A):
Pn. II, Year 8, Si 7
Psus. III, Year 5 8
Ape, Year 49 13, 25 (3rd), 29
Ape, Year [x] + 3 29, 30
Cairo Cat. 559 266
Cairo Cat. 42213 279
Cartonnage, Hori s. Iaꜥo 257, n. 304
Chronicle of Prince Osorkon 148, 162, 292–4

Commemorative scarab, Shabako 340
Gebel Silsila stela 100 260
Jubilee, Osorkon II 279, 280
Karnak, Nile-level texts:
No. 6 68
No. 23 68
No. 24 106
No. 33 137
Karnak Priestly Annals, Fragment No. 4 242

495

2. Index of Biblical References

3. General Index

Taneshet, w. Besenmut i, 190 gn

Tanis, pl. n, in Ro-nefer, 328, n. 710; as Delta capital, 213, 223, 236, 333; works at, of Psus. I, 224 (with Pn. I, 5 (17), 219); of Si, 234; of Sh. I, 248; of Os. II, 71, 75, 277; Tk. II, 76; of Sh. III, 304; of Pimay, 308; of Sh. V, 315; local kings, 124, 357, 361, 423ff. (CycP), Table 23B; cults, 395–6; Maps 1, 3A, 4, 5, 7, 10

Tanodjmet, 166 gn

Tantamani, kg, dating, etc., 116, n. 259; 120, 138, 139, 141; account of reign, 354–5, 359; with Taharqa, 120, 139, 354; slew Necho I, 117, 354 & n. 883; & Assyria, 355; not in Manetho, 421; Tables 4, 11

Tanutamun, Tanwetamani, 120, 421, see Tantamani

Taperet i, w. Hor vi, 166 gn, 170 & gn

Taperet ii, 196 gn

Tapeshenese, 90 (C. 741), 91 & gn

Tappuah, pl. n, 254, 404, n. 89; Map 2

Tar(a)cos, for Taharqa, 120, 421

Taremu, 102, is Leontopolis, q.v.

Tarqu, Assyr. for Taharqa, 120

tartannu, turtan, 'commander', 333, 335

Tarwa i, w. Ankhpakhered ii, 180 2 x gn

Tarwa ii, w. Hormaat i, 180, n. 109 & 2nd gn; 190 gn & n. 139

Ta-sasai, 191 gn

*Tasdamani, for Tantamani, 120, n. 276

Ta-set-mery-Thoth, pl. n, 171, end

Tashakheper A, d. Os. II, 281; Table 10

Tashakheper B, GW, 282, 318, n. 650; Tables 10, 13B

Tashedkhons, m. Tk. I, 76, 85 gn, 93, 270; Tables 10, 19

Tashemsyt (Djed-Mut-es-ankh i), 166 gn, 168, 170 & gn, 181, n. 109

Tashepenbast, d. Sh. I, 166 gn, 171, 245, 249; Tables 10, 12

Tashepenkhons, 190 gn

Tashepenmut, 88 gn

Tasher(it)enese i, 262; ii, 319; Table 10

Tasherenmut (Shepenese), 181, n. 109; 183 & gn; 184 gn; 274, end

Taweret, pl. n, 328, n. 717

Tayu-heret, 54, G; 397; Table 9

Tchet-Chensu-af-ankh, 392

Tefnakht (I), Ch. & kg, dating, etc., 84, 112 (kg), 115, 118, 142, 145, 148, 149; not Stephinates, 117; ctp. 'So', 149, but not him, 333; not on 'Pian-khy blocks', 202 ff.; history, 316,

324–8, 332; 425; Tables 4, 6, 21A

Tefnakht 'II', 116–18, 356; Table 4, see Stephinates

Tefnakht 'III', 357

Tefnakht, of CycP, 429 & n. 156

Tell Abu Hawam, pl. n, 258, n. 308; 401, n. 72

Tell Arad, 406

Tell Balamoun, 394, n. 20

Tell Balla (& varr.), 328, n. 710

Tell Beit Mirsim, 258

Tell (el) Farah, S., 258 (Sharuhen?)

Tell Jemmeh (Yemmeh), 258, 407, n. 101

Tell el Maskhuta, 248, 277, end

Tell el Milh, 406

Tell Moqdam, see Leontopolis

Tell es-Shalaf (Eltekeh?), 346, n. 815

Tell Slihat, 256, n. 300

Tell Umm Harb (Mostai), 304

Tell el Useifir, 404

Tell Yaham, 401

Tell el Yehudiyeh, 67, 98, 262, 302, 315, Maps 4, 5, 7

Tell Yemmeh (Jemmeh), 258, 407, n. 101

Tennis, pl. n, 225

tensions in Thebes, 217, 291 ff.

Tent[. . .], w. Osorkon B, Table 10

Tentamenope, qu Sh. III, 305; Table 10

Tentamun, w. Sm. I, 41, 42, 209, 212, 214, 216; Tables 7–9

Tentkat[. . .], qu. Iu. I, 98, 302; Table 10

Tent-nau-bekhnu, 54, B; Table 9

Tent-pahau-nefer, 238, n. 242

Tentremu, see Leontopolis

Tentsai, m. Tk. III, 76, 100, 157, 312; Table 10

Tentsepeh A, m. Sh. I, 85 gn, 88, 90 & gn, 91 & gn, 239; Tables 10, 19

Tentsepeh B, 90 (C. 741), 91 & gn, 236, end, 239; Tables 10, 12

Tentsepeh C, w. Nimlot C, 85 gn; Table 19

Tentsepeh D, d. Tk. II, 291; Tables 10, 12, 19

Teos, kg, size of forces, 253, n. 289

Teos, in CycP, 424, 428

Terraneh, pl. n, 79

Teudjoi, 226, 429; see El Hibeh

Tewosret, qu, 144, 206

Thebes, pl. n, twin to Tanis in Dyn. 21, 1, 395–6; accepted Dyn. 22 to early

THE THIRD
INTERMEDIATE PERIOD
IN EGYPT
(1100-650 B.C.)

SUPPLEMENT

K. A. Kitchen

ARIS & PHILLIPS LTD

Warminster England

1986

Contents

of

Supplement

ADDITIONAL   ABBREVIATIONS

AMNRJ	*Archivos do Museu Nacional do Rio de Janeiro.*
Beltrão/Kitchen, *Catalogo Rio*	Prof. Maria d. C. Beltrão, K. A. Kitchen, *Museu Nac- ional: Catalogo dos Monumentos do Egito Antigo/ Catalogue of the Ancient Egyptian Monuments,* [forthcoming]
Bierbrier,LNKE	M. L. Bierbrier, *The Late New Kingdom in Egypt (c.1300-664 B.C.)*, 1975.
BSEG	*Bulletin de la Société d'Egyptologie, Genève.*
GM	*Göttinger Miszellen.*
Graefe,Unt. Inst. Gottesgemahlin	E. Graefe, *Untersuchungen zur Verwaltung und Ge- schichte der Institution der Gottesgemahlin des Amun vom Beginn des Neuen Reiches bis zur Spät- zeit,* I, II, 1985.
JSSEA	*Journal of the Society for the Study of Egyptian Antiquities.*
JWAB	K. Jansen-Winkeln, *Ägyptische Biographien der 22. und 23. Dynastie,* I, II, 1985.
Munro, *Totenstelen*	P. Munro, *Die spätägyptischen Totenstelen,* I,II, 1973.
OMRO	*Oudheidkundige Mededelingen uit het Rijksmuseum van Oudheden te Leiden.*
OrAnt	*Oriens Antiquus.*
Vittmann,PBTS	G. Vittmann, *Priester und Beamte im Theben der Spätzeit,* 1978.

Prefatory Note

In the last fourteen years, study of Late Period Egypt has flourished. So, it is hoped that reissue of this book (including fresh discussions of problems, and reference to new data, in this Supplement) will be of service to Egyptologists and all students of antiquity. For references and counsel, my warm thanks go to Prof. A.F. Shore, Mr. A.R. Millard, and especially to Dr. M.L. Bierbrier for valued help; thanks, too, to my publishers for their patience!

Woolton, Liverpool, March, 1986.   K. A. Kitchen

PART   ONE

S 431   TWENTY-FIRST   DYNASTY

In terms of reigns and total years, most figures are agreed, with only two
or three points of continuing doubt. Unexceptionable is Smendes I at 26
years (highest date, Year 25), Amenemnisu at 4 years (Years 1 to 5 of the
'Banishment Stela'?), Amenemope at 9 years minimum (a possible Year 10;
cf. above, p.421, **S** 388:55), Osochor at 6 years (Year 2 attested) and Siamun
at 19 years (Year 17 attested, p.423 above; this corrects Niwinski, JEA 70
(1984),77, n.17). Psusennes II at 14 or 15 years shows minimal variation;
14 years should be retained provisionally, as Year 13 is the highest probably
attested date so far - *15 years depends solely upon emending 35 to 15
years in the Eusebius/Armenian versions of Manetho's text, often (but not
always) inferior to that of Africanus (here, 14 years). Psusennes I ruled
at least 48 years, but was certainly coregent with Amenemope. A 2-year
coregency would leave to Psusennes I a sole reign of 46 years agreeing with
Manetho (Africanus), giving 124 years (or, with Hornung, 125) for the whole
Dynasty.

However, two scholars have sought to rehabilitate the overall total of
130 years given in Manetho (all versions) for the Dynasty: W. Barta, MDIK
37(1981),35-39, and J. von Beckerath (unpublished; cited by Barta, p.36, n.5).
As the totalled individual years of the rulers only amount to 124/125 years,
there is a discrepancy with the transmitted total of 130 years. Harmonisat-
ion would require finding another 5/6 years that could legitimately be added
to a reign or reigns to turn 124/125 into 130 years.

S 432   Here, attention has been focussed upon the reigns of Psusennes I
and Amenemope. A coregency between these two kings seems certain in
view of the bandage-epigraph, [Year x of] King Amenemope, Year 49 [of
King Psusennes I], discussed above, pp.29 (**S** 25) and 411-416 (**SS** 371-8), a
point that has met with wide acceptance (e.g., Barta,MDIK 37(1981),38).

S 433   The Manethonic figures for Psusennes I vary at 46 years (Africanus)
or 41 years (Eusebius/Armenian), but are constant for Amenemope at 9
years. As Barta proposes (p.38), one might suggest that 5 years of co-
regency has been overlooked in the Africanus version - i.e., Psusennes I,
46 years, plus Amenemope at 14 years (5 coregent; 9 sole reign), or else

emend to 51 years for Psusennes I (e.g., from the 41 years in Eusebius) and have 9 years for Amenemope. This is possible - but this also entails a further error in Manetho (either 9 years for 14; or 41 for 51). Yet another option textually would be to emend Amenemope's 9 years to *19 years; combined with 41 years for Psusennes I, a 130-years' total would be reached by having a 10-year coregency between these two kings, an idea that few may feel inclined to adopt. In other words, just for the sake of justifying the supposed total of 130 years for the Dynasty, one is compelled to import new (and unsubstantiated) emendations at some point into the text of Manetho's figures for regnal years that do not otherwise need any alteration. Previously, the only emendation absolutely needful was *19 for 9 years for Psinaches (Siamun), because of 17 years monumentally attested. Now the figure either for Psusennes I or for Amenemope would have to be changed also, merely to retain the supposed total of 130 years.

But what is so special about this figure of 130 years? The fact that it recurs in all three versions of Manetho's text (Barta, p.36) does not prove its veracity, and is therefore absolutely meaningless. After all, Psinaches has 9 years in all three versions - and it is totally wrong! And elsewhere in Manetho, unanimity in numerical readings in totals and individual regnal years alike is no guarantee of correctness. Thus, 453 years for the 13th Dynasty (all versions) will be believed by nobody; and 13 years for Takelothis II (all versions) is very quickly emended to 33 years by Barta himself without compunction (RdE 32(1980),12), and so ad libitum. So why should this particular figure of 130 years be held so sacred? Why waste time trying to justify a figure that clashes with regnal figures that correspond so well with the first-hand monumental and documentary evidence? For these reasons, it is infinitely better (and better methodologically) to stay with the 124/125 years that genuine evidence justifies.

S 434   Basing himself on von Beckerath's diktat, Barta has proposed also that the ending of the 20th Dynasty in 1075/73 B.C. requires 130 years for the 21st Dynasty (1075-945 B.C.), cf. MDIK 37(1981),36 and n.5. This argument is also fallacious, because there is not one scrap of hard evidence that the 20th Dynasty indubitably ended in 1075/73 B.C. - or in any other precise year B.C. Highest and lowest limits can be set, between 1085 and 1068 B.C., owing to the known permissible flexibility of regnal data between the accession of Ramesses II (1279 B.C. at latest) and the beginning of the 21st Dynasty. Anything more precise is opinion, not hard fact. In the table

that follows, A = minimal regnal years, giving highest dates B.C.; B = maximal regnal years, giving lowest dates B.C.:

King	A	B
Ramesses II	66	66
Merenptah	9	10
Amenmesses	-	4
Sethos II	6	6
Siptah/Tewosret	7	7
Setnakht	1	2
Ramesses III	31	31
Ramesses IV	6	6
Ramesses V	4	4
Ramesses VI	7	8
Ramesses VII	7	8
Ramesses VIII	1	3
Ramesses IX	18	18
Ramesses X	3/9	9
Ramesses XI	28	29

Totals,   194/200,   211, years respectively,
        = 1279-1085/1079,   1279-1068 B.C., respectively.

Therefore, the regnal figures for the 19th and 20th Dynasties cannot be
used to determine the precise date of the beginning of the 21st Dynasty.
In the light of these facts, there is no reason whatever to prefer the summary 130 years to the well-founded 124/125 years (Hornung, Kitchen) for
the 21st Dynasty, and the dates 1070/1069 - 945 B.C. may stand.

§ 435   In   JARCE 16(1979),56-59, Niwinski has raised again the issue of
"Year 48 n̲ High Priest of Amun, Menkheperre" from the bandage-epigraph
found on mummy no.105 of the priestly burials in Western Thebes. It is, by
now, a well-attested fact that no Theban governor (not even "King" Pinudjem I!) had independent regnal years of his own. As the presence of Nefer-
kheres in the kinglist of Manetho indicates that Amenemnisu did have some
independent reign (and not wholly a coregent as Niwinski suggests, p.59),
the appointment of Menkheperre to high-priestly office was not coeval with
the accession of Psusennes I. However, thanks to Niwinski's stimulus, it is
possible to offer a much simpler solution for this "Year 48 n̲" that has good

analogies in earlier Egyptian history. Namely, that as high priest and shadow "king", Menkheperre at the end adopted (or was attributed) the regnal years of Psusennes I - precisely as also Hatshepsut used as hers the regnal years of Tuthmosis III, or Tewosret continued the regnal years of Siptah, using in each case the years of an already-reigning king. So, Menkheperre may later have used (or been assigned) the years of Psusennes I in a precisely similar way. This avoids the gratuitous assumption of needless anomalies either in the bandage-epigraph 105 or in regnal usage.

§ 436   On the main genealogy of the successors of Piankh, High Priest of Amun, there is close agreement in most quarters, including the possibility that Psusennes I and his queen Mutnodjmet were the offspring of Pinudjem I and Henttawy A: so, Wente, JNES 26(1967),175 (in contrast to above, Tables 7, 9), and also Niwinski, JARCE 16(1979),66-67.

Minor corrections to Table 9 (p.475, above) can be made as follows, thanks to observations by various scholars. Thus, Nespaneferhor should appear underneath [f]Nedjemmut, as offspring of Pinudjem I, and not under Ankhefenmut B - correction owed to Niwinski, JARCE 16(1979),63, n.32. We may now add a 'new' son of the High Priest Menkheperre, namely a prophet of Amun and Seth named Hori, alongside Gautsoshen and her siblings in Table 9; cf. Niwinski, p.54, § B.   In Table 9 perhaps add as son of [f]Fai-a-en-mut (daughter of Piankh) the priest Menkheperre C; certainly one must correct the reference to him (p.66 end, above, and n.326) to 'C' from 'B', following Niwinski, p.63, n.32.

The lady Istemkheb B, as daughter of Masaharta (above, p.62, § 50B; Table 9) should probably be abolished. She can now be identified with Istemkheb D, daughter of Menkheperre; on the catafalque, the names of Pinudjem I (grandfather) and Masaharta (uncle) would simply attest her family antecedents; cf. M. Dewachter, BSFE 74(1975),20-21 and n.12, who further noted the links with Akhmim of both Istemkheb D and "B".

§ 437   In Table 9, the conjectural link between Amenemope and Osochor should be deleted, and replaced by an entirely new link-up, thanks to the brilliant paper by Yoyotte, "Osorkon, fils de Mehytouskhé, un pharaon oublié?", in   BSFE 77-78(1977),39-54. Re-studying a pair of now lost inscriptions from the roof of the Temple of Khons at Karnak (LD,III,258c; Daressy RT 18(1896),51-52), which can be attributed to Year 7 of Takeloth III, Yoyotte was able to give a reconstitution of the vital part of the second text (p.41), and to derive from it the following genealogy.

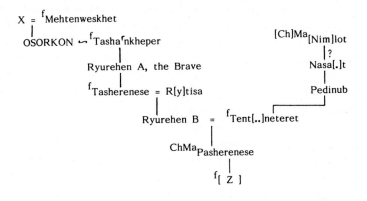

As Yoyotte clearly pointed out, none of the known kings Osorkon I-IV had a Mehtenweskhet for mother (but were sons, respectively, of the ladies Karamat A, Kapes, Ka(ro)ma F, and Tadibast). See Table 10. Conversely, the well-known lady Mehtenweskhet A (wife of Shoshenq A, mother of Nimlot A, and grandmother of Shoshenq I) is entitled mwt-nsw, 'King's Mother' on the famous Pasenhor stela (see p.112, above). As her grandson became king (as Shoshenq I) after Psusennes II's 14/15 years' reign, her son Nimlot A would have been a contemporary of Siamun and Psusennes II, and also of Osochor before them.   Hence, the king Osochor (successor of Amenemope) would be her younger contemporary. If "Osochor" is in fact "Osorkon", then as Yoyotte suggests (like others in the past) the two pieces of the puzzle fit: she was indeed 'King's Mother' to 'Osochor', third-last king of the outgoing 21st Dynasty, the Pharaoh Osorkon son of Mehtenweskhet of the Khons Temple genealogy being the 'Osochor' of Manetho. The whole fits perfectly, and serves to complete the genealogy on p.112 end, above; to correct that given on p.115 (substituting Osochor/Osorkon the Elder for the ^{f}x = Psusennes I [read II]); and should be added at the top of Table 10, p. 476.   For other portions of the Khons Temple genealogy, see E. Graefe, Unt. Inst. Gottesgemahlin,I,1981, 112-114, S n130. Cf. also S 505 below.

S 438   However, no such brilliant solution can be recorded for the problem of relationships at the beginning of the 21st Dynasty in either the Theban or Tanite lines.

One gain since 1972 is a negative one. Full study and publication of the reliefs in the forecourt in the Temple of Khons at Karnak has shown that the first son of Herihor and Nodjmet was not Piankh (as long thought on the basis of LD,III,247a), but a man Ankhef, perhaps an abbreviation for Ankhef(enmut), who is present in a directly neighbouring scene. Cf. Epigraphic Survey, The Temple of Khonsu,I,1979, pls.26,44, and Wente's remarks, pp.x-xi, following on his paper, "Was Paiankh Herihor's son?", in Drevnii Vostok (Volume for M.A. Korostovstev),1975, 36-38. Hence, we now have no proven parentage for the High Priest Piankh.

On the other hand, a positive gain may balance this: it seems clear that Hrere B was the wife of Piankh (p.45, above), as shown by M.L. Bierbrier, JNES 32(1973),311, and cannot by any means be identical with Hrere A, mother of Nodjmet and hence mother-in-law of the previous high priest Herihor. Thus Niwinski's suggestion to identify the two Hreres as one , so making both Nodjmet and Herihor actually younger than Piankh (JARCE 16(1979),52, 62 n.21), would reverse the historical sequence of Herihor and Piankh, and must be discarded as unworkable. However, there is a real possibility that Hrere B (Piankh's wife) was a daughter of Nodjmet and Herihor, and so a granddaughter of Hrere A (feminine version of papponymy). This situation would readily explain the situation of Piankh conducting correspondence with (and about) Nodjmet as his mother-in-law, on his (and his wife's) absence from Thebes, campaigning in Nubia (above, p.41). We may therefore have:

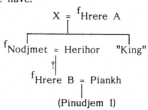

S 439   Beyond this point, unfortunately, no further progress can be recorded. Those by Wente (1967) and this writer (here, 1972, Table 9) remain the two most plausible reconstructions for the relationships of Smendes I, Tentamun, Ramesses XI, of Henttawy(s), Psusennes I and Mutnodjmet (plus Amenemnisu) and the Theban successors of Piankh. The highly ingenious attempt to break the impasse, by Niwinski (JARCE 16(1979),49ff.), is not convincing. The genealogy offered on his p.51 brings together Henttawy Q and A, allows for Ramesside blood in the 21st Dynasty, and would account for Tentamun's presence alongside Smendes - which all seems ideal.

But there are serious drawbacks. First, Niwinski's view requires that the lady Tentamun of the Wenamun account who sits alongside Smendes in Tanis (Year 5 of the Renaissance) is not his wife, but a queen of Ramesses XI! Such a role for an Egyptian queen-consort - living away from her royal spouse, and accompanying a mere official (however distinguished) as co-administrator in a seaport - is surely totally unparalleled in all that we know of the roles of even the most prominent queens-consort in the New Kingdom (or any other period). As Niwinski notes (p.50), the names are so closely linked that not even the conjunction ḥnꜥ, 'and', separates them. Unless very good reason indeed could be produced to justify so glaring an anomaly, this scenario seems out of the question. Second, Niwinski's whole reconstruction of relationships leaves Smendes I, founder of the 21st Dynasty, totally isolated and having no identifiable link with either the 20th Dynasty or the Theban commanders and high priests.

S 440   A happier solution along the lines of Niwinski's approach would have been to make Tentamun a daughter of Ramesses XI, wife of Smendes and later his queen. Then, if Henttawy A = Q, marrying Pinudjem I, they in turn (with Wente) might be the parents of Psusennes I and Mutnodjmet with Ramesside blood in their veins (Kitchen). However, there is one item that opposes this simple solution: the sobriquet <u>ỉr.n</u> (s3b) <u>Nb.sny</u>, "begotten of (the hon.) Nebseny" - who was possibly the scribe and priest Nebseny whose coffin was found in the great cache near Deir el-Bahri. As Tentamun could not have been daughter of both Nebseny and Ramesses XI, this appears to preclude the solution just outlined. To understand the phrase <u>ỉr.n</u> <u>Nb.sny</u> as a dedication seems very unlikely, occuring as it does as a randomly repeated filiation in a funerary papyrus. So, as Wente's solution did not sufficiently allow for the Ramesside element in the 21st Dynasty, and as this writer's solution was inferior to his in accounting for female titles, and as Niwinski's solution involves unrealistic assumptions about Tentamun and Smendes, while the occurrences of <u>ỉr.n</u> <u>Nb.sny</u> oppose a variant of his theory (just offered above), stalemate is promptly reached.

S 441   Is there any other way out?   There is, perhaps, just one avenue which has not previously been explored, or not for a very long time. There is a way to unify the two Henttawys A (= wife of Pinudjem I) and Q (= daughter of Ramesses XI), to account thus for the Ramesside link claimed by Psusennes I and his son Ramesses-Ankhefenmut C, to cover the parent-

age of Smendes, Amenemnisu, Psusennes I and Mutnodjmet, to account for
the importance of Tentamun alongside Smendes in Tanis, and for Tentamun
daughter of Nebseny, plus the queen-motherly roles of Hrere A and Nodjmet
(besides Henttawy A). The key to this highly desirable solution is to opt for
two Tentamuns, not one: the elder, a queen of Ramesses XI, daughter of
Nebseny and mother of Henttawy A=Q; the younger, a daughter of Ramesses XI and wife (later, queen) of Smendes I. However, this solution can take
two forms, - A and B - depending on whether Hrere A is taken as being
queen-mother of Smendes or of Herihor; correspondingly, Nodjmet would be
queen-mother of either Amenemnisu or Smendes I. These two variant solutions are best presented in genealogical form.

Scheme A

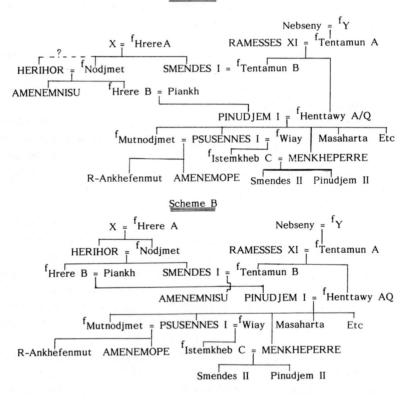

§ 442   The difference between these two schemes is essentially a matter of which two kings should be regarded as sons of Hrere A and Nodjmet respectively. On Scheme A, they would be Smendes (as brother of Herihor) and Amenemnisu (as son of Herihor). On Scheme B, they would be Herihor, and Smendes (as Herihor's son). On Scheme B, Smendes I along with Tentamun B and Henttawy A/Q (as daughter of Ramesses XI) all come one generation later than on Scheme A.

The main advantage of B over A is that it offers a smaller generation-jump (one in B; two in A) between Pinudjem I and his (younger) royal wife, Henttawy A/Q. But in either case, the simple answer must be that Henttawy A/Q would have been a younger (or youngest) daughter of Ramesses XI (10 or 12 years younger than Tentamun B), married-off to Pinudjem I later than Tentamun B was to Smendes, especially as Ramesses XI reigned almost 30 years. So, the supposed advantage of B over A might just be illusory.

As Piankh is no longer to be regarded as a son of Herihor, we are now free to consider him as having been a younger contemporary of Herihor (not of the same generation) who early on married Herihor's eldest daughter Hrere B, fathering Pinudjem I by her.

If on the basis of Scheme B, Smendes I be considered (with Wente) as a son of Herihor (not needfully the eldest), Smendes might have been 30/40 years of age during the decade of the Renaissance Era in Tanis, and then have reigned 26 years, dying as king aged about 66. On Scheme A, as a younger brother of Herihor Smendes might have been up to 10 years older, giving an equally viable result.

On the basis of Scheme B, with Smendes as a son of Herihor, Smendes would belong to the generation following Herihor, well suiting the length of his 26-year reign from just a few years after Herihor's death. But if Smendes really was the son of Herihor (either eldest, or at least among the earlier sons), then it still seems well-nigh incredible that he is not to be found in the long procession of sons of Herihor and Nodjmet in the Khons Temple at Karnak. Wente's suggestion (Temple of Khonsu,I,p.xiii) that Smendes' absence from Thebes in faraway Tanis led to his omission sounds very unconvincing - he would still be Herihor's son, regardless of where he travelled! One might theorise that Smendes was son of Herihor by some woman other than Nodjmet, hence was omitted at Karnak; but as no-one but Nodjmet ever accompanies Herihor as spouse, this is perhaps a desperate ploy. It would be one way to rescue Scheme B.

S 443   This particular problem is automatically solved on Scheme A, where Smendes I features as a much younger brother of Herihor - he would then not be found in a procession of Herihor's sons. Moreover, if Amenemnisu was in turn a very young son of Herihor and Nodjmet, his name might originally have been carved as 18th in the series of sons, where a name was later on erased in favour of a son of Pinudjem I (cf. Temple of Khonsu,I, pl.26 with p.12, and p.13 with note on line 39). Or he might have been son of Herihor by some lesser wife or concubine of Herihor. Nodjmet herself (if she was Amenemnisu's mother) would have died very old within the short reign of Amenemnisu, as 'King's Mother' on her funerary effects.

The possible and postulated existence of two Tentamuns, as wife and daughter of one ruler, would not be exceptional; quite the reverse. Suffice it to mention Ramesses II as husband of one Nefertari and father of a daughter Nefertari, or as husband of one Istnofret and father of a second (the daughters, see KRI,II,916:Nos.3, 6, in list). Or at this very period (21st Dynasty), the high priest Menkheperre as husband of one Istemkheb (C) and father of another (D); or, Pinudjem I himself, as husband of one Henttawy (A/Q) and father of another Henttawy (B). And the proliferation of ladies with the same names is one of the marks of this whole epoch. So, there is no special reason why Ramesses XI should not have been husband of Tentamun A, daughter of Nebseny, and father of a younger Tentamun (B), the one that eventually married Smendes. Her exalted origin would explain her prominence by the side of Smendes in the Wenamun report, thus accounting for Niwinski's observation of this fact.

S 444   It but remains to draw attention to certain other facts and possibilities only partly-realised hitherto: the Libyan connections of Herihor's family, and his non-Theban origin.

The names Herihor, 'Horus is chief', Nodjmet, 'Sweetie', and Hrere, 'Flower', are purely Egyptian and anodyne enough to raise no special comment. The same applies to the names of his first six sons at Karnak and several others. However, the seventh (Masaharta), eighth (Masqaharta), sixteenth (Mawasun), seventeenth (Osorkon) and probably nineteenth (Madanen) are indubitably of Libyan stamp, a fact already noted by others, e.g. by Wente (Temple of Khonsu,I,p.xiii with n.27, references). Hence at the very least, there may have been a Libyan strain in Herihor's family; but it may be more likely that he came from a family background of Libyan militia incorporated into the Egyptian army and garrisons earlier on in the 20th Dynasty under Ramesses III.

In any case, Herihor suddenly appears in Thebes during the Renaissance Era under Ramesses XI. But clearly he came there from elsewhere, especially if he was of Libyan stock. If he really was linked with Smendes, and the latter with Ramesses XI, then it would be in order to offer the hypothesis that Herihor had originated in the North, and quite possibly in the East Delta, where Libyans had been press-ganged into military establishments by Ramesses II (KRI,II, 206:15-16), and even more explicitly by Ramesses III (KRI,V, 91:5-7). Eventually, it was from just such a cantonment at Bubastis that the family of the 22nd Dynasty sprang. Intercourse between Tanis (outpost of decaying Pi-Ramesse) and Memphis (real capital) and Delta cities along that route would have given opportunity for Herihor's family to enter the service of the later Ramesside rulers at Memphis. Hence, as a trusted servant of Ramesses XI, Herihor would have been sent to the South, to rule both the Thebaid and Nubia, and having his northern headquarters at Teudjoi (El-Hibeh).

S 445 Such origins would also shed light on the occurrence of Osorkon the Elder (Osochor) as successor to Amenemope during the 21st Dynasty, if some antecedent link had already been forged back in the Delta between the family of the Great Chief of the Ma, Shoshenq A and the Tanite/Theban ruling clan. The name Osorkon was not new, witness its occurrence as the name of Herihor's seventeenth son, a century before Osochor. Only the family affiliations of Siamun now remain in doubt - a son of Osochor? Shoshenq A's son Nimlot A was thus full brother of king Osochor, and in the next generation Shoshenq B (future Shoshenq I) was consequently nephew of Osochor and brother-in-law of Psusennes II, becoming his natural successor when that king seemingly died without male issue.

TWENTY-SECOND TO TWENTY-FIFTH   DYNASTIES

§ 446   The first major matter concerns the kings Iuput I/II of the 23rd Dynasty, their identification and effect on chronology. The data come conveniently under four heads as follows.

1. A clearly-attested king Iuput I, Meryamun, no prenomen, whose Year 2 was equivalent to Year 16 of his senior coregent Pedubast I, founder of the 23rd Dynasty, about 812 BC (Nile level text No.26).

2. The equally clearly-attested king Iuput II, no prenomen, named as ruler of Tentremu (later Leontopolis, Tell Moqdam) by Piankhy, about 728 B.C.

3. The stela dated to Year 21 of a king Iuput, no prenomen, featuring Smendes son of Harnakht, ruler of Mendes, now fully published by J. Chappaz, Genava 30(1982), 71-81.

4. A group of monuments of a king Usimare Setepenamun (var. Setepenre), Iuput Si-Bast, Meryamun, from the Delta; list, see above, pp.124-5, § 98.

In theory, items 3. and 4. could be attributed to either Iuput I or II; in 1972, I had opted to assign them to Iuput I, as being potentially the more important ruler of the two Iuputs, through his association with the founder of the Dynasty.   However, later studies have shown that the opposite solution is preferable, i.e. that monuments under 3. and 4. - with the Usimare prenomen - probably belong to Iuput II, not I. In 1975, I also changed over to that option (CdE 52(1977), 42-44, and cf. foreword to Bierbrier,LNKE, 1975,p.x).

§ 447   First of all, in his work   Die Libyschen Fürstentümer des Deltas, 1974, F. Gomaa (p.120) correctly pointed out (as Petrie had done) that the Hood Plaque (Brooklyn 59.17) shows the king in a style of dress closer to that of the 25th Dynasty than the 22nd; hence, it is better attributed to Iuput II rather than I.   As the Iuput of the Hood Plaque also has the prenomen Usimare Setep[enre], it is a very short step then to attribute to Iuput II the other monuments bearing the closely similar prenomen Usimare Setepenamun, namely the bronze fragment from Leontopolis itself, and the barque-stand from Tell el-Yehudiyeh. For the Hood Plaque, see also E. Riefstahl, Ancient Egyptian Glass & Glazes, 1968, No.59; and R. Fazzini, Miscellanea Wilbouriana 1(1972), 64f. and fig.36.

§ 448   Of greater chronological importance is item 3., the Mendesian stela.

On genealogical grounds, Bierbrier noted that the interval between Pedubast I and Osorkon III needed to be shorter than the 16 years allowed in this work in 1972 (10 years for Iuput I as sole ruler; 6 years, Shoshenq IV); cf. LNKE, 100, and cf. 78 and 103. If the Mendes stela be attributed to Iuput II, then Iuput I (on present knowledge) would have been a short-lived co-regent of Pedubast I, probably dying within the latter's reign without any sole reign of his own. As a result, the supposed 16 years before Osorkon III shrinks to a mere 6 years (Shoshenq IV), and subsequent dates for the 23rd Dynasty would be raised by 10 years.

Instead of	we have
818-793: Pedubast I	818-793: Pedubast I
804-783: Iuput I	804-803?:Iuput I
783-777: Shoshenq IV	793-787: Shoshenq IV
777-749: Osorkon III	787-759: Osorkon III
754ff. : Takeloth III	764ff. : Takeloth III.

S 449   Turning to the rulers of Mendes, Table 22A (p.491, above), Nes-khebit(?) remains unaffected ($\underline{c}$.830-810 B.C.), and his son Harnakht A very largely so, $\underline{c}$.810-792 B.C. (Kitchen, CdE 52(1977), 44), including now a new correlation with Year 30 of Shoshenq III, $\underline{c}$.790 B.C. from the Strasbourg stela No.1379 of Har[nakht], as was well suggested by Gomaa, Die Libyschen Fürstentümer des Deltas, 76-77. Then, Smendes (IV) son of Harnakht (A) of the first text of the jamb Cairo JdE.43339, would follow during $\underline{c}$.792-777 B.C. (i.e., 10 years earlier than previous dating). Then we should have his son Harnakht (B), inducted in a Year 11 probably of Osorkon III, now 777 B.C., down to perhaps $\underline{c}$.755 B.C. For the jamb J.43339, see now JWAB,I, 229-238, and II, 571-5:A.22 (cited as 43359). Then may be placed Smendes V (son of Harnakht B) of the stela of Year 21 of Iuput (II), neatly filling the gap between $\underline{c}$.755 and $\underline{c}$.730 B.C., just before the ruler Djed-Amen-ef-ankh attested for Mendes by Piankhy in about 728 B.C. Correspondingly, the accession of Iuput II would be (at latest) 20 years before, in $\underline{c}$.748 B.C. For a possible statue of Smendes V, cf. Brooklyn Museum 37.344E, edited in JWAB,I, 239-241, and II, 576-77:A.23. If Djed-Amen-ef-ankh was followed by his son, Ankh-hor may have ruled $\underline{c}$.720-700 B.C., then Djed-hor (cf. LNKE, 141, n.266) could be dated down to $\underline{c}$.700-680 B.C., leaving the Buiama of the Assyrian records at $\underline{c}$.680-665 B.C.

S 450   Returning to the 23rd Dynasty, the Wadi Gasus graffito has the correlation: Year 12, Adoratrix of the God, Amenirdis (I); Year 19, the God's Wife, Shepenupet (I). The identification of those regnal years as pertaining to Piankhy and Takeloth III no longer applies (p.178, above). Instead, one may better understand these dates as for Year 12 of Piankhy and Year 19 of Iuput II, cf. Kitchen, CdE 52(1977), 44, following on Bierbrier,LNKE, 100 end. With Year 20 of Piankhy in c̲.728 B.C. (stela, Year 21, in 727), and his 12th year then in 736 B.C., this latter date will also have been Year 19 of Iuput II. Hence his Year 21 would fall in 734 B.C. (Mendes stela of Smendes V), and his accession in 754 B.C. His reign may still have lasted to c̲.720/715 B.C., depending on the questionable existence of Shoshenq VI. This leaves, finally, the brief interval 759-754 B.C. for the sole reign of Takeloth III (after his 5-year coregency, 764-759, with Osorkon III), and for Rudamun. Hence, 2 years for Takeloth III as sole ruler (total reign, 8 years), and 3 years for the ephemeral Rudamun (757-754 B.C.) may well fit the case.

§ 451   However, the initial dates for the 23rd Dynasty depend on the correlation of Pedubast I with Shoshenq III of the 22nd Dynasty (pp.130-136, above), from Year 8 of Shoshenq III set at c̲.818 B.C. In turn, that date depends on the dates assigned to Shoshenq III's predecessors.

Here, Shoshenq I's 21 years c̲.945-924 B.C. seem reasonably assured within narrowest margins. The supposed mention of a Second Jubilee (cf. Wente, JNES 35(1976), 277) is illusory, because the formula s̲p̲ t̲p̲y̲ w̲ḥ̲m̲ ḥ̲b̲-s̲d̲ does not indicate a second jubilee - in contrast to the proper and well-authenticated formula, w̲ḥ̲m̲ ḥ̲b̲w̲ s̲d̲; rather it is merely an anticipatory formula, without any independent historical value - see Kitchen, Serapis 4 (1978), 72-74. So, the Year 33 bandage of Nakhtefmut cannot be referred to Shoshenq I, but rather to Osorkon I as originally suggested (p.110 above). Furthermore, the tag [w̲ḥ̲m̲] ḥ̲b̲w̲ s̲d̲ apparently applied to Osorkon I (see Epigraphic Survey, RIK III, pl.13 bottom) is the known specific formula that is actually used for real second jubilees! This is so for Amenophis III and especially Ramesses II; cf. Kitchen, Serapis 4(1978), 74 with references, nn. 29,30; Hayes, JNES 10(1951), fig.12 after p.40; KRI,II, 384:5; 386:1,5; 390: 10; 391:2,13. As a first jubilee would fall in Year 30, and a second jubilee in Year 33 or 34, this would imply a minimal reign of 32/33 years for Osorkon I, exactly in accord with the Year 33 bandage, with Manetho's *35 years (emended from erroneous 15), and with a group of other indications for a relatively long reign for Osorkon I. Hence the reign of Osorkon

I should be retained at 35 years, c.924-889 B.C.

S 452   Similarly, the basic position has not changed on Shoshenq II, as a possible coregent of Osorkon I who predeceased his father. The simplest and least objectionable solution to the problem of the otherwise unattested king Heqakheperre Shoshenq still is to identify him with the former High Priest of Amun, Shoshenq son of Osorkon I, briefly elevated to coregency with his father but dying first, with the result that the kingship then passed on to his brother Takeloth I, and so into a parallel branch of the family. There is no good reason why Shoshenq I should suddenly be credited with a new prenomen at his death, if the Tanite burial of Heqakheperre were really his (cf. Edwards, CAH^2,III/1, 1982, 549, citing Gardiner, Egypt of the Pharaohs, 1961, 448, and H. Jacquet-Gordon, BiOr 32(1975), 359).

As Edwards acutely notes (loc.cit.), we actually possess fragments of canopic jars and a heart-scarab of Shoshenq I, found in the tomb of Shoshenq III (Montet, Chéchanq III, pl.49a, and p.76), to which should be added the Canopic chest, in Berlin since 1891 (No.11000), kindly brought to my notice by Mr. Aidan Dodson (see Roeder, etc., Aeg. Inschriften, Mus. Berlin,II, 332 top). These objects are clearly inscribed for Hedjkheperre Shoshenq I. Thus, there is no clear reason why a coffin for him should have been inscribed differently for him as Heqakheperre.

It should be noted that, already, on the statue British Museum No.17, the High Priest of Amun Shoshenq son of Osorkon I openly uses a cartouche - Shoshenq Meryamun - precisely the same as that adopted by Heqakheperre. His ephemeral 'kingship' may well have justified the claims of the later High Priest Harsiese A to royal status, as nominal co-ruler with Osorkon II (as with Pinudjem I and the Tanite kings). But the high-priestly role of Shoshenq (II) was what in fact justified Harsiese's own real position as high priest of Amun, - hence his filiation from Shoshenq as high priest rather than king.

S 453   Again, there seems no reason to change the attribution of the 'nameless' Years 5, x, y, 8, 13/14, to Takeloth I (p.311 above), as otherwise we would have an almost impossibly-rapid turnover of high priests of Amun within the modest 23/24 years' reign which is all that we are currently justified in assigning to Osorkon II. He was already served by three men in that capacity (Harsiese A; H's son; Nimlot C). To add further years to this reign is also a gratuitous luxury for the present.

§ 454   Exactly   the   same   applies to the 25 years of Takeloth II. But here, the issue of 22nd Dynasty chronology has been bedevilled by recent attempts to reassert a role for a non-existent mention of a supposed lunar eclipse in this reign. In the Chronicle of Prince Osorkon, son of Takeloth II, in an entry dated to Year 15, 4th Month of Shomu, Day 25 of his father, one reads: n [negative sign] ꜥm pt iꜥḥ, "a convulsion .. broke out in this land."   For over a century, scholars have been divided between those who sought to interpret the transliterated phrase as an allusion to a lunar eclipse,   and those who have denied that any eclipse is required by this passage,   given the crystal-clear negative n sign before the verb and nouns. For references, see latterly Kitchen, RdE 34(1982/3), 59, nn.4,5; Barta [see next], pp.3-6.   The other n (followed by a book-roll determinative) is often emended to read ꜥꜣ, "great", applying to nšny, "storm, convulsion". Hence the clear, straightforward rendering: "the sky did not swallow the moon, (but) a great(?) convulsion broke out in this land".

Recently, Barta has attempted to revive the eclipse hypothesis (RdE 32 (1980), 3-10), boldly emending (or at least interpreting)   the negative n to be ordinary n, it then signifying the conjunction "because", and treating the n plus bookroll after nšny as a related adverb ni, "on account (of it)". In theory, as I have fully stated (RdE 34(1983), 61), this interpretation is possible.   But is it even remotely likely?

§ 455   First, there is the point of chronic 'ambiguity inherent in reading a negative n as if it were an ordinary n, "because".   What person, reading this text later, could possibly know that this 'negative' hieroglyph was not really a negative particle, but a positive conjunction?   By this arbitrary reading, the whole point of this section of the text is lost in total ambiguity: "not swallowed the sky the moon", or "because swallowed the sky the moon"?   If the scribe had really intended a simple "because", why did he not just write a plain n (undotted in hieratic, so marginally quicker to write)?   Why write a totally misleading negative sign needlessly?   In short, there is no merit whatever in reading the negative sign as anything other than a simple negative sign, unless some other feature in the text had imperatively demanded the positive "because" interpretation. Surely, nine out of ten readers (ancient or modern) on seeing the negative sign would in such a case expect to read a negative meaning. The straight interpretation as a negative admits of no confusion or ambiguity - unlike the conjunctional interpretation. Hence the latter lacks merit.

Secondly, the supposed adverbial nỉ with bookroll determinative. It is perfectly possible to retain this reading and suggestion, with the rendering: "The sky did not swallow the moon, (yet) a convulsion therefor broke out in this land" - i.e., a convulsion worthy of an eclipse, or (in modern terms) trouble of such status that befitted a premonitory sign of the importance of an eclipse - "a convulsion (appropriate) to such broke out...". But in any case, and despite Barta's advocacy of this adverb (RdE 34, 8; GM 70 (1984), 9), (i) his translation "because (weil) .... on account of it (deshalb)" remains essentially tautologous (despite his denial, GM 70, 9), and is not the only possible translation, as shown just above. (ii) Also as shown above, the nỉ can be readily construed with a negative first clause, rendering the eclipse hypothesis entirely superfluous. (iii) But, despite Barta's appeal to Edel, ZÄS 84(1959), 27-28, the specific adverb nỉ is not so far attested with the bookroll determinative (even if mỉ is); (iv) this adverb occurs principally in the older phases of Egyptian, especially the Pyramid Texts, and in the 18th Dynasty hardly beyond the narrow confines of the Pyramid Texts' ultimate successor, the Book of the Dead (RdE 34, 61, n.12), a point ignored by Barta - such a recondite antique is not so likely to occur in the time and context of Prince Osorkon's Chronicle. (v) Taken as adverbial nỉ, this word would be a total hapax in Osorkon's texts. How can this situation possibly be any better than emendation to ꜥ3 (a word commonly used in this text) having just once a bookroll determinative? A simple error of one thin sign for another and one extra sign in spelling, yielding a straightforward, uncomplicated meaning, is surely far preferable to the conceptual gymnastics and linguistic archaeology that Barta's nỉ requires.

§ 456   Thirdly, if Barta's eclipse interpretation were to be accepted, placing Takeloth II's 15th year in 850 B.C., this requires us to raise the date of Takeloth II's accession by 14 years, to 864 B.C., with consequent and inevitable compression of the preceding reigns of Osorkon I, Takeloth I and Osorkon II. As Osorkon II cannot be set at less than 23 years, the difference must come from the reigns of Osorkon I and Takeloth I. No valid reason has yet been found for materially reducing the 35 years of Osorkon I; all the points given above (pp.110-111) remain valid, and new factors can be added to them (just above, §451, p.544). Thus Barta is compelled to reduce the reign of Takeloth I to 1 year, at most 2 years (RdE 32, 14; cf. RdE 34, 60).

As hinted above (§ 453, p.545), such a result has drastic consequences for the high priests of Amun in Thebes under Osorkon II (cf. already, RdE 34(1983), 61).

Osorkon II	High Priest	Incumbencies	
Year 5	: Iuwelot	*Years 1-7	(7)
Years 8-14,x	: Smendes III	*Years 7-15	(8)
Year x+1?	: Harsiese A (HP)	*Years 15-18	(3)
Year x+1+y?	: Son of " (now King)	*Years 18-20	(2)
Years 16+z-24	: Nimlot C (into T.II)	*Years 20-24	(4)
		(plus Tak.II, Yrs.1-10).	

Such a compression is physically just possible - but is it remotely likely? Yet, short of adopting different but equally unrealistic options, there is no escape from some such situation on Barta's eclipse-chronology.

§ 457   Fourthly, Barta is obliged to add 14 years to the chronology after Takeloth II's accession. He first adds 8 years to Takeloth II's reign (33 years instead of 25), boldly emending the hopelessly corrupt text of Manetho from 13 to *33 years, scattering the other six years amongst later reigns. Immediately, the very long career of Prince Osorkon - already at least 53 years on the minimal chronology adopted in this work - is lengthened to 61 years at least, and longer if he were appointed before Year 11 of Takeloth II. As for age, on this showing (as noted in RdE 34, 62), in Year 39 of Shoshenq III, Prince Osorkon would at the age of 81/86 be still actively campaigning, "overthrowing his foes"! Possible, but unlikely. Barta's comparison with Pepi II and Ramesses II (GM 70, 10) misses the point, because neither of these men in their extreme old age was known to be actively ruling Egypt in person; both had viziers and high officials to run the state (while they sat back) - and witness the roles of Khaemwaset and Merenptah in the last decades of Ramesses II. Prince Osorkon, by contrast, was still actively running his own affairs (and vendettas) late under Shoshenq III.

§ 458   Fifthly, the matter of the (needlessly) lengthened lives of the Apis bulls remains cogent. It is perfectly true (Barta, GM 70, 9 and n.8) that even on my chronology, two out of six bulls were aged 26 at death (rather than 15 or 20). But the whole point is that Barta's dating leads to a far worse result, of two bulls living till 26, one to 27, and one to 23/24, leaving only two bulls to die within the attested norms of 16/20 years old. Four out of six bulls living too long is a clear trend in the wrong direction, and constitutes a clear warning that something is wrong with a chronological scheme that requires such anomalies.

§ 459 Sixthly, recent discussion of Urk.VI,121:18ff. (GM 70, 7-8) has not advanced matters - this very passage was already dealt with by Caminos (CPO, 88-89), along with a further Demotic reference.

Seventhly, the assumption of 9 years for Tefnakht and 6 (for 5) for Bakenranef is purely the gratuitous result of "stretching" the chronology to match the over-high date for Takeloth II required by the eclipse-hypothesis. Monumentally, Tefnakht remains attested only up to Year 8; 6 full years for Bakenranef could only be justified if it were proved that Shabako had taken over from him when more than 6 months of Bakenranef's 5th year had already passed.

§ 460 Eighthly, the basic structure of Barta's chronology shows trends in two opposite and wrong directions.

A. Over-compression: (i) Over-reduction of reign of Takeloth I to almost zero; (ii) too-heavily-compressed careers for the high priests of Theban Amun in the early 22nd Dynasty.

B. Over-stretch: (i) artificial lengthening of the already-long career (and active old age) of Prince Osorkon; (ii) the suspicious anomaly of two-thirds of the mid/late 22nd-Dynasty Apis bulls living unusually long lives; (iii) the need, gratuitously, to lengthen the reigns of Takeloth II by 8 years (on which the contemporary data are curiously silent), and of five other rulers from Piankhy to Bakenranef by 1 to 6 years.

Ninthly, Barta's entire assumption of an eclipse in the first place falls fatally foul of a cardinal principle in the proper assessment of detailed textual evidence - i.e., that of economy of assumptions. When faced with two (or more) theoretically possible interpretations of a particular text, one should always opt for the one that leads to the most 'banal' result, insofar as no other factor renders it inferior to some rival interpretation. In this way, one may avoid historical (or other) "conclusions" that are likely to be shown up as fallacious by future discovery. And if the 'banal' solution is later proven wrong, then the result is pure gain, not the exposure of fallacy. Given the choice between "eclipse" and "no eclipse" interpretations, if the options are equally unobjectionable, it is methodologically preferable (indeed, needful) to opt for the most banal choice, "no eclipse", to avoid foisting onto Egyptian chronology and history a possible eclipse (and consequences) that later knowledge may show to have been fallacious after all. But if an eclipse is not present here in the first place, then there is nothing to disprove. But if in due time future finds were to desiderate a chronology that did correspond to Barta's eclipse-hypothesis dating, then that hypothesis would merit reconsideration on the basis of fresh and independent evidence. However, as the previous eight points should have made abundantly clear, we in fact do not have a choice between two options of equal value; the eclipse-hypothesis and its dependent chronology is shown to be an inferior option, both factually and methodologically, nine times over.

§ 461   Therefore, the experimental maximum dates based on Barta (RdE 34(1983), 68-69) for the 22nd-23rd Dynasties are just that - experimental - and nothing more. The best dates for the 22nd Dynasty are still as given in Table 3A, p.467 above. For the 23rd Dynasty, see the revised dates given above, §§ 448, 450, pp.543-44 above, and gathered in the new Table 3B to Part Six, below. Dates one year later for the 24th Dynasty than in Table 4 are possible (RdE 34, 69), but are not needfully any better - the same remark applies to the possible extension of the reign of Osorkon IV to 713 B.C. (ibidem).

§ 462   The Kushite (25th) Dynasty has also come in for renewed scrutiny. Here it should be remembered that we have four sources that bear on the chronology of the period.

(i) Actual first-hand regnal years of the Kushite kings from the monuments and original documents.

(ii) The absolute base-line of 664 B.C. for the beginning of the 26th Dynasty, and the firm framework of dates of Assyrian involvement with Egypt from 725 B.C. to 663 B.C.

(iii) The perfectly clear Old Testament narratives in 2 Kings 18-19 and Isaiah 36-37, in which real problems are minimal.

(iv) The hopelessly garbled data in the surviving versions of Manetho, plus a few other and later classical allusions of very little worth.

Among several recent contributions, that by F. Yurco (Serapis 6(1982), 221-240) may especially be mentioned for its judicious and careful treatment of most of the data for this Dynasty generally, and of the clash with Assyria in 701 B.C. in particular. If a minimal chronology (with coregency of Shabako and Shebitku) is eventually shown to be anything more than hypothetical, then his presentation will probably be found to be closest to the truth. If the higher dates prove preferable (see below), then - excluding the coregency - most of his observations would still retain their value. For Kush in cuneiform documents, cf. the summary by W. Röllig in Reallexikon der Assyriologie, VI, 1983, 374-5, which betrays no acquaintance with the first edition of the present work, using hyper-minimal dates for the 25th Dynasty wholly uncritically.

(i) Thus, monumentally, Shabako's dates run up to Year 15 (14 full years and possibly 15); for Shebitku, we have only a Year 3, which is nowhere near his real length of reign on any calculation. Taharqa had definitely 26 years. See already above, pp.153-172, and RdE 32(1983), 63-67.

§ 463   (ii) The scala of Assyrian interventions runs as follows.

726/725 B.C.   So, king of Egypt (2 Kings 17:4) was appealed to by Hoshea of Israel , rebelling against Shalmaneser V of Assyria. The long series of reasons for taking So to be Osorkon IV of Tanis retain their full validity; Goedicke's objections (WZKM 69(1977), 7-8) are captious, and refuted by the following facts. (1) Sais in the far west of the Delta played no part whatever in Egypt's relations with the Near East in the eighth century B.C. (2) The Hebrew prophets condemn the sending of envoys to Tanis and Memphis in Egypt, never Sais. (3) The abbreviation So for Osorkon is of a piece with (e.g.) Shosh for Shoshenq, and need not be a merely familiar or disrespectful form. (4) Relations between the Hebrew monarchies and the 22nd Dynasty are known to go back to Osorkon II (giving ample precedent for Hoshea's appeal); no such relationship had existed with Sais. Hence we have no warrant whatsoever for reading So as Sais, which imports a gratuitous and unjustified emendation into the text; in this error, Goedicke is followed by Redford, Biblical Archaeology Today (Jerusalem Congress, 1984), 1985, 197 and n.56. As Osorkon IV was pharaoh by 730 B.C. on independent grounds, he is the obvious candidate for identification as So barely five years later. See already pp.372-375 above. The interesting note by Redford in JSSEA 11(1981), 75-76, adds nothing to the case for Sais.

720 B.C.   The army-commander Re'e came from Egypt to support Hanun of Gaza against Sargon II (cf. above, pp.375-6). Re'e's chief was probably still Osorkon IV. As Pir'u of Musri, he sent presents ("tribute"), ANET, 285a, top.

716 B.C.   Shilkanni king of Musri (Egypt) sent a gift of 12 large horses to Sargon II at El-Arish (above, p.376). There can be no serious doubt

that this Shilkanni is (U)shilkan, Osorkon IV, which in turn would clinch
the latter's contemporaneity with the episodes of 726/5 and 720 B.C.
that fall after Osorkon IV's accession c̲.730 B.C.

S 464

713/712 B.C.   In 712 B.C., Sargon II had to suppress a rebellion by Iamani
at Ashdod. Iamani had previously ejected Ahimiti, former Assyrian
vassal-ruler of Ashdod, then tried to organise a coalition of local princes against Assyrian rule, and to raise help from "Pir'u of Musri" - an
Egyptian dynast, not a Kushite ruler, as Spalinger observantly pointed
out (JARCE 10(1973), 100); he further dug a moat at Ashdod, etc. All
these activities, the transmission of news of the conspiracy to Assyria,
and the organising and leading of an expedition westward by Sargon II
would imply that Iamani's career as rebel leader began in at least 713
B.C., to be crushed in 712 B.C. As in that same year Iamani fled into
Egypt, to the border of Meluhha (Nubia), it would appear that his
"Pir'u" (pharaoh, Egyptian dynast) was no longer there to succour him,
so that he fled instead to the king of Nubia, who in turn extradited
him to the Assyrian ruler. This Nubian ruler is now generally admitted
to have been Shabako.

As a result, 713/712 B.C. is the probable lower limit for the end
of the reign of Osorkon IV (but not certainly). In turn, 713/712 is certainly the very latest possible date for the establishment of the rule
of Shabako in Egypt. But it is important at this stage to stress that
this date is only the bottom minimal date, and not necessarily the correct date, quite a different matter (contrast Yurco, Serapis 6, 221); it
is certainly not the maximal date.

S 465

701 B.C.   In this year, indubitably, Sennacherib invaded Judah and neighbouring kingdoms; he mentions the participation of the (unnamed) ruler
of Nubia (Meluhha). So far, no-one has produced one scrap of hard,
first-hand evidence for any later Palestinian campaign by Sennacherib
subsequent to 701 B.C., a fact now admitted by most scholars (e.g.,
Spalinger, CdE 53(1978), 39; Yurco, Serapis 6(1982), 223, n.22, cf. 222).
An ingenious attempt was made by H. Tawil (JNES 41(1982), 195-206)
to understand the Masor of 2 Kings 19:24 (=Isaiah 37:25) as the Mount
Musri north-east of Nineveh, drawn on by Sennacherib for his irrigat-

ion scheme in 694 B.C., and so to prove that a second western campaign of Sennacherib fell after 694 B.C. However, this remains fanci-
ful. Tawil has to admit that in fact Isaiah and Micah do use the word
Masor as a variant for Misraim, Egypt; and y^eor is above all else the
Hebrew word for the Egyptian Nile, not other streams. In the plural,
it may be understood of the Delta branches. Sennacherib's "drying up
the Nile" is simply metaphorical for his defeating the Egypto-Nubian
force at Eltekeh, and nothing more. The attempt by D. Livingston
(The Law and the Prophets, Volume for O.T. Allis, 1974, 402-412) to
have Taharqa as ruling king in Kush in 701 B.C. (parallel with Shabako/
Shebitku in Egypt) founders on the explicit passage in Kawa stela IV:7ff
that clearly describes Taharqa as a mere youth and king's brother (not
himself a king) when summoned north by Shebitku his senior.

674, 671 B.C. Esarhaddon marched against Taharqa of Nubia and Egypt.
667-665 B.C. Assurbanipal warred against Taharqa in Egypt.
664/663 B.C. Assurbanipal took action against Tantamani, the successor of
Taharqa.

S 466 As the death of Taharqa in 664 B.C. and beginning of the 26th
Dynasty is an agreed datum, we may work backwards, combining the Assyrian and Egyptian evidence. The 26 years of Taharqa are universally admitted
to have covered 690-664 B.C. Shabako took over Egypt not later than
713/712 B.C. and possibly earlier; his 14/15 years (Year 2, vanquished Bakenranef) in Nubia and Egypt would have fallen at latest during 714/713 or
713/712 B.C. to 700/698 B.C. - quite possibly earlier, but not before 716/
715 B.C. as Shilkanni was ruling in the East Delta in 716 B.C. (see above).
Hence Shabako's accession in Nubia was 717/716 at earliest, 714/713 at
latest; his conquest of Egypt came in 716/715 at earliest and in 713/712
at latest. This would set his duration, at 14/15 years, between 703 and 697
B.C. at the most extreme limits, giving his successor Shebitku (if not co-
regent) between 13 and 7 years' reign.

S 467 (iii) This brings us to our third source, the Old Testament data. For
2 Kings 17:4, tied to the reign of Shalmaneser V, see above **S 463** (p.551).

In 2 Kings 18-19 and the mainly parallel Isaiah 36-37 we find the principal Hebrew account of the Assyrian invasion of Palestine of 701 B.C.
Among the anti-Assyrian allies, these accounts specifically include "Tirhaqa,

King of Kush" (2 Kings 19:9; Isaiah 37:9). That Taharqa was not king of
either Egypt or Kush in the year 701 B.C. is all but universally recognised
- Shabako, Shebitku or both ruled the Nile valley then. However, Taharqa
could well have been involved while still a prince - a possibility that cannot be factually denied or excluded, especially in the wake of the total dis-
credit of the old ultra-low chronologies of Macadam and Albright (cf. above
pp.154-161; also Spalinger, JARCE 10(1973), 98). The naming of Taharqa as
"king" in relation to an event in 701 B.C. (eleven years before his accession) has led various commentators to view this reference as an anachronism
or a source of confusion (e.g., Spalinger, CdE 53(1978), 39-40; Redford, Biblical Archaeology Today, 1985, 197/204, n.58), even when the real explanation has long been clear and available. "A text taken out of context becomes a pretext", as one early writer long since remarked; and sometimes,
so here. The brutally simple truth about "king" Taharqa of 701 becomes
amply evident if one simply takes the trouble to read right through the
entire Old Testament narrative about Sennacherib to the end. The last
event recalled in that narrative (as pendant to Sennacherib's retreat from
the Levant in 701) is the murder of Sennacherib and succession of Esarhaddon (2 Kings 19:37; Isaiah 37:38) - events known to have occurred in 681
B.C. That single fact dates the present Hebrew narrative to not earlier
than 681/680 B.C., in the form that we now possess - ten years after the
accession of Taharqa as King in 690 B.C. It is, then, absolutely clear that
the writers of Kings and Isaiah (in 680 at earliest) thus refer to Taharqa
by his then current title, by prolepsis of a kind that is universal in both
ancient and modern times, and used by Taharqa himself (Kawa stela IV),
see above, p.160. Hence, the whole artificial Taharqa problem melts into
thin air; any confusion remaining belongs in the minds of those who might
gratuitously choose to have it so, - for whatever reasons.

The one main question that remains to be reviewed is: who was king in
the Nile Valley in 701, when Taharqa was prince? The answer to this
question is entirely a matter of the internal Egyptian evidence, including
the late and unreliable data now to be considered, and has nothing more
to do with the Old Testament narratives.

§ 468   The surviving Manethonian versions of the 25th Dynasty are (as
they now stand) absolutely riddled with errors from end to end, as the following brief tabulation should make crystal clear.

Sabacon,   8 yrs (Af.),   12 yrs (Eu);   contrast Shabako, Year 15.

Sebichos, 14 yrs (Af),   12 yrs (Eu);   ? (Shebitku, Year 3, + x...).

Tar(a)cos, 18 yrs (Af),   20 yrs (Eu);   contrast Taharqa, 26 years.

Total, 40 yrs (Af), 44 yrs (Eu);   contrast 50 yrs from 714 to 664 B.C.

As these figures stand in the existing text, NOT ONE FIGURE IS COR-
RECT. They are WRONG. It is, therefore, preposterous to claim to base
a sound, factually-grounded chronology of the 25th Dynasty upon these
faulty data. Only by emendation can any plausible chronology be wrung from
them. And emendation automatically removes objectivity and reduces the
whole set of adjusted numbers into modern hypothesis having no ancient
authority whatsoever. One man's guess is then as good or bad as another's,
with no objective criterion to judge between them, if no monumental or
other external first-hand evidence can be adduced to provide an objective
means of control over idle speculation. It is because of the totally unsound
methodology (inter alia), that such misguided attempts as Barta's to manipulate the Manethonic data by free emendation, and against contrary indications from better sources, for this Dynasty (e.g., RdE 32, 17; GM 70, 10-12)
must be firmly rejected.

There is no way of rescuing the 18/20 years' figures for the reign of
Taharqa, or the 40/44 years' total for the Dynasty - such numbers are just
rubbish, the detritus from copyists' errors in textual transmission. It is irrefutable that Taharqa reigned 26 years, and the Dynasty ruled Egypt for
some 50 years. Yurco has made the ingenious suggestion (Serapis 6(1982),
230, n.71) that Manetho or his source only allowed 18 years' rule in Memphis to Taharqa, assigning the last 8 years of rule there to Necho I. However, this theory is contradicted by two points. First, the first-hand evidence of the Apis stelae (up to Year 26 of Taharqa) prove that his rule was
recognised there to the end. Second, Manetho recognises the entire line of
four Saite rulers from Ammeris to Necho I (cf. pp.145-7, §§ 116-7 above),
and they are specifically given as rulers of Sais, not Memphis.

As has long been recognised, sense can only be made of Africanus'
other figures (8, 14 years) by arbitrarily reversing their order, in order to
bring 14 years for Sabacon (not 8) into line with Shabako's Year 15, leaving
8 years for Sebichos/Shebitku. This could give a minimal chronology, 712-
698 and 698-690 for Shabako and Shebitku respectively. However, the first-
hand inscriptional data well-nigh certainly condemn this solution as wrong;
cf. § 469 below. Alternatively (and with equal justification), one may allow
12 years each for both Shabako and Shebitku with Eusebius' variant, which

can only be made to work by inventing a 2-year coregency between Shabako
and Shebitku, in order to square Shabako's known minimum of 14 years with
a Manethonic 12 years. These kings would then have reigned in Egypt during
714-700 and 702-690 B.C., respectively, with Shabako's accession in Nubia
falling in 715 B.C. In general, this is a far better option than the previous
one because it is consistent with other, first-hand data (Kawa IV; titles of
Shebitku, etc.) whereas   the   previous theoretical scheme (*14, *8 years)
is not. And while Africanus often appears to preserve figures that are closer to those required by first-hand data, this is by no means always so, and
figures are sometimes more accurately transmitted in Eusebius' version.
As an example close to this period, one may cite the nonsense-entry 'Petubates, 40 years' in Africanus, as against the entirely superior figure of 25
years given in Eusebius' version for the founder of the 23rd Dynasty. So,
using Eusebius' version for these two reigns, and inventing a coregency to
harmonise 12 years with 14 for Shabako, we may accept this scheme as a
possible chronology, although lumbered with a totally theoretical coregency
lacking external attestation, already admitted as possible (cf. Murnane, Ancient Egyptian Coregencies, 1977, 189-190). Some such scheme is also envisaged by Redford, in Biblical Archaeology Today, 1985, 196 (his location of
'Sabaco at Eltekeh' is obviously a slip of the pen; no Assyrian source requires this presence of Shabako on campaign in his penultimate year of
life, while no fact exists at present to refute the combined inscriptional and
Old Testament evidence that would bring prince Taharqa into Palestine at
Shebitku's behest in 701 B.C.).   On behalf of the coregency, it is possible
to interpret the plural reference to "kings" in later recensions of Sennacherib's annals as a reflection of Assyrian consciousness of the coregency of
Shabako and Shebitku - so, Yurco, Serapis 6 (1982), 225. However, two
points speak against this interpretation. First, Near-Eastern rulers never
normally recognise Egyptian coregencies. Second, in the Assyrian text, the
clear distinction is made between "the kings of Egypt" (Musri), and forces
from "the King of Nubia" (Meluhha) - precisely the distinction between
Egyptian local dynasts and the Kushite pharaoh that obtained in 713/712
B.C. as well as in later Assyrian texts. Despite Yurco, there is here a
clear distinction between political entities, not merely an adjectival description of Nubian troops. So this supposed evidence is fallacious, leaving
the coregency still wholly theoretical. It should also be stressed that the
unity imposed on Egypt by the Kushite kings was wholly superficial - most
lines of petty dynasts remained in place and in power right through from

the 22nd/23rd Dynasties to the early years of the 26th Dynasty; cf. above, pp.395-98.

So, the thesis of a Shabako/Shebitku coregency is a possibility that still lacks any clear supporting evidence to justify forcing the first-hand evidence into a Manethonic strait-jacket to fit 12+12 years. But there is a third manipulation of Manetho that is no whit inferior to the two just reviewed; it has the advantage of fitting all the first-hand data, without inventing any imaginary coregencies. This would be to adopt the reattributed *14 years for Shabako from the Africanus version, and the 12 years for Shebitku from the Eusebius figures, and assume no coregency. The dates for the two kings are then 716-702 and 702-690 B.C., as arrived-at in this work originally. Novelty is not the arbiter of truth, and a solution which best fits the first-hand data while avoiding theoretical rearrangements and hypotheses (such as unattested coregencies) should be accorded preference over solutions that do depend on these species of modern gematria.

S 469   (v) There must now be considered certain first-hand Egyptian data for this period under three heads.

(1) The significance of Taharqa's bringing an army-force all the way north from Nubia into Lower Egypt at the behest of his brother Shebitku, newly-acceded as King (whether as sole ruler or as Shabako's coregent). This was amply dealt with above, pp.154-8, plus RdE 34, 65-66. For what reason, other than the deliberate intervention in Palestine in 701 B.C., need such a force be levied so peremptorily and be taken so far?   To this question (if the occasion of 701 be disallowed) there is no clear or logical answer (none is given, e.g., by Barta, GM 70, 11, who does not account for this event). Thus, Taharqa's bringing this army north is not absolute, mechanical proof of his being summoned in 702 B.C. (or even in 701, with Yurco, 223, 225-227), but it is the best possible indirect evidence that Shebitku as king planned and organised the Egypto-Nubian intervention in Palestine in 702/701 B.C., hence should be accorded a reign of not less than 11 years, and better 12 years (agreeing with the Eusebius figure from Manetho).

S 470   (2) The variant titulary of Shebitku, with its nakedly imperialistic pretensions; see above, p.383, nn.809-811, and RdE 34, 65; - a point total-ly misconstrued by Barta (GM 70(1984), 11 and n.13). The whole point is that, for the first and only time in 70 years, a king openly took such a titulary - and the phenomenon never thus recurred again during Egypt's re-

maining dynasties. So clear an ancient manipulation of such formularies cannot be dismissed or evaded as just accidental. That Shebitku failed in his
ambition, or did not persist with it after the 701 debacle, is beside the
point.

§ 471   (3) In the wake of an important study by Vernus (BIFAO 75(1975),
1-66, pls.1-7), also commented on by Spalinger (CdE 53(1978), 22f., 41ff.),
it is now clear that a series of blocks adjoining the barque-sanctuary at
Karnak should be attributed to Taharqa - and not (except in two cases)
to either Shoshenq I or Osorkon II (in contrast to my earlier attribution to
Shoshenq I). Thus the Nubian references noted on p.293 above (with n.285),
along with the mention of Khurru/Palestine, p.302 and n.319 above, should
be removed from the account of Shoshenq I, and be referred to the reign
of Taharqa. The mentions of Nubia need occasion no surprise; Amun might
expect to draw revenues and products from Nubia - once more ruled by a
pharaoh (even though he came from there!) - as was the case in New
Kingdom times. The reference to Khurru (Vernus, pp.29:16, 31:16, 45-46,
note nnn) is fleeting and not very informative: "when(?) I made/will make
it as your (=Amun's) tribute of the land of Khurru, which had turned away
/which one has turned away from you." This allusion could apply to tribute
gained already in Khurru by Taharqa, who had brought it for Amun after
Khurru had earlier experienced Egypto-Nubian power. This could imply a
successful campaign of some kind by Taharqa. The future-tense rendering
(with Vernus) would imply merely that Taharqa intended to regain Khurru
as a source of tribute - which it had not been for some time. Either way,
very little can be made of this mention; it certainly cannot be dated
specifically to the first decade of Taharqa's reign (Spalinger) or to his
Years 14/17 (Vernus) on current knowledge. Compare the cautionary note
by Yurco, Serapis 6(1982), 240, n.246.

§ 472   So to conclude. In short, the full chronology for the 25th Dynasty
originally given above (Table 4) remains superior to the lower dates recently advocated, because it gives preference to primary sources interpreted
with a minimum of theoretical elements or of manipulation, whether of
Manetho or any other source. Whatever is taken from Manetho's text in its
present confused state must be fitted to the first-hand data, not the other
way round. Hence, 14 years for Shabako plus 12 for Shebitku remains the
most economical solution. As an alternative, one may offer the theory of

a 2-year coregency of Shabako and Shebitku, to accomodate the 12+12 years in the Eusebian version of Manetho, and still retain compatibility with all the available first-hand data; the assumption must also be made that, as soon as he became coregent, Shebitku in effect took over effective power from a perhaps ailing Shabako - hence the sudden change to an aggressive policy in Assyrian-dominated Palestine. As a non-viable option, we do best to reject the attempt to assign only 8 years to Shebitku, with 14 for Shabako; this clashes badly with all the indications that Shebitku was the moving force in Egyptian foreign affairs from 702/701 B.C. Nor can one use the specious argument that Shebitku must have reigned fewer years than Shabako, because his monuments are fewer (e.g., Barta, GM 70, 10). On that basis, surely Takeloth II at 25 years (to whom Barta would attribute 33 years!) should, by his paucity of monuments, have reigned far less than Osorkon II, ruling for 23 years; or compare the monuments under Shoshenq I in 21 years, compared with those of Smendes I reigning 26 years; and so on. Frankly, one cannot crudely "read off" the length of a reign merely from the total of surviving known monuments! There are too many random factors involved.

S 473 <u>A.</u> Before the conquest of Egypt by Shabako, the reign of Piankhy may safely be left at about 31 or 32 years (or just over). The notorious scrap of bandage in the British Museum should by preference be read Year 30 (not 40), as being two 'tens' over a 'ten' and a '<u>t</u>'-sign (in contrast to Baer, JNES 32(1973), 7f., n.1); see above, 152 and n.292, and 370, n.732, and parallels with <u>t</u>-sign in datelines. If desired (in agreement with Barta), the odd year could easily be added at need to the reigns of Tefnakht (8 for 7 years) or just possibly Bakenranef (6 for 5 years).

<u>B.</u> One proposed change to the genealogy of the 25th Dynasty is to make Tantamani the son of Shabako, not of Shebitku - hence a cousin of Taharqa, not his nephew; see A. Leahy, GM 83(1984), 43-45.

OFFICIALS OF THE REALM

§ 474   MEMPHIS: High Priests of Ptah

To **§§** 151ff. (pp.187ff.), little need be added. See briefly Bierbrier, LNKE,
48-49. On Shedsunefertem, officiant under Shoshenq I, cf. A.R. Schulman,
JNES 39(1980), 303-311, publishing a further Memphite lintel (his fig.1) from
the temple of Siamun, dedicated by Shed(su)nefertem and (his son) Pahemneter, each entitled (among other things) Chief of Secrets of Ptah and
Prophet of Ptah. Pahemneter occurs as holder of these in the Berlin genealogy, and there as son of Shedsunefertem given the same titles. The identity of the two men on this new lintel with the like-named father and son
of the Berlin genealogy and stela Louvre 96 seems beyond any reasonable
doubt. The reason for the difference in titulary on these two monuments
(which puzzled Schulman, op.cit., 310) may be quite simple. Louvre 96
shows the long line of high priests of Memphis, down to two generations
that lost that title but who perhaps cherished the (vain!) hope of its eventual restoration, and cited it out of ancestral pride. The Berlin genealogy's
author was perhaps more concerned to retain in the family the specific
functions of Chief of Secrets of Ptah, etc., which had come down through
Pahemneter, realistically making no vain claim to the high-priestly office.

     On points of detail. At p.189 & n.7: translation of CGC 741, see JWAB,
I, 243-245:B.1; for Cairo JdE 86758, ibidem,I, 246-248:B.2. At p.189, n.10,
read c.1230 to c.1080/1060 B.C., .. (courtesy, E. Hornung, OrAnt 13(1974),
335). At p.194, n.27, CGC 1212, translated in JWAB,I, 302:B.27. For a further Memphite statue of this period, cf. S. Sauneron, BIFAO 77(1977), 23-
27, pls.1-3; also, JWAB,I, 306-7:B.29.

THEBES

§ 475   The Neseramun/Nesipaqashuty Family (pp.202-211, above).
Here, cf. C. Traunecker, BIFAO 69(1971), 219-237, and Bierbrier, LNKE, 60-
67, 68-73, both with some additional data and full discussions, Bierbrier being able to improve on Traunecker's treatment of relationships. Several
statues are modernly re-edited and translated in JWAB, thus: CGC 42230/1,
JWAB,I, 170-182, II, 530-5, pls.44-46:A.15; CGC 42221, JWAB,I, 183-192, II,
536-540, pls.47-48:A.16; CGC 42231, JWAB,I, 193-204, II,542-551, pls.49-53:
A.17; CGC 42232, JWAB,I, 210-215, II, 556-60:A.19; CGC 42220, JWAB,I,
278-82:B.17; CGC 42219 (§ 168), JWAB,I, 295:B.23; CGC 42222, JWAB,I,

296-7:B.24; CGC 42224, JWAB,I, 298-9:B.25; Karnak column-base, JWAB,I, 258-9:B.8.

S 476 The Nebneteru Family (pp.211-213, above).

Here, one should add full discussion by Bierbrier, LNKE 73-78, and note his identification of Hor vii/viii/ix/xi as one person (pp.76-77), correcting my dating of Hor, and pointing out that his statue (Berlin 17272) dedicated by Nebneteru iv (cartouche of Osorkon III) was probably posthumous (pp.75,77, 78); this statue, also in JWAB,I, 300-1:B.26. For CGC 42228, see R. El-Sayed, ASAE 65(1983), 111-125, pls.I-IV; JWAB,I, 156-167, II, 520-26, pls.37-40:A.13.

S 477 The Family of the Fourth Prophet Djed-Thut-ef-ankh B called Nakhtefmut A (pp.217-224, above).

Again, see full discussion by Bierbrier, LNKE, 79-83, with refinements and adjustments in detail, including the need to give an earlier date to Osorkon III (cf. on this, p.543f., **SS** 448-450). New publications of relevant statu-ary as follows. CGC 42206/7, R. El-Sayed, ASAE 69(1983), 219-39,pls.I-II; JWAB,I, 25-34 (A.2), 35-43 (A.3), II, 441-6 (A.2), 447-452 (A.3). CGC 42208, JWAB,I, 274:B.15. Statue, Montu temple (T.35), JWAB,I, 275-77:B.16. This book, p.219, n.120, **S** 184, above, add jamb of Harsiese C, JWAB,I, 283:B.18.

S 478 Notables of the Family of Montemhat (pp.230-233, above).

Again, see Bierbrier, LNKE, 104-6, also in Glimpses of Ancient Egypt (H.W. Fairman Volume), 1979, 116-118. Most elements of the main genealogy are well assured. Add Babai i as wife of the vizier Harsiese F, and complete fTjes[....] as fTjes-Ese-peru, as the name of Montemhat's maternal grandmother. Similarly, Khamhor A's wife was Tabetjet i, leaving Pediamun i's daughter to be Tabetjet ii.

S 479 The Vizier(s) Nakhtefmut and the Ankhpakhered Family (pp.214-217 above).

By contrast with the four preceding genealogical groups, this group (plus those of the Besenmuts and Pediamunnebnesttawys, dealt with below) has occasioned considerable differences of opinion over its composition and relative dating. Thus, initially, the careful discussion by Bierbrier (LNKE, 86-91) showed up possible weaknesses in the treatment given on pp.214-217 above.The crux of the matter was that, if only one Vizier Nakhtefmut (C)

was to be postulated, then my early dating for the Besenmut family (i.e.,
with Besenmut iv as husband of the famous Montemhat's cousin Tabetjet
ii) could no longer be maintained. Conversely, a unitary Vizier Nakhtefmut
C would require a later dating of the Besenmut family (i.e., with Besenmut
iv's grandfather Besenmut ii as the husband of Tabetjet ii). At that time,
Bierbrier opted for two viziers Nakhtefmut: either C-i and C-ii/iii/iv, four
generations apart (LNKE, Chart XX, and p.90), or possibly C-ii/iv two generations before C-i/iii (Chart XXI and p.91), as he then retained the early
dating of the Besenmut family. Vittmann (next S), p.12, simply expressed
caution.

S 480   Later, in a valuable review of G. Vittmann, Priester und Beamte
im Theben der Spätzeit,1978, published in BiOr 36(1979), 306-309, Bierbrier
offered a fresh table of relationships embracing the Besenmut and Montemhat families and the vizier(s) Nakhtefmut. Here, he provisionally operated
with Vittmann's late date for the Besenmuts, but retained the option of two
viziers Nakhtefmut, but this time grouped as C-i/iv and C-ii/iii, four generations apart (BiOr 36, 307 and Table I).

Still more recently, the wheel has come full circle, as J.H. Taylor (CdE
59(1984), 41-42 and 41f., n.1) once more raised the possibility of just one
vizier Nakhtefmut (C), allied to the late dating of the Besenmut family,
a dating espoused by Vittman, and now favoured by Taylor on the basis of
the additional indications afforded by the stylistic development of wooden
stelae set up by P. Munro, Die spätägyptischen Totenstelen, 1973), and
latterly by his own study of the changes in forms and decorative schemes
of coffins c.1100-650 B.C. (Taylor, The Development of Theban Coffins
during the Third Intermediate Period: A Typological Study, forthcoming).

On this basis, the (one) vizier Nakhtefmut (C) would have had two wives
(as adopted above, p.214), the younger one being Istweret, a younger daughter from the later years of her father Takeloth II (Taylor, CdE 59(1984),
41f., n.1, a possibility envisaged by Bierbrier, LNKE, 89 end). Of three possible permutations (I-II-III, Charts B,C,D), Taylor in CdE 59, 42-46, provisionally opts for his second (II, Chart C), which gives a genealogical result
in many respects concordant with this work, pp.214/215, above. One important difference is that he distinguishes Ankhpakhered ii, son of [f]Tamit and
Nakhtefmut D, from the like-named husband of Tarwa i, denoting him as
Ankhpakhered viii, a son of the 4th Prophet of Amun, Nakhtefmut B; this
results from fresh data obtained from the interior of coffin BM 24958

(Taylor, CdE 59, 40-41; and cf. Bierbrier, JEA 70(1984), 84-86). For an edition of CGC 42229, see JWAB,I, 205-209, II, 553-555, pls. 54-57:A.18.

S 481 The Besenmut Family (p.224-230 above) and the Pediamennebnest-tawys.

As noted above, there seem now to be very good reasons for adopting the later dating of the Besenmut family. This has been argued in detail by Vittmann, PBTS, 3-61 in particular. With caution, and some appropriate corrections in detail, this dating was employed also by Bierbrier, BiOr 36(1979), 307-8. Further support comes from the stylistic studies of stelae by Munro and of coffins by Taylor, see **S 480** above. Therefore, this later dating of the Besenmuts will also be adopted here, as the best solution currently.

Most of the basic genealogy of the Besenmuts as given on p.225 above still remains correct. Two important points should be added here from Vittmann,PBTS. First, on his pp.9,10 (and 51), he adds two new sources (the Cairo statues JdE 36957 and 37878) for the earliest generations of the family, both extending it back earlier in time, and offering a variant: Nes-amun - Penmaat - Djed-Khons-ef-ankh before Pestjenef/Nesamun, instead of the series Nebneteru - Djed-Khons-ef-ankh - Penmaat before Pestjenef. The 'new' sequence may prove to be more accurate (so also, Bierbrier, BiOr 36 (1979), 307 top). Certainly (as Vittmann, p.10, correctly points out), Neb-neteru ix was not a vizier as given in the genealogy, p.225 above.

Second, in my genealogy (p.225 above), a clear error should be corrected - Besenmut i fathered Nespasef ii (husband of Tashepenkhons) not by his wife Taneshet, but by his other wife Itawy iii (omitted in that genealogy); see Bierbrier, LNKE, Charts XXII, XXIV, p.92,96, and Vittmann, PBTS, 18f. For Cairo JdE 36957, see also R. El-Sayed, BIFAO 83(1983), 135-143, pls. 24-25A.

S 482 However, the biggest changes affect the Pediamennebnesttawys (pp.227-230, above); the works of Vittmann and colleagues go well beyond my rather scrappy treatment; cf. Vittmann, PBTS, 66-91, with Bierbrier, BiOr 36(1979), 308. For an additional monument of Pediamennebnesttawy D, conserved in the School of Archaeology & Oriental Studies at Liverpool, see S. Snape, CdE 59(1984), 230-232, **S** 18, and fig.1; while yet another monument linked with this family was published by J. Berlandini, Cahiers de Karnak VI, 1980, 235-245.

One may now set out the main family in genealogical form as on the next page.

DjedMutefankh ^{3PA}Pediamen(etc.) A+B $=^{f}$Ankh-karoma   Besenmut i

Hor xv $=^{f}$DjedMutesankh ix   Mentuhotep   Nespasef ii

^{f}Shepenmut $=^{3PA}$Pediamen(etc.) C/i ^{f}Gautsoshen iii = Irt-Hor-rou i

^{3PA}Hor xvii $=^{f}$Istenkheb

(Yr. 14, Ps.I,
651 B.C.)

^{3PA}Pediamen(etc.) D

NB: Pediamen(etc.) is used above for Pediamennebnesttawy.

S 483   For a fresh branch of the Besenmut clans, see the studies of Hor 'A' and family by Vittmann, PBTS, 54-58; Bierbrier, BiOr 36(1979), 308 with corrections, likewise M. Raven, OMRO 62(1981), 10 (also with corrections); and now Taylor, CdE 59(1984), 28-34, cf. 35-40 and Chart A (p.30).

On p.228 above, **S 194**, correct the number JdE 86908 to 36908 as is given by B.V. Bothmer, Kêmi 19(1969), 15, n.4 (courtesy E. Hornung, OrAnt 13(1974), 335).

Notes affecting Tables in Part VI

S 484   Changes to Table 12: Princesses wedded to commoners. Under marriage No.12 (p.479 above), read now Ankh-Karoma, daughter of Takeloth III, not II, to the 3rd Prophet of Amun, Pediamennebnesttawy B. (**S 193**, now corrected by Bierbrier, LNKE, 83, n.186, and by Vittmann, PBTS, 89 & n.5, 90), as Djed-Thut-ef-ankh D should also be regarded as a son of Takeloth III, not II. One should probably add a 16th marriage (but after No.13), of the princess Tentsai (a daughter of Takeloth III) to an official of Khons, called Nakhtefmut, attested on the statue Vienna 5085 of their son, the Prophet of Montu, Ankh-Takeloth; see H. De Meulenaere, CdE 57(1982), 218-222.

S 485   Changes to Table 13A: High Priests of Amun at Thebes (p.480). At the entry '754-704', change text to read: Half-century interval during which the office may have been left vacant, at least the last 30 years , c.734-704, as no pontiff greeted Piankhy at Thebes in 728 B.C. But c.754-

734 B.C., may have seen a further high priest, Osorkon F, in office. Two indications would favour this view. First, the stela Turin 1632 of a lady Shepenupt, daughter of a high priest Osorkon is of a type datable to c.720/ 700 B.C. (Munro, Totenstelen, 261), as was noted by Vittmann, PBTS, 62, which would put her father in office c.750/740 B.C. Second, with this would agree the genealogy of the priest Ankhnahebu and his son Djed-Amen-ef-ankh on the statue Cairo J.37163, published by H. De Meulenaere, SAK 6 (1978), 63-68, pl.20. The son reappears in 651 B.C. in Papyrus Brooklyn 47.218.3 (cf. ibidem, 67), hence his father Ankhnahebu must have flourished c.680 B.C., and his grandmother Mutmose c.700 B.C. She was daughter of a King's Son and High Priest of Amun, Osorkon - who, again, could then be set at c.740/750 B.C., i.e. precisely the same date as our Osorkon F of Turin 1632; he was presumably a son of Takeloth III, and named after his grandfather Osorkon III (cf. also De Meulenaere, p.68). The only obscurity is whether Mutmose was married to Wennufer (Ankhnahebu's father) or to a further Djed-Amen-ef-ankh (Ankhnahebu's father-in-law), but this has no bearing on the date of Osorkon F.

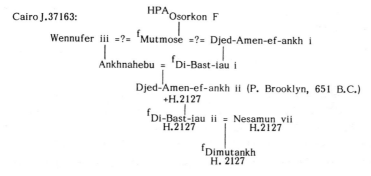

H.2127 = Hildesheim 2127 (De Meulenaere, p.67).

S 486   Changes to Table 14: 2nd, 3rd, 4th Prophets of Amun.
A. 2nd Prophets of Amun. At c.835, delete Djed-Ptah-ef-ankh D (S 290), as he should be taken as a son of Takeloth III, not II; Bierbrier, LNKE, 83 & n.186, and Vittmann, PBTS, 89 & n.5, 90. Instead, insert: c.830ff., Djed-Khons-ef-ankh C who was also 4th Prophet (q.v.), Bierbrier, loc.cit.

At c.740ff., delete Neshorbehdet, and substitute Djed-Ptah-ef-ankh D, son of Takeloth III (references just above). After Montemhat, add an entry: c.650-640: Neshorbehdet, see Vittmann, PBTS, 65, 176.

S 487   B. 3rd Prophets of Amun.

c.850? - delete Pakhuru, vizier (S 314), and substitute Pimai (ASAE 7(1906), 52A; cf. H. De Meulenaere, CdE 53(1978), 229).

Possibly add: c.760/750, Amenhotep, on whom see Vittmann, PBTS, 91, 92, 123, following on Kees, ZÄS 84(1959), 54-67; and c.750-725: Wennufer A, cf. Vittmann, PBTS, 90.

At c.750ff., delete Pediamennebnesttawy B, and substitute: c.725-700, Pediamennebnesttawy A/B, cf. Vittmann, PBTS, 87-90, and Bierbrier, BiOr 36(1979), 308. At c.725ff., delete present entry; and at c.695ff., read instead c.700-675, Djed-Anhur-ef-ankh, cf. De Meulenaere, CdE 38(1963), 71-77, and Vittmann, PBTS, 90. At c.675-653, read Pediamennebnesttawy C/i, cf. Vittmann, PBTS, 87,89. Then, read: c.653-603, Hor xvii, see Vittmann, PBTS, 86,89, this Hor being father of Pediamennebnesttawy D, in office c.603-590. Then delete c.610-590, Pekhelkhons (S 193), and substitute: c.590 ff., Djed-Khons-ef-ankh G (references, Vittmann, PBTS, 91, 93).

S 488   C. 4th Prophets of Amun.

At c.960ff., Nesamun, a shabti of his in Hungary, M. Ciho, GM 72(1984), 91-95, and fig.1. Change entry at c.790ff., Nakhtefmut B (etc.) to: c.800ff :Nakhtefmut B (cf. SS 187,188,191,314), father of - c.780ff. - a Djed-Khons-ef-ankh F, postulated by Bierbrier, BiOr 36(1979), 307 top & Table I, as father of c.765, Nåkhtefmut G (ibidem), father of (c.750ff.) Djed-Khons-ef-ankh D, etc.

After Montemhat and Nesptah B (to 640), one may add several fresh entries.

Thus, c.640-635, perhaps Hor xxiii, son of (a) Montemhat, cf. Vittmann, PBTS, 97,99,l00; c.635-630, Nesmin (ibidem, 97-100). Then, c.630-625, Udjahor (ibidem, corrected by Bierbrier, BiOr 36(1979), 307); c.625-620, Nespamedu, father of (c.620-610) Nesipaqashuty (ibidem).

S 489   Changes to Table 15: Viziers.

A. Southern Viziers

At c.930/900; probably re-date Padimut A to c.940, and Ia-o to c.925, as it was perhaps Ia-o's son Hori (not his father) who went on Shoshenq I's Palestinian campaign in 925; cf. JWAB,I, 254.

At c.890, delete Nebneteru ix, as he was never vizier; cf. Vittmann, PBTS, 10 & n.4.

Delete entry c.840, Nesipaqashuty B, etc.; see 745 B.C., below.

After the entry at c.760 B.C., Hor x, a new entry: c.755, Ankh-Osorkon, a grandson of Osorkon (III), is named on the coffin BMFA 72.4824, on which see Bierbrier, JEA 70(1984), 82-84. After the entry at c.750: Harsiese F, should now be added: c.745, Nesipaqashuty B, son of Pediamonet (S290), who married a daughter of Takeloth III (not II); documentation on him includes a spelling of the name of the god Osiris only current from c.740/730 B.C., on which see A. Leahy, SAK 7(1979), 141-153, esp. 148f.

After c.660, Nesipaqashuty D, a new entry - c.650/640(?), Iry; see Vittmann, GM 15(1975), 47-52; PBTS, 159-160, 163. Of quite uncertain date there remains the vizier Hori son of Iutjek, of Cairo statue J.37512, published by Kees, ZÄS 83(1958), 129-138, pl.12a; now in JWAB,I, 216-222, II, 561-5, pls. 58-60:A.20.

B. Northern Viziers

S 490   a. Mentuhotep, Vittmann, PBTS, 145; as a son-in-law of Taharqa, he may have officiated early in this reign - say c.685-675 B.C.

b. Harsiese R (c.675-660?) - see Vittmann, PBTS, 39-43,, 148, following on his paper, Orientalia 44(1975), 376 & n.10; Bierbrier, Glimpses of Ancient Egypt (Studies H.W. Fairman), 1979, 118; idem, BiOr 36(1979), 307; idem, JSSEA 12(1982), 153-4; De Meulenaere, JEA 68(1982), 139-144, esp. 141-2.

Perhaps the data on this much-discussed vizier may be worked out as follows. Item 1: From Thebes come the Theban coffin and stela (Vittmann, PBTS, 41) of Naneferheres, married to the Prophet of Montu, Nesamun of the notorious Besenmut clan. She was the daughter of a vizier Harsiese and his wife Sheta.

Item 2: This vizier is there given distinctively northern cult-titles: Great of Seers (i.e., high priest) in Heliopolis, wn-r priest in Letopolis, and Sem-priest in the House of Ptah in Memphis.

Item 3: On the statue from Giza (Univ. Museum Philadelphia, E.16025), the title Sem-priest of Ptah recurs (plus titles referring to Apis), and Middle/Upper Egyptian titles appear: Chief of prophets of Osiris in the Thinite province, and 'Great Chief' of Djufy.

S 491   These facts may be taken to indicate the following scenario. (i) That Harsiese's family origins were in Upper/Middle Egypt, and that his family early on had links with Thebes. As his daughter's stela belongs to the end of the 25th Dynasty (Munro, Totenstelen, 19 (cf. 31ff.), Abb.13), this vizier probably officiated during the 25th Dynasty, most likely under Taharqa.

(ii) As this vizier's official cult-titles include three related to the major sanctuaries in Heliopolis, Memphis and Letopolis, he has been regarded as a northern vizier (so, Vittmann and Bierbrier). This seems the best solution to his sphere of office. He may have married-off his daughter Naneferheres to the Theban priest Nesamun before Taharqa went on to appoint him as northern vizier (perhaps as successor to Mentuhotep?). The provenance of his Philadelphia statue - Giza (originally from Memphis?) - would also supp- ort the theory that he went to officiate in the north.

S 492   Item 4: There is also known a high priest of Heliopolis, Harsiese, who became father-in-law to Psammetichus I, the latter marrying his daughter Mehtenweskhet C; see Vittmann, Orientalia 44(1975), 376-77 and references. This wife of Psammetichus I had her tomb-chapel in Western Thebes (at Medinet Habu).

The last fact has been accounted-for as stemming from the fact that Psammetichus I's daughter Nitocris went (as God's Wife of Amun) to live (and die) at Thebes. But if this father-in-law Harsiese was in fact the northern vizier Harsiese (already having Theban family roots), then the presence of his second daughter's tomb in Western Thebes becomes even more fully intelligible.

The possible identification of the Heliopolitan high priest Harsiese, father-in-law of Psammetichus I, with the vizier and Heliopolitan high priest Harsiese R would imply that, even during the reign of Taharqa, Har- siese had entered into relations with Necho I as prince of Sais, in marrying off his other daughter to Necho's son Psammetichus (I). Thus, Harsiese was able to continue in office as a northern vizier, into the early years of Psammetichus I.

S 493   c. Djedkare, see Vittmann, PBTS, 148; Bierbrier, JSSEA 12(1982), 154.Given on later monuments as son of Harsiese, he may have directly succeeded him as northern vizier (660ff.?).

d. After these two viziers may come a series of viziers under the long reign of Psammetichus I and under his two successors: Sisobek (Vittmann, PBTS, 147); Nasekheperensekhmet (ibidem, 145/6); Bakenranef (p.146); Gem- enefhorbak (p.147); Harsomtusemhat (p.148).

e. Then under Amasis II, two viziers, Psamtek-Meryneit and Pasherienta- ihet (both, p.147).

OUTLINE HISTORICAL SURVEY

S 494   General works: J. Černý, 'Egypt: from the Death of Ramesses III to the End of the Twenty-first Dynasty', first issued in 1965, was reprinted in CAH[3],II/2, 1975, 606-657, with slightly augmented bibliography, pp.1004-1009. For works embracing the 22nd Dynasty onwards, see below Addenda to Ch.18 (for pp.287ff.). Outlines, Ramesside decline to 21st and Libyan Dynasties, cf. Kitchen, Pharaoh Triumphant, 1982, 215-221; in French, Kitchen, Ramsès II, pharaon triomphant, 1985, 291-301; C. Lalouette, L'Empire des Ramsès, 1985, 265-363.

S 495   Chapter 15

On **S 206**, to p.244. On the second factor of potential vulnerability of the Ramesside empire on its western flank, see Kitchen, RdE 36(1985),177-179, concerning the demographic pressures that forced the Libyans over this long 'border' the length of Egypt and Nubia; this topic is also handled separately in a wider context by Amin A.M.A. Amer, Continuity & Change in New Kingdom Egypt (PhD thesis, Liverpool, 1983), 172-180 passim.

On **S 207**, p.246: to n.15 (late-Ramesside family-relationships), add Kitchen,JEA 68(1982), 116-125, and Kitchen, SAK 11(1984), 127-134, which supercedes J. Grist, JEA 71(1985), 71-81 (dating Queen Tyti much too early, on indecisive stylistic grounds). For Eastern Desert expeditions for gold and galena under Ramesses VII, see Y. Koenig, Hommages à Serge Sauneron,I, 1979, 185-220, pls. 30-37 (=KRI,VI, 397-403), completed by Koenig, BIFAO 83(1983), 249-255, pls. 52-54. The document of Year 2 of Ramesses IX (p. 246 & n.20, above; KRI,VI, 517-522) also dealt with such gold-prospecting.

S 496   On **S 210**, p.251: for Herihor as merely 'King of Karnak', cf. also M.-A. Bonhême, BIFAO 79(1979), 263-287; Herihor's texts in the Great Hypostyle Hall, cf. A.M. Roth, JNES 42(1983), 43-45 (=KRI,VI, 730). P.252, above, the scenes by Herihor in the Temple of Khons at Karnak were fully published by The Epigraphic Survey, Temple of Khonsu, 1-2, 1979/1981; on pp.252/3 above, the references to Piankh being Herihor's son should at present be deleted, as the supposed evidence from the Khons-temple is illusory; see above, **S 438**, pp.535-6. On Piankh, see survey of monuments by R. El-Sayed, BIFAO 78(1978), 197-218 & pl.66. Texts of Herihor in Khons-temple, some also in KRI,VI, 709-723, plus 843-8 with other relics; Piankh, KRI,VI, 848-9.

S 497   Recent new translations of Wenamun (cf. p.252) include those by
E.F. Wente in W.K. Simpson (ed.), The Literature of Ancient Egypt[2], 1973,
142-155; H. Goedicke, The Report of Wenamun, 1975; and M. Lichtheim,
Ancient Egyptian Literature,II, 1976, 224-230.

On **S** 212 (p.254): for the possibility of two Tentamuns, and the equivalence of Henttawys A and Q, see just above, **SS** 441-3, pp.537-540.

S 498   Chapter 16

For the titularies of all kings in compact, up-to-date form, see J. von Beckerath, Handbuch der Ägyptischen Königsnamen, 1984 (Münchner Ägyptologische Studien, 20); pp.97-111, 253-273, for the 21st to 25th Dynasties. For
a summary of inscriptional sources for the 21st to 24th Dynasties, see H.
Jacquet-Gordon, in Textes et Langages de l'Egypte pharaonique,II, 1973, I
107-122; for the 25th Dynasty, Leclant, ibidem, 123-135; Saite period, H.
De Meulenaere, ibidem, 137-142 passim.

At p.258, n.80: on the colossus of Pinudjem I, cf. also L. Habachi,

On **S** 215, p.257: It is possible that, after reaching advanced old age,
'Queen' Nodjmet was buried in a Year 1 later than that of Smendes
(of Amenemnisu, or even Psusennes I?), if the style of her coffin required
it to have been made closer in time to those of Pinudjem I and Henttawy
A; cf. Niwinski, JARCE 16(1979), 52 (but discount his taking Nodjmet as
a sister of Pinudjem I). Butehamun has been studied by Niwinski, SAK 11
(1984), 135-156.

At p.258, n.80: on the colossus of Pinudjem I, cf. also L. Habachi,
Second Stela of Kamose, 1972, 16ff., and E. Hornung, OrAnt 13(1974), 335.
On **S** 216, p.259 with n.88: For the notable private stela Cairo J.71902 from
Coptos, showing Pinudjem I and Henttawy A as King and Queen, see Aly
O.A. Abdallah, JEA 70(1984), 65-72 and pls. 16-17. The apparent epithet
'real(?) King's Daughter'(idem, p.66 lunette 5, pp.66/67 note a) may well
imply direct descent from Ramesses XI, as suggested **SS** 441-443 just above.
The stela was set up by Wenennufer, a native of Coptos and 2nd Prophet
of Min there; the autobiographical text is of interest in narrating his pride
in Coptos, his career covering a variety of priestly duties, and in incidenta-
lly illustrating the already considerable 'Osirification' of the local cult.

S 499   The accession to kingship by Pinudjem I had its fluctuations, on the
evidence of the entry portal at the Temple of Khons in Karnak, in the light
of careful investigation of Pinudjem's reliefs there, see K.R. Weeks in
Temple of Khonsu,2, 1981, pp.xviii-xix. Thus, reliefs showing Pinudjem I in

royal style with high-priestly titles were altered back to exhibit him with
solely high-priestly attributes, as though his initial kingly claims were to
be minimised. However, this was all eclipsed by Pinudjem's achievement
of the full outward trappings of kingship (full titulary, cartouches, etc.)
- excluding regnal years - from Year 15 of Smendes onwards. His possible
parentage of Psusennes I and consort could only have strengthened his
status.

S 500   On **SS** 216/7, pp.259-60: To the time of the kingship of Pinudjem
I and the incumbency of his daughter the God's Wife of Amun, Maatkare
A, may most probably be attributed the career of Hori, whose coffin is in
the collection of the Museu Nacional at Rio de Janeiro (Inv.525/526; PM^2,
I^2, 832); publications, A. Childe, AMNRJ 25(1925), 283-326, and in Beltrão/
Kitchen, Catalogo Rio [forthcoming], ad loc. He was priest at the front
(when carrying) Amun, Royal Scribe, Royal Cupbearer, Chief of Harim of the
God's Wife of Amun, and more fully Royal Scribe of Documents in the
King's Presence/at Court (sš ^{r} nsw, n̠   h̠ft h̠r nsw), as most spellings prove,
thus amending the interpretation in E.   Graefe,Unt. Inst. Gottesgemahlin,I,
129, h 115/P 10 (Titel, end). Beginning as a priestly bearer of Amun's
image in festal processions, Hori went on to become Cupbearer to the
"King", and Royal Secretary "at Court", and chief of harim to the God's
Wife of Amun. In the functions of Scribe, Cupbearer and harim-chief, Hori
followed his father Panehsi who had borne the loyalist name Sai-dwat-neter-
em-petri-Amun, "The God's Wife is satisfied by contemplating Amun". As
Hori's coffin is of the brightly painted type on yellow ground that is typical of the period from late Ramesses XI to c.1000 B.C. (on criteria worked
out by Dr. J.H. Taylor, The Development of Theban Coffins [forthcoming],
to whom I am indebted on this point), so Panehsi and his son Hori would
in succession have served their Theban "King" Pinudjem and his 'court', and
his daughter the God's Wife of Amun, Maatkare, say c.1060-1020 B.C. in
round figures. A second monument of Hori is appositely published by Graefe
(op.cit.,I, 129:2; pl. 2*:P.10, and pl.7a,b:P.10), namely a wooden figure of
the god Sobek in Florence (No.134).

S 501   On **S** 219, p.262: Menkheperre's kingship. Here, fresh evidence indicates that Menkheperre's use of the prerogatives of kingship - while not
as full as Pinudjem I's - at least matched Herihor. First and foremost may
be cited the bronze statuette (PM^2,I^2 794) in the Museu Nacional at Rio

de Janeiro (Inv.81), published by Childe, AMNRJ 32(1930), 80-81 and plate;
also Beltrão/Kitchen, Catalogo Rio [forthcoming], ad loc. This statuette is
the epitome of Menkheperre's priestly 'shadow' kingship. He is shown in
kneeling posture (as if offering), wearing proper pharaonic royal kilt with
traditional triangular forepart. Down the centre of this, a text reads: 'Made
/dedicated by the High Priest of Amun, Menkheperre' (name in indubitably
clear cartouche). But on his head, this priestly shadow-pharaoh wears simply
the close-fitting priestly 'skullcap' so familiar from the reliefs of Herihor,
but no uraeus on his brow.

   The genuine use of cartouches by Menkheperre can now be better documented, thanks to recent work at Karnak. Here, the Canadian excavations
by the east side of Amun's vast precinct have produced two bricks stamped
with clear cartouches of Menkheperre and his wife Istemkheb C (see Redford, JARCE 18(1981), 17, pl. 3d; idem, JSSEA 13(1983), 221, pl. 30b - the
two examples facing opposite ways), while a whole series of bricks has been
recovered (texts oriented either way), bearing twin cartouches "High Priest
of Amun" and "Menkheperre" (Redford, JARCE 18(1981), 17, pl.3c; cf.
JSSEA 13(1983), 221), giving a pair of cartouches exactly like those of
"High Priest of Amun", and "Herihor", of roughly half a century earlier.
Thus, the Rio statuette, the plentiful supply of stamped cartouches on
bricks, and the occasional use of the title of "King of Upper and Lower
Egypt" (above, p.262 and n.110) illustrate clearly beyond any doubt that
Menkheperre laid modest but firm claim to limited use of kingly style,
though less than Pinudjem I. It is just possible that, in the last years of
Psusennes I, Menkheperre or his subordinates occasionally used the Tanite
king's regnal years but attributing them to Menkheperre; cf. above, S 435.

S 502   On S 222, pp.265-7, the Court of Psusennes I. For the family of
Nesy(en)amun - not necessarily Theban - and his descendants, see the valuable paper by F. von Kaenel, BSFE 100(1984), 31-43. Four generations can
be traced, from Nesyenamun to Khons(em)hab, all roughly contemporary
with the long reign of Psusennes I and perhaps later. It should be noted
that the fragment illustrated by von Kaenel, p.36, fig.2, does not belong to
the man Sa/Sia of this family, but reads: "The Steward Sau-Per'o-em-bah-
Amun, justified before ⟨ the great god⟩ , the venerated one." The name
"Sated is Pharaoh in presence of Amun" is of precisely the same type as
that of the Theban Hori's father Panehsi: Sai-Dwat-neter-em-petri-Amun,
"Satisfied is the God's Wife by contemplating Amun" (S 500 just above) of
this time.

S 503   Late in the reign of Psusennes I (by the high regnal year), in a Year 49, 3rd month of Akhet, Day 5, at Kom Ombo in the far south, there took place the reburial of a marine warrior - the Troop-Commander of the Warship "Great of Voice(?)" (i.e., 'The Thunderer'!), and Chief of the (twin-ned) Crew, confidant of His Majesty, close to his (royal) feet, Wenentawat. Perhaps he had fallen in some internal conflict (if we remember Menkheper-re's dissidents in the oases); published by S. Wenig, Forschungen und Berichte 10(1968), 71-94, pls. IV-VII, 11-15.

On **S** 226(i), p.269/270: From El-Hibeh comes a papyrus-fragment (now in Moscow, No.5660) of a letter from(?) the high priest Menkheperre, possibly to the god Amun of El-Hibeh in relation to an oracle; it gives especially full military titles to Menkheperre - "Generalissimo of the South and North, the Army-leader Menkheperre, who is at the head of the great army of all Egypt"; see Posener, JEA 68(1982), 134, 138, pl. 14:1. For the property-settlement inscribed in the Temple of Khons at Karnak (above, p.270, n.162), see Epigraphic Survey, Temple of Khonsu,2, 1981, pl.133, pp.17-20; the high priest Menkheperre consulted the oracle of Amun in the presence of Khons; cf.also Kitchen, BiOr 41(1984), 85.

S 504   On **S** 228, p.271: In JEA 68(1982), 136, Posener has suggested that the splendid palette of the High Priest of Amun, Smendes, in the Metropolitan Museum of Art, New York (Hayes, JEA 34(1948), 47-50) should be ascribed not to Smendes III (contemporary of Takeloth I, 22nd Dynasty) but to Smendes II, son and successor of Menkheperre - handwriting is remarkably similar, and likewise the fulness of military titulary. To this attractive suggestion, the one objection is that, while Menkheperre was commander of all Egypt, the Smendes of this palette is commander over all the South-land only (^{r} rsy r-dr.f) - a more restricted command more typical of the 22nd Dynasty than the 21st.   For Smendes II as High Steward of Amun under Menkheperre, see Goyon, Cahiers de Karnak VII, 1982, 275-280.

Chapter 17

S 505   On **S** 230, p.273: Osochor can now be identified as an Osorkon - best entitled (for historical purposes) as Osorkon the Elder, following Yoyotte, to avoid the endless confusion that would result from trying to re-number all the Osorkon-kings at this stage. For the identification, see above **SS** 437, 445, following on Yoyotte, BSFE 77/78(1977), 39-54, using two now lost genealogies from the roof of the Temple of Khons at Karnak; for other parts of these genealogies, see Graefe, Unt. Inst. Gottesgemahlin,I, 112-114: n 130. It is now clear that a childless Amenemope was succeeded by an Osorkon, son of the Great Chief of the Ma, Shoshenq A; the new ruler was brother of Nimlot A, and so an uncle of the future Shoshenq I. Whether Siamun was a son of this Osorkon, we do not know.

S 506   At **SS** 235-6, pp.279-83; notes on this period also by Redford, JAOS 93(1973), 3-5, but largely superseded by the present work. P.279 & n.220: Louvre sphinx of Siamun, see J.D. Cooney, ZÄS 93(1966), 45 (courtesy, Hornung, OrAnt 13(1974), 335). At **S** 235 (ii), p.280/1: The role of Siamun in Philistia is also admitted by A.R. Green, JBL 97(1978), 353-367, who adds nothing new. Contrary to his p.366, conquered foes in Egyptian triumphal reliefs do hold real weapons and (despite Lance) there is no reason to doubt the presence of a crescentic axe-head in the Siamun relief. The admitted north-west origins of the Philistines are quite sufficient to account for the Mycenean and related background observed by Lance.

On pp.282, 285 (**SS** 236, 239), delete references to the supposed marriage of Psusennes II to a daughter of Shoshenq A. Mehtenweskhet was royal mother to Osochor, hence her title; thus one scion of this family occupied the Egyptian throne over a generation before their definitive accession in the person of Shoshenq I.

Chapter 18

S 507   For the epoch of the 22nd to 24th Dynasties, see also the outline by I.E.S. Edwards in CAH[2], III/1, 1982, Chapter 13, pp.534-581, and bibliography, pp.966-974. See also two stimulating essays: (i) by D. O'Connor, in B.G. Trigger, B.J. Kemp, D. O'Connor, and A.B. Lloyd, Ancient Egypt: A Social History, 1983, 232-249; and (ii) by A. Leahy, in Libyan Studies 16 (1985), 51-65.

S 508   At **SS** 244, 245, pp.288-9: For Iuput's granite cenotaph, etc., at Abydos, see Vernus, BIFAO 75(1975), 67-72, pls. 6-10; its blocks were in part later reused further north by Amasis II. At **S** 244, p.289: On the great royal cache at Deir el-Bahri, see the successive discussions by M. Dewachter, BSFE 74(1975), 19-32; A. Niwinski, JEA 70(1984), 73-81; and C.N. Reeves, Studies in the Archaeology of the Valley of the Kings [forthcoming], knowledge of the content of which, I owe to the kindness of the author.

At **S** 244 end (p.289), the statue of Nesy (CGC 42218) is now edited and translated in JWAB,I, 112-115, II, 490-93, pls. 24-27:A.9.   **S** 246, p.290 & n.266: add here the statue Vienna 5791, translated (with earlier references) in JWAB,I, 249-250:B.3 - note his correction of reading of the name of Nimlot B's mother: Patoreshnes (p.249), not Penreshnes. At **S** 247 (iii), p.290 & n.269, add D.B. Redford, in Studies on the Ancient Palestinian World (for F.V. Winnett), 1972, 141-156, esp. 153ff., with which cf. H. Cazelles, RdE 26(1974), 158-161. At **S** 249, p.291: For the name Niumatiped (perhaps from Nimlot-iped), see H. Jacquet-Gordon, BiOr 32(1975), 359, § 4; E. Graefe, Enchoria 5(1975), 13-17.

S 509   At **S** 251 (ii), p.293, Nubia: The supposed Nubian campaign of Shoshenq I is illusory, because the blocks in question can be shown to belong to inscriptions of Taharqa; see Vernus, BIFAO 75(1975), 1-66, pls. 1-5.

S 510   At **SS** 253ff. (pp.294ff.), on Shoshenq's Palestinian campaign. Some corrections to identifications and locations of lesser toponyms in particular in Shoshenq's great list can be gleaned from S. Ahituv, Canaanite Toponyms in Ancient Egyptian Documents, 1984, although not every suggestion will prove convincing.   At **S** 257, p.299, n.304: For the cartonnage of Hori (in Fitzwilliam Museum, Cambridge, as E.8.1896), see translation and notes in JWAB,I, 252-4:B.5. With Müller and Jansen-Winkeln, the restoration [šms] is to be preferred to [r-gs]; and it was Hori rather than his father who probably went on the campaign. At **S** 260, pp.301/2: The treatment of Shoshenq I's reign, campaign and buildings by A.R. Green (JBL 97(1978),353-367) adds nothing new, and labours under some misapprehensions; e.g., the court of Shoshenq I at Karnak is <u>not</u> a jubilee-hall, but a 'court of millions of years', or memorial-foundation. The jubilee-wishes for Shoshenq I are purely formal, and <u>not</u> a record of actual jubilees - see Kitchen, Serapis 4(1978), 72-74; and E. Hornung, E. Staehelin et al., Studien zum Sedfest, Aegyptiaca Helvetica 1, 1974, on formulae for wishes (pp.63-65) as distinct from mentions of real jubilees.   Again, despite Green, the chronology of the 21st/22nd Dynasties is not totally dependent upon Hebrew chronology; dead-reckoning from the base-line of the 26th Dynasty and upper limits set by the 19th/20th Dynasties also serve to set tangible limits for the 21st/22nd Dynasties. Furthermore, the texts of the great triumphal relief <u>explicitly</u> refer to Shoshenq's building-project (see pp.301/2 above); hence, the court, gate and triumphal relief are all part of one undertaking. The entire project was left unfinished, and there is no other explanation needed for the rough state of the colonnades of the court.   At p.302, n.320: For fragments of the triumph-scene of Shoshenq I from El-Hibeh, of very fine work and now in Freiburg & Heidelberg, see E. Feucht, SAK 9(1981), 105ff., pl.2. For other reliefs from this temple, see Feucht, SAK 6(1978), 69ff., pls. 21-22.   For a recent brief exploration at El-Hibeh, see R.J. Wenke et al., Archaeological Investigations at El-Hibeh, 1980: Preliminary Report, 1984.   At S 262, p.304 & n.335: The titles Count and dignitary belong not to Djed-Ptah-ef-ankh C, but to his immediate superior who is lost except for the merest traces on the Munich lintel; see J. von Beckerath, OLZ 74(1979), 10, S 4.

S 511   At p.306, n.350: The statue Cairo J.37881 does not belong to the high priest Shoshenq; see Jacquet-Gordon, BiOr 32(1975), 359, S 5.   At S 265 (pp.306/7): In an early year of his reign, Year 2+x (Year 4, 5, 6, or 12?), Osorkon I commissioned work for the Temple of Khons - [doors?] of conifer wood, ornamented with [precious metals?], commemorated by a graffito in the temple forecourt - see the Epigraphic Survey, Temple of Khonsu,2, 1981, pl.134, pp.20-21; cf. Kitchen, BiOr 41(1984), 85, where it is suggested that, if Year 4 were the date, Osorkon's bounty may have been part of his vast largesse to Egypt's temples in his first four years (see S 262).

S 512   At S 266, p.308: For translations of the texts on CGC 559 of Djed-Khons-ef-ankh A, see M. Lichtheim, Ancient Egyptian Literature,III, 1980, 13-18; with full edition, JWAB,I, 9-24, II, 433-440, pls. 1-3:A.1. For full translations, etc., of texts on statues, etc., erected in Karnak by this priest and his descendants, see: CGC 42206, JWAB,I, 25-34, II, 441-6, pls. 4-7:A.2; CGC 42207, JWAB,I, 35-43, II, 447-452, pls. 8-11:A.3; CGC 42208, JWAB,I, 44-62, II, 453-61, pls. 12-14:A.4; CGC 42210, JWAB,I, 63-82, II, 462-69, pls. 15-17:A.5; CGC 42211, JWAB,I, 83-99, II, 470-81, pls. 18-21: A.6; CGC 42213, JWAB,I, 100-07, II, 482-87:A.7; CGC 42214, JWAB,I, 108-111, II, 488-89, pls. 22-23:A.8; Karnak N., T.35, JWAB,I, 275-77:B.16.

For a small chapel of Thoth and Amun south of the Sacred Lake at Karnak, renewing one of Haremhab, see Goyon and Traunecker in Cahiers de Karnak VII, 1982, 355-66; the simple form of cartouche, Osorkon Beloved of Amun, suggests that Osorkon I built the present edifice; the otherwise unknown 2nd Prophet of Amun, Bakenamun, whose son helped decorate the tiny edifice, might well belong to the long reign of Osorkon I.

At S 270, p.311, n.385: BM 1224, brief notice by JWAB,I, 257:B.7.

Chapter 19

S 513   At **S** 273, p.315: New translations of statue CGC 42225 of the aged Nebneteru iii, see M. Lichtheim, Ancient Egyptian Literature,III, 1980, 18-24; full ed., JWAB,I, 117-135, II, 494-505, pls. 28-29:A.10. For the hitherto unpublished statue CGC *42252 belonging to the Scribe of Correspondence , Prophet of Amun, and Treasury-Scribe of Amun's Estate, Nesamenope, see JWAB,I, 272-3:B.14.

At **S** 274, p.315: A further private statue that bears the cartouches of Harsiese is the unpublished CGC *42254 (J.37374), JWAB,I, 263-66:B.10. Also here (plus at **SS** 157:6, 160), on the Coptos monument of Harsiese A's son, see Yoyotte, Annuaire de l'Ecole des Hautes Etudes, Ve Section, 86(1978), 163-9, with its hymns to Hathor, Osiris, etc.   At **S** 275, p.316 & n.404 end: For the cult of Harsiese A attested in the 25th/26th Dynasties, add the statuette of Wenennufer in Cambridge (Fitzwilliam Museum, E.11.1937), published by C. Insley, JEA 65(1979), 167-9, pls. 30-31. At **S** 278 (p.317): The Pyudu as Libyans in Libya; see on this term, E. Graefe, Enchoria 5 (1975), 13-17.

S 514   At p.319 (**S** 277(iv)): For the officer Harmose, add the Louvre item published by Barguet in Melanges Maspero,I:4, 1961, 7-10, as pointed out by Jacquet-Gordon, BiOr 32(1975), 359, **S** 3. Statue BM 1146 (p.319, n.416), cf. JWAB,I, 267:B.11, plus the block, ibidem, 268:B.12. For the statue BM 1007 of Ankhrenpnefer, cf. ibidem, 269-71:B.13. At **S** 278, p.320: For text of Osorkon II at Karnak, add Vernus, BIFAO 75(1975), 2, **S** B, and pl.2. At **S** 279, p.320f., & n.424, on jubilee of Osorkon II, add W. Barta, SAK 6 (1978), 25-42.

At **S** 282 (p.323 & n.445): Jacquet-Gordon (BiOr 32(1975), 360, **S** 6) would refer Basa's mention of a Karomama to the Queen of Takeloth II, "as . . assured by her titles". This, I fail to see, as the texts on Berlin 2278 (Aeg. Inschr.,II, 206/LD,III, 256h) clearly read: "Daughter of the King's Wife of the Lord of the Two Lands, Mistress of the Two Lands", with cartouches above and opposite (the latter with an obscure text before it). At the base, surely read: "[God's Wife of] Amun (obelisk-sign), Karomama Merytmut. Hence one expects the God's Wife, not the Queen.

S 515   At **SS** 284/285, pp.324f.: In the cultural field, Levantine ivory-carvers made extensive use of Egyptian motifs in the decorations that they turned out to adorn furnishings, often looted and appreciated by Assyrian kings warring in the Levant. On these, see now G. Herrmann, Ivories from SW 37, Fort Shalmaneser (=Ivories from Nimrud (1949-63), Fasc. IV), 1986, esp. Chapter VI.

S 516   At **S** 290 (iv), p.328 n.468, family of the vizier Nakhtefmut C, - see just above, **SS** 479-480. For statues CGC 42226-8, see JWAB,I, 136-167, II, 506-526, pls. 30-40:A.11-13. The "Cairo block" (Cb of p.211, nn.95,97 & genealogies above) is J.29248, on which see now JWAB,I, 168-9, II, 527-9, pls. 41-43:A.14.   The ladies Ir-Bast-udja-tjau and Di-Ese-nesyt (above, p.328 end) are better regarded as daughters of Takeloth III, not II; see just above, **S** 489. At **S** 291, p.330: On Chronicle of Prince Osorkon, add JWAB,I, 290-294:B.22.   At **S** 292, p.331, n.485: Add E. Hornung, Altägyptische Höllen-vorstellungen, 1968, 27f. Again p.331, n.486: For Year 11 block Louvre E. 3336, cf. also JWAB,I, 287-9:B.21. And p.331, and n.488: Despite recent attempts to assert the contrary, a plain reading of the Chronicle of Prince Osorkon does <u>not</u> permit with any degree of likelihood the reading into it of a supposed lunar eclipse under Takeloth II; see above, **SS** 454-461 with full discussion. This was also endorsed by J. von Beckerath, OLZ 74(1979), 10, **S** 1.

Chapter 20

S 517   AT **S** 296 end (p.335): Pediamennebnesttawy A was grandson-in-law of Takeloth III, not II; see just above, **S** 487, references. Perhaps one may add here the donation-stela of a Niuma(r)tiped C (titles lost), of Year 4 of [prenomen, lost] Shoshenq Beloved of Amun, Si-Bast, Neter ⟨heqa Iunu?⟩ , published by Graefe, Armant 12(1974), 3-9 with 2 pls. As Shoshenq V usually eschewed such epithets until late in his reign, this Year 4 perhaps belongs to Shoshenq III (not to IV, who was not Si-Bast). At p.337, n.518, reverse the numbering of Iuput I and II (as II is now Usimare, leaving the prenomen of Iuput I unknown). At **S** 298, p.337/8, nn.521,523,524: For Karnak Priestly Annals Nos.1-2, see JWAB,I, 223-8, II, 566-70:A.21. Possibly to the early decades of Shoshenq III, during the continued rivalry of Prince Osorkon and Harsiese B, may belong the appeal at Karnak to Amun by the wḏ-priests of Amun in the presence of a Harsiese as governor in the South - see Vernus, Cahiers de Karnak VI, 1980, 215-233, and pl.53. At **S** 302, pp.341/2: The prenomen Usimare Setepenamun/re is now generally attributed

to Iuput II, so all monuments in this name must likewise best be assigned
to him, not Iuput I; see just above, SS 446-450, pp.542-4. At S 305, pp.343-
344 & n.566, see now P. Vernus, BIFAO 76(1976), 3-15, pls. 5-6 (Cairo, J.
36728) for this monument.

S 518   At S 306, p.345: Under Mendes, delete mention of Smendes in Year
21 of Iuput I as son of Harnakht A. This Smendes lived under Year 21 of
Iuput II, hence was probably great-grandson of Harnakht A; cf. just above,
S 449 (p.543); Table 22a revised (below), following Kitchen, CdE 52(1977),
42-44.

Chapter 21

S 519   At p.350, n.604: delete mention of Smendes and his dating by the
23rd Dynasty, as this is a later Smendes (under Iuput II). At S 311, p.351
and n.610: On Ker's stela, see now Y. Koenig, ASAE 68(1982), 111-113, a
revised text and transcription (improving on YMM).

   At S 312, p.351: In late 1985, Dr. A.J. Spencer very kindly made known
to me his view that the 23rd Dynasty (at least in part) was based not at
Leontopolis, but probably at Hermopolis; he was sceptical of the Leontopolis
royal tomb; see his paper, JEA 72(1986), in press. His suggestion is worthy
of consideration, but not necessarily convincing. The tomb found at Tell
Moqdam (ASAE 21(1921), 21-27, see its plan, p.22, fig.1) has all the marks
of a typical royal burial of the 21st/22nd Dynasty era, having twin burial-
chambers with the queen in the south chamber; her husband may have occupied the north chamber (burial, destroyed). This is all very reminiscent of
the twin-chambered tomb of Psusennes I, albeit on a smaller scale. That
we have here a proper tomb is clear from the presence of mythological
scenes on the walls of the south chamber at least (ASAE 21, p.23), like
what is found in the tombs at Tanis (Psusennes I to Shoshenq III). The
queen's name, Kama, is closest of all to Kamama (rather than Karomama),
Kamama being the form best attested for the mother of Osorkon III; Kama
need be nothing more than an abbreviation used in the limited space of a
scarab-base. The contents of her water-ruined but unplundered burial are
fully consistent with it being a royal burial of this period: a series of splendid gold jewels of excellent workmanship; a massive granite sarcophagus,
of reused stone, and a set of four canopic vessels, at least one being
second-hand (of a lady Pipu). The burial of Shoshenq IV may well have oc-

cupied the other chamber (traces of a smashed coffin were found). If all this be so, then there seems no reason to doubt that other rulers of the 23rd Dynasty were both based there and buried there; since Naville's dig, no proper full-scale excavation has ever been conducted at Tell Moqdam, and much will have been destroyed, as all too often in the Delta.

It should also be remembered that the 23rd Dynasty was not recognised only in Upper Egypt (Thebes, Hermopolis, etc.). It was also recognised by people at Memphis in the north, under Pedubast I (see above, **S** 300, p.339f. - two stelae of Ewelhon A and probably Pimai). And from the Delta probably comes a statuette of Pedubast I (p.341, above), and a stela from Bubastis. Osorkon III was seemingly tacitly recognised by Harnakht B at Mendes (Year 11 text), while his son Smendes V dated in Year 21 of Iuput II. So, this Dynasty was acknowledged in the North alongside the 22nd Dynasty (as befitted a parallel, neighbouring line) and not only in the South.

S 520   At **S** 313 (ii), p.352: Additional monuments of Osorkon III hail from Middle Egypt. The British Museum excavations at Hermopolis have produced the shattered remains of a once-splendid donation-stela of Year 15 of Osorkon III, showing also his queen Karo-atjet and a prince [name lost]; see A.J. Spencer et al., British Museum Expedition to Middle Egypt, Ashmunein (1982), 1983, 12-13, 88, fig.26 and pls. 6a/b (No.1983/77). In a Bulletin of the recent Japanese excavations at Tehneh (Acoris) is illustrated their find of a further stela of Osorkon III, [Year 6?/12?], concerning a land-endowment for Amun, Lion foremost upon the River-bank.

S 521   At **S** 314, p.353, n.621: Delete the 2nd Prophet Neshorbehdet here. On the 3rd prophets of Amun (p.353), delete present text, and substitute: Holders of the 3rd Prophetship of Amun are also veiled from our view after Pimai (c.850 B.C.?) until c.775 B.C. with Nebneteru iv, possibly followed by Amenhotep (c.760/750), and then Wenennufer called Iryiry (c.750-725), all these three during the reign of Osorkon III to early Iuput II. See Table 14 revised below, and just above, **S** 487, p.566.

For the 4th Prophets, after Nakhtefmut B, read now 'contemporary of Pedubast I to Osorkon III, then to a probable Djed-Khons-ef-ankh F and Nakhtefmut G (under Osorkon III and Takeloth III), and ultimately to Djed-Khons-ef-ankh D (under Iuput II).' At **S** 316 (ii), p.355: Between Ker and Ankh-Hor now comes a chief Rudamun (c.745-740; see Table 21A revised, below) - stela, Year 30 of Shoshenq V, Berlandini, BIFAO 78(1978) 147-163.

At S 316 (iii), p.355 & n.647: For the Louvre aegis (E.7167) of Osorkon (IV) and Tadibast, see J. Berlandini, Hommages Sauneron,I, 1979, 98-109, pl. 16. At S 314 (iii), p.352f., and S 317, p.356: Osorkon III and his son Takeloth as high priest of Amun appear on intercolumnar panels reused in the foundations of Taharqa's colonnade before the Temple of Khons; see Traunecker in Cahiers de Karnak VI, 1980, 55-56, pl. 13b, and cf. Cahiers de Karnak VII, 1982, 321-23 passim.

At S 318 (ii), probably add now a new high priest of Amun, Osorkon F, who may have officiated under Takeloth III (coregent and king), Rudamun and Iuput II until shortly before Piankhy's visit to Thebes; see above, S 485. At S 319 (iii), p.357: Twin genealogies on roof of Khons Temple, see Yoyotte, BSFE 77/78(1977), 31-54, and Graefe, Unt. Inst. Gottesgemahlin,I, 1985, 112-114:n 130. For a statue-base probably of Takeloth III, with a queen Betjet, see J. Berlandini, Hommages Sauneron,I, 1979, 92-98, pl. 15. Delete reference here to Neshorbehdet as 2nd Prophet of Amun at this date, and likewise to Pediamennebnesttawy B as 3rd Prophet then. Instead, insert: By this reign, Amenhotep was perhaps 3rd Prophet of Amun, to be followed by Wenennufer A/Iryiry. Under 4th prophets, read: Nakhtefmut G was probably succeeded by Djed-Khons-ef-ankh D in the seventh generation; see above, SS 486-88 on all these people, and Table 14 revised, below.

S 522   In the Thebaid, Takeloth III probably married-off two daughters to local worthies: Ir-Bast-udja-tjau to Pakhuru, and Di-Ese-nesyt to Nesipaqashuty B (who each became vizier).   A third daughter Tentsai (named after her grandmother) was progenitor of an 8th-century Theban priest appropriately named Ankh-Takeloth (statue Vienna 5085); cf. H. De Meulenaere, CdE 57(1982), 218-222, figs. 1-2.

At S 320, p.358 & n.666: On the names and reign of Kashta, see K.-H. Priese, ZÄS 98(1970), 16-23.

At S 321, p.360: The double date of Wadi Gasus, Years 12/19, should be referred to Piankhy and Iuput II respectively (in 736 B.C.); see Kitchen, CdE 52(1977), 44 and references, and just above, S 450.   At S 323, pp.360/1: Iuput II - to whom should now be attributed all data previously referred to Iuput I (pp.341/2, S 302, above), except for Nile level No.26, Karnak.

Chapter 22

S 523   At S 325ff., pp.363ff.: Inscriptions of 25th Dynasty period, cf. Leclant in Textes et Langages de l'Egypte pharaonique,II, 123-135. Also sur-

veys of the 25th Dynasty, cf. Leclant, Annuaire, Collège de France 82
(1982), 497ff.; 83(1983), 527ff.; 84(1984), 585ff.   At p.364 & n.699: The
Stela of Piankhy and his campaign in Egypt have received much attention.
See K.-H. Priese, ZÄS 98(1970), 24-32; language of the Napata stelae, idem,
ZÄS 98(1972), 99-124; T.J. Logan and J.G. Westenholz, JARCE 9(1972), 111-
119. Full publication of the great stela, N.-C. Grimal, La stèle triomphal
de Pi(ankh)y au Musée du Caire,.., 1981; recent translation, M. Lichtheim,
Ancient Egyptian Literature,III, 1980, 66-84. Other studies, see: A. Spalinger, SAK 7(1979), 273-301; RdE 31(1979), 66-80 (negative forms); JSSEA 11
(1981), 37-58 (army and its orthography). Also, D. Kessler, SAK 9(1981),
227-251.

S 524   At S 330, p.370 & n.73): On the name of Pi(ankh)ye, see more
fully K.-H. Priese, MIO 14(1968), 166ff., and G. Vittmann, Orientalia 43
(1974), 12-16; it may be that Piye is the real, Nubian name of the ruler,
the ankh-sign serving as determinative, and also to express an Egyptian
equivalent of the Nubian name, i.e. Piankhy.   Here, delete mention of Neshorbehdet.   For translation of texts on one of Harwa i's statues, see M.
Lichtheim, Ancient Egyptian Literature,III, 1980, 24-28.   At p.370, n.731:
P. Leiden F.1942/5.15, see B. Menu, RdE 36(1985), 74-75 (following on S.P.
Vleeming, OMRO 61(1980), 1-17 & pl.1; P. Vatican 10574, cf.Menu, RdE 36
(1985), 75-76.

S 525   At S 331, p.371: Delete the supposed local king Menkheperre
Khmuny; rather, one should read Menkheperre Pi(ankh)y on the famous stela
Louvre C.100 (i.e., Piankhy himself); see J. von Beckerath, OLZ 74(1979),
10, S 3, after collation; so also, in his Handbuch der Ägyptischen Königsnamen, 1984, 108 (T.1/E.2), 111 n.7, and 269 (T.1/E.2). Mutirdis would then
have been a daughter of Piankhy. I foresaw this possible solution long ago;
see already, above, p.98, n.71 end, and p.371, n.739 end!

   Instead of Khmuny, we should add the kinglet Pedinemty (or Pedi'anty),
at Hermopolis or elsewhere, for whom see Weill, BIFAO 49(1950), 57-65; von
Beckerath, Handbuch, 107 (XXIVA/d) & n.4, 268. For Thutemhab, cf. also
H. Wild, RdE 24(1972), 209-215.   On Heracleopolis, cf. general account, M.
G. Mokhtar, Ihnâsya El-Medina, 1983.

S 526   At S 332, p.372, n.741: For Athens stela of Tefnakht, see full edition by R. El-Sayed, Documents relatifs à Sais et ses Divinites, 1975, 37-

53 and pl. 7. At SS 333-334, pp.372-375: Osorkon IV as So; see additionally
above, SS 463, 464 end. For a possible Sî who might even have been an
(O)so(rkon), cf. already above, pp.97/98:XVI, and especially p.342, n.551
(abbreviation for Osorkon III?). The study by D.E. Schwab, ZÄS 104(1977),
131-141, adds nothing new, except for wrongly doubting the correct reading
Re'e (for Sib'e) established by Borger; as my cuneiformist colleague Mr. A.
R. Millard kindly showed me, Schwab had failed to recognise archaic forms
of signs used to write Re'e. At S 336, p.376: The death or disappearance
of Osorkon IV could have fallen in 715, 714, or 713 B.C.; early 712 is the
bottom limit merely, not a definitive date, cf. already S 464 just above.
On Nahal Musur, cf. A.F. Rainey, Tel Aviv 9(1982), 31-32. On Assyrian
interest in trade with Egypt, cf. M. Elat, JAOS 98(1978), 20ff.

Chapter 23

S 527   At SS 339/340: The dates given are still a valid option; the alternative is to date the reign of Shabako up to 2 years later (he dying in 700
B.C.), ending in a 2-year coregency with Shebitku (702-690). See above, S
468 for full discussion. As there shown, the coregency hypothesis is possible
but is neither essential nor preferable. The hard fact remains that Egyptian
policy changed over to the offensive in 702/701 B.C., indicating a new hand
in control; so either Shebitku succeeded Shabako directly then (the best
view), or became full coregent, taking over the direction of affairs from
a presumably ailing Shabako.

At S 341, p.380: With Spalinger, JARCE 10(1973), 100, the "Pir'u of
Musri" ('Pharaoh of Egypt') with whom Iamani of Ashdod made alliance in
713 B.C. should probably be identified with a local Delta dynast, perhaps
Osorkon IV, but not with his Nubian overlord Shabako - particularly in view
of the altered translation of the passage "which (land) belongs (now) to
Kush" as "(the border of Egypt) which is (at) the border/territory of Kush",
cf. Spalinger, p.97 & n.17. Or with my colleague Mr. A.R. Millard, one may
render:"to the border of Egypt which is at the territory of Meluhha (Nubia),"
and cf. Chicago Assyrian Dictionary, 7:I/J, 1960, 313b (itû, 1-3). Certainly
in 712 B.C., with Osorkon IV dead and gone, Iamani fled to Shabako. On
p.380, in n.778, all that is said there still holds good, except that Pir'u
is not used of the Nubian ruler. P.380, n.779: Yurco (Serapis 6(1982), 237-
238) re-activates an old suggestion by Olmstead that Shabako's seals from
Nineveh might have come from documents sent to Sennacherib in 701,

rather than to Sargon II in 712. But this is all theoretical and uncertain. One also notes a seal-impression found in Stratum III at Megiddo, and atrributed to Shabako on Rowe's authority (Lamon & Shipton, Megiddo I, 1939, 132, pl. 115:4 and notes); the proposed reading Neferkare as Shabako's prenomen is possible, but frankly uncertain.

At S 342, p.381, n.780: Shabako's works at Memphis, cf. E.R. Russman, Brooklyn Museum Annual 10(1968/69), 87ff. (statue); Leclant, MDIK 37(1981), 289-292, fig.1, pl. 44a-c; Berlandini, BSEG 9/10(1984/85), 31-40 (fragments of Mut-chapel). At S 344, p.382: Year 10 of Shabako, in legal documents of a family also attested under Taharqa, cf. Menu, RdE 36(1985), 76-77.

S 528   At S 345.2, p.383: Shebitku. On the importance of the "imperialising" tone adopted by Shebitku in stark contrast with the simpler, archaic style of titulary dominant for the previous 70 years and for the rest of Egypt's independent history thereafter, see above S 470 with references; this was not accidental.

At S 346, pp.383-6: The clash with Assyria in 701 B.C. For a fuller and improved account of the clash of the Assyrian forces under Sennacherib with the petty states of Judah and Philistia and Egypto-Nubian forces, see Kitchen,"Egypt, the Levant and Assyria in 701 BC" in Fontes atque Pontes, Festgabe für Hellmut Brunner, 1983, 243-253 with two slightly revised maps (improving on those given above, p.384), especially in the light of fresh additional Assyrian data dealt with by N. Naaman, BASOR No.214(1974), 25-39, and in VT 29(1979), 61-86. On the role of Taharqa as prince, and only termed 'king' in references written after 681 B.C., see also above, S 467, 469; the charge of 'untold confusion' here (cf. Redford, Biblical Archaeology Today, 204, n.58) is merely its author's personal misconception. And clear, unambiguous cuneiform evidence for any further Palestinian campaign by Sennacherib after 701 has yet to be produced. Cf. also M. Elat, in Y. Aharoni (ed.), Lachish V, 1975, 61ff. (now partly overtaken by more recent studies). An important study (based on the minimal acceptable chronology for Shabako/Shebitku, invoking a coregency) is that of F. Yurco, Serapis 6(1982), 221-240. He too notes (p.224) - as I did - the strategic use of separate army-divisions by both Assyrians and Egyptians. On the Assyrian and Hebrew narratives, see the careful study by A.R. Millard, Tyndale Bulletin 36(1985), 61-77, in contrast to the outmoded, 19th-century, and unscientific treatment by R.E. Clements, Isaiah and the Deliverance of Jerusalem, 1980; the paper by D.N. Fewell, JSOT 34(1986), 79-90, examines some literary usages of the narrative in 2 Kings 18-19, but wildly out-of-date on historical aspects. At p.385, n.818: For the reliefs of the seige of Lachish and correlation with the remains found at Tell ed-Duweir (almost certainly the site of ancient Lachish), see D. Ussishkin, The Conquest of Lachish by Sennacherib, 1982. The Lachish destroyed by the Assyrians is almost certainly that of Tell ed-Duweir level III, which ended in a massive destruction; cf. (e.g.) D. Ussishkin, Tel Aviv 4(1977), 28-60; and A.F. Rainey in Y. Aharoni (etc.), Lachish V, 1975, 47ff.

S 529   At S 349, pp.388-9: Taharqa erected stelae on the western desert routes beyond Dahshur, on which he boasts of reviewing his troops and of going on military exercises with them, to the Fayum and back to Memphis; see H. Altenmüller and A.M. Moussa, MDIK 37(1981), 331-337, and more fully in SAK 9(1981), 57-84. This perhaps dates to the king's early years, before his clashes with Assyria. At p.388, n.836: The abnormal hieratic documents of Years 3, 5, 6 of Taharqa, see Menu, RdE 36(1985), 77-81, with earlier literature. At p.389 & n.840: On translation of stelae Kawa IV and V, see Rainey, Tel Aviv 3(1976), 38-41. At p.389, n.846: For a stela of Taharqa decreeing the restoration and re-endowment of a small temple of Amun in the Estate of Ptah at Memphis, see D. Meeks, Hommages Sauneron,I, 1979, 221-259, pl. 38. Also at Memphis, add to p.386, n.825: A block of Taharqa, Leclant, MDIK 37(1981), 292-4, & fig.2. At Thebes, a donation stela of Year 21 commemorates a private chapel for "Osiris who delivers his servant in the Netherworld", see Graefe and Wassef, MDIK 35 (1979), 103-118, pl. 17. At S 350, p.390: Additional monuments of the God's Wife of Amun, Shepenupet II, Leclant, MDIK 37(1981), 294-6, pl. 45a/b. For the 'high temple' of Taharqa north of the sacred lake at Karnak, see R.A. Parker, J. Leclant, J.-C. Goyon, The Edifice of Taharqa by the Sacred Lake of Karnak, 1979.

S 530   At SS 352ff., pp.391ff.: The relations of Egypt and Assyria under Taharqa have called forth several recent studies: A. Spalinger, Orientalia 43(1974), 295-326 (on Esarhaddon); idem, JAOS 94(1974), 316-328 (on Assurbanipal); idem, CdE 53(1978), 22-47 (Taharqa; clash of 701); A.K. Grayson, JSSEA 11(1981), 85-88 (general outlines only). In Spalinger's paper in CdE 53, most of the supposed evidence for the military pose of Taharqa is mere traditional formulae, reflecting no known reality. And a statue-fragment found in Assyria is nothing more than Assyrian loot. His treatment of the events in 701 B.C. (CdE 53, 39ff.) is careless and misleading (e.g., wrongly attributing two campaigns for Taharqa to this author); for other shortcomings in Spalinger's CdE study, see (e.g.) Yurco, Serapis 6(1982), 228 n.19 end 224 n.24, 225 n.40, 229 n.70, 230 nn.73,74, 231 n.80, 232 n.89.

§ 531   Rather more interesting (as Spalinger also realised) are the fragments of texts near the barque-sanctuary of Amun at Karnak, formerly taken to be of Shoshenq I, and now known to belong to Taharqa (Vernus, BIFAO 75(1975), 1-66, pls. 1-5). In the East text, Taharqa addresses Amun in all his majesty (Vernus, p.30), and reflects on his role as pharaoh, invoking Amun's care and aid (p.31). We read: 'O Amun, what I have done in/for the land of Nubia . . . [? benefaction]s, when (m-dỉ) I do/did it/them, for/with your tribute of the land of Khurru, which they had turned aside from you, O Amun . . '. In the even more broken West text (Vernus, pp.49ff.), Taharqa mentions: '[. . . .] Nubia; grant that I may bring it to you from the land of Nubia [. . .] Kush.' Later on is mentioned: '. . . everything which comes to you, (pertaining) to Nubia - your [. . .], (your) red bulls, . . (and other products...)'.

§ 532 The gleanings for knowledge of Taharqa's activities are very limited. Fleeting references to Nubia and Khurru (Palestine) are often too broken or obscure to permit of any definite historical conclusions. Revenues for Amun from Nubia might be expected (as from within Egypt itself); but tribute from the Levant must have been more an aspiration than a reality.

§ 533   At p.392, n.875: On Nespamedu (Assyrian Ishpimatu), as ruling at Thinis not Aswan, see H. De Meulenaere, CdE 53(1978), 230-231, and A. Leahy, GM 35(1970), 31-39.

At § 354, p.393: Tantamani may have been a distant cousin of Taharqa, as a son of Shabako, not Shebitku; see A. Leahy, GM 83(1984), 43-45. At p.393 & n.880: The pyramid WT.1 asigned to Taharqa at Sedeinga should be noted (with Hornung, OrAnt 13(1974), 336); see M. Schiff-Georgini, Kush 13 (1965), 116-125, and J. Leclant, CRAIBL:1970, 249-252. But later excavation (1982) has shown reuse of Taharqa fragments utilised to block the entry to another pyramid-tomb. Hence, his fragments at WT.1 might also be a reuse, which could date tomb WT.1 later than Taharqa, and have no bearing on the location of Taharqa's own burial. See Leclant in Studien zu Sprache und Religion Ägyptens (Festschrift Westendorf),II, 1113-1117, esp. 1116f. At § 351, p.390: Texts from CGC 42237 and Berlin 17271 are translated by M. Lichtheim,Anc. Eg. Literature,III, 30-33. At § 356, p.395: Later Greek

traditions about Nechepsos, see J. Ray, JEA 60(1974), 255-6. On name Pasenhor (p.397 above), cf. Leahy, GM 62(1983), 37-48.

At p.393, n.881: For the Dream-stela of Tantamani, and the later Napatan stelae, see the new edition by N.-C. Grimal, Quatre stèles napatéennes
au Musée du Caire (JE 48863-48866), 1981, with further volume(s) to follow.

Chapter 24

S 534   At S 359, p.399 & n.923: Tomb of Tantamani, cf. now Ali Ahmed
Gasm El-Seed, RdE 36(1985), 67-72. At S 360ff., pp.400ff.: The rise of
Psammetichus I is further considered by Spalinger, JARCE 13(1976), 131-
147; the later years, idem, JARCE 15(1978), 49-57. At SS 365ff., pp.404ff.:
On the Saite Dynasty, cf. Spalinger, Orientalia 47(1978), 12-36. At S 366,
p.405: Cf. also for Psammetichus I and Nubia, S.M. Burstein, JSSEA 14
(1984), 31-34.

At pp.404/5: A further statue of Aba, high steward of the God's Wife
of Amun, Nitocris, see S. Abdel-Hamid, Cahiers de Karnak VII, 1982, 367-
375 (including illustrations).   The statue of a 4th Prophet of Amun, Nesmin,
published by J.-C. Goyon, Cahiers de Karnak VII, 281-287, is considered to
belong to the period from the 30th Dynasty to the early Ptolemies (ibidem,
281); hence, it will not be of the Nesmin of c.630 B.C. (Table 14 revised,
below).

At S 369, p.407 & n.969: For accession of Amasis II and interventions
by Nebuchadnezzar II, cf. E. Edel, GM 29(1978), 13-20.

PART FIVE
Excursus B

S 535   Additions. At S 381, after No.11: Add Year 7 (+x), O. CGC.25,575/6
here. At S 382, No.22: Add Graffito 3492 (A.F. Sadek, Graffiti de la Montagne Thébaine, IV/4, 197). And after No.25: Add Year 14, O. CGC.25,577.

Excursus E

S 536   Many suggested corrections for identifications of mainly lesser sites
will be found in S. Ahituv, Canaanite Toponyms in Ancient Egyptian Documents, 1984, passim; despite his p.21, this list is not boustrophedon.

REVISED TABLES

TABLE *3 Revised

The 22nd and 23rd Dynasties

About B.C.:   *22nd Dynasty*

  945-924: Shoshenq I, Hedjkheperre Setepenre (21 y)

  924-889: Osorkon I, Sekhemkheperre Setepenre (35 y)

     *c.*890: Shoshenq II, Heqakheperre Setepenre (*x* yrs; co-rgt only)

  889-874: Takeloth I, [*Prenomen unknown*] (15 y)

  874-850: Osorkon II, Usimare Setepenamun (24 y)

*c.*870-860: Harsiese, Hedjkheperre Setepenamun (*c.*10 y?; co-rgt only)

  850-825: Takeloth II, Hedjkheperre Setepenre (25 y)

  825-773: Shoshenq III, Usimare Setepenre/amun (52 y)

              [*Start of Dyn. 23*]

  773-767: Pimay, Usimare Setepenre/amun (6 y)

  767-730: Shoshenq V, Akheperre (37 y)

  730-715?/713?: Osorkon IV, Akheperre Setepenamun (15/17 y)

23rd Dynasty

  818-793: Pedubast I, Usimare Setepenamun (25 y)

  804-803?: Iuput I, [*Prenomen unknown*] (co-rgt only?; *x* yrs)

  793-787: Shoshenq IV, Usimare Meryamun (6 y)

  787-759: Osorkon III, Usimare Setepenamun (28 y)

  764-757: Takeloth III, Usimare (Setepenamun) (7 y; 5, co-rgt)

  757-754: Rudamun, Usimare Setepenamun (*c.* 3 y?)

  754-720: Iuput II, Usimare Setepenamun (*c.* 34/39 y)

  (or 715)

(720-715: Shoshenq VI, Wasneterre Setepenre (*c.* 5 y??);

        existence, doubtful).

TABLE *4 (Revised Parts)

The 24th-26th Dynasties

About B.C.:   *24th Dynasty: Preferred Dates*

727-720: Tefnakht I, Shepsesre (7 or 8 y)
720-715: Bakenranef, Wahkare (5 y)

24th Dynasty: Alternative Dates

727-719: Tefnakht I (8 y)
719-713: Bakenranef (6 y)

Proto-Saite Dynasty

715- or
713-695: 'Ammeris' - Nubian governor? (18/20 y?)
695-688: Stephinates - 'Tefnakht II?' (7 y)
688-672: Nekauba - Nechepsos (16 y)
672-664: Necho I, Menkheperre (8 y)

25th Dynasty: Preferred Dates

*c.*780-760: Alara (*c.* 20 y?)
*c.*760-747: Kashta, Maatre (*c.* 13 y?)
  747-716: Pi(ankh)y, Usimare, Menkheperre, Sneferre (31 y)
  716-702: Shabako, Neferkare (14 y)
  702-690: Shebitku, Djedkaure (12 y)
  690-664: Taharqa, Nefertemkhure (26 y)
  664-656: Tantamani, Bakare (8 y, in S. Egypt)

25th Dynasty: Alternative Dates

(- Alara, *Kashta,* as above)
  747-714: Pi(ankh)y, (33 y)
  714-700: Shabako, (14 y, 2 as co-rgt)
  702-690: Shebitku, (12 y, 2 as co-rgt)
  690-664: Taharqa, (26 y)
  664-656: Tantamani, (8 y, S. Egypt)

TABLE *6 Revised

Ready-reckoner: Contemporary Years of the Twenty-second to Twenty-fifth
Dynasties

Date B.C.:	Dyn. 22: Shoshenq III	Dyn. 23: Pedubast I	Dyn. 23: Co-regents
825	1		
824	2		
823	3		
822	4		
821	5		
820	6		
819	7		
818	8	1	
817	9	2	
816	10	3	
815	11	4	
814	12	5	
813	13	6	
812	14	7	
811	15	8	
810	16	9	
809	17	10	
808	18	11	
807	19	12	
806	20	13	
805	21	14	*Iuput I*
804	22	15	1
803	23	16	2
802	24	17	?
801	25	18	
800	26	19	
799	27	20	
798	28	21	
797	29	22	
796	30	23	
795	31	24	

Date B.C.:	Dyn. 22: Shoshenq III	Dyn. 23: Pedubast I	Dyn. 23: Co-regents
794	32	25	
793	33	26	
		Shoshenq IV	
"	"	———— 1	
792	34	2	
791	35	3	
790 ————	36	4	
789	37 ————	5	
788	38	6	
787	39	7	
		Osorkon III	
"	" ————	1	
786	40	2	
785 ————	41	3	
784	42	4	
783	43 ————	5	
782	44	6	
781	45	7	
780 ————	46	8	
779	47	9	
778	48 ————	10	
777	49	11	
776	50	12	
775 ————	51	13	
774	52	14	
773	53 ————	15	
"	*Pimay*		
"	———— 1	"	
772	2	16	
771	3 ————	17	
770 ————	4	18	
769	5	19	
768	6 ————	20	
767	7	21	

Date B.C.:	Dyn. 22: Shoshenq V	Dyn. 23: Osorkon III	Dyn. 23: Co-regents	Dyn. 25: Nubia
	Shoshenq V			
767	1	21		
766	2	22		
765	3	23	Takeloth III	
764	4	24	1	
763	5	25	2	
762	6	26	3	
761	7	27	4	
760	8	28	5	
759	9	29	6	
758	10	Takeloth III, alone.		
"	"	7		
757	11	8		
		Rudamun		
"	"	1		
756	12	2		
755	13	3		
754	14	4		
		Iuput II		
"	"	1		
753	15	2		
752	16	3		
751	17	4		
750	18	5		
749	19	6		
748	20	7		Piankhy
747	21	8		1
746	22	9		2
745	23	10		3
744	24	11		4
743	25	12		5
742	26	13		6
741	27	14		7
740	28	15		8
739	29	16		9

Date B.C.:	Dyn. 22: Shoshenq V	Dyn. 23: Iuput II	Dyn. 25: Piankhy	Dyn. 24: Sais
738	30	17 ———	10	
737	31	18	11	
736	32	19	12	
735	——— 33 ———	20	13	
734	34	21	14	
733	35	22 ———	15	
732	36	23	16	
731	37	24	17	
730	——— 38 ———	25	18	
	Osorkon IV			
"	——— 1	"	"	
729	2	26	19	
728	3	27 ———	20	*Tefnakht I*
727	4	28	21 ———	1
726	5	29	22	2
725	——— 6 ———	30	23	3
724	7	31	24	4
723	8	32 ———	25 ———	5
722	9	33	26	6
721	10	34	27	7
720	——— 11 ———	35 ———	28	8
		(Shoshenq VI?)		*Bakenranef*
"	"	——— (36/1?)	"	——— 1
719	12	(37/2?)	29	2 (1?)
718	——— 13	(38/3?) ———	30	3 (2?)
717	14	(39/4?)	31	4 (3?)
716	15 ———	(40/5?)	32 ———	5 (4?)
			Shabako	
"	"	"	1	6 (5?)
715	——— 16 ———	(41/6?) ———	2 ———	(6?)
714	17		3 (1?) ———	(6 end?)
713	18		4 (2?)	
712			5 (3?)	

Bracketed numbers under 24th/25th Dyns. are on alternative dates.

TABLES   7-11

Tables 7-9: 21st Dynasty Genealogy. Changes, see above SS 436-441

Table 11: 25th Dynasty Genealogy. See above, S 473B.

TABLE *12

(Revised Parts)

Marriages of Princesses to Commoners

22nd Dynasty

4. Tashepenbast, d. of Shoshenq I, to 3PA Djed-Thut-ef-ankh A (S   166, 245)

5. Istweret A, d. of Harsiese, to 2,4PA Harsiese C (S 184)

6. Tjesbastperu, d. of Osorkon II, to HPM Takeloth (SS 81, 281)

7. Shepensopdet B, d. of Takeloth II, to 4PA Djed-Khons-ef-ankh C (SS 184 290)

8. Istweret B, d. of Takeloth II, to vizier Nakhtefmut C (SS 180, 290, 480)

9. Tentsepeh D, d. of Takeloth II, to Ptah-udj-ankhef (S 291)

10. Ankhes-en-Shoshenq, d. of Shoshenq III, to one Iuf-o (S 305,ii)

23rd Dynasty

11. Ir-Bast-udja-tjau, d. of Takeloth III, to vizier Pakhuru (S 489)

12. Di-Ese-nesyt, the d. of Takeloth III, to vizier Nesipaqashuty B (S 489)

13. Ankh-Karoma, d. of Takeloth III, to 3PA Pediamennebnesttawy A/B (S 484)

14. Tentsai, d. of Takeloth III, to official Nakhtefmut (S 484)

15. Ir-Bast-udja-nefu, d. of Rudamun, to Pef-tjau-awy-Bast who became local king in Heracleopolis (S 318)

(Under 26th Dynasty, No.15 is now No.16).

TABLE *13A (Part-Revision)

Theban High Priests of Amun

About B.C.:

754-734: Osorkon F (S 485)

734-704: Unattested pontiff, or office left vacant?

TABLE *14 (Revised)

Theban 2nd, 3rd and 4th Prophets of Amun (21st-26th Dynasties)

2nd Prophets	3rd Prophets	4th Prophets
	'Renaissance Era' and 21st Dynasty	
c. 1074: Nesamun(re?) S 211	-	*c.* 1075: Pare-Amun-en-Amun S 211
c. 1070: Heqanufer, S 211	-	-
c. 1040: Amenhirpa-mesha? Kees, *Pr.*, 318	*c.* 1040: Amenhirpa-mesha? Kees, *Pr.*, 318	*c.* 1040: Amenhirpa-mesha? Kees, *Pr.*, 318
-	-	*c.* 1020: Nespaherenmut, S 232; father of
-	*c.* 1000: Nesishuenopet (MMR, 572-3)	*c.* 1000: Tjanefer A SS 226-7; father of
-	*c.* 991-986: Tjanefer A, SS 232-3; father of	*c.* 990/980: Pinudjem, S 232
c. 985?: Tjanefer A?, S 233	*c.* 985: Menkheperre B, S 232	-
-	*c.* 950/940?: Neseramun A, SS 266,273 (vzr)	*c.* 960: Nesamun (Kees, *Pr.*, 170)
	22nd and 23rd Dynasties	
c. 945-935: DjedPtahef-ankh A, S 244; Kees, *Pr.*, 168, n.3	*c.* 945-935: DjedPtahef-ankh A, S 244	*c.* 945: Nesy, Ch. Mahasun, SS 188,244,266; father of
-	*c.* 925ff.: DjedThutef-ankh A, SS 166ff., 245, 266	*c.* 930ff.: Nesankhefmaat, SS 188, 244, 266
c. 910: Bakenamun, S 512 end	-	*c.* 920ff.: Pashedbast A, Ch. Mhsn, SS 263, 266
	-	*c.* 900ff.: DjedKhonsefankh A, SS 183ff., 245, 266; father of next

	c. 875ff.:Pedimut B (Patjenfy), **SS** 184, 270	*c.* 880ff.:DjedThutefankh B (Nakhtefmut A), **SS** 183 ff., 273; father of
c. 855: Harsiese C, **S**274 (*pro temp.*?)	*c.* 850?: Pimai, **S**487	*c.* 860ff.: Harsiese C, **SS** 183ff., 274; father of
c. 830ff.:DjedKhonsefankh C, **S** 486A		*c.*830ff.:DjedKhonsefankh C, **SS** 290,314, 486; father of
-	-	*c.* 800ff.: Nakhtefmut B, **SS** 187, 188, 191, 314; father of
-	*c.* 775: Nebneteru iv, **SS** 177, 314	*c.* 780:*DjedKhonsefankh F **S** 488C, as father of
-	*c.* 760-750:Amenhotep, **S** 487B	*c.* 765: Nakhtefmut G, **S** 488C; father of
c. 740ff.: DjedPtahefankh D, **S** 486A	*c.* 750-725:Wennufer A, **S** 487B	*c.* 750ff.:DjedKhonsefankh D **SS** 187/8, 191, 319

25th/26th Dynasties

c. 720-700: Patjenfy, **SS** 330, 342, & Vittm,PBTS, 64f.	*c.* 725-700:Pediamennebnesttawy A/B, **S** 487	*c.* 725ff.: Kelbasken, **S** 344
c. 680:Nesishutefnut, **S** 351	*c.* 700-675:DjedAnhurefankh, **S** 487B	*c.* 705ff.: 2 unattested incumbents ?
c. 664: Montemhat (*pro temp.*?)	*c.* 675-653:Pediamennebnesttawy C/i, **S** 487; father of	*c.* 680-650: Montemhat A, **SS** 196, 351, 365; father of
c. 650-640:Neshorbehdet, **S** 486	*c.* 653-603: Hor xvii,**SS** 193, 365, 487; father of	*c.* 650-640: Nesptah B, **SS** 196, 365
-	*c.* 603-590:Pediamennebnesttawy D, **S** 487	*c.* 640-635: Hor xxiii, **S** 488
	c. 590ff.:DjedKhonsefankh G, **S** 487	*c.* 635-630:Nesmin, **S** 488
-	-	*c.* 630-625:Udjahor, **S** 488
		c. 625-620:Nespamedu, f. of
		c. 620-610:Nesipaqashuty,**S** 488

TABLE *15 (Revised)

A. Southern Viziers, 21st-26th Dynasties

| *Vizier* | *References* |

'Renaissance Era' and 21st Dynasty

c. 1075: Herihor	*G3*, 232, I,I
c. 1070: Pinudjem I	*G3*, 245,IX, 247, XIII
c. 1040: Amenhirpamesha?	Kees, *Pr.*, 318
c. 960: Neseramun A	SS 266, 273

22nd and 23rd Dynasties

c. 940: Padimut A	SS 184, 270, 489A
c. 925: Ia-o	SS 257, n.304, 489A
c. 880: Rudpamut	Karnak Priestly Annals, frag-ment 12 (*RT* 22, 57, and *RT* 26, 88, n.2)
c. 876: Hor[y]	Year 14, Takeloth I? (Möller, *Zwei äg. Ehevertråge, Vorsait-ische Zeit*, 1918, 4)
c. 845?: Hori son of Iutjek?	JWAB,I, 216ff.; S489 end
c. 835: Nesipaqashuty A	SS 169-172; prob. 'retired' under Shoshenq III
c. 825: Harsiese D, son of above	SS 171f.
c. 820: Hor xviii, father of next	
c. 815: Pentyefankh	S 298 (Year 8, Pedubast I, 811 B.C.)
c. 790: H a r s i e s e E	S 300 (Yr.39, Shoshenq III, 787 B.C.)
c. 780: DjedKhonsefankh E	Cf. CdE 33(1958), 196
c. 775: Nakhtefmut C	S 290 (twice), SS 479-480
c. 770: Hor x, son of above	S 180 (temp. Os. III); perhaps cf. ASAE 7(1906),50-51? (Also CdE 33, 194-195)
c. 765: Pamiu, father of next	See next
c. 760: Pakhuru, mar. d. Takeloth III	S 290, corr. by p.594:11 above.
c. 755: Ankh-Osorkon	S 489
c. 750: Pediamonet son of Pamiu, above	Cf. S 489

*c.*745: Harsiese F   §§ 196, 330, cf. 489

*c.*740: Nesmin A, son of above   §§ 196-7, 330

*c.*730: Ankh-hor   YMM, § 60; temp. Piankhy and

*c.*725: Nesipaqashuty B, § 489.   Akunosh A

*c.*720: Pediese, son of Harsiese (F?) §§ 196-197

25th and 26th Dynasties

*c.*715: Khamhor A, son of Harsiese F §§ 196, 330, 344

*c.*700: Pahrer/Harsiese G, son of above §§ 196, 344

*c.*690: Nesmin B, s. of Khamhor A §§ 196, 344

*c.*680: Nesipaqashuty C   § 351

*c.*670: Nespamedu, son of above   § 351

*c.*660: Nesipaqashuty D, son of above Yr. 14, Psam.I, Parker,
                                       Saite Oracle Pap., 651 B.C.

*c.*650-640?: Iry   § 489

B. Northern Viziers, 25th-26th Dynasties

*c.*685-675: Mentuhotep   § 490a

*c.*675-660: Harsiese R   § 490b-492

*c.*660ff. : Djedkare   § 493c

*c.*650-610: under Psammetichus I, order not
                (ff.)
        known: § 493d; Leahy,GM 65(1983),

        : Sisobek,   51-56 (Harsomtusemhat)

        : Nasekheperensekhmet

        : Bakenranef

        : Gemenefhorbak

        : Harsomtusemhat.

*c.*550-525: Psamtek-Meryneit,   § 493e

        : Pasherientaihet,

        both under Amasis II.

TABLE *16B (Part Revision)

B. Hermopolis

Delete Khmuny (who is simply Piankhy); add Pedinemty? See § 525

TABLE *17 (Revised)

Index of Genealogies of Theban Officials in Part III
plus Supplement

Neseramun Family: §§ 166, 170, 171, 173, plus 475
Nebneteru Family: §§ 177, 178, plus 476
Vizier Nakhtefmut C, etc.: §§ 180 (three parts), plus 479-480
Djed-Thut-ef-ankh B, 4PA: §§ 183, 184 end, 186-188, plus 477
Montemhat Family: §§ 196, plus 478
Besenmuts & Pediamennebnesttawys: §§ 190-192, 193 (2 pts), 195 (2 pts),
plus 481-483.

TABLE *21A (Part Revision)

Delta Chiefs: West & South

A. The West: Chiefs of Libu

*c.*750-745: Ker,   Yr. 19, Sh.V, 749 B.C.; **S** 311
*c.*745-740: Rudamun, Yr. 30 (Sh.V), 738 B.C.; Berlandini, BIFAO 78(1978),
147-163, pls. 49-50 (stela IFAO, No. sq. 14456).

TABLE *22A   (Revised)

Delta Chiefs: Chiefs of the Ma (North-Central, East)

A.   Mendes

*c.*830-810: Nes-khebit(?), father of following
*c.*810-792: Harnakht A, father of following
*c.*792-777: Smendes IV, son of Harnakht A
*c.*777-755: Harnakht B (son of Smendes IV??)
*c.*755-730: Smendes V, son of Harnakht B
*c.*730-720: Djed-Amen-ef-ankh, temp. Piankhy, 728 B.C.
*c.*720-700: Ankh-hor, son of preceding
*c.*700-680: Djed-hor (position, hypothetical)
*c.*680-665: 'Buiama' (Akk. form), **S** 356.

For all the foregoing, see above, **S** 449, following on CdE 52
(1977), 44.

All references are to paragraphs and the new Tables; the conventions used are the same as those given before the main Index, above, p.495.

1. General